ALSO BY BERYL SATTER

Each Mind a Kingdom

FAMILY PROPERTIES

Mark J. Satter with unidentified woman (probably a client, probably around 1958). Date, place, photographer unknown.

FAMILY
PROPERTIES

HOW THE STRUGGLE OVER RACE
AND REAL ESTATE TRANSFORMED
CHICAGO AND URBAN AMERICA

BERYL SATTER

Picador

A METROPOLITAN BOOK

Henry Holt and Company

New York

FAMILY PROPERTIES. Copyright © 2009 by Beryl Satter. All rights reserved.
Printed in the United States of America. For information, address
Picador, 175 Fifth Avenue, New York, N. Y. 10010.

www.picadorusa.com
www.twitter.com/picadorusa • www.facebook.com/picadorusa

Picador® is a U.S. registered trademark and is used by Henry Holt and Company
under license from Pan Books Limited.

For book club information, please visit www.facebook.com/picadorbookclub
or e-mail marketing@picadorusa.com

Maps by James Sinclair
Designed by Kelly S. Too

The Library of Congress has cataloged the Henry Holt edition as follows:

Satter, Beryl, 1959–
    Family properties : race, real estate, and the exploitation of Black urban America /
Beryl Satter.—1st ed.
        p.   cm.
    Includes bibliographical references and index.
    ISBN-13: 978-0-8050-7676-9
    ISBN-10: 0-8050-7676-X
 1. African Americans—Housing—Illinois—Chicago—History—20th century.
2. Discrimination in housing—Illinois—Chicago—History—20th century.   3. Housing policy—
Illinois—Chicago—History—20th century.   4. African Americans—Illinois—Chicago—Social
conditions—20th century.   5. African Americans—Relations with Jews.   6. Chicago (Ill.)—
Social conditions—20th century.   7. Chicago (Ill.)—Race relations—History—20th
century.   8. Satter, Mark J., 1916–1965.   9. Lawyers—Illinois—Chicago—Biography.
10. Landlords—Illinois—Chicago—Biography.   I. Title.
    HD7288.76.U52C434 2009
    363.5'9996073077311—dc22   2008033005

ISBN 978-0-8050-9142-7 (trade paperback)

First published in the United States by Henry Holt and Company

D   10 9 8   7   6   5

To my brother, Paul Satter

and

in memory of Maureen McDonald

CONTENTS

CONTENTS

FAMILY PROPERTIES

THE STORY OF MY FATHER

When an elderly woman erupts into shouts of rage at the mere mention of events now forty years past, you know there is a story there. In the winter of 2000 I asked my aunt what had become of my father's buildings after he died. I should have known by then that nothing connected with my father—or with property, especially property owned by Jews in black neighborhoods, and especially in Chicago—was simple.

I was six years old when my father died. He had a heart condition that slowly destroyed him. On his third hospital stay, with his wife and one of his sons at his side, Mark J. Satter went into convulsions. At around 2:00 a.m., he called out words of warning: "Look out! Later! Watch it!" And then he died. It was July 12, 1965. He was forty-nine years old.

A period of confusion followed. At first, my mother tried to talk to me and my older brothers and sisters about the man my father had been. He was an independent attorney who used the law to help the poor—black people in particular; our family was on the side of black people. He was respected in our city, and we should be proud to be his children. Although my mother was never very specific about my father's accomplishments, I had reason to believe her. She framed an editorial obituary that was published in the *Chicago Daily News:* "Satter was the kind of man who made enemies—big and comfortable ones, not poor and weak ones."[1] I supposed that was a good thing. And then there were the condolence letters. There were stacks of them. They praised Mark J. Satter as the city's conscience. They told my mother that her loss was the city's loss as well. They insisted that her husband was a great man and that his legacy would not be forgotten.

It wasn't long, however, before discussion of my father ceased almost entirely. My sisters and I squirmed with discomfort on the occasions that our mother mentioned him. He had "passed away," my mother said, so why did we need to hear about him? The rare comments my aunts and uncles made about him grew increasingly negative. He left my mother in a terrible state, bankrupt and dependent on Social Security checks, Jewish social services, and one of my uncles for financial support. How could he do that to her? The recollections of my two older brothers, who had been sixteen and seventeen when my father died, turned bitter. "He was driven to run a race that he could not win," my brother David recalled. "Unfortunately, he pulled the rest of us into it with him."

And then there were the buildings. My father had owned several apartment buildings in Lawndale, an old Jewish neighborhood on Chicago's West Side that had become almost entirely black by the late 1950s. They had been sold, I eventually learned, shortly after my father's death. A friend of his named Irving Block had helped my mother get rid of them. But the sale had brought nothing to the family, not even money to pay the properties' coal bills.

The talk about the buildings confused me. I had heard scraps of discussion about these mysterious structures from earliest childhood. My brother Paul would mention them to my mother, it seemed to me, mainly to upset her. "Why did you sell the buildings? Everything would have been fine if you hadn't sold them!" I would chime in, too: "What buildings?" I would press. "Nothing, never mind, don't bother me! Don't talk to me about those buildings!" my mother would respond, her voice sharp with irritation and pain. It was one of the few topics that could shake her composure.

It was hard to reconcile the tales of my father's prominence with the financially cramped circumstances of my childhood—and with my relatives' odd reticence about him. As I got older I tried to learn about him on my own. My main source of information was a notebook filled with newspaper clippings that Paul compiled soon after my father's death. The articles, some by my father but mostly written by others, dated from the late 1950s and early 1960s. "Credit Reform Fanfare and Flop," "Contract Buyers at Mercy of Sharpies," "Federal Curbs Urged on Wage Assignments"—as a child of eleven, twelve, or thirteen, I could not follow the arguments these articles contained.[2] I gave up in frustration. By the time I got to college I told friends that my father had been some sort of "civil rights attorney," but that was the extent of my understanding of his work.

Given the mysteries of my family's past, perhaps it is no surprise that I became a historian. But it was not until some thirty years after my father's death that I decided to find out more about him. I wanted to understand the source of his public prominence—and discover, as well, the reasons my relatives steadfastly refused to laud him for his activism. I could not ask my mother—she had died in 1983. But my brother Paul again came to the rescue. It turned out that he had compiled not one but close to a dozen large notebooks full of newspaper articles, letters, speeches, and other documents pertaining to my father's career. I read through them systematically. Then I started calling people who had known my father—reporters, friends, fellow activists, clients, and legal partners. They weren't hard to find—many were still listed in the Chicago phone book. Most remembered him instantly, as if his death had occurred a week rather than over three decades earlier. Each person I called gave me contact information for several others. Then I retrieved my father's legal files. I scoured archives and manuscript collections, examining the papers of civic organizations he'd belonged to and those he'd opposed. Slowly, the picture came clear.

The first thing I learned was that my father had represented scores of African Americans who had been grossly overcharged for the houses they had bought. For him, it all began in April 1957, when a black couple, Albert and Sallie Bolton, showed up at his office. They were being evicted from their home and they wanted him to delay the proceedings. My father agreed to look into the matter. He asked what they had paid for their property. When they told him, he was astounded. They had paid the enormous sum of $13,900 for a cramped, one-hundred-year-old wood-frame house. My father investigated the property records. He discovered that the white real estate agent, Jay Goran, who had sold the cottage to the Boltons in the fall of 1955, had himself purchased the building only the week before—for $4,300.

Clearly my father's clients had been given a raw deal. But the scam went deeper than that. Goran never told the Boltons that he was the building's owner. He convinced them to make their down payment and to sign some complicated documents that stipulated that the building would remain the legal property of its current owner until they had entirely paid off the property's cost, plus 6 percent interest, through high monthly installments. The contract they signed left the Boltons in a horribly vulnerable position.

In Chicago, as across the nation, most banks and savings and loans refused to make mortgage loans to African Americans, in part because of the policies of the Federal Housing Administration (FHA), which "redlined"—that is, refused to insure mortgages—in neighborhoods that contained more than a smattering of black residents.[3] Therefore, the Boltons could not do what most whites would have done—obtain a mortgage loan and use it to pay for their property in full. Their only option was to buy "on contract," that is, more or less on the installment plan. Under the terms of most installment land contracts, the seller could repossess the house as easily as a used car salesman repossessed a delinquent automobile. With even one missed payment, a contract seller had the right to evict the "homeowner" and resell the building to another customer. If the contract seller happened to be a speculator who charged a wildly inflated price for the building, then a missed payment—and subsequent quick eviction and resale for profit—was practically guaranteed.

This is what had happened to the Boltons. After a year of prompt payments, they had missed one installment and were now threatened with the loss of their entire investment—the down payment, plus all that they'd paid in monthly contract payments and for repairs, insurance, interest, and maintenance. And they were not the only ones. My father found that the speculator who sold the Boltons their home had recently filed repossession claims on over twenty properties. Another speculator working nearby had filed for sixty-nine repossessions in 1956 and an additional fifty-nine repossessions in the first half of 1957. And these were only two of at least a dozen major operators pursuing similar activities.[4]

By the 1950s, contract selling was common in many American cities where black populations had skyrocketed as a result of post–World War II migration from the South. In Chicago, my father estimated that 85 percent of the properties purchased by blacks were sold on contract. He calculated that by selling buildings to housing-starved African Americans on such exploitative terms, speculators were robbing Chicago's black population of one million dollars a day.[5] These sales stripped black migrants of their savings during the very years when whites of similar class background were getting an immense economic boost through FHA-backed mortgages that enabled them to purchase new homes for little money down.

The speculators' profits were stunning. As one contract seller bragged, "If anybody who is well established in this business in Chicago doesn't earn $100,000 a year, he is loafing."[6] My father saw it differently: these profits were the product of machinations that deserved to be labeled criminal. Contract sellers do not in fact "sell the home to a Negro," he told a journalist. They "use the home as a 'bait' to defraud the Negro out of a substantial sum of money and then push the Negro out into the street [in order to] defraud another party."[7]

While contract sellers became millionaires, their harsh terms and inflated prices destroyed whole communities. Because black contract buyers knew how easily they could lose their homes, they struggled to make their inflated monthly payments. Husbands and wives both worked double shifts. They neglected basic maintenance. They subdivided their apartments, crammed in extra tenants, and, when possible, charged their tenants hefty rents. Indeed, the genius of this system was that it forced black contract buyers to be their own exploiters. As my father explained, the black contract buyer was forced to "defraud his own people in order to feed the hungry mouth of the speculator."[8]

The resulting decline of racially changing areas fed white racism. If black contract buyers saw themselves making heroic sacrifices against impossible odds to keep from falling behind on their payments, this was not how their white neighbors viewed the situation. Whites saw population densities doubling, while garbage collection and other municipal services stayed the same or declined. They saw unsupervised children flooding the neighborhood. They noted that buildings bought by African Americans rapidly decayed. Small wonder that whites blamed their black neighbors for the chaos they observed.

Contract selling was another version of a condition that has victimized African Americans from the sharecropping era to our current sub-prime mortgage crisis—namely, their lack of equal access to credit.[9] Yet its full implications—fabulous enrichment for speculative contract sellers and their investors, debt peonage or impoverishment for many black contract buyers, and an almost guaranteed decay of the communities in which such sales were concentrated—have never been explored.[10] Instead, conventional wisdom on why so many aging urban neighborhoods deteriorated once their populations shifted from white to black has been blind to the issue of speculators and their profits. In the 1950s and 1960s, mainstream thinking was divided between those who blamed blacks for their pathological behavior in destroying their own residences and those who blamed racist whites for hysterically fleeing long-established neighborhoods at the first sight of a black face. By the 1980s and 1990s, the division had shifted only slightly, to one between those who blamed the devastation of urban black neighborhoods on the "culture of poverty," or the degraded culture of inner-city blacks, and those who argued that such conditions were the product of "deindustrialization," or the flight of industrial jobs overseas. Up to the present, even commentators who are sympathetic to the plight of inner-city residents frequently blame "the riots" for the eerie emptiness they observe there—seemingly unaware that they are fostering yet another variation of the "blacks destroy their own communities" theme. At best, all of these interpretations point to a lack—of culture, of jobs, of resources, or of courage to fight one's racist impulses and stay put in a racially mixed area.

My father's papers suggested an entirely different reading. The reason for the decline of so many black urban neighborhoods into slums was not the absence of resources but rather the *riches* that could be drawn from the seemingly poor vein of aged and decrepit housing and hard-pressed but hardworking and ambitious African Americans. The real threat to "changing" urban neighborhoods was a sobering economic truth: a single investment by a speculating contract seller of $1,000 could turn into $3,000 in one year; that investment could be multiplied by thousands across the city; and its profits could be shared widely, as the contract paper that enforced draconian monthly payments was frequently sold off at a discount to middle-class and professional residents of the city.[11] The problem was not that racially changing neighborhoods were unprofitable. On the contrary, the problem was that the pickings were too easy, and the scale of profits too tempting, for many of the city's prominent citizens—attorneys, bankers, realtors, and politicians alike—to pass up.

Although the devastating effects of speculative contract selling have been erased from popular memory, I discovered that in Chicago they were discussed, for a time at least. The source of much of the discussion was my father. His immersion in the heartbreaking details of his clients' lives led him to embark on an impassioned public crusade against Chicago's real estate speculators and the white professionals, mortgage bankers, and politicians who enabled them to thrive. He gave speeches, wrote essays, and made radio addresses and television appearances. He believed that if white Chicagoans could only understand the financial processes at work, they would accept black neighbors.

More significantly, he was convinced that the decay of Chicago's neighborhoods could be stopped. "I claim that Chicagoans will not object to Negro neighbors. I claim that Negroes are welcome in every community in Chicago *if they come in without a corresponding instant deterioration of the home they occupy and the block they occupy*. This deterioration will be guaranteed to accompany Negro arrival . . . so long as we do not pull the fangs from the evil speculators who prey upon Negroes only," he charged.[12] He also warned working-class black Chicagoans about the dangers they faced from housing speculation and other credit-abuse schemes. He pursued this latter course through a biweekly column he wrote for the famed black newspaper the *Chicago Defender* titled "All That Money Can Buy"; a weekly column in a West Side community organization newsletter titled "So You're Buying a Home"; and a weekly broadcast on a black radio program titled *The Cost of Your Dollar*.[13]

He offered solutions as well. My father called upon the Illinois Department of Registration to "revoke the license of any broker who engages in the consistent practice of speculation." He lobbied officials to revise Federal Housing Administration practices so that "minority people will profit from the same program of government insurance as is available" to white Americans. He called upon bankers to set up a fund of "at least 50 million dollars for the sole purpose of lending money to Negro people in competition with the contract dealers." This would "result in an immediate return to the Negro community of the fantastic sums now being drained" by the speculators.[14]

It would have been easy to use my father's papers simply to detail the ugly story of how Northern white mortgage, legal, and real estate professionals impoverished African Americans and enriched themselves—a very different story from the culturally-deficient-Southern-rural-blacks-moved-North-and-couldn't-make-it narrative that continues to inform both scholarly and popular literature.[15] But as much as that information needed to be revealed, it didn't fully address the complexity of the situation. As I gradually learned from my father's papers—and from the sometimes wrenching private interviews with which I supplemented them—speculators' exploitation of mid-twentieth-century black Chicagoans' desperate need for housing unleashed two separate processes. The first was a widely discussed though poorly understood public event—the rapid racial turnover of Chicago neighborhoods, usually followed by devastating economic decline. The second was the more private experience of people, both black and white, who inhabited those neighborhoods and who found themselves fighting to hang on to the homes on which they had gambled their futures. This latter, bitter tale was one my father's personal tragedy left me uniquely situated to explore.

Because there were terrible ironies in my father's life—ironies that were most brutally exemplified by the fate of his buildings. At the same time as he was waging his crusade against speculators and contract sellers, he was also managing his own properties, which consisted of four West Side apartment buildings that he had purchased in the 1940s and 1950s. As my father urged others to protect their investments, his own deteriorated. Determined to avoid becoming the sort of slum landlord he denounced, he poured every cent he earned into the buildings, to no avail. Tenants refused to pay their rents. The buildings were repeatedly vandalized. Our family began to suffer financially and my mother offered to find work to help pay the bills, an offer that enraged my father and caused fights between the two of them.

As the bills and the pressures mounted, the end result, as my brother David later told me, was that my father was "caught in his own trap." All of his buildings were in Lawndale, an area that had been heavily Jewish (my father was born and raised there) but that was rapidly becoming black. When he rented to black tenants, he was called a "blockbuster." If he were to refuse to rent to them, he would be a racist. Given his public posture, my father could not sell his buildings as blacks were beginning to move in; to do so would make him a hypocrite. If he sold after the neighborhood had become all black, he'd find no buyers except the speculators he was denouncing. Of course he would not participate in the plunder engaged in by these men and women. He would hold on, then, and try to maintain his properties while the surrounding area crumbled. But if his efforts to maintain them failed, then he was a slumlord. If the buildings were damaged by tenants, he was a slumlord as well.

During the last year of his life my father lived in almost unbearable tension. The buildings were a relentless financial drain. He had plenty of clients, but they were so broke that they couldn't meet their contract payments, much less pay their attorney. He had a certain degree of fame, but he had also incurred the enmity of lawyers throughout the city who could not forgive him for turning against "brother attorneys." He desperately sought to bring in more money, but nothing worked: applications to teach law school, efforts to obtain political jobs, even attempts to get his essays published in national outlets were all met with rejection. His health was failing. In March of his final year, as my father lay in the hospital recuperating from a pulmonary embolism, he was tormented by the possibility that his attempt to live by a code of even minimally fair dealing would result in his leaving his wife and five children destitute.

My brother David told me that toward the end of my father's life he reconsidered his radical politics. But did he? If he had, it would help make sense of a troubling piece of family history. In July 1966, just one year after our father's death, David published an article titled "West Side Story" in the *New Republic*. It was an analysis of conditions in my father's old neighborhood of Lawndale. David was then a precocious eighteen-year-old sophomore at the University of Chicago. Our family was proud that my brother, so fresh from the trauma of his father's death, had published an essay in such a major journal. Yet when I read the article as an adult, its content surprised me. Instead of an analysis of the evils of real estate speculation, it appeared to be a defense of slum landlords. "'There's really no such thing as a slum landlord—only slum tenants,'" David quoted a realtor. "Lawndale real estate . . . is unprofitable," David concluded. "How else can one explain the abandoned buildings all over Lawndale, or the fact that it is impossible to borrow money for a first mortgage on the West Side?"[16]

David's "West Side Story" seemed to invert every argument my father made in his public life. Yet that wasn't my brother's view. "I wrote the article to defend our father," he told me. In fact, after it was published some of David's fellow students at the University of Chicago had sneered to his face, "Your father was a slumlord."

Who had started these rumors? Were they spread by the "enemies—big and comfortable ones," that my father's *Daily News* obituary had described? Or was there more to it than that? I wondered, because of what I'd learned about Irving Block, the attorney who had helped to settle my father's estate. About six weeks before his death, my father had written to his sister Helen, "I would suggest for help regarding any aspect of the building you call IRVING BLOCK. . . . I have a deep affection for him and trust him to advise you with utmost fidelity."[17] Of all the attorneys my father knew well, and there were surely scores of such men, why had he chosen Irving Block to look after his family? It was an odd choice, given that Block had been well known in Chicago circles for his impassioned defense of contract sellers and slumlords, the very people my father considered the scourge of the city. I learned about this side of Block when I found an old booklet among my father's papers, a reprint of a 1960 Illinois appellate court decision. The case at hand was an egregious but not atypical contract sale. A real estate agent had sold a house to a black couple on contract for $11,900—after having purchased it himself, shortly before, for $3,000. Although my father's complaint alleged numerous fraudulent acts committed in the course of the sale, he lost the case. The speculator got off, in part, because of the vigorous defense launched by his attorney, who not only dismissed count after count as "scandalous, impertinent, and not germane to the issues in the case" but also asked the bar to censure my father for his "cold blooded character assassination . . . against . . . brother lawyers." That attorney was Irving Block.[18]

My father's unexpected reliance on Block was an indication that within the tangle of forces and personalities that created slums the sides were not always clear-cut. Not all slum landlords, for example, were exploiters. Speculators were indeed reaping massive profits and destroying sections of Chicago's West and South sides—the two parts of the city where African Americans were purchasing homes on contract—but there were also some owners who were ruined financially by their properties. Mark J. Satter was hardly the only Chicago landlord to find himself dragged down by his real estate investments. An experience recounted by Nicholas von Hoffman, the right-hand man of famed community organizer Saul Alinsky, made this chillingly clear. As he worked to organize a South Side neighborhood in 1962, von Hoffman realized that pressure on landlords was not going to stop the decay of area housing. At one important meeting, a reviled slumlord turned up with his lawyer, who announced: "I'm the attorney, and here is the deed of conveyance, and you tell us who to fill it out to and the building is yours." As everyone cheered, von Hoffman found himself thinking: "Oh, this is *not* a good sign; these guys know something I haven't figured out yet. . . . I said, 'Saul, there aren't any more slumlords, there are just people stuck with turkeys.'"[19]

But of course there were still slumlords. Major contract sellers loved telling the media that their properties' state of disrepair had been caused solely by their tenants' behavior. They frequently denied their immense profits, which averaged in the 75 percent range, claiming instead that owning buildings in minority communities was simply not profitable. Indeed, the tragic experiences of small landlords were used as a smoke-screen behind which these more sinister forces could hide. Chicago's racially changing and all-black neighborhoods contained both: slumlords who milked their properties and landlords who struggled to maintain them, willfully destructive tenants and also tenants whose sincerest efforts at decent living were thwarted by their landlords' criminal neglect. Yet many made no distinctions, thereby obscuring the underhanded behavior of exploitative contract sellers who owned hundreds of properties by identifying them with the elderly widow who could no longer pay the bills on her building—or with the man like my father who got in over his head by owning more than one property in a redlined neighborhood. Such commentators used a small truth about individuals to cover up a much larger and more significant truth about federal mortgage insurance programs that excluded black buyers, about the lawyers and real estate brokers who found ways to manipulate them, and about the black home buyers who were their victims. The fates of all of these players, landlords and slumlords, decent tenants and criminally destructive ones, were intertwined—sometimes grotesquely so.

Another handy smokescreen concealing the injustice at work was religion and ethnicity. The whites who used violence to keep pioneering black families out of their communities were often Catholic. A significant proportion of exploitative contract sellers were Jewish. Although it was federal-level decisions about credit flows that most damaged black home buyers, the disastrous results of those decisions stoked sometimes bitter tensions over religion and ethnicity. This was true everywhere, but perhaps most intensely in Chicago. A Catholic-run city and home to the largest archdiocese in the country, Chicago had a Protestant banking and business elite, powerful Jewish, Catholic, and African American traditions of left-wing Popular Front organizing, and equally entrenched Jewish, Catholic, and African American traditions of illicit dealings that ran the gamut from occasional graft to organized crime. Within the various communities, battles raged between the respectable but powerless and the shady but well-connected, as well as between those who sought to prop up a system in which they thrived and those who sought to overturn a system they viewed as exclusionary and immoral. Each community had to negotiate its internal conflicts under the harsh light shone by outsiders, who had ugly stereotypes ready to wield against them no matter what actions the group ultimately embraced.[20]

The greatest injuries were borne by ordinary Chicagoans, especially ordinary black Chicagoans—the janitors, mechanics, steelworkers, clerks, laundry workers, and domestics—whose dreams of owning a family property so often turned sour. Black Chicagoans hardly found their Northern city to be a promised land where they could start anew, leaving behind the blood-soaked history of their Southern past. Rather, black Chicagoans would have to fight for their rights in the North's most segregated city, a complex terrain already scarred by decades of ethnic, racial, and religious battle.

My father's story could guide me through the corrupt and serpentine world of mid-twentieth-century Chicago, a city where wheeling and dealing created both millionaires and devastation as severe as that found in war zones. Yet Chicago was also the one city that produced activists tough and savvy enough to expose and contain the actions that formed the foundation of that ill-gotten wealth and wholesale destruction—namely, the racially biased credit policies of the nation's banking industry.

This resistance is part of the story, too. In the late 1960s, thousands of black homeowners who had bought their buildings on contract—many of them residents of my father's old Lawndale neighborhood—organized the Contract Buyers League (CBL). Their goal was to stop exploitative contract sales, renegotiate their existing contracts, and open new lines of credit to black home buyers. They picketed realtors and banks. They drew national media attention to the role that the FHA played in the creation of ghettos. Their efforts led to the filing of two massive federal suits aimed at abolishing the nation's dual housing market and ensuring that in the future "a dollar in the hands of a black man" would have the same purchasing power as "a dollar in the hands of a white man."[21] In the mid-1970s, Chicago activists drew upon the CBL's groundwork to create some of the most critically important pieces of urban-focused federal legislation passed in the twentieth century—legislation that led to the investment of billions of dollars in scores of U.S. cities and provided some of the few tools we have for documenting the racial biases and destructive impact of the contemporary subprime mortgage crisis.

Back in the winter of 2000, though, I was just starting to investigate the nagging questions I had about my father's life. I thought I would begin with the buildings, my father's four rental properties in Lawndale. I wanted to know how he had purchased them, why he could not maintain them, and why and to whom they were sold upon his death. These were the concerns on my mind when my brother Paul and I visited our aunt Theresa that winter day. I trusted Theresa. She was liberal; she was tolerant. She had worked most of her life as a teacher in some of the city's toughest schools and then retired to a condominium in one of the Chicago area's few racially integrated neighborhoods. But when I asked her a simple question about the fate of my father's buildings after he died, Theresa turned red with anger. For the first time in my life I heard her raise her voice. "You want to know what happened to the buildings? I'll tell you what happened. Mark should have gotten rid of them long ago. He kept them and they dragged him down, they killed him! People were animals out there, animals! I can tell you, I saw with my own eyes. They chopped down the porches for firewood! They ripped out the toilets and took them with them when they were evicted! But Mark wouldn't sell!" Paul cut in, now highly agitated himself. "How could he sell? He couldn't sell! It was impossible to sell!" Theresa fired back: "He *could* sell. Anyone could sell! You just couldn't be picky about who you sold to. And you better not expect to make a penny!"

My aunt's outburst was typical of the emotion-charged response I would hear from many Jews who had once lived in Lawndale. It was the bitter residue of a larger history—one that encompassed the mass population shifts of Southern blacks, second-generation immigrant Jews, and urban Catholics; moneymaking schemes, urban renewal, and turnabouts in federal policies; Martin Luther King Jr.'s Chicago campaign, street riots, arson for profit, and arson born of despair. One could start this story in many different places, but I will start with the community of Lawndale. By the mid-1960s, Lawndale would become a national symbol of black ghetto violence and desolation. But in the 1920s, it was still Jewish Lawndale—a teeming immigrant neighborhood that bred radicals and hustlers in equal measure.

PART I

PART I

ONE

JEWISH LAWNDALE

Growing up in Lawndale, children learned the word *gang* as soon as they learned to talk, my father wrote of his West Side home in the 1920s. "Their neighborhood taught them little cultural. There was more of a constant fight so as not to be afraid to be outside the house."[1] In years to come many would bemoan the transformation of Lawndale from a middle-class haven to a rough working-class ghetto, but in truth Lawndale was never the respectable enclave whose loss they lamented. The neighborhood's first developers, who laid it out in 1870, had certainly hoped to attract a middle-class population. They gave it the fanciful name of "Lawndale"— fanciful because the only grass to be found there was in its two city parks. But fate soon altered their plans. The Great Chicago Fire of 1871 forced the McCormick reaper plant to relocate west, to an unincorporated area near Lawndale. The workers, mostly Dutch, Irish, and German, followed, giving Lawndale a working- and lower-middle-class character from the start.[2]

Lawndale's Irish and German residents did not welcome the Polish and Russian Jews who started moving into the neighborhood in the early 1910s. They refused to rent to the newcomers. But unlike the residents of more well-to-do areas, Lawndale's working-class population lacked the time and expertise to form legally enforceable restrictive covenants against selling land to Jews. And so, while Jews found it difficult to rent in

Lawndale, they could buy. Beginning in the 1910s, Jews purchased much of the community's vacant land. Though the area was known for its "two-flats," or two-story, two-family apartment buildings, the newer inhabitants constructed larger buildings that contained ten, twenty, or even thirty units. The result was a massive population increase. Lawndale contained 46,000 people in 1910. By 1930, it had a population of 112,000, of whom the great majority—75,000—were Jewish. As one neighborhood historian observed, "While the tough Chicago [communities described in] the novels of Nelson Algren and James Farrell had 25,000 humans per packed mile, Lawndale had 51,000." By 1930, another notes, "North Lawndale achieved the dubious distinction of having the highest population density of all local communities in Chicago save one, Grand Boulevard, in the heart of the *Black Belt.*"[3]

In some ways, the 1920s were an optimistic time for immigrant and second-generation Jews moving into urban Jewish enclaves such as Lawndale. The neighborhood quickly sprouted institutions and businesses that reflected the varied identities of its Jewish residents. In 1922, the Hebrew Theological College opened on Douglas Boulevard, the proud, sweeping avenue with a grassy strip down its center that ran through the heart of Lawndale. Next door to it, the Jewish People's Institute opened in 1927. A vibrant community center, the JPI offered a library, sports, educational forums, instruction in art, music, and dance, clubs, a theater, and a roof-top garden where dances were held. Nearby stood the Labor Lyceum, which provided spaces for Jewish labor unions, as well as the Douglas Park Theatre, which featured many of the day's top Yiddish performers. Lawndale had a Jewish hospital, Mount Sinai, for Jewish physicians who were still excluded from residency in Christian-run hospitals. It had a Jewish orphanage, the Marks Nathan Orphan Home, where indigent or orphan Jewish children could be cared for without being subjected to Christian proselytizing. The Midwest edition of the *Jewish Daily Forward* was published in Lawndale. Along Roosevelt Road were shops providing for every need, from kosher butchers to social halls to funeral chapels, as well as restaurants that served regional foods to nostalgic immigrants from Hungary, Poland, or Romania. By 1930 Lawndale contained approximately forty Orthodox synagogues. Douglas Boulevard alone boasted almost half a dozen synagogues, including Congregation Anshe Kneseth Israel, also known as the Russishe Shul. With 3,500 seats, it was the largest synagogue in the city.[4]

But Lawndale in the 1920s was hardly paradise. It was an overcrowded working-class immigrant neighborhood surrounded by industrial areas, poorly served by public transportation, and almost bereft of parks, lawns, or single-family homes. As my uncle Charlie recalled, the Lawndale of his youth was nothing more than "semi–all right." Still, the neighborhood's Jewish character provided a shield of sorts from the anti-Semitism that typified 1920s America—years in which Jews were excluded from many of the nation's universities, business and law firms, and even low-level clerical jobs.[5] And for most of the area's Jewish residents, Lawndale represented a step up. Many had moved there from the Maxwell Street neighborhood, also known as "Jew Town," a ramshackle, overcrowded quarter even more lacking in grass and parks than Lawndale.[6] In contrast, Lawndale was a residential area, with wide avenues and solid two-story apartment buildings that had amenities like windows and bathrooms.

My father's family was part of the movement that transformed Lawndale from a German and Irish neighborhood into a heavily Jewish one. Like almost half of Lawndale's residents, they were foreign born. My grandfather Isaac was brought from Russia to the United States in 1890, when he was four years old. He worked as a laborer and in a trunk factory. My grandmother Yetta Dunkleman was born in Manchester, England, the daughter of Polish Jewish immigrants. She came to the United States in 1908 and worked as a shopgirl in a Chicago department store. She met Isaac her first year in the States, and the couple married in 1910.

After his marriage Isaac opened his own small trunk manufacturing company. Yetta and Isaac's first child, Helen, was born in 1912. Their second child, Nathan, was born in 1914. By 1916, the year of my father's birth, Isaac was able to buy a small building for his family and his business at 1227 South Spaulding, on the eastern border of Lawndale.[7]

As the third child in what would soon be a family of six, with a younger brother, Charlie, born barely a year later, my father could easily have been lost in the shuffle. Instead, an accident changed his life. When he was three years old Mark fell out of a second-story window. Except for a sore leg, he seemed uninjured. Yet the leg would not heal. By the age of five, he was walking with a limp. He was taken to specialists who put him in a body cast that immobilized him from the waist down. He remained in that cast for a year. He had to be wheeled about in a baby carriage, subject to the mockery of other children. My father described the experience in a short autobiography that he wrote, curiously in the third person, when he was around twenty years old. "At these times ridicule and pity were mixed to such an extent that it became almost impossible for the small boy to distinguish between them," he wrote. "He began to desire to get away from people, [with] their caustic comments about the 'cripple.' . . . His helplessness . . . troubled him. . . . At night he imagined fiends who speedily pursued him as he tried to hobble away."[8] After a year in bed, my father was given a club shoe and a pair of crutches. One year after that, he discarded the crutches. But his recovery was never permanent. He would burst from his restraints, his dammed-up energy fueling frenetic play. Then there would be a relapse. He would be taken out of school and confined to his bed for weeks at a time.[9]

My father's invalidism made him the undisputed center of the household. His mother read to him for hours and told him long, colorful stories about her childhood in England. While this doting attention helped my father develop intellectually, his infirmity wounded him emotionally. It fueled an aggressive need to prove himself against all comers. But it also contributed to his lifelong sympathy for the underdog. My father knew what it meant to be the helpless object of other people's ridicule and contempt.[10] He would fight to protect others from such treatment, no matter what the odds.

In 1924, my father's family moved deeper into Lawndale. With the birth of their fifth child, Theresa, Isaac and Yetta realized that their family had outgrown their home on Spaulding Avenue. They hoped that the building they purchased at 4112 West Roosevelt Road would answer their needs. It had a storefront on the first floor for Isaac's trunk business, cold-water two-bedroom flats on the second and third floors, and three more small apartments in the back. They rented the back and top-floor apartments. Isaac, Yetta, and their children lived in the two-bedroom apartment on the second floor, above the store. Their apartment was crowded, especially after their sixth child, Joseph, was born in 1926, but the building brought income and security to the family.[11]

Then came the Great Depression, which put an end to many immigrant dreams. Chicago was particularly hard-hit. Over 160 of the city's banks failed. Home foreclosures rose by 500 percent. Chicago's economy was heavily dependent on manufacturing. By the early 1930s manufacturing employment in the city was down by 50 percent, and up to one-third of the population was unemployed. Manufacturing plants and the small businesses that relied on the workers from these plants as customers collapsed.[12] My grandfather's trunk business was one of them.

With his business destroyed, Isaac's assets (that he was literate, responsible, and hardworking) could not offset his deficits (that he was a man in his forties with a wife and six children to support). Isaac was terrified that he would lose his building. He sat home among his children, consumed with anxiety. But like many others in Lawndale, my father's family got by. Yetta did piecework sewing ruffles onto aprons. Isaac took a job that one of Yetta's brothers found for him, selling insurance for Metropolitan Life. The company set brutal quotas for weekly sales, along with harsh penalties for those who failed to measure up. Isaac developed a serious ulcer. Each evening he returned from work and collapsed into his living room chair, his body trembling from exhaustion and suppressed rage.[13]

Perhaps it was his family's economic struggles that instilled in my father a grim determination to succeed. For his first three years of high school he made the honor roll every semester. He ran for school office and was elected each time. The verbal sparring of high school election campaigning appealed to him, and he considered a future career as a lawyer. To help ease his family's severe financial straits, he took a paper carrier route, which required him to wake at 3:30 a.m. To maintain his position on the honor roll, he stayed up till midnight studying. Then came a series of blows. During the fall of 1932 my father decided to take out an insurance policy. He was rejected, not because of the leg injury but for something potentially more serious: a systolic heart murmur. My father was shocked to learn of this new and potentially crippling condition. Between his exhaustion over the paper route and his anxiety over his health, he could not maintain his grades. A scholarship he had counted on went to another boy. Without a scholarship, college was out.[14]

Troubles followed troubles. In the spring of 1933, Yetta fell ill. The diagnosis was colon cancer. The disease would hospitalize her every year or so until it killed her in 1944. Since my father's sister Helen had married, as had his brother Nate, it fell to him and his brother Charlie to watch over the two youngest siblings. Then the only free college in the city announced it was closing, putting an end to my father's last chance for an education. He volunteered as a speaker and organizer for a group formed to challenge the decision and was present at meetings that were violently broken up by the police. When the group petitioned the city's Board of Education, board members promised that the school would stay open—and then quietly shut it down months later, after the protesters who were mostly students had disbanded for the summer.[15]

This was my father's first taste of political activism—and of the behind-the-scenes maneuvering that enabled those in power to subvert their public promises. Determined to devote himself to social justice, he realized he would have to attend college to acquire the necessary skills. For a year he held odd jobs and saved his money. Then in 1934, while continuing to work at a wholesale market, he started night school at the People's Junior College, which was run out of the Jewish People's Institute.[16] His field was prelaw, and though he had doubts about the morality of following "a hypocrite profession in an artificial world," he thought that putting his talents in the service of "the labor element" might be of some use.[17]

In part, my father's desire to fight for the disenfranchised grew naturally from his upbringing. Isaac had taught his children that society was threatened by unbridled wealth, and not by the occasional missteps of the workingman. "If there's no limit to how much a man can make, and it doesn't matter how he makes it, God help us," he would say.[18] My father's dedication to aiding the "workingman" had another source as well: his encounters with Communist Party activists. His exposure to Communism was not surprising. Though few in number—nationally, Communist Party USA membership in the 1930s peaked at a mere 82,000—party members could seem omnipresent in urban areas.[19] When a family was evicted, they moved them back in. When relief ran out, they demanded that funds be reinstated. If workers at a plant wanted to unionize, the most dedicated organizers were often Communists. When activists were censored, CP members fought for their right of self-expression. And when a school that served the poor was closed, they demanded that it reopen.

That was how my father first encountered CP members—during the campaign to prevent the closing of Chicago's free college. Though he rejected their vision of a revolutionary utopia, he shared their anger at gross social inequality and was drawn to their understanding of class as the primary divide in society. He admired the intellectual elegance of Marxist thought and the idealism that seemed to drive it.[20] The party's anti-racism and its unflinching support of "foreign" cultures within the United States was probably an equally powerful draw, giving second-generation Americans like my father a way to value their own heritage and engage with others in a common "American" cause of upholding democracy.[21]

In 1936 my father received a scholarship to DePaul University, a local Catholic college whose law school was one of the few in the city that accepted Jews. By this time he had fallen in love with Clarice Komsky, the woman he would eventually marry. Like my father, my mother was the child of hard-pressed Jewish immigrants. She was a rosy-cheeked, raven-haired young woman who loved to socialize. "Such exotic beauty will get you somewhere," a friend wrote in her high school yearbook. My father claimed not to notice her appearance. He valued her, he wrote, because she was a "willing listener" to his views. He was one of many to note that Clarice was a "zieseh neshumah," a sweet soul in whom others naturally confided their troubles.[22]

Their relationship was rocky from the start. My father was tortured by jealousy when anyone so much as "looked at" Clarice.[23] "*My* Clarice," he wrote in her yearbook. My mother found his moodiness and possessiveness too much and broke up with him but then had second thoughts.[24] Mark was a strikingly handsome young man, with large, heavily lashed gray green eyes and dark wavy hair that framed his powerful forehead. He was smart and ambitious, and he loved her. Though Clarice worried about Mark's temperament, she admired his drive and supported his values. The two were married in the fall of 1939, after my father graduated from DePaul University with his law degree. The final words of his autobiography summed up his surprisingly uncertain mood. "He can only speculate as to the weather which lies ahead," my father wrote. "His sturdiest craft may flounder, and his greatest calculations come to naught. Ancient sailors called it 'The will of the Gods.'"[25]

My father's somber mood was surely colored by the fact that he embarked on married life just as the Second World War broke out in Europe. His bad heart disqualified him from military service, but he helped the war effort by working nights in a munitions factory. My parents anxiously followed the war news. It was probably the horrific reports of the mass murder of the Jews of Europe that led my father to join the Communist Party in 1945. As he later told my brother David, "If it weren't for the Russians, every Jew in Europe would have been murdered."[26]

My father did not last long in the party. The discipline and personal subservience that the party demanded was not for him, and he quit one year after he joined, leaving just as international events gave rise to the Cold War and its domestic shadow, McCarthyism.[27] Only a few pieces of evidence remain about my father's political activities during these years. Among them is a 1948 telegram from Henry Wallace wishing my father a happy birthday and thanking him for helping Wallace's presidential campaign. Dubbed "the American dreamer" by his biographers, Wallace had been vice president under Franklin Delano Roosevelt and was now running for president under a new party, the Progressive Citizens of America.[28] When Wallace proposed that the United States send aid to all war-torn nations, including the Soviet Union, Winston Churchill publicly called him a "crypto-Communist." Red-baiting of this sort, along with Wallace's principled refusal to purge Communists from his party, doomed his campaign and he received just over one million votes—less than 3 percent of the national total. In December 1948, the House Committee on Un-American Activities (HUAC) published a report highlighting the role of Communists in the Progressive Citizens of America. The PCA was added to the attorney general's list of subversive organizations, and its most active members were put under FBI surveillance.[29]

My father himself was the subject of an FBI investigation. He came to the bureau's attention as a member of the National Lawyers Guild (NLG), a group founded as an alternative to the American Bar Association, the professional organization of the nation's attorneys.[30] In these years, the guild repeatedly ran afoul of the FBI. In January 1950, just as the NLG was about to release a report detailing the FBI's illegal spying, bugging, and burglary operations, Senator Richard M. Nixon called for an investigation of the guild "to determine the truth or falsity of charges that it is being used as a Communist front organization." Simultaneously, HUAC published its own report, prepared long in advance, titled *The National Lawyers Guild: Legal Bulwark of the Communist Party*. The NLG was discredited, its account of FBI illegalities was ignored, and mass resignations from the guild followed, since staying in the organization meant risking one's professional future. "Only about a dozen of us were left by 1954," a member of the Chicago NLG recalled. "We figured about half of us were spies." That estimation was probably correct. One of my father's guild colleagues was in fact an FBI informer. He passed on some of my father's comments to the bureau, adding that he believed that Satter might well be a Communist sympathizer.[31]

Based on this information, the FBI launched an investigation of my father. They noted his height (5'6"), weight (150 lbs.), hair color (black), eye color (green), and complexion ("sallow"). They listed every apartment he'd inhabited and every school he'd attended since kindergarten. They noted that he had been in the Communist Party in 1945 but had fallen "out of favor with the Party because of insisting upon following his own dictates in handling cases." They also noted his suspicious activities since that time: joining the Progressive Citizens of America and playing a role in what became known as the "Peoria street riot." The riot began in November 1949, when white residents of a South Side Chicago neighborhood observed that a new neighbor, Aaron Bindman, had black people in his home. The rumor quickly spread that Bindman planned to sell his home to blacks. Bindman's explanation that his guests were members of his union invited to meet a visiting union official did nothing to calm the crowd. For three nights hundreds of people stoned the Bindman home, shattering windows and screaming "Burn the house," "Nigger-loving kikes," and "Communists." Bindman contacted members of the Progressive Citizens of America to come to his aid. When they showed up, roving gangs beat the outsiders bloody.[32]

My father was one of several NLG attorneys who represented the victims of this riot, the FBI file noted. In 1949 as well, the file claimed, the Chicago police observed that his car was parked in the vicinity of a hall where the Chicago Council of Arts, Sciences and Professions, which they labeled a Communist-front organization, was meeting. In 1950, he attended a rally held by the Civil Rights Congress, allegedly another Communist-front organization.

However troubling my father's activities, in the FBI's view the picture that emerged did not add up to that of a committed revolutionary: "The subject is not being recommended for the Security Index"—that is, for the FBI's secret list of individuals to be rounded up for detention in case of a national emergency. After all, the Chicago FBI office noted, "there has been no allegation that he is presently a member of the Communist Party." J. Edgar Hoover disagreed. "You are instructed to submit an FD-122 recommending that the subject be included in the Security Index," Hoover wrote back.[33]

My father's inclusion in the Security Index meant that he was subjected to ongoing surveillance. In 1955, the FBI decided that since he was in "disfavor" with the Communist Party yet still moved in left-wing circles, he might be receptive to working for the bureau. "It is expected that, if cooperative, SATTER is in a position to furnish information concerning Communist Party activities . . . in the Chicago area," an agent wrote to Hoover, requesting permission to interview my father. The FBI showed up at my father's law office on April 14, 1955. In May, they returned three times. In June, they showed up six times. Each time my father refused to speak with them. They tried again on July 14, 18, 20, and 22. On August 2 a Chicago agent wrote to request additional permission to interview my father. This time, Hoover denied the request. "It is noted that relet [*sic*] reflects fifteen dates on which unsuccessful attempts were made to contact Satter. It is believed that future expenditures of man power . . . to interview the subject would not be justified." But the FBI kept my father under surveillance for the rest of his life. They were attentive enough to note that in 1958 he was "cold-shouldered" out of the National Lawyers Guild. The reason, they reported, was NLG members' belief that Satter was an informer for the FBI.[34]

In the hothouse imagination of the FBI, my father was a small but potentially significant player in a global struggle between Communist tyranny and capitalist freedom. In the real world, his life was not nearly so dramatic. He devoted most of his time to his family, his law practice, and his own economic future. By the early 1950s he was sharing a suite with half a dozen other young attorneys. My father didn't specialize. He was drawn to litigation that was complex. He loved legal research and was good at it. He enjoyed courtroom arguments, and was good at that, too. His suite mates viewed him as a liberal and a freethinker. Though he was a small, wiry man, he was so energetic that his friends were sometimes left awkwardly lumbering in his wake. He had a certain charisma, especially in court. But he could also be abrupt, even rude. As a journalist friend of his recalled, "If you didn't agree with him, you were automatically his enemy."[35]

In 1954 my father hired attorney Favil Berns, a skinny young man from the neighborhood, as his assistant. Their office at 134 North LaSalle was so cramped that Berns had to set up his desk practically on top of my father's. My grandfather Isaac came by most days and sat in a small chair just to the right of Berns, waiting for Mark to give him something to do. Money was so tight that Berns supplemented his income by working nights in a downtown parking garage.[36]

While my father built his law practice, he had another occupation—that of landlord. There was a desperate housing shortage in Chicago during the war and immediate postwar years. Real estate was a hot commodity. In 1943, my father "flipped" a building—that is, he bought it and then resold it one year later for a profit.[37] There was money to be made in real estate, but the experience convinced him that he didn't want to be a speculator. Instead, he would acquire a few buildings, keep them well maintained, and charge reasonable rents. He would make a fair profit on his investments and render a service to the community. The buildings would also provide for his family's security. Isaac had held on to his building on Roosevelt Road throughout the Depression, and now it was the source of a consistent if modest income. My father's heart ailment meant that he could not count on working forever, so he too turned to real estate as a source of income.

In 1944, he purchased a six-flat on Congress Street in Lawndale. He and my mother moved to one of the apartments, and he rented the rest to friends or family members. In 1947, Mark and Clarice had their first child, a son they named David. Fourteen months later their second child, Paul, was born. In 1953 they had their third child, a daughter named Julietta.

In 1952, my father bought a second building, a twelve-flat on Jackson Boulevard. He purchased another twelve-flat on Gladys Street in 1955 and went in as part owner on another, on Kilbourn, in 1958.[38] My father took the maintenance of his properties seriously. He rose early each day to check the coal heat in each of his buildings. He put in long days at his law office and then checked on the buildings again each evening. As his holdings expanded, more of his immediate family moved into his buildings. His sister Theresa and her family lived in one of the Congress Street apartments. His brother Joe and his wife moved into the building on Jackson. Clarice's sister and her family rented another of the Congress Street flats, while Clarice's parents lived just down the street.[39]

He also rented to black tenants. He sometimes presented his willingness to do so as strictly pragmatic. As he once told a hostile white reporter, "I'm simply going along with a trend—a trend that can't be stopped. These Negroes are moving into all neighborhoods and they have as much right to live decently as we have."[40] But in fact, he was passionately, ideologically dedicated to the ideal of an interracial community in Lawndale. And he had reason to believe it could happen. Small numbers of blacks found their way into Lawndale in the 1940s: by 1947, over 1,400 blacks had settled there, and only two minor racial incidents had resulted.[41] Several of Lawndale's first black families were encouraged to seek housing there by Jewish friends. If viewed without prejudice, they had the makings of ideal neighbors. Most were Chicago-born middle-class men and women who purchased their buildings with substantial down payments. They managed to get modest mortgages to finance their purchases, and several paid off their mortgages early. The new black residents of Lawndale not only maintained their buildings but upgraded them.[42]

Lawndale had other features that made an interracial community seem possible. One was the presence of Sears, Roebuck. The merchandizing giant had its corporate headquarters there and so had an interest in committing substantial resources to "stabilization." Another was the area's liberal Jewish institutions. The Jewish People's Institute (JPI) threw its support behind integration and in 1950 formed the North Lawndale Citizens Council to organize residents, revitalize local businesses and institutions, and transform Lawndale into a "'pilot community' for interracial living."[43] To be sure, there were sporadic outbursts of violence against black residents throughout the early 1950s, especially in Polish, Italian, and Czech sections of South Lawndale. When my father rented some units in his twelve-flat at 3901 West Jackson to black tenants, whites broke fifteen windows on the building and a police guard had to be stationed there for several months.[44] But there was nothing like the attack on the Bindmans.

As my brother Paul recalled it, the early 1950s were halcyon days in Lawndale. The immediate area around our family's Congress Street apartment was bursting with cousins, friends, and relatives. On Sundays, my father would lead about a dozen kids on bicycle rides through nearby Garfield Park. "I was so proud that the landlord was my father," Paul recalled. "He was *everybody's* landlord. All the relatives, at any rate, and other people as well. . . . Everybody knew that landlords were bad guys. But everybody liked him! He was the greatest father, and the greatest landlord."[45]

Like all other halcyon days, these were brief. By the early 1950s, Jews were already beginning to leave Lawndale. Although racism surely played a role, Jews' abandonment of the area was not just about resistance to sharing their neighborhood with blacks. As a man who was proud of his working-class origins, my father didn't seem to recognize that Jewish Chicagoans might not want to remain in a neighborhood that had always been viewed as "lower middle class" at best.[46] Lawndale was dominated by multiunit dwellings. It was overcrowded. It was surrounded on three sides by industrial areas. It was far from the educational institutions upon which the families of Jewish Lawndale pinned hopes for their children's future. Most of all, it was tarred by its very success as a way station for Jewish migrants. It was the home of numerous institutions that had helped those migrants adjust to American life. Now that the Jews were adjusted, they didn't need the institutions. Instead, they scorned them as embarrassing reminders of an outsider status they hoped to outgrow. By the 1940s, Chicago Jews were mockingly referring to Lawndale as "Lower Slobovnia." As soon as the postwar housing shortage eased enough to allow them to leave, Lawndale's Jewish population started to shrink.[47]

One day in 1953, my brother Paul looked out the window of his home and saw something frightening. Wrecking crews were ripping down the building across the street. For a five-year-old boy, it was an awesome sight. "Buildings as big as ours, blocks and blocks of them, as far as you can see, just being destroyed—but not ours!" Paul recalled. "You sure they're not going to get us?" he asked his father.

Paul was witnessing the "clearance" of hundreds of Lawndale properties to make way for the Congress Street Expressway (later renamed the Eisenhower Expressway). Its construction was a physical manifestation of Jewish Chicagoans' political powerlessness. While church leaders' lobbying sometimes changed the routes of expressways or even kept highway construction out of Catholic communities altogether, Lawndale's Jews could not prevent the Congress Street Expressway from bisecting their neighborhood.[48] For Paul, the massive construction marked the end of the stable world of his childhood. For Lawndale, it signified something much worse. It sliced the neighborhood in two and essentially destroyed it. Routines that had marked daily life were now impossible. The walk to the newsstand for the Sunday morning paper? Forget it; what used to be a peaceful stroll now entailed crossing eight lanes of traffic. The corner tailor? Gone. The baker? Out of business. My brother David summarized the mood of mid-1950s Lawndale: "There was an air of impending catastrophe. The neighborhood had been ripped open and was ripe for the kill."[49]

In 1954, Clarice had news for her husband; she was pregnant with their fourth child. Shortly thereafter, my father shocked her with news of his own; they were moving. He'd purchased a single-family home in a Chicago neighborhood known as South Shore. The move to South Shore meant that they wouldn't be raising their four children in a three-bedroom apartment across from an expressway. Still, my mother was hurt and angry that Mark had given her no say in the selection of the house or the neighborhood. She felt that he was uprooting her from her friends and family. True, many of them were leaving Lawndale, but they were all moving to Jewish enclaves on Chicago's far North Side.[50] Mark had chosen instead a largely white South Side neighborhood that, while gracious and elegant in character, was close to the South Side's so-called Black Belt. That proximity alone was enough to hint to white Chicagoans that South Shore too might soon share Lawndale's experience of an almost wholesale population shift from white to black residency.

For this was indeed Lawndale's situation by 1955. That year Lawndale's Jewish People's Institute, the Hebrew Theological College, and the Labor Lyceum all shut down and relocated to the far north neighborhoods of Rogers Park and Skokie. The white and Jewish population of Lawndale was plummeting, proving what would soon become common wisdom in Chicago—that integration was nothing more than "a term to describe . . . the period of time that elapses between the appearance of the first Negro and exit of the last white."[51]

The increased availability of housing brought a new influx of blacks to Lawndale. Here, too, 1955 marked a turning point. The African Americans who moved to Lawndale before 1955 were largely Chicago-born. But from 1955 onward, those moving to Lawndale were mostly recent migrants, many from Mississippi. Long-term residents noted with disapproval the migrants' large families and "countryfied" ways. They noted the decay that seemed to follow the newcomers' arrival on a block. As former sharecroppers and rural folk, the migrants simply didn't know how to maintain a building, their more established neighbors assumed.[52]

But if many Lawndale residents were unsettled by the new arrivals from Mississippi, a small group of men saw something else in the faces of the hardworking new people now streaming into the area. They saw an opportunity.

Lawndale's operators, its schemers and hustlers, had much in common with the area's idealists. Like my father, several of them were first- or second-generation immigrant Jews. Their early years, like those of my father, were marked by anti-Semitism and poverty. But while my father's childhood disability and exposure to his father Isaac's social idealism inspired in him a profound empathy for the oppressed, these men drew very different conclusions from the harsh realities they had witnessed during the Depression. They had observed a world of victims and of victimizers, of those who "worked the system" and those who were destroyed by it. And they knew which side of that divide they wanted to be on.

By the early 1970s, the names of some in this group—Moe M. Forman, Al Berland, Joseph Berke, Lou Wolf, and Gilbert Balin—would be well known to the city. Their faces would be plastered across newspapers under banners proclaiming them "the most ruthless slumlords in Chicago." They would be damned as a force that "moved like a reaper thru north Lawndale . . . leaving behind a wasteland of abandoned buildings, rubble-strewn lots and crushed hopes."[53]

But back in the 1950s, they were just starting out. Though my father had no connection to these men, Favil Berns, who worked in his office, knew some of them well from his childhood in Lawndale. Berns's father, David Bernstein, was the manager of the silk department in a downtown Chicago clothing store. By the late 1920s, Bernstein had become a property owner as well, purchasing a two-flat in Lawndale. Then came the Depression. Bernstein lost his job. In October 1935, he sickened and died, leaving his widow and nine-year-old Favil in a precarious state. But Mrs. Bernstein had an entrepreneurial spirit. Her two-flat was near the Blind People's Institute, and one day Mrs. Bernstein came up with a plan. She would turn her building into a rooming house for the blind. As Berns recalled, "We loaded up the two-flat building with blind people, and . . . my mother got the state monthly checks. She beat the system. Wasn't that clever?" Young Favil, too, benefited from the arrangement. He earned two cents a trip when he carried home the blind tenants' groceries.[54]

In the midthirties Favil and his mother faced difficult times, but there were others who had it worse. Among them were the Berlands. Mrs. Bernstein had met Mrs. Berland when both were out strolling with their babies. The women remained close, and the two boys, Favil Bernstein and Al Berland, became inseparable. Berland's father was an unemployed barber who cut hair in the couple's kitchen for five cents a head. It was not enough to support the family, and Mrs. Bernstein often sent Favil over on his roller skates to deliver extra food to the Berlands. She realized that the Berlands would not survive much longer on five-cent haircuts and scraps from their friends' tables. "You must do something!" she told Mrs. Berland. There were rows of empty storefronts on the nearby commercial strip of Ogden Avenue. "Why not make a try at a business again? What could you lose?" Mrs. Bernstein wanted to know.

The Berlands followed her advice. In 1936, they opened a small paint store. To everyone's surprise, it prospered. "If there ever was a touch of gold that rained upon people, it was that particular item," Berns recalled. By 1936, the Depression had eased and people who had put off renovations for years were ready to spruce things up. All the formerly out-of-work painters and contractors made a beeline to P. G. Berland Paints. Mrs. Berland "started increasing the number of rings on her fingers," Berns recalled. "Nobody could touch the cash register but her, see?"[55]

She also became even more indulgent of her son. Al was always a bit lazy and eager to cut corners, a bit antisocial. Even in grade school he formed a separate little group, the "Berland Gang," of which Favil was a member. The boys were apolitical, but it would be inaccurate to say that they grew up without an ideology. They believed in the "American way." They understood this "way" in its simplest terms: to succeed, one had to "make a buck" and "beat the system."[56] They had no thought that hard work and integrity would be rewarded. Instead, they assumed that the system was stacked against them. This was a reasonable assumption. Chicago's West Side was notoriously corrupt and had been so for generations. Small businessmen were prey to extortion from politicians as well as from criminals. "America isn't so different from Russia," one West Side merchant explained in the 1920s. "Of course we haven't any pogroms, but we have *rishes* [prejudice] just the same, and we have to buy our right to make a living from the grafters and the politicians, instead of the Tsar and the bureaucrats." As sociologist Louis Wirth observed in his 1928 study *The Ghetto*, many West Side Jews "take it more or less for granted that they do not possess equal rights before the law. They feel that they must rely to a large extent upon political pull and fixers to obtain 'favors' and achieve their ends."[57]

For favors, one turned to those one trusted: to friends and to family. There was no reason to study and sacrifice. If you knew the right people, you could fall into a profitable business without even trying.

That was how Al Berland and his childhood friend Lou Wolf made their fortune. After one semester at the University of Illinois, Al went to work at his father's paint store. Meanwhile, Lou drifted from job to job. He sold used cars. He ran a tavern. He worked as a theatrical booking agent.[58] Then Wolf found a new profession: real estate. His brother-in-law Joseph Berke had already opened a real estate office in Lawndale, and now he introduced Wolf to the inviting prospects of low prices in "changing" neighborhoods. Following Berke's advice, Wolf set out to acquire some properties. He would buy a building, immediately mortgage it, and use the loan to buy another.[59] He offered his growing list of Lawndale properties to eager black customers on contract. His customers paid little money down, but Wolf kept the deed to the property and had the right to repossess with one missed payment. He often exercised this right, which meant that he could sell the same building over and over.[60]

Wolf shared his new knowledge with Al Berland, who had lots of his own contacts with real estate people through his father's paint store; P. G. Berland was where all the real estate guys on Roosevelt Road purchased their supplies. It was in the paint store that Berland met a Greek American named Lou Fushanis, with whom he and Wolf would soon co-own numerous properties.[61] Fushanis had been a used car salesman, a tavern owner, and a restaurant owner. In the early 1950s, he turned his attention to real estate, opening the Friendly Loan Corporation, and soon he, too, was buying up properties in Lawndale.[62]

Perhaps it was through Fushanis that Berland and Wolf met another important local entrepreneur, Moe Forman. A Russian Jewish immigrant who had come to the United States with his parents in 1929, at the age of twelve, Forman exemplified the American success story. He started out with nothing. He went to public schools, the Central YMCA College, and then John Marshall Law School. He married a local girl, Mildred Greenfield, whose father owned a real estate company. Then he opened his own office, Lidsker and Forman Realty Company, at 3803 Roosevelt Road. In the early 1950s, Forman began working closely with Lou Fushanis. The two set up a company, F & F Investment. Forman was Fushanis's attorney, his financier, his accountant and record keeper, and secretly the co-owner of many of Fushanis's buildings. Forman performed the same multiple roles for Al Berland, for Berland's friend Lou Wolf, and for Wolf's brother-in-law Joe Berke.[63]

Forman's access to financing and his thorough knowledge of real estate law made him indispensable to the men he worked with. "Anyone I am handling, he can't do without me. I have all the records and all the papers. . . . All he has to do is double-cross me once and he's thru," Forman bragged.[64] As a *Chicago Tribune* exposé written twenty years later would explain, "If there has been a Mr. Big in Chicago's West Side slum operation, it has been Moe Forman." According to the *Tribune*, "Forman apparently used his intimate knowledge of Lawndale and its financial institutions to help build the biggest individual slum empire in the city's history." He was the "nucleus of a small group of men who, working together, exploited the West Side."[65] By 1973, this small group of men—Berland, Wolf, Berke, Forman, and a young protégé, Gil Balin—controlled up to two thousand buildings in Lawndale.[66] The area was riddled with abandoned buildings, and Moe Forman, the immigrant boy, had become a millionaire.[67]

Forman and his circle were hardly the only group of friends and relatives who used "intimate knowledge" of their neighborhood to loot their neighbors and enrich themselves. From the late 1940s on, scores of such groups were at work in "changing" neighborhoods on Chicago's South and West sides. Within Lawndale, Forman's group faced stiff competition from several other combines. For example, a Greek American named John Karras opened his office, Community Realty, just up the road from Fushanis's Friendly Loan Corporation.[68] Karras specialized in areas of racial transition. Another group, the Peters Brothers, was run by Chicago Real Estate Board member Warren J. Peters, who, with his mother, Sylvia, and brother, Charles, controlled about sixty buildings.[69] Also big players were attorneys Jay Goran and Gerald Crane, who together controlled hundreds of buildings on the city's South Side.

"Amateurs," too, got involved—lawyers especially, but also doctors, dentists, merchants, and other members of Chicago's professional classes. As Berns recalled, "When they found how easy it was to make a buck . . . everybody got on the bandwagon." You had to watch yourself, he cautioned, because you never knew which lawyers were "involved in this game."[70]

Favil Berns had fond memories of the Berland gang, but he took a different path. After high school, he studied engineering and then went to John Marshall Law School. He got his license to practice in 1952. Just as he was starting out he was drafted, but with the help of an uncle who knew the arcane rules governing the draft, Berns got an honorable discharge.

In 1954, he was a young attorney with little experience, no office, and no clients. When answering the ads brought him no job offers, Berns stopped in at 134 North LaSalle, where scores of attorneys had their offices. That was how he came to meet my father. The building manager told Berns that there was a lawyer who needed someone to help him out. His name was Mark J. Satter, and he was on the fourth floor.[71]

Berns's work with my father was eclectic. They handled everything from labor law to criminal cases to real estate disputes. Perhaps their most notorious case was that of a "spinster" who embezzled almost half a million dollars from the bank where she'd worked for thirty-three years. (She gave the money to hard-pressed customers and kept nothing for herself. My father got her off with two years' probation.) There was an intellectual excitement in their small office, and Berns was grateful to my father for giving him an opportunity to be part of it.[72] He didn't yet realize that his new boss and his old friends were on a collision course.

TWO

THE NOOSE AROUND
BLACK CHICAGO

The cause of that collision could be witnessed at the Illinois Central train station, a short walk from my father's office. Every day African American migrants, mostly from Mississippi, poured out of that station. Between 1940 and 1960, Chicago's black population skyrocketed, from 277,731 to 812,637. Most newcomers to Chicago could find accommodations only in the two neighborhoods that were open to African Americans. Many went to the South Side's Black Belt, a neighborhood that was bursting at the seams. Apartments there were frequently divided into smaller units with makeshift kitchens. "Kitchenette" apartments often lacked electricity, forcing residents to rely upon kerosene lamps, and one bathroom per floor sometimes had to accommodate as many as nine families. These were the conditions *before* the Second Great Migration, as the post-1940 northern movement of Southern blacks has been called. With the arrival of hundreds of thousands of migrants, conditions became considerably worse. The other area was a small section of the West Side's former "Jew Town"—a neighborhood located a few miles east of Lawndale, where some of the city's poorest Italians, Mexicans, and Jews still lived and where the housing stock was even more decayed than that typically found in the Black Belt.[1]

Through most of the 1940s the city as a whole suffered a severe housing shortage. No new residences had been constructed there since the onset of the Great Depression in 1929. Workers of all races who migrated to Chicago to take jobs in wartime industries had to compete for extremely limited housing. When World War II ended and hundreds of thousands of veterans returned home, the city faced what one contemporary described as the "most critical housing shortage since the Chicago fire."[2]

For white Chicagoans, the crisis began to ease in the late 1940s as new suburban properties were constructed. For black Chicagoans, the situation was quite different. The new suburbs generally excluded them; similarly, within the city limits most African Americans who sought to rent or buy outside of the Black Belt or Near West Side were curtly informed by white real estate agents that the apartment or building they had inquired about was no longer available. In short, while white "ethnics" like my parents were free to live anywhere in the city that their income allowed, most black Chicagoans of all income levels were confined by an interlocking set of forces to the most overcrowded and run-down sections of the city.[3]

In the late 1940s and early 1950s, however, the city's hardened racial status quo began to crack. The pressure produced by a combination of intense overcrowding in black neighborhoods, rising black incomes fueled by Chicago's thriving wartime and postwar economy, and the existence of vacancies in adjoining white neighborhoods destabilized the city's racial boundaries and created the phenomena of racially "changing" communities.[4]

Sallie and Albert Bolton's trajectory was probably typical. Both had been raised in Chicago. In 1939 they married and moved to a small kitchenette in the Black Belt. The following year they managed to get a four-room cold-water apartment. It was located over a furniture repair shop. Every summer it was permeated with the sickening smells of wood-stripping fluids. In 1955 they were still living in that apartment, now with four children, two of them teenagers. Their children were bright and hardworking, but the local schools were among the city's worst. If the Boltons could get out of the neighborhood, their children would have a chance.[5]

Then in the fall of 1955, the Boltons found a way out. A white real estate agent named Jay Goran had a house available for purchase. It was in Hyde Park, a liberal-minded, predominantly white South Side neighborhood located east of the Black Belt that was home to the University of Chicago. The local schools were excellent. The price was high ($13,900, "on contract") and the terms were steep ($750 down and $110 a month). What finally convinced the Boltons to buy was Goran's reassuring approach. When they said that the house seemed too small, they were promptly reassured that when they were ready to move again, Goran's office would credit them for all the money they'd invested into the property. "All the money that you pay in on this home can be applied to any other house you like. . . . It is just like putting money in the bank," they were told. That sounded good to the Boltons—how could they lose? They said that they would consult an attorney and return to finalize the details.

For some reason their mention of consulting an attorney seemed to anger Goran. Without deigning to look at the Boltons, he leaped from his chair and said to an assistant, "Well, they do not want to buy the house. Let them go! We'll get someone else!" It was quickly explained that "Mr. Goran is an attorney, you do not need a lawyer." He had all the papers they needed right there at the office. Albert turned to his wife. "Do you think we can handle it?" "We're both working. I think we can make it," Sallie whispered back. They signed. Within two weeks they had settled into their Hyde Park home.[6]

The story of how the Boltons escaped the Black Belt was repeated a thousandfold since, by the late 1950s, 85 percent of the buildings that black Chicagoans purchased outside of the Black Belt and Near West Side were sold in a similar manner.[7] Also typical was the way in which the family's deal went sour. After the Boltons signed their installment contract papers, Goran added extra charges to their monthly payment. When they called to ask about the fees, he refused to speak to them. Then they were deluged with housing code inspectors. First they were ordered to take down the wooden shutters. Then the front porch had to be rebuilt. Next it was the back porch. Then a fire broke out in the basement; the men must have spilled some oil when they refilled the battered old furnace. If Sallie and Albert hadn't noticed the smoke right away, the house could have gone up in flames. Sallie began to feel that things were going wrong a bit too often. "What did other people do when *they* lived in this house?" she asked Albert.[8]

Soon the expenses became too much and the Boltons fell behind on a payment. Goran's response was immediate. He filed an action of forcible detainer against them. "Action of forcible detainer" was a complex phrase to cover a simple process: they were being evicted. They would lose close to $3,000 in down payment, fees, and improvements that they had invested in the house. Future buyers were already showing up at their door.[9]

Sallie can't quite recall how it happened, but the couple ended up consulting a pair of white attorneys, Mark J. Satter and Favil D. Berns. Satter and Berns agreed to look into the matter. Evictions were straightforward affairs that did not require a great deal of legal expertise.

But as the Boltons and their attorneys would soon realize, their case was not fundamentally about eviction; it was about residential segregation, which was anything but simple. Chicago had pioneered methods of black containment that would be copied nationally and that turned it, not coincidentally, into the nation's most segregated city by 1957.[10] The Boltons were in for a battle that would be far more difficult than they ever imagined.

Chicago had not always been a segregated city. Black Chicagoans traditionally lived on the city's South Side, with much smaller numbers scattered through parts of the West Side. Yet in the early years of the twentieth century much of the "black" South Side was actually racially mixed; only about a dozen blocks were exclusively inhabited by African Americans. As late as 1910, Chicago's African Americans were less set apart from native-born whites than Italian immigrants were.[11]

This situation changed dramatically during the 1910s and 1920s, when tens of thousands of Southern blacks migrated to Chicago—among them Sallie's and Albert's parents. This First Great Migration unsettled Chicago's relatively open racial system and led to the creation of the city's black ghetto. As the number of blacks in Chicago more than doubled, crowding forced them over invisible racial boundaries into adjoining white neighborhoods, where they were met with threats and violence. A 1919 study on race relations in Chicago noted that "a kind of guerilla warfare" was raging at the boundaries of black neighborhoods. Between July 1917 and March 1921, there were fifty-eight recorded bombings of properties rented or purchased by blacks in white Chicago neighborhoods.[12]

White Chicagoans also used nonviolent methods to contain African

Americans. They formed "neighborhood improvement associations" to pressure white owners and realtors into refusing to rent or sell to blacks.[13] Most of these associations were organized by the Chicago Real Estate Board (CREB), the professional association of white Chicago realtors. At a fateful meeting in 1917, the board formulated its response to the "invasion of white residence districts by the Negroes." Rather than allowing blacks to purchase property wherever they wished, CREB decided to confine such sales to blocks immediately adjoining neighborhoods that already contained black residents. No new areas would be opened until these blocks became entirely "black." "Inasmuch as more territory must be provided, it is desired . . . that each block shall be filled solidly and that further expansion shall be confined to contiguous blocks," the board declared.[14]

CREB attempted to enshrine this policy in a city ordinance, but a 1917 Supreme Court ruling thwarted its plan by outlawing racial zoning laws. CREB then decided to organize "voluntary" block clubs in white neighborhoods. The goal of these clubs was to ensure that no homes were sold to blacks except in the "contiguous blocks" identified by CREB. "Resolved, that this board . . . recommend owners societies in every white block for the purpose of mutual defense," CREB decreed in November 1917. In 1924, the National Association of Real Estate Boards adopted CREB's code of refusing to sell to blacks outside of specific areas. Real estate boards across the nation recognized CREB's pioneering work in maintaining all-white communities and looked to CREB for advice as they crafted their own racially restrictive plans. Chicago's realtors were thus instrumental in the creation of a dual housing market both locally and nationally—that is, a "white" market of low prices and expansive neighborhood choices and a "black" market of high prices and extremely limited options.[15]

Whites also adopted restrictive covenants to confine black Chicagoans to small sections of the city. These legally binding documents limited the ways that a property could be used or disposed of. Most restrictive covenants prevented the sale of property to blacks, although some targeted Jews and Asians as well.[16] A typical covenant read, "At no time shall said premises . . . be sold, occupied, let or leased . . . to anyone of any race other than the Caucasian, except that this covenant shall not prevent occupancy by domestic servants of a different race domiciled with an owner or tenant."[17] Restrictive covenants were introduced in the 1920s. By the 1940s, Chicago led the nation in their use. Racial deed restrictions covered approximately half of the city's residential neighborhoods.[18] Together, the bombings, "neighborhood improvement associations," realtors' sales policies, and restrictive covenants helped create Chicago's first all-black ghetto on the city's South Side. As historian Allan H. Spear explains, the ghettoization of Chicago's blacks "was not the result chiefly of poverty; nor did Negroes cluster out of choice. The ghetto was primarily the product of white hostility."[19]

The Second Great Migration intensified the overcrowding long characteristic of the Black Belt. It also coincided with the solidification of federal policies that exacerbated racially motivated segregation—particularly the biased appraisal policies of the Federal Housing Administration (FHA) that shaped the nation's banking and savings and loan industries. The very federal housing programs that would enable Chicago's white ethnics, along with millions of other white Americans, to purchase new homes in the suburbs worked to fortify the black ghetto in Chicago and in cities across the nation.

Created by Congress in 1934, the FHA offered insurance for the mortgages that banks and savings and loan institutions granted to home purchasers. It thereby helped inaugurate a new era of cheap and easy credit. Because banks faced so little risk with an FHA-insured loan, their interest rates on mortgage loans dropped from 6 to 8 percent to 4 percent. They made mortgage loans that covered 90 percent of a building's sale price, rather than the previously typical 50 to 70 percent. As a result, from 1939 onward it was often cheaper to buy a new home than to rent. At a time when city rents were approximately $50 a month, one could purchase a new $5,000 home in the suburbs for a down payment of $550 and mortgage payments of $29.61 a month.[20]

Unfortunately, this option was not open to couples like Albert and Sallie Bolton. This was because the FHA uncritically incorporated racist ideas then current in the home appraisal industry. In the 1930s, the U.S. appraisal industry opposed the "mixing" of the races, which it believed would cause "the decline of both the human race and of property values." Appraisers ensured segregation through their property rating system. They ranked properties, blocks, and even whole neighborhoods according to a descending scheme of A (green), B (blue), C (yellow), and D (red). A ratings went to properties located in "homogenous" areas—ones that (in one appraiser's words) lacked even "a single foreigner or Negro." Properties located in neighborhoods containing Jewish residents were riskier; they were marked down to a B or C. If a neighborhood had black residents it was marked as D, or red, no matter what their social class or how small a percentage of the population they made up. These neighborhoods' properties were appraised as worthless or likely to decline in value. In short, D areas were "redlined," or marked as locations in which no loans should be made for either purchasing or upgrading properties.[21]

The FHA embraced these biases. It collected detailed maps of the present and likely future location of African Americans, and used them to determine which neighborhoods would be denied mortgage insurance.[22] Since banks and savings and loan institutions often relied upon FHA rating maps when deciding where to grant their mortgages, the FHA's appraisal policies meant that blacks were excluded by definition from most mortgage loans. The FHA's *Underwriting Manual* also praised restrictive covenants as "the surest protection against undesirable encroachment" of "inharmonious racial groups."[23] The FHA did not simply recommend the use of restrictive covenants but often insisted upon them as a condition for granting mortgage insurance. While the FHA generally refused to insure mortgages of blacks moving to white neighborhoods, it was sometimes willing to insure loans in all-black areas. There was a catch, however; it would grant insurance only when the surrounding neighborhood was not "blighted," that is, overcrowded or containing aging properties. Since black enclaves were often marked by just such conditions, most were excluded from FHA insurance. Through its appraisal system, its enthusiasm for racial covenants, and its refusal to insure mortgages for blacks moving to white neighborhoods, the FHA effectively standardized and nationalized the hostile but locally variable racial biases of the private housing industry.[24]

Black activists were quick to challenge these discriminatory policies.[25] Typical was the attack by black Chicago attorney and NAACP member William Robert Ming Jr. "Most if not all banks, insurance companies, and other lending institutions are unwilling to loan money for the purchase . . . of housing for Negro . . . . occupancy in areas not now occupied by Negroes," Ming wrote in a 1949 essay. "Even the Federal Housing Administration's practices in approving loans which it will underwrite manifest the same attitude." Although these loan and insurance refusals were based on the "widely held notion that Negro occupancy reduces the value of property," he pointed out that "no evidence exists" to support this claim. The solution was achingly simple: "Application to both Negroes and whites of the same rules as to personal credit standing as a prerequisite to making loans would appear to solve much of the concern over comparative risks."[26]

This logic was never followed. Although a 1948 Supreme Court ruling, *Shelley v. Kraemer*, rendered racially restrictive covenants legally unenforceable, FHA commissioner Franklin D. Richards insisted that *Shelley* would "in no way affect the programs of this agency."[27] If the FHA was resistant to change, private industry was even more so. In 1948, black banker Robert R. Taylor told the national convention of the U.S. Savings and Loan League that he had lent millions of dollars to black home buyers in Chicago without a single foreclosure. The league nevertheless declined to change its policies, and the question of lending to black home buyers was not addressed at the convention again until the 1960s. In 1954, FHA official George W. Snowden told the Mortgage Bankers Association that since black home purchasers had an excellent credit record, it would be logical for mortgage bankers to use a "uniform, single-standard lending policy" for blacks and whites. The association's trade journal, *Mortgage Banker*, derided Snowden's comments as "one of the most remarkable statements ever heard from an MBA rostrum." In short, on the rare occasions that private bankers and savings and loan officials were presented with evidence of black creditworthiness, they rejected the information.[28]

One way for blacks to evade the racism of the mortgage industry might have been to set up their own mortgage companies, but that path was extraordinarily difficult. The Mortgage Bankers Association was an all-white organization; African Americans were barred from both the national organization and its local subsidiaries. Since mortgage banker training courses were open only to members of the MBA, blacks were excluded from these courses as well.[29]

The experiences of Dempsey J. Travis, a black real estate agent who tried to set up his own mortgage company, give a concrete sense of those barriers. When Travis got his real estate license in 1949, there was an immediate demand for his services among black families eager to leave the Black Belt. There was one major problem: he couldn't find mortgages

for his customers. Travis saw that speculators who were buying properties from whites and reselling them to blacks on contract at 100 to 300
percent markups easily obtained mortgages from the same financial
institutions that rejected him. He also saw that he could get all the business he wanted—if he was willing to work for white speculators. "I starved
the first nine months I was in the real estate business," Travis recalled,
"because I refused to become a 'bird dog' for white speculators . . . who
were plundering the black housing market with land contracts." He was not
opposed to contract sales per se, just to their abuse. "The land contract is
intrinsically a good document," he observed. "It was white speculators'
exploitive use of the instrument which gave it a slaveship stench."[30]

To survive in the real estate business, Travis had to find his own mortgage sources. It was a challenge. The city's two black-owned savings and
loan institutions were overwhelmed by the demand. Travis decided that
the way around this "mortgage bottleneck" was to create his own, black-
controlled mortgage corporation. In 1953, he formed the Sivart (Travis
spelled backward) Mortgage Corporation. He hoped that it could tap the
"billions in black savings" now held in white banks, savings and loans,
and pension and insurance institutions, thereby giving blacks access to
"the community's own wealth." His first step was to apply to be a loan correspondent for the FHA—that is, he asked the FHA to accredit Sivart so
that the company could make FHA-insured loans in the Chicago area. His
application was turned down that year and every subsequent year for the
rest of the decade. Sivart went nowhere because, as Travis recalled, "the
Federal Housing Administration would not approve an application for a
black mortgage banking company" in the 1950s.[31]

Travis persevered. He ran for president of the Dearborn Real Estate
Board, an organization of black real estate brokers that was formed
because the Chicago Real Estate Board excluded African Americans. The
group had a reputation for being polite, even staid, but under Travis's
presidency it took an activist turn.[32] First, it undertook a detailed survey
of the racial record of Chicago's lending institutions. Travis drew upon the
results when he testified before the United States Commission on Civil
Rights about racial discrimination in the mortgage loan industry. In 1959,
he told the commission that out of 243 savings and loan institutions in
Cook County (only two of which were black-owned), only twenty-one
were willing to make loans to blacks wishing to purchase homes within

black neighborhoods. Blacks hoping to move to white areas faced even more daunting obstacles. Out of the 241 white-operated savings and loans in Cook County, only *one* was willing to grant a mortgage loan to a black family moving to a white neighborhood.[33] These "institutional barricades" were "directly responsible" for the thousands of blacks "who are exploited annually by unscrupulous speculators," he pointed out. He also proposed remedies. He called for new laws that would prohibit discrimination by any mortgage lender whose loan was guaranteed by the FHA. He urged the creation, by presidential executive order, of an agency that would make direct mortgages to low-income families displaced by urban renewal.[34]

Travis knew that such demands were publicity exercises. Despite his extraordinary optimism, energy, and perseverance, by the late 1950s he had made no perceivable dent in the wall that blocked black Chicagoans' access to credit and to fairly priced housing. It was a "sour time," he recalled.[35]

Biased FHA policies further inflamed white resistance to black neighbors. In the FHA's view, the presence of a single black family was reason enough to refuse to insure mortgage or home improvement loans to an entire block. The redlining of a block could spell its doom, since property owners there could neither obtain loans to improve their homes nor sell them to the typical buyer who used a mortgage to purchase property. Whites now had a motive to keep blacks out that went well beyond amorphous anxieties about the "decline of the human race"—racist fears that could potentially be countered by knowledge and goodwill. Instead, since the presence of a single black family usually led to mortgage redlining, whites had a powerful *economic* incentive to keep such families out.

Perhaps it is not surprising, then, that the late 1940s saw an upsurge of violence against the black families who moved into white neighborhoods. While the first black home buyers in Jewish sections of Lawndale generally remained unmolested, those who moved to white South Side areas were not so lucky. Many were subject to arson, vandalism, and shotgun blasts—vigilante attacks that sometimes escalated into full-scale white riots.[36] In July 1946, a black physician purchased a home in Park Manor, a white South Side neighborhood. In response, a mob of two to three thousand whites set fire to his garage and stoned his building. In December, the families of two black war veterans—John Fort, who had earned four battle stars and fought in the Battle of the Bulge, and Letholian Waddles, who had served in the Philippines—attempted to move into the Airport Homes, a temporary veterans' housing project located in another white South Side area. Chicago Housing Authority officials had hoped that a small percentage of these apartments could be rented to black residents without much controversy. After all, the housing was temporary, for war veterans only, and offered only to tenants who had been rigorously screened. Instead, Fort and Waddles were met by a mob of three thousand whites, who stoned their moving van, burned a cross outside their building, and battled the police who tried to disperse them.[37]

This was only the beginning. As one liberal white Chicago priest recalled, "About 1947 . . . we began to dread the long summer evenings."[38] That August, five thousand whites rioted for three nights in a row after a small number of black veterans attempted to move into the Fernwood Park Homes, another temporary South Side housing project constructed for veterans. At least thirty-five blacks were assaulted by white gangs, and approximately a hundred automobiles driven by blacks were attacked. It took over a thousand police to calm the area.[39] In 1949, two thousand whites attacked a two-flat building that had been purchased by Roscoe and Ethel Johnson, a black couple, in Park Manor, also on the South Side.[40] The harassment of the Johnsons and other black pioneer families in Park Manor continued through 1950.[41]

Violence broke out again in the summer of 1951, when five thousand whites spent days looting and tossing Molotov cocktails at a building in suburban Cicero—just west of Lawndale—where a single unit had been rented to a black family. Nineteen people were injured in that riot, which was quelled only when the state governor summoned the Illinois National Guard.[42] The "Cicero uprising" was followed by "Trumbull Park," the blanket term for the years of white harassment of blacks who moved to the previously all-white Trumbull Park housing project on the South Side. In response to the arrival of one black couple in 1953, two thousand local whites mobbed their building. In 1954, hundreds of whites gathered to stone the police convoy that moved a few more black families into the project. CHA officials noted that "bombings are a nightly occurrence" and that they "have increased in number and power." Low-level harassment by whites that sporadically spiked into pitched antiblack battles continued in Trumbull Park throughout the 1950s.[43]

These ongoing white attacks on black home buyers might have been one reason the Boltons took the deal offered to them by Jay Goran, despite the steep price. White Hyde Parkers, after all, were unlikely to greet the Boltons with violence. What the Boltons did not realize was that their move placed them directly in the path of plans made by two of the city's most powerful entities—the Metropolitan Housing and Planning Council (MHPC) and the University of Chicago—to minimize the black presence in Hyde Park.

The MHPC, a "quasi-official" body founded in 1934 to improve the city's housing, was that ambiguous creature—an *elite* reform organization. Its policy was set by its board of governors, which, as realtor and council member John W. Baird described, largely consisted of "the major mortgage bankers, realtors, commercial bankers, industrial and retail leaders of the region."[44] These power brokers hoped to look after their own interests as well as those of the city.

In the early 1940s, the MHPC began studying a problem that concerned many of the prominent businessmen on its board—the fact that Chicago's downtown Loop shopping district was surrounded on its west and south sides by dilapidated housing. These slums created a physical barrier between Loop businesses and their middle-class customers. Slum dwellers not only did not patronize these upscale department stores but scared off those who did.

In 1947, the MHPC proposed a solution. Its members drafted and steered into law the Illinois Blighted Areas Redevelopment Act, which pioneered what would soon be called "urban renewal." The act created a new public agency, the Land Clearance Commission, empowered to acquire land in "blighted" areas, demolish existing structures, and then sell the land—at a huge discount—to private investors who promised to build new, more profitable structures on the site. Theoretically, this extraordinarily generous "one-time subsidy" would eventually be offset through taxes on the revenues produced by the new structures.[45]

The scheme's generosity to private business interests was vividly on display in the first redevelopment project completed under the new law.

In 1948, the Land Clearance Commission used its power of eminent domain to condemn a long-established black community that bordered the southern edge of downtown. The neighborhood was slated for demolition in part because developers wanted land with a prized lakefront view. Black homeowners made the rational point to Chicago's City Council that the urban renewal plan "ignores actual slum areas completely and plans the demolition of a well-kept Negro area where the bulk of property is resident owned, its taxes paid, and its maintenance above par." Their warning did no good: the area was razed. Where a black neighborhood once stood, private developers constructed "Lake Meadows," a middle-class housing complex whose units rented at prices entirely out of reach of the area's former residents. The cost of purchasing and "clearing" the land was $16 million. Of that, $12.6 million was paid for by the commission—a munificent gift from the state to Lake Meadow's developers.[46]

Although the Blighted Areas Redevelopment Act was designed by businessmen in order to subsidize private development, its supporters justified this state largesse in moral terms. They insisted that the razing of older communities would improve the lot of slum dwellers by forcing them to leave the slums.[47] Yet the bill made only the stingiest provisions for residents of areas targeted for demolition. The Illinois Relocation Act, passed as a companion measure to the Redevelopment Act, allocated money to build public housing for just 15 percent of those displaced by urban renewal. Based on statistics about available housing in the Chicago area, the legislature argued, the remainder of the displaced would find housing without aid from the state.[48]

This was at the very least disingenuous, given the city's dual housing market. As John H. Sengstacke, publisher of the *Chicago Defender*, put it, basing relocation funding on the vacancy rate of the whole city "suggests pure hypocrisy. The city's vacancy rate is totally unrelated to the availability of housing for Negroes."[49] Statistics about available housing were meaningless if those displaced were black—which many were.[50]

Even the public housing allocation was disingenuous. The Relocation Act gave the City Council veto power over all public housing sites, which meant that white Chicagoans were legally able to keep public housing that was open to black residents out of their communities.[51] As Chicago Housing Authority commissioner Robert R. Taylor noted, this veto power was explicitly intended to "prevent the influx of Negroes into white neighborhoods." Taylor also accurately predicted that this stipulation spelled "the end of public housing sites in good residential areas."[52] From the late 1940s on, public housing was constructed exclusively in black areas that were already densely overcrowded. This led to Alice in Wonderland convolutions: to build public housing for those displaced by urban renewal, the CHA first had to clear land in the Black Belt, but by clearing this land it displaced yet more black people, who were left to seek housing in a city where the vast majority of neighborhoods were closed to them.[53]

Perhaps even more troubling was the fact that the Blighted Areas Redevelopment Act set the pattern for federal urban renewal legislation. President Harry Truman's Housing Act of 1949 incorporated many of its key features. Title I allocated federal money to cities to enable them to purchase, raze, and resell slum land to private developers at greatly discounted prices. To get this federal money, cities needed only to assure the federal government that the slum clearance was part of a broader plan for the area, that the new, privately funded project would be constructed within a "reasonable time," and that the developer would find "decent, safe and sanitary" housing for the displaced. Title III authorized the building of more public housing, but the allocations were so inadequate that most displaced people were left on the streets.[54] What's more, since the act allowed the location of federally funded public housing to be determined by local authorities, whites nationwide were given the power to exclude such housing from their communities. As a result, Title III public housing, as in Illinois, was constructed in densely overcrowded black neighborhoods, where desperately needed existing residences were destroyed to make room for public housing units.[55]

Once the Housing Act made federal funds available for urban renewal and public housing, cities across the nation began petitioning for the money. Chicago was among the first in line, seeking Title I aid for the acquisition and clearing of land for the Lake Meadows project and Title III funds to build public housing for those displaced. The federal official overseeing Chicago's request noted that most of those displaced by Lake Meadows were black and that the sites chosen for public housing ignored vacant land near white areas in favor of sites located in overcrowded black neighborhoods. The Chicago proposal "not only displaces Negro families to a degree smacking of 'Negro Clearance,' but at the same time buttresses up existing patterns of segregation," he noted. Robert C. Weaver, then chairman of the National Committee against Discrimination in Housing, also railed against the Chicago proposal. Chicago stood as a "laboratory" from which standards of either integration or segregation would "spread" to the nation as a whole: "Should this [plan] be permitted, federal sanction would be given to a policy of minority containment."[56] The Chicago plan was approved. Weaver's concern proved prescient. By the early 1950s, the NAACP reported examples of the misuse of Title I and Title III programs to displace blacks and increase segregation in cities across the nation.[57]

It was a second wave of urban renewal legislation, designed by University of Chicago and MHPC leaders, that directly threatened the Boltons. When the land for the Lake Meadows complex was cleared in the late 1940s, many inhabitants of the destroyed black area moved farther south to Hyde Park, where the University of Chicago was located. University leaders feared that the school might lose its student base if Hyde Park became black. Yet the university could hardly sell its physical plant, in which it had invested approximately $200 million, and move elsewhere; there was no market for secondhand universities.[58]

Instead, the school decided to contain the local black population. University chancellor Lawrence A. Kimpton and his legal counsel, Julian Levi, worked on legislation that would extend and refine the public land clearance powers created by the Illinois Redevelopment Act and the federal Housing Act. Enlisting MHPC support was easy enough, since over one-third of the MHPC's Board of Governors had Hyde Park or University of Chicago connections. After working closely with the university, the MHPC proposed legislation that would empower the state to raze sections of neighborhoods that were not yet "blighted" but appeared in danger of becoming so. Those sections were usually areas of black residency; privately, Levi and Kimpton admitted as much.[59]

Levi and Kimpton called their new approach "conservation" since it would preserve urban neighborhoods by targeting "pockets of decay." But in fact, their proposition was even more radical than the original Illinois redevelopment legislation, since it justified the demolition of buildings for reasons other than physical deterioration. The city now could "eliminate *standard* as well as substandard structures in those cases where their *location* or condition was inimical" to general neighborhood improvement or conservation.[60]

The MHPC's proposal formed the heart of Illinois's Urban Community Conservation Act of 1953, which made the prevention of "blight" a "public purpose" and therefore a legitimate justification for city governments to invoke the power of eminent domain.[61] It was quickly followed by the federal Housing Act of 1954. Described by one historian as among "the most significant pieces of federal legislation ever passed that affected U.S. cities," the act offered localities federal funding for rehabilitating older structures and "conserving" areas that seemed threatened by decay.[62]

The strong resemblance between the state and federal legislation was not accidental. As historian Arnold Hirsch has shown, MHPC and University of Chicago leaders realized that local sources could not provide enough funding for their urban renewal goals; federal funds were needed. They therefore assisted in drafting the Housing Act of 1954, which was, in effect, "the Illinois Urban Community Conservation Act writ large." And this time too—just as in 1949—Chicago "was well prepared to meet the legal requirements for aid and was first in line for the federal largesse."[63]

The most stringent legal requirement was the passage of a new housing code. After a year of behind-the-scenes labor by the MHPC, Chicago's was passed in 1956.[64] It required Chicago properties to have such basics as running water. It set new space-per-occupant stipulations in an effort to stop overcrowding. It outlawed crash panels—partitions containing glass panels, which had been widely used during the postwar housing crunch to divide large apartments into two smaller ones. The penalty for thwarting the new code was set at $200 a day.[65]

The code's supporters claimed that it would force slum landlords to upgrade their buildings. Unfortunately, in Chicago's closed housing market, the code also threatened to intensify the viselike pressure on the Black Belt, where the vast majority of "cut-up" apartments were located. As a Chicago building department official admitted in 1958, "We don't try to enforce the overcrowding provisions in the housing code too strongly in Negro Neighborhoods. After all, where would the people go? We'd have to put at least 75,000 out on the streets."[66] The code also increased housing pressure on black Chicagoans for another reason—its expedition of urban renewal. Despite its humanitarian trappings, the housing code's true purpose was to get federal urban renewal dollars for Chicago. And in Chicago, more money for urban renewal usually meant further demoli-tion of black neighborhoods.

The first Chicago community to petition for and receive federal con-servation funds was Hyde Park. By 1958, the conservation of Hyde Park was well under way. Most of the homes that were destroyed were located in its southwest section, which had the heaviest concentration of black residents. Although 2,100 new homes were constructed, the conservation plan left the area with almost 4,000 fewer housing units. The cost of Hyde Park's "renewal" was $50 million, and it was largely paid for with state and federal funds. As one Chicago alderman noted at the time, the Illinois Urban Community Conservation Act "look[ed] like a U[niversity] of C[hicago] bail-out."[67]

For Sallie and Albert Bolton, the new urban renewal and conservation laws meant that when they moved to Hyde Park in the fall of 1955 they were met not by a mob of angry whites but by a swarm of housing code inspec-tors. While the two "welcoming committees" surely felt very different, the results for the Boltons were the same. They were driven from their home because the cost of remaining there was suddenly made too high. Instead of aiding those who most needed housing, state and federal legislation tightened the noose around black Chicago.

The Boltons and other black residents might have expected some support from Chicago's black political establishment. By the late 1950s, however, Chicago's black politicians had been effectively neutralized, aware that whatever power they had was contingent upon the Democratic machine that ran the city.

Chicago was composed of fifty wards, each of which elected an alder-man to the City Council and a committeeman to the Democratic Central Committee of Cook County, where Chicago is located. Ward committee-men distributed a hefty share of the approximately 30,000 patronage jobs that were controlled by the Central Committee—jobs ranging from street sweepers to assistant corporate counsel. They allocated these jobs in ways that solidified the party's hold within the ward. Often they left the distribution of jobs to aldermen, who handed them down to precinct captains, who in turn were expected to deliver their precinct on Election Day. The best way to deliver a precinct was by meeting the practical needs of those living there. As political scientist Milton Rakove observed, the ward structure forced "every individual in the organization to think locally, to concern himself almost exclusively with his bit of turf." As he explained, the machine in Chicago was not really "one citywide organization, but, rather, a composite of approximately 3,148 local precinct organizations, each under the control of an individual responsible for his organization. There is no room in such a system for ideology, philosophy, or broad social concerns."[68]

What was true of the Chicago machine—that structurally it was pragmatic and antithetical to social concerns—was equally true of the black submachine that developed within it. William L. Dawson, leader of this submachine, served as a ward committeeman and a U.S. congressman from 1942 until his death in 1970. Like most black politicians in Chicago, Dawson spurned "status" issues such as the fight against discriminatory housing practices that kept well-to-do blacks out of white areas; he preferred to "gild the ghetto rather than break it up." According to Rakove, the power held by Dawson and other black machine Democrats was predicated upon the existence of a segregated black community. The geographical concentration of black voters ensured black politicians' "own tenures of office, indebt[ed] their constituencies to them, and enable[d] them to advance themselves within the Democratic machine . . . and to garner unto themselves the political and economic perquisites of their positions."[69] These "perquisites" allowed politicians like Dawson to attend to the daily needs of their constituents—"welfare" needs such as dispensing jobs and emergency loans or guiding them through tangles with the law. They had little reason to challenge housing segregation, especially if doing so meant risking the loss of patronage jobs dispensed by the Democratic machine.[70]

The 1955 election of Richard J. Daley as mayor initially looked like a step forward. His predecessor, a millionaire businessman named Martin Kennelly, had treated the city's black population with near-open contempt. When black residents protested their forced removal from the Lake Meadows area, Kennelly ignored them. When antiblack riots erupted at the Trumbull Park homes in 1953, Kennelly took no action. These were among the reasons black Chicagoans overwhelmingly supported Daley.[71]

But he proved to be a far more difficult adversary than Kennelly ever was. Determined to consolidate power, he served as chairman of the Cook County Democratic Central Committee as well as mayor until his death in 1976, with the result that for the first time both city and party patronage derived from a single source. Ward committeemen were not cut out of the picture altogether. They still had plenty of jobs to distribute. But now, like aldermen, they became mere middlemen between their constituents and the real center of power in Chicago, Mayor Daley.[72]

Among the first to feel his iron hold was William Dawson. While previous mayors accepted Dawson's role as power broker for black Chicago, Daley viewed his strength as a threat. He stripped Dawson of many of the patronage positions he had formerly been allowed to distribute, handing them over to men who were more malleable.[73]

Typical of the new black political leadership was Alderman Claude Holman, who was willing to do Daley's dirty work—and do it in public. When, in 1958, a white liberal alderman from Hyde Park named Leon Despres sponsored an "open occupancy" ordinance that would have forbidden property owners and real estate agents in Chicago from acts of racial discrimination in the sale or rental of housing, Holman derailed it by adding numerous stipulations, helping to delay its passage until 1963. By then the ordinance had been watered down to what Despres described as a "tiny, bumbling, almost penalty-free, largely ineffectual step," and Holman had become the most verbally violent opponent of Despres, the City Council's lone independent alderman.[74]

Holman's willingness to serve Daley's ends brought him power.[75] The price, however, was silence on issues of civil rights and housing discrimination. And Holman wasn't alone. By the early 1960s, he was one of six black aldermen in Chicago's City Council who were dependent upon Daley for patronage positions and who repaid their debt to him with unquestioning obedience. Black Chicagoans mockingly referred to them as the "Silent Six." In contrast, they praised white independent alderman Leon Despres as the City Council's "only Negro."[76]

The city's black civic organizations were similarly weakened. The fates of the local branches of the NAACP and the Urban League offer sobering lessons in the difficulties of mounting overt challenges to racism in 1950s Chicago.

The Chicago Urban League began the decade as a forum for activism.

Its head, Sidney R. Williams, was known as a "militant exponent of controversial causes."[77] Williams believed that the city's response to the 1949 Peoria street riots had been weak; its goal had been to silence discussion about the violence. He created a new group, the Committee to End Mob Violence, to address the causes of such outbreaks. But because the committee accepted members who were leftists and Communists, the industrialists who supported the Chicago Urban League (and who, as one scholar reports, "kept their own file on Sidney Williams's activities") withdrew their funding. The league was thrown into such a financial crisis that it shut down entirely in 1955. When it reopened six months later, it had solid business support as well as a new, less threatening agenda that highlighted "stay in school" campaigns and youth counseling projects. It also had a new leader, Edwin C. Berry, who was far more skilled in fund-raising and politicking than his predecessor had been. By the late 1950s, Urban League officials admitted their weakness. As one staff member explained, "We, the Urban League, are of the 'do-good' type of organization. We can't compete with a machine."[78]

The Chicago branch of the NAACP suffered equally serious damage. Its president in 1956 was Willoughby Abner, a charismatic and militant official of the United Auto Workers union. That year, Abner denounced Congressman William Dawson for his silence over the murder of fourteen-year-old Emmett Till in Mississippi and the Montgomery bus boycott in Alabama. Abner also attacked Mayor Daley for ignoring the NAACP's evidence that Chicago's schools were segregated and its black schools underfunded.

When Abner organized a mass rally and picket at City Hall in 1957, Dawson decided that he'd had enough. He would not allow the NAACP to attack either himself or Mayor Daley, whom he then still perceived as a friend. Dawson secretly purchased memberships in the NAACP for approximately six hundred of his precinct captains. These men and women, all of whom owed their jobs to Dawson, showed up at the NAACP's annual meeting, denounced Abner as a "front man" for left wingers, and voted him out of office. As one defeated NAACP leader recalled, "The invaders . . . were elected to make sure that no one in the . . . NAACP hierarchy or their successors would ever rock Daley's political boat, and they didn't."[79]

The black leaders who survived in the late 1950s tended to be politically savvy individuals who valued pragmatism over purity. Typical, perhaps, was Dempsey Travis, who became president of the NAACP in

1959.[80] His years of struggle to create an independent black mortgage company had left him remarkably clear-eyed about what was and was not possible in Chicago. Perhaps it was this sense of futility that led Travis to describe his tenure as Chicago's NAACP president as a failure. During those years, he wrote, "the most segregated city in the United States was without an effective mainstream civil rights organization. The Chicago Branch of the NAACP, the largest branch in the nation, had been co-opted by the Daley Democratic machine and, therefore, ceased to articulate the black experience except in toothless rhetoric that was designed not to offend Mayor Richard J. Daley or the Chicago business establishment."[81]

This, then, was the context that shaped the Boltons' experience. From 1939 until 1955, they had suffered the outrageous overcrowding typical of the Black Belt and no doubt had read about the white mob violence that met African American families brave enough to leave its boundaries. When the opportunity to move to a seemingly safe neighborhood outside the Black Belt finally emerged, they were shut out from mortgage money but offered easy terms by a speculator selling on contract at an enormous markup. The house they purchased was in Hyde Park, where a conservation program was under way that aimed at stopping the very rise in black residency that they represented. They lived in the house from November 1955 through the fall of 1958, long enough to be caught by the city's newly restrictive housing code, which brought an army of inspectors swarming over their property. Their bad experience with Jay Goran coincided with the election of Richard J. Daley as mayor and with the undercutting of virtually every organized source of black power in Chicago, from the Dawson submachine to the Chicago Urban League and the NAACP.

Perhaps this was why in April 1957 the Boltons turned for help not to any local black organization, but to my father and Favil Berns.

My father filed a motion to delay the Boltons' eviction. Then he went out to see the house. He found a cramped, one-hundred-year-old wood-frame structure that lacked central heat or a finished basement. He went to the County Building vault and checked the revenue stamps affixed to the deed. His research revealed that Jay Goran co-owned the property with one Gerald Crane.[82] As Berns recalled, Goran "had a multitude of buildings, and when

I checked out the court docket, that name kept appearing all the time." He saw that the Boltons weren't the only people being evicted by Goran; he and Crane had filed almost thirty eviction notices in the past year alone. Then my father got a copy of the *Chicago Defender* and looked at the real estate ads. There he saw that Goran and Crane had "page after page of advertisements of real estate for $500 to $700 down. Not one listed a price."[83]

By May 1957, my father and Berns had pieced the story together. Because blacks were excluded from conventional sources of mortgage financing, they were forced to buy on contract. But installment land contracts (or "articles of agreement for warranty deed," as they were technically called) left buyers like the Boltons in a highly vulnerable position. Like homeowners, they were responsible for insurance and upkeep—but like renters they could be thrown out if they missed a payment. While it cost from $100 to $300 to instigate foreclosure proceedings against those defaulting on a mortgage, a forcible entry and detainer (that is, eviction) action against a contract buyer cost only $4.50.[84] Worst of all, evictions in Illinois were extraordinarily difficult to challenge in court. Those facing evictions were asked two questions: Did you receive the notice? and Did you make the payment? If the answer to the first question was yes and the answer to the second was no, then the eviction was allowed to proceed. Arguments providing the reasons for a failure to make a payment were off-limits. Any attorney who attempted to make such an argument would be reprimanded by the judge for "not knowing the law."[85]

Berns recalled the effect this information had on my father: "Your father kept on saying it was outrageous, and I kept on saying it's unconscionable. People taking advantage of others, working on the backs of black people, and everything else, you know."[86] Yet it was all legal. Although the Boltons had been misled and exploited, no laws had been broken in the process. As a liberal Catholic magazine summed up the situation: "If the Negro buyer has signed the contract, it holds, and he must continue to make the exorbitant payments or lose the house and all the money he has put into it."[87]

But Berns found an angle. "I came across a concept called *judicial fiat*," he recalled. "If a court on its own order thought something was unconscionable, they could on their own motion stop it." When Berns mentioned the concept to my father, "Boy, he snapped it up. . . . He says,

'That's it!' That's the match that lit the fuse. 'Cause you needed *something* to start an explosion, you know. And from there you couldn't stop him."[88]

Instead of petitioning to stop the Boltons' eviction, my father and Berns filed a complaint against speculators Jay Goran and Gerald Crane. Acknowledging that the Boltons were "without an adequate remedy at law," they nevertheless charged that the behavior of the two men had been so "unconscionable" that it should be stopped by the court. They began by presenting the context. In Chicago, a "great housing shortage" and a "pattern of racial segregation" had created a situation in which only "a very small part of available housing" was available to blacks. Knowing that this situation left black would-be home buyers vulnerable, Goran and Crane "devised a scheme to defraud Negro persons in matters of securing housing." They played on racial fears to convince whites to sell their property "at or below market prices." In this manner they acquired "hundreds of properties . . . in areas immediately contiguous to areas occupied by Negro persons." Then they resold these properties to black buyers "at prices that would shock the conscience of a court of equity."[89]

The complaint charged Jay Goran with numerous procedural abuses. He claimed to be merely a broker for the property, when he was in fact its owner. He misled the Boltons about the property's value. His unethical behavior continued after the sale, when he demanded from the Boltons "additional sums, which sums plaintiffs paid, all without any basis for said charges." He promised the couple that "an accounting would later be furnished" to them explaining these mysterious fees but never provided it.[90]

What made these actions all the worse was Goran's betrayal of the Boltons' trust. Attorneys and real estate brokers have a "fiduciary relationship" with their clients; they are authorized to transact business for their clients' benefit, not for their own. As the Boltons' broker, Goran had a duty to secure "real estate at the best prices and on the best terms available." Instead, he sold them his own property for four times its value. Goran pressured the Boltons into accepting him as their attorney. Once Goran began to act in that capacity, my father and Berns argued, he was obligated to "deal fairly and openly with the plaintiffs, without fraud and without overreaching." In short, Goran's and Crane's actions bore little resemblance to the "usual functions of attorneys and real estate brokers." Instead, the two men used their authority as a tool for "manipulating Negro persons in such a way as to exact a commission for themselves equal [to] or greater than the true value of the properties involved."[91]

The suit was filed in April 1957. It was still working its way through the court in 1958. Meanwhile, throughout 1957 my father tried to interest the press in the Boltons' case. The reporters he spoke with rejected the story. They felt that Goran and Crane were simply bad apples. My father disagreed—advertisements in the *Chicago Defender* showed numerous brokers selling homes in "changing" neighborhoods on similar terms. He also realized that the circle of those profiting from exploitative contract sales went well beyond the contract sellers themselves. This was because contract selling was intimately tied to a secondary industry—the sale of contract paper.[92]

Here's how it worked. After contract sellers made healthy sums of money through contract buyers' down payments and a year or so of high installment payments, many sold off their contracts to other investors for a price that was less than what the contract buyer owed on the building (though well above what the contract seller had originally paid for the property). The investors thus acquired an income-generating contract at a nice discount, while the speculators received more cash, which they could use to purchase more properties. My father was sure that those buying the contract paper were largely members of the city's professional classes—physicians, attorneys, and the like.[93] He knew this in part because he himself had been solicited by a speculator, who dropped off a circular at his office that offered "a selection of installment contracts secured by real estate" at "maximum discounts."[94]

My father assiduously followed the "Homes for Sale" notices in the black press that listed down payments but not the full asking price—a sure sign of a building's being sold on contract—and located the addresses on a map. Multiplying the number of homes by the typical "speculator's tax," or the additional charges that blacks paid for their homes because they were excluded from the conventional mortgage market, he came up with the figure of one million dollars a day—the cost, he said, of being black in Chicago. He wrote up his findings in an article for the *Chicago Bar Record* titled "Land Contract Sales in Chicago: Security Turned Exploitation." What he really wanted, however, was a much broader audience. As a result of a series of tragedies in January 1958, he got it.

• • •

On January 20, Louana Walker was awakened from a deep sleep by heat and smoke. She grabbed her baby daughter, Stephanie, and ran to the bedroom door, but her way was blocked by flames. She set Stephanie down in order to break a window. When she turned to pick her up, the baby had vanished in the thick black smoke. "A neighbor outside cried, 'Throw me the baby! Throw me the baby!' but I couldn't find Stephanie. She must have crawled away," a hysterical Walker told reporters. Walker survived with severe burns on her face. Stephanie and three adults in the building—Herman McNeil, his wife, Virginia, and Virginia's brother, Robert Gillard—were consumed by the flames.[95]

An investigation revealed the full dimensions of the tragedy. The fire had broken out in a once-elegant South Side mansion that had been converted into a rooming house. The building's third floor—a space originally designed as a ballroom—had been partitioned into five small apartments, divided by a locked door into two main sections. This door blocked the McNeil-Gillard family's efforts to escape the flames via a rear stairway. No permit had been filed for converting the third floor into apartments. In fact, such a permit would surely have been denied, since the front part of the space had no fire exit. "This is one more case where money has been put ahead of human lives," Chicago's coroner, Walter E. McCarron, commented.[96]

Then on January 23 another apartment house, this one located just blocks away, erupted into flames. The building had been constructed in 1884 as an eight-flat but had been "cut up" into twenty-seven apartments. Seven children were killed. Four days later, yet another fire broke out in a nearby basement apartment. Two children suffocated to death.[97]

This was carnage, even by Chicago standards. The *Chicago Sun-Times* called for "a change in public attitudes" toward "the buildings and neighborhoods where families are crammed into unsafe, unhealthy cubicle flats, paying exorbitant rents for the privilege of dying like cattle caught in a barn." The *Sun-Times* as well as the rest of the city's white press argued that the only solution was increased housing code inspection. Many also blamed the city's municipal court, which winked at slumlords by levying fines for code violations that were one-tenth or less of the limits imposed by law.[98] Mayor Daley asked the city's mortgage and insurance leaders to help him shut down "fire traps" by recalling mortgage loans and canceling insurance on structures with major code violations or illegal conversions. He also asked that bankers refuse loans to customers who wished to make illegal conversions. Within weeks a consortium of twenty-eight Chicago bankers and savings and loan officials agreed to the new policy.[99]

Dempsey Travis was one of several black leaders to point out a basic flaw in this plan: if housing codes were enforced, there would be no place for those displaced from code-violating buildings to go.[100] "What are you going to do? Put the people into the street?" the *Chicago Sun-Times* asked— and answered, "Yes. . . . *They would be safer in the streets.*" The *Sun-Times* failed to mention that the buildings and neighborhoods in question were inhabited exclusively by African Americans. Nor did it acknowledge that the reason code enforcement would leave many of them homeless was that African Americans were barred from large swaths of the city. The black-owned *Chicago Defender* made precisely this point. Overcrowding would lead to "more fires and more deaths" as long as black Chicagoans remained "hemmed into a ghetto by the relentless pressure of residential segregation." While code-enforcement and increased municipal court fines would help, the city could best cramp "the slumlords' lush operations" by unlocking the ghetto itself.[101]

The *Defender* was evasive about one critical fact: in at least two of the three fires, the "slumlords" were African Americans. Their operations were hardly "lush." The building where Stephanie Walker and three adults died was owned by Charles and Alice Butler, an African American couple. Charles worked as a Chicago Transit Authority car washer, and Alice managed their building. They were not absentee landlords; they lived on the building's first floor. As one newspaper reported, on the night of the fire "Charles Butler and his wife, Alice, led many of the roomers past shooting flames and through a curtain of smoke to the street."[102]

A closer look at the Butlers' experience revealed that code inspection would not only have failed to solve the problem but might even have provided further opportunities for exploitation. Alice Butler had converted the third-floor ballroom because, it turned out, a code inspector had told her she could. He assured her that permits had been filed, when in fact they had not.[103] A second inspector then convinced her to hire construction workers from a firm that he happened to own. As the work proceeded, the building inspector occasionally stopped by. "I see you have my men at work here," he told her approvingly.[104]

The building where seven children died was a sad reminder of the dangerous consequences of contract sales. Its African American owner had bought the structure for the inflated price of $75,000 from two white speculators, who had paid a fair price only months before. Even after packing the building and hiking his tenants' rents, the building's new owner was hard-pressed to keep up his payments. My father summed up the situation: the speculators had sold the property "for a price so high, at terms so impossible to perform, that they need only have collected a few months [payments] . . . and then by simple forfeiture proceedings, reclaimed the property, to make their sale to another unwitting victim. Only here fire and death had intervened, and the scheme failed."[105]

The media's response to the slum fires of January 1958 solidified my father's conviction that Chicagoans were using the wrong model to understand the slum problem. Their misguided emphasis on code enforcement provided him the opening he'd been waiting for—the chance to shift public discussion toward the real culprits: mortgage redlining and the abuse of contract sales. For the rest of 1958, he gave numerous speeches on those two topics. Addressing Chicago's legal and political elite at the City Club, he offered a blistering condemnation of Daley's plan to involve mortgage bankers in slum prevention: "The bald hypocrisy of this position is shown by one simple fact. These men make no loans in any of the areas about which we are concerned. They have declared 'out of bounds' whole sections of our city." A *Chicago American* headline succinctly summarized the speech: "Loan Bankers Make Slums."[106] In a talk at a local synagogue, my father stressed that banks and savings and loan organizations' refusal to lend to blacks meant that "a white man may live in the suburbs in a home of his own for only $500 down, but a Negro may not have his own home" in the city "for even $5,000 down."[107] In a speech to the National Catholic Conference for Interracial Justice, he demonstrated that as a result of mortgage redlining, "the Negro people pay double and triple [for their homes], and haven't enough left to provide the barest upkeep of their property. How wicked are those who sneer at the Negro as a home owner. What other people would long bear so frightful a burden?"[108]

My father saved his most scathing speeches for black audiences.[109] In

March 1958, he spoke at two "giant mass meetings," one on the city's West Side and one on the South Side. Both were sponsored by Dempsey Travis's Dearborn Real Estate Board.[110] At each he described the "$1 million a day" contract sale penalty, a "ruthless and wicked speculators' tax that has been added as a burden only upon the Negro people." He outlined the Boltons' sad experiences. He explained that he and his partner were now asking "the courts to say that real estate . . . is one price and that the price is the same to a Negro man as to a Caucasian man."[111] But he stressed that "until fair and reasonable financing" was made available to black property owners, exploitative contract sales would continue. He targeted bankers for refusing to lend the money that they gathered from urban depositors back to redlined urban communities. Chicagoans, he said, had "an obligation to demand of the savings and loan association that the money be loaned . . . in the community from which it comes." He told the crowds that he would be meeting with members of the Chicago Mortgage Bankers Association to demand that a fund of $50 million be made available for loans in black sections of the city. He pointed out that $50 million was "less than two months' loss to our community."[112]

My father got what he had hoped for—his numerous speeches were widely covered by the press. Black families read the coverage, or attended the open meetings, or heard about Mark J. Satter through their friends. Many realized that they had fallen victim to the contract sale scheme and contacted him for legal representation. Many were also willing to go public with their experiences. Soon dramatic accounts of the cases he brought to court began appearing in the newspapers.[113] By the summer of 1959, he had settled "several dozen" cases in his clients' favor. "These boys are thieves and they settle fast," he told reporters.[114] Those who wouldn't negotiate found themselves summoned to court. My father looked forward to these courtroom battles. He hoped that the principle of charging one price for an item, no matter what the race of the purchaser, might become a reality.[115] He would soon learn whether justice could be had in the courts of Chicago.

THREE

JUSTICE IN CHICAGO

Since my father was unable to challenge the legality of a signed contract, his courtroom strategy was to highlight the contract sellers' ethical violations. He would show that their behavior toward their black customers flouted both the ethics of a free market, in which price was determined by value, not racial bias, and the professional codes governing real estate, law, and banking, which obliged practitioners to aid, not exploit, those who engaged their services. The problem, he believed, was that the professional bulwarks of a stable community—bankers who loaned, realtors who guided, and attorneys who advised—all turned into predators when the client was black.[1] While the Boltons' suit gave him his first example of these abuses, by 1960 he had dozens of African American clients who had been mistreated by the professionals they turned to for guidance. While his cases all resembled one another, each had its own heartbreaking details.

Some were notable for the size of the down payments that the purchaser stood to lose. In 1953, for example, Sallie Bottom and her daughter, Jessie Jackson, bought a two-flat apartment on contract for $28,000, with a hefty down payment of $6,000. Their broker, Frank Bishofberger, concealed the fact that he was the building's owner and that he had purchased it only a few weeks before, for $17,000. By 1959, Bottom and

Jackson had paid Bishofberger an additional $16,800. At that point, despite having made a down payment of over one-third of the building's true value—plus additional monthly installments that more than covered what Bishofberger had paid for the building—the two women fell behind, and Bishofberger moved to evict them.[2]

Other cases were notable for the extremes that contract sellers went to in order to repossess the buildings they "sold." Henry Taylor Shelton and his wife, Elizabeth, purchased their home on contract in January 1951. Their complaint alleged that the week before they bought it for $9,950, their broker, Adolph B. Lewis, had acquired the building for $3,500. Lewis also hid his ownership and convinced the Sheltons that the building was a "real buy." Telling them that they did not need a lawyer, he then provided them with one who was secretly in his employ. The lawyer assured them that the deal was sound, and so the Sheltons agreed to the price Lewis asked.

While all of this behavior was typical, there was a vicious twist to the Shelton case. By 1957, the Sheltons had lived contentedly in their home for six years, not missing a single payment. This meant that Lewis was at risk of actually losing control of the building, so, the Sheltons' complaint alleged, he snuck into their house and changed the locks the night of September 10, 1957. He explained to the Sheltons that they had fallen behind on money owed not to him but to the federal government. If they signed a contract he had prepared, he said, they would be released from these charges. The Sheltons signed. They soon learned that the contract was a quit-claim deed for the house—that is, a document giving up any claim to ownership of the property. By the time they realized their mistake—February 5, 1958—the completion of their contract for $9,950 was well in sight. They had paid $8,473, plus $2,300 for improvements, on a house worth $3,500. Now they had somehow lost it all.[3]

Some contract sellers planned to repossess homes by promising to help buyers get mortgages once they had paid a certain percentage of the contract price; the sellers knew, of course, that mortgages would be impossible to get. This practically ensured that the purchaser would lose the home after paying a set amount. Johnnie and Marylue James faced such a situation. According to the Jameses' complaint, in August 1955, they bought a building on contract from Charles M. Peters, who told them that the structure was owned by "an old white couple" and that the asking price of $13,500 was reasonable.[4] In fact, Peters was the owner; he had purchased the building thirteen days earlier, for $8,000.[5] The Jameses' contract called for $1,000 down, with monthly payments of $105 for the following three years. When the three years were up, the Jameses would pay a remaining balance of approximately $10,500 with a regular bank mortgage. Peters told Marylue that while she might have difficulty getting a mortgage "because [you are] colored," he could "get it a little easier" and would "take care of that" for her when the time came.

In 1958, the Jameses tried to get a mortgage. They went to six banks but were refused by each one. Banking officials explained that they couldn't lend them the additional $10,500 since the property was not worth anywhere near that amount. In desperation, the couple went to Peters for his promised help, but, they alleged, he turned them away, saying that he no longer had an interest in the property and could not care less what happened to it. Two years earlier, Peters had sold the Jameses' contract to a liquor store owner, Arthur Krooth, at a substantial discount. Now Krooth was free to evict them and resell the property on contract to another family.[6]

Even those few black buyers who obtained mortgages for properties outside the Black Belt were not necessarily protected against exploitation. In June 1953, a real estate agent named George Kotas showed Mary Moore a home in Lawndale. He told her that the owners wanted $20,000 for it and asked for a down payment of $2,500. As for the remaining $17,500, Kotas gallantly offered to help her execute two separate mortgages—one for $11,500 and the other for $6,000—with General Federal Savings and Loan, located in the nearby all-white (and notoriously racist) suburb of Cicero. Kotas knew a good attorney who would assist her. Grateful for the help, Moore agreed to purchase the home on these terms.

Kotas, in fact, was not a licensed real estate broker. The building's former owner had asked for $14,000, not $20,000. The first mortgage, for $11,500, covered the actual purchase cost. The second mortgage of $6,000 was a fraudulent charge tacked on by Kotas. He went to great extremes to prevent Moore from learning the home's true price, providing her with an attorney who was in on the scheme, orchestrating her movements at the time of the closing to ensure that she and the building's former owner were never together in the same room, and affixing tax revenue stamps on the deed that made it look as if the building's value was $20,000, not $14,000.

The officers of General Federal Savings and Loan were also involved. The complaint alleged that the extraneous second mortgage of $6,000 was arranged by the bank's president, Harold A. Pinkert, and the general counsel for the bank, Joseph M. Dvorak. These men were happy to make the loan because after Kotas took his cut—approximately $1,811—he turned the remainder over to Dvorak. At that point, Dvorak took over from Kotas in collecting entirely unwarranted payments of $219 a month from Mary Moore.

This wasn't the end of these men's interest in Moore. In January 1954, a few months after she took possession of the property, Kotas showed up at her door offering to build her a basement apartment to increase the building's income. He pressured her to sign a "promissory note" for $2,874.50—far in excess of the value of the bits of carpentry service he eventually performed. In October 1956, Kotas again offered his services. He said he would get her a new mortgage—presumably a home equity loan—for $14,000 from Victory Mutual Life Insurance, an African American–owned company. The price for negotiating the loan, he told her, was $900. In fact, Victory Mutual charged no such fee; the $900 was pure profit for Kotas. But this still wasn't enough for him. In March 1958, he informed Moore that she owed him an additional $3,500 and that she had already signed a document indebting herself to him for that amount. Moore was dumbfounded. She had no memory of signing any such document. It was possible, she realized, that he was charging for some light plumbing work he had done for her over the past few years, but that, too, didn't seem right—she had paid Kotas for that work up front.

That was when Moore realized that she was in trouble. By April 1958, she had retained my father as her attorney, and her complaint, *Mary Moore v. Harold A. Pinkert, Joseph M. Dvorak, Anthony Broccolo and George Kotas*, began working its way through the Circuit Court of Cook County. In addition to her legitimate mortgage debt of $11,500, Moore had been induced to ring up an additional debt of approximately $11,300, in return for which she'd received nothing but a bit of help with plumbing. Moore had avoided purchasing on contract by obtaining a mortgage, but, her complaint alleged, that hadn't protected her from relentless exploitation by a small combine operating out of Cicero's General Federal Savings and Loan.[7]

My father's suits put special emphasis on the violation of the broker-client relationship. Instead of acting as an intermediary between the buyer and the seller, the suits alleged, Frank Bishofberger, Adolph Lewis, and Charles Peters had, like Jay Goran and his partner, Gerald Crane, hid their ownership of the properties they sold to their clients. Just like Goran and Crane, Lewis obscured the fact that he was acting as broker for a property that he owned by putting it in a "land trust." This legal document conveyed the title of a property to a trustee, who then managed the property on behalf of the beneficiaries of the trust—that is, the actual owners of the property. Because the trustee was not required to reveal the name of the property's owner unless ordered to do so by a court of law, land trusts were extremely useful to those hoping to keep their ownership secret.[8] Goran, Crane, and Peters also set up dummy corporations for the same purpose. Thus Gerald Crane claimed to be selling the property of "Bart Realty Company"—even though the owner of Bart Realty was Crane himself.[9] These men then sold their buildings on contract for double, triple, or even quadruple the properties' worth, collecting not the usual broker's commission of 5 percent but rather profits of close to 100 percent of their buildings' value. In all of these ways, my father argued, these men violated the "confidential and fiduciary relationship" between broker and client, a relationship in which a broker was to "deal fairly and openly with the plaintiffs without fraud and without overreaching [and] . . . to communicate to plaintiffs all information which had come to him or which was in his possession relating to the said property."[10]

The terms of that relationship were spelled out in the Chicago Real Estate Board's Code of Ethics, which stipulated that realtors were to keep themselves current on real estate values in order to better guide their clients toward sound purchases, protect their clients against fraud or misrepresentation, and protect the property values of the neighborhoods in which they operated. As a National Association of Real Estate Boards (NAREB) official explained, "We want to encourage ownership. A homeowner is a father, a husband. He has stability. He makes a good citizen."[11]

My father was right that the speculators he took to court had warped every aspect of this code. They misled their clients, fostered the decline of property values, and sold properties on terms that made home ownership almost impossible. But he failed to understand that the city's white professional class saw his clients as entirely outside the bounds of ethical consideration. In the white-dominated fields of real estate, law, and banking, professional ethics applied to whites only. And in this context, the treatment that his black clients received broke no rules at all.

Of course, most white real estate brokers did not openly discuss their racial attitudes. However, in the early 1950s a white University of Chicago graduate student named Rose Helper set out to discover their views for her Ph.D. thesis. In 1955 and 1956, she conducted 121 detailed interviews with Chicago-area brokers. On the promise of complete anonymity they spoke freely. The resulting study, *Racial Policies and Practices of Real Estate Brokers*, provided an unparalleled view of the dynamics shaping the business practices of both speculators and legitimate real estate brokers at precisely the moment when contract selling in Chicago was at its height.[12]

The picture was not pretty. As Helper's study showed, legitimate realtors—that is, those who did not engage in real estate speculation— were well aware of the contract sellers' activities. They knew that banks generally refused to grant any more than "1 percent or 2 percent" of their mortgages to African Americans who sought homes outside of already black areas.[13] They knew that anyone who sold property to blacks outside the ghetto did so on contract, and for grossly inflated prices. They were not surprised by the huge profits the speculators made from such sales.[14]

If they chose not to deal in contract sales—and most did not—their reasons had nothing to do with scruples about overcharging African Americans. In fact, most white real estate brokers felt that blacks *ought* to pay more for their property. Ignoring evidence to the contrary, some claimed that blacks should pay more because they always made smaller down payments. Others argued that blacks had to pay higher prices because they bought on credit. Overlooking the fact that blacks were forced to buy on credit since they were excluded from the mortgage market, they insisted that "if you buy for cash you always get a better deal than if you have . . . extended credit." Yet others claimed that speculators were right to inflate prices when they sold to blacks because the sale was inherently risky. As one broker explained, the white speculator is "just the middle man. He finances the Negro in the deal, and he's entitled to some money for the gamble."[15]

The reason these brokers stayed away from contract-selling speculation, they told Helper, was to avoid introducing black residents into white neighborhoods—a practice known as "blockbusting" or "breaking a block." The Chicago Real Estate Board's Code of Ethics forbade the sale of property to any person whose ownership would cause adjoining properties to depreciate. Given the redlining policies of the FHA, this meant no sales to blacks in white blocks. White real estate agents understood this implicitly. A realtor "won't break a block," said one, "because of his responsibility . . . to the white people. . . . It's an unwritten law." Another explained, "I would not [sell to an African American] because a broker is a member of a licensed profession. One of the greatest things is honesty and integrity and fair dealing. Can a man live up to the code of the profession and go into a neighborhood where he knows the Negro is not wanted . . . and sell property to them without violating the trust and respect that people have . . . for a member of the real estate profession?"[16]

Thus, for white brokers, ethical behavior entailed *not* selling to African Americans in "white" areas. "I'd have made a fortune around here if I had sold to colored," said one Chicago realtor, but "for a measly few dollars I certainly don't want to make people unhappy, to put people in there whom [whites] think they don't like." This refusal to deal with black customers was cast as valiant behavior that protected white communities. A realtor explained, "We all know what they do. One family moves in, but soon you have 5 or 6 families in the same house. . . . The colored tear down good neighborhoods once they get in." Real estate agents described the increase in crime—sometimes real, but often pure fantasy—that followed black residency. For example, one broker described African Americans' mundane daily routines as a "calculated procedure" aimed at creating a "psychosis of fear" among white residents: "Yes, Negroes come in deliberately to shop in the stores. They also drive up and down the streets for no apparent reason. They'll also utilize some of the public playgrounds on a limited scale once in a while, and parks if there are any." Another explained, "They scare you when you look at them. . . . They seem to carry a hand in the pocket as if they had a gun. They frighten people."[17]

Occasionally an interviewee might grant that it was African Americans who had the most to fear: "After all, any colored person going into an area where there is a crystallized [antiblack] feeling, he is taking his life in his hands." But mostly, white real estate agents saw the dangers to themselves. A broker "wants to stay in business," one explained. "If he tries to sell [to blacks] in a white area . . . white people would stop doing business with him." Or worse. "I could get killed," said one. "My wife and children could get killed, and it's no exaggeration whatsoever." As another put it, "I had no qualms about doing that other than getting my head bashed in."[18]

Speculators who engaged in blockbusting took heat not for exploiting blacks but for being too close to them. "As a result of my business dealings, I have been cursed, called 'nigger lover,' 'vulture,' and 'panic peddler,'" complained one. Another described arriving at his club and hearing the other brokers say, "Here comes the biggest colored real estate broker in the city." Jay Goran's colleagues mocked him as the "Moses of the black people," deriding his deals as efforts to lead blacks to a promised land: white neighborhoods.[19]

Besides "nigger lover," men and women who sold to blacks were called something else—"Jew." Many white gentiles assumed that anyone who sold to a black must be a Jew. This perception was not based on the existence of large numbers of Jewish speculators. As one non-Jewish speculator admitted, "Though we hear 'the Jews are coming in and buying,' only a normal percentage are Jews. The rest are white gentiles." Rather, the association of blockbusters with Jews derived largely from anger at Jewish people who rented or sold to blacks on fair terms, out of principle. Jewish real estate agents who were ideologically committed to integration considered themselves the polar opposite of their coreligionists who exploited blacks. Yet both were excoriated as blockbusters by whites to whom the unforgivable crime of speculators was not exploitation but integration on any terms.[20]

In fact, although speculators who sold to blacks were damned as "nigger lovers," real estate brokers knew that their practices aided whites far more than blacks. In redlined neighborhoods where homeowners could not sell their properties—since most prospective buyers could not get mortgages to purchase in such areas—speculators "provide[d] a necessary function." As a realtor explained, they could buy the properties with cash: "A white man sold a 6-flat for $30,000 all cash. It was worth $35,000 to $40,000. . . . But at least [the speculator] gave the man his $30,000. . . . He was very happy to get it." While $30,000 may not have been full value, it was more than enough to cover the down payment for a nice new home in the suburbs.[21]

Speculators also helped whites "save face." Homeowners who wanted to leave their neighborhoods could sell to a white speculator rather than directly to a black family.[22] Speculators performed a similar function for "legitimate" real estate brokers who felt social pressure to avoid selling to blacks yet were pulled to do so by the lure of huge profits. They solved their dilemma by dealing secretly with speculators. In public, they retained their respectability; in private, they made the sales and split the commissions. As one speculator explained, he bought many of the properties that he resold to blacks at "a pretty cheap price" from "the established real estate firms, some of the biggest firms in the city." They sold to him because they had a policy "that they won't sell directly to Negroes. That way they keep their skirts clean." Some speculators had a great deal of contempt for those who dealt with them on the sly. "You know what those firms did?" one said. "They wouldn't sell it direct. They work with every broker so as not to sell it direct, and then they blame it on the Jews."[23]

Although many brokers were happy to use speculators as go-betweens, they nevertheless attacked speculators for violating the profession's ethical code as it pertained to the treatment of white sellers. Indeed, no matter how badly the contract seller treated his black customers, the brokers Rose Helper interviewed remained rigidly focused on the harm that he did to whites. "He makes the [white] seller think he has another buyer and the seller will sell to him completely unaware that he is selling to the speculator and that the speculator is going to sell to colored afterwards. . . . No buyer is supposed to buy property from a seller without informing him that he himself is buying it. . . . [This behavior] breaks all real estate ethics and codes," one broker explained.[24]

Given the social opprobrium they faced, why did white speculators stay in this line of work? The money, of course, but also the thrill. In the classic novel *The Old Bunch*, Meyer Levin depicts a pair of loan-sharking West Side real estate agents: "Each dollar was loaned, borrowed, loaned, till it served a dozen ways." There was something almost magically compelling about such activity. "And each time the sum left an increasing part of itself as interest, and yet was whole." One could "feel the ceaselessness, the relentlessness, of this incessant squirming, gnawing, bickering. And it was a lust with them! They enjoyed it [and] lived for it."[25]

Gerald Crane, whom my father described as "a very handsome man, with dark, piercing eyes, very neatly dressed," used his earnings to live the high life. He had a fashionable Lake Shore Drive apartment and devoted his free time to tennis and golf. As a later newspaper exposé reported, Crane's "fun-filled private life sometimes puts him on the society pages."[26] For Jay Goran, contract sales profits bought different benefits. The money enabled him to be a good husband and solid provider to his wife and children and established his respectability.[27] Favil Berns, who knew many men like Goran, explained their way of thinking: "I can make money now . . . and I can make contributions to my synagogue, . . . and I can join the Highland Park country club, and I can do all these upward-mobility things. I can send my family to Miami and buy a condo. Enjoy the good things in life, you know?" Any nagging sense that respectability was purchased through shady dealings was easily quashed. The speculators didn't "have to tell their families about it," Berns noted. And they could evade the fury of whites in "changing" neighborhoods, since most did not live in the areas in which they sold.[28]

Like all people, however, speculators needed a justification for engaging in behavior that they knew was socially unacceptable. Some insisted that they were simply capitalists who, like any good investor, bought low and sold for as high as they could get away with.[29] Others put a moral spin on their work, depicting themselves as problack. While most brokers refused to serve blacks who dreamed of buying a home outside the Black Belt, contract sellers welcomed them as clients. They were polite and gracious to their black customers, at least at first. They even cast contract selling as a favor for the less fortunate. As Jay Goran insisted, by selling on contract he was giving "people of little means" a "chance at home ownership."[30]

Some salesmen employed by speculators were troubled by the repercussions of their work. One of contract seller Lou Fushanis's salesmen admitted that "if you sell for him, you'll have to sell . . . garbage and it will make you sick—unless it makes you hard." After watching Fushanis inform a "stunned" and "bewildered" black couple that their home was being repossessed, he had enough. "I'm leaving today, there's one of the reasons," he said.[31]

Most of the men my father brought to trial put their customers through scenes like this routinely. In such situations their paternalistic talk of giving their customers "a chance" shaded into something more predatory. According to Favil Berns, the speculators saw their customers as "on their own. If you can survive in the wilderness, survive. If you can't, you go by the wayside, that's all. It is survival of the fittest." Selling on contract was closer to a blood sport than a livelihood. As Berns said, explaining why speculative contract sellers kept at the business despite having already made huge amounts of money, "It was like people who like to go out and shoot lions in Africa. It was the same thrill. . . . The thrill of the chase and the kill."[32]

For contract sellers who needed a further justification for their actions, mid-twentieth-century racism provided one. In the 1950s, mainstream opinion held that blacks in cities like Chicago struggled because of their faulty culture.[33] This theory, which was articulated by leading scholars, asserted that problems facing African Americans—lower earnings across occupational categories, feelings of alienation from mainstream U.S. life, and the "physical and . . . moral deterioration" that characterized the growing Northern black ghettos—had two sources. The first was a warped family structure: female-headed households—a legacy of slavery—created weak men who were unable to assert their masculinity in an appropriate manner. The second, related cause was the cultural inferiority of "relatively backward Southern agricultural communities"—the supposed origin of the urban blacks now jammed into decaying housing in Northern American cities. Rural customs emphasized immediacy and pleasure over the careful planning, hard work, and deferred gratification required to succeed in modern industrial society. Blacks were not exploited, conventional wisdom held. They simply lacked the character structure needed to handle Northern urban life.[34]

The facts were different. Many black migrants to 1950s Chicago were actually "urban-born Mississippians." More striking, Southern black migrants to Northern cities tended to earn *higher* incomes than Northern-born blacks. As recent studies document, on average Southern-born African American men in Northern cities earned 9 to 10 percent more than comparatively educated Northern-born men. This should not be surprising: as one scholar of the Second Great Migration observes, black Southern migrants, like most immigrants, were "self-selected for ambition and commitment to work."[35] But whites tended to cast all blacks as backward "rural people" no matter what their background or behavior.[36] Contract sellers told themselves that those whose homes they repossessed were simply unable to handle the complexities of urban living, from maintaining their boilers to paying their property taxes. If they failed at it, that was their own fault: "How are you going to educate dumb animals?"[37]

Finally, contract sellers were fully aware of how central their actions were to the economic functioning of Chicago. Like many other seemingly marginal operators, they knew that their activities were not marginal at all. Speculators worked with, and brought considerable profits to, many of the city's banks and savings and loan associations. When speculators sold their contracts in order to raise cash to purchase more properties, the circle of those profiting from their business expanded. "I can raise cash by selling my contract paper at a discount to some of the most reputable doctors, dentists, lawyers, and other business and professional men in town," one speculator boasted.

As the speculators understood, responsibility for their practices was shared by everyone who created the explosive market in black housing— from the Federal Housing Administration, redlining banks, and the Chicago Real Estate Board to the ordinary white Chicagoans who harassed black families who dared to move into their neighborhoods. This broad range of complicity enabled speculators to view themselves not as predators but as level-headed professionals who approached their profit-making activities with open eyes. As one explained, "Whatever my faults and whatever the social stigma I endure, I don't believe I am hypocritical in all this."[38]

Although no Ph.D. student recorded the views of lawyers involved in contract selling, these are not hard to tease out. Many speculators were also attorneys. My father argued that it was "unconscionable" for speculator-attorneys to mislead their own clients. But here, too, his assumption that attorneys should treat black clients as they did white ones ran up against a different understanding of ethics. Indeed, these attorneys' sense that they were playing by the rules—and benefiting numerous people by doing so—might explain their stunned reaction to my father's legal suits. Some initially assumed that he simply wanted a cut of the action. "'Come on in—there is enough money in this for all of us," they told him.[39] When he spurned such overtures, some turned nasty. For example, when he tried to work out a settlement with an attorney, Samuel Aronfeld, who had sold his own clients a building on contract, Aronfeld responded with a threat. "We know who you are and we're taking appropriate steps to take care of you because you're in more trouble than you think," he said. Aronfeld's attorney, Irving Block, added menacingly, "It would be wiser to stop what you're doing."[40]

Other speculator-attorneys ostracized Favil Berns and my father. "Some of them weren't generous enough to extend their hand to me if they knew that I was working for your dad," Berns told me. My father returned the snub, sometimes storming off in midsentence when one of these men approached him. "What gives, Mark?" "I don't fraternize with the enemy," he'd snap back. Berns found this discord disturbing. The legal community was an intimate circle in those days: "There was a big dining room at the Chicago Bar Association. A lot of us guys used to eat there and talk, you know, common tables and so forth." Berns understood that by taking on attorneys who engaged in contract selling his partner was breaking yet another powerful rule: "You don't sue other lawyers." He warned my father that going after other lawyers would expose him to "all types of abuse." "You've got to be very careful. If you're going after lawyers, they'll countersue you, and you don't even know who they're related to or who's on the bench that's related to them," Berns said. "Well, that did not faze your father," he told me. "He was bullheaded. He figured 'social justice should prevail in this world.'"[41]

Tensions that played out in the Bar Association dining room were also on display in the courtroom. The litigation of the Boltons' case was typical. Attorney Morris C. Shaps, who represented Goran and Crane, seemed mystified by the suit. As my father described, "We were as two persons in a dense fog. Nothing that either of us said seemed to reach the other." My father said that Goran "was so unfair as to be evil." Shaps said, "Who is going to stop two people from selling property to each other?" My father tried to make the issue concrete. "'Tell me, Mister Lawyer, would you buy such a cottage for your daughter and son-in-law for $14,000, and then would you add another $12,000 in interest?'" Shaps's reaction showed his inability to put himself in the Boltons' situation. Shaps turned to him "in horror. 'What,' he said, 'buy a junk like that for $14,000; do you think I'm crazy?'"[42]

The speculators were particularly outraged that my father dared take them to court over their treatment of black customers. The Boltons' case is again indicative. As the pretrial deposition of Jay Goran revealed, Goran saw the issue as one of betrayal—not his betrayal of the Boltons but my father's betrayal of the code that attorneys not bring suit against one another.

While Goran's manner with the Boltons had been benevolent and bountiful, at his deposition he was surly, evasive, and, most of all, angry. He denied that his main occupation for the past decade had been the purchase and sale of real estate. When asked directly if he had told the Boltons that he was a real estate broker, Goran spat back, "I did not. As a matter of fact, I never said that to nobody." He admitted that he "probably" told the Boltons "I am a lawyer and I represent the owner of this property," but he denied that he was the true owner of the property. Of course, he "may have" at one time had an interest in the property sold to the Boltons—"I really, I can't recall." He denied that he had told the Boltons that they "would exercise good judgment in purchasing the property." Although he could not quite recall the details of his conversation with the Boltons, he was sure of one thing: "I didn't say what you state in your complaint there." When my father admonished, "It is not what I state. It is what Mr. Bolton says," Goran exploded. "You are the one that is putting words in his mouth. Why sugarcoat it? You don't have to hide behind his tales." He finally came to the source of his rage. "You are slandering a couple of lawyers here. Why not be a man and stand up on it?" he snapped.[43]

By the time the Boltons' case went to trial in the summer of 1958, Goran and Crane had replaced the mystified Morris Shaps with a new attorney, John F. McCarthy. McCarthy's motion to dismiss focused on hairsplitting the facts. Goran's discussions with the Boltons did not constitute a "fiduciary relationship." The price he placed on the building was not a "misrepresentation of fact" but merely a statement of opinion. "Plaintiffs seek to reform the contract . . . for misrepresentation or fraud. Reformation of a contract may not be made on that ground."[44]

The judge found these arguments convincing. In November 1958, he ruled in favor of Goran and Crane. The Boltons were ordered to vacate the property by January 5, 1959. By 1960, another black family inhabited the house. They purchased the house, which was still worth about $4,300, on contract for $14,000, with a down payment of $1,000.[45]

From the late 1950s on, the same arguments that defeated the Boltons were used repeatedly, and usually successfully, against my father's other clients. The case of the Sheltons, who paid $8,473, plus $2,300 for improvements, on a house worth $3,500, was dismissed with costs assessed to the plaintiffs. There was "no misrepresentation of fact" in the case, and "no fiduciary relationship between plaintiffs and this defendant, and no duty to plaintiffs by this defendant, which would permit this Court to grant plaintiffs any of the relief which they seek."[46] The court ruled against the Jameses, who had simply asked for a delay in Arthur Krooth's order of eviction so that they could come up with the $10,500 mortgage. The complaint's allegation of Charles Peters's hidden ownership of the property, his gross inflation of the price, and his willingness to sell the property at one price to Krooth while using an entirely different price scale for the Jameses had "no bearing" on Krooth's right to evict them. My father pleaded that the history of Peters's financial dealings around the property "is the heart and soul of my case"—but in vain.[47] Even Mary Moore's case was dismissed. Although the complaint alleged shocking behavior by her brokers, the judge ruled in favor of them and General Federal Savings and Loan. There was no fiduciary relationship. A contract was a contract. However mysterious the second mortgage, Moore had signed for it and would have to fulfill its obligations. The judge did more than support the defendants: in a punitive flourish, he ruled that Moore had to pay all costs associated with the case.[48]

Still, the clients kept coming in. In December 1958, only one month after the Boltons' case was dismissed, my father had Crane and Goran back in court. The plaintiffs were William H. Coleman, a fifty-nine-year-old janitor, and his wife, Wilma. In 1956, the couple had purchased a home on contract from a South Side real estate broker. The price was $11,900. Two years later, after indebting themselves for over $3,000 worth of repairs to correct housing code violations, the Colemans gave up. They stopped making their payments, and the property reverted to the contract seller. When my father had the house appraised, it was valued at not $11,900 but

$4,200—*after* the $3,000 worth of repairs put in by the Colemans. It turned out that their broker, William F. Smith, was employed by the building's owners, Goran and Crane. Now the two men stood to get back the house and all the money and labor invested in it.[49]

The case of *William H. Coleman and Wilma R. Coleman v. Jay Goran, Gerald H. Crane, and W. F. Smith* demonstrated the problems—some of them self-inflicted—involved in trying such suits. My father was an independent, financially strapped attorney whose supporting staff consisted of Favil Berns, his secretary, and his elderly father and two young sons, who occasionally ran legal errands for him. He had to act quickly since his clients were under the threat of eviction. But he could get the full history of his clients' properties, which were usually held in land trusts, only if he subpoenaed the records of the banks that acted as trustees; this took time his clients didn't have.

As a result, the initial complaint was hastily written and weak on supporting facts. It spent more time explaining Goran and Crane's general operations than their specific interaction with the Colemans. Goran and Crane took advantage of a black housing shortage that was caused by racial segregation, manipulated the "fears and prejudices" of white property owners in order to buy properties low and resell them for two to three times their value on contract to blacks, and perverted their fiduciary relationship with their clients into a source of immoral gain. My father alleged in his complaint that the Colemans' broker, William Smith, had acted not on their behalf but on that of Goran and Crane. Smith convinced the couple that they could trust his professional judgment, misled them as to the value and condition of the property, and dissuaded them from hiring their own attorney, thereby leading them into a scheme that ultimately left them homeless and bereft of their life savings.[50]

By now Goran and Crane had a new attorney—their third in fighting Mark Satter's clients: Irving Block. A tough-talking, chain-smoking fighter with thirty years' experience, Block proved a powerful adversary. His "motion to strike and motion to dismiss plaintiffs' suit" ripped my father's complaint to shreds. The complaint presented no evidence that Crane or Goran had ever spoken to the plaintiffs, nor did it explain what interest, if any, Crane or Goran had in the plaintiffs' property. The assertion that the price the Colemans paid would "shock the conscience of a court of equity" was absurd, a mere "conclusion of the pleader." It ignored the distinction between the "cash market value" of a building and the cost of the same building on credit and with a mere $375 down payment. Block pointed out that the Colemans lived in the property for two years before realizing that they had made a "bad bargain" with Smith. For the court to permit a change of contract "would foreclose any purchase . . . from ever being final."

Block reserved his most vehement language for my father's attempts to explain the broader scheme engaged in by Goran, Crane, and Smith. The complaint's "allegations" of a housing shortage and a pattern of racial segregation were "inflammatory in nature, scandalous, impertinent . . . and not germane to the issues in the case." Allegations about an "artificial manipulation" of the resulting conditions by the defendants and about their "scheme to defraud Negro persons" were "libelous and defamatory." The complaint provided no names, dates, places, or supporting details to substantiate its claims about Goran and Crane's business practices. Block went over each phrase: "The use of the words 'fears and prejudices of white property owners' assumes that the white property owners are both preju-diced and fearful. . . . Said paragraph fails to explain how the arrival of Negro persons would cause an owner to 'lose his entire equity in his prop-erty.'" After a page of this, Block concluded, "We have only finished ana-lyzing one-half of paragraph seven (7), but we submit that a further word by word analysis would be redundant. The balance of the paragraph con-sists of a methodical, cold blooded character assassination indulged in by a member of the bar against two brother lawyers."[51]

My father responded to Block's onslaught with several amended com-plaints. He subpoenaed the property records and was able to show that Goran was indeed the owner (the records showed that Gerald Crane did not co-own this particular property with Goran, so Crane was dropped from the suit). He documented the Colemans' efforts to reach Goran once they realized that the contract they had signed left them financially respon-sible for a severely deteriorated property. Smith had told them to contact Goran—to "make your complaint downtown where you pay your money." They called Goran's office repeatedly for the next five months, from May 1957 through October 1958, but Goran refused to speak to them.[52]

Block fought back harder. Smith was not the Colemans' "agent"— indeed, he met the couple only twice. His claims about the value of the property were his opinion only. Block pointed out that the Colemans had lived in Chicago for at least thirty-seven years, were literate, and had both attended two years of high school. They read their contract before signing it and so presumably understood its terms. They also had a chance to inspect the property before purchasing it. How could they not realize it was in a "deteriorating condition"? By what leap of logic did their confusion over the worth of their purchase become the fault of Smith? Once taking possession, why did the Colemans wait a whole six months before realizing that something was wrong? They were guilty of laches—neglecting to assert their rights in a timely fashion.[53]

In December 1959, Judge Walker Butler delivered his ruling. The plaintiffs had failed to "disaffirm their contract" at the earliest possible moment after discovering the alleged fraud. Therefore, there was no cause of action. Case dismissed.[54]

My father appealed. The cause of action, he clarified, was fraud and deceit. The problem was not the contract that the Colemans signed but the false representations that induced them to sign it in the first place. He insisted that Smith did have a fiduciary relationship with the Colemans since he had told them they could rely upon his professional advice: "Where a relation of trust and confidence obtains between the parties there is a duty to disclose all material facts and failure to do so constitutes fraud." He challenged the argument that the Colemans had waited too long to bring their suit. The couple had made repeated efforts to contact Goran. "Is it honorable for Goran, an attorney, to hide behind his telephone and his secretary, and now complain that the plaintiffs were not prompt in their complaint about his fraud?" The court should have permitted the plaintiffs to present proof that "Goran was an artful dodger and had for years engaged in exactly such practice as this." Despite refusing their calls, Goran had continued to collect money from the Colemans. Their ongoing payments should not be taken as proof that they accepted the terms of their purchase. Since the plaintiffs could be evicted if they missed a single payment, they had no choice but to continue paying, even as they sought "satisfaction from the elusive Goran."

The amended complaint concluded by begging the court to go to the heart of the issue—the use of land contracts as a means of exploiting minority buyers. In the hands of men like Goran, my father argued, land contracts were "especially evil," distorting "the normal uses" of the legal process "to exact enormous profits on the one hand, and frightful over-charging with attendant community decay on the other."[55]

The appellate court of Illinois's ruling was handed down on June 14, 1960. The question, as the judges saw it, was whether the "fraudulent misrepresentations" of Smith and Goran justified the cancelation of the Colemans' land contract agreement. They did not. There was no fiduciary relationship between Smith and the Colemans. "A mere assertion of faith and trust in Smith" because of his "superior knowledge" did not create a fiduciary relationship. "Statements as to the value of a property are . . . mere expressions of opinion and, for that reason, are not sufficient to warrant a rescission of the contract, even though they are false and relied upon by the other party." The court added that this case was not the appropriate context to discuss "unfair practices by speculators in transitional communities."[56]

"'Let Buyer Beware'" was how the *Chicago Daily News* summarized the decision. "'A misrepresentation with respect to value or condition is not sufficient to constitute fraud and deceit,'" the paper quoted the ruling. "That is the law," Goran commented. "If it weren't the law there would never be an end to litigation." The paper described Mark Satter as "seemingly crushed by the decision." The ruling gave a "green light" to exploitative contract sellers, he told the *Daily News*.[57]

Despite these repeated defeats, my father continued to appeal negative rulings. One small victory involved the case of Mary Moore. In November 1960, the appellate judges delivered their verdict. They seemed genuinely shocked by the defendants' "flagrant disregard of the law and the principles of fair dealing." They supported the argument that the defendants had a duty to Moore: "The rule is well established . . . that the relation existing between principal and agent for the purchase or sale of property is a fiduciary one, and the agent in the exercise of good faith is bound to keep his principal informed on all matters that may come to his knowledge" about the property's value. They dismissed the bank officers' claims that their involvement with Moore was too indirect. They also rejected the argument that Moore was obligated to pay the bogus $6,000 second mortgage. "It is just as logical to say that an entrepreneur selling a sham gold brick to an innocent from the hinterlands can defend himself by saying that he never asked any greater price than was agreed to be paid to him by the victim," the court ruled.[58]

• • •

This victory buoyed my father for his next court battle, which had been years in the making. The initial target of the suit was West Side realtor and attorney Moe Forman. But the ultimate target was General Federal Savings and Loan—the same institution whose officers had entangled Mary Moore—and the discriminatory lending practices of savings and loans across the country.

Mary Lee Stevenson and her sister Joeanna Williams migrated to Chicago from Vicksburg, Mississippi, in 1941. One year later they were joined by Joeanna's seventeen-year-old-daughter, Bertha. After that Joeanna sent for her remaining three children, all boys. In Chicago Joeanna was first hired as a domestic servant. Then she and Mary Lee found work at a laundry. They performed grueling physical labor in intense heat, wearing homemade masks over their faces to shield them from the dust and noxious smells. Nevertheless, they made time for other pursuits. In 1944, Joeanna and Mary Lee were among the half dozen people who founded King David M. B. Baptist Church. It started in a basement, then moved to a storefront. Before long the church had its own structure, at 728 West Peoria on the city's South Side.[59]

The two sisters and their extended family started out as boarders on the South Side. Then they moved to a house of their own. It was "a little place, and all of the family couldn't fit in," Bertha recalled. In 1953, Bertha married Lawrence Richards, a Tennessean who had served in the military during World War II and then moved to Chicago. A mature, loving man, he adored Bertha and was devoted to her mother, Joeanna. But with his arrival, their small house became impossibly overcrowded. By 1954, the extended family needed to find more comfortable surroundings.[60]

More neighborhoods had opened to black buyers. One of them was Lawndale. In November 1954, Joeanna Williams and her daughter and son-in-law visited the Lidsker and Forman Realty Company, where they were served by Moe Forman himself. To Bertha, Forman "seemed like a good person." A tall, handsome black-haired man, he was kind and solicitous, a real "sweet talker." He showed the family a beautiful yellow-brick three-flat at 3920 West Grenshaw. The price was steep—$29,500, with $2,500 down and payments of $275 a month. But all three of them were working, Joeanna in the laundry, Lawrence as a forklift operator, and

Bertha doing piecework at a tailor shop. Besides, Forman and his associate Nathan Elkin assured them that "this is the best house you can get for that price." A few days later, Joeanna, Bertha, and Lawrence bought the building on contract. They were so thrilled with the purchase that they convinced Mary Lee Stevenson to buy a building from Forman as well. Both families moved into their buildings in January 1955. As Bertha later realized, "We just walked right on into the trap."[61]

Joeanna, Mary Lee, and their families made their monthly payments for three years, but it was a struggle. They began to sense that they had been cheated. Then came the newspaper coverage of exploitative contract selling in the spring of 1958. A friend read the stories and advised them to contact Mark J. Satter, a white man who "would help the black people."[62]

Joeanna Williams and Mary Lee Stevenson showed up at my father's office in May 1958. When my father investigated the history of their buildings, he discovered that both of them were already part of a lawsuit. To his amazement, the court records of the suit neatly laid out all of the information he would need to help the sisters—and take on one of the biggest contract sellers in Lawndale. He had hit a gold mine.

The earlier suit had been initiated by a real estate investor named Morris Gans, who had agreed to purchase the contract paper of twenty-six properties from a combine of contract sellers headed by Moe M. Forman. Then Forman and his group backed out of the agreement. Now Gans was bringing Forman's group to court to force them to honor the deal.

As supporting evidence, Gans supplied detailed documentation about each of the twenty-six buildings involved. All were in Lawndale, most within a two-block area. He listed the price that Forman's group had paid for each property, the price for which they sold it on contract to a black buyer, and the price for which they agreed to sell the "paper" before changing their mind about the sale. The numbers confirmed everything my father had assumed about how speculators made their money. Forman's group sold the properties to black buyers at an average markup of 70 percent. In these two blocks of Lawndale alone, the twenty-six black families that purchased on contract paid Forman's group $155,000 more for their structures than they were worth—a "speculator's tax" that the speculators could collect simply because black families had no choice but to deal with them.[63]

My father told his clients that shortly before selling Joeanna Williams her building for $29,500, Forman's group had purchased it for $18,500. In Mary Lee Stevenson's case, Forman had purchased the building for $16,500, with a down payment of $1,500; shortly afterward he sold it to Mary Lee for $26,500—with a down payment of $2,000. My father explained to them that Forman had treated twenty-four of their close neighbors in a similar fashion.[64]

Mary Lee Stevenson and Joeanna Williams did not think of themselves as particularly political people—that is, as Bertha recalls, "until they found out what Moe M. Forman was up to and what he was doing to us." They confronted Forman and found that their formerly warm and solicitous real estate broker now behaved "stuck up," with an attitude of "I will if I want to and I won't if I don't." Soon he refused to see them at all.

Stevenson and Williams decided to contact the other families that had purchased from Forman. My father provided the addresses, and they did the footwork. Eventually six families agreed to join their suit. "They all got together and whatever they did they did it together," Bertha told me. "They had meetings, at the different houses. And then my mother and my husband would take it to your dad, whatever they talked about. Then he'd know how to write it up."[65]

In *Mary Lee Stevenson et al. v. Louis Lidsker, Nathan Elkin, Moe M. Forman, Morris Gans, and the Chicago National Bank,* my father documented the financial and personal interactions that the seven families had had with Forman and his salesmen. (Chicago National Bank was included as a defendant because some of the Forman group's properties were held "in trust" there.) All had been assured by Forman or his agents that the buildings were an exceptional buy. Most were told that the buildings would generate far more in rental income than was the case. None had realized that their "real estate agents" were the buildings' owners and that the prices they paid were close to double the buildings' worth. Most made down payments on their contracts that were well above the down payments that Forman's syndicate had made on its own mortgages—the syndicate made a $21,000 yearly profit from that difference in down payments alone. The complaint alleged that all had only learned of the fraud perpetrated upon them in April or May 1958, when Forman, Lidsker, and Elkin sold their contracts to Morris Gans for prices only somewhat higher than what the three men had paid a few years before.

The complaint my father drafted provided details of fraud and abused fiduciary relationships and once again set these underhanded interactions within the context of an "acute housing shortage among Negro persons" caused by Chicago's pattern of racial segregation. The immense profits Forman and his associates extracted from the plaintiffs "represents an unconscionable drain upon the Negro community, and a calculated plan on the part of the defendants . . . to foster the growth of slums . . . in the City of Chicago." He asked that the court change the contracts to reflect the buildings' "real value" and that it appoint a receiver for all the properties "pending a final determination of the rights" of all parties to the suit.[66]

Forman called the suit "ridiculous." "We have been in business in the area for fifteen years and deal only in that neighborhood," he told the *Chicago Daily News*. He could buy low and sell high, he explained, because he bought for cash and then sold on credit with "a small down payment." His attorneys marshaled the usual arguments. A court of equity had no authority to remake a contract. An expression of opinion as to value did not constitute fraud. The defendants' statements that they were brokers when they were in fact owners did not constitute fraud because the "plaintiffs could not have been damaged by such a representation." The judge agreed with the Forman group's attorneys. On June 22, 1960, he dismissed the suit.[67]

But some of the plaintiffs were not ready to give up. Six months later, Mary Lee Stevenson and Reginald Kent, one of the six neighbors who had joined in the earlier suit, were back in court, again represented by my father. By now, both had defaulted on their contracts. Stevenson, sixty-one, had invested $13,500 in her building, which, though valued at $16,500, had been sold to her for $26,500. Reginald Kent, thirty-nine, an unemployed machinist, had invested $11,000 in his building, plus $1,200 in improvements. Although the building was worth about $14,000, Kent's contract obligated him to pay $21,000 for the property. To pay off their contract debts, both Kent and Stevenson had applied for mortgage loans from General Federal Savings and Loan. Both had been turned down. Now they faced foreclosure and the loss of all they had invested.

This time, my father tried a different approach. Instead of going after Forman, he would go after General Federal, the savings and loan that generously funded Forman's speculation. Instead of basing his arguments on equity laws about unconscionable behavior or the obligations of fiduciary relationships, he would go to the heart of the matter: civil rights.

My father dug up an old Reconstruction-era law, the Civil Rights Act of 1866 (now codified as Section 1982 of Title 42 of the United States Code), which stated that "all citizens . . . shall have the same right . . . as is enjoyed by white citizens . . . to inherit, purchase, lease, sell, hold, and convey real and personal property." It gave him grounds to go after the racially discriminatory practices of most savings and loans. If "all citizens," that is, African Americans, had the same right to purchase property as "white citizens" and if discriminatory loan policies denied them this right, then the discriminatory loan policies of General Federal Savings and Loan were illegal.

"Negroes File Suit Alleging Gouge," ran a February 1961 *Chicago Daily News* front-page headline on the case. Kent and Stevenson's suit would be based on "statutes barring conspiracy to deprive people of their civil rights and on laws governing the operation of federal savings and loan associations," reporter Nicholas Shuman wrote. He pointed out that the suit, "the first such known case filed in the country," could have huge implications: "If successful, it could serve as a model for a legal attack on profiteering against Negroes."[68]

My father crafted his argument carefully. As a savings and loan organization, General Federal was chartered by the federal government to "provide for 'the sound and economical financing of homes,'" he wrote. Instead, General Federal had "knowingly participated in a practice which was calculated to make" such financing of homes "well nigh impossible." It had engaged in "active conspiracy" with speculators by providing them with loans that enabled them to purchase property in areas open to "Negro and other minority persons" for the sole purpose of reselling it at an "artificially inflated price." Since the right to hold real property was "controlled almost entirely by the federally insured savings and loan industry," General Federal, by refusing loans to black customers, denied Stevenson and Kent the same right to purchase property that white citizens had, a right guaranteed them by federal law. The "arbitrary and unreasonable decision" of the federally insured savings and loan industry "to withhold funds" from his clients and instead "provide funds [to white speculators] for purposes utterly repugnant to sound purchase of homes is a denial of the rights guaranteed to these plaintiffs under Section 1982 of Title 42 of U.S.C.A."[69]

General Federal's counsel, Daniel S. Jorgenson, answered my father's conceptually sweeping arguments with an equally sweeping rejoinder. The U.S. District Court did not have jurisdiction over his client because, as numerous rulings made clear, Section 1982 barred only *governmental* interference with the right of "all citizens" to purchase property. "It is settled beyond cavil that the act does not protect one from invasion of private rights by individual action," one such ruling asserted. Despite General Federal's status as a federally chartered and insured savings and loan, Jorgenson insisted that it was a private, not a governmental, actor.

The complaint's allegations that General Federal Savings and Loan had engaged in conspiratorial actions against black Chicagoans were once again mere "conclusions of the pleader." As Jorgenson noted in a reply brief supporting his motion to dismiss, the idea that all Chicago federal savings and loans have "*by agreement* refused to grant financing in the entire area of the city in which the plaintiffs seek to make their home" was "absurd"; indeed, it was "an example of the wild accusations made by the plaintiffs." Finally, Stevenson and Kent had waited too long to bring their suit. The statute of limitations lasted five years, and it was now six years since they had taken the fateful step of signing a contract with Moe Forman, thus entangling themselves, in a roundabout manner, with General Federal Savings and Loan.

The hearing was held on June 19, 1961. My father's innovative attempt to use the Civil Rights Act of 1866 to stop the discriminatory practices of the savings and loan industry failed. The court ruled in favor of General Federal and the case was dismissed.[70]

The truth was that for cases of this kind justice was rarely to be had in the courts of Chicago. Judges repeatedly ruled in favor of the speculators. To a large extent, the rulings reflected the cleverness of the speculators, who kept most of their actions just within the law. But the structure of the judiciary in Chicago was also a factor. Judges were political appointees who were nominated not for their legal expertise but for their loyalty to their aldermen and to the Cook County Democratic Central Committee. Although some judges ruled fairly, many used their position to pay back those who helped them get there in the first place. As journalist Mike Royko summed up, "Most of the judges came up through the Machine;

many are former ward bosses themselves. This doesn't mean cases are always rigged, but one cannot underestimate the power of sentimentality."[71] The speculators, on the whole, were wealthy men; they had ties to aldermen who were, in many instances, close to the judges.

A final reason for the dismissive rulings was cultural. The judges were comfortable and the plaintiffs were working class. The judges were established and the plaintiffs were newcomers. And of course, the judges were white and the plaintiffs were black. These differences might have made it difficult for the judges to empathize with my father's clients. At least this was my father's view. As he ranted in a letter to a journalist friend, he was furious at the judges' attitudes, furious that his clients' fates were determined by men who had "neither grasp nor concept of the tremendous burden carried by the Negro people." Those few blacks who brought their predators to trial found that "the Court . . . treats them with a callous contempt and our Judges act as though the Negro deserves the punishment he gets. It is hard to imagine any other society in which the Courts and Judges are so brutal to the needs of the people as are the Judges of Cook County to the needs of the Negro."[72]

My father's clients, not surprisingly, were less free to express their anger. Their reactions ran the gamut from acceptance to bitterness. To Sallie Bolton, the house was "a trauma." She never forgot that the down payment she and Albert gave to Jay Goran could have been saved for their children's college education. But the Boltons refused to let the loss crush them. Some of their resilience was temperamental. While Sallie tended to be a worrier, Albert was an easygoing type. In Sallie's words, "He wore life as a loose garment. He flowed with the ways of life." Between the two of them, the couple managed to make peace with adversity. Their treatment by Goran was but part of a continuum of difficult experiences they'd had with white Chicagoans. When Sallie applied for a job with the publishing company R. R. Donnelly, for example, the woman behind the desk took one look at her and announced, "I won't hire you." Sallie cried all the way home, but Albert told her, "Sal, that's O.K., it's not the end of the world," and sure enough, the next day she found a job at Revere Camera, where she stayed for twenty-five years.

Albert took a similar view of the house they'd hoped to own. "You didn't lose an eye and a limb, so just let it go," was his attitude. Sallie, too, realized that "if I let that house hurt me, it'd be a monkey on my back."

The financial loss was something they could surmount. "We enjoyed it while we were there," she said. The Boltons remained as renters in the Hyde Park area, with its safer streets and superior schools. They paid a high price for doing business with Goran, but as Sallie put it, the encounter with him ultimately led them out of the dismal conditions of the Black Belt. "The house brought us out of the depths of poverty," she reasoned.[73]

William and Wilma Coleman did not fare as well. The couple spent two years fighting Jay Goran, only to find themselves held responsible for their own exploitation.[74] The final ruling came on June 14, 1960. Two weeks later, William Coleman was dead. He died of a heart attack brought on, the press reported, by the "strain and anguish of trying to meet [his] debts." Coleman was sixty-one years old. According to his widow, "He seemed to age 10 years in the last two years. It was just worry, worry, worry." The house "took everything we had," she told Chicago Daily News reporters: "I will be lucky to find work to support myself."[75]

Joeanna Williams, Mary Lee Stevenson, and Bertha and Lawrence Richards found a way to move forward. Bertha said that after Moe Forman "messed up" her family's life, they "fought till they couldn't. All of them went into bad health. Lawrence had about three heart attacks." Bertha, however, ultimately came to terms with her family's financial and political loss: "I feel sorry that they were so cruel, to treat us like that. . . . Nothing . . . didn't go like we wanted it. . . . We just felt sorry in the heart, that's it." Her family tried not to let the experience poison their lives. Joeanna, Mary Lee, and Lawrence had "no bitterness" about their battles with Forman, Bertha recalled, because "they was Christians."[76]

As his lawsuits made their way through the courts, my father continued to look for ways to inform black Chicagoans directly about the dangers of contract buying. Julio Vivas, the executive director of the Greater Lawndale Conservation Commission (GLCC), had closely followed the unfolding drama of my father's crusade against exploitative contract sales.[77] In the summer of 1958, Vivas invited my father to address a GLCC-sponsored community meeting on the problem.

Unfortunately, even so small a step as sponsoring a community meeting was too much for some commission members. Among those most passionately opposed to the gathering was board member Al Weinberg—

perhaps because Weinberg was himself a contract seller. Weinberg and his attorney, Michael Kalika, both "highly irate," showed up at the GLCC offices shortly before my father was scheduled to speak and "condemned the Commission's action [in inviting Mark Satter to discuss contract sales] as destroying their business." Eager to placate them, the board agreed to allow Kalika and a savings and loan representative, Al Ropa, to present their view as well.[78]

The forum was held on June 17, 1958. It was, in some ways, a great success. The neatly dressed, overwhelmingly black audience of 150 people listened with expressions of shock, concern, and anger as my father laid out the extraordinary price that black Chicagoans paid for their exclusion from the legitimate mortgage market. The "one million dollars a day" that speculators extracted from black Lawndalers was "money that is lost to the grocer, the shoemaker, the clothier, and to colleges for higher education for Negroes. This is money that is taken out of the community for good." The blame for this "intolerable situation" lay with "the mortgage bankers of our community," he insisted, and he predicted that the evil would "persist so long as Negro people are unable to borrow money in order to buy a home."[79] In rebuttal, Kalika stated that contract sellers had every right to buy low and sell high: "Aside from the theory of Communism, there is nothing wrong with investing in a legal venture in the hope of gaining the highest possible profit."[80] Al Ropa, executive vice president of People's Federal Savings and Loan and the director of the Cook County Council of Savings and Loan Associations, chose to ignore evidence that many black contract buyers made larger down payments on their properties than white speculators did. He insisted that savings and loans were prevented from lending money to African Americans because of regulations that barred loans to those without sufficient down payments. "We're hamstrung," he told the audience. "We have to refuse the loan." He suggested that Lawndale's black residents form their own savings institutions, which would presumably be able to avoid the problems that "hamstrung" his associations.[81]

Julio Vivas was pleased with the forum, which was well covered in Chicago newspapers.[82] Immediately afterward he offered my father a place on the board as well as a monthly column in the GLCC newsletter. The column, "So You're Buying a Home," ran from July 1958 to February 1961. During these same years my father was also writing a biweekly column in the *Chicago Defender* titled "All That Money Can Buy." In both, he explained the contract sales trap, analyzed the repercussions of the mortgage "blacklist" of Lawndale, and warned against other forms of predatory credit sales that could lead to bankruptcy.[83]

The GLCC's compromise of supporting both my father and the mortgage lenders and contract sellers he condemned was bound to fall apart eventually. As my father put it, the "merchants in the community complained about my writings and . . . since the group was dependent on financial contributions," Vivas saw "fit to discontinue the type of advice I offered." On the black-oriented radio program *South Side Lights,* my father offered a more brutal summary. The GLCC, he said, was "against educating the people because they were looking to the merchants who were fleecing these people for money."[84]

But there was a deeper conflict. My father believed that Lawndale's greatest need was for access to mortgage money. The GLCC, essentially an urban renewal organization, believed that middle-class housing was the priority. In 1959, the GLCC sponsored a not-for-profit corporation that would acquire vacant land in the area, build middle-class housing, and then market the units interracially. The development, called "Kedvale Square," would be the first new construction in Lawndale in thirty years. Its planner, one Jack Meltzer, had worked closely with University of Chicago leaders on Hyde Park's urban renewal and, like them, he viewed urban renewal as a way to reduce black residency.[85]

My father spoke vehemently against the Kedvale Square project. He told *South Side Lights* radio show host Wesley South that the development diverted "funds contributed in $1.00 and $3.00 amounts by the poor people of the community"—that is, the dues paid by locals who had counted on the GLCC to fight slum landlords—to the "pockets of a private builder" who had "nothing to offer the community." He complained about the project to the *Chicago Daily News:* "I regard 'Kedvale Square' development as a highly improper departure from the stated purposes of the organization supposedly sponsoring it," he wrote.[86] In fact, Kedvale Square was very much in keeping with the GLCC's fundamental purpose as a "conservation" organization. But my father was probably right about the folly of believing that new middle-class housing was the answer to Lawndale's problems. The Kedvale Square development cost $1.5 million. By 1962, only six of its eighty-nine units had been sold.[87] The middle class didn't want to move to Kedvale Square; Lawndalers couldn't afford to.

The leaders of the GLCC continued to passionately support the idea that urban renewal could save Lawndale. "Kedvale Square will help bring about a new image of Lawndale as a good place to live," Vivas wrote in 1964.[88] While the GLCC devoted itself to a vain pursuit of urban renewal funds, Lawndale spun out of control.

The cycle of "blockbusting," white violence, urban crime, white flight, and community decay that beset Lawndale from the late 1950s on was depressingly familiar to anyone who had followed the processes of racial change in Chicago. First, Lawndale's streets were canvassed by speculators soliciting sales. "It was learned that [speculator Lou Fushanis's] Friendly Loan Corp. has been visiting home owners and raising fears of a changing community in an attempt to purchase homes," a GLCC member noted in 1959. The company's salesmen told whites that "the only persons who will rent a vacant apartment [in Lawndale] are Puerto Ricans, Mexicans, or Negroes," she added. Knowing that the rumored or actual presence of African Americans would depress prices, Fushanis also rented units in his own buildings to black tenants.[89]

As more black families moved in, some whites responded with mob attacks on black properties. For example, in July 1957, approximately a thousand whites surrounded a building that had been purchased by an African American in an Italian section of Lawndale. They shattered the building's windows until they were dispersed by the police. The next night two hundred white teenagers gathered near the home, chanting, "We want blood." In another 1957 incident, over one hundred black Lawndale residents flooded the street to rescue four black youths who were being chased by a gang of approximately twenty young white men. While more dramatic than most, this was merely one of numerous incidents throughout the 1950s in which black adults confronted white teenagers who were harassing black youth.[90]

Smaller-scale acts of harassment against African Americans became increasingly common. Blacks moving into Polish and Italian sections of Lawndale were particularly likely to suffer threats and indignities. Whites set the cars of their new black neighbors on fire, threw torches on their roofs, and smoke-bombed their apartments. One apartment building purchased by blacks had its windows shattered so consistently that the owners could not find tenants willing to live there. Another black family endured four years of harassment by local whites and received no help from the police.[91]

Racially motivated violence was only part of a larger wave of crime that engulfed the neighborhood. Crime was nothing new in Lawndale; it had had the highest crime rate in Chicago since the late 1940s, when it was overwhelmingly Jewish (in the north section) and Polish and Italian (in the south section). Even at that point, as one resident noted, Lawndale had "been going downhill for a long time." But once Lawndale began to experience rapid racial change, things got a lot worse. There were robberies, stabbings, and beatings as well as gang murders and shakedowns of local businesses. Many of these crimes were committed by youths; by the late 1950s Lawndale produced the largest number of juvenile offenders of any neighborhood in the city.[92]

Although few noted the connection, the youth crime wave may well have been yet another painful consequence of exploitative contract sales. To manage their high monthly contract payments, black residents had to overcrowd their properties. For Lawndale, which had always been a densely packed neighborhood, the resulting increase in population was a disaster. In 1960, when Chicago's average population ratio was 17,000 people per square mile, the ratio in Lawndale was 29,000 people per square mile. Lawndale's schools suffered especially. Between 1951 and 1965, school enrollment increased 286 percent. Bryant School, which my father had attended as a child, was typical. Its enrollment soared from 1,546 students in 1954 to 3,218 in 1957. In 1955, Lawndale was approximately a hundred classrooms short of what its youth population required.[93]

The city responded to the shortage of classrooms by placing the students on "double shifts," with half of the students attending an early shift and half a later one.[94] Double-shift schools denied Lawndale's children more than a basic education; the truncated school day also meant that many went without adult supervision. As the executive director of a local community center reported in 1957, in three-quarters of the families they served, "both parents or all the adults in the home are working" in order to meet the "high cost of living."[95] The director offered no explanation for why the cost of living should be so unusually high in this particular neighborhood, but undoubtedly primary among those costs was housing purchased on contract.

Left to fend for themselves, Lawndale's black teenagers gravitated toward gangs, which provided some structure—and unleashed violence. "The kids learned if they got together they could control the neighborhood," one resident noted. As early as the mid-1950s, gangs appeared to be "all powerful" in Lawndale. They battled one another, and local residents were caught in the crossfire.[96]

In the summer of 1958, Chicago newspapers reported a "rising wave of brutal assaults" in Lawndale. The violence accelerated white flight and definitively ended the Jewish presence in the area. That July a local rabbi, Dov Warshawsky, announced that he was leaving after he had been beaten and slashed by two men. "We have been thinking of moving for a long time because of the neighborhood," he explained, but "the beating was the last straw."[97]

The complex crosscurrents in Lawndale may have best been captured by the events surrounding one particular contract sale. In August 1959, a black couple, Josh and Barbara Hargrave, purchased a building on a block that had been all white. They made the extraordinary down payment of $9,000 on the "modern" yellow-brick three-flat that was sold to them on contract for $29,000. The Hargraves had been displaced from their previous home by the city's land clearance office and hoped to start a new life with their four children in Lawndale. Instead, menacing white crowds gathered in front of their building for four nights in a row. On the worst night, 500 police confronted a mob of 4,000 rock- and bottle-throwing whites. The real estate dealer who expedited the contract sale, Harry Gaynor, was also threatened repeatedly. "I hope you remember what happened to Melchiorre, so you be prepared," an anonymous writer threatened. The reference was to Mario Melchiorre, who had been murdered three weeks earlier; rumor had it that he'd been killed for selling to blacks in a white neighborhood.[98]

Yet the sale was not what it seemed. The building had been sold on contract not by a ruthless Lawndale speculator but by its owner, a Mrs. Rosen, who had no choice but to sell under those terms. She had kept the building on the market for two years but received no offers that were even close to its worth. Finally she agreed to sell to the Hargraves. Even though they could not get a mortgage, their $9,000 down payment was so generous that she was willing to defer payment of the remaining $20,000 at a reasonable rate of interest. Mrs. Rosen saw nothing wrong with selling to a black family. As she told the GLCC, when she'd moved to the neighborhood thirty years earlier, she, too, had "received threats from people who said the presence of a Jew would lower property values." Harry Gaynor, the dealer who arranged the sale, made no extraordinary profit on it. He was a former Communist Party member who felt that "you didn't have to exploit people" to work in the real estate business and that "all men are created equal in the image of God."[99]

In short, the broker, the seller, and the buyers in this contract sale were all principled people maneuvering in difficult circumstances. But by the late 1950s, the structural problems besetting Lawndale forced even well-meaning individuals to participate in an odious system. Bank redlining made it impossible for a property owner to make a normal mortgage sale. As a result of the outrageous sums charged by real estate speculators operating in the increasingly black northern section of Lawndale, that decaying area was degenerating further into an overcrowded, violence-ridden slum. No white person would consider moving to the adjoining white section of Lawndale, where Mrs. Rosen's building was located. Nevertheless, in the eyes of that section's whites, any sale to a black person would compound the credit squeeze that was strangling their community and bring with it the host of social ills they observed in North Lawndale—social ills whose causes they misunderstood but whose results they rightly deplored.

The perspectives of all concerned in this painful downward spiral were articulated in the media response to the harassment of the Hargraves. First the *Chicago Daily News* printed an essay by Theodore A. Jones of the NAACP, who denounced the threatening white mob as a "social blight." Instead of gaining sympathy for the Hargraves, however, Jones's essay prompted white readers to express their own despair and rage. "The people who were protesting have seen what happens to so-called 'changing neighborhoods,'" wrote Elsie Weigert, a white Chicagoan. "A case in point is the [North] Lawndale district. It was a nice-looking section of Chicago. Mr. Jones should drive through it now and he would really see blight. . . . People do not object to the color of [African Americans'] skin. It is the mess a neighborhood gets into once it has changed that people object to." Her views were seconded by Harry Berry, another white Chicagoan. "Mr. Theodore A. Jones asks the question: 'How can the myth that Negroes drive whites out of a neighborhood be exploded?' . . . It was not myth that moved my family from a changing neighborhood," Berry countered. "Fear and filth were the factors."

Their comments prompted a rebuttal by Benjamin F. Bell Jr. of the NAACP. Bell noted that, while Weigert and Berry had "much seeming truth" in their complaints, they ignored the fact that "housing is the only salable commodity in Chicago that black Chicago citizens cannot buy on the open market." He laid the blame for the deterioration of the area on "real estate interests—black and white"—who "mercilessly" hiked rents and sales prices while reducing "maintenance and inducing overcrowding which result in atrocious crimes and conduct." The final word came from Welton I. Taylor, a self-described "middle-class Negro homeowner." He agreed that Weigert and Berry's objections were "all too true. However, all decent people, Caucasian and Negro, share their hatred of the fear and filth, purse-snatching, dope raids and blight." People like him, who "deposited our life savings to buy into these changing neighborhoods at premium prices, hoping to form stable, respectable, interracial communities," were dedicated to "keep[ing] their property free of blight." But he and his kind confronted immense obstacles. "Face it! Racial prejudice is profitable in Chicago. Every time a new parcel of land is added to the Bronze Ghetto, millions of dollars in real estate profits are made!"[100]

By 1959 everyone from aggrieved whites to the NAACP agreed that changing areas like Lawndale were prone to crime and decay.[101] Two years later local clergy reported that South Lawndale was "experiencing something of a 'sense of siege'" as the "Negro community to the North gradually expands southward." They reported residents' concerns about overcrowding, housing decay, dangerous parks and streets, and the fact that "the police do not respond when you call them." Soon South Lawndale's remaining white residents were fleeing in droves.[102]

My father observed the devastation in Lawndale with increasing anxiety. By the time I was born in January 1959, my parents' finances were already stretched so thin that my mother worried over how they would accommodate this final baby. The family needed whatever extra income the Lawndale properties could bring in—income that was threatened by the decline of the neighborhood.

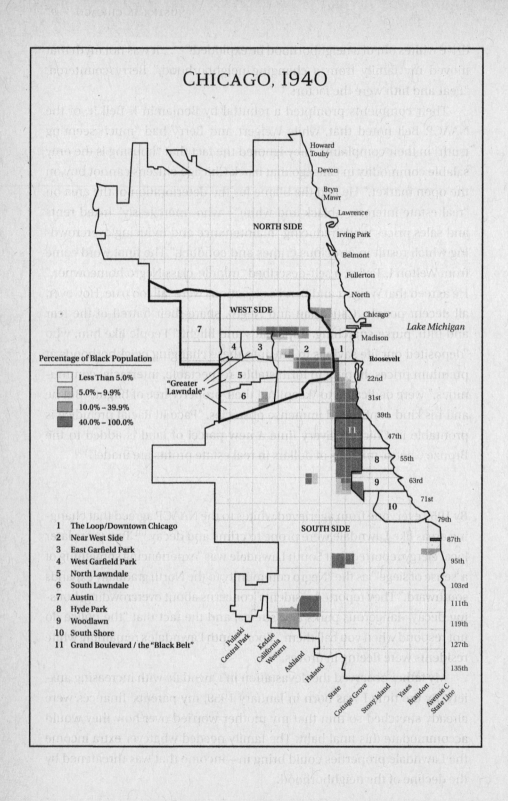

CHICAGO, 1940

Howard
Touhy
Devon
Bryn
Mawr
Lawrence
Irving Park
Belmont
Fullerton
North
Chicago
Madison
Roosevelt
22nd
31st
39th
47th
55th
63rd
71st
79th
87th
95th
103rd
111th
119th
127th
135th

NORTH SIDE

WEST SIDE

SOUTH SIDE

Lake Michigan

Percentage of Black Population

- Less Than 5.0%
- 5.0% – 9.9%
- 10.0% – 39.9%
- 40.0% – 100.0%

"Greater Lawndale"

1   The Loop/Downtown Chicago
2   Near West Side
3   East Garfield Park
4   West Garfield Park
5   North Lawndale
6   South Lawndale
7   Austin
8   Hyde Park
9   Woodlawn
10   South Shore
11   Grand Boulevard / the "Black Belt"

Pulaski
Central Park
Kedzie
California
Western
Ashland
Halsted
State
Cottage Grove
Stony Island
Yates
Brandon
Avenue C
State Line

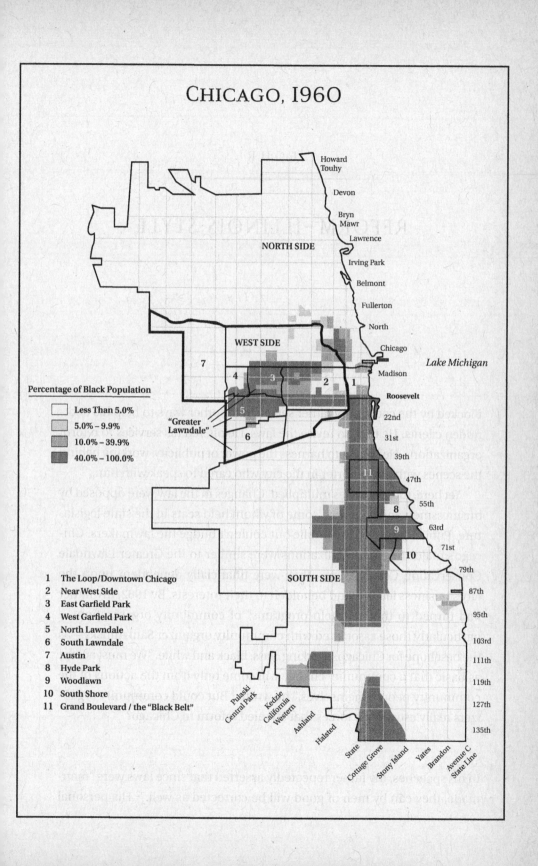

CHICAGO, 1960

Howard
Touhy

Devon

Bryn
Mawr

Lawrence

NORTH SIDE

Irving Park

Belmont

Fullerton

North

Chicago
Lake Michigan

WEST SIDE

Madison

7

Roosevelt

4
3
2
1

Percentage of Black Population

	Less Than 5.0%
	5.0% – 9.9%
	10.0% – 39.9%
	40.0% – 100.0%

5

22nd

"Greater
Lawndale"

31st

6

39th

11

47th

55th

8

63rd

9

SOUTH SIDE

71st

10

79th

87th

95th

1   The Loop/Downtown Chicago
2   Near West Side
3   East Garfield Park
4   West Garfield Park
5   North Lawndale
6   South Lawndale
7   Austin
8   Hyde Park
9   Woodlawn
10   South Shore
11   Grand Boulevard / the "Black Belt"

103rd

111th

119th

127th

Pulaski
Central Park

Kedzie
California
Western

Ashland

Halsted

135th

State

Cottage Grove

Stony Island

Yates

Brandon

Avenue C
State Line

FOUR

REFORM—ILLINOIS-STYLE

Blocked by the courts, my father searched for other ways to help his debt-ridden clients. He tried to revise the laws. He offered his services to reform organizations. He sought to harness the power of publicity, working behind the scenes with any reporter in the city who cared to speak with him.

Yet here, too, obstacles multiplied. Changes in the law were opposed by businessmen and creditors, some of whom held seats in the state legislature. Publicity roused the public but couldn't budge the lawmakers. Chicago's major reform organizations were similar to the Greater Lawndale Conservation Commission—they were financially dependent upon the city's business leaders and beholden to their interests. By 1962, my father had turned to the "self-help programs" of community organizations—particularly those associated with community organizer Saul Alinsky—as the best hope for Chicago's working class, black and white. "We must accept as basic that a community change will come only from the actions of the community people themselves," he wrote.[1] But could community organizers really escape the forces that stymied reform in Chicago?

In his speeches, my father repeatedly asserted that since laws were "man-made, they can by men of good will be corrected as well."[2] His personal effort to reform Illinois law began in earnest in 1960, and it concerned not contract selling but what contemporaries called the "sell-and-garnishee credit racket."[3]

The two were related. Brokers and attorneys were not the only white professionals who preyed upon Chicago's African Americans. They were also hurt by merchants who sold them overpriced, high-interest items on credit and then garnished their wages when they missed a payment. The obvious common denominator between the contract sale of property and the installment sale of smaller items lay in white professionals' ability to manipulate African Americans' desperate need for credit.[4] Both created debt peonage, and both would have to be stopped if Chicago's burgeoning black population was to have a fair chance to prosper.

For my father, the issue was not simply that merchants charged high prices and outrageous rates of interest on goods that they sold on credit but rather that the law gave them the right to *collect the wages* of their delinquent customers. In Illinois, creditors were allowed to lay claim to over a quarter of their debtor's paycheck—a stark contrast to the laws of New York, which allowed only 10 percent of weekly wages to be subject to garnishment.[5] Illinois law also made wage garnishment extraordinarily easy. It permitted the use of "wage assignment" forms—contracts in which the customer promised that if he or she was late with a payment the merchant could go directly to the customer's boss and collect a portion of his or her wages. No court order was necessary. Illinois also allowed retailers to require customers to sign "confession of judgment" forms, which nullified in advance their right to defend themselves in court should their creditors pursue legal action against them.[6]

Of course, an individual was in principle free to choose whether or not to sign a wage assignment or confession of judgment form. In reality, the choice was not so evident. The forms were usually buried within long, complicated installment sale contracts. People believed that they were making some small purchase—a watch, or a ring, or dancing lessons—for a mere "five dollars down." They rarely realized that by signing these forms, they were putting their wages at risk.[7]

The result was a situation ripe for abuse. By the late 1950s, the actions of "credit racketeers" who stood outside factory gates and combed Chicago's black and immigrant neighborhoods, selling cheap or worthless items for little money down, were well known among advocates of the poor.

The credit racketeers' goal was not to make sales per se but to get signatures on wage assignment forms. Once they had the signatures, unscrupulous merchants could go to their victims' employers and ask for whatever sum of money they thought they could get away with. The city's largest employers of unskilled labor noted the results. When the Inland Steel Company's "garnishment administrator," Dorothy Lascoe, began to investigate some of the garnishments she was processing, she found merchants who demanded sums of $550 when their customers owed only $250 and creditors who collected wage garnishments for months without ever applying the money they were collecting to the debt they claimed to be owed. As Lascoe explained: "The debtor is not properly protected by the law because, under Illinois law, the merchant does not have to prove to the judge how much a person still owes him."[8]

My father believed that the worst injustice of the credit-garnishee racket was its violation of a fundamental human right: the right to collect a wage for one's labor. He felt strongly that Illinois law should not allow this right to be waived for any reason. He also pointed out that the state's garnishment laws compromised a debtor's ability to hold a job. Employers who did not want to go through the bother of dividing up a garnished paycheck often chose to fire the employee instead. And an employee who had several garnishments on his or her record became virtually unemployable. Since unscrupulous merchants congregated in black neighborhoods, African Americans were disproportionately subject to wage garnishments—and unemployment. My father found this outcome particularly abhorrent. "A job is all a poor Negro has," he wrote. "Take that away and you leave him nothing."[9]

Black Chicagoans who were victimized by both real estate speculators and unscrupulous credit merchants were left to face devil's choices. Take my father's client Reginald Kent. By 1961, when Kent joined Mary Lee Stevenson in a suit against General Federal Savings and Loan, his problems had ballooned well beyond the loss of a building into which he had sunk $11,000 in less than five years. Apparently he had purchased various items on the installment plan, possibly to save money for his house payments. But when he fell behind on his payments, his creditors garnished part of his wages. Kent's employer, unwilling to deal with the paperwork of dividing up his paycheck, simplified matters by firing him.[10] Kent could not find a new position because of the garnishments on his record.[11]

Robert Wilson was another client who experienced the brutal economic facts of life for those at the bottom. Wilson's wife believed that she was getting a low-priced refrigerator and some free canned food in return for joining a "club"; she needed only sign some documents. The forms she signed indebted her and her husband for $1,536 and included a wage assignment. The Wilsons couldn't make the payments, so the company garnished Robert's wages. Since he already had garnishments on his record, his employer threatened to fire him. The only way he could have the wage garnishment removed was by declaring bankruptcy. However, the bankruptcy declaration would enable his creditors to take his house. As my father noted of Wilson, "He's in a deadly spot. He loses his home if he goes bankrupt, he loses his job if he doesn't. He has a wife and four children. Jobs can't be found. The end of the line usually is the relief rolls."[12]

In 1959, my father wrote an article for a legal journal in which he argued that Illinois law must be reformed to make the garnishment of wages illegal in all circumstances. That year he also wrote numerous articles on the subject in his *Chicago Defender* column—many describing the bitter experiences of his own clients.[13] But try as he might, my father and the handful of others who hoped to interest Chicagoans in the perils of the sell-and-garnishee credit racket got nowhere.

This situation changed suddenly in February 1960. As usual in Chicago, the catalyst for change was an avoidable tragedy.

On February 5, 1960, a Puerto Rican Chicagoan named William Rodriguez purchased some rat poison and gulped it down as he walked the streets. Within hours he went into convulsions. Rodriguez, who had a wife and four children to support on his earnings as an order filer at Sears, Roebuck and Company, had already had his paycheck garnished three times. He had just learned that his wages were about to be garnished once again. From his hospital bed he told policemen that he was "tired of being hounded by creditors." By the morning of February 6, he was dead.

Rodriguez's suicide made headlines. It also prompted an explosion of media coverage on the wage garnishment problem. Within weeks, Mayor Richard Daley directed his Committee on New Residents to study the problem of credit exploitation. He also appointed a Subcommittee on

Legislative Action to propose changes to Illinois law. Among the business, labor, and welfare leaders invited to join was my father.[14]

Some in the Legislative Action group argued that Illinois should follow New York's example and make wage garnishment less worthwhile for creditors by exempting a larger proportion of a worker's wages. My father passionately disagreed. He insisted that the damage of wage garnishment lay less in the money it deducted from the paycheck than in the threat it posed to the debtor's ability to hold a job—any job. As he put it, "The exemptions are basically meaningless; once an employer is involved in his employee's troubles, he tells the employee to pay up or get out." The only solution was to outlaw the garnishment of wages, as Britain had done almost a century earlier.[15]

On November 22, 1960, the members of the Legislative Action committee made their official recommendations. First, they proposed that wage garnishments, hereafter to be referred to as "wage deductions," be limited to 15 percent of a worker's wages, instead of the 25 percent that was previously allowed. Second, while currently creditors were forced to file a separate request for each week that they wished to garnish a salary, the committee proposed that creditors be allowed to garnish workers' wages for as long as eight weeks with a single request—this last in order to simplify the bookkeeping for employers forced to deal with wage deductions. The committee's final two proposals called for the abolition of the wage assignment and confession of judgment forms, which were the two documents most easily abused by unscrupulous merchants.[16]

The committee's chairman, Ely Aaron, admitted that the proposals were not as forceful as they might be. But he pleaded expediency: the task was "to get a set of proposals together that would stand a good chance of being enacted into law." My father disagreed. "Our stand must be based upon our own concepts of what is right," he insisted, not on what will pass.[17] He also resigned from the committee, explaining in a letter that he had believed the committee's purpose was to rectify the exploitative credit laws that had led to a victim's death—not to make debt collection easier for creditors.[18]

Determined to fight the proposals, my father went to the press. He told reporters that "Inland Steel betrayed the trust" of Chicagoans, apparently by privately convincing some on the Legislative Action committee to vote for the plank granting creditors the right to garnish two months' worth of wages with a single request, even though the committee had rejected that proposal in several earlier meetings.[19] The result was a rush of negative publicity for the mayor's committee. "Calls Credit Law Proposals 'Fraud,'" read a *Daily News* headline reporting my father's resignation. *Kup's Column,* the city's premier gossip source, reported that "Mayor Daley's Committee to correct credit abuses" was "strife-torn with the resignation of attorney **Mark Satter**," adding that "Chicago has the worst record on garnishments in the nation."[20]

My father used the attention to continue his battle against wage garnishment. During a June 1961 appearance on the television show *City Desk,* he was accused by host Len O'Connor of trying to "tear down the whole house" of credit simply because a few "used car dealers . . . are taking advantage of some poor chump who needs a keeper." My father answered: "I am in favor of credit and I believe that neither these people nor I could live without credit." He wanted only "to remove the ability of the creditor . . . to grasp the wages of the man who works," a change that would "put the buyer and seller on more of an even basis." "What you're trying to do is . . . to legislate economic protection," O'Connor protested. "It would not be the first time in the history of our country," my father fired back.[21]

His efforts had little effect. That summer, the Illinois legislature passed credit reform bills that closely followed the proposals of the Legislative Action committee. Chicago newspapers praised the new bills and promised that they would drive the "sell-and-garnishee retailers" out of the state.[22] My father, of course, shared none of their optimism. Although gratified that the legislature had outlawed confessions of judgment and made wage assignments far more difficult to use, my father deplored the remaining changes. He mocked the legislators for their courageous action in abolishing the word "garnishment" from the legal statute of the State of Illinois—and replacing it with the words "wage deduction," which meant "precisely and exactly" the same thing. He minimized the significance of raising the percentage of wages exempted from garnishment from 75 to 85 percent: the problem was the threat to a worker's employment posed by any wage garnishment whatsoever. He argued that the one substantive change—the extension of a single garnishment action from one week to four weeks—would hurt rather than help debtors. This change "will be responsible for a general lowering of the earning powers of hundreds of thousands of our people," my father told a Chicago community group. The *Daily News* reported his demand that the U.S. Congress take action to outlaw wage attachment, since "no honest remedy can be expected" from the Illinois legislature.[23]

It seemed, however, that a corner had been turned in public toleration for the sell-and-garnishee credit racket. In the spring of 1961, Chicago's municipal court appointed a special commissioner to investigate credit abuses. The commissioner, attorney John J. King, worked closely with two undercover detectives to establish a highly effective sting operation. A downtown Chicago jeweler sold a 21-jewel watch to a black janitor newly arrived from Mississippi for $56.85 on credit. The watch was actually worth nine dollars, and the janitor, it turned out, was Detective Sylvester Rhem, who promptly arrested the jeweler. A suburban car dealer sold a "Mexican newcomer" a car with a blank sales contract that would have allowed him to write in any price and conditions he wished. The "newcomer" turned out to be Detective Aurelio Garcia, and the auto dealer ended up in court for fraud.[24]

King received powerful additional support when Illinois created its first Bureau of Consumer Credit Protection in the summer of 1961. Charged with revoking the charters of firms that repeatedly engaged in unethical credit practices, the bureau received four hundred complaints within two weeks of its establishment. Many were related to a vending machine scam that was ensnaring hundreds of working-class Chicagoans, this time mainly white.[25]

The scam was a classic. People in need of cash responded to phone solicitations and advertisements promising part-time work servicing vending machines. Instead of being hired to service the machines, they were pressured into purchasing them. Some believed that the long and confusing forms they signed were contracts of employment, only to find that they had signed papers indebting them for $700 vending machines—as well as wage assignment forms, still legal that spring, that enabled the companies to garnish their paychecks if they fell behind in their payments. Others realized that they were purchasing an expensive vending machine sight unseen but were convinced by the salesmen that the machines "pay for themselves" and would soon be making a profit.[26]

The $700 vending machines turned out to be shoddy contraptions—primitive hot-water heaters accompanied by packets of instant coffee or soup—worth less than $100. Purchasers found it impossible to cancel their contracts, which were legal and fully binding. They also discovered that their contracts had been sold to collection companies within hours of their signing. Those who called to complain were told: "We are definitely not interested in your problems, only in your monthly payments." When they missed a payment, the collection companies garnished their wages. The victims—mostly low-wage workers who had sought extra employment to cover their overdue bills—found themselves burdened with a useless new debt and, worse, with the threat of garnished wages. Meanwhile, the companies selling the machines were netting $6,000 a day.[27]

Commissioner King tried to stop the racket. His undercover detectives were only able, however, to catch careless salesmen who had violated technicalities. As reporters explained, the "vending machine companies appear to be legal in themselves and it is difficult to prove criminal intent."[28]

Despite the legal shakiness of their position, vending machine victims found an attorney who would champion their cause: in July 1961, my father filed a complaint on their behalf.[29] As the case was publicized, more defrauded people stepped forward. Within three months the number of plaintiffs had swelled to 223. The number of defendants was widened to include several closely linked or jointly owned vending machine and collection companies.

In May 1962, the case came to trial and was quickly dispatched. Judge Cornelius Harrington ruled that the complaint set forth no cause of action, since the contracts that the plaintiffs signed were binding. Furthermore, the victims had no common grievance to justify being bound together. If each individual had brought a suit separately, they could have been heard, but because they brought suit as a group, they were dismissed. By now the original vending machine companies had "vanished into thin air." The victims, however, were left with the garnishments on their wages and their debts.[30]

My father appealed the ruling.[31] He argued, first, that his complaint did set forth a cause of action—namely, that the defendants had engaged in "fraud and deceit practiced in conspiracy."[32] Second, the injuries suffered by the plaintiffs were similar enough to justify a joint suit. "No plaintiff is possessed of funds to conduct alone a protracted legal battle with his despoilers," he added. Given this situation, "refusal to permit joinder is equal to a denial of redress."[33] But the most essential issue was the right to collect wages for work performed. My father drew upon an earlier ruling, *Van Kleek v. Bente,* which stated that a defendant's action was particularly vile because it involved a threat of wage garnishment and it was "common knowledge" that "employees causing such annoyance" were often dismissed. The situation here was similar. The finance companies knew that their power to collect a fraudulently induced $700 debt depended on the debtor's fear of wage garnishment and loss of employment: "An attack upon wages, carrying with it so devastating a threat to the very economic survival of the wage-earner . . . is . . . the greatest single offense committed by the defendants here, in a series of dishonorable offenses."[34]

The appellate court of Illinois rejected these arguments and dismissed the case. The plaintiffs' experiences were too distinct to be joined in a single suit. There was no proof that the finance companies were engaged with the vending machine companies in a "fraudulent scheme."[35] Finally, the court turned to the assertion that workers had a right to a wage for labor performed. To my father, the loss (or potential loss) of the right to be paid for one's labor was the essence of the injustice his clients had suffered. To the court, there was no such problem. Citing the revised Illinois credit laws of 1961—the very laws that my father had so strenuously denounced as useless—the court held that the threat of losing one's job because of wage garnishment "no longer exists." Given these new protections, the court held, there was no need to "consider the other points raised" by my father's appeal.[36]

The *Garfieldian,* a neighborhood paper that had given extensive coverage to the vending machine racket, added a nasty twist to my father's defeat. Not only had he bungled the case, the paper's reporter hinted, but he had exploited his clients as well. "The victims . . . can add another $75 to their list of debts. Each paid $25 to Mark Satter, attorney, for fighting the initial case and another $50 for being included in the appeal. Thus far Satter has been paid nearly $10,000," observed the *Garfieldian.*[37]

Who was right about the 1961 reform of Illinois's consumer credit laws—Satter or the court? Did the revised laws offer new protections, or didn't they? Within months of the laws' passage, Commissioner John King reported that garnishments had dropped by 20 percent. Evidence indicates, however, that this rosy view was premature. The number of garnishments filed in municipal court soon shot up again, from 19,742 for the last six months of 1961 to 31,187 for the last six months of 1962.[38] Moreover, since the period for each garnishment action had been extended from one week to four, the actual number of paychecks garnished was undoubtedly significantly higher. Meanwhile, the political will to fight credit scams evaporated. In February 1963, Commissioner King's sting team was dismantled, effective "immediately." As King told a *Daily News* reporter, "I tried to find out why, and was told there are 12,000 rapes a year in this city." King resigned a month later; the job, he said, "no longer had teeth."[39]

Faced with statistics proving that the 1961 reforms were ineffective, Illinois governor Otto Kerner decided that new laws were needed. In February 1963, he appointed a sixty-four-member advisory committee to propose stronger consumer credit laws. Unfortunately, the committee was well stocked with credit industry representatives. Apparently even the minimal reforms enacted in 1961 had "triggered panic in the credit industry." This time, Inland Steel's Dorothy Lascoe explained, "they banded together—the banks, loan companies, finance companies—to make sure 1963 wouldn't hurt them."[40]

Here is a sample of the changes recommended by the committee and enacted by the Illinois state legislature. Before the reforms, interest rates on small loans were limited to approximately 13 percent. After, the ceiling was raised to 19.56 percent (for comparison, New York and Pennsylvania both limited small-loan interest rates to 12 percent). Before the reforms, small-loan companies were forbidden to take homes as security on a loan. After, they could. Where the reforms didn't improve the prospects of creditors, they maintained the status quo. Before 1963, there was no legal limit to the interest rates charged on goods bought on installment; the interest rate could reach 200 percent, as long as the sales form included some explanation for it. Afterward, such exorbitant rates were still legal, since the bill proposing limits on installment sale interest rates was defeated. Similarly, prior to the changes a merchant could repossess an item sold on installment—say, an automobile—and still collect monthly payments on it, even though it was no longer in the debtor's possession, on the grounds that the customer had depreciated the item's value during the time he or she owned it. After the reforms, such actions were still legal;[41] the bill to outlaw the so-called deficiency judgment had been defeated.

Daily News reporter Lois Wille sarcastically summed up the changes as "reform Illinois-style." Democratic state representative Abner Mikva, a Kerner advisory committee member who had tried to safeguard consumer interests, had an even more scathing assessment. "We tried to solve burglary problems by legalizing burglary," he told Wille. "The credit companies are the single most powerful and influential lobby in Springfield." But credit companies weren't simply lobbyists. Some state legislators, such as Republican Dwight Friedrich of Sedalia, also owned small-loan companies. As one observer noted, "With legislators like him, the credit industry doesn't need lobbyists."[42]

Needless to say, my father was outraged. In letters to journalists he denounced the credit industry's ability to "use drives for reform as further springboards to oppress the poor." His 1963 article "Outlaw Garnishments" described both the mayor's Committee on New Residents and the governor's committee as consisting of "major economic interests with a sprinkling of neutral members." By participating in such efforts, the reformers had played "into the hands of the exploiters." The mayor's committee had produced thousands of pages of proposals, he said, when all that was needed was a three-line law outlawing garnishment. "The right to work is a basic human right. To take that right away by making it impossible for [a person] to find employment is oppressive and barbaric, whether sanctified by Illinois law or not."[43]

While my father found little legislative support for his reform crusades, he had somewhat more luck with the press, in particular the *Chicago Daily News*.[44] His most valuable contact there was Maurice "Ritz" Fischer, the paper's city editor.[45] My father did not need a personal relationship with a city editor to get his ideas into print, of course. As Favil Berns recalled, cub reporters often spent their time hanging around the County Building, "all waiting for tidbits of news from the lawyers who would drop by" with stories of scandal and the case records to provide the juicy details.[46] But my father's friendship with Fischer did expedite matters. He wrote Fischer long, detailed letters that documented the abuses his clients had suffered. He offered full access to his files for any verification that reporters

might need. Direct quotations from his letters found their way, sometimes acknowledged and sometimes not, into *Daily News* articles published only days later.[47]

In October 1959, the *Daily News* ran a series called "The Panic Peddlers." Researched and written by reporters M. W. Newman, Jack Willner,
and Harry W. Swegle—who was taken to the County Building by my father
and personally shown how to do property-records research—it detailed
the "nasty bag of fear tricks used to 'bust up' blocks," that is, to scare whites
into moving so that their homes could be resold to blacks at marked-
up prices.[48] From my father's perspective, the series was timid. It focused
on tactics used to hound whites from their homes rather than on the
devastating effects that race-based refusals of mortgage funding had on
blacks. Still, the series was a bombshell. It added a new phrase, "panic
peddler," to the language used to make sense of racial change.[49]

On December 7, 1960, two weeks after his noisy resignation from the
mayor's Committee on New Residents, my father sent Fischer a seven-
page letter detailing the brutal experiences of one of his clients. Onyx
Judon, a factory worker and father of five, had signed a note to enable a
friend to purchase a car. When the friend skipped town, the car company
garnished Judon's wages, sucking Judon into a disastrous sequence of
escalating indebtedness.[50] My father explained that all of the actions that
entrapped Judon were "entirely legal" and that "unless a tremendous house-
cleaning is instituted in regard to the financial transactions [affecting]
minority peoples, even worse conditions will arise." He concluded with
the usual postscript—"Should you see fit to further explore the truth of
these statements, for inclusion in a 'Panic-Peddler' type series, I can furnish examples of each practice, with the names of both perpetrators and
victims."[51]

Fischer took him up on the offer. Several weeks later, the paper began
a five-part series, "One Million Underdogs," that made connections
between contract selling and other forms of credit exploitation. "Economic oppression takes many forms, but the most vicious is in housing
and the installment credit-wage attachment racket," reporter Nicholas
Shuman announced in the January 23, 1961, opening article. He started
with housing. On January 24, the *Daily News* ran a photo of Joeanna
Williams's building on its front page, with the caption "Three-flat at 3920
Grenshaw—bought by white real estate dealers for $18,500 and sold to a

Negro for $29,500." The accompanying article explained the dangers of contract selling, under which the purchaser's "investment can be wiped out and his home repossessed as easily as his auto if he misses a payment or two." Dempsey J. Travis, president of the Dearborn Real Estate Board, explained that, in the Chicago neighborhoods that were opening to blacks, 75 percent of the properties were sold on contract. "A contract buyer can't afford anything more than his installments, so he just lets the property go. No grass. No paint. Maybe he'll make his apartments smaller to get more income. That's the beginning of a slum."[52] Shuman emphasized that mortgage companies were ultimately responsible for the problem. "Mortgage Credit Refusals Squeeze Minorities Here: Loan Practices Force Them to Buy Homes on Contract," read one headline. His next article took on the state's wage garnishment laws.[53] Even after going through bankruptcy court to free one's wages from garnishment, Shuman quoted my father, the laws allowed the "one single asset the debtor has sought to wrest free—his paycheck—[to be] subject anew to garnishment. . . . This man is marked for the relief rolls."[54]

"One Million Underdogs" was in many ways a triumph for my father. It drew upon his research, quoted him extensively, and reframed the credit racket and contract sales issues as he saw them. It was also a triumph for Nicholas Shuman, who received accolades from the Associated Press for the series.[55] But while the articles spurred discussion, they were unable to influence Illinois's 1961 credit reform laws, which followed the script of the mayor's committee.

A year later, another journalist entered the fray. Early in 1962, Alfred Balk showed up at my father's bare-bones office. He noted the long line of clients waiting there. Most were black. All were poor. Some had forlorn, desperate expressions and frightened, runny-nosed children in tow. "This fellow is in the front line of this thing," Balk thought. He had been following the blockbusting issue and was struck by the inadequate coverage of what was, after all, a national problem. But he had an idea. He would tell the story from the perspective of the blockbuster. He would also place the blockbuster's practice in its broadest context, so that Americans could go beyond demonizing individual real estate agents to the deeper problems of banking, mortgage, and federal government complicity in neighborhood redlining and decay.[56]

What Balk needed was a blockbuster who was willing to talk. My father was happy to help. The names of the city's worst real estate speculators were no secret, he told Balk. "Just check the *Daily Defender*."[57] After a bit of digging, Balk found his man. The big boys downtown benefit from your work, Balk told the speculator, but let you take the heat for it. I'm willing to tell your side of the story—and to keep your identity secret. That was all it took. Once Balk showed some sympathy, the speculator "poured his heart out." "They all get down on me," he raged. Let the country hear the real story. They could decide who was really to blame.[58]

"Confessions of a Block-Buster," by "Norris Vitchek as told to Alfred Balk," appeared in the July 14, 1962, edition of the *Saturday Evening Post*. It caused a sensation. "Vitchek" described the petty bigotries of white residents and the ease with which he exploited them. He would pay a fair price, or close to it, for the first house he "broke" on a block. After that he easily cleaned up on his purchases of the remaining houses and on their resale, on contract, to black families. "I make four times the profit I could for the same amount of effort in all-white real estate," he stated.[59]

The effectiveness of Balk's *Saturday Evening Post* exposé was magnified by its fortuitous timing. Another bombshell was released that same week, a Chicago Commission on Human Relations (CHR) study titled "Selling and Buying Real Estate in Racially Changing Neighborhoods." This "dynamite-packed" report detailed the real estate transactions of every building on a single square block that had changed from white to black residency. In January 1953, the block was exclusively white and not one of its buildings had been purchased with an installment land contract. Then black families moved in. By 1961, most of the buildings on the block (twenty-four out of twenty-nine) had been sold on installment contracts. The average profit to speculators making these sales was 73 percent. The names of the most active speculators on the block, Jay Goran and Gerald Crane, were familiar ones, at least to people who knew of my father's work. This was not surprising, since he had secretly participated in the report's preparation.[60]

The CHR's report was shocking (and meticulously documented), but its recommendations for stopping exploitative contract sales remained mild. It suggested a "strong program of consumer education" to teach black Chicagoans "the disadvantage of dealing with real estate speculators" and "the advantage of mortgage financing"—ignoring altogether the mortgage industry's refusal to grant loans to black applicants. As the *Chicago Defender* put it: "Negroes resort to installment contract buying, not as a matter of choice . . . but because commercial banks and trusts will not make loans to them." While "consumer education may do some good," those most truly in need of education were the "real estate and mortgage industries."[61]

Ultimately the CHR was forced to respond to the public outrage generated by the "Block-Buster" piece and its own "Selling and Buying Real Estate" report. In August 1962, it held a daylong public hearing on the contract sales problem. From the outset, the CHR was determined to preserve goodwill and declared that the hearing would not be "accusatory." Nevertheless, most of the twenty-seven speakers agreed that a "dual housing market" existed in Chicago that forced "Negroes [to] pay as much as 100 percent more for property than would be charged for similar property in a white neighborhood."[62] The hearing, widely publicized, led to yet more media attention. *Dateline Chicago* ran a television special titled *The House on Congress Parkway,* which focused on the travails of my father's clients Artiste and Angel Bowan. Despite having an "excellent" credit rating, Artiste Bowan, a war veteran and post office worker, had been refused a bank loan. The Bowans then bought a code-violation-ridden building on contract from speculator Lou Fushanis for $21,500, not knowing that Fushanis had recently purchased the property—on borrowed money (since redlining didn't seem to apply to white slum landlords with kickbacks to offer)—for $8,500. *The House on Congress Parkway* was so popular that *Dateline Chicago* ran a second show about the Bowans.[63] The shows generated their own followup press, including a hard-hitting series in the *Chicago Courier* on contract selling, installment credit buying, and my father's work, titled "The Million Dollars a Day Cost of Being Black."[64]

Although my father contributed to every part of this wave of coverage, he was not satisfied with it.[65] The Commission on Human Relations report does not "come to the heart of real estate difficulties in Chicago," he insisted. The *Saturday Evening Post* exposé also "failed dismally to complete the story," since it didn't fully explain contract sales or the high prices routinely paid by black purchasers. The CHR's public hearings were doomed from the start: "A hearing which does not probe in an 'accusatory' manner is simply not a hearing at all." My father listed the questions he felt ought to be asked. "Are there men in our city who make a profession of buying up property," who then offer it "for sale only to Negroes, and on terms which indicate a conspiracy to cheat and defraud whole communities?" "Do the Federally Insured Savings and Loan Associations of our city have an agreement to loan money to real estate speculators and to refuse money for the purchase of a home to the Negro people themselves?" "Is there a connection between gross gouging and crime in the Negro community? Is there an abdication of leadership on the part of Negro community organizations and Negro leaders? What responsibility does the Negro community itself bear for the conditions uncovered?"[66]

My father wanted an open fight—and he got one. The first to take a swing at him was Len O'Connor, who invited him back to *City Desk* in late July 1962. My father knew that O'Connor was not particularly progressive when it came to racial issues. On an earlier program O'Connor had criticized the "Selling and Buying Real Estate" study for its "implication that the Negroes and not the Whites are being fleeced" by real estate speculators. Ignoring the survey's proof that most African American contract buyers would have been able to afford traditional mortgages—indeed, speculators annually took in $10,730 more from contract buyers than they paid on their own mortgages—he also blasted the report for hinting that mortgages were denied to blacks because of racial bigotry rather than for the simple economic reason that blacks were "economically deprived."[67]

Nothing prepared my father, though, for what awaited him on O'Connor's show. Instead of hosting an "accusatory" investigation of mortgage bankers and speculative contract sellers, O'Connor turned the show into an accusatory investigation of Mark J. Satter. He flashed photographs of broken windows on the screen and identified my father as the owner of the photographed properties. Completely unprepared, my father was left to state weakly that "I try to replace the windows, but the tenants keep breaking them"—sounding no different from the average slumlord.[68] O'Connor also informed viewers that about a year earlier Satter had been given a suspended fine of $25 for failing to repair "defective plumbing fixtures" in one of his buildings. Finally, he asked a series of complicated questions that somehow gave the impression that my father sold buildings on contract. My father was too stunned by this unexpected personal attack to adequately defend himself.[69]

After the broadcast my mother sent an anguished letter to *City Desk*. "If you were seeking truth, you should have made an honest investigation before this broadcast, instead of wasting valuable time . . . which left the viewing audience wondering . . . about the character of Mark Satter instead of the real issue which was Real Estate speculators and the resulting decay of our neighborhoods," she wrote. "The fact that Mark Satter has enemies is no secret. . . . Many of these individuals would go to great lengths to do harm to my husband in whatever way they could."[70]

My mother was right; Mark Satter had enemies. They included members of the United Property Group, an organization of whites living in Lawndale and the adjoining West Garfield Park neighborhood, who came together in 1959 to hold the line against black occupancy. The UPG despised blockbusters, but like many other whites they had an expansive definition of the term, applying it to any person who rented or sold property to an African American, no matter what the terms or conditions. My father's long history of renting his apartments to black families meant that he fit the bill. Now the UPG accused him of being the blockbuster who "confessed" in Balk's piece. The *Garfieldian* supported this rumor by printing stories about Mark J. Satter's buildings and about the fees he charged as an attorney. My father's response had an embattled tone. A *Garfieldian* reporter described how "Satter grabbed him by the arm" as he rose to leave after an interview. "Let's be fair about this thing. If you're going to call me a blockbuster, come on out and say it—quit beating about the bush," my father insisted. "I demand that in subsequent stories about my practices and myself, you either clear my name or come right out and say I'm a no good panic peddler. Then at least I'll have something tangible on which to base my future movements in this thing."[71]

If my father felt cornered, this seemed only to make him more aggressive. He launched an attack on a new target. In a barrage of letters to reporters, he argued that Chicago's reform organizations were corrupted by their financial dependence upon the very people who profited from laws that exploited the poor. Credit merchants had "reached far into the ranks of the organizations set up to protect the credit victims," he wrote to *Daily News* reporter Nick Shuman, making "inevitable dependents of do-good people and groups." Therefore "the entire reform program is doomed from the start."[72] He made a special target of the Chicago Urban League, accusing the black civic group of kowtowing to the interests of its funders, including the "State Street Jewelers" and "used automobile dealers." He went further. "I am equally sure," he wrote, that the league "has not overlooked the gold in the hills of real estate speculators."[73]

In truth, the Chicago Urban League had stopped being an activist group years earlier, becoming, in its own words, a "'do-good' type of organization."[74] Under Edwin C. Berry's leadership, the CUL lobbied for improved housing and job opportunities for blacks and turned out carefully researched studies on the effects of housing segregation, mortgage redlining, and urban renewal. Berry believed that the best way to achieve progress was to win the support of the city's power brokers. He was successful: during his presidency, the CUL's board included men associated with Inland Steel, International Harvester, Sears, Roebuck and Company, Carson Pirie Scott and Company, and other major Chicago business interests, as well as politicians like Marshall Korshak, who was part of Daley's "machine inner circle" of ward committeemen.[75] Not surprisingly, such a group avoided the credit reform issue—and exemplified the tangled alliances that made Chicago so resistant to reform.[76]

My father was absolute in his condemnation. "The time has come for the Negro community to shake off the many, many charlatans who have in the name of improving the lot of the Negro merely feathered their own nest," he said during a fall 1962 appearance on black activist Wesley South's radio show *South Side Lights.* As examples he named the Chicago Urban League, the NAACP, the Commission on Human Relations, and the GLCC. "We must pull out of existing organizations and start over," he said. The only hope lay in activist community organizations. My father lauded the work of one in particular—the Temporary Woodlawn Organization, known as TWO, which had recently been established in an almost entirely black neighborhood near the University of Chicago. "Here is a militant group of people . . . [who] stand on their feet and say you are cheating. And name names, and demand that slum tenement operators pull out of their community," he told South.[77]

By 1962, when my father made this statement, two men had distinguished themselves as the city's most forceful proponents of community activism: Saul Alinsky, a Jewish organizer, and his close friend John J. Egan, a Catholic priest. Their methods of bringing people together to fight for their own interests were copied by community organizations across the nation. But it was not certain whether even these two men would succeed in persuading Chicagoans to stand up to the forces that were rapidly destroying the city's neighborhoods.

Like many other Chicagoans of his generation, Saul Alinsky was the child of immigrants. He liked to tell friends that he'd been raised in "one of the worst slums in Chicago."[78] In fact, Alinsky, who was born in 1909, grew up in Douglas Park, a reasonably comfortable, largely Jewish neighborhood adjoining Lawndale. His father, who ran a tailor shop, did well enough to purchase a new nine-flat apartment building; his mother, an intense and energetic woman, was fiercely protective of Saul, her only son.[79]

As a child Alinsky was not a particularly good student. But when a football accident at the age of fourteen left him incapacitated for nearly a year, he turned to intellectual pursuits as a form of escape. By the time he recovered he had acquired a lifelong habit of reading. Alinsky did well in high school and with financial support from his father went on to do undergraduate and graduate work at the University of Chicago, where he studied sociology and social work. He particularly thrived in "participant observer" studies that required him to join in the daily life of some of Chicago's rougher communities to learn the unspoken rules that structured their social interactions.

After graduate school Alinsky worked for sociologist Clifford Shaw, an innovative thinker who believed that the crimes plaguing poor and immigrant communities were the result of social disorganization rather than any innate criminal tendencies. If social chaos and anomie led to crime, Shaw believed, then the antidote was social cohesion, which could be achieved through citizen participation. In 1938, Shaw was asked to set up a delinquency prevention program in the Back of the Yards, an impoverished, mostly Catholic, but ethnically divided neighborhood bordering Chicago's stockyards. Shaw sent his associate, Saul Alinsky.

Instead of setting up a program for teenagers, Alinsky joined with local labor activists from the radical Congress of Industrial Organizations (CIO) to create a community organization. The Back of the Yards Neighborhood Council (BYNC) aimed to combat unemployment as well as juvenile delinquency and to upgrade housing, health, and education. But its underlying premise was that any specific agenda mattered less than the fact of citizen participation. Drawing upon his mentor Shaw and the ideology that animated the CIO, Alinsky believed that such activity could unite people across ethnic divides, undercut fascist appeals then on the rise in Europe, and promote participatory democracy.[80]

Alinsky soon developed his own philosophy and method of community organizing. First, he insisted that potential groups be fully funded before their work could begin; to that end, he created the Industrial Areas Foundation, whose purpose was to fund future organizing efforts, in 1940. Second, although he continued to believe that an organization's specific agenda was less important than the benefits that grew from citizen involvement, he insisted that the issues addressed must arise from the community itself. Third, he believed that the chosen goals must be achievable: one should never embark on a battle that was not winnable. Alinsky's pragmatism informed every aspect of his program. He did not think it worthwhile to organize the very poorest members of a neighborhood; such a focus, he feared, would only divide the larger community.[81] He was convinced that all activity must build upon a community's self-interest rather than upon notions of right and wrong. Finally, he proudly proclaimed his adherence to power politics. He believed that the ends justified the means; he told organizers that a good way to rouse apathetic citizens was to "agitate to the point of conflict," "fan resentments," and "rub raw the sores of discontent." His tactics could shade perilously close to bullying.[82]

Alinsky and his team began by poring over census records, planning commission reports, and other municipal sources to gain an accurate picture of the community. Next, they compiled a list of every institution in the area, from churches to pool halls. Then they interviewed as many people as possible to identify local leaders. Only after this groundwork had been laid did they take the final step, which was to bring all of the groups and leaders into a single, representative neighborhood council that was charged by the community to address its interests. These steps, which Alinsky followed successfully in the Back of the Yards Neighborhood Council, became the foundation of all of his organizing campaigns.[83]

From the start, Alinsky forged close relations with the Catholic Church. Committed to including a neighborhood's major institutions, Alinsky was naturally drawn to establish a partnership with the churches in the heavily Catholic Back of the Yards. But there was also a certain compatibility between his ideas and the progressive Catholic view of community action, which, according to Jacques Maritain, a Catholic theologian and friend of Alinsky's, also began with "selfish interest" leading to a "sense of solidarity and finally to an unselfish devotion to a common task."[84]

Alinsky's equivalent on the Catholic side was Monsignor John J. Egan. An exemplary representative of progressive Catholicism, Egan embraced the principles of Catholic Action, which called upon believers to observe (or gather facts), judge (in the light of the Gospel), and then act (as Jesus would).[85] But while Catholic Action shared Alinsky's emphasis on gathering facts in order to understand a community, it also stressed the importance of formulating a moral response to a situation—a difference that would have significant consequences.

By the early 1960s, Monsignor Egan was known as an "insider's insider," but he didn't start out that way. Born in 1916 to Irish immigrant parents, Jack Egan entered the St. Mary of the Lake Seminary in 1935. There he came under the influence of Monsignor Reynold J. Hillenbrand, the seminary's rector and an advocate of Catholic Action. Hillenbrand taught that the Church was the earthly embodiment of the Mystical Body of Christ and thus a vehicle for connectedness between all Catholics. He viewed *human* connectedness and mutual obligation as the essential core of Jesus's message. Racism, anti-Semitism, and nationalism were dangerous, since they could divide humanity and thus rend the Mystical Body of Christ.[86]

"Monsignor Hillenbrand opened up a whole new world for us," Egan recalled. But opposition to racism and other forms of social inequality was more than an intellectual position for Egan. He felt an almost instinctual anger about oppression, especially racial oppression. Egan explained his sympathy for African Americans in terms of a few childhood experiences— his affection for a black housekeeper, Mrs. Bishop, who helped care for his family when his mother was ill, and his horrified observation of a white streetcar conductor's abusive treatment of an elderly black man. But the roots of his identification with the oppressed lay deeper. Egan was raised by a father who "lacked understanding, and lacked forgiveness, and was very, very strict," he recalled. His father's authoritarian ways left him with a deep-rooted anger at behavior that was arbitrary and discriminatory.[87]

Egan's "wary appraisal" of his father's moods also left him highly sensitive to the feelings of others. "He was an artist at listening," one of his parishioners noted. Egan's empathetic tendencies were reinforced when he studied counseling with pioneering humanist psychologist Carl

Rogers.[88] Rogers believed that you couldn't change people by simply telling them what to do. Instead, the counselor should practice "unconditional positive regard for the client," who would then grow to the point of self-direction.[89]

Egan embraced this idea and applied it to his parishioners at St. Justin Martyr parish, where he was assigned after his ordination in 1943. In 1947, Egan was appointed to head the Chicago archdiocese's Cana and Pre-Cana programs—marriage and premarriage counseling services intended to help couples view the complexities of married life in the light of spiritual principles. Part of Egan's job was to visit each of the 250 rectories within the Chicago archdiocese and convince the pastors to organize Cana programs. Not surprisingly, Egan brought Catholic Action tenets to his Cana work. If faith meant anything, he believed, you had to live it. He encouraged Cana participants to follow the principles of observe, judge, and act within the marital relationship. But he also helped them to see how those principles, once integrated into one's life, could easily be applied to the broader community. In short, they could lead to spiritually informed political action. Thus Egan saw no conflict between encouraging Catholic lay people to explore the spiritual meanings of marital love and advocating for Chicago's burgeoning Puerto Rican community: both arose from the same emphasis on understanding others and taking actions to address their needs. As his biographer notes, throughout the 1950s Egan's full-time work in marriage preparation went hand in hand with his growing reputation as a priest who was deeply "responsive to social issues."[90]

At first, Egan's progressive, antiracist approach enjoyed significant institutional support. He had the backing of Samuel Cardinal Stritch, who had earned the nickname "Bishop of the Poor" when he'd used funds some thought should go toward repairing his church's damaged roof to help the impoverished in his community instead. As archbishop and later cardinal of the Chicago archdiocese, Stritch promoted the interests of immigrants and the poor, spoke out against anti-Semitism, and encouraged Catholics to view racism as antithetical to Catholic spirituality.[91] Egan also found support in the Chicago branch of the Catholic Interracial Council (CIC), an archdiocese-sanctioned national organization that promoted spiritual reflection on racial justice and encouraged Catholics to act against racist bigotry. By the 1950s, the Chicago chapter was among the nation's most vibrant. It sponsored numerous seminars and study groups to combat racism.[92] Typical was a High School Study Day on Race Relations, which brought together six hundred Catholic Chicago-area students to analyze racial prejudice. "When whites are prejudiced," one student explained, "it helps tear down their whole moral structure." Another described the "Catholic position" on racism as "We believe with the conviction of our hearts that we are all blood brothers with souls that come directly from the hands of God." The students were echoing a powerful 1958 statement by the bishops of the United States that condemned racism in schools, jobs, or housing: "Discrimination based on the accidental fact of race or color . . . cannot be reconciled with the truth that God created all men with equal rights and equal dignity."[93]

Egan's politically engaged Catholic faith soon confronted a very different Catholic reality. It escaped few people's notice that the neighborhoods where whites harassed, bombed, and sometimes burned out black families were overwhelmingly Catholic. The Catholic Interracial Council even observed the "use of parish halls for anti-racial meetings." As one CIC member noted, "The mobs are entirely white, many of them Catholics. . . . It seems that it has come to the point where Catholics believe our Church condones and approves segregation."[94]

One scholar explains this vehement white Catholic response as an understandable defense of the parish as sacred space.[95] A more likely explanation lies in the fact that the arrival of blacks meant that the neighborhood would be redlined and property values would decline. For the white working class in general, property—the investment of a lifetime, often representing decades of sacrifice—was their only security for old age. For working-class white Catholics, home ownership was particularly charged. As one churchman noted of the suburban, all-white community of Cicero, "The god worshipped in Cicero is the unencumbered deed, and . . . the town's real churches are its savings and loan associations." Home ownership represented stability, respectability, status, and community—all things that ethnic Catholics had been denied during the early decades of the century, when they were often derided by the nation's Protestant leaders as disloyal or "hyphenated" Americans.[96] Small wonder, then, that many experienced the arrival of blacks in their communities as an assault upon their hard-earned status. "How did they even find their way into the last beautiful neighborhood in Chicago?"

Pastor F. J. Quinn wrote, in his parish bulletin, of black families. "Sometimes we feel like Christ weeping over the City of Jerusalem. If we lose this, we have lost everything."[97]

Other churchmen had a different response. As one Chicago pastor noted of urban renewal in 1956, "The real diabolical part is that all of this hatred will be thrown back upon the colored people that haven't one blessed thing to say about it." Cardinal Stritch summed up his sorrow and shame over Catholic antiblack actions. Referring to the outbreaks in Trumbull Park, Stritch told a Catholic audience that "the Mystical Body of Christ is being torn limb from limb in many neighborhoods populated by Catholics who practice racial injustice."[98]

Egan thought that Saul Alinsky could offer a way out of this Catholic conundrum. When they first met in 1954, Egan immediately felt he'd found a kindred spirit in Alinsky, who told him, by way of explaining his devotion to community organizing, "Oh Jack, I hate to see people pushed around."[99] Alinsky convinced Egan that community organizing could stop or at least modify the cycle of violent resistance, panic selling, deterioration, and resegregation that plagued Chicago neighborhoods. The two men worked together to persuade the Chicago archdiocese to fund an Alinsky-style community organization in a racially transitional area, or at least to fund a feasibility study to determine if such an organization was worth launching. In 1956, Cardinal Stritch arranged for the archdiocese to give Alinsky's Industrial Areas Foundation (IAF) a three-year grant totaling $118,800 to study "changing communities resulting from population shifts." Stritch also arranged for several priests to receive training in community organizing techniques. One priest was given leave to work practically full-time with the IAF—Monsignor Egan.[100]

Cardinal Stritch was particularly interested in the repercussions of the Lake Meadows development and the construction of the Dan Ryan Expressway, which ran through the center of the South Side. "I would like to find out how those people survived and where they moved to," he told Egan. To answer that question, Egan and organizer Lester Hunt visited practically every building in the Grand Boulevard neighborhood—that is, the heart of the South Side Black Belt—and met with everyone from barbershop owners to Congressman Bill Dawson. Each night Egan wrote up a summary of what he had seen and whom he had met and gave these to Alinsky, who would barrage him with questions: "Well, you saw these people on Monday. . . . Did you do anything to follow up . . . on Wednesday? . . . Did you really believe what these people told you? Did you check this with anyone else?" As Egan recalled, "It was real training in the analysis of organization."[101]

Egan and Hunt's final report so impressed Stritch that he named Egan executive director of the Cardinal's Committee on Conservation and Urban Renewal, a group formed to articulate a Catholic response to urban renewal issues. Thus, when the University of Chicago announced its "conservation," or urban renewal, plan for Hyde Park in 1958, it was Egan's job to respond to it.[102] And he did —critically.

To Egan, the flaws of the Hyde Park urban renewal plan were obvious. While the proposal envisioned the destruction of 20 percent of Hyde Park's buildings and the displacement of 20,000 people, it contained no comprehensive provision for public housing or for relocating the displaced. Egan had seen the "pitiful, pathetic, and deplorable" housing conditions endured by many black Chicagoans; any plan that further limited their housing options was unconscionable.[103] With support from Stritch and Alinsky associates Nicholas von Hoffman and Lou Silverman, Egan campaigned to stop the Hyde Park plan until provisions for black housing were in place. In a series of articles in the archdiocesan newspaper the *New World,* Egan condemned the Hyde Park urban renewal proposal because it required "the demolition of buildings that people live in," which, in the absence of alternatives, "must, by simple arithmetic, mean overcrowding." Egan was explicit about the reasons for Chicago's apparent housing shortage: "There is no open housing market for Negroes. We all know very well [that] one fifth of the population of Chicago . . . is the victim of a gigantic silent conspiracy." Since blacks were shut out of the mainstream housing market, they became the victims of "speculators and unscrupulous landlords." Will we address these basic problems, Egan asked, or must we continue to "endure the cycle of deadly slum fires in the winter and murderous racial disturbances in the summer?"[104]

Egan's stance made front-page news. It also brought a great deal of anger down upon him and demonstrated, once again, the difficulties of reform in Chicago. First to attack Egan were the "enlightened business-men" on the Metropolitan Housing and Planning Council (MHPC). They held a press conference in which they accused the Archdiocese of Chicago of "doing a great disservice by fighting urban renewal." Liberal Protestant and Jewish clergy also opposed Egan after University of Chicago counsel and MHPC board member Julian Levi asked them to stop the "Catholic attack" on conservation.[105] Mayor Daley was furious with Egan for interfering with the university's plans. So were many prominent Catholics with close connections to the Daley administration. "I used to fight with Jack," recalled attorney Thomas Foran, who had been hired to use the power of eminent domain to clear land for Hyde Park's conservation project. "When he'd say we were driving blacks out, I'd tell him, 'You don't know your [ass] from your elbow. What we're trying to do is save the place. What's there? Terrible stuff like Bombay or Calcutta, filthy rotten terrible buildings without interior plumbing, filthy drug addicts, rats—if you think that's helping the blacks . . .' Whatever was done was better than what was there." He told Egan, "The best thing you can do for me, Jack, is shrive me for my sins and stick God in my mouth. I don't need your advice on social issues."[106]

More upsetting to Egan were the attacks he endured from other progressive Catholics.[107] Jerome Kerwin, a Catholic University of Chicago faculty member, supported the renewal plan and made sure that his complaints reached Monsignor Hillenbrand, Egan's mentor. Hillenbrand arranged a meeting of Catholic activists, purportedly to discuss the Church's stand on urban renewal, but as Egan recalled, the real agenda was "to kick the hell out of Jack Egan." Hillenbrand led the charge. "You had no business there because you are a priest," he lectured Egan. "And not only that, what do you know about urban renewal? You're a disgrace to the Roman Catholic Church and the priesthood. You should be in favor of that plan just because the University of Chicago is there."[108]

Perhaps most shocking of all was an attack from a truly unexpected quarter—Saul Alinsky. He had been in Europe during most of Egan's campaign. Once back and confronted by the uproar, he immediately summoned Egan, von Hoffman, and Silverman. As Silverman recalled, Alinsky got right to the point. "What the fuck are you doing, you assholes?" he asked them. According to von Hoffman, Alinsky was furious over their tactical blunder in taking on so large an issue. "While he was away, his little mice had blown up the city. It wasn't that he disagreed with our position. It was 'What are you guys doing? You can't possibly win.'"[109]

Alinsky's upset might also have been traceable to something that linked his community organizing to more mainstream reform groups: financial dependence upon the contributions of wealthy board members. Among the Industrial Areas Foundation's most generous contributors was Hermon Dunlop Smith, a Chicago businessman who was also a trustee of the University of Chicago. Smith raged to Alinsky about Egan's opposition to the Hyde Park project. Egan was certain that Smith's intervention fed Alinsky's fury. "Never underestimate it," he said about the power of the university and its trustees. "In those days it was frightening."[110]

The final blow to Egan was the sudden death of Cardinal Stritch in the spring of 1958. Egan was left with no institutional support for his position. "I never felt more lonely in my life," he recalled. His battle against the conservation plan delayed its implementation, but only for a few months. It was ultimately approved—with no provisions for the displaced. "It's tragic," one uprooted Hyde Parker told reporters. "We have no say in our future."[111]

Alinsky's shying away from "unwinnable" issues did more than torpedo resistance to the displacement of black Hyde Parkers. It also sabotaged his own effort to create a community organization in a mostly white but changing Chicago neighborhood.

In 1959, Alinsky sent three of his top people—von Hoffman, Ed Chambers, and Joe Vilimas—to organize Chicago's Southwest Side. The prospect was not promising. A *Daily News* reporter noted that many residents "are frankly interested in keeping Negroes out at all costs." Black "new arrivals" were frequently met by "a bomb or a torch" tossed onto their front porches, accompanied by whispered threats of "We'll get you yet." Still, some whites seemed open to a different approach. "Sure, you can burn people out, but suppose you burn the wrong house? It's too risky," one white housewife told reporters. Another added, "There is nothing to be gained by running away. And where can we replace this house at a reasonable cost? We are staying."[112]

Building on this less than enthusiastic mandate, Alinsky's representatives set out to create a community organization that would encourage residents, black and white, to work together to prevent the decay of their neighborhood. The task took enormous energy and physical courage. Monsignor Egan experienced the risk firsthand. He gave a talk to a Southwest Side block club that was in the immediate vicinity of St. Justin Martyr, where he had been a much-loved pastor. When the man who invited Egan realized that he would be advocating integration, Egan recalled, "he went to the bathroom and you could hear him retching. He knew he would probably be fired." At the end of Egan's talk, four large men—"fellows I'd married or baptized their children"—quickly hustled him out the door. "You better get out of the neighborhood, Father," they told him. "If I'd been totally foreign [to the community]," Egan recalled, "it would have been a good bit worse."[113]

Yet after months of intensive activity, the work seemed to bear fruit. In October 1959 a thousand delegates met to form the Organization for the Southwest Community (OSC). Organizers proudly touted the harmonious, interracial character of the OSC—at least to outsiders.[114] Within the OSC, they followed a different line. Terrified of scaring off whites, they made the pragmatic decision of claiming that their organization was "neither 'integrationist' nor 'segregationist.'" In fact, the OSC was essentially a white outfit. Of the initial 104 groups participating, only one—from a Methodist church—was black, and even this lone affiliate was barely tolerated by many white delegates.[115]

Although the threat to this neighborhood lay in redlining and in the financial exploitation of black families, the OSC's opening convention tried to soothe its overwhelmingly white membership by scrupulously avoiding any mention of racism.[116] The OSC thereby refused to face the racial discrimination that lay at the root of community decay—an issue that Alinsky viewed as "too complicated." Instead, the OSC's agenda reflected the concerns of its majority constituency. Among the group's first acts was the distribution of 25,000 copies of the *Daily News'* 1959 "Panic Peddlers" series, which highlighted the costs to whites rather than blacks of blockbusting. OSC goals included increased housing code enforcement, which often backfired against black contract buyers. The group drew up a "Code of Realty Ethics" that condemned realtors who used blockbusting sales tactics to "induce fear and panic" among whites, but it made only passing and somewhat obscure reference to realtors who refused to show properties to blacks. Finally, the OSC announced the creation of a

$2 million home loan program. The recipients would not be loan-starved blacks. Rather, the money was earmarked for whites who were willing to "move into 'fringe' areas" (that is, areas where African Americans had already taken up residence).[117] Crucially, the OSC made no effort to provide fair mortgage funding for blacks, who had no choice but to continue to deal with real estate speculators.[118]

The OSC's effort to evade the "race question" was doomed to fail. It simply made the organization seem out of touch. "You know how the South Side was then," one white Methodist minister recalled. "The race thing was like grit. . . . You could never wash it out of your food. It just impregnated everything." Internally, much of the OSC's energy was consumed by "*the* question: is the OSC pro-integration or anti-integration?" When more radical members finally pushed the OSC to go on record as supporting a proposal for open occupancy legislation in March 1961, the move was so controversial that it almost split the organization. The neighborhood, too, showed no sign of coming together. By 1963, whites were fleeing. By 1970, the area had become overwhelmingly black.[119]

While his organizers struggled in the OSC, Alinsky began considering a different approach. He would sidestep the perils of interracial organizing and instead build an all-black community organization. In the fall of 1960, he finally amassed the funds he needed to launch a community organizing project in Woodlawn, an all-black neighborhood just south of Hyde Park that included areas that were well maintained as well as slums. He immediately set up headquarters in a South Side storefront manned by his key organizer, Nicholas von Hoffman, and Bob Squires, a young black Chicagoan who had worked for a settlement house on the West Side. The two men walked the streets of Woodlawn daily for months. They talked to every resident, retail merchant, police officer, or street person they encountered and dictated nightly reports on what they had learned.[120]

By January 1961, Alinsky's organizers identified five local groups that agreed to unite as the Temporary Woodlawn Organization (TWO), later renamed The Woodlawn Organization. The group quickly embraced an issue that my father had identified as one of the heaviest burdens on minority people: credit exploitation. The community itself had brought the issue to the fore. "The grievance that stood out above all others was the exploitation . . . by some of the businessmen in the area," recalled Arthur M. Brazier, an African American minister who became the president of TWO. "Credit buying was enslaving some of the residents of Woodlawn."[121] In response, TWO embarked on a "Square Deal Campaign" to stop cheating by local merchants. The campaign got a push from the "One Million Underdogs" series, which had appeared only weeks earlier and was lauded by a TWO spokesman as "'instrumental' in the birth of the campaign."[122]

TWO launched its attack against sell-and-garnishee credit retailers with a mass parade down Sixty-third Street, the central retail strip of Woodlawn. They investigated residents' stories of being overcharged and organized boycotts against the offending merchants. People brought faulty goods to public meetings and recounted their tangles with shop owners. After confronting these shop owners, representatives returned to tell the group of the "square deal" they'd negotiated. They also created a "Code of Business Ethics" for merchants to sign.[123]

TWO's next target was slum landlords. They organized rent strikes against landlords who neglected basic upkeep. They also tried a radical new tactic. Black Woodlawn residents traveled to the white neighborhoods where some absentee landlords resided, picketed the slumlord's home, and passed out flyers to his neighbors. "Do you know that one of your neighbors is a slumlord? He is Julius Mark, 2409 East Seventy-third Street. He leases and won't fix a slum at 6434 South Kimbark, where the residents are so mad they've called a rent strike," read a typical flyer. This method capitalized on white anxieties about black bodies in white spaces. "For this assignment, we practically use a color chart in Woodlawn to recruit pickets. We wanted only the darkest Negroes," Alinsky joked.[124] TWO members also picketed banks that held slum properties "in trust," in order to pressure the banks to release the names of the buildings' owners. It may have been reports of these sorts of actions that led my father to praise TWO on Wesley South's radio show as "a militant group of people . . . [who] stand on their feet and say you are cheating."[125]

But beneath TWO's radical surface lurked confusion about goals and tactics that sabotaged its effectiveness. Initially, the cause of credit exploitation seemed "made to order" for TWO. It was a "dramatic, indigenous issue; it was relatively small; [and] it was a battle that TWO could probably win," explained Brazier. In fact, the credit exploitation issue was neither "relatively small" nor easily winnable. Perhaps this is why TWO quickly dropped the Square Deal campaign, infuriating its constituents. Most of the Puerto Rican members quit the organization because of its failure to pursue a "tough enough" strategy against the credit-and-garnishee racket. Von Hoffman was not overly disturbed by their departure; they were too narrowly focused on this "single issue," he felt. Though "purists" might find such a turnaround "intolerable," TWO had to drop its campaign against credit exploitation, he argued, because "you need his [the merchant's] money which you will get if he fears you, but not if he hates you. You will also get his money . . . if the organization's progress includes objectives that are worth something to him."[126] The net result was that, instead of blazing a new path for community activism, TWO became yet another demonstration of the perils of reformers' financial dependence on the very people they needed to challenge.

According to Alinsky's biographer, the Square Deal campaign was "intentionally terminated by Alinsky and von Hoffman" because TWO wanted the financial support of merchants when it turned to "larger issues such as urban renewal." But with dizzyingly circular logic, Alinsky often cast urban renewal as an "unwinnable" issue to be avoided.[127] TWO's attitude toward housing was similarly confused. The group apparently felt that the redlining policies that forced black Woodlawners to buy on contract were too complex for effective community mobilization.[128] Instead, they focused on the seemingly straightforward problems facing renters. But as TWO president Arthur Brazier explained, since TWO had to win, it bypassed Woodlawn's major slumlords to focus on the "less affluent slum owner" who "does not keep his building up but is small enough to need the money from it." Brazier conceded that rent strikes against marginal landlords were "not the answer to deplorable housing in the ghetto." Only "the city" had the power to "deal effectively with the situation," he concluded, in a tacit admission of TWO's lack of strategy.[129]

Von Hoffman was caught in the same bind. After noting with shock the response of one small landlord targeted in an early TWO rent strike who simply offered to hand the building over to the tenants, von Hoffman concluded that the "housing issue" was of limited potential as an organizing tool. "I said, 'Saul, there aren't any more slumlords, there are just people stuck with turkeys.' So we knew early, but we didn't know what to do about it."[130]

Alinsky's refusal to battle the Hyde Park urban renewal plan, as well as the ineffectiveness of the OSC and TWO, highlighted the two major flaws in Alinsky's model of organizing: his insistence that organizing efforts be fully funded before they could be launched, which left him vulnerable to pressure by the wealthy donors, and perhaps more serious, his belief that they should tackle only issues that were "winnable."[131] This stance was in stark contrast to the attitudes of African American activists in Mississippi, who in the early 1960s were risking their lives for a goal that seemed impossibly utopian: the end of a reign of white supremacy that had been in place for generations.[132] That same fearless attitude was needed in Chicago, where community groups in changing and black neighborhoods faced wealthy and entrenched opponents who were highly adept at evading moral, legal, and economic pressure. Unfortunately, Alinsky's insistence on fighting only for winnable ends guaranteed that his organizations would never truly confront the powerful forces devastating racially changing and black neighborhoods.

During TWO's first year my father supported the group. He even wrote an article explaining how outsiders could lend a hand. Although "community change will come only from the actions of the community people themselves," he wrote, this was a far harder proposition in areas where people's economic burdens left them no time to contribute to neighborhood betterment. He listed a number of things "interested young people" could do to jump-start the community organizing process of "self-help." They could do background research that would bring financial exploitation to light. They could get buildings in the area appraised. They could calculate the costs of running a typical apartment building, compare those costs with the fees taken in by slumlords, and call these slumlords to task for their drain on the community. "Knowledge of the real value of housing is the weapon most urgently needed in order that minority peoples may deal on equal terms with speculators and profiteers in our midst," he wrote.[133] He followed his own advice, offering TWO leaders detailed figures on the purchase price, resale price, tax and operating expenses, and income-generating potential of a twenty-four-apartment complex in Woodlawn.[134]

Very soon, however, my father soured on TWO. In a letter to a *Daily News* reporter, he complained about the organization's "inconsistent approaches" and expressed his irritation over the group's refusal to make use of information that he had provided about the Woodlawn apartment complex. But in truth, my father's ideas seemed out of step with those of Chicago's progressive community. His article on how young people could aid groups like TWO was rejected by all of Chicago's small reform periodicals.[135]

But by 1963, my father realized that, whatever their flaws, the city's reform and community organizations were hardly the biggest obstacles to change in Chicago. Instead, he saw the liberal establishment that dominated the debate about race and housing as his most dangerous opponent. This establishment consisted of the Metropolitan Housing and Planning Council and all of those that followed in its wake. In contrast to Alinsky's organizers, whose face-to-face immersion in "ghetto" issues left them wondering—privately, at least—precisely "what to do" about slum conditions, this liberal establishment, which kept a safe distance from the people and conditions it pronounced upon, was confident that it knew how to solve Chicago's many problems. My father developed a "violent philosophical antipathy" to the views of this establishment on virtually every issue.[136] His struggle against a solidifying liberal consensus would consume the final years of his life. His arguments were impassioned in part because they sprang from a very intimate source. While he battled the "exploiters," some applied that label to my father. And while he fought the forces that sucked well-meaning people into a quicksand of debt, he was drawn ever more deeply into financial ruin.

FIVE

THE LIBERAL MOMENT AND
THE DEATH OF A RADICAL

In April 1961, Favil Berns took leave of my father. The split, he believed, was amicable. "I cannot devote my time to you any longer," Berns told him. "I appreciate everything you did for me—you gave me an opportunity." Berns had a chance to open his own law office in Northlake, Illinois. The economic prospects for a lawyer in the growing town were excellent, and after years of working for my father the time had come to "make a living."

There were other issues, of course. Among them were conflicts of temperament. "I wanted to learn how to practice law, but I didn't want to get bashed!" Berns recalled. "Everybody wanted to give Mark a hard time, see? I said, 'Give him a hard time, but don't give me a hard time!'" As Berns saw it, Mark Satter brought a lot of the hostility upon himself. "You're not diplomatic!" he warned him. My father's politically charged language also bothered Berns. There had been murmurings among the city's lawyers about Satter for years—that he was a leftist who couldn't get rid of his "pinko ideas"—and his impassioned statements about "working people" only heightened their distrust. Berns, who was "innocent as can be" of such matters, tried to ignore the talk, but he couldn't help it; it got under his skin.

Berns and my father also disagreed on a more concrete issue: how to respond to the increasingly chaotic conditions on the city's West Side. Both men owned properties there. Berns had purchased his two buildings shortly after his marriage. "It was a way to make a buck and make a living." When that was no longer true, as the neighborhood deteriorated and the buildings lost their value, Berns got out. "I sold the buildings to a speculator. I took my loss. I was happy to be rid of them. I told your dad to do the same, but he wouldn't do it," Berns told me. "He still wanted to be the do-gooder. He was going to show them."[1]

Berns's departure occurred at a moment when the housing crisis on Chicago's West Side had become acute. The area was now largely black. Much of the property there was held by absentee owners who included the city's worst slumlords. According to a 1962 study, building inspectors found that "rats and roaches infested the structures; garbage and debris was prevalent; leaking water, sewer pipes and dripping roofs caused rank living quarters; rotted and broken floors, walls and stairways, faulty electrical wiring along with improvised heating and cooking facilities caused peril to the life and safety of the inhabitants; and faulty plumbing not only caused inconvenience to the occupants of the buildings, but also threatened to contaminate the drinking water of the city of Chicago."

The "peril to life and safety of the inhabitants" of slum buildings was often of a gruesome sort. Residents were injured on poorly lit stairways or ones with broken banisters. They were knocked out by falling plaster. They were scalded by the escaping steam of malfunctioning radiators. They perished in fires in buildings where fire escapes had collapsed from neglect. Their infants' limbs were gnawed by rats. Each year approximately twenty-five Chicago children died from eating lead-filled paint chips. Others survived lead poisoning but were left mentally disabled.[2]

Chicago's Metropolitan Housing and Planning Council, which had pioneered urban renewal and conservation policies for both Illinois and the nation, believed that it knew just what to do about such horrific conditions. Even as organizers like Alinsky and crusaders like my father fought to voice the perspective of those at the bottom, the MHPC offered a solution that unapologetically derived from those at the top. As MHPC president John W. Baird explained, racial change and the decay that followed were "a big problem which needs big people from all segments of community life, big money, and a determination to work on a lasting solution."[3] The MHPC, representing "big people" and "big money"—that is, the city's business elite, including some of its most powerful mortgage bankers and real estate companies—thought it had come up with just that. It was a solution that would be wholeheartedly embraced by the liberal establishment and one that would—not surprisingly, given its origin—utterly fail to address the true causes of Chicago's slums.

The MHPC proposed a tripartite solution to the problem of slum housing: code enforcement, urban renewal, and open occupancy. Code enforcement would force slum landlords to maintain their buildings, thus halting "blight." The high fines levied on noncompliant slumlords would cut into their profits and thereby enable the city to drive them out of business. Either way, strict code enforcement would take the profits out of slum housing, thus encouraging slumlords to sell their properties at a reasonable price to city agencies. This would clear the way for the ultimate solution to the slum problem: urban renewal. As the MHPC summed up in a private report, urban renewal "is the only way to destroy blight," and "code enforcement is the primary tool for urban renewal."[4]

Of course, by the early 1960s African Americans had been attacking urban renewal as "Negro removal" for almost two decades, since all too often it led to the razing of black housing and the displacement of black families.[5] For this unfortunate consequence, the MHPC had a simple solution: open occupancy, or "fair housing," legislation.[6] If laws were passed making it illegal for brokers to refuse to show listings to African Americans, then the entire city would be opened to black residency. Displaced families would no longer be forced into the city's few black or "changing" neighborhoods, thereby creating new slums. Instead, open occupancy would enable them to disperse across the city, replacing Chicago's dual housing market with one that was truly free. "The development of the normal operation of a free market in private housing must be given a top priority. A free market obviously does not exist when 15% of the population is effectively denied the right to buy or sell in over 97% of the metropolitan area. Real estate practices which inhibit the normal operations of a free market must be changed if slums are to be eliminated," the MHPC resolved.[7]

On the face of it, the MHPC's solution seemed logical. Given the emphasis on open occupancy laws, it also seemed progressive and antiracist.

Perhaps that explains why so many liberal, faith-based housing groups in Chicago and throughout the nation embraced this approach. The Unitarians led the way with the creation of the Fair Housing Service for Greater Chicago, followed by the American Friends Service Committee's Home Opportunities Made Equal (HOME), the interfaith but Catholic-organized National Conference on Religion and Race, and the Chicago-area umbrella organization Freedom of Residence. These groups were particularly fervent in their support of open occupancy legislation. They also hoped to make white neighborhoods available to black families in advance of such legislation by persuading individual whites to rent or sell to blacks. Typical was the "fair housing pledge" circulated by the Fair Housing Service. "'I am happy to welcome any neighbor who seeks to maintain good standards and a healthy, democratic community without regard to race, religion, color, or national origin,'" the pledge read. "Segregated . . . patterns will change only when *individuals* change them," a HOME pamphlet declared.[8]

But religious liberals should have thought more carefully about following a reform agenda dictated by "big money." After all, the view from the top is by nature cloudy and indistinct. Whether because of MHPC members' social distance from the working poor or as a result of simple self-interest, the organization's reform program was seriously compromised. It overlooked the fact that as long as credit redlining continued, open occupancy legislation could have no real effect on African Americans' ability to escape deteriorating black neighborhoods. The main reason that African Americans bought from speculative contract sellers or rented from slumlords was not that bigoted real estate brokers refused to show them homes in white neighborhoods but that they could not get mortgage loans to purchase homes in those areas, no matter what their credit history. The emphasis on code enforcement, urban renewal, and open occupancy was in many ways a smoke screen promoted by redlining bankers and mortgage brokers—and one that, not coincidentally, entirely elided their own contributions to the creation of the city's slums.

This is not to say that all who promoted these reforms were insincere. MHPC president John Baird, for example, was genuinely committed to open occupancy legislation. Scion of one of Chicago's oldest and most upstanding real estate families, he ran Baird and Warner, the mortgage finance firm founded by his great-grandfather. Even though his background was not particularly liberal, he held antiracist convictions that originated, he felt, in his childhood relationship with a black man who worked for his family as a caretaker. "He taught me how to play baseball. He taught me a whole bunch of things," Baird recalled. One night when Baird and his sister found themselves locked out of the family summer home, the youngsters spent the night with African American friends of the caretaker. The shocked response of Baird's mother taught him a lesson about the absurdity of racism, and he continued to challenge racial boundaries as an adult. When he built his new home in suburban Winnetka in 1950, he scandalized his family by having it constructed in the suburb's Jewish section.[9]

But there were limits to his liberalism. "We were in the mortgage business and there were certain sections of the city we weren't to make mortgages in," Baird said. Given the reigning perception that blacks drove down land values, "if you saw blacks moving into an area, . . . why, you were leery about putting a mortgage on that house." To Baird, redlining racially changing neighborhoods was a matter of fiscal responsibility. "The lenders were lending . . . other people's money and they were responsible for that," he said. "If they lent money in those areas, why, they might lose it."[10] That the "other people's money" being so carefully guarded included the savings of black families—who deposited in lending institutions but were denied the right to borrow from them—did not occur to Baird or other MHPC members.

The result was a liberal reform consensus that ignored widespread credit discrimination. Baird explicitly opposed any strategy that advocated changes to installment land contracts or additional mortgage funds for black home buyers. Instead, he focused on psychology. "What is at issue here is the non-acceptance of the Negro as a full-fledged citizen," he said. The answer was legislation that would allow "all persons regardless of race or color to reside in any locale of their choosing." Baird also viewed the problem as one of education—that is, of educating blacks. The most important immediate step would be an "educational program" that would "acquaint Negroes with opportunities which currently exist . . . and . . . with the consequences of entering into agreements which they cannot possibly fulfill."[11]

For my father, responses of this sort were enraging. As he pointed out in one of his many speeches, the urban renewal agenda was dictated by savings and loan executives who "participate loudly and publicly on all forums of community improvement" while their "financial practices drive minority peoples into the hands of the speculator." He begged his listeners to reject a useless "sociological approach" that focused on individual acts of prejudice in favor of a realistic examination of the "dollar-packed economics" of the speculator's trade.[12] In particular, my father strove to heighten public awareness of the false hope offered by open occupancy legislation. "In the absence of honest free flow of mortgage money into all areas of Chicago," he told one audience, such legislation would effect not "the slightest change upon the present patterns of segregation and worse yet, upon the present deteriorated condition of the great majority of housing occupied by Negro people in Chicago."[13] He also wrote a scathing article titled "Open Occupancy Legislation—Who Are the Hypocrites?" that dismissed such legislation as "precisely" as useful as throwing a "drowning man . . . a steel life preserver."[14] (My father spent three years pitching the article to liberal journals, to no avail. He could give speeches against such laws till he was blue in the face, but he could not get his challenge to this cornerstone of the era's solidifying liberal consensus in print.)[15]

My father's disgust with the bankers' reform proposals was grounded, once again, in the personal experiences of his clients. He had often encountered the limits of liberal bankers and mortgage brokers, most vividly when he tried to secure a mortgage for Bertha and Lawrence Richards and Bertha's mother, Joeanna Williams. The family's years of litigation had ended in failure. The only way they could get out from under was to find the money to pay Moe Forman in full. My father agreed to negotiate a bank loan on their behalf. He contacted Al Ropa, the executive vice president of the People's Federal Savings and Loan Association. Ropa knew the entire history of the Richards-Williams family's dealings with Forman, having heard it recounted at the panel sponsored by the Greater Lawndale Conservation Commission in 1958. In case Ropa had forgotten the details, my father repeated the story to him and to his attorney, Walter Rojek. Yet Rojek and Ropa rejected the loan application.

Perhaps my father should have expected as much. After all, Ropa's speech at the panel had included the false statement that "no loans are made to speculators"; this despite the fact that his own bank had lent Forman the money to buy the very property that he then sold "on contract" to the Richards-Williams family.[16] But my father was still furious. "You notice that although People's Federal readily made its money available for speculative purposes, they have refused to lend any money to Mrs. Williams," he wrote to Rojek. "I am at a loss as to any further steps to take to help Mrs. Williams. I do believe the actions of [People's Federal] have made possible the unconscionable burden under which she has labored and has failed during the past six years." Rojek responded with an angry letter of his own: "It may interest you to know that People's Federal Savings has made many loans to folks without prejudice. A charge . . . such as yours does not warrant a reply in that the undersigned personally has been a staunch defender of the rights of all minorities." Nevertheless, People's Federal stood firm in its decision to deny the loan.[17]

With "staunch defenders of the rights of all minorities" taking stands such as these, my father knew better than to trust liberal bankers' promises. He was not alone in this regard. Another person with intimate knowledge of the double-talk of white bankers was Dempsey J. Travis.[18] His efforts to establish the Sivart Mortgage Company had revealed the usually invisible walls that kept capital in white hands and had highlighted the duplicity of white bankers who refused loans to qualified African Americans and then blamed resulting credit problems on the weak economic position, poor education, or faulty character of blacks themselves.[19]

Determined to increase the flow of mortgage loans to black would-be home buyers, Travis had first applied to be a loan correspondent for the FHA back in 1953. Finally, after his seventh annual attempt, the FHA said yes. Starting in January 1961, Sivart Mortgage Company would be able to make FHA-insured mortgage loans to black home buyers in black areas.[20]

Next, Travis set out to create the capital base that would allow the company to grant mortgages. Of course, Sivart needed to borrow that money, but Travis should have had no trouble raising the funds since Sivart's loans would be FHA insured. In addition, the company already had a respectable grounding; its initial liquid net worth was $100,000. On that basis, Travis tried to get an additional $500,000 line of credit. The reactions he got were humiliating. At Exchange National, Jerome Sax, the bank's executive vice president, agreed to lend Sivart interim financing of up to $15,000 per building. But the terms were unacceptable: thirty to sixty days for repayment, and on top of the company's $100,000 base, Travis and his wife would also have to add their personal assets as collateral.[21]

Travis was stunned by the grotesque imbalance of the conditions. After all, Exchange National regularly made generous loans to speculators; indeed, it was one of three banks that controlled the mortgages for most of the properties held by slum landlords on the West Side.[22] Yet Sax seemed to think that he was being benevolent. "May I also say that it is a pleasure to do business with people like yourself," he wrote to Travis.

Travis continued his search for financing. Finally, in March 1962, a friend's personal intervention convinced the chairman of Central National Bank to give Travis a $200,000 line of credit.[23] His mortgage loan company was "good news for Negro homeowners who are struggling to pay high interest rates, or to pay off exorbitant real estate sales contracts," an article announced.[24] But the funding was still not enough. Travis realized that he "could not survive in the mortgage banking field without black support." In 1962, blacks controlled a minute fraction of the nation's lending institutions—a total of ninety-four. Nonetheless, Travis saw a benefit in unity. To that end, he created a new organization, the United Mortgage Bankers of America (UMBA). There was profit to be made in lending to blacks, and Travis felt that black-owned institutions should be the ones to make it.[25]

In addition to encouraging the formation of more black banks and insurance companies, Travis and the UMBA also pressured the white financial industry to grant more loans to blacks.[26] They undertook national surveys to document, once again, that there was racial discrimination in the loan industry. Inasmuch as 85 percent of black savings were in white financial institutions, one UMBA member reasoned, "they can't just take Negro savings and not offer loan services in return." The association appealed to these institutions' financial self-interest. Between 1950 and 1960, the number of black households earning over $5,000 a year—that is, earning a middle-class income—had increased almost twentyfold. "Commercial banks, union pension funds and life insurance companies are scouting all over the country looking for sources of higher investment earnings, but they're almost completely overlooking a market that is screaming to be discovered—mortgage loans on Negro housing," Travis told a *Wall Street Journal* reporter. One weapon under consideration by the UMBA, Travis announced, was a boycott. He warned that blacks would refuse to place their money in white institutions that wouldn't loan to them.[27]

As a result of these efforts, in 1963 white savings and loan institutions made "oral commitments" to loan $400 million to qualified black applicants. Unfortunately, Travis found, "none materialized."[28] Obviously, blacks' lack of credit left them vulnerable to exploitative contract sales.[29] But Travis also understood this refusal of credit to African American home buyers in the broadest terms. "Within the system there is a willingness to lend all you need to buy a car," he told an interviewer. "A car can't appreciate. . . . When you want to buy a house, however, you get only a big frown. . . . The house represents a method of capital appreciation in the ghetto community. And a strong capital base is a threat to the white community."[30]

Travis's struggles exposed the hollowness of white bankers' claims that only the personal bigotry of homeowners and real estate brokers prevented blacks from purchasing homes in white areas. The key to fixing the dual housing market was ending the structural, industry-wide blockage of credit to African Americans. Without that, enacting fair housing legislation would be a symbolic gesture only, tantamount to doing nothing.

For one prominent Chicagoan, Mayor Richard J. Daley, this was precisely the appeal of open occupancy legislation. It could pacify the African American community—which by the early 1960s was showing significant signs of unrest—while posing no real threat to his white voters.

Open housing proposals had been kicking around the legislature since 1958, passed back and forth like a hot potato between city and state bureaucracies. Chicago's first municipal open occupancy ordinance banned discrimination in the sale or rental of real estate by property owners and real estate agents. Drafted by Alderman Leon Despres in 1958, it was still stalled in the City Council in 1961. In May of that year, Chicago corporate counsel John C. Melaniphy reported that Chicago did not have the power to pass an open occupancy law. "Cities are not autonomous governmental bodies," he wrote. "They have no home rule powers" to regulate "the right of contract for use of private property for lawful purposes." He recommended instead that the matter be addressed on the state level.[31]

Mayor Daley, primarily concerned with placating his white constituency, was eager to move the issue out of his city. He happily agreed with Melaniphy's recommendation, which meant that the City Council went along as well. So, in the spring of 1961, an open occupancy bill was submitted to the Illinois General Assembly. It specified that antidiscrimination laws would apply only to structures that included five or more units—a bizarre stipulation, since the vast majority of housing in Chicago consisted of single-family homes, two-flats, or three-flats. Despite these exemptions, the Illinois General Assembly defeated the bill in June 1961.

Since the assembly met only every two years, the next time that a statewide open occupancy bill could be submitted was in 1963. This new "fair housing" bill included more exemptions for owner-occupied buildings and was therefore weaker still than the one proposed in 1961. Even the MHPC, which supported the bill, recognized its limitations. "We regret that the freedom of residence bill is not more inclusive," John Baird said, adding that he hoped it would provide a "beginning" or "legal foundation for a single housing market." Yet this watered-down bill also failed to pass.[32]

With this second defeat on the state level, proponents of open occupancy decided that it was once again time to push for a citywide bill. During the summer of 1963, Alderman Despres tried anew, proposing legislation that would outlaw discrimination by both property owners and real estate brokers. His cosponsor was Charles Chew, an African American who had recently defeated a white, machine-sponsored candidate to become the new, independent alderman of the Seventeenth Ward—a formerly white area that was now 90 percent black.[33]

Despres and Chew now found an unexpected source of support for their bill—Mayor Daley. There were several reasons for Daley's sudden about-face. First, Chew's defeat of a white machine candidate was one of many signs of unrest among the city's African Americans. The Southern civil rights movement was in full swing, and black Chicagoans, who followed the movement closely, were increasingly dissatisfied with local black leaders who evaded civil rights issues. Daley would have to take immediate steps to assuage them if he wished to maintain the credibility of his "silent six" aldermen and prevent the emergence of more militant spokesmen. He needed to make a gesture of goodwill right away.[34]

A municipal ordinance could be just the thing. It would be useful in another way as well: federal funds for urban renewal and public housing contained stipulations that steps be taken to provide housing for those displaced. Daley could use the measure to prove that Chicago was taking such steps and was therefore a worthy recipient of the federal housing funds that were important sources of patronage and power. Most important, Daley understood that a municipal fair housing law would barely make a dent in the racial segregation so intensely valued by his white supporters. A 1960 national study of the effects of open occupancy ordinances by the Chicago Commission on Human Relations (CHR) had confirmed that municipal open occupancy laws in other cities had resulted in "neither drastic political consequences nor substantial population shifts."[35]

But Daley decided to go Despres and Chew one better and pass his own alternative ordinance—one that was, Daley biographers report, a "pale imitation of the Despres-Chew proposal." Corporate counsel Melaniphy provided the key: although the city had no right to stop discrimination by private owners, it could limit discrimination by real estate brokers. Since the city had the power to license brokers, it could use that power to regulate their operations.

The Chicago City Council passed the Fair Housing Ordinance on September 11, 1963. It targeted real estate agents—exclusively. The bill also prohibited panic peddling. Real estate agents were not to pressure people into selling their homes at a reduced price because of claims of "loss of value due to the present or prospective entry . . . of . . . persons of any particular race." Enforcement was left to the Commission on Human Relations, which was given the right to initiate complaints against ordinance violators. Instead of acting on this power, though, the CHR focused on facilitating "conciliation" between aggrieved individuals and real estate brokers. At most, it threatened to revoke a discriminating or panic-peddling real estate broker's license. (By 1967, the CHR had recommended the suspension of a broker's license in exactly one case. It involved a black real estate agent who was accused of panic peddling after he sold a home on a white block to a black family.)[36]

To pass even this anemic fair housing bill, Mayor Daley was forced to use all his political capital. Instead of the usual 49 to 1 City Council vote, the ordinance passed by a vote of 30 to 16. The loyal alderman whom Daley chose to help draft the bill, James C. Murray, initially resisted the mayor's pressure to act as one of its sponsors. Murray ultimately decided that the fair housing bill was "the right thing to do" to relieve the housing pressure that blockbusters exploited, but his constituents never forgave him. "This guy would be a great alderman if he wasn't such a nigger lover," said one. Angry whites picketed his home and deluged him with threatening phone calls. "People would call and say they were going to throw acid in my mother's face," Murray's son recalled. "My brothers had police bodyguards watching them." The situation left Murray distraught. "My family's going through hell," he told the press. He was voted out of office at the next election.[37]

So much for open occupancy. The politics of code enforcement were similarly compromised. In May 1963, the *Chicago Daily News* ran an in-depth series, "The Story of Chicago's Slums," which raised public awareness about improving code enforcement as a means of addressing the problem of deteriorating housing stock. For once, my father had nothing to do with the story. The *Daily News*' behind-the-scenes collaborator for the series was the MHPC.

In 1962, the organization had completed a study of Chicago's housing court that revealed that the city's code enforcement had failed abysmally. The MHPC then made a secret deal with the *Chicago Daily News* and CBS TV to turn over all its "raw materials and findings." In return, the *Daily News* and CBS agreed that they "would give the MHPC . . . ample opportunity to comment and make recommendations" and that, without attributing research or conclusions to the MHPC, the series would "place the emphasis where it belongs—on the *judicial system*."[38] The underlying goal of the series was quite specific: to expose corruption and inefficiency in the city's Building Department and municipal courts and thus improve enforcement of the housing code. This would then ease the way for urban renewal as the final answer to the problem of Chicago's slums.

As a result of this secret collaboration, in May 1963, Chicagoans were subjected to a week of shocking, coordinated television and newspaper stories. "Life in the Chicago Slums—An Ugly Mosaic of Degradation, Misery and Filth," a headline screamed. In dozens of related stories, Chicagoans learned about the crumbling, overpriced hovels where families lived without heat or electricity, with broken toilets and plumbing, and with rodent infestations so severe, tenants reported, that "we take the dog with us to the bathroom to keep the rats away."[39]

The *Daily News* did not march in lockstep with the MHPC. It allowed slum landlords ample opportunity to present their side of the story. They claimed to be caught in a three-way squeeze: vacancies were rising, taxes were rising, but profits were declining, they said, because of tenant damage on the one hand and increased building code prosecutions on the other. They put most of the blame on the tenants. Mrs. Jacob Hammer, who managed about ten buildings with her husband, explained, "They steal everything that can be taken away. They strip the apartments. They even take the plumbing." The problem, she believed, was lack of family cohesion: the children "grow up like weeds—their parents are indifferent." Contract seller Warren J. Peters, my father's old opponent, also complained about the dysfunctional behavior of welfare, or Aid for Dependent Children (ADC), tenants. "If I take in 12 ADC families this month, we will have evicted nine or 10 of them in six months for non-payment."[40]

Peters neglected to mention the role that he sometimes played in forcing people onto public aid. An apparently unrelated story that appeared in the *Daily News* around the same time described how Peters cheated Mrs. Elizabeth Bennett, a seventy-three-year-old African American widow, out of two buildings: a six-flat building she purchased on contract from Peters for $40,000 (appraisers valued the property at $20,000) and an older property that she had owned outright but deeded to Peters in partial payment for the six-flat. Taking advantage of Mrs. Bennett's age and naiveté, Peters convinced her that the six-flat would provide for her in her final years. In a now familiar refrain, he said that she "did not need a lawyer" and assured her that through the rental income the building would pay for itself, which was untrue. When Mrs. Bennett fell behind on one of her grossly inflated installment payments, Peters evicted her and reclaimed the six-flat. Now she lived on public aid. "I lost both buildings," Mrs. Bennett told *Daily News* reporters. "I don't know how they done it to me."[41]

On the whole, however, the exposé followed the MHPC's blueprint. It named the city's major slum landlords and described the numerous code violations in their buildings. It highlighted the inefficiencies of the municipal housing court by describing a typical day there. "Cases are heard at the rate of nearly one a minute. Many of the usual legal formalities are overlooked," the *Daily News* reported. The paper noted that code violators routinely paid only a tiny fraction of the fines levied against them: Lou Fushanis, for example, owed some $100,000 but had paid only $430. When reporters suggested that perhaps time pressures had led Judge Eugene L. Wachowski to let Fushanis off easy, Wachowski defended his ability to handle one to two hundred housing code violation cases in a six-hour workday. "Wachowski feels that only on days when he has 300 or so cases is the load 'rather heavy,'" the *Daily News* noted.[42]

From the MHPC's point of view, the series was effective. Among the first changes to be enacted after its appearance was the addition of a second housing court judge to help handle the load formerly carried solely by Judge Wachowski. The *Daily News* then ran an article presenting further solutions that the MHPC had outlined in advance. It called for a national search for a new building commissioner, the establishment of a modernized code violation record center, the issuing of certificates by the Building Department identifying which structures were up to code, and new legislation forcing banks to disclose the names of beneficiaries of land trusts within ten days of being notified of a building code violation.[43]

While these proposals were all reasonable in themselves, as strategies for ending slums they were too narrow and politically naive to make a substantive difference.[44] Focused exclusively on strengthening enforcement of the city's housing code, such efforts were doomed from the start by Chicago's political machine, which transformed any additional powers given to the city into sources of patronage and profit. The housing code was particularly handy in this regard. As one community activist explained, building codes functioned primarily to enable aldermen to line up votes: "If you vote the right way and know the right people, you can get away with [housing code violations]. If you vote the wrong way, though, they'll throw the book at you."[45]

Corruption was a major problem throughout the system. The Building Department had long been known for "doing little except shake householders down," an observer noted. The municipal court, too, was rife with opportunities for bribery. Landlords often paid off the judges, but they were also known to bribe bailiffs, clerks, and other court personnel in order to "stall the proceedings, misinform witnesses, and do other things which eventually result in the charges being quashed." The courts also went light on slumlords because many slumlords were themselves attorneys. As *Daily News* editor Maurice Fischer pointed out, "Members of the bar have been known to extend courtesies to each other—even from the bench."[46]

Chicago's politicians were also unlikely to challenge slum profiteering, since some of them owned slum buildings. The *Daily News* exposé mentioned a few such cases. Perhaps the most striking example was U.S. congressional representative Roland Libonati, whose district encompassed much of the city's West Side. Libonati and his sister Ellinore, who was employed by the municipal family court, jointly owned at least six slum buildings. Since 1950, code violations in their properties had led to the filing of approximately seventy-three court cases. They had also neglected to pay $30,406 in real estate taxes—not counting penalties and interest. The Libonatis' tenants complained that their children were eating paint chips that flaked from the walls, that they often lacked electricity, and that the landlord refused to repair a broken water pipe that left them without water for several months. "They won't even buy a carpet tack," tenants lamented. When a neighbor begged the city to tear down one of the Libonatis' buildings "before it falls down on my place," the city ignored her request. A possible reason for the delay was discovered by reporters, who found a handwritten note in assistant corporate counsel Louis A. Wexler's file on a Libonati building. The note, signed by corporate counsel John C. Melaniphy, instructed Wexler to "hold until further notice." Neighborhood residents were not surprised: "Try to get it torn down," they scoffed to reporters. "That building belongs to a politician."[47] Problems like these would not be alleviated by the appointment of an extra judge to housing court.

The most basic problem with the MHPC's approach was that it ignored the consequences of code enforcement for ordinary Chicagoans. Since the city didn't have housing for those who would be displaced if statutes on overcrowding were enforced, both slum landlords and slum residents had a stake in resisting such enforcement. Furthermore, given that most of those displaced would be black and that their search for new housing would inevitably take them to adjoining white neighborhoods, white aldermen pressured the building commissioner to prevent such an occurrence. This explained, an observer noted, why Chicago's building commissioner had publicly stated that "the code is unenforceable" and "he has no intention of enforcing it."[48]

The debate over code enforcement crystallized around the issue of "crash panel fire doors." These partitions, widely in use during the housing shortage to subdivide apartments, had been outlawed by the city's 1956 housing code, but property owners had been given five years to remove them. As the ban's effective date grew closer, opposition began to organize. In the fall of 1960, 230 property owners came together to form the Income Property Owners Association (IPOA), whose goal was to repeal the city's ban on crash panels.

In my father's view, the group was a front for slum landlords—an easy guess, given that the group's leader, attorney Samuel Bass, also represented several of the city's most notorious slumlords.[49] Now they were openly fighting for their right to overcrowd their properties. Crash panels allowed a landlord to charge "minority and uneducated families . . . as much for half an apartment . . . as . . . his former tenant [paid] for the entire apartment," my father noted. But he also pointed out that the simple enforcement of this "entirely proper ordinance"—the approach favored by urban renewal proponents—would cause great harm to African Americans who had bought their homes on contract. Having paid inflated prices, they were forced to install crash panel dividers, "if only to be able to take in enough money to make their monthly payments," he wrote to news reporters. "Should the 'crash panel' ordinance be enforced," he added, "the great bulk of Negro contract purchasers will be wiped out." The solution was to fine "*only* . . . the title holder owners of the properties" in question, and not the resident contract buyer, and to make low-interest government loans available to minority homeowners so that they could comply with housing codes.[50]

Suggestions such as these aimed to make code enforcement a more just and nuanced tool. But neither the MHPC nor the news media seemed much interested.[51] At the end of 1961, the IPOA launched a legal challenge to the crash panel ordinance. It was argued by the group's lead attorney—Favil Berns.

Berns's involvement with the IPOA started modestly. "I'm home watching television, and I see this show about an apartment building on the South Side of Chicago. A whole television crew is up there at night, going through it, and they say, 'The city is now enforcing its new housing ordinance, and the slumlords in Chicago are in for big trouble.'" Berns sat up and paid closer attention, in part because he recognized the news reporter; he was "the same one that your father was always in concert with, giving him information," Berns told me. The next day, as he was running an errand at City Hall, whom should he bump into but his friend Ray Podolsky. Podolsky was practically family—Podolsky's mother had fixed Favil up with Marcia, his wife. Podolsky looked absolutely crushed. "And I said, 'What happened, Ray?' He says, 'Did you see television last night?' He says, 'You know, that was my building!'"

Berns took Podolsky for coffee and heard the whole story. Podolsky was not a contract seller; he rented the units in his thirty-one-flat building. Out of the blue, with no warning whatsoever, he had been ordered to deconvert the building. He didn't know how he would handle the expense of the deconversion much less the 50 percent loss of his rental income. "I'll help you if I can," Berns promised. He looked into the matter and came up with an angle. While Podolsky had been subject to a court injunction ordering him to deconvert, Berns told the judge, he had never been given a chance to defend himself in court. This was unfair, Berns argued. The judge agreed. He removed the deconversion order. Observers were stunned by the outcome. "All of a sudden I'm a hero!" Berns recalled. His victory brought him to the attention of Samuel Bass, who headed the IPOA. "He said, 'Look it, there's an organization needing some help understanding why people have to deconvert their buildings and lose their investments.'"

Berns was willing to help. He joined Bass's group and became a bit of an activist. He was soon delivering speeches to the IPOA. "Your father used to have an expression. . . . 'What man makes he can unmake,'" Berns told me. When he gave speeches to IPOA members, he added, "I was thinking of Mark." An article titled "Landlords Tell Their Side of the Story" confirms his recollections. It describes Berns as "the only attorney to win a reversal of a deconversion order in court involving the city of Chicago. . . . 'These laws are man-made and they can be undone,' Berns said while property owners applauded."[52]

Berns coauthored the IPOA's test case against the crash panel ban, *Adolph Kaukus et al. v. City of Chicago.* The plaintiffs, Adolph and Vera Kaukus, were a Lithuanian couple who owned a single, well-maintained building. They had spent $16,000 to remodel their building just before the 1956 housing code was passed. The changes they made were in accordance with the laws then in place but were rendered illegal by the new housing code. Berns and his coattorneys argued that the couple would now be forced to undo all of their remodeling by fiat, at immense cost to themselves and with no recourse.[53]

The superior court judge ruled in favor of the IPOA, writing that "forcing owners to remodel is tantamount to taking property without just compensation to the owner."[54] However, the Illinois Supreme Court overturned the judge's ruling. Its decision drew heavily upon a friend of the court brief filed by the MHPC, the Chicago Mortgage Bankers Association, the Chicago Association of Commerce and Industry, and the South East Chicago Commission (a Hyde Park urban renewal group closely associated with Julian Levi). The city had the legal right to compel changes to buildings that were originally "to code," the appellate court ruled. Although this presented some burden to the property owners, previous supreme court rulings established that legislatures had the right to "adopt the most conservative course" when creating codes aimed at saving human lives.[55]

In response IPOA members published two scathing pamphlets attacking the MHPC as a "front for the Urban Renewal promoters," real estate syndicates, and the University of Chicago. They argued that the housing code under dispute had nothing to do with public health and safety. Rather, it was designed "to meet the requirements of the Federal Urban Renewal law," which insisted that codes be in place before granting the city much desired federal dollars. Had the housing code been aimed at improving the city's existing buildings, it would have earmarked renovation loan money for small property owners, who were crippled by the costs of deconverting. Instead, "only the multi-million dollar institutions and real estate syndicates receive a gift of your tax dollar." Why must only small owners make financial sacrifices, and not those who "make millions for themselves" out of urban renewal? Because "the very persons and institutions like the Chicago University [*sic*] who drafted the laws and lobbied for their passage, designed them for their benefit."

The IPOA's self-presentation as "innocent victims" who were "harassed more than the actual true slum landlord" was, at best, only partially true, since its members included slum landlords. Yet the group's most damning charges—that the MHPC was a front for urban renewal advocates, that the business leaders promoting urban renewal made "millions for themselves" while small property owners were denied loans for routine maintenance and deconversion, and that urban renewal promoters received huge subsidies from taxpayers—were accurate.[56]

The morality of the situation, though, was complex. Building code enforcement could be used to shake down property owners or to rein in slum landlords; it could wipe out black contract buyers or save human lives. Berns learned something of these complexities when he became involved, in a roundabout way, with James Johnson, aged seven. James lived in a West Side three-flat that had been cut up into nine units. The building was repeatedly cited for code violations, but the city had difficulty tracking down its owner because it was held in trust by Oak Park National Bank. When the bank finally turned over the names of the owners—Arthur Vigott and his wife—the city proposed that, instead of paying a fine, Vigott should fix the 127 code violations found in his building.

Vigott believed that doing so would bankrupt him, and he hired Favil Berns to plead his case. As with the Kaukuses, Berns argued that it was unjust to make the 1956 housing code retroactive; to do so would amount to confiscating the building from its owners. Because the Illinois Supreme Court was then hearing the identical argument in the Kaukus case, the judge agreed to wait for the outcome before deciding on the Vigotts'. The Kaukus ruling came on February 6, 1963. Five days later, on February 11, 1963, Judge Julian P. Wilamoski ordered Vigott to correct his building's code violations within ninety days.

The order came too late. At 3:00 a.m. on March 10, 1963, a fire broke out at the Vigott building. The exits of the third-floor rear apartment, where James Johnson lived, were cut off by flames. The seven-year-old died in the fire. It was impossible for reporters to learn much about James, since George and Fannie Johnson, his grandparents, who had raised him since birth, also perished. The only information they were able to obtain about the boy was that at the time of his death he was four feet tall and weighed fifty pounds.[57]

Berns's activism on behalf of the IPOA greatly strained his relationship with my father and may well have precipitated the break between the two men. That he ultimately ended up battling the same groups that my father despised—the bankers and businessmen who dictated housing policy in Chicago—was just the final, ironic twist. Indeed, the situation in early 1960s Chicago was replete with ironies. Mortgage bankers fostered urban decay by granting the loans that enabled speculators to take over neighborhoods.

Their representatives in the MHPC then targeted small landlords and slumlords alike to force them to comply with housing codes, which would result only in further exploitation of those who purchased on contract. The group that devised the housing code erased from its agenda the one thing that would have made it workable—that is, granting mortgage or improvement loans to small property owners, black and white. The crusading journalists who might have offered an honest appraisal of the MHPC's purpose served instead as the council's mouthpiece. In a response to the *Daily News* series that must have pleased the MHPC, Mayor Daley announced that the only answer to slum conditions was "more money and more personnel for demolition, enforcement of the building code and urban renewal."[58]

With all its flaws, the *Chicago Daily News* series did, however, expose the business practices of one of the city's most important contract sellers—Lou Fushanis. In the spring of 1963, Fushanis hired an Irish immigrant to help him sell homes on contract to black Chicagoans—actually an undercover reporter named John Culhane. On May 24, 1963, the *Daily News* published "I Was Hired to Sell Slums to Negroes," in which Culhane revealed all he had learned about Fushanis.

Readers were taken inside Fushanis's West Side office, where seventeen of his employees labored in what looked like a converted 1920s dance hall, an airy room whose "swank black and silver décor" provided temporary distraction from its state of disrepair. Culhane had initiated contact with Fushanis by telling him that he had $5,000 cash to invest in a building. Fushanis responded with warm personal interest. "'Whether or not I sell you a building, I'm going to give you some good advice," he told Culhane. "I'm an immigrant myself—from Greece, so I know your problems." When Culhane said that he was interested in starting his own business, Fushanis ran down the list of options. A grocery store was a bad idea because of competition from the new supermarkets—unless he wanted to start an all-night store, where people who wanted to shop late would have no choice but to pay higher prices. He could start a "colored tavern," but that could be dangerous—"Knifings and shootings all the time." Better would be a "hillbilly tavern," Fushanis advised. "The hillbillies are the lowest rung of our society, but a tavern catering to them, with country music—that's very profitable." Ultimately, though, he believed Culhane would be best off working for him. "I can put you in real estate right now," Fushanis said. For a "small downpayment" he was willing to give Culhane five buildings and show him how to run them. He would also hire him to sell "on contract." If Culhane was willing to work "16 or 17 hours a day," he could make good money. "And if you're smart, you'll draw $50 a week to live on, and leave the rest to pile up. . . . That way, you'll save money to buy more buildings. That's the way to start."

Culhane's tasks would be simple. "You'll take prospective buyers to the buildings, then bring 'em back here. When you get back here, you shut up and let me do the talking," Fushanis advised. "When you can talk the way I do, you can do the talking," he added. "It's not hard to sell buildings to colored people," he reassured Culhane. "They're the easiest people in the world to sell to." Culhane accepted the offer. "Mr. Fushanis is going to put me in the real estate business!" he babbled to one of his new cowork-ers, who turned out to be considerably more jaded. "Don't buy any prop-erties from him. They're garbage, I tell you." The coworker turned to one of the secretaries. "Lou's going to keep this kid till he gets all his money." Culhane observed that "she laughed uncomfortably."[59]

Culhane worked for Fushanis for two days—long enough to observe the basics of Fushanis's operation. He accompanied one of Fushanis's sales-men as he showed a building for sale on contract to prospective buyers, a black trucker and his wife. The tenants in the basement apartment com-plained that they'd been without heat the entire winter. The second-floor apartment had broken plumbing, a malfunctioning toilet, and crumbling plaster. The first-floor apartment was occupied by the building's current owners, who were in the process of being evicted after falling behind on a contract payment; furious, they refused to allow the salesman to see the place. Fushanis was asking $19,000 for the building—$500 down and pay-ments of $190 a month. "The salesman was obviously embarrassed by the dilapidated condition of the building," Culhane wrote. "'I'll have our con-tractor right in here to look at this place,'" he told the couple, adding that "'I might be able to knock $500 off the purchase price against repairs.'" Later the salesman explained to Culhane, "'That's just something you say to pacify 'em. . . . Lou fixes some things, but he makes sure the purchaser gets stuck with most of the repairs.'" When Culhane asked the couple why they wanted the building, they had a rational reply. "'We have been leasing for so long, we've about paid for the building we're in,'" they explained. "'We decided we wanted to own a place.'" Their deal with Fushanis was not likely to bring them to that goal. "'He loads them up with payments they can't meet, then he takes the property away from them. He's sold some of these buildings three or four times,'" an office secretary told Culhane.[60]

As it turned out, Fushanis didn't have to bear the heat from Culhane's exposé. On May 23, the day before the first installment was to appear in the *Daily News*, Fushanis collapsed from a heart attack and died. He was forty-two years old. His employees reported that Fushanis knew that the *Daily News* was about to publish an exposé about him. "He just laughed," one of his secretaries commented. Fushanis's obituary was frustratingly vague. Although he was of Greek descent, he was no immigrant: he had been born in Ohio. Employees believed that Fushanis had a wife and two teenage children in Florida, but no one knew their names. He kept one apartment near his West Side office and a second, more elegant residence on the city's North Side. At the time of his death Fushanis owned over six hundred buildings, mostly in Lawndale, plus an additional 269 buildings that he co-owned with Moe M. Forman. His estate was estimated to be worth $3 million.[61]

My father left no record of his reaction to the death of his longtime opponent. However, by 1963 his sense of who were his friends and who were his foes was shifting. He was disgusted by most liberal housing groups' obsession with passing an open occupancy ordinance. He was stunned that many of these groups still supported urban renewal.[62] He was dismayed by the failure of efforts to reform Illinois's wage garnishment laws. He was frustrated by the insensitivity of the courts to the desperate plight of his clients. He was irritated with the city's mainstream black leadership, whom he viewed as "charlatans" who simply "feathered their own nest."[63] Finally, he was alienated from most of his fellow attorneys. "He didn't have a close relationship with any of them," his secretary, Sandy Gatto, recalled. "They didn't share his passion for helping people. They were out to make a good living, you know. They thought that he was just spinning his wheels for nothing."[64]

At the same time, my father was battling to improve his own perilous financial situation. The fact that he did not make much money was well known. "Satter's been labeled the patron saint of Chicago's poor," one gossip columnist noted, "which means he has more poor clients than dollars."[65] Gatto confirmed this assessment. "Because his clients were in trouble, they couldn't afford to pay," she recalled, "but he took them on anyway."[66]

The personal repercussions of this admirable stance were harsh, as Favil Berns sadly witnessed. The two men had managed to maintain a fragile relationship. Although my father was angry at Berns, he contained his feelings. For his part, Berns struggled to remain in my father's life even after he opened his independent practice in Northlake: "Favil maintained a certain loyalty to him," my brother David said. The two sometimes met for breakfast on Saturday mornings, and here Berns observed my father's precarious circumstances. "If people came to see your dad," Berns told me, it meant "they had no money to pay their contract. They certainly had no money to pay for attorney's fees. So your dad would take a token payment, $50, but that wouldn't support his family."[67]

My father's Lawndale properties offered no relief. When he first bought them, David told me, he'd viewed them as "a portal to wealth." He used to say, "'If we make it to such and such a year, then all the buildings will be paid off and we'll be fortunate, and pretty wealthy,'" David recalled. "He had become an owner of property because it seemed to him that his father had had a piece of property, had held onto it through thick and thin in the Depression, and that had kept his family afloat."[68] By the early 1960s, my father had struggled for almost twenty years to keep up his buildings, and the mortgages were almost paid. He couldn't lose them now.

Yet his grip on the properties was increasingly tenuous—largely because of their maintenance costs. As he told his sister Helen, the buildings required "tremendous repairs" that caused him "tremendous losses in income." My brother Paul explained the losses: "People didn't pay rent. That was the main thing. They'd stay there, they'd pay the first month, maybe the second month, and then they'd freeload . . . until the legal system got rid of them." By that point, Paul recalled, "everything would be stripped. Bathrooms with the toilet gone, the sink gone, the kitchen smashed . . . just really vicious." Berns also witnessed my father's tenant troubles. "The repairs were unending. The tenants weren't paying the rent, and he was trying to support this family of his, which was very difficult." The situation was "so distressing—that's why the beads of sweat kept coming out of his forehead."[69]

There were problems with the buildings' managers as well. After discovering that a management company he had used had "bilked him out of a large amount of money," my father arranged to have one of his tenants collect the rents. The tenant, it turned out, was also untrustworthy, so he turned to yet another company, Balin Realty. Although Gilbert and Ralph Balin, the two men heading it, were young and new to the business, my father was running out of options; there were only so many management companies still operating in Lawndale.[70] What he did not know, in all likelihood, was that one of the Balin brothers, Gilbert Balin, was a protégé of contract seller Moe Forman.[71]

The stress began to eat away at my father. He took out his frustration on the nearest target, which was my mother. "You can't bear the idea of our getting out of debt, can you?" he snarled at her when she asked for money. Though she was subjected to his sarcasm and temper, my mother was entirely cut out of his financial decisions. He confined his attacks to harsh words, but there was, my brother David recalled, an "undercurrent of physical aggression in it." It could border on violence. "I remember once he got in an argument with Mom about something, and she was sitting there holding a glass in her hand," David said. "He swung his hand and sent the glass flying." At that point my mother considered leaving him.[72]

Then one Saturday morning in the spring of 1963 my father went to collect the rents from his properties. After gathering the money, he was robbed and beaten. He pulled himself together and went directly to a breakfast meeting with Favil Berns. He was "black and blue," Berns recalled. "Oh, it was devastating what they did to him." Later that morning David was shocked to see our father entering the house in torn clothing. David stared awkwardly until he looked up and snapped, "Get away from me!" It is not clear who was responsible for the beating. Was it a random attack by local thugs? Or was it a paid job, on behalf of others—white speculators, perhaps—who wanted Mark J. Satter out of the neighborhood? There is no way to know. To add to my father's humiliation, details of the attack were written up in the press.[73]

It is an old joke that a conservative is a liberal who has been mugged. This can be true enough; if one's empathy toward the poor is based on sentimental fantasies about their inherent goodness rather than on a realistic appraisal of the forces impinging upon them, then a sound beating could overturn one's worldview. But my father's thinking was radical, not liberal, and the beating only deepened his commitment to understanding the roots of the criminal behavior that he observed and experienced in Lawndale. Initially, he believed that some West Siders committed crimes because they felt that crimes had already been committed against them. As a result of the ruthless actions of speculators and unethical credit merchants, they or people they knew struggled under immense economic burdens. While they might not understand precisely how their families or friends had become economically entrapped, they did sense that the law gave "systematic protection" to the men and women who exploited them—a knowledge that fueled rage as well as contempt for law itself.[74]

By 1962, my father had added "public assistance" to the forces that he believed fostered crime in minority communities. By then, Aid to Dependent Children (ADC), or "welfare," was a hot topic.[75] Conservatives argued that black Southerners had migrated specifically to take advantage of Northern states' more generous welfare provisions, that the rolls were full of "chiselers," and that women on ADC had babies in order "to get a bigger monthly check."[76] Liberals countered that welfare rates were rising because many of the jobs formerly held by African Americans had vanished, while the industries that were thriving did not hire black workers.[77] As Raymond Hilliard, director of Chicago's Public Aid Department, summarized, "If there were no racial discrimination in employment or housing, the relief rolls would melt to 40% of their present size." The problem had nothing to do with "immorality or laziness," he stressed. "The basic solution is adequate jobs at adequate salaries."[78]

Of course my father understood that many black Chicagoans ended up on relief because of plant closings, wage garnishments, and other scams such as exploitative contract sales. But he felt that however unfair the processes that landed people in penury, the provision of "dole" was the wrong solution. He insisted that all people had a basic human right to support themselves through their own labor and to keep the wages that they earned. In his view, both wage garnishment and welfare payments took away this right to a wage for labor performed. The result was an irrevocable shattering of self-esteem. "Men on dole know that society considers them useless and react savagely against the brutal manner of feeding, and at the same time, degrading them," he wrote in a 1964 article. "We are entirely too complacent" about the "complete disintegration of a human being attendant upon long periods of idleness."[79]

My father also rejected the liberal claim that "education and jobs" would solve the welfare problem. Such a claim overlooked a crucial structural fact: private industry had no need for the minority workers who made up most of the nation's unemployed. Even with "American industry functioning at peak levels," he pointed out, there remained millions of Americans "for whom our economy has no place."[80] Other sources supported his assertion that the jobs held by black Chicagoans were those least valued by private industry. Between 1950 and 1960, housing, highway, and skyscraper projects had generated jobs for Chicago's African Americans, both native born and migrant. As a result, black family income had increased by 50 percent.[81] But this economic progress had recently slowed. A 1961 Urban League study reported that almost two-thirds of black Chicagoans worked "as semi-skilled operatives, service workers, or general laborers. These are occupations that are least desirable, lowest paid, [and] most often affected by extended periods of unemployment." They were also the jobs being phased out in "advanced industrial economies" like Chicago's.[82]

Rather than waiting for private industry to find places for the city's unemployed, my father argued, the federal government needed to create "job opportunities for all who would work" through a program similar to the Depression-era Works Progress Administration. His dream of a revived WPA was probably based on *Minister of Relief*, a biography of New Deal administrator Harry Hopkins that he had recently reviewed. Hopkins had created the WPA because he believed that unemployed Americans needed work, not dole. The WPA "produced employment and restored self-respect to millions. These are people who would otherwise have been the predecessors of today's ADC recipients," my father wrote.[83]

In the last piece he wrote on the subject, titled "Jobs vs. Dole—A Suggested Approach"—which remained unpublished despite numerous journal submissions—my father's arguments about welfare and joblessness revealed a deep identification with men who struggled to support their families.[84] Indeed, he wrote this impassioned defense of economic independence at a time when he himself was desperately struggling to keep his family solvent, and inklings of his personal situation are evident throughout. Writing of the problems facing welfare tenants, he shifted to the devastating effects of the welfare system on the small property owner: "Unable to collect even a portion of the monies necessary to maintain his property and overwhelmed by unfortunate tenants who cannot cope with even rudimentary financial problems, the would-be real estate owning resident is either wiped out or abandons his efforts to be a contributing member of the community." The contract buyer who hoped to rent out part of his building was caught in an even tighter squeeze. He was hurt by his seller, who charged him "unconscionably high monthly payments," *and* by his tenants, that is, by "his inability to cope with men and women" whom "joblessness and welfare" had reduced to "community liabilities rather than assets."[85]

My father's description of small property owners who suffered from their "inability to cope" with destructive tenants was obviously autobiographical. More than anyone, he understood the array of forces that dragged down so many of his black clients and that wreaked havoc in Lawndale. Yet his intellectual understanding did not mitigate his personal anguish over the impoverished men and women who abused his property. As he wrote in a 1965 letter to his sister Helen, "My greatest fear is that . . . the people available to us as tenants are so disintegrated as responsible human beings that no matter how much we try, we will be constantly in court actions to put them out, and will be constantly repairing broken windows and other destruction." In another letter to his sister his comments were even more bitter: "You must remember that it is not easy as I watch the efforts of twenty five years threatened by people turned animal, and [by] forces which I never learned to handle."[86]

By 1964, my father's struggles to keep afloat financially took on an almost feverish intensity. He applied for a night job teaching law at the University of Chicago. His application was brushed off in a condescending letter.[87] He continued to write articles on urban problems, both to express his ideas and in the hope that his writing could lift him out of his financial morass, but more often than not the articles were rejected. By the end of the year his usually boundless energy was flagging. "I seem exhausted every day beyond anything I have ever known," he wrote his sister. Gatto noticed the change. "I saw him slowing down, and walking slower, his shoulders down and his head down."[88]

He continued to put in long hours representing his clients. He wrote even more articles on the need to outlaw wage garnishment, as well as an essay criticizing the generous insurance the Federal Deposit Insurance Corporation provided for savings and loan companies—insurance that allowed them the "freedom to injure."[89] He gave speeches attacking the hysterical anti-Communism that paralyzed intellectual discussion by equating any questioning of the status quo with subversion. "The Right Wing has made of our country a nation of intellectual cowards," he said.[90]

The subject closest to him remained the law. He criticized the sporadic crusades that focused on "lawyers who skirt the ethics line." The problem was not these individual deviations; it was "the very law itself." Exploitation would end only when "our laws are re-designed to serve rather than despoil our people."[91] He pointed out that most lawyers didn't care about the impoverished because they were ignorant of the realities of poor people's lives. He told a graduating law class of 1964 that the graduate of 1934 was "brother" to the destitute, aware that "he was responsible for the poor around him." In contrast, "the poor man today to the young lawyer is at most a distant and unrelated thing. . . . Our country is the loser because of this failure of our would-be leaders to know the pulse and heart of the poor among us."[92]

Perhaps my father's sense of distance from the younger generation of attorneys explains the relationship that developed between him and Irving Block. Block had been my father's toughest opponent in several cases brought against exploitative contract sellers.[93] But by 1964, the two had become trusted friends, in part owing to their mutual expertise. "They were really different," Sandy Gatto recalled, yet "they both had a great love for law. . . . If you were Block's client, you knew he would go to bat for you." Block was an immensely likable, fiercely loyal, and profoundly cynical man. As he once told my brother David, "Mark would no sooner step out of a case because a client couldn't pay than I would enter into one unless I was sure that he could." For my father, who was irritated by what he viewed as the facile and hypocritical solutions offered by liberal reformers, Block's humor and cynicism was refreshing. "Block was not false," David said of him. "He didn't pretend to be anything different than he was. Whereas Dad knew that a lot of wealthy people were pretending." And according to Block, most liberal attorneys were "just a bunch of phonies," while my father lived by the words that he preached.[94]

Toward the end of 1964 my father suffered a series of blows. His older brother, Nate, died of a heart ailment. Shortly thereafter his father, Isaac, passed away. Isaac's death left him with one more building to manage—the cold-water flat on Roosevelt Road that Isaac had held on to since the 1920s. His financial situation was so precarious that he could barely keep up the mortgage payments. "No matter what area you look, 1964 was not an easy year," he wrote to his sister Helen.

But he was optimistic that 1965 would be better. David, then seventeen, was completing his freshman year at the University of Chicago, and sixteen-year-old Paul was applying for early admittance that coming September. My mother had gotten a secretarial job in the university's Biophysics Department, which brought a 50 percent reduction in the boys' tuition and also gave her a new sense of confidence. "Clarice is so proud of her ability to handle the job . . . that she is absolutely impossible to live with," my father joked. "The entire arrangement seems to have worked wonders for our home. For the first time in maybe two years, the pervading atmosphere of despondency seems to be gone. We all leave together in the morning . . . and the teamwork is terrific."[95]

My father's professional life was looking up as well. The *Chicago Daily News* launched another investigative crusade about credit exploitation, which led to my father's giving testimony on credit fraud before the City Council. Why not give the abolition of wage garnishment a two-year trial run, he proposed, and see if the claim that it would hurt consumer credit was borne out or not? This time, over half a dozen witnesses supported his position. His testimony also brought an expression of interest from the University of Chicago Law School. "Perhaps the day will come that I will leave this animal trap and get into a slower life," he wrote to Helen about the law school solicitation. "The plain truth is that this is an erratic way of life; December was the most destructive month I ever knew, and January in every way has been the most productive and gratifying. . . . In the midst of the sense of good feeling is the wonder about what the next month will bring."[96]

Nine days later, on February 5, my father collapsed at his office. He was rushed to Chicago's Woodlawn Hospital, where physicians spent weeks trying to determine how best to treat his damaged heart. Later that month, while he was still hospitalized, my mother noticed a lump in her breast. She, too, was admitted to Woodlawn Hospital. In March, Paul and David visited their parents on two different floors of the institution. Clarice's case was serious, potentially graver than Mark's. "She went up for a biopsy and they said if it's cancer we're going to remove the breast," David recalled. They put her under for the biopsy. "When she came down she was still smelling of ether and her face was completely drained." This was hard for a boy of seventeen to witness. "It was obvious from the way the sheet was laying that the breast was gone, and part of her arm was gone," David told me. "She was crying."[97]

Clarice's illness was almost more than Mark could bear. Both of his sons were present when the doctors arrived to tell him about his wife. "He cried when they found it was cancer," David said. It was the only time he had ever seen our father in tears. Both of my parents were released from the hospital by the end of March. The doctors believed that my father would recover with rest and drug treatment; my mother would have to undergo radiation for the next several months. My father returned to work, but it was a struggle. Clarice's illness was a "big blow to him," Sandy Gatto recalled. "I saw a big change in him after that." As the weeks passed, my father's exhaustion increased. "He couldn't make it up the stairs," Paul said. He would walk up to the first landing and then rest until he mustered the energy for the second. "He was an invalid."[98]

By May it was clear that my father wasn't simply exhausted; he was suffering from advanced heart failure. He flew to Minnesota's Mayo Clinic on May 20. With Mark gone, Clarice was left to fend off creditors while caring for five children and completing radiation treatments. "I called Carson's [Department Store] to ask for more time but they refused and threatened legal action," she wrote to my father. "We owe them $439.80. If we send a substantial payment that might hold them off—but where will it come from?"[99]

At the Mayo Clinic, Mark learned the full extent of his deterioration. His aorta valve was calcified and the mitral valve was badly damaged. He had a mysterious congestion in his lungs and what appeared to be a tumor in one kidney. He was too anemic for physicians to risk the onlyoperation that they believed would save him: a daring open-heart surgery in which two of his four heart valves would be replaced. So he waited. Although he kept the truth to himself, he knew that his chances of surviving the surgery were not high. He was also facing the complete impoverishment of his family. He had no idea what would happen to his five children. His brother Charlie tried to encourage him by suggesting a vacation after his operation. "Vacation? I'm facing the most difficult time of my life. If I survive, that will be a vacation enough," my father responded.[100]

He tried to continue his legal work from his hospital bed. He received support from friends, especially John King, the attorney who had headed the sting operations against credit-and-garnishee racketeers. He sent my father joking letters every day. If you are sent home with "a new heart," would you "come back the same?" he asked. "Or is it your rotten diseased organs that have caused us to love you? . . . We don't want you to come home a new man who we wouldn't like," such as the "president of a temple, the owner of a loan company, a conservative and a good driver." King rallied others to support my father. Monsignor John J. Egan wrote that he'd heard "the news" from King. "May God give you patience and courage during this ordeal." Maurice "Ritz" Fischer reported hearing from King that "you had encountered all kinds of complications, but it seemed to me . . . that you weren't nearly so trussed up . . . as when you were in the midst of the credit reform fight. . . . We've got you in our prayers—and while mine may not count much, I assure you that [my wife] Elvera's are most effective."[101] My father's spirits were also lifted by a tribute to his work that appeared in an unlikely place—the Nation of Islam newspaper *Muhammad Speaks.* Its glowing two-part series on his battles against credit racketeers lauded him as the "Clarence Darrow of the Bankrupt."[102]

Mostly, Mark and Clarice tried to encourage each other. "I think of you constantly and miss you more than I can say," my mother wrote. "You must have faith that you will pull through all this successfully and we will help each other to regain our health. I never needed you as much as I do now." My father replied, "The strength I get from you and the children would carry me through far more than this; you must believe the same way, and the sweetness of the touch of your hand, and your face, will be mine again, and soon." But behind his words of love lurked a profound anxiety about his family's future. "You must remember that we both have a duty to live," he wrote my mother.[103]

Should he die, he told her, everything possible must be done to keep hold of the West Side buildings. "Far more important than visits and phone calls . . . is the need to keep our family group in economic life. All the house mortgages must be paid, and there will be some who will use this time to try and take by exploiting our fears, the things we have tried to build," he wrote Clarice.[104] He made sure that as many people as possible knew his desires. He wrote to David, "It is my judgment that we hold the buildings, no matter how rough it may be."[105] He reminded his sister that his buildings would be "paid in full" in three years. They would then provide the income to "keep the family together." He also appointed someone to look after his family and properties in case of his death—Irving Block. Decades later Sandy Gatto recalled his words. "'You can trust him,' he would tell me, 'you can trust him.'"[106]

Finally the physicians at the Mayo Clinic determined that my father's condition had stabilized. They performed open-heart surgery on him on June 8. My mother flew to Minnesota for the operation. On June 22, she returned to Chicago, expecting my father to remain in the hospital another ten to fifteen days, or at least until his fever was under control. Instead, the hospital discharged him five days later.[107]

He never recovered. On July 7, he was taken to Michael Reese Hospital. For five days the physicians there struggled to help him breathe. On July 11, my father told Max Berg, his physician, "Max, I'm losing ground." Berg agreed. He took my mother and my two brothers aside. "I'm afraid Mark's not going to make it," he told them. "There comes a time to face these things."

That evening the three sat vigil. My father's pulmonary cavity was filling with fluid, preventing his lungs from fully expanding. The pain was agonizing. He was drowning, but very slowly, over hours instead of minutes. He asked who was looking after the girls. Clarice and his sons assured him that the younger children were being cared for, but Mark wouldn't let the matter rest until David and Paul drove back home to tuck the girls in. When they returned, Mark looked up at them in bewilderment. "Where's Berg?" he asked. They were too upset to answer. "Where's Berg, what did he say?" Mark repeated. Clarice left the room in tears. Mark knew by then what Berg had said.

The pain increased as the evening wore on. That night, for the first time in over five months of illness, he asked for relief: "Miss, I'm sorry, I'm in pain, can't you do something?" he called to a nurse. Around midnight he began to drift into a coma. By 1:00 a.m. he was delirious. "He kept repeating, 'Look out,' and 'I don't understand,'" David recalled. David had taken a break from the hospital room when my mother approached him at around 2:30 that morning. She took his hand and held it tightly. "I think he's gone, my poor baby, I think he's gone."[108]

My mother had no time to grieve. Her first order of business was to fight off creditors, starting with those at the Mayo Clinic. "I must say that I feel his post-operative care was inadequate," she wrote to the clinic. "He was discharged too soon. This was very evident to me that first week at home. Now he is gone at age 49. I am a widow with 5 minor children. I too underwent major surgery twice, during the month of March of this year. . . . My husband had no insurance since he had a heart murmur and was not acceptable for insurance. Whatever security we had was from his earnings as an attorney. Although nothing can bring this dear man back to his wife and children, I hope you can do something to help me for I cannot afford to pay the hospital bill which I received." Even as she battled with outsiders to keep her family afloat, my mother did her best to project confidence to her children. But beneath the calm was enormous shock and grief. "I remember only one time when Mom freaked out," Paul told me. "She had a nightmare after Dad died, and she was screaming."[109]

For Paul, the grief was overwhelming. When our father was hospitalized in Minnesota, Paul missed him terribly. "I'm looking forward to that day in the near future when you'll drive up in the De Soto, step out with the paper under your arm, and greet me and the kids," Paul wrote. He tried desperately to help. "If it's in any way possible for me to assist in administering the buildings . . . please let me know, because I realize that there is much to be done in these respects and I am both willing and able to help out," the sixteen-year-old boy had written. He hoped to make financial contributions to the family through his job as a busboy. "I'm still working because the money's got to come from someplace. I wish I could do more." On hearing of our father's kidney tumor, Paul was shaken. "I can't quite understand this new complication. . . . Anyway it couldn't be serious because we've already had more than our share of hideous coincidences. One more is simply mathematically impossible. . . . Don't worry about anything (that's my job)."[110]

The night after my father's death Paul disappeared. The family searched for him, fearing that he had gone wandering in an unsafe part of town. In fact, Paul had walked alone to the funeral home. He sat next to the body and sobbed while an employee tried to comfort him. "I'll never get over this," he told David.[111]

Mayor Daley sent a telegram of condolence to my family. Other sympathy letters poured in from Chicago's journalists, politicians, and reformers. Most echoed the sentiments of Alderman Leon Despres, who described my father's death as a "terrible shock" and wrote of the "wonderful legacy of character and achievement" he left behind.[112] The *Chicago Daily News* published an editorial memorializing him. "Mark Satter, the Chicago lawyer, was at once a fighting man and a gentle man. He fought the money lenders who preyed on the poor. He fought blockbusters poisoning the housing market. He found time to plead the cause of the helpless and friendless when other lawyers shied away," it read.[113]

At the funeral, Rabbi B. A. Daskal praised my father as a "prophet."[114] Hundreds attended. Mary Lee Stevenson, Joeanna Williams, and Lawrence and Bertha Richards were there. So were Favil and Marcia Berns and Irving Block and his wife. Attorney George W. Hansen attended; he was both a neighbor and one of the biggest contract sellers in Chicago.[115] The manager of my father's buildings, Gilbert Balin, paid his respects. Balin must have entered the funeral home just before radio host Wesley South, whose signature in the condolence book immediately follows Balin's. A number of *Daily News* reporters—including Maurice Fischer, M. W. Newman, Edmund Rooney, and Bob Schultz—who made it their business to investigate companies like the Balins' also attended.[116]

Wesley South was on his way to my father's funeral on July 14, 1965, when he heard on the radio that Adlai E. Stevenson II had died that day. With the deaths of these two white progressives, South sensed the end of an era.[117] He was right. On August 12, exactly one month after my father's death, Lawndale exploded.

PART II

PART II

SIX

KING IN CHICAGO

It started with a freak accident. On August 11, 1965, a fire truck hit a stop sign, which fell over and killed a twenty-three-year-old woman standing nearby. The woman was black, as was the neighborhood where the accident occurred; the local fire station employed only whites and had been the target of protests earlier that summer. The next day several hundred African Americans gathered to protest the incident. When the police attempted to control the crowd, fighting broke out and quickly escalated into a full-scale riot. By August 14, 65 people had been injured and 104 arrested. Although the Lawndale riot has been obscured in popular memory by one that broke out in Watts, California, over the same few days, its impact in Chicago was profound. Observers were stunned by the crowds of teenagers who "shouted, screamed, looted, and laughed hysterically as they tossed bricks, bottles, stones, and Molotov cocktails towards the police." A *Chicago Daily News* reporter was among those beaten by roving gangs. "Innocent people were being injured everywhere," he wrote. "I have never before witnessed such horror."[1]

The riot was shocking, but not all that surprising. By this time Lawndale was in a state of advanced decay: 80 percent of its housing stock had been constructed before 1900, and 40 percent was substandard. The overcrowding in some sections reached over three hundred people per acre. Lawndale was also now part of a continuous stretch of slums that extended for one mile north and two miles east of its boundaries, encompassing the East Garfield Park, West Garfield Park, and Near West Side neighborhoods. This larger area, known as "the West Side," or "Chicago's newest ghetto," was home to 300,000 African Americans, the majority Southern-born.[2]

The ghetto's residents faced numerous social and economic problems. Between 10 and 25 percent of the adult population was unemployed. For young people, the statistics were far worse: 25 to 50 percent were unable to find jobs. Those who were employed received very low wages. While the median family income for Chicago as a whole was $6,738 per annum, Lawndale's median family income was $4,981, and almost 25 percent of the area's inhabitants earned under $3,000 a year. Over 31 percent were on some form of public aid, giving the neighborhood the largest concentration of people on welfare of any part of the city.[3]

The public schools were abysmal, with many young adults barely able to read at a sixth-grade level.[4] These educational handicaps may have been less a cause than a symptom of broader problems. Among the obstacles facing local children was their "lack of nutritious food," as one report delicately phrased it. More bluntly put, they came to school hungry. Parents could not afford eyeglasses for their children. The high schools were "jammed" at up to 50 percent overcapacity, and dropout rates reached 60 percent. Crime rates, especially for juveniles, were high. The most common crimes were runaways, burglaries, and shoplifting, but gang violence was also a problem.[5]

Though the West Side was overwhelmingly African American, it was firmly under the control of white ward officials, many of whom claimed "ghost addresses" in their wards but in fact lived elsewhere.[6] West Siders believed that this problem was "most severe" in the city's Twenty-fourth Ward, that is, in Lawndale. As one reformer explained, people "simply feel they have no adequate representation from their political leaders. . . . One phrase you hear continually . . . is 'We don't pick them—they're handed to us.'" While the August 1965 riot shocked many Chicagoans, others were ready to admit the truth: in the absence of real political representation, a riot was one of the few means West Side residents had to express their anger over the conditions in which they lived.[7]

The riot gave new impetus to efforts to organize the West Side, and specifically to developing leadership within the community. The Interreligious Council on Urban Affairs (IRCUA), an ecumenical organization of Catholic, Jewish, and Protestant leaders founded by Monsignor John J. Egan, declared that "moral imperatives with deep Biblical roots compel the religious community to mobilize its resources to side with the exploited minorities of the community."[8] According to Egan, one achieved this goal not through offering outside help, which "is resented and often repudiated," but through funding "trained, competent community organizers" who can enable local people to "generate their own social structure, strength, and direction." The IRCUA also offered seminars in which Saul Alinsky or his associates trained clergy as community organizers. The council's relationship to Alinsky was so close that Rev. Kris Ronnow, its executive director, described the IRCUA as a "front group" for Alinsky's Industrial Areas Foundation.[9]

The Jewish Council on Urban Affairs (JCUA), launched by Rabbi Robert J. Marx, also stressed "self-determination" rather than "social service." The purpose of the JCUA, like the IRCUA, was to funnel financial resources and labor power—in this case, of specifically Jewish origin—to local community groups.[10] By maintaining a positive presence in black urban neighborhoods, the JCUA also hoped to counter the activities of exploitative Jewish slum landlords and merchants, who, though representing only "an infinitesimal fraction of the American Jewish economy," nevertheless contributed to a rise in black anti-Jewish anger and to a splintering of the black-Jewish civil rights alliance. "Slum landlords and those who earn their living through the abuse of credit have no role within the Jewish community," Marx declared. Among the first projects undertaken by the JCUA was an investigation of the estate of contract seller Lou Fushanis, whom they mistakenly believed to be Jewish.[11]

While these associations explicitly adopted Saul Alinsky's organizing philosophy, several Protestant groups sought an alternative approach. They were uncomfortable with Alinsky's call for organizers to "rub raw" local resentments—that is, his enthusiastic use of anger at an outside villain as a means of building community cohesion. They also opposed his emphasis on self-interest. "Can anyone be a follower of the gentle Christ and at the same time play the game of power politics?" asked a writer in the Protestant journal the *Christian Century*.[12]

Thus the West Side Organization (WSO), founded by Congregationalist minister Archibald Hargraves, rather than fomenting community anger, sought to prepare the "poor themselves" to understand their rights and negotiate common complaints. Soon several unemployed local men— among them Chester Robinson, William Darden, and Gene Harris— emerged as leaders, organizing one of the first and most successful welfare rights groups in the nation. Hargraves viewed the WSO's achievements as an overt challenge to Alinsky, who had warned him against organizing the very poor—an action that Alinsky believed would divide the larger community.[13]

Most notable among the groups that sought an alternative to Alinsky's approach was the West Side Christian Parish (WSCP), a small coalition of storefront churches that had been established as the "urban ministry" branch of the Congregational Church. Although its executive director, Robert Mueller, admired Alinsky, he was more attracted to the morality-centered efforts of the Southern civil rights movement. In the spring of 1965, he replaced two staffers trained in Alinsky's method with the Reverend James Bevel, a charismatic Mississippi-born African American who had participated in virtually all of the major Southern civil rights crusades.[14] In Bevel's view, too, Alinsky "simply taught how to, within the context of power, grab and struggle to get your share." His own approach was to teach people "to be nonviolent," which would lead them to "become totally resourceful and intelligent and creative." One white Chicago activist, William Moyer, an American Friends Service Committee member who began working closely with Bevel in 1965, pointed out that "Alinsky was trying to organize people on the basis of their hate. . . . The rest of us were trying to organize people on the basis of love."[15]

Bevel's involvement heralded more than a shift in approach. He was, it turned out, the advance guard of a far greater presence from the Southern civil rights movement—Martin Luther King Jr. On September 1, 1965, King announced that the Southern Christian Leadership Conference (SCLC) had chosen Chicago as the focus of his long-anticipated "Northern campaign." As a first step, he assigned ten SCLC activists to work directly with Bevel. Their goal, in the short run, was to support a coalition of Chicago organizations that were fighting school segregation. Their larger ambition was to apply the tactics of the Southern civil rights movement to the problems of the North. "The only solution to breaking down the infamous wall of segregation in Chicago rests in our being able to mobilize the white and black communities into a massive nonviolent movement," King explained. Alinsky, who was then in the midst of a community organizing project in Rochester, New York, had his doubts. As he told *Harper's* magazine, "In the North you need a more sophisticated approach. The segregated practices in the South are a kind of public butchery. It's visible. There's bleeding all over the place. Up here we use a stiletto, it's internal bleeding, it's not visible, but it's just as deadly."[16]

This indirect but public debate between King and Alinsky was indicative of something broader. By announcing a civil rights crusade in Chicago, King ensured that a long-simmering contest over competing visions of social change would be tested, in view of the world and in a city that exemplified intransigent residential segregation and ghetto decay. Would love or power triumph in Daley's Chicago? Could either love or power reverse the complex forces that had looted Lawndale and transformed the West Side into Chicago's worst ghetto?

By the time King arrived in Chicago, his vision of social change through nonviolent resistance had come to define the struggle for black equality and was celebrated as a strategy that had led to historic successes. Indeed, the national media coverage of assaults on peaceful black marchers and civil rights workers in places like Birmingham, Alabama, and small-town Mississippi—where protesters were smashed against walls with the spray from fire hoses, attacked by police dogs, beaten, and even killed—pushed President Lyndon Baines Johnson to sign the landmark Civil Rights Act of 1964. The act, which outlawed racial and gender discrimination in public accommodations and employment, offered powerful federal backing to ongoing desegregation struggles. In January 1964, King was *Time* magazine's "Man of the Year," and that December, he received the Nobel Peace Prize.

In early spring 1965, when King expanded his campaign to secure suffrage for African Americans—a right not covered by the Civil Rights Act of 1964—he outlined his now-familiar strategy for change: (1) "nonviolent demonstrators go into the streets to exercise their constitutional rights"; (2) "racists resist by unleashing violence against them"; (3) "Americans of conscience in the name of decency demand federal intervention and legislation"; and (4) "the Administration, under massive pressure, initiates measures of immediate intervention and remedial legislation."[17] The target city to bring blacks to the ballot box was Selma, Alabama, where clergy and activists from around the country marched with the local African American community, including representatives from Chicago's Jewish Council on Urban Affairs, the West Side Organization, and the West Side Christian Parish. Also marching in Selma was Jack Egan, who described the unsettling experience to Chicago reporters. Selma was "the first time that I've been afraid, wearing a Roman collar, to walk through a white neighborhood. It's the first time I've . . . heard a policeman say, 'I'd like to put my club through that priest's skull.'"[18] King's tactics were resoundingly successful, although not, predictably, without human cost. Televised attacks on hundreds of peaceful marchers by Alabama state troopers, as well as the murders of several civil rights supporters, unleashed a surge of national outrage. On March 15, 1965, President Johnson called for the passage of the Voting Rights Act. Congress passed the bill, and Johnson signed it into law on August 6.[19]

King's movement achieved momentous results, but the doctrine of nonviolence was proving hard to sustain. In the spring of 1963, Ku Klux Klansmen had bombed the Birmingham headquarters of the SCLC as well as the home of King's brother. This was the final provocation for working-class black residents of Birmingham, who had suffered months of police and Klan abuse. They poured into the streets and pelted police and firemen with rocks. When King's advisers tried to calm the mob, they shouted back, "They started it! They started it!" When an SCLC leader begged them, "Please. Please go home," they responded with defiance. "Tell it to 'Bull' Connor," they yelled, referring to the avowedly segregationist Birmingham police commissioner who had ordered numerous violent attacks on peaceful black demonstrators. "This is what nonviolence gets you."[20]

By this time the civil rights movement had sustained nine years of harassment, beatings, shootings, bombings, and murders by white vigilantes, as well as several murderous, full-scale white riots.[21] Yet the Birmingham riot of 1963 marked a turning point. It was the first riot not by whites against blacks but by blacks against whites. That same year Malcolm X, spokesman for the Nation of Islam, roused blacks and angered whites with his insistence that the "day of nonviolent resistance is over." In 1964, in the midst of an ongoing campaign of white terror against civil rights workers, young blacks in Jacksonville, Mississippi, rioted against city police and firemen. Riots also broke out that summer in black sections of several northern cities: Harlem and Rochester, New York; Jersey City, Elizabeth, and Paterson, New Jersey; Dixmoor, Illinois; and Philadelphia, Pennsylvania. All of the Northern riots occurred in entirely black enclaves where people suffered from overcrowded and decaying housing, high unemployment rates, and pervasive despair—problems that were unaddressed by the antisegregation and voting rights campaigns of the Southern civil rights movement.[22]

Then in August 1965, Chicago's West Side and Watts, a black section of Los Angeles, erupted. Watts residents engaged in "extensive firebombing" of white-owned property "in order to drive white 'exploiters' out of the ghetto"; property damage was estimated at $35 million. When King toured Watts in the aftermath of the riot, residents defiantly told him that the violence had been worthwhile. "How can you say you won when thirty-four Negroes are dead, your community is destroyed, and white people are using the riot as an excuse to accelerate a white backlash?" King asked incredulously. "We won because the whole world is paying attention to us now," a resident responded. King pondered the man's words. Here was someone who was "so fed up with . . . powerlessness" that he would "rather be dead than ignored."[23]

These experiences contributed to King's sense that the civil rights movement had to shift its focus to the Northern ghetto if it was to remain relevant and demonstrate the efficacy of nonviolence. The only question remaining was where to launch the new campaign. In addition to Chicago, SCLC leaders considered New York, Philadelphia, Washington, and Cleveland. But black leaders in Philadelphia and New York told SCLC leaders that they were not wanted. Cleveland was too small, and Washington was too politically risky.[24]

This left Chicago. For Southern activists accustomed to Selma (population 20,000) or Birmingham (population 200,000), Chicago—a city of three million people, one third of them black—was overwhelming. As King's longtime ally Reverend Ralph Abernathy recalled, "As we drove through the South Side . . . we kept waiting for the slum tenements to give way to warehouses, vacant lots, and then country stores and open fields. . . . Instead we saw more slum blocks. And more. And more. And more. We had the feeling that if we drove much further south we were going to see the Gulf of Mexico. 'That's nothing,' said Jesse [Jackson]. 'Wait till you see the West Side.'"[25]

The sheer size of the city was not the organizers' only problem. They were also troubled by the demoralized condition of the local black clergy. Chicago was the home of the Reverend Joseph H. Jackson, head of the powerful National Baptist Convention. Jackson had been King's enemy since 1961, when King had supported the unsuccessful candidacy of a man who hoped to unseat Jackson and shift the convention to an activist, pro–civil rights position. Those black clergy who were not under Jackson's sway were kept in line by Mayor Daley's machine. As the Reverend Clay Evans, one of the few black Chicago ministers who welcomed King to Chicago, recalled, "Many ministers . . . had to back off [from supporting King] because they didn't want their buildings to be condemned or given citations for electrical work, faulty plumbing or fire code violations."[26]

The city's black aldermen were even more beholden to Daley, and they did not hesitate to attack King at Daley's behest. As Abernathy put it, Daley liked to play the part of the "benevolent and rational servant of all the people" while "his black henchmen were denouncing us at every turn." Ordinary black residents who were dependent upon the city in any way— for welfare payments, for example, or for a public housing placement— also feared to support King's group. In the view of Dorothy Tillman, a SCLC staffer, Chicago's blacks were "worse off than any plantation down south. You know, down south you lived on the plantation, you worked it, and you had your food, clothing, and shelter. Up here they lived on a plantation with Boss Daley as slave master. Their jobs, their clothes, their shelter, food, all that depended on Boss Daley." Some black Chicagoans, such as the Black Muslims, prided themselves on their independence from Daley, but they rejected the SCLC for being too prowhite.[27]

For all these reasons, King's trusted adviser Bayard Rustin had warned him away from the city. "You don't know what Chicago is like. . . . You're going to be wiped out," he said.[28] Yet Chicago's reputation as the "Birmingham of the North," that is, as the North's most segregated community, made it a natural target for a nonviolent civil rights campaign. SCLC staffers also saw a positive side to Daley's awesome power. It enabled Daley to stifle dissent, but it also implied that he could make real changes if pushed to do so. Although the black clergy was cool to King, Chicago's white religious leaders were supportive and highly organized.[29] In any case, problems with local black leadership were nothing new. SCLC activists had faced similar opposition in Birmingham and had managed to overcome it.[30]

Still, to avoid unnecessary conflict with black leaders, most of whom were based on the South Side, SCLC activists decided to focus on the West Side. James Bevel's appointment as program director of the West Side Christian Parish gave them an institutional base. There were other benefits as well. First, the West Side housed the poorest of the city's black population, the very people King felt he had to reach if he was to prove his movement's relevance. Second, many West Siders had migrated from Mississippi. As Southerners themselves, SCLC activists felt they would have a natural bond with them.

In sum, King and his associates saw the very difficulty of organizing in Chicago as an opportunity. "If we can break the system in Chicago, it can be broken any place in the country," King said. He warned that the stakes were high: "The future of the SCLC will depend on Chicago."[31]

School segregation was the first target. The NAACP and other black organizations had struggled for years to remedy the problems of double shifts, inexperienced teachers, and overcrowding that were endemic to schools located in black neighborhoods. They understood the relationship between school overcrowding and residential segregation: the confinement of black Chicagoans to a few areas of the city inevitably led to packed conditions in those neighborhoods' schools. As an alternative to double shifting, they had urged that black students be allowed to transfer to schools in neighborhoods with underutilized classrooms.

Their main opponent was the superintendent of Chicago's public schools, Benjamin C. Willis. No matter what solution they proposed, Willis, a Daley appointee, refused to cooperate. When an NAACP report provided hard statistics proving that Chicago's public schools were segregated in contravention of *Brown v. Board of Education,* Willis replied that he was not required to know the racial composition of Chicago's public schools, and since he didn't have information on the schools' racial balances, he couldn't be responsible for them. When black activists presented the Chicago Board of Education with a seven-page list of schools in white neighborhoods that had underutilized classrooms, Willis denied any knowledge of empty classrooms or double shifts.[32]

In response to this intransigence a coalition of groups concerned about school segregation formed the Coordinating Council of Community Organizations (CCCO), including Chicago's NAACP, Alinsky's Woodlawn Organization, and the Catholic Interracial Council. But their efforts were equally ineffectual. In the wake of the 1963 Armstrong Act, which compelled local school boards to make "racial head counts" of their students as a first step toward ending school segregation, Willis had finally authorized a plan that allowed a very limited number of black students to transfer to nearby underutilized white districts. But faced with protests from whites, Willis dropped fifteen schools from the plan, leaving only nine. When frustrated black parents got a court order to compel Willis to carry out the transfers, he resigned rather than carry out the order. To the shock of these parents, the Chicago Board of Education voted not to accept Willis's resignation.

By now, black parents and activists were so infuriated that they engaged in mass protest. They held sit-ins at Board of Education meetings; they organized a school boycott to protest school segregation and to call for the removal of Willis as school board superintendent. Organizers expected 75,000 students to boycott; instead, 225,000 did so. Yet the Board of Education refused to budge from Willis's extremely limited transfer plan. By the summer of 1964, a total of twenty-eight black students had been transferred.[33]

Willis's reappointment as superintendent of Chicago's schools in May 1965 triggered a new wave of protests. Al Raby, an African American activist and schoolteacher who was passionately dedicated to his Lawndale students, led almost daily marches against Willis and for integrated schools. The first of the marches disrupted traffic in the city's downtown. When police told protesters to move, they sat down in the street. Most were then arrested. By early July, over six hundred Chicagoans had been arrested in anti-Willis marches. That same month the CCCO filed a complaint with the U.S. Office of Education that accused the Chicago Board of Education of violating Title VI of the Civil Rights Act of 1964. The complaint warned that the "means of creating and perpetuating segregation in Chicago may become the handbook for southern communities seeking to evade the 1954 Supreme Court ruling" and requested that the federal government withhold financial assistance from the Chicago school board until it ended its policy of de facto segregation. The U.S. Office of Education verified most of the group's charges and added a few of its own.[34]

The prospects looked good and seemed to get even better once King's SCLC organizers allied with the CCCO. More groups joined in, including the United Packinghouse Workers of America, the West Side Federation, the American Jewish Congress, and the Friendship House. The newly expanded, combined forces of the SCLC and CCCO had great hopes. School segregation was just the beginning, they said. Their overriding goal, they reported, was "solving Negro problems in the ghetto."[35]

They were, perhaps, overly optimistic. The CCCO seemed to win a victory in September 1965 when the U.S. commissioner of education, Francis Keppel, announced that Chicago schools would be denied $32 million in federal funds because the city was in "probable noncompliance" with Title VI of the 1964 Civil Rights Act. Al Raby told reporters that he "felt wonderful. I hope that this is the first step toward building a school system that will make every Chicagoan proud."[36]

But this wasn't the end of the story. On October 3, Daley attended a gathering with President Johnson in New York City. He took the opportunity to tell Johnson how upset he was about Commissioner Keppel's action. Johnson immediately called Keppel into his office, gave him "unstinted hell," and demanded that a compromise be reached that would be acceptable to Daley's friends on the Chicago Board of Education. The compromise was simple. Instead of having the CCCO's complaint investigated and enforced by the federal Department of Health, Education and Welfare, Keppel agreed to allow the Chicago Board of Education—that is, the defendant in the case—to investigate its own noncompliance. The board was to report back in sixty days with its findings and suggestions for remedial action, "if any is called for." Of course, according to the Chicago Board of Education, none was called for.

In short, it took Daley less than a week to destroy one of the most important test cases of how federal power could be used to bring urban school systems into compliance with *Brown v. Board of Education*. And as the CCCO had warned, the repercussions were national. Chicago pioneered a way for all states, Northern or Southern, to resist school integration.[37]

With school segregation no longer a viable cause, the SCLC and CCCO were left to search for an alternative focus for their joint campaign to "break the system" in Chicago. King wanted the civil rights movement to target economic inequality and pushed Chicago activists to concentrate on remedying slum conditions. But as Bevel pointed out, there was a core problem. "What is a slum? How is it created? Most people in the CCCO don't know and thus can't deal with it," he said, adding that "it takes time to think this out."[38]

SCLC organizers spent much of that autumn attempting to do so. It did not take long, in the course of their probing, to come across one of the primary factors in Chicago's slum creation: exploitative contract sales. The issue was brought to their attention by John L. McKnight, head of the Midwest office of the U.S. Commission on Civil Rights. McKnight was thrilled when the group he called "the Revs"—that is, King and his most prominent assistants, Bevel, Abernathy, and Andrew Young, all Protestant ministers—came to Chicago. Their presence in the city offered an unparalleled opportunity, he believed, to reform the system that he believed to be at the root of Chicago's racial ills.

McKnight did not seem like a person who would know much about slum conditions. He was a white Protestant who had been raised in small towns in Ohio where "sundown laws"—that is, unspoken but enforced rules that no black person be allowed in town after dark—still existed. But there was a radical edge to McKnight's background that led him to question established norms, especially those involving minority rights. "I come from a group of dissenters," he said. His family were "Covenanters"— Scottish Presbyterians whose historic resistance to religious coercion had left them with an enduring self-image as an embattled minority. McKnight's grandfather was a Covenanter minister and dedicated Populist. He taught McKnight that "if the majority of people agree with you, you must be wrong."

In 1956, McKnight went to work for the Chicago Commission on Human Relations (CHR). His job was to report on outbreaks of white violence in neighborhoods then in the midst of "racial transition." "I was inside the houses when they were throwing stones through the windows, burning down the back porch, that sort of stuff," he recalled. Part of his work involved easing racial tensions by calming the fears of longtime residents. "What we were saying was, if people of good will work together, we can create stable integrated neighborhoods." Following conventional wisdom, he believed that the problem was primarily cultural or psychological.[39]

McKnight's perspective changed after he heard a Chicago attorney

Mark J. Satter at his
law school graduation, 1939

Clarice Komsky on
her wedding day, 1939

The six-flat at 3846-48 W. Congress St., purchased by Mark and Clarice Satter
in 1944

Satter addresses panel on contract selling sponsored by the Greater Lawndale Conservation Commission (GLCC), June 1958. *Photograph by Marshall Marker. Copyright Jeffery Marker. Reprinted with permission*

Shocked Lawndale residents listen to Satter's speech at GLCC meeting, 1958. *Photograph by Marshall Marker. Copyright Jeffery Marker. Reprinted with permission*

ATTY. MARK J. SATTER, whose column, "All That Money Can Buy," begins Monday exclusively in the Daily Defender. The column, dedicated to the problems of the working man, will run twice weekly — on Monday and in the Weekend edition of the Chicago Defender.

Advertisement for Mark J. Satter's column in the *Chicago Defender*, "All That Money Can Buy," 1958. *Courtesy of the* Chicago Defender

Satter with (*left to right*) Frank London Brown, author of novel *Trumbull Park*, real estate broker Leslie Word, and Dempsey J. Travis, Dearborn Real Estate Board president, June 1959. *Courtesy of the* Chicago Defender

Albert and Sallie Bolton in their Hyde Park house, 1957. *Courtesy of Sallie Bolton*

Favil David Berns, 1960.
Reprinted with permission

Joeanna Williams and her sister, Mary Lee Stevenson, who led neighbors in a suit against Moe M. Forman in May 1958. *Photographs taken from obsequies, courtesy of Bertha Richards*

Contract seller and attorney
Moe M. Forman, 1973.
Tribune *file photo by William Yates.*
Chicago Tribune *file photo. All rights*
reserved. Used with permission

Contract seller Lou Fushanis,
1963. *As published in the*
Chicago Sun-Times *LLC.*
Reprinted with permission

Contract sellers Albert Berland and Louis Wolf, 1970, 1973. *As published in the* Chicago Sun-Times *LLC. Reprinted with permission*

Contract seller Al Weinberg.
New World, 1968.
Reprinted with permission

Martin Luther King Jr. addresses residents of Chicago's West Side, 1966. *Photo by John Tweedle. Copyright Dianne Tweedle. Reprinted with permission*

Coretta and Martin Luther King greet neighborhood children in their Lawndale apartment, 1966. *Photo by John Tweedle. Copyright Dianne Tweedle. Reprinted with permission*

named Mark J. Satter explain at a meeting of the CHR's Housing Advisory Committee how blacks excluded from conventional mortgages were compelled to buy overpriced homes on contract. The talk was a revelation: he was left feeling privy to the "under-the-table" secret that "ruined Chicago racially." "Here we were . . . in the middle of this stuff without understanding why it was happening. We thought the only problem was the racist attitudes of working-class whites. And all of a sudden Mark walks in and explains that what's really going on is a systematic plan of profit-making activity. Well, this was huge. It gave order and meaning and a way of understanding the outbreaks other than just plain old bigotry."[40]

McKnight then sought, but failed, to reorient the commission. He suspected that the CHR would not touch contract sales because "a lot of the elite of Chicago" had money invested in highly profitable contract sales "paper." McKnight left the CHR in 1960, taking positions first as the executive director of the Illinois division of the American Civil Liberties Union and then as the head of the Midwest Equal Employment Opportunity Office Army Material Command, where he pioneered one of the first affirmative action contracts.[41]

In 1965, McKnight was newly returned to Chicago as head of the Midwest division of the U.S. Civil Rights Commission. He believed that the first step toward ending slum conditions would be to "get the regular money, standard rate money, flowing" into black communities; to that end, he met with the heads of several lending institutions and assured them that, if they made mortgages on the West Side, the FHA would back their loans.[42] But he was also determined to "resurrect" this idea of the destructive effects of contract sales. While the issue was technical, he felt that he could make its importance clear if given the chance.[43] "When Dr. King came to town," he saw the opportunity he'd been waiting for. "I wanted to tell him the land contract story because I thought if he took this on, boy, it would really blow this thing up." McKnight met with James Bevel. He started with his standard explanation of how contract sales drained money out of black neighborhoods. Then he took Bevel on a tour of the West Side and showed him some buildings, explaining the true reason for their decline. Bevel seemed "really taken by this thing." "I'll tell them about it and see if we can't make this our issue," McKnight recalled him saying.

When Bevel returned to McKnight's office, he had bad news: "It didn't sell." The SCLC leadership believed that, if contract buyers had enough money to buy a home, then they were a cut above the people King wanted to represent. "These were not the poorest people," in the view of the SCLC, "and they were here to support the poorest people," according to McKnight.

There were other issues at play. One was the character of Bevel himself. McKnight realized too late that Bevel, though smart and passionately committed, was also "a little mystical" and therefore not the best messenger for this very structural story of credit exploitation. "If I had got to Andy Young, it might have been different," he speculated. Then, too, the workings of exploitative contract sales, McKnight knew, were "very difficult" to get across to the public.[44] If the SCLC wanted an issue that would instantly demonstrate the problem of ghetto life, this was probably not it. Finally, by the time Bevel explained contract sales to the SCLC, King had decided to focus not on homeowners, however tenuous their hold, but on renters who inhabited the city's most impoverished structures. To illustrate this commitment to the "poorest," King took a dramatic step in January 1966. He and his wife, Coretta, moved into a slum building in the worst part of the city. They rented an apartment in Lawndale.

King's move to Lawndale was entirely tactical. His assistant, Reverend Ralph Abernathy, had expected conditions on the city's West Side to be better than those on the South Side. Instead, the West Side was considerably worse. "The apartment houses reminded me of buildings I had seen in Europe right at the end of World War II—windows broken out and mounds of rubble instead of yards," he recalled. "And the odor was unbearable. . . . There was no escaping it. The hallways were filled with rotting food and piles of feces, and always you could see the rats patrolling— so large and bold that you wondered if they weren't going to attack you. Indeed, I was told that sometimes they did." Since King and Abernathy wanted to spotlight the "worst possible housing" in the city, they had SCLC organizers rent them apartments in the heart of the West Side ghetto. The two apartments they chose on Hamlin Avenue in Lawndale were, according to Abernathy, "the epitome of filth and disrepair."[45]

In line with the movement's decision to focus on tenants rather than contract buyers, organizers targeted large apartment buildings with absentee landlords and attempted to set up tenant unions. "The Chicago problem is simply a matter of economic exploitation," King told a gathering of CCCO and SCLC members. "Every condition exists simply because someone profits by its existence. This economic exploitation is crystallized in the SLUM."[46] In a sense, this focus reflected a colonial model, in which local resources are exploited by distant powers. In fact, the situation on Chicago's West Side more closely resembled a neocolonial model, in which local resources appear to be controlled by indigenous people but are in fact subject to outside interests through debt peonage. The miscalculation would prove costly for King and his people.

That same January, the SCLC's Chicago organizers and the CCCO formally consolidated into a joint organization, the Chicago Freedom Movement (CFM). They also announced their "Chicago Plan." King explained that although their original goal had been to "get rid of Willis," the new target was nothing less than the slums themselves. He listed twelve contributing components of slum conditions: educational institutions, discriminatory building trade unions, real estate, banks and mortgage companies, slum landlords, the welfare system, federal housing agencies, the courts, the police, the political system, the city administration, and the federal government. The list was broad, but this was inevitable given Chicago's political complexity. "In the South concentration on one issue proved feasible because of a general pattern of state and local resistance," King explained. "However, in Chicago we are faced with the probability of ready accommodation to many of the issues in some token manner. . . . Therefore, we must be prepared to concentrate all of our forces around any and all issues."

In phase one of the Chicago Plan, slated to begin in February 1966, the CFM would "awaken the people" through a campaign of educating and organizing. In phase two, commencing in March, they would hold demonstrations "at points which should reveal the agents of exploitation and paint a portrait of the evils which beset us in such a manner that it is clear the world over what makes up a slum." The final phase would begin around May 1 and consist of a "massive action" that would "create the kind of coalition of conscience which is necessary to produce change in this country."[47]

King's program began right on schedule. In late January, the CFM organized a meeting of five hundred Lawndale tenants who spoke out about the miserable conditions of their buildings. Then in February, in an act that King labeled "supralegal," his organization and a local group called the West Side Federation jointly "assumed trusteeship" of a building at 1321 South Homan, where tenants had gone without heat for a week in sub-zero weather. They announced their intention to clean up the building, collect the rent money themselves, and use it to make necessary repairs. That spring the CFM spearheaded an effort to organize slum tenants into "Unions to End Slums." Tenants engaged in a rent strike to pressure Condor and Costalis, a firm that managed over thirty West Side buildings, to sign an agreement promising to address their grievances. Lifting a tactic from Alinsky, organizers also picketed slum landlords' offices and homes.[48]

Activists also tried to organize Lawndale on a "block-by-block" basis. They worked with the United Auto Workers, one of the few unions in Daley's Chicago to support King's crusade, to create the Lawndale Community Union, a job training and referral service. They held educational workshops for mostly white high school and college students on organizing and on the history of Chicago slums, in which they pinpointed as the primary culprits the discriminatory policies of the Chicago Real Estate Board and the refusal of banks to make mortgage loans in black areas.[49]

They even reached out to local gang leaders. "We had no idea that such gangs existed in Chicago and we were really at a loss when it came to dealing with them," Abernathy recalled of the "young hard-eyed black boys" who were "terrorizing whole neighborhoods." But King believed that he could communicate with them. He invited leaders of the Roman Saints, the Cobras, and the Vice Lords to his Lawndale apartment and spent hours arguing with them about the relevance of nonviolence. Organizers also showed the young men films of the devastation wrought by the Watts riot, so they could see the failure of violent attempts at social change.[50]

Taken separately, these were modest actions. Yet the goal of the Chicago Freedom Movement remained grandiose: "the renewal and re-democratization of the social order itself," as one organizer put it. Another, C. T. Vivian, lauded the transformative power of the philosophy of nonviolence: "Nonviolence is the only honorable way of dealing with social change because if we are wrong, nobody gets hurt but us, but if we are right, more people will participate in determining their own destinies than ever before. A new man is the end product. . . . We are seeking a kingdom of God in twentieth-century terms." Bevel best summed up the group's political-psychological orientation. "You fight a machine by making people grow so that they don't fit into the machine any more," he explained.[51]

The CFM faced hard obstacles that quickly threw their neat three-phase plan of action into disarray. Their organizing efforts were repeatedly undermined by bad luck, poor planning, or strategic accommodation by their enemies. King's move to a slum apartment was a prime example. The building's manager, Alvin M. Shavin, resisted the role of the vicious slumlord called for by the script. When asked how he felt about having King as a tenant, he replied, "I'm delighted to have him. What else can I say?" Once Shavin discovered the identity of his new tenant he repainted the building. As Abernathy recalled, King's repainted apartment was hardly "House Beautiful, but it was clean and bright—probably the best looking quarters within fifty blocks of that location. Not a place you would show the press to let them know how bad life in the slums could be." Some reporters joked that King could clean up the slums simply by moving from one apartment to another. (Shavin didn't bother to renovate Abernathy's apartment, which remained filthy and rat-infested. After spending a few nights there to "make a point," Abernathy moved to a black-run hotel.)[52]

The CFM confronted a different problem with its takeover of 1321 South Homan. There was no question that the building was in terrible shape and that the tenants suffered. But the owner, John B. Bender, turned out to be a childless eighty-one-year-old invalid who relied on the building as his sole source of income. Bender wished King well and, furthermore, was eager to let King buy the building. "All I want . . . is maybe a thousand dollars more than the mortgage," he told the press.[53] Even the concessions that the CFM wrung from slum managers Condor and Costalis had their ambiguities. "We're with you, believe it or not," John Condor told tenants at a mass meeting. He also tried to redirect the crowd's anger. The problem was "the big boys" downtown who redlined black neighborhoods. "Don't fight the wrong fight," he pleaded.[54] The CFM never seemed to consider the possibility that Condor could be correct.

Mayor Daley was a particularly cagey adversary. King's people expected Daley to fit one of two models: either he'd oppose them, like Birmingham's Bull Connor, and thereby provide a focal point for resistance or he'd support them. They didn't realize that Daley typically followed neither approach. As one local noted, Daley "has always beaten his enemies by taking their programs and running with them." Accordingly, on January 31, 1966, Daley unveiled his own antislum program, explaining, "All of us, like Dr. King, are trying to eliminate slums."

Daley declared that he would clean up every slum in the city by the end of 1967. He promised to greatly increase building code inspections. He launched what he called "the most massive and comprehensive rodent-eradication program ever undertaken in this country." Public Aid Department head Raymond Hilliard threatened that the city would withhold welfare rents from any slum operators who did not upgrade their buildings.[55] As if in answer to King's effort to rehabilitate a single slum building through a takeover, or "trusteeship," the Chicago press announced a "breakthrough" in May 1966: $3 million in mortgage funds would be made available for slum rehabilitation, allowing for the renovation of some five hundred apartment units.[56]

Daley's plan rested heavily on the code inspection favored by urban renewal proponents, and it had all the same problems: the corruption of the Building Department—which, as Dempsey Travis noted, often functioned as "the plain clothes arm of the police department and was frequently used to keep black ministers and real estate owners in line politically"—and the ease with which slum landlords evaded code violation suits in municipal housing court.[57] Most important, since inspectors fined contract buyers and not the sellers who still held title to the properties, the burden often fell squarely on those who could least afford to bear it. As the *Chicago Sun-Times* reported, while Daley's program led to the inspection of 2,874 Lawndale buildings between March and May 1966, the result was that "thousands of buyers with only a tiny equity" in their homes were ordered to bring their buildings up to code but denied the loans they needed to do so. Most were "already beleaguered by sizable monthly mortgage—usually contract—payments," the paper reported. For these struggling families, code inspection was an unexpected calamity. "'Why are they picking on me?' And 'My house was this way before I bought it,'" they told reporters.[58]

In any case, black contract buyers were not eligible for the headline-making $3 million low-interest loans set aside for slum rehabilitation. This money would be loaned not to blacks hoping to purchase their homes (or buy themselves out of exploitative contracts) but to a city agency that would own the structures it rehabilitated. The Chicago Dwellings Association (CDA) said that it would "either rent or sell" the structures it rehabilitated, but its talk of rent ceilings implied that the former was more likely. A bias toward rental units meant that, no matter how beautifully the units were renovated, they would produce no equity for anyone but the CDA.[59]

In short, Daley's bold initiative to end slums by 1967 was mostly smoke and mirrors. Abel Swirsky, the deputy city building commissioner, acknowledged that despite the hopeful statements of the CDA, "very, very few West Side buildings have been rehabilitated." He also admitted that while 5,400 code violation notices had been sent out since March, only 300 had gone to court. Of all the antislum actions launched by Daley—rat control, receivership, welfare-rent withholding, or building inspection— the only program to have a major impact was rat control.[60]

Still, Daley's initiative managed to subvert King's enterprise. As one commentator noted, "Before [Daley's] through, his crusade will make King's look minor league." Thomas Curtin of the Sears YMCA in Lawndale was impressed by Daley's strategy: "They yell about rats one day, and the next day Mayor Daley announces 40 rodent control teams have been sent to the West Side." Sister Mary William, who was the director of a Lawndale community center, observed that residents had been "all gung ho" about King's organizing efforts until they learned that "if you call the Department of Streets and Sanitation and say you're from East Garfield Park, you can get two pickups a week." Then, people weren't "half as mad at the city" as they had been. Watching it all from Rochester, Saul Alinsky couldn't help but gloat over King's naiveté. King "moves into a slum and Daley has the place fixed up on him. Every time Daley has taken the issue away from him."[61]

On another front, activists kept coming up against the relentless hostility of some black Chicagoans. Reverend Joseph H. Jackson, for example, warmly supported Daley and condemned King's advocacy of civil disobedience as "not far removed from open crime." King responded, "I don't think Dr. Jackson speaks for one percent of the Negroes in this country." But Jackson was not alone in his opposition to King's movement. SCLC activists recalled their shock and hurt when well-placed Chicago blacks "told us to go back down South where we came from." They were especially troubled by what they saw as widespread passivity. As SCLC activist Hosea Williams put it, "The Negroes of Chicago have a greater feeling of powerlessness than I've ever seen. . . . They are beaten down psychologically. We are used to working with people who want to be free." Even King commented on the apparent lethargy of the city's blacks. Dorothy Tillman, another SCLC staff member, recalled his saying, "You ain't never seen no Negroes like this, have you, Dorothy? . . . Boy, if we could crack these Chicago Negroes we can crack anything."[62]

Black Chicagoans, for their part, probably resented the SCLC organizers' arrogant attitude. As one civil rights scholar has noted, "You cannot organize people you do not respect." Many viewed the SCLC as both purist and naive. Some referred to the activists as "romantic, disorganized tin gods." *Chicago Daily News* reporter M. W. Newman summed up the problem: "They talk moral and religious principles, but this town moves on political principles."[63]

Even without Daley's opposition and local black rejection, the SCLC might well have floundered. Despite their experiences in Southern communities that often resembled war zones, the organizers felt crushed by the "formidable task" they faced in Chicago. The group was underfunded and understaffed. The herculean project of block-by-block organizing in Lawndale, for example, fell to a staff of four, aided by three volunteers. Organizers became dispirited. A few began "talking about going back to the relative tranquility of being a civil rights worker in Alabama."[64]

The CFM's most basic problem, however, remained one that had plagued it since King's January 1966 announcement of the Chicago Plan: its inability to decide on a concrete program of reform.[65] By late spring, Al Raby was losing patience. The CFM was planning a mass rally at Chicago's Soldier Field stadium on June 26. Unfortunately, as Raby pointed out, by late May it still had no precise demands to make at the rally. We must come up with some issues we can mobilize around, he insisted, so that after the rally we can "send one thousand people to do this thing or that thing." The CFM finally formulated a draft program in June 1966. Its fifty-three demands covered all the factors that might contribute to the creation of slums, broken down into headings of employment, finance, housing, education, the welfare bureaucracy, and health care. Even within the CFM, the response was tepid. Many felt that this "laundry list" of demands was so broad as to lack any focus whatsoever.[66]

• • •

In early June, just as organizing for the rally at Soldier Field reached full steam, King was pulled away. James Meredith, the first black person to enroll at the University of Mississippi, had begun a solo 220-mile "walk against fear" from Memphis, Tennessee, to Jackson, Mississippi. His goal was to encourage Southern blacks to take advantage of their new protections under the 1965 Voting Rights Act and turn out to vote. On June 6, the second day of his march, Meredith was shot from an ambush and rushed to a local hospital. On June 7, King and other civil rights leaders arrived in Memphis and announced that they would continue Meredith's march. The Soldier Field rally was postponed until July 10, when the Meredith march would be concluded.[67]

Participants in the Meredith march—the numbers varied from twenty to two hundred—faced continuous state-sanctioned white harassment along the route. Then on June 16, marcher Stokely Carmichael and two others were arrested for trespassing when they attempted to set up a sleeping tent on the grounds of a black high school in Greenwood, Mississippi. Released on bail, Carmichael went directly to a meeting called to protest police harassment of the marchers. "This is the twenty-seventh time I have been arrested," he raged, "and I ain't going to jail no more! The only way we gonna stop them white men from whippin' us is to take over. We been saying freedom for six years and we ain't got nothing. What we gonna start saying now is Black Power!" He led the crowd in a passionate new chant: "We want Black Power!" The rallying cry made national headlines.[68]

The term "black power" would become a blanket phrase to advocate everything from guerrilla warfare to voter registration to small-business self-help strategies. At the time, however, it was understood as a challenge to King's philosophy of nonviolence. King himself feared that black power supporters would undermine his vision of an interracial society united in justice. "I do not think of political power as an end. Neither do I think of economic power as an end. They are ingredients in the objective that we seek in life. . . . That objective is a truly brotherly society, the creation of the beloved community," King told reporters.[69]

Animated by a renewed sense of the importance of nonviolence, King went directly from the traumas of the Meredith march to deliver a round of last-minute speeches aimed at boosting attendance at Soldier Field. His efforts bore little fruit. Though organizers expected 100,000 people, no more than 40,000 showed up. "Martin's staff always had this problem of thinking that Chicago was Selma, and anything could happen by just saying 'you all come,'" said one local activist. The weather was no help. July 10 was brutally hot and humid. People stood or sat for hours on unshaded seats; over twenty collapsed from heat prostration.[70]

Still, the rally was a powerful event. "Mahalia Jackson sang that day as if the heavens were coming down. . . . You felt that God was with us," one participant remembered. There were other striking moments: at one point the Blackstone Rangers, a Chicago street gang, challenged the mood of the gathering—and King's leadership—by holding up signs with the words "Freedom Now" etched over the image of a submachine gun. At another, a powerful antisegregation statement was read on behalf of Chicago's new archbishop, Cardinal John Patrick Cody. "Wherever there is segregation, no man can be truly free," Cody wrote. King also addressed the crowd. "Freedom is never voluntarily granted by the oppressor. It must be demanded by the oppressed," he exhorted. "This day, we must commit ourselves to make any sacrifice necessary to change Chicago. This day, we must decide to fill up the jails of Chicago, if necessary, in order to end slums."[71]

At the conclusion of the rally, King led some 5,000 sweat-drenched people on the mile-long march from Soldier Field to Chicago's City Hall. There, following the example of his namesake, he posted the CFM's demands on one of the building's doors. Though pared down from the original fifty-three, the list remained comprehensive. The CFM called for the desegregation of Chicago's schools and "the abolition of garnishment and wage assignment." It asked for "increased garbage collection, street cleaning and building inspection services in the slum areas," an ordinance to facilitate "ready access to the names of owners and investors for all slum properties," and the construction of new public housing "outside the ghetto." It demanded the creation of a citizen review board to investigate complaints of police brutality and the "replacement of absentee precinct captains" with representatives who actually lived in their districts. Another set of demands aimed at remedying one of Chicago's most timeworn strategies for evading civil rights obligations. White authorities often claimed that since no records were kept that tabulated employees (or customers or students) by race, there was no way to determine whether discrimination actually existed. To undercut this maneuver, the CFM insisted that unions, city and state departments, and private employers provide racial "head counts" so that discrimination could be documented and challenged. The CFM also sought to improve black access to mortgages. It asked for "federal supervision" to guarantee that financial institutions insured by federal monies did not discriminate in their lending policies. It even called for "special loan funds for the conversion of contract housing purchases to standard mortgages."

But the two key issues that topped the CFM's lengthy list were surprising. First, the CFM demanded that all real estate brokers immediately make their listings available "on a non-discriminatory basis." Second, it wanted the city's brokers and real estate boards to declare their "endorsement of, and support for, open occupancy."[72] In an odd turn, the CFM had come to prioritize open occupancy—the very issue that had been embraced by Chicago's urban renewal advocates and, for his own purposes, Mayor Daley himself. It seemed unaware that open occupancy had long been promoted by the city's wealthiest business interests precisely because it did not challenge their customary practices—which included racially redlining areas that open occupancy ordinances would supposedly make accessible to black home buyers.

The decision to focus on open occupancy was the product of many factors—but the desires of the people who were most affected were not among them. It had been suggested by William Moyer, a CFM coalition member whose parent organization, the American Friends Service Committee, had long embraced the liberal establishment's analysis of housing problems.[73] Admitting that he "was as lost as" Bevel on the question of how to end Chicago's slums, Moyer argued that real estate discrimination obviously restricted black housing choices, thereby fostering segregation, overcrowding, and the growth of slums. He pointed out that, unlike more institutional forms of racism, real estate discrimination was easily demonstrated. He saw it as the perfect parallel to the lunch counter segregation that propelled black student activism in 1960. In both cases at issue was the right of an American citizen to be "served" at a place of business regardless of his or her race.[74]

Bevel embraced the cause of open occupancy, even though he knew that most slum dwellers did not particularly care about it.[75] He understood that the "forces that create slums" went well beyond a discriminatory board of realtors, but he believed that it didn't really matter where one intervened in the "cycle" of exploitation. As his coworker Mary Lou Finley put it, Bevel felt that "one point would be as good as another, providing one could gain successes which would encourage the Negro community to take up the next battle."[76]

Besides, open occupancy had promising psychological ramifications. When a black man is turned away from a real estate office, Finley explained, "the affront to his dignity is sharp, direct, insulting." Since, in Bevel's view, ghetto residents' despair was among their greatest enemies, there was much to be said for any action that encouraged a black man to "stand up and be a man, to declare that he was a human being and would hence-forth expect to be treated like one." If confronting racist realtors would make black men feel like men, then greater social change was sure to follow.[77]

Bevel also felt that, unlike other Northern problems such as school segregation or unemployment, housing discrimination offered a clear path, with clearly delineated villains and victims. Real estate brokers who refused to show black customers their listings were, after all, in violation of the law according to Chicago's 1963 open occupancy ordinance and subject to the revocation of their licenses.[78] The Chicago Real Estate Board's (CREB) bad intentions were indisputable. Having been instru-mental in the creation of the dual housing market, it now dedicated itself to overturning existing open occupancy legislation and to supporting laws that would preemptively outlaw future ordinances. As an Illinois Association of Real Estate Boards official plaintively explained, "All we are asking is that brokers and salesmen have the same right to discriminate as the owners who engage their services."[79]

There was one additional reason for the Chicago Freedom Movement to spotlight the bad behavior of real estate brokers. The issue of open occu-pancy had become the linchpin of the latest national civil rights battle, and CREB's parent body, the National Association of Real Estate Boards (NAREB), was in the midst of a campaign to roll back fair housing legisla-tion nationwide. NAREB's efforts began in 1963, when, in response to a fair housing ordinance passed by the city of Berkeley, the California Real Estate Association launched a referendum campaign, "Proposition 14," to make the right to discriminate in the sale or rental of housing part of the California state constitution. Californians voted 2 to 1 to pass Proposition

14. As Governor Edmund G. "Pat" Brown noted ruefully, the state's whites "voted their prejudice."[80]

NAREB had worked hard to duplicate its California victory elsewhere, even developing "Forced Housing" kits that provided detailed instructions on how to wage a campaign against local fair housing or open occupancy laws. The result was a string of successes. In 1964, Detroit passed an anti–fair housing measure, and open occupancy ordinances were overturned in Tacoma and Seattle, Washington, and in Akron, Ohio. Twenty-two states allowed residents to make laws by referendum. If real estate boards continued their efforts to repeal or ban fair housing initiatives, they could have a significant impact.[81]

NAREB targeted federal legislation as well. It was one of the very few business associations to oppose the Civil Rights Act of 1964, specifically Title VI, which outlawed discrimination on the basis of "race, color, or national origin" in any "program or activity receiving Federal financial assistance." But NAREB needn't have worried, since Title VI exempted one extremely critical form of such assistance: loan or mortgage insurance programs underwritten by the federal government. This meant that the Federal Housing Administration's mortgage insurance programs did not need to comply with nondiscrimination laws. In short, while states and municipalities across the nation battled over whether real estate agents should be allowed to "steer" blacks away from white neighborhoods, the U.S. Congress ensured that the underlying problem of racially based FHA mortgage redlining was left untouched.[82]

Many civil rights leaders had been concerned that the 1964 Civil Rights Act was not sufficient to fight housing discrimination, and they had pressured President Johnson to take further action. In response, Johnson pushed Congress to draft a truly comprehensive open housing plank as part of its proposed 1966 Civil Rights Act—one that banned racial discrimination not only by real estate brokers but also by property owners, developers, lending institutions, and "all others engaged in the sale, rental, or financing of housing." Johnson offered strong verbal support for the bill. "The time has come to combat unreasoning restrictions on any family's freedom to live in the home and neighborhood of its choice," he proclaimed.[83]

Unfortunately, the plank, Title IV, had extremely weak enforcement mechanisms. Like most housing antidiscrimination laws, it left responsibility for enforcement to the individual who suffered the discrimination. Furthermore, by the summer of 1966, President Johnson had been forced to agree to amendments that would exempt all privately owned dwellings containing less than five units from the bill—that is, 60 percent of the nation's housing. Meanwhile, NAREB's lobbying bore fruit. By June 1966, congressional mail was running 100 to 1 against the fair housing bill. In such a context, a CFM victory over CREB and NAREB would draw national attention and could have national ramifications.[84]

On July 11, the day after the Soldier Field rally, King and Raby met with Daley. They tried to negotiate on all of the issues they had presented to City Hall—not just on open occupancy. Daley appeared receptive but somewhat perplexed. Citing his own "war on the slums," he asked King and Raby, "What would you do that we haven't done?" The meeting went downhill from there. By its end Daley was "scarlet faced" with anger. He told reporters that, while he had given King's group a hearing, "they have no solutions." King is "sincere," Daley added, but "maybe, at times, he doesn't have all the facts on the local situation. After all, he is a resident of another city. He admitted himself they have the same problems in Atlanta."

Adding to the CFM's disappointment were the statements released by Chicago's realtors, its public housing authority, and its business leaders, all of whom rejected the group's demands. The only official who had a positive response was Charles H. Percy, Republican candidate for the U.S. Senate, who enthusiastically endorsed the call to get rid of absentee precinct captains. Of course, this was an expedient stance for Percy, since the politicians in question were exclusively Democratic.[85]

With little to hope for from the Chicago establishment, King and his group began to prepare for direct action. By the time of the July 10 rally, the CFM had documented approximately fifty cases of blatant discrimination at real estate offices. It had made several efforts to convince the Chicago Real Estate Board to change its behavior, to no avail. Meanwhile, to ensure the efficacy of its action, the CFM had done careful research. It used census data to choose its targets: Gage Park and Marquette Park, all-white Southwest Side neighborhoods where solid and comfortable housing was available at prices that many black ghetto residents could afford.

The group planned to organize interracial picnics, shopping trips, and especially church visits in these neighborhoods, followed by vigils in which black ministers would lead interracial protest groups in "prayers that the people of the community might be moved to act with justice and to recognize their brotherhood with all men." It also planned pickets and marches around the offending real estate offices. As one CFM participant explained, such actions would "expose and . . . dramatize the fact that this city has two separate housing markets."[86]

CFM leaders knew that the presence of black protesters in these all-white bastions might provoke white violence, but that, too, was part of the strategy. White Southerners had resisted the integration of public accommodations, but their violent reaction to blacks' peaceful protests aroused the nation's conscience to the point where white Americans supported federal legislation to remedy the injustice. "Now I think the same thing must happen in housing," King believed.[87]

On Tuesday, July 12, before King and the CFM could make their next move, a riot broke out on the Near West Side, the second in less than a year. The trigger was a seemingly innocuous event, a tug-of-war between policemen and children over the opening of a fire hydrant. That day temperatures exceeded ninety degrees, as they had each day for the past week. On several blocks West Side children opened fire hydrants in order to play in the water. On one corner, though, police decided to close the hydrant. When a young man named Donald Henry defiantly reopened it, the police arrested him. As a crowd gathered, Henry called out to them, "You are not going to let these policemen arrest me. Why don't you do something about it?"[88]

The crowd grew angry. The police called for reinforcements. Fifteen police cars descended on the corner, and soon thereafter the crowd turned violent. By late afternoon people were hurling rocks at police cars, smashing shop windows, and looting. Particularly hard-hit was the Liberty Shopping Center, where eight of the nine shops had their windows smashed in. The one left untouched was a restaurant owned by a black man.

The next day, Wednesday, July 13, nine hundred police officers were sent to quell the riot. The presence of an almost entirely white police force further inflamed the crowds. While some residents raged against the local teenagers whom they blamed for the trouble, complaints of police brutality dominated. Witnesses described people who were attacked by police as they stepped out of buses or simply tried to walk home from work. Searching for rioters and looters, police pushed their way into houses and beat any inhabitant who protested. Locals reported that the police used vicious racial epithets and seemed to be "enjoying" the free hand they'd been given. In one West Side police station someone taped a handwritten sign to the wastebasket: "Drop badges here." Anonymity gave the police carte blanche. "They treat us like we were animals, like we are less than dogs, like we are inhuman!" one West Side resident told a community activist.[89]

By Thursday, July 14, two people had been killed in the riot, including a pregnant fourteen-year-old girl who was standing on her porch when she was hit by a stray police bullet. Fifty-six people were injured and there were 282 arrests. Still the rioting continued. On Thursday night, it spread to Lawndale. Before long Roosevelt Road, the commercial center of Lawndale, "looked like a tornado had churned through." That evening fifteen hundred National Guardsmen descended upon the area. They were met by taunts, jeers, and mock applause from West Siders. By Friday night, when the riot ended, newspapers reported the tally as sixty-one police injuries and 533 arrests. They did not note the numbers of citizens who had been injured, nor did they mention the two black West Siders who had been shot to death.[90]

For King, the riot was a disaster. On Tuesday, July 12, he and his wife, Coretta, had been driving to a mass meeting on the West Side when he noticed a group of people dashing down the street. "Those people—I wonder if there's a riot starting," he commented. King tried to quell the violence. He drove to a nearby police station to get six recently arrested teenagers out of jail. There he paced, muttering, "I told Mayor Daley, I told Mayor Daley something like this would happen if something wasn't done." King headed back to his meeting, taking the six teenagers with him. He tried to turn the occasion into a speak-out where locals could express their anger instead of acting on it. But he was heckled by some youths. Many "refused to hear King, declaring they did not want to be talked to about nonviolence in the face of what they were convinced was police brutality," one observer noted. The next evening King attended a community meeting, where police officers listened uncomfortably as locals spoke about the authorities' overreaction to the hydrant openings and about police brutality. The police responded by lecturing the audience on the importance of law and order. With that, several gang leaders stormed out, perhaps to join other teenagers who were making Molotov cocktails in nearby alleys. As the meeting dispersed, the sound of firearms and home-made bombs could be heard in the surrounding streets.[91]

On the third day of the riot, King called together 150 Chicago clergy, black and white, to walk the streets in order to calm the seething West Side. Quoting President Kennedy's famous statement that "those who would make a peaceful revolution impossible make a violent revolution inevitable," he added emotionally, "I'm trying desperately to lead a nonviolent movement. I must say I need some help in getting this faith across."[92]

On Friday, as the looting on the West Side continued and Daley called in the National Guard, King received another blow. Daley blamed the SCLC for the riots. "I think you cannot charge it directly to Martin Luther King," the mayor granted, before continuing in his famously garbled syntax, "but surely some of the people came in here and have been talking for the last year in violence and showing pictures and instructing people in how to conduct violence." The reference to "showing pictures" was an allusion to Bevel's attempt to convince gang leaders to embrace nonviolence by showing them films of the havoc wreaked by the 1965 Watts riot. The Reverend Joseph H. Jackson seconded the mayor's attack. "I believe our young people are not vicious enough to attack a whole city," he told the press. "Some other forces are using these young people." King responded immediately: "This is absolutely untrue. It is very unfortunate that a mayor of the city would perpetuate such an impression. My staff has preached nonviolence. . . . The films showing the Watts riot were to demonstrate the negative effect of riots."[93]

Later that same day, King and a small delegation that included Al Raby and Edwin Berry of the Chicago Urban League met with Daley to discuss the riots. Daley asked the group what they "thought could be done." His question seemed to catch them off guard. According to an observer, one of the civil rights leaders stood up and said, "The riots started because you had black youngsters seeking relief with water from a fire hydrant, so obviously they need swimming pools." The observer continued, "They didn't really know what to ask for. So they asked for swimming pools and they got swimming pools and the meeting was over." Daley also responded to King's demand for a police civilian review board with a compromise promise that he would appoint a citizens' committee to "advise him and make recommendations to the police department." It was "an important step," King told reporters, but one that "falls short" of the civilian review board he had requested.[94]

These concessions effectively sidelined the broader issues raised by the riots. As Rabbi Robert Marx noted, Daley offered nothing to address West Siders' sense that "they have no access to the political power necessary to change the environment within their communities." Chicago columnist Mike Royko mockingly summarized the agreement: "City Hall embarked on a crusade to make Chicago's blacks the wettest in the country. Portable swimming pools were being trucked in. Sprinklers were attached to hundreds of hydrants, and water was gushing everywhere. . . . One cynical civil rights worker said, 'I think they're hoping we'll all grow gills and swim away.'"[95]

After the riots, the attacks on the CFM came from all sides. "I think King is finished," Saul Alinsky told the *Washington Post* on July 17. "He's trapped. He can't get out of [Chicago] in less than ten months to a year and he doesn't know what to do if he stays." On July 21, Ernest E. Rather, a black entrepreneur close to Daley, publicly called upon King to go back to the South. Other Daley supporters continued to hammer at the SCLC for causing the riots.[96]

If the movement were to survive, King would have to take immediate action. As Andrew Young understood it, "the trouble here is that there has been no confrontation" of the kind "they interrupted the network TV programs" for. The SCLC had been too cautious in Chicago: "We should have waded right in."[97]

On Friday, July 29, the CFM initiated direct action. An interracial group of protesters gathered for an all-night prayer vigil in front of Halvorsen Real Estate, a Gage Park office against which the CFM had documented numerous acts of racial discrimination. By 10:00 p.m., however, the crowd of whites surrounding the kneeling protesters had grown so large and threatening that the vigil was called off. The protesters returned the next day. This time white residents were prepared. Two hundred and fifty interracial marchers carrying signs reading "End Slums" and "A Prejudiced Child Is a Crippled Child" were met by a mob of whites carrying signs embossed with "Nigger Go Home" and "White Power." White residents cursed at the marchers and pelted them with rocks and bottles.[98]

That was just the beginning. The next day, Sunday, July 31, while King was out of town for a speaking engagement, approximately five hundred demonstrators marched from Marquette Park, an adjoining all-white bastion, back to Gage Park. According to one marcher, who recalled the "four-hour nightmare," the mood of the crowd "had definitely changed from hating us—but mainly just wanting us to go away—to wanting to kill us." Rocks and bottles rained down. Raby was struck four times. The people of Gage Park, "the most heavily Catholic neighborhood" in Chicago, seemed particularly infuriated by the Catholic clergy who participated in the march. They raged against Chicago's Archbishop Cardinal Cody for his stand against segregation. When a nun was knocked unconscious by a rock to her head, the crowd howled in approval.[99]

Marchers were particularly upset by the composition of the crowd. In the South, hecklers were mostly the "rabble element." In Chicago, mobbing interracial protesters was a family affair. Little boys waved nooses and chanted, "I'd love to be an Alabama trooper / That is what I'd really like to be / For if I were an Alabama trooper / Then I could hang a nigger legally." Ten-year-old girls pelted protesters with whatever objects they could find. Teenagers screamed "White power" and "Burn them like Jews." Young couples helped each other to rocks for stoning the marchers. Older women seemed particularly venomous. As one marcher recalled, they spat and "ranged a long list of sexual perversion charges against us."[100]

By the time the protesters made it back to their cars, which had been left under police protection, twelve of the automobiles had been burned, two had been pushed into a lagoon, and dozens of others had been overturned or seriously vandalized. Over fifty of the approximately five hundred marchers had been injured by the mob, as had two police officers. Many more would have been hurt if not for three black street gangs—the Cobras, the Vice Lords, and the Roman Saints—who acted as marshals, "batting down with their bare hands hundreds of bricks and bottles." Despite the open violence, police made only fourteen arrests. Their inaction was documented for the world to witness. There was "a very large contingent of police who were not deployed for our protection and in fact simply sat and waited until everything was over," Raby recalled. "When that showed on national TV, that embarrassed the city and I think put the mayor on the spot." Black West Siders angrily noted that neither the police nor Mayor Daley referred to white mob violence as a "riot."[101]

The week of August 1 remained tension-filled as the city debated the meaning of the weekend's white riot. Most white newspapers blamed the protesters for the violence that had been inflicted upon them. Violence "will happen as long as there is incitement," the *Chicago Tribune* intoned. "The demonstrators knew they were asking for trouble when they invaded the Gage Park community." The *Chicago Sun-Times* sympathized with the Gage Park mob, whom it described as "understandably concerned when their area is made the target of demonstrations." The *Chicago Daily News* argued that the protesters deserved police protection, but it also condemned the equally "mistaken" notions held by both sides: the white view that their homes "would be in jeopardy if their community were 'invaded' by Negroes" and the black view "that brute force, alone, can wrest the Negro's birthright from whites"—an odd interpretation of a nonviolent march. While all three white papers linked the Gage Park mobs to the recent West Side riots, only the *Chicago Defender* traced the violence to segregation. "Illinois as well as the rest of the nation must soon or late come to the grim realization that residential segregation is a root cause of racial unrest," the paper editorialized, tying the Gage Park riot to white violence against civil rights demonstrators in Mississippi and Alabama.[102]

White anger over the marches began to threaten Daley's power. On August 3, the CFM marched against a discriminatory real estate office in the all-white Northwest Side neighborhood of Belmont-Cragin. To prevent further disorder, Daley made sure that the three hundred protesters were protected by a large police presence. Now furious whites raged not only against the marchers but against the police, Cardinal Cody, and Daley. Elections were scheduled for three months hence. If Daley wanted to win the votes of white Southwest and Northwest Side neighborhoods, the marches would have to stop.[103]

Instead, the marches continued. On Friday, August 5, King led an interracial march of six hundred protesters back to Gage Park. They were met by a mob of between four and eight thousand people. Once again the demonstrators suffered a hail of rocks, bricks, bottles, and cherry bombs. Whites stood on their front steps shrieking "Cannibals" and "Go home, niggers," waving signs proclaiming "The only way to stop niggers is to exterminate them." Nine hundred and sixty police officers could barely control the crowd. The sight of King particularly incensed them. Shouts of "We want King" and "Kill him, kill him" filled the air. King was hit in the head by a fist-sized rock that knocked him to his knees. "I have never seen such hostility and hatred anywhere in my life, even in Selma," he said. "The people from Mississippi ought to come to Chicago to learn how to hate."[104]

Even the police were shocked by the mob's vehemence. "The outrageous cop-fighting we experienced here was about the most vicious I've ever seen in thirty years of service," one officer recounted. Black policemen came in for particular abuse, as did the white clergy who joined the march. John McDermott of the Catholic Interracial Council noted that "we had priests and nuns in our march . . . and the insults, the vulgar language which they were subjected to [were] just unbelievable." He was stunned by the "anger and hate, the swastikas which were held up, the housewives who turned their lawn sprinklers on you." McDermott found himself thinking that white people had "never experienced the kind of change from acceptance to hate" that can happen by crossing the boundary between black and white neighborhoods. "For the first time in their lives they were walking in the shoes of black people."[105]

The violent response of white Chicagoans to nonviolent marchers convinced the CFM that it had chosen the right approach. Finally, it was able to "dramatize a problem so that the injustice is visible for all to see."[106] With great courage, Chicago activists continued their marches. On Sunday, August 7, about one thousand protesters returned to Belmont-Cragin for a prayer vigil. Only the rain prevented the taunts of the angry white crowd from escalating to violence. By Wednesday of that week, Daley, Cody, and numerous Chicago editorials were calling for a halt to the marches. Chicago police superintendent Orlando W. Wilson predicted a race riot should they continue. Following a line that was already worn with use by white authorities in Birmingham, Alabama, and Albany, Georgia, Wilson asserted that crime in the city had risen by 25 percent—supposedly because police had been diverted from their usual duties in order to protect the marchers. But Raby refused. In his view, it made no sense to end the protests before a single demand had been met.[107]

The CFM escalated its actions. On Friday, August 12, James Bevel led about six hundred marchers back to the Southwest Side. One thousand policemen guarded the marchers from an estimated five thousand white onlookers. On Sunday, four simultaneous marches were held in all-white neighborhoods. Black activist Jesse Jackson, who led one group of 350 through the all-white neighborhood of Bogan, quipped, "We took an educational tour. We wanted some of our people to see the homes they will be living in soon." That same day members of the American Nazi Party addressed a thousand-strong white crowd in Gage Park. Ignited by the racist rhetoric, the crowd poured into the streets, where they attacked police and passing black motorists.[108]

Nevertheless, Gage Park residents felt that they were the victims. One local woman stated, "I wouldn't go and live somewhere I wasn't wanted. Why do they? Why don't they clean up the slums if they want nice places?" Another Gage Parker cast the violence as self-defense. He'd fled a changing neighborhood once before. "Now they want to come in and drive us out again. Well, we have to protect our neighborhood. This is a matter of self-preservation." Residents also accused liberals who supported open occupancy of gross hypocrisy. As one Gage Parker wrote to Illinois governor Otto Kerner, "Because people like you and President Johnson have large estates, you don't need to worry who lives next door or whether your child or daughter will be raped or stabbed when they leave their home." Another seconded, "IT IS EASY TO TELL SOMEONE ELSE WHAT TO DO, WHEN YOU DON'T HAVE TO DO IT YOURSELF."[109]

By the middle of August, Chicago had suffered two weeks of nearly constant protests. The marches were threatening the city's image nationally. CFM activists realized that they had built a "box" for Daley: "If he didn't protect us he was in serious trouble with the blacks. . . . If he did protect us it would hurt him in his white constituency." This was an accurate assessment. As one Chicago precinct captain mourned, "We lose white votes every time there's an outburst like this."[110]

And things were about to get even worse. On August 8, Jesse Jackson had unexpectedly announced that the next area to be targeted for open housing marches would be Cicero, an all-white, mostly working-class suburb that had a well-deserved reputation for using violence against any black who dared set foot there.[111] The last time a black family had attempted to move to Cicero, a white mob smashed windows and ripped down the trees around their apartment complex. The riot stopped only when police flooded the area. That was in 1951. By 1966, little had changed. In May of that year, a black teenage honors student named Jerome Huey had gone into the neighborhood to apply for a job. He was attacked by four white teenagers who smashed his head so severely that his eyes were beaten out of his skull. The boy died. "Cicero, you don't know what Cicero meant to people in Chicago," said Clory Bryant, a black Chicagoan. "You didn't walk through Cicero alone. You didn't let your car break down in Cicero. . . . You just didn't go to Cicero if you were black."[112] Jackson's announcement of a march in Cicero sent chills through whites as well. Cicero residents made panicky calls for the deployment of the National Guard. Cook County sheriff Richard B. Ogilvie told the press that, according to his informants, the violence in Cicero "would make Gage Park look like a tea party."[113]

Daley could not ban the marches. That would only swell the protesters' numbers and threaten his voting base among Chicago's blacks. He had to find some way to meet the protesters' demands. Luckily, the marchers were demanding nothing more than the enforcement of fair housing laws regarding real estate listings. That should not be difficult to accommodate. Daley was on record as supporting open occupancy. After all, he had personally pushed through Chicago's Fair Housing Ordinance of 1963.

Daley set out to resolve the crisis. After a few false starts, the Chicago Conference on Religion and Race convened a meeting charged with responding to the CFM's demands and ending the demonstrations. The participants would be the CFM on one side and Chicago's notables on the other. The fifty-six men who gathered for the "summit negotiation" on August 17 were a distinguished group. Religious leaders included Archbishop John Patrick Cody, Rabbi Robert J. Marx, and Dr. John Gardiner of the Church Federation of Greater Chicago. Edwin Berry of the Urban League was present, as was William R. Ming Jr., perhaps the most prominent black attorney in Chicago. Many of the city's top business leaders attended, including John W. Baird, William G. Caples of Inland Steel, and several representatives of the city's banking and mortgage broker industries. Union leaders and heads of various city agencies also came, as did four representatives of the Chicago Real Estate Board. Speaking for the Chicago Freedom Movement were Martin Luther King Jr., James Bevel, Al Raby, Jesse Jackson, Andrew Young, and Reverend Arthur Brazier of The Woodlawn Organization. John McKnight, a designated observer representing the U.S. Commission on Civil Rights, took detailed notes on the proceedings.[114]

Al Raby presented the CFM's demands. First, Mayor Daley must acknowledge that Chicago's 1963 open occupancy law was toothless and "immediately launch a new program to enforce the Chicago Fair Housing Ordinance." Second, the Chicago Real Estate Board must stop fighting fair housing legislation. Third, the Chicago Housing Authority must stop building public housing complexes exclusively in poor black neighborhoods. Fourth, the Cook County Department of Public Aid must end its "containment policy" of placing welfare recipients exclusively in "ghetto communities." Fifth, the city's urban renewal program must use relocations to break down rather then reinforce racial segregation.

Raby then turned to the issue of home financing. His sixth demand was that "Savings and Loans and other financial institutions" embrace a "policy of equal service and lend mortgage money to qualified Negro families." Seventh, the Federal Deposit Insurance Corporation must use its power to enforce nondiscriminatory lending by financial institutions. The FDIC should "suspend from membership any bank or savings and loan association which is found guilty of practicing racial discrimination in the provision of financial services to the public." The remaining two points called upon business, labor, and religious leaders to pledge moral support for these reforms and financial support for the creation of "integrated low- and middle-income housing outside the ghetto."[115]

There seemed to be an immediate breakthrough. Clark Stayman of the Chicago Mortgage Bankers Association stood up and made the dramatic statement that the CFM's crucial sixth demand—that mortgage funding be made available on a nondiscriminatory basis—was "absolutely accepted" by his group.[116] Oddly, this historic statement seemed to pass almost unnoticed. Daley immediately shifted the discussion to his own primary concern: stopping the protest marches. If the movement's demands were met, would the CFM stop its protests? he wanted to know. Ralph Abernathy sarcastically described what happened next: "Warily Martin suggested that we might, whereupon Daley went down the list of demands and quickly agreed to every one of them. Presto! The race problems in Chicago had been solved, and after only a few minutes of discussion." As Abernathy noted, Daley had revealed his basic strategy: "Promise them anything so long as they stop the marches; later we can figure out ways to circumvent the granting of their demands."[117]

Abernathy's prediction turned out to be accurate. There was a fair amount of verbal maneuvering to be gotten through first, however. Daley and most of the other gathered dignitaries took turns pressuring CREB into dropping its opposition to Chicago's 1963 Fair Housing Ordinance. CREB's chairman, Ross Beatty, would agree only to "freedom of choice in housing"—an ambiguous statement that could easily support the right of homeowners to discriminate—and to the even more convoluted promise that CREB would drop its opposition to "the philosophy of open occupancy" while retaining its right to criticize "the details as distinguished from the philosophy" of open occupancy laws. After several hours of such discussion, Al Raby tried to get at least one concrete concession. At the next City Council meeting would Daley ask for legislation requiring brokers to post nondiscrimination ordinances in their windows? Daley said he would consider it—on the condition that Raby stop the demonstrations.[118]

This caused the normally cool Raby to show his first flash of anger. "Some day, I hope I can come before the Mayor of Chicago with what is just and that he will implement it because it is right rather than trading it for a political moratorium," he seethed. He pointed out how amorphous each of the mayor's promises had been. "The Real Estate Board hasn't done anything meaningful here. I'm not clear on what the Chicago Housing Authority is really going to do about high-rises. The Cook County Department of Public Aid has got to change; it can't tell us that it has all Negro recipients in one area and all white recipients in another area and that's an accident. That's an insult to our intelligence. The Urban Renewal program is going to have to do something about its relocation policies. I want to hear the details about what the Savings and Loan people are going to do. . . . I am not going to go back to our people with a philosophical program. We want a real program." He summed up, "A moratorium on discrimination will bring a moratorium on marches."[119]

King spoke next. "I hope we are here to discuss how to make Chicago a great open city and not how to end marches." He pointed out that the marches were not illegal. "We haven't even practiced civil disobedience," he reminded Daley. Now "we are being asked to stop one of our most precious rights, the right to assemble, the right to petition."[120]

Daley was unmoved by King's plea. He remained rigidly focused on stopping the marches. Realizing that negotiations were at a deadlock, summit chairman Ben Heineman suggested that a subcommittee be appointed, consisting of Daley, representatives of the CFM and the Real

Estate Board, and representatives of business and labor. It was agreed that the entire group would reconvene in ten days, on Friday, August 26, to discuss the subcommittee proposals.

The next day, Thursday, August 18, King and his advisers met to discuss their strategy for the final summit meeting. They were still uncertain what they should ask for in order to create an "open city." Bevel insisted that the Real Estate Board was key. "We should ask the board of realtors to have a delivery plan for opening up every community in Chicago," he argued. King stressed that whatever came out of the upcoming meeting, it must be "a real plan" which "sees that five Negro families move into Gage Park." Perhaps it was hearing this extraordinarily modest goal of new homes for five black families that led Kale Williams, a member of the AFSC, to end the meeting on a somber note. "No one knows how to deseg-regate," he said.

Then on Friday, just two days after the first meeting, Daley shocked CFM members by obtaining an injunction against future marches. His injunction did not ban their demonstrations, but it severely limited them to no more than five hundred marchers, no more than one demonstration per day, and only with a twenty-four-hour advance warning to the police. The excuse was the old claim that the police presence needed to ensure the safety of larger marches would make it impossible for the police department to protect "the life and property of the more than 3½ million [Chicagoans] who are not participating" in protests or counterdemon-strations. King was enraged by the move. He called it "grossly unjust, ille-gal, and unconstitutional" and attacked Daley for his "bad faith" in taking out an injunction while negotiations were still in process.[121]

King was now under pressure from many sides. Some CFM members encouraged him to defy Daley's injunction and thereby commit the move-ment more firmly to civil disobedience. Others felt that the CFM would lose what public support it had if it resisted the injunction. King settled on a compromise. He agreed to abide by the injunction until the summit committee reconvened on August 26. At the same time, King continued to challenge Daley. He announced that the CFM would resume its marches in suburban areas, which were not covered by the injunction. He also said that if the summit meeting was not productive, the injunction would be defied—dramatically. The CFM would carry out the threat made by Jesse Jackson two weeks earlier: it would march in Cicero.

The prospect of a showdown in Cicero created panic. Cook County sheriff Richard B. Ogilvie called it "awfully close to a suicidal act." The *Chicago Daily News* called King's threat an attempt to "blackmail" the members of the summit meeting. But King held firm. "We're not only going to walk in Cicero, we're going to work and live there," he told a rally.[122]

In this tense atmosphere, the fifty-six negotiators reconvened on August 26 to hear the subcommittee's recommendations. The results were anticlimactic. The Chicago Commission on Human Relations pledged to continue implementing the city's 1963 Fair Housing Ordinance. The Chicago Real Estate Board restated its commitment to "freedom of choice in housing." The Chicago Housing Authority agreed to "take every action within its power to promote the objectives of fair housing," and the Cook County Department of Public Aid similarly pledged to "make a renewed and persistent effort" to house welfare recipients in "the best housing" available, regardless of location. A U.S. Department of Justice official agreed to "inquire" into the possibility of asking the FDIC and FSLIC to refuse service to financial institutions that engaged in racially discriminatory loan practices. "While the matter is a complex one, it will be diligently pursued," he promised. The closest the subcommittee came to actual implementation was in its call to the Chicago Conference on Religion and Race to help create a "continuing body" of city leaders who would "accept responsibility for the education and action programs necessary to achieve fair housing."[123]

John McKnight, who was once again present to observe the proceedings, deemed the subcommittee's program, contained in a ten-point document, "so vague as to be an unreliable instrument for securing significant progress." CFM leaders struggled to pin down specific actions from the various representatives who pledged "commitment to the principles of open occupancy." Al Raby asked the religious leaders present to say "whether or not the churches will take responsibility for a specific number of Negro families in each all-white community." Raby was fighting for any commitment, however modest, as long as it was concrete. "Will we be able to have one percent Negro occupancy in every community in Chicago by 1970?" he asked. In response, the church and synagogue leaders present each stood and reiterated their commitment to working toward that end. As McKnight caustically summarized, these "statements of good will" were "not significant" since they lacked "any specific content."[124]

To the last, CREB's Ross Beatty equivocated about his organization's willingness to show its listings on a nondiscriminatory basis. "We'll do all we can," he said to the group, "but I don't know how to do it." He added pathetically, "The last two weeks have been the most confusing of all my life. I think that there are a lot of specifics that we just aren't going to be able to work out here. But I hope everyone will understand that we are all not bums."

As the meeting neared its close, King made a final attempt to get Daley to withdraw his injunction. "We feel that injunction is unjust and unconstitutional," he said. By limiting marches to groups of no more than five hundred, the injunction "denies freedom of assembly." Daley responded emotionally: "I was raised in a workingman's community in a workingman's home. My father was a union organizer and we did not like injunctions. I know the injustice of injunctions." Nevertheless, Daley continued, it was his job to protect 3½ million Chicagoans from crimes that might possibly be committed if the city's police force was distracted by protecting the marchers. His ultimate argument for inaction on the injunction, though, was completely pragmatic. "If this agreement is made and everybody keeps to it you will have no worry about the injunction because you won't need to march," he told King.

At this point the CFM representatives must have realized that nothing of substance could be expected from this gathering. When the chair called for a vote on the ten-point proposal, it passed unanimously. King made a short conciliatory speech, emphasizing that "we seek only to make possible a city where men can live as brothers." Summit chair Ben Heineman issued a triumphant statement to the press. "This is a great day for Chicago," he said. "We are all gathered here and through the great democratic process, we have worked out an agreement." At the very last moment, CFM member Al Pitcher added his own gloss to Heineman's words. "Democratic process, shit," Pitcher murmured to McKnight. "It was forced out of them."[125]

• • •

King tried to put the best face on the agreement. He called it "the first step in a thousand-mile journey, but an important step." Others, black and white, were less diplomatic. The white suburban real estate boards were furious with Beatty for even the very limited promises he had made. Some white Southwest and Northwest Siders picketed City Hall, carrying signs proclaiming "Daley Sold Out Chicago" and calling for an end to "the forced housing ordinance." Many black Chicagoans recognized that the agreement was so vague as to be meaningless. Chester Robinson of the West Side Organization charged King and Raby with selling out black interests for "empty promises." He was irritated that wealthy Chicagoans believed they could privately determine what was best for the people of the West Side. "How do they know what we need? . . . They ain't never been into this community. They don't even know what the streets look like." The Chicago branch of the Student Nonviolent Coordinating Committee (SNCC) asked, "Is token integration the solution to our problem? Would you move your family into Gage Park? Who is kidding who?"[126]

Even some white liberals were angry over the agreement. Alderman Leon Despres dismissed it entirely. It was "a treaty to cover Martin Luther King's retreat from Chicago," he said. Privately, Ralph Abernathy seconded Despres's view. Shortly after the summit meeting, Abernathy received a call from Carl Stokes in Cleveland, who wanted to know if King and his staff would help him campaign to be the first black mayor of a major city. Abernathy pressured King to accept the invitation. "What can we hope to achieve?" King asked. To Abernathy, the answer was obvious. "The most important goal I can think of," he replied. "We can get the hell out of Chicago." As two scholars of the 1966 Chicago crusade summarized, "Marching into neighborhoods was the only behavior the summit agreement actually stopped."[127]

Still, the protests didn't stop right away. The immediate issue facing the CFM was whether or not to hold the march on Cicero. King was against it. Other CFM members, especially those who felt that black interests had been ignored, passionately insisted that it go forward.[128] They argued that the murder of Jerome Huey, the unofficial rule that blacks working in Cicero had to be out of the area by sunset, and the ongoing humiliation of being excluded from a section of the city "as if blacks were a lesser form of humanity" were all reasons for the march to proceed. As the WSO's Chester Robinson summarized, "We have to go. There ain't no question about that, 'cause Cicero is just like the Berlin Wall. It's got to be knocked down."[129]

On September 4, 1966—Labor Day weekend—the Cicero march finally took place. Daley dispatched 2,000 National Guardsmen and 1,000 police to protect 250 marchers from a mob of 3,000 whites. Cicero's whites shouted, "Go back to Africa!" and "Two, four, six, eight! We don't want to integrate!" The marchers called back, "Black power! Black power!" They stopped at the site where Jerome Huey had been murdered. Huey's parents, Isaac and Ruth, were present. Mrs. Huey wept as one of the marchers, a theology student, said a prayer in her son's memory. While the group prayed, hundreds of whites crowded around them, waving swastikas and shouting taunts.[130]

As the marchers were leaving Cicero they were attacked by rock- and bottle-throwing whites. This time, some of the marchers hurled the missiles back at their tormentors. Their actions further enraged the mob, who tried but failed to crash through the police lines. One persistent white heckler was grabbed by the police and clubbed into submission before being carted away. Six white teenagers were bayoneted by National Guardsmen. Thirty-two whites were arrested.[131]

The marchers felt that they had achieved a moral victory. They had courageously committed to marching in Cicero, and they had followed through on their commitment. "That in itself was a triumph, because people just didn't do that in Cicero," one marcher recalled. Others felt that the march helped sharpen the demand that had emerged as the heart of the CFM: "We marched in Cicero . . . not because we want to live in Cicero, but because we believe beyond a doubt in open occupancy."[132]

White press reaction to the Cicero march was considerably murkier. The *Chicago Sun-Times* called it "an irresponsible and pointless act." While acknowledging that the "hoodlums who tried to break it up are irresponsible lawbreakers who deserve the rough treatment from the police and national guardsmen," the paper insisted nevertheless that "there should have been no march in the first place." National press reaction was even more skewed. Papers across the country printed headlines like "Guards Bayonet Hecklers in Cicero's Rights March." They published photos of heavily armed guardsmen menacing white teenagers, reinforcing the idea that the violent white mob had been the victim and not the oppressor.[133]

There was another group that saw the Cicero march, and all the other CFM marches into white Chicago neighborhoods, in a negative light: the U.S. congressmen who were in the midst of debating the proposed 1966 Civil Rights Bill. The bill came up for debate in the House of Representatives in August. Six references were made to the CFM's actions in Chicago—all of them negative and most equating King's nonviolent activism with the black ghetto riots of the previous summer. The comments of a North Carolina congressman were typical. "Are not many of those on the scene of the current Chicago outbursts of violence the same ones responsible for the gleeful cries of 'burn, baby, burn' in Watts?" he asked.

The House passed the bill nevertheless—though not with a wide majority—and sent it on to the Senate, which began deliberations two days after the Cicero march. The key person was Illinois Republican senator Everett Dirksen. This prickly but eloquent Senate minority leader had opposed both the 1964 and 1965 Civil Rights Acts, only to change his mind at the last minute and instead convince his fellow Republicans to provide the margin of victory. Now, though, his opposition remained firm. The sticking point for Dirksen was the Title IV open housing provision, which would have outlawed racial discrimination in housing by a wide range of actors, though with extremely weak enforcement requirements. He denounced this provision as "a package of mischief for the country." He specifically condemned the civil rights "leaders who've gone into white areas of Chicago," accusing them of "calculated harassment" of the city's whites.[134]

Dirksen's view was supported by Southern senators, some of whom went so far as to equate the bill's passage with an endorsement of black rioting. That defeating the bill would constitute an endorsement of white rioting did not occur to any of the senators. The combined opposition of Southern Democrats and Northern Republicans who followed Dirksen doomed the measure. On September 19, the Civil Rights Bill of 1966 died. It was the first proposed civil rights bill *not* to pass since 1957. Many were not surprised at its failure. Commentators openly discussed the white backlash against racial liberalism that had begun in 1964 and was now in full bloom. As NAACP head Roger Wilkins noted, "it would have been hard to pass the Emancipation Proclamation in the atmosphere prevailing now."[135]

By the fall of 1966, King had turned his attention to other concerns, including the escalation of the Vietnam War, and to what he saw as the fundamental problem confronting the nation: that it "harbors 35 million poor at a time when its resources are so vast that the existence of poverty is an anachronism." In Chicago, the remnants of the CFM tried to carry on their struggle to end segregation. It was disheartening work. In September, the Chicago Urban League released a new study on school segregation in the city. It showed that schools were even more segregated in 1966 than they had been in 1964. In October, the AFSC's William Moyer issued a report claiming that there had been virtually no progress in desegregating housing since the summit agreement of August 1966: the city's realtors had continued to discriminate, the CHR had taken no further enforcement action, and there had been no changes in the policies of the Chicago Housing Authority, the Public Aid Department, or the Department of Urban Renewal. In November, the Holmeses, a black family who had recently moved to Marquette Park, the white neighborhood adjoining Gage Park, were forced to move again after their home was bombed. The Holmeses had three sons on their way to Vietnam. The case received some publicity, but no official action was taken.[136]

The Holmeses' experiences were extreme but hardly unique. Throughout the fall of 1966, there was "violence every day in racially changing blocks," Moyer noted. As Al Raby reviewed the situation: "Since the summit meetings, the only officially reported change is that eight Negro families have been moved out of the ghetto. We are trying to verify this report." He placed this news in its appropriate context: "Eight families moved out of the ghetto is no tangible change for a city of one million Negroes!"[137]

By the mid-1960s many black Chicagoans, like inhabitants of other Northern black enclaves, held views that shattered "widely held assumptions" about the wishes of ghetto dwellers. According to a 1966 survey of mostly male residents of black sections of Chicago, Baltimore, Watts, and Harlem, the average ghetto resident "loathes welfare programs," which were blamed for "causing degeneration and forcing families to separate." Most were not interested in school integration. They felt tyrannized by "a small minority—the dope addicts, criminals" who were "making decent living all but impossible." In addition to ghetto inhabitants' overwhelming desire to stop street crime, "an equally important response was the need for better housing."[138]

In short, black Americans wanted what white Americans wanted: intact families, decent homes, and safe communities. But the CFM's failure in Lawndale—where conditions were as brutal as in any ghetto in the country—led many outsiders to assume that West Siders simply could not be organized to achieve these basic goals. Some SCLC organizers felt confirmed in their belief that West Siders' passivity was to blame. As one staffer recalled, he could not imagine how "you could get people in some of these buildings to actually organize, to withhold their rent, to put it into an escrow account, and try and force meaningful changes."[139]

In fact, the problem lay not with West Siders but with the SCLC's vision of change. Instead of listening to those it claimed to represent, the SCLC had chosen a primary focus—open occupancy legislation—based upon national strategic concerns and upon its superficial similarity to the demand for service in restaurants and public accommodations that had mobilized young people in the South. The SCLC had long based its activism on community mobilizing—that is, the organization of large-scale, somewhat short-term public events designed to demonstrate the existence of an injustice that authorities would then be pressured to correct. This was in sharp contrast to the community-organizing methods embraced by other activist organizations, from Chicago's Woodlawn Organization and West Side Organization to the Southern-based Student Nonviolent Coordinating Committee (SNCC), which believed that change happened not simply through turning out large numbers of people to make demands but rather through developing the leadership abilities of ordinary people, who would then take charge of local struggles against targets that they themselves determined.[140]

SNCC members had followed this policy in Mississippi, where against overwhelming odds they enabled local people to emerge as leaders of their own communities. The same strategies could have been followed in Chicago.[141] Instead, SCLC organizers' engagement with West Siders was scattershot rather than intensive, as it needed to be. Their distance from the people they hoped to mobilize was epitomized by their decision to foreground open occupancy.[142] Their early, exhaustive list of demands was evidence that they had a sophisticated understanding of the complexity of the forces that created slums. To be successful, however, a movement had to grow from the desires of those it claimed to represent. When SCLC organizers chose their central issue based on the advice of liberal housing experts rather than on the wishes of West Siders, they doomed their movement.

Despite King's nationally visible failure, change would come to Lawndale. Where King's organizers had seen only hopelessness, others saw a community on the brink of positive change. "Lawndale is fascinating. The intense, teeming crowds, the swarms of bright-eyed little Negro boys; what is their future?" one visitor asked in the summer of 1966.[143] That future would be shaped not by "outsiders" but by Chicagoans.

SEVEN

THE STORY OF A BUILDING

While Martin Luther King Jr.'s crusade was unfolding in my family's former Lawndale neighborhood, most of us were too involved in our daily lives to pay it much mind. My few memories of that first year following my father's death mostly concern adjusting to the first grade; as a child of six, I was too young to realize that my father's absence was permanent. My sisters and I continued to attend the nearby public school in Chicago's South Shore neighborhood. My brother Paul received early admittance to the University of Chicago; he started there that fall at the young age of sixteen.

The exception was my older brother, David, who was then an eighteen-year-old second-year student and an editor of the University of Chicago student paper, the *Chicago Maroon*. In March 1966, he wrote a long and ambitious essay for the *Chicago Maroon Magazine,* which he had recently launched. The essay, titled "The West Side, and the Plight of the Urban Poor," was a vividly written, in-depth critique of Martin Luther King Jr. and the Chicago Freedom Movement.

David began with an exegesis of King's January 7, 1966, statement about the root of slums: "The Chicago problem is simply a matter of economic exploitation. Every condition exists because someone profits from its existence. This economic exploitation is crystallized in the slum." King's view, according to David, was based on the "Alinsky concept," which had "clear advantages over logical thinking." It was attractive because its axioms were so simple. Slums are the result of oppression; organize people against oppressors; "eradicate the oppressors; and presto-chango, no slum," he summarized.

David argued that the greatest factor in the devastation of Chicago's black ghetto was not "economic exploitation" but the destructive behavior of black welfare recipients, mainly from the rural South. David discovered this harsh truth, he wrote, after talking to West Side landlords and tenants. He was also taken on a "revealing tour" of slum properties by Norris Morris of Acme Realty, a man David contacted after seeing him listed as a major slumlord. "'When they come up here from Tennessee, they're not quite housebroken,'" Morris explained, as he took David into a building with "an indescribably foul hallway." Their first stop was the apartment of Minnie Jackson. "For absolute filth, I had never seen anything like it," David reported. Jackson's idea of cleaning up after a meal was to push everything off the table onto the floor. "'Then they wonder why there are rats,'" Morris commented. He gave Jackson a notice telling her that, since she had not paid her rent in three months, she would have to move. Jackson stuffed the notice "into a dirty cloth bag full of crumpled papers. . . . From where I stood, I could see forms from the department of public aid and more five day notices," David noted.

Their next stop was the apartment of Fanny Lou James, which was located directly above Jackson's. "The apartment was literally an island of warmth, spotlessly clean, it was a reasonable place to live," David wrote. The two apartments rented for the same amount—$100 a month. "'You see,'" Morris told David, "'there's really no such thing as a slum landlord, only slum tenants.'" He added that, because of tenant destructiveness, "the individual landlord doesn't have a prayer in Lawndale.'" As David concluded, every "loan office in the city" knew that landlords couldn't make their mortgage payments out of slum rents. This was why it was "impossible to borrow money for a first mortgage on the West Side."

David's essay emphasized the role of public aid recipients. Because they were barred from paying over $105 a month for rent, it followed that any building whose rents exceeded that amount would be free of tenants on welfare. David observed that such buildings "remain in as good condition as they were in before Lawndale itself became a slum." But apartments that rented for $105 or below, and hence were open to welfare recipients, were often devastated. "Apparently, the presence of welfare people in a building is the factor that makes it a slum even though most of the building's residents are conscientious people," he concluded.

To back up his claims, David referred to a small scale study he had undertaken, which found that aid recipients were far more hostile toward merchants, landlords, and "society" than their employed counterparts. He also drew support for his position from leaders of the West Side Organization, who were then in the midst of organizing welfare recipients. According to a WSO official, "'The system works to dehumanize the recipient.'" David added, "It is this dehumanized recipient that rents an apartment in the slums of the West Side from slum landlords." It was no surprise that such a person, one who lacked a job and therefore a "stake in the economic life around him," caused so much trouble for those who provided shelter.

The implications were obvious. To end slums, far more was needed than simply "crucifying the slum landlords and ending exploitation." Instead, David suggested "education for the poor newcomer to the big city," a "restructuring of public aid," and, most broadly, "a concerted effort by society to . . . salvage the welfare poor who play such a large role in making the slums." Martin Luther King would not leave the West Side "one iota better than he found it," he concluded, "because the answer to ending the slums lies in helping the people who make slums." The alternative was "the kind of wishful nonsense that King proposes for the West Side."[1]

One might expect that an article criticizing Martin Luther King Jr. and published in an obscure, newly launched campus magazine by a college sophomore would have little impact. Instead, the essay quickly reached a citywide and then a nationwide audience. As a result, my brother accomplished at eighteen something that our father never accomplished in a lifetime. He contributed to the national debate on race and housing in America.

Within weeks of the essay's publication, David received a flood of congratulatory letters. Typical was one from George W. Beadle, a Nobel Prize–winning scientist who was then the president of the University of Chicago. Beadle praised David for examining the slum problem "objectively and without over-simplification." He added that he'd recently learned of a new city program to "teach public aid recipients something about housekeeping. It is a long job and, as you say, many changes are necessary."[2] Housing administrators far and wide enthused over the article. The *Housing Affairs Letter,* a Washington, D.C., newsletter, praised David's piece as "the best report we've seen in a long time." Peter G. Burns, the director of the city of Ottawa's housing code program, wrote that he agreed with "almost every point and theory advanced by Mr. Satter in his article."[3]

That was just the beginning. In July 1966, David published a slightly revised version of his essay, now titled "West Side Story: Home Is Where the Welfare Check Comes," in the *New Republic.* Once again David warned against taking "the easy way of attacking the 'exploiters' and doing little else"—as Martin Luther King Jr. was doing. Instead, King must "acknowledge some awkward facts." These were, first, that ending the slums would require "teaching poor rural Negroes how to live in a big city" and, second, that the very "theory and methods of public welfare in Chicago" would need to be recast. "Welfare recipients and other desperately poor people have learned to trick the system that tricked them," David warned. "They are one of the most potentially destructive forces in urban America and the salvation of Northern cities will depend on how their anger and energy are channeled."[4]

The *New Republic* article won David further accolades. He received letters of praise from senior editors at the *Atlantic Monthly* and the Little, Brown publishing company as well as a note from Houghton Mifflin expressing interest in any "book-length manuscript" he might have "either at hand or in mind." (Immensely flattered, David demurred since, as he explained, "I am now only eighteen and my ideas are still percolating.") David also received a letter from conservative *Washington Post* columnist Joseph Alsop, who offered his "very warmest congratulations" on the *New Republic* essay. "I take it you have studied the problem you describe for a very long time," Alsop wrote—to a teenager.[5]

In one of his nationally syndicated columns, Alsop described the "existing welfare system" as a "cancer that threatens our great cities," citing David's article as perhaps the "most poignant single piece of evidence" supporting this view. "Satter, who is a young Chicago liberal, originally set out to do a searing exposé of 'slumlords.' But his study turned into an even more searing exposé of the social effects of welfare as now administered," Alsop wrote. In his telling, the nuances to be found in David's broadly drawn arguments disappeared altogether. Although David described only one clean slum apartment, Alsop had him visiting "many" slum apartments in "the worst parts of Chicago's Negro ghetto" that were "scrupulously clean" and "regularly and properly maintained." While these apartments "*always* rented for a few more cents per room" than Chicago authorities authorized for public aid recipients, in "welfare-eligible buildings . . . Satter invariably found conditions of such filth and misery as hardly exist outside the slums of Calcutta," Alsop wrote—overlooking the fact that the one "spotless" apartment described in David's essay was located in just such a building. According to Alsop, "Satter further found that in such buildings, clean-up and maintenance were quite useless" because welfare tenants destroyed any repairs their landlords attempted. "This, plus nonpayment of rents, was why Martin Luther King gave up his private slum clearance experiment," Alsop informed his readers.[6]

The acclaim that greeted my brother's article was puzzling, since anyone who had followed press coverage of the slum issue would have seen nothing new in it, and much that was questionable. David's claim that even major slumlords like Norris Morris made no money from their investments had been effectively debunked over the years.[7] Numerous exposés dating back to the mid-1950s had contested David's assertion that banks refused to make mortgage loans in black areas like Lawndale because slum properties were not profitable.[8] The "rural" origins of the migrants was yet another point in dispute. Complaints about tenant destructiveness had also been made, and challenged, many times before.[9] Finally, David's dramatic presentation of a calculus by which the condition of a building could be predicted by its rent level cried out for verification, especially since he never indicated the welfare status of the woman who kept her low-priced apartment "spotlessly clean."[10]

Instead of a pathbreaking analysis of the cause of slums, David's essay was a variation on a common theme in slum journalism: the shocking discovery of the clean slum apartment. "A Slum Home CAN Be Clean," a typical story reported. This particular article, which was part of the *Chicago Daily News*'s 1963 slum series, featured a photograph of Mrs.

Clytie Fleming in her simple but dazzlingly clean kitchen. That story, however, undermined conventional wisdom about the flawed culture of rural Southern blacks and the destructive force of welfare. Fleming was both a migrant from Arkansas and an ADC recipient. Her son, an eighth grader, was an altar boy.[11]

For those whose memories did not reach back to 1963, more recent news reports made identical observations. In June 1966, the *Chicago Daily News* reported on an often overlooked but "vital factor" of the West Side's antislum crusade: "the tenants who have been waging their own slum wars for years and almost invariably losing." Typical was Mrs. Dorice Jones. "The flat is spotless and bright with framed pictures from magazines, bed quilts she has made and pillows she has covered," the paper noted. Yet there were problems beyond Mrs. Jones's control. Despite her strenuous efforts to block every rat hole she could find with scavenged concrete, she reported that rats "ran at night over our beds" until the Board of Health's rodent control team came to patch her walls. Mrs. Jones lived in the apartment with her five children. She was also, like Mrs. Fleming, a public aid recipient. "'A lot of places around here, it's the tenants that tear the building down,'" she commented. "'But there's also a lot where the tenants have done everything they know how, and it's still a slum.'"[12]

Examples of welfare tenants who maintained their apartments were not included in David's essay. David told me that he never intended to indict all welfare recipients, only a "destructive minority which . . . created havoc for the whole community." Yet by emphasizing welfare as the sole source of tenant destructiveness, David left himself open to criticism. His opponents, however, avoided rational debate about welfare, or even about bad tenants' contribution to slum conditions, in favor of a more personal approach. Soon after the essay's publication, David was confronted by a group of student activists. "It's well known that you're the son of a slum landlord," they flung at him.[13]

Although these taunts were cruel, they were in one sense accurate. By 1966, Mark J. Satter's former buildings were in dismal shape. The student activists had also hit on an emotional truth: David's essay was an attempt to defend our father. "By explaining the true forces" that led to the decline of the properties, David told me, he hoped "to protect his reputation."[14]

Indeed, the relationship between David's essay and our father's life and work was more intimate than anyone imagined. The buildings upon which David based his claims had not been chosen randomly: they had belonged to our father. David visited them in the fall of 1965 not to research the cause of slum conditions but to collect back rents. "I went out there to see if I could do anything to help Mom. I mean, she was desperate," David said. He was let into the apartments not by Norris Morris but by a black man who worked for Balin Real Estate, the company that managed our father's buildings along with many other slum properties. As for Norris Morris, there was no such person: the most vivid "character" in David's supposedly nonfiction essay was a "composite" figure—based mostly on Irving Block.[15]

The buildings had suffered "a period of neglect," David recalled. During the last months of our father's life, the money ran out and "he couldn't maintain the properties the way he wanted to." Now David saw the results. The building he based his essay on was the twelve-flat at 3901 West Jackson, which was in the worst shape. Some of the windows were broken. The stairways were shabby, and there was an overpowering smell of urine in one of the hallways. The whole experience was a shock for David, who had already witnessed the shocking destruction wrought by his father's worst tenants, and who now could not help but blame their rapacious behavior for his father's untimely death. While he was impressed by how some tenants maintained their apartments, other apartments were the picture of slovenly disorder.[16]

Our father's smallest building, the six-flat at 3846–48 West Congress, by contrast, was in fairly good shape: "There were definitely things that needed repair. But it was basically a sound, comfortable place to live, and the people who lived there paid their rent regularly," David said. It was this dramatic disparity that led him to the claim that while nothing could save a building that contained welfare tenants, buildings free of such people could remain clean and well maintained.[17]

David saw his article as more than a defense of our father and other well-meaning building owners from accusations that they were slumlords. He also viewed it as a posthumous tribute to our father's views on the destructive effects of welfare. Indeed, David told me that the sentence in his *New Republic* article about how welfare recipients "learned to trick the system that tricked them" was a direct quote from our father.[18]

Both David and our father believed that people without jobs understood and acted upon their social marginality. But David argued that destructive tenant behavior derived from the culture of "rural Southern blacks." In contrast, our father was acutely aware of the forces—legal chicanery among bankers, real estate agents, attorneys, and merchants; plant downsizings and closings—that combined to strip people of their savings and push them out of work, leaving them to take their fury and frustration out on the buildings and communities in which they lived. In his view, the group in need of "education" was the federal government, which should reform exploitative credit and wage garnishment laws and shoulder its responsibility to provide work for all who sought it, as it had during the Great Depression.[19] My father's belief that destructive behavior was a response—however confused—to bad treatment explained why even his harshest words about welfare recipients were leavened by sympathy. "*Already brutalized by factors which would destroy the strongest of us,*" my father wrote in an unpublished essay, "the unwanted recipient spreads a wide path of destruction wherever he goes."[20] David too expressed sympathy for the victims of racial discrimination, but he implied that discrimination was enacted exclusively by whites in the "most backwards parts of the South." He thereby overlooked the heart of our father's work—the brutal *Northern* experiences that left so many black Chicagoans dependent upon welfare in the first place.[21]

My brother's essay fit in well with an emerging consensus about the "culture of poverty." This, more than anything, accounted for its rapturous reception. The approach had considerable support among professors at the University of Chicago. For example, a paper on the hostility of welfare recipients that David wrote for his sociology class—the "small scale study" he alluded to in his *Chicago Maroon Magazine* article—had originally echoed our father's thinking. "It has long been my feeling that relief should be given only when a man refuses to work," David wrote. "Harry Hopkins, Franklin Roosevelt's 'Minister of Relief,' had vision that today's administrators lack. He gave men work instead of dole and lifted not only the economy but also the men involved in the old WPA." His professor disagreed. In response to David's conclusion that "the institution of relief" robbed a person of "the self-respect that is a necessary part of . . . social integration," his professor argued: "Not proved. Absence of self-respect may lead to avoidance of work."[22]

David's horrified observation of our father's ultimately futile struggles with destructive tenants, combined with the intellectual atmosphere at the University of Chicago, predisposed him toward a psychological and cultural—rather than economic—interpretation of welfare recipients' antisocial behavior. His resulting essay was lauded because it reflected what was fast becoming conventional wisdom about the roots of urban decay. After all, even Martin Luther King Jr. couldn't remedy Chicago's slums, the argument went. Clearly the problem must lie deeper, in the slum residents' own background. This fit with convention goes a long way toward explaining the lack of skepticism that greeted a teenage boy's article, with its many undocumented claims.

Nothing signaled David's intention to defend our father and other landlords as much as his choice of Block to play the starring role in his piece. Block's feelings about the limited options available to landlords were no secret. The character's silly name was a hint to those in the know. "Norris Morris" was David's play on "Norris Vitchek," the sympathetic blockbuster described in Alfred Balk's 1962 essay "Confessions of a Block-Buster." And "Morris" was much like Irving Block himself: a salty, plainspoken man who happily punctured liberals' most revered beliefs. But David's choice also expressed a new closeness that had developed between Block and our family, having to do—as always—with the buildings.

In June 1965, Block received a letter from my father, just before his surgery at the Mayo Clinic. If the surgery's outcome wasn't good, his wish was for Block to look after his family's interests. "Otherwise," my father added, "I'll be back to abuse you myself." Block was badly shaken by his friend's death and took seriously his responsibility not only to advise Clarice but to watch out for her children. David described Block's attitude toward him as "avuncular." For Block—a man who enjoyed mentoring young people and who had three daughters but no sons—the feeling might have been more paternal. Block often spoke to David about our father. He told him that it was not Mark's fault that his buildings decayed. No small landlord had a chance in Lawndale—not with tenants as destructive as those typically found in that neighborhood. As Block explained, our father's fate was proof, if any more was needed, that tenants, and not landlords, were the cause of the slums.[23]

Block even served as David's legal counsel. On August 25, just after Martin Luther King Jr. announced the march in Cicero, David and another reporter from the *Chicago Maroon* went there to find out what the "man in the street" felt about King's plan. When a Cicero woman complained to the police that she had found their questions upsetting, the two were arrested for disorderly conduct. Irving Block defended the boys. Despite the vigorous attack of the opposing counsel, who baited the University of Chicago undergraduates for thinking that they are "so intelligent, but you are not intelligent enough to realize what you are doing to this poor lady," Block got the charges dropped. A *Maroon* article about the incident included a photograph of the two boys and their lawyer, with Block standing protectively close to David.[24]

Block also did his best to help Clarice. This was a difficult time for my mother. She had to find a way to support herself and her five children. Probate records show that my father's estate was valued at $2,603, which was not enough to cover legal fees and the cost of his funeral, much less our debts or daily expenses. At the time of Mark's death, Clarice was forty-seven years old. She had a high school education and the only paid job she'd ever held was secretarial.

What the records did not reveal was that, although Clarice had no money, she did own property: the single-family South Shore home as well as four Lawndale buildings. My father had put the properties "in trust" in Clarice's name; they did not appear as part of his estate because legally Clarice already owned them. These buildings were Mark's sole legacy, passed on with one piece of financial advice: Clarice was to hold on to them, the product of twenty years of shared struggle, "no matter how rough it may be."

It was a hard legacy to honor. By the fall of 1965, Clarice was thousands of dollars in debt to the painters, contractors, coal providers, and pest control companies that Mark had hired in his ongoing efforts to maintain his buildings.[25] She owed mortgage payments on all of them. She had no money to cover the upcoming winter's coal bills. She was concerned that a manager for the buildings had allowed in tenants who vandalized the apartments and didn't pay their rent. In sum, the buildings were quicksand. Every month she held on to them dragged her further into debt. They also presented an even worse prospect. David told me that one of our father's anxieties toward the end of his life was that "a fire might break out" and "he might be blamed."[26] After his death, a small fire did break out in one of the apartments; apparently a tenant had thrown a lit match into an overstuffed closet. My mother faced the dreadful possibility that the buildings might not only bring her financial ruin; they might implicate her in an innocent person's death.[27]

Clarice decided to sell the buildings. It was an agonizing decision that meant going against her husband's dying request—though Mark himself had realized that it was not possible to hold on to all four properties. In the year before his death, he tried to sell the Kilbourn Avenue twelve-flat. But after several months, he wrote his sister Helen, he had not "even received a call" expressing interest.[28] The decision to sell also meant a huge financial loss. My parents may have paid close to $50,000 for the six-flat they owned on Congress Street, and more than that for the other buildings, all of which were twelve-flats.[29] They had come within three years of paying off the mortgages completely. Clarice knew that she was unlikely to get anywhere near the amounts they had paid. Indeed, given the difficulties Mark had encountered trying to find a buyer for the Kilbourn Avenue building, she was not sure she'd be able to sell them at all.

Irving Block, however, ran in different circles than Mark. He couldn't exactly sell the buildings for Clarice, but if she wished, he could do something else. He could "take the buildings off her hands." It was not a complete giveaway. Block's buyers were willing to pay Clarice something for the four multi-unit structures: they offered her two thousand dollars—in total.

My mother was shocked. She knew that the properties had declined in value, but she believed that they were easily worth $10,000 each. She suggested that Block sell off the twelve-flats on Gladys, Kilbourn, and Jackson, which were the most difficult to manage and the most expensive to maintain. She would hold on to the smallest building, the six-flat on Congress Street, where she and her family had lived for many years. The Congress Street mortgage was almost entirely paid off, the building was in reasonably good shape, and it was currently rented out to responsible tenants. It had the potential to provide my mother with the small but steady income that she desperately needed.[30]

But Block's buyers had their conditions. They were willing to take over the larger buildings, but only if the well-maintained six-flat was thrown in as well. "She felt really crushed by that," David recalled. "All those years of sacrifice, all those years of counting on the buildings eventually providing some security, only to lose it all." The precise process by which the property transfer occurred remained opaque to him: "To this day it's a mystery. She was presented with a fait accompli." Irving Block "advised her to go ahead, or even set it up in such a way that she had no choice, and she did not have the strength to oppose him. . . . He was appointed by Dad. We had to assume he was looking out for our best interests."[31]

My mother's harsh experience was similar to that of other Jewish residents of Lawndale who stayed "too long." Whatever their personal convictions, they were ultimately forced to sell or even give away their property to slumlords. Their financial loss—as well as their overwhelming feelings of powerlessness—left many embittered. But the ironies in my mother's case were particularly brutal. Shortly after she sold the twelve-flat on Kilbourn for approximately $500, it came into the possession of Margaret Balin, the wife of West Side property manager Gilbert Balin. He immediately put the property into a trust with Exchange National Bank. A few months later, it had been resold on contract for $13,000. The sales agent was Moe Forman, who had recently taken on Gil Balin as a business partner and protégé.[32]

Block was certainly aware of my father's battles against exploitative contract sellers like Moe Forman. But he must also have believed that in an imperfect world he had done the best he could by Clarice. He relieved her of properties that were dragging her down, and if, in the process, he helped some small businessmen make a reasonable profit, that was fine, too. As the Norris Morris figure explains in David's article, Lawndale landlords were able to make a modest living out of buildings that housed destructive tenants solely because they had paid so little for the buildings in the first place: "'The only way I can make a profit is because I buy buildings from landlords who are desperate to get out. I agree to take over and finish paying off the mortgage and the building is mine for a song.'" Although Morris complains about the difficulties of managing slum buildings, apparently these difficulties lessened if one managed *many* such buildings. "'I own enough buildings, so that I can make a living by devoting full time to running them,'" David has Morris explain. "'But it's nothing I can retire on—just a pretty reasonable living.'"[33]

Given David's knowledge that Block was selling our father's buildings "for a song," it was probably comforting for him to believe Morris/Block's argument that there were no evil slumlords in this scenario, only over-whelmed individuals "desperate to get out" and rough but pragmatic men who had the stomach to make a "pretty reasonable living" by running such buildings. David's desire to believe this version of events might explain why he gave strong editorial backing to Morris's argument that owning slum property was no longer profitable, not even yielding enough money for owners to pay their mortgages. Morris's claims had to be true. "How else can one explain the abandoned buildings all over Lawndale?" David wrote.[34] Left unsaid was a bitter truth: Lawndale real estate was indeed still profitable, but only for those who had no intention of maintaining their buildings.

David's involvement with Lawndale ended in 1967. That year, in part as a result of an enthusiastic letter of recommendation written by Joseph Alsop, David won a Rhodes Scholarship. He left for Oxford the following fall, and although he pursued a career in journalism, he never returned to the preoccupations of the essay that first earned him recognition.[35] He also never learned of the surprising developments at 3901 West Jackson—the building where he witnessed the shocking contrasts of filth and clean-liness that so vividly demonstrated to him the destructive effects of welfare. What happened at our father's former building ultimately under-cut the conclusions of David's article as well as mainstream arguments about welfare recipients and the culture of poverty.

By 1967, the Jackson Street building was in the hands of L. J. Epstein, an attorney and long-established neighborhood slumlord.[36] The building's tenants, who were, as David had believed, mostly on public aid, soon experienced the repercussions of the sale. In January, when Chicago was hit by a storm that buried some sections of the city in six feet of snow, their new landlord neglected to heat the building. The main water pipe froze and then burst, flooding the basement. A woman was living in that basement with twelve children, two of whom were ill and needed a doc-tor immediately.[37]

One tenant, a Tennessee migrant and mother of four named Ruby Kirk, heard that a new priest at a nearby church, Monsignor John J. Egan, helped people in bad situations. She called him, and he contacted Sears, Roebuck, asking them to provide the women and children of 3901 West

Jackson with blankets. Nuns from his church waded through the snow and retrieved the two sick children, whom they carried to paramedics. Egan also called a coal company and demanded that they deliver coal to the building. When the company said their trucks could not get through the snow-buried streets, he told them to carry the sacks in by piggyback if they had to; the people in the building needed heat and they needed it right away.[38]

The immediate crisis passed but the property remained in dismal shape. Kirk and some other women from the building traveled to Epstein's home in suburban Lincolnwood and talked to his neighbors about the building's condition. In response, Epstein made a few repairs, but it was only "minor patch work." Inspectors cited Epstein for numerous code violations, but as one tenant recalled, "A day before we'd go to court, a workman would come and drive a nail or two. So the case would be continued on the ground that work was in progress." Finally, Kirk had an idea. She suggested that the tenants collect the rents, put the money in a special account, and use it to fix up the building. She pointed out that public aid officials sometimes withheld rents from particularly bad landlords, so why shouldn't they do the same? With the exception of a sole holdout, the rest of the building went along with the plan.[39]

Meanwhile they kept up the pressure on Epstein to make necessary repairs. In September 1968, the tenants held a "Chicago Slum Open House," inviting clubs and civic organizations to see the condition of their building. Kirk was "amazed" by the "number of white people" who showed up in response to their invitations. "They walked over our rotting floors and touched the soft plaster and said they had never seen anything like it," she recalled. Still, the real turning point came only in 1969. One day that January, Kirk was sitting in her living room, removing her boots. Moments later she was knocked out cold by a blow to the back of the head. When she came to, she realized what had happened—a chunk of the wall, about two feet wide, had come loose and fallen upon her. This was the final straw. After that, Kirk insisted that Housing Court Judge Franklin I. Kral visit the building. Kral was so horrified by what he saw that he decided to take the property away from Epstein and appoint a court receiver to manage it. Convinced that "the tenants were the only ones who cared" about the building, Kral took the highly unusual step of naming Ruby Kirk the receiver of 3901 West Jackson. "You'll never get the repairs done," Epstein snarled at Kirk. "What would you bet on it?" she replied.[40]

Like open occupancy, the placing of buildings into receivership was a solution to slum conditions that had been knocking around for years. The semipublic Chicago Dwellings Association had been created in 1966 to act as a receiver for slum buildings, with the idea that it would use rents to make repairs. By June, director Ira Bach reported the agency's accomplishments to date: "We've been named receiver for three or four buildings that are in bad shape, and we did get one torn down."[41] Toward the end of that year, the Community Renewal Foundation, a group affiliated with the Congregational Church, received a $4 million loan from HUD to rehabilitate apartment buildings in Lawndale and in the South Side neighborhood of Kenwood, which were then to be turned over to joint ownership by the tenants.[42]

But these receivership projects were all too little, too late. Receivership might have worked in the 1950s, when Chicago slumlords were just beginning their buying sprees and the properties they grabbed were still solid enough to make renovations possible based on rental income alone.[43] By the time the idea was implemented, however, the buildings had degenerated past the point of repair. In addition, adequate resources were never put behind the receivership-and-rehabilitation program. In 1969, the Chicago Dwellings Association was shut down. It had been so severely underfunded—its budget allocated a laughable $20 per apartment for rehabilitation—that it never stood a chance.[44]

It was in the spring of 1969, in the midst of press stories about the death of the receivership idea, that Judge Kral put Ruby Kirk in charge of Epstein's twelve-flat. Kirk and eleven other tenants formed a corporation, Chicago's Best Landlord, Inc., to serve as the official receiver. The *Chicago Daily News* noted that their control of the building could be the answer to "one of the city's toughest problems: Who will repair the slums?" Kral added, "Nothing like it had ever been done before, but I realized that if the slums are ever to be eradicated the people who live there must do the job."[45]

The first challenge facing the tenants was the repairs. An architectural firm estimated that rehabilitating the building would cost $75,000. With the help of an attorney who showed Kirk "how the system really worked," the tenants got a loan to cover the costs. Kirk also made herself the general contractor for the project. Those who doubted that the women of

3901 West Jackson could handle the challenge didn't know much about Ruby Kirk. Back in Tennessee, her father had made his living hauling logs, cutting timber, and making lumber. Although he told her that this was men's work, she had insisted that it was "everyone's work" and convinced him to teach her everything he knew. She discovered that she "loved to fix and nail stuff." So instead of suffering incompetent repairmen she hired her own, that is, people she trusted. She also taught some of the other women in the building to do repairs.[46]

The tenants' second step was to obtain ownership of the building, which required that a group of Lawndale women, most of whom were on public aid, receive fair access to credit. Judge Kral noted the low odds: "Imagine a black woman who is on welfare with six kids and no husband asking for a loan. . . . Impossible," he commented. But Kirk (who had four children, not six) had a large imagination. When First National Bank refused her request for a mortgage loan and suggested that she look else-where for help—to a charitable foundation, perhaps—she set them straight. "I told them that we are different," she recalled. "We know the rules of society and one of those rules requires you to borrow money and pay it back. We want to be part of the system." She would not back down. "We said, 'You're the First National Bank, and we're the "First Tenants" to say that we'll run our own building'"—it was only natural, then, that the First should loan to the First. When the bank asked how the tenants would pay off their loan, Kirk explained that they would use the rent money. After all, "That's how Mr. Epstein said he did it." Ultimately First National arranged for Chicago's Best Landlord, Inc., to get an FHA-backed mort-gage to buy the building outright. As Alan Boles, a young man who lived in the building, commented, Kirk achieved the "impossible" because "white people were kind of intimidated by her and impressed because she would make these demands and refuse to take no for an answer."[47] To mark their triumph, Kirk and the other tenants had the words "Chicago's Best Land-lord, Inc." inscribed in stone over the building's entrance, where it is visible to this day.

Boles observed that Kirk was an "amazing woman" of awesome deter-mination. Slender and delicately built but fearless, "she would chase after the drug dealers on the corner with a kitchen knife. She decided she was going to whip this building into shape." When Boles moved into 3901

West Jackson, the building whose "rotting floors" and "soft plaster" had shocked visitors only a year before now appeared solid and well maintained.[48]

Alongside Kirk's determination, there were two other reasons for her success. The first was that by 1969 the policies of the Federal Housing Administration had changed. Partially in response to the riots of the mid-1960s, the FHA now insured mortgage loans in black urban neighborhoods like Lawndale. The possibility of obtaining FHA insurance made the First National Bank's loan economically feasible. The second reason was the condition of the building. Many structures in Lawndale had been milked by slum landlords for years, but this was not the case for 3901 West Jackson. L. J. Epstein had neglected it for two years, but before that my father had done his best to maintain it. The result, as Judge Kral noted, was that despite the smelly hallway and crumbling plaster, 3901 West Jackson was "structurally sound." The tenants, too, saw the possibilities in the gracious, well-built redbrick twelve-flat. "We care about the building," Kirk told reporters that year. "We want it to be beautiful, the way it once was."[49] She succeeded. "We fixed it up and kept it up—it's a solid building," Kirk, still a resident, said in 2001.

The building that had once housed tenants who had contributed to my father's financial ruin turned out to have a better future. Within three short years it became a symbol not of the inherently destructive nature of welfare recipients, but of the inspiring resourcefulness of such people. In 1966, in the wake of our father's death, my brother probably would have had a hard time conceiving of such an outcome. The outsiders who lauded David's essay never acknowledged the institutional obstacles that prevented ghetto residents, especially women on welfare, from upgrading their communities. Nor did they recognize that grit and determination, along with a few strokes of good fortune, could sometimes overcome those obstacles.

There was one commonsense point on which David Satter and Ruby Kirk agreed: you couldn't upgrade a building if it contained bad tenants. As Alan Boles recalls, although Kirk was a single mother on welfare, she could be "very disdainful" of other aid recipients. When they didn't follow the rules, she "kicked a lot of them out." Those who remained "were people that got along with her and met her standards."[50] Destructive tenants could doom a building—but as Ruby Kirk clearly understood, destructive behavior bore no direct connection to whether or not an individual was receiving aid from the state.

When David's article came out, Irving Block sent him an effusive letter. "Not only have I read it, but my partner has read it and I have had other people sit down and read the article," he wrote. "I wonder whether I could obtain half a dozen reprints for which I would be happy to pay."

Block's letter also hinted at deeper feelings. "Taking into consideration your natural liberal tendencies on the one hand, balanced by the horrible experience that your mother is having in the area on the other, I think you have been quite objective," he wrote. "I only feel sad as I read the article at the thought that the forces involved and the emotions involved are such that there may be no solution in my time. I hope there is in yours."[51]

For Block, the story was hardly over. In 1969, he was sixty-nine years old. He was a chain smoker with a hacking cough that would soon turn into emphysema. He had spent his life building up a small but respectable local practice. And he was about to embark upon the most public case of his life. Whether he liked it or not, Block would soon be enmeshed in highly public confrontations with one of the most beloved priests in Chicago. He would experience for himself both the "forces" and the "emotions" involved in a battle over Lawndale's future.

EIGHT

ORGANIZING LAWNDALE

Ruby Kirk's triumph was part of an activist surge that would transform Lawndale, and this time it would be insiders who would play the major role. A not inconsiderable factor in this surge was the appointment in January 1966 of a new pastor to Lawndale's Presentation parish. The job—hardly a plum position—happened to have fallen on one of the city's most prominent Catholic liberals—Monsignor John J. Egan.

Ironically, the move was ordered by Cardinal John Patrick Cody, the recently appointed head of the Archdiocese of Chicago, as part of an effort to halt the social activism of Chicago's priests. Although Cody came with the reputation of a Church liberal, he deemed the city's wealth of priest activists as a movement to be stopped at all costs. "I understand there are some troublemakers in this city," he told a conservative crony. He would "put them in their proper place."[1]

Among the first of the "troublemakers" whom Cody moved to contain was Monsignor Egan, who was in charge of the archdiocese's Office of Urban Affairs, an innovative, nationally known body that trained pastors in community organizing. The forty-nine-year-old Egan had participated in practically every agency in Chicago that dealt with either urban or religious matters, transforming the OUA into what one commentator called "the light and the power of the Church's city apostolate."[2] To Chicagoans, his sudden appointment to Presentation parish was clearly an effort to silence him. Egan's transfer was a "blow to liberalism," the *Chicago Daily News* reported. It was probably meant as "the first step in 'phasing out' the influential archdiocesan Office of Urban Affairs." "Put to Pasture?" read its headline about Egan's new job assignment.[3]

Presentation parish was as far from a center of influence as one could get. In 1950, it had been an all-white parish of 1,600 families, but by 1966, the area was 100 percent black and only 400 families remained associated with the church. Presentation Church was a decrepit structure with peeling paint, a filthy basement, and a fragile furnace that gave out regularly during the winter months. It was also in dire financial shape. To run its programs and maintain the plant, Presentation's former pastor bequeathed to Egan a cash balance of $382.

But as Cody would soon learn, the idea that Jack Egan could be silenced simply by putting him in charge of a declining parish in an impoverished, non-Catholic neighborhood was profoundly misconceived. "Archbishop Cody had an unbelievable power of underestimating people," Egan recalled. "We were Chicagoans. We understood power. We were survivors." Egan arrived in Lawndale just as Martin Luther King's Chicago crusade was focusing national attention on the West Side. If Cody didn't understand the significance of the moment, Egan did. "I'm living with black people for the first time in my life," Egan recalled. "Archbishop Cody couldn't have given me a greater gift. I don't think he thought of it that way. I think he thought he was getting rid of me."[4]

Despite being a white Irish Catholic, Egan brought to Lawndale a body of experience that Martin Luther King Jr.'s Southern-based SCLC cadre inevitably lacked: a lifetime's worth of connections to local social networks, a decadelong immersion in every aspect of Chicago housing activism, and a deep commitment to the direct engagement with the local community favored by James Bevel's rival, organizer Saul Alinsky.

Just months before his new assignment, Egan explained his approach to a national gathering of Catholic Social Action adherents. "In a democracy, it is presumed that people generate their own social structure, strength, and direction. If the ravages of unemployment, segregation and family collapse atrophy this ability," he said, others, including the Church, must step in to "develop and train competent, knowledgeable community organizers" who can help create "indigenously powerful" community groups. Local action would benefit not only the poor but "*the entire urban democratic fabric.*"[5] Egan encouraged religious activists in impoverished neighborhoods to "hit the pavement and start knocking on doors" in order to learn from the community. The poor "are as smart as you," he reminded his listeners, but "their diction is not the diction that makes the secretary at the other end of the phone pay very close attention to what is being said." It was therefore essential that Church activists and "deprived" community members cooperate: they supply "the facts and all sorts of insights . . . [and] you can be the mouthpiece."[6]

Egan's transfer to Presentation gave him the chance to put his beliefs into practice. He immediately set about transforming the church into a hub of community life. He had the great fortune to be aided by Peggy Roach, a lay activist who devoted her talents to supporting his work. As Egan's biographer put it, Egan was "the steam engine, spitting out visionary schemes [and] subtle maneuvers. . . . Peggy was the steel in the engine, . . . keeping his drive focused and his projects on track." Another talented laywoman, Ann Coe Pugliese, came up with a brilliant solution to the church's material needs. She launched a newsletter, titled *Friends of Presentation,* which was sent to the 1,500 people on Egan's personal mailing list. It described the most pressing problems facing Presentation and suggested that readers pledge $2 a month toward solving them. The appeal netted $4,000 a month, which was enough to cover the parish's immediate expenses (but not enough to replace the faulty furnace).[7]

Next, Egan moved to the issue closest to his heart: training community organizers. He divided Lawndale into "parishes" of one block each. He told Chicago-area seminarians that, if they wanted to have a true "inner city experience," they could take one of these mini-parishes as their own. They were to show up at Presentation Saturday mornings at nine and spend the day immersing themselves in the world of their block. The goal was to transform that block into a community. "You've got to get to know every person in every house or apartment," Egan told the seminarians. "You're to find out who is ill; who is out of work; who has housing problems; whose kids aren't in school. At the end of the day, you're to report to me on every problem you uncover. We'll discuss then what we are going to do about it."[8]

Egan called his program Operation Saturation. By the fall of 1966, he had recruited thirty seminarians to make weekly visits to one-block areas in Lawndale.[9] He also brought in volunteers from all over Chicago to help with everything from sweeping the streets to distributing clothing to neighborhood children. Egan's enthusiasm for Lawndale was contagious. "It was like an ad for Florida," one participant recalled of a notice Egan posted at one of Chicago's Catholic colleges. "'We need your talents, your competence, your compassion. Come, live with us and learn from the people. Let yourself be touched and let your heart be opened. Feel the joy here,'" the notice beckoned.[10]

The reality was somewhat more mixed. "I don't think there was a day that went by there wasn't a shooting," one Presentation worker recalled. Volunteers confronted conditions that shocked them: glass-strewn streets, abandoned buildings, and kitchen walls covered with cockroaches that wriggled into motion with the switch of a light. They faced verbal threats from teenage boys who were upset that "a bunch of grays" were infiltrating their neighborhood.[11] Most depressing, perhaps, was the reaction of some older Lawndale residents to the sudden influx of young white Catholics knocking on their doors. "People would say we were in peril," a volunteer remembered. "They would say 'What are you doing? You'd better get out.'" Still, according to another volunteer, although "there was reluctance to talk," in the end "there weren't very many [seminarians] told they couldn't come in." And Egan had not misled them. As Presentation's school principal noted, "Everything important going on in the country was reflected on the West Side of Chicago."[12]

Among those most profoundly affected by Egan's call was Jack Macnamara, a tall, slender thirty-year-old Jesuit in training from Skokie, Illinois. Macnamara's family had experienced its share of hardship. When Macnamara was in high school, his father was diagnosed with multiple sclerosis. Then he developed cancer. Until his death six years later, Macnamara's father was unable to work, and Macnamara, the oldest of five children, helped support the family. At eighteen he enrolled as a full-time student at Loyola University, while also working forty hours a week at Delta Airlines—the midnight to 8:00 a.m. shift. Macnamara next entered the University of Chicago Law School, but after one year he quit law school and entered the Society of Jesus. In the fall of 1966 Macnamara had just concluded a mandatory year of teaching Latin at a Jesuit high school in

Cincinnati, and was now completing his studies to be a Jesuit at the Bellarmine School of Theology.[13]

After hearing Egan's pitch at his seminary, Macnamara committed himself to visiting a Lawndale block every week. He learned the rules of community organizing from Tom Gaudette, who had been trained by Alinsky and who was now helping Egan's volunteers get their bearings. First, the organizer must learn to listen, because "the people . . . know better what their situation is than anyone." Second, "the people have to be involved in solving their own problems," since they "have the capacity within themselves" to do so. These principles made sense to Macnamara, but he was increasingly frustrated by the necessarily limited results produced by once-a-week visits. Macnamara was being taught at the seminary that "love" was the solution to the plight of the ghettos, but his encounter with the people of Lawndale brought him to a different conclusion: "What struck me is that they know how to love better than we do. What they need is some accomplishments, . . . a victory." And only committed organizers would help deliver that victory. With Egan's support, Macnamara got permission from his Jesuit supervisor, Father Robert F. Harvanek, to rent an apartment in Lawndale and move there for the summer of 1967. Using his apartment as a base, he would devote himself full-time to community organizing.[14]

Thus was born the Presentation Church Community Organization Project. To staff it, Macnamara reached out to some of the students he had taught at St. Xavier High School in Cincinnati. Macnamara "was not your usual Jesuit Latin teacher," as one class member put it. He had rushed them through the required Latin and then spent the remainder of the year discussing cutting-edge theological works such as Harvey Cox's *The Secular City,* which called for the Church to take its place at the forefront of social change. To his students, Macnamara was "an extraordinary guy who was opening our tiny narrow Catholic middle-class brains" to the pressing issues of the day. He helped them realize that their dreams were possibilities. When Peter Cassady, a student leader, announced that he wanted to get everyone in the school socially involved, Macnamara worked with him to engage the students in community life. Ultimately a remarkable 400 out of 1,300 students volunteered with social service organizations.[15]

On hearing Macnamara's plan for Lawndale, Cassady volunteered to join him and to bring some others along. Soon Macnamara had a "staff" of ten former students, all of them white, under twenty, college freshmen or sophomores. The young men agreed to spend the summer in Macnamara's cockroach-infested apartment close to Presentation, "next door to the Red Rooster grocery store, where they used to pour red [soda] pop on the meat to make it look good."[16] One bedroom had two sets of bunk beds sleeping four. In the other, the bunk beds were triple height, sleeping six. The students' instructions were vague: they were to go door-to-door and to "listen." Their weekly pay was "five dollars and unlimited cigarettes."[17]

Over the summer, Macnamara and his students set out to organize Lawndale. They didn't know much about the neighborhood's history. Until about 1963, Chicagoans still spoke of Lawndale as an "old, worn-out Jewish area" or "ghetto" whose population had always been "very poor." But by 1967, the myth that Lawndale had been "an area of middle-income Jews" that inexplicably decayed once "low-income Negroes" moved in was already in place. Sometimes the fanciful elevation of Lawndale's past was even more extreme. According to an early newspaper story about Macnamara and his organizers, the young men hoped to learn why the walls were now crumbling in "homes that, a generation ago, had been among the finest in the nation."[18]

The organizers were energetic and resourceful. They challenged neighborhood kids to basketball: if the teenagers won, they each got two dollars, but if the college boys won, the losers had to volunteer two hours of their time or bring other boys to a meeting to plan a summer program.[19] On learning that Lawndale received less garbage collection than other neighborhoods despite its greater population, Macnamara's boys staged a "dump-in" during which they deposited uncollected, overflowing bins of garbage on the steps of City Hall. Shortly thereafter, the city began regular garbage pickups in Lawndale. When the students realized that there was no playground for area children, they bussed local youngsters to a playground in Mayor Daley's all-white Bridgeport neighborhood. After three tense "play-ins" in Bridgeport, the city suddenly found the resources to construct a playground on one of Lawndale's many empty lots. Construction began on July 3 and was completed by July 18.[20]

These small victories weren't enough, however, to mobilize the neighborhood. The Presentation Church Community Organization Project did a lot of listening during the summer of 1967, but the complaints the students heard from residents didn't add up to any single issue they could organize around. "It was total frustration," one student recalled.[21]

Then one day something changed. Macnamara was making a routine visit to a parishioner named Ozirea Arbertha, who lived with her mother and four children in a two-flat building. Arbertha's husband, David, had been killed in an automobile accident a year before. Now she endured a three-hour daily commute to work nights at a far South Side post office, where she earned $5,800 a year. Her mother worked full-time as a nurse's aid, earning $3,400 a year. Despite their combined annual income of over $9,000, Arbertha was in a financial quagmire. "If I just didn't have this big house payment every month, I think I could make ends meet," she told Macnamara, as tears streamed down her cheeks. She told him that she paid $240 a month for her building. Macnamara was shocked. His own family had struggled to make mortgage payments of $108 a month on a $12,000-a-year income. He understood immediately that "there was something really out of line" with Arbertha's payments.[22]

In subsequent meetings Arbertha told Macnamara more of her story. She and her husband had purchased their building on contract in 1959, for $28,000, from the real estate firm of Fushanis and Forman. "Yes, we knew it was an awfully high price," she told him. "But we had looked so long. Out South, all over the West Side—in every neighborhood that would take Negroes. . . . And this was the best we could find. So we decided to make the sacrifice." The Arberthas spent an additional $8,000 to replace the building's ancient furnace and rickety back porch and to add new sewer and water lines, new plumbing, and new floors for the kitchen and bathroom. Still, they had managed to make every payment, until David's sudden death. Without his salary of $9,000 a year, the family's income was cut in half. Life had been a desperate struggle ever since.[23]

At first Macnamara did not understand the full complexities of Arbertha's position. "I did not know what a real estate contract was," he admitted.[24] If Macnamara didn't have the larger picture, however, his friend and spiritual mentor Jack Egan did. He told Macnamara that it was "absolutely necessary" for his organizers "to get their facts and to do their homework" on this issue. He also asked John McKnight, the Midwest director of the U.S. Commission on Civil Rights, to educate the group on the contract sales problem.[25]

With McKnight's help, Macnamara soon mastered the "fairly complicated and painful" technicalities of conducting title searches to uncover the real owners of a building and what they paid for it. On investigation, he learned that three months before selling the building to the Arberthas for $28,000, Fushanis and Forman had purchased it for $15,000. He also learned that this transaction was typical of the vast majority of buildings on her block. "I was horrified," Macnamara recalled. "Not so much that people would do this sort of thing but because of the way it affected the lives of the people who were victimized."[26]

Next, his group decided to research the property records for buildings in an eight-block area in Lawndale. They found that almost every building had been sold to the current residents on contract at grossly inflated prices. They were stunned not only by the devastating financial consequences of contract selling for Lawndale's residents but by the enormity and ease of the speculators' profits. As Mark Splain, one of the former St. Xavier students who joined Macnamara in Lawndale, recalled, "you could flip these properties with no cash," making it "an unbelievable capitalist dream" of easy riches.[27]

Here finally was an issue that could mobilize Lawndale, and Macnamara was eager to begin. But Egan was skeptical about using contract sales as an organizing focus. Exploitative contract selling was "the worst-kept secret in Chicago," he told Macnamara. "City Hall knows about it. Real estate firms know about it. But no one is saying anything about it because the power behind contract buying is so great some people have been killed who have tried to correct the situation." Saul Alinsky was equally discouraging. "If I were you I would leave it alone," he said, adding that a friend of his had "died trying."[28]

These odd mentions of people who had "died trying" to stop exploitative contract sales were probably distorted references to my father, who, as Egan and Alinsky knew, had devoted years to that battle and had died, exhausted, at the age of forty-nine.[29] Their hesitancy to tackle contract sales had to do less with personal fear than with the enormity of the undertaking. As one of the college students pointed out, echoing Egan, the scale of contract selling was so huge that it simply "could not have happened without the permission and the complicity of the Democratic Party." As another discovered, the city's judiciary—in all likelihood the place where challenges to the contract system would end up—contained numerous patronage workers who "themselves speculated in 'contract properties' . . . or represented those who did."[30] Alinsky and Egan were savvy enough to know that open challenges to Daley's machine were doomed to failure.

But Macnamara would not be deterred. "To hell with you," was his immediate reaction to Alinsky's discouraging comments. He vehemently disagreed with Alinsky's requirement that an organization's focus be readily comprehensible, easy to mobilize around, and ultimately winnable—a perfectly logical strategy if issues were simply a means to the end of creating group solidarity. "My feeling is that if you get involved in something . . . it's not simply about building the organization," Macnamara said. "Maybe we have to go after some things even if we're not sure of the outcome." He added, "Here were these people who we had gotten started on this . . . who really wanted to do something about it." He wasn't going to drop the issue because it was too difficult.[31]

As the summer drew to an end, Macnamara felt he had just scratched the surface of the problems plaguing Lawndale. He couldn't leave now. So, for the second time, he petitioned his Jesuit supervisors for a postponement of his theological studies. For the second time, they granted his request. His staff, however, had to return to school. Several of the boys were eager to continue working with the project, but in the fall of 1967, nineteen-year-olds who were not in college might be drafted and sent to Vietnam. This was a risk Macnamara could not ask them to take.

He came up with a solution. He met with the deans of his volunteers' colleges and proposed that the students receive college credit for community organizing. Almost to his own surprise, he succeeded. "We're very conservative here," the dean of Holy Cross College said, "but I think this is something we should do."[32]

Macnamara's band now returned with renewed dedication to the task of organizing Lawndale. Some worked with the tenants of several slum buildings to pressure landlords into improving property maintenance. Others supported Lawndale resident Ruby Kirk, who had just begun to organize her building at 3901 West Jackson.[33] But contract sales remained a priority. Following Egan's command to "get their facts and to do their homework," they spent most of their time—"hundreds of hours"—conducting "brain-numbing title-searches" in the basement of City Hall, or what student organizer Michael Gecan described as "the sixth rung of hell at the Chicago title and trust offices." They went "building by building, day after day, that's what we did," he recalled. The result was a rock-solid factual grounding. "I mean, we had this thing down cold."[34]

Armed with detailed financial information on practically every building in Lawndale, Macnamara's organizers walked the neighborhood. The months they had already put in paid off: "People would talk to us on their stoop or they'd invite us in," Splain recalled. Eventually the organizers "got around to asking fairly direct questions about when people bought their house and whom they bought it from, how much it cost, and what their monthly payments were." It soon became apparent that, although almost everybody on the block had bought on contract, nobody really talked about it. Their silence wasn't a matter of denial, Splain said, but simply a conviction that "this was the way the world worked. That's how people bought. They basically worked two jobs or more to try to keep the property up and not lose the property."[35]

In January 1968, after months of one-on-one discussions, the students convinced about a dozen Lawndale contract buyers to come to a meeting at Presentation, where Macnamara explained all he had learned about the exploitative structure of contract sales. His talk was met with "absolute, dead silence." No one wanted to admit publicly that they had been "taken."[36] But Ruth Wells, a Lawndale resident who had already been working with Macnamara on the issue, would soon put an end to this reticence.

For several months Wells had been tangling with her contract seller, Moe Forman, over a $1,500 fee he had added to her already high monthly payments. She and her husband, James, had bought their two-flat in 1959 and never missed a payment. Their contract specified that after half the balance was paid the couple could switch to a regular mortgage. But now that they were half paid up, Forman had come up with a mysterious additional charge. Wells was outraged. "If this man could just put $1,500 on my bill out of the sky like this, I'll never finish paying," she said. "It's just like blackmail, only I don't know what I've been blackmailed for." As she recalled, she was "tired of being cheated every way I turned—whether it was for purchases of the home or of groceries. . . . I'd had this bad, tight feeling all these years and now I was going to do something about it."[37]

Wells talked to Father Egan, who put her in touch with Macnamara's group. With the help of Sister Andrew, a nun who had formerly worked as a real estate agent, Macnamara found out that Wells's building, which she and her husband had bought for $23,000, had been purchased by Forman only the month before, for $13,500. They convinced Wells to get an FHA appraisal of her home's current value. To her shock, her $23,000 building, in which she and her husband had installed a new bath and kitchen, a new roof, new wiring, a new back porch, fencing, new front steps, and a sidewalk, was now valued at just $14,750.[38]

Macnamara and Sister Andrew encouraged Wells to act on her own behalf. "Go and see the man yourself. Tell him what you know and ask for something off," they urged. Wells finally agreed to confront Forman in his office. It was a cold day in December 1967. She was accompanied by Macnamara, Sister Andrew, and Father Egan. This eased her nerves. With all those people there to back her up, she felt protected: "In case he comes across the desk, I believe they'll catch him."

Wells's first impression of Forman was that he didn't look good. "You could tell he ate all the wrong stuff. . . . He just looked like that," she recalled. Forman was recalcitrant. He told her that the $1,500 was for insurance. Wells struggled to contain her fury. "Maybe you got us mixed up with one of your other properties. I don't live on North [Lake] Shore Drive," she told him, referring to an elegant white neighborhood. "I live in *Lawndale*. We don't have any mansions out there to be paying $1,500 for insurance." Wells asked how he slept at night. "He said he slept very well except when he worked a little too hard at the office," she recalled. And why not? "He's getting checks in the mail every month, educating his kids, and if you're ragged and hungry that's *your* business. But I told him *why* I thought he slept pretty good. He said when he got ready for spiritual advice he definitely would not come to me. I thanked him and told him I wouldn't go to him either."[39]

Wells demanded to see a copy of the insurance policy. As Forman reached across the table to hand her the forms, Wells noted that "his hand began to quiver like a leaf in the wind." In years of dealings with Forman, this was the first time she had ever seen him nervous. Earlier that day, Wells had prayed to God for a sign. "I wanted to know if I was wrong. If I was wrong I would not return to this man, but if I was right I would like to go ahead and fight this thing to the bitter end." Forman's shakiness was the sign she needed. "I thought, 'Somebody done touched him and let him know. He's feeling something he's never felt before: *guilt!*' He's all trembling and shaking, really upset. And I thought to myself, 'I didn't upset him, but I know *who* did.'"[40]

In the end, Forman refused to budge on the insurance charge, but he agreed to cut $1,000 off her contract payment. "One thousand dollars!" she gasped as soon as she was out of his office. This was serious money. Since buying their building in 1959, she and her husband had been "going like mad just to keep up. I was afraid to miss a day's work and my husband was the same. . . . Sometimes I'd have one dollar to last all the week. I'd keep it in my wallet. I'd be afraid to break it." Macnamara congratulated her on her success: "That's the first time you ever made one thousand dollars in an hour!"[41]

Invigorated by this experience, Wells was among those attending the small gathering of contract buyers that Macnamara arranged at Presentation. She sat through that first tense meeting thinking, "*Something* is missing there, but I don't know what it is." Then she figured out what it was. When Macnamara gathered people for a second meeting, in January 1968, the featured speaker was not Macnamara but Wells. She had never addressed an audience before. Other than Macnamara, she didn't know a soul in the room; between her long hours at work and her responsibilities at home, she'd never had time to get to know her neighbors. She was so frightened that she held on to the back of a chair just to steady herself. But when Wells spoke, she was eloquent. She detailed her history with Moe Forman. She told the audience how she had been overcharged. Then she asked "if any of them was in the same boat."[42]

The effect was electric. Practically every hand in the room shot up. Wells encouraged the people gathered there to "tell your family and your friends, your neighbors, the people you work with, if they bought on contract they should come out."[43] At the next meeting approximately two dozen contract buyers decided to form an organization, the Contract Buyers of Lawndale (CBL). Within months, attendance at the CBL's Wednesday night meetings had snowballed beyond the wildest expectations of Presentation organizers.[44] The group expanded so quickly in part because it had a perfect target for its anger—Moe Forman.

On February 3, Wells returned to Forman's office. Since Forman said he wouldn't see her "if any of those church folks are with you," she brought along some twenty Lawndale residents instead, as well as several Presentation Church Community Organization Project workers who were not in religious orders. Of the Lawndalers, Wells recalled, "I picked out the ones I knowed had bigger mouths than mine. . . . Some of the ladies . . . love to get at people like him." Forman tried to cancel the meeting when he saw the size of the group, but they pushed their way into his office. Wells asked Forman to repeat his refusal to negotiate "so all my friends could hear it." At this point, Forman quickly offered to "deduct the $1,500" from Wells's bill along with another few thousand off the contract balance.[45]

But Wells and the others were no longer interested in individual gestures. With the help of Macnamara and his organizers, the group now had quite a bit of information on F & F Investment. They knew that Forman held contracts on several hundred buildings in their neighborhood. They knew that he had charged most of the buyers double to triple the price that he himself had paid for the buildings shortly before reselling them. They were also aware that FHA appraisals now estimated the buildings' worth as only marginally above what Forman had bought them for.

There was only one action that Forman could take to make up for what he had done. The group demanded that he renegotiate the price of every building he held on contract in Lawndale. They proposed a "fair price" formula, which consisted of his original purchase price plus an additional "fair profit" of 15 percent. They wanted credit for what they had already paid on the principal and their interest rates lowered to what they would have been on a standard mortgage. In short, they wanted Forman to reduce the debt of each contract buyer by approximately $10,000 to $15,000.[46]

Wells and her group understood that they had no legal case against Forman. "We cannot fight you through the courts because the law does not protect us," they told him. But now that his dealings were public knowledge, they expected him to negotiate.[47] When Forman refused, Wells lost her cool. "How would you like to be on television, explaining to the people coast to coast what kind of louse you are?" she blurted out. She unnerved Forman further by mentioning his daughter in college "down state," at the University of Illinois. "What is she going to tell her friends down there when she find out that what her father do for a living is beat down poor people?" she asked.[48]

The group left Forman's office that day with no promises. But Forman was shaken. He had never confronted anything like this, Wells supposed:

"All these black folk knowing the answers. And all these white folk living in Lawndale where he don't think it's safe for a white man to go."[49]

A week later, Wells attempted to meet with Forman again. This time, he was not available, the group was told. Luckily, they had a backup plan. With signs prepared and the police notified, they picketed Forman's office in the zero-degree cold. They also visited Forman's North Side neighborhood. In groups of twos, Lawndale residents knocked on his neighbors' doors. They passed out flyers that described the high price that Forman had charged them for their homes. Picketing and leafleting in downtown Chicago or in a white Chicago neighborhood was frightening. "I was a good deal scared. . . . My lips was dry. . . . I thought I was perpetrating evil," recalled Lawndale resident Clyde Ross of his first experience on a picket line. But there was no trouble. "In Forman's neighborhood several residents invited the pairs who visited them in for coffee. Many expressed sympathy with the cause," the group reported.[50]

The CBL's next move was to invite Forman to meet with Lawndale residents in a public forum to be held at Presentation Church. There they would discuss further the renegotiation of his contract holdings. They very much hoped he would attend. If he refused, they told him, they would picket his home and his office until he changed his mind.[51] Forman waited until the day before the meeting to reply, but he agreed to their request. In Lawndale, news of Forman's forthcoming appearance had an explosive effect. Over four hundred residents packed Presentation's community room, eager to confront him in person.

Forman never showed. He did, however, have a letter messengered to the meeting. It explained that he held only a partial interest in his hundreds of contract properties. The remaining interest was held by the "Estate of Lou Fushanis, deceased," which was currently tied up in probate court. Any changes to contract balances would have to pass through the Probate Division of Chicago's judicial system. Nevertheless, Forman wanted to show his good faith. "I individually am acceding to your request that the contract balances be renegotiated and that the guide lines . . . for the renegotiations are appraisals to be secured from F.H.A.," he wrote.

This news brought "a shout of joy" from the crowd. Lawndale residents would soon discover that Forman had no intention of renegotiating his contracts, but for the moment they felt a new sense of power and possibility. Once Macnamara was able to tell the media about the CBL's "million-dollar victory" over Moe Forman, "the phone rang off the hook with reporters."[52] CBL membership expanded dramatically. By April 1968, 500 Lawndale residents regularly attended the group's Wednesday night meetings. By November, participation had grown to over 1,000.[53]

The key to the CBL's success in organizing the community may well have been the commitment and maturity of its activists.[54] Within weeks of its founding, four neighborhood residents emerged as the "indigenous leadership" of the CBL. All were migrants from Mississippi and Alabama—the very people whose degraded "rural culture" both white and established black Chicagoans blamed for Lawndale's decay. Through the CBL, these migrants finally talked back to the city that had entrapped them economically and then blamed their background for their problems.

Clyde Ross, one of the four, was born in Farrell, Mississippi, in 1923, the seventh of his sharecropping parents' thirteen children. Despite growing up in a culture in which "every white man was the jury, and every white man was the policeman, and every white man was the governor," Ross wasn't raised to hate white people. His parents told him, "Don't classify all white people as the same. . . . Pick out who is a friend and who is against you." Ross's Southern background gave him important insights into the shaky foundations of white power. "White kids will attack you, but they'll never attack you by themselves. So I found out that, hey, they're afraid of me." White anxiety derived not from a fear of black violence, he concluded—after all, "black people have no police, they have no power, they have no guns, they have no murderous organizations, no Klan groups"—but from guilt. "They're afraid that someday they're going to get paid back for what they done."[55]

Ross moved to Chicago in 1947. "After you come out of the army," he said, "you couldn't stay in Mississippi no more" without a constant fight. But finding a good-paying job wasn't easy. "I had spent so much time working in the South that I didn't have no time for education. So you come here, you had to take less of a job." He found employment at the Campbell Soup Company. The work was difficult. Hot cans had to be guided down the assembly line. Workers could get badly burned. Still, it was better than the alternatives. "Campbell's Soup was a cheap job, but it was a steady job," he recalled. He started at Campbell's in 1948 and stayed there for the next twenty years.[56]

In 1961, Ross and his wife, Lillie, were expecting a child. The apartment they shared with Ross's extended family was already overcrowded, so he set out to find his own place. When he asked about a modest-looking home in a white neighborhood, the realtor told him the price was $50,000. Though the prices he was quoted in Lawndale were also outlandish—in the $25,000 range—he thought he might be able to swing it. But when he tried to apply for a mortgage the loan officer told him flatly, "We don't finance in that area." Ross recalled the humiliating experience. "He closed his little window when he said that and he never looked up again. I stood there for about five minutes to see what he was going to do. He acted like he was busy" and left Ross waiting there, as if he were invisible.[57]

Ross ended up buying a two-flat on contract from Joseph Berke. The white real estate agent showed up at Ross's home in a Cadillac with a black female secretary, ready to ferry Ross and Lillie around Lawndale. "I thought the guy must be all right if he's got all black help," Ross recalled. He put $1,000 down and paid $260 a month for a $27,500 Lawndale two-flat. When he joined the CBL and got the building appraised seven years later, he learned that its true value was $15,000. But by then Ross already knew he'd been exploited. One day the building's original owner, an Italian American, came back to sell Ross some radiator caps; he had taken them from the apartment when he moved, but they didn't fit the radiators in his new place. He spoke so fondly of the building that Ross asked why he'd sold it. "They gave me $12,000 for it," the man said. "They made me, they threatened me. They was in here every day. They were gangsters, bad men." Then he asked what Ross had paid for the place. When Ross said "$27,000," the man sat silently for a long time. When he finally spoke, his concern wasn't for Ross. "They cheated me," he said.[58]

Ross's experience was typical. Soon after he and his wife moved in, the furnace broke down. He was forced to pay an extra $40 a month to replace it. "I was already paying [Berke] $260 a month," he recalled. "My wife was furious. . . . I had no money for food or medical expenses—my wife was pregnant and I couldn't get a doctor." Ross faced the bitter truth: "I realized then that I was stuck for life." He took a second job, working four hours a night for two dollars an hour. "Man, that was work. I did it for three years. When I'd leave for work in the morning the baby would be asleep.

When I'd come home at night he'd be asleep too. One day I realized that I was really messing up my family. I picked up my kid and he pulled away. . . . My own kid didn't even know me."[59]

In late 1967, Ross heard "some talk in the neighborhood" that a "young white fellow" named Macnamara had been researching the real estate situation in Lawndale. He attended the first meeting at Presentation Church, and he saw the shame in his neighbors' eyes when Macnamara described how their contract purchases had been rigged. Ross decided that the time for shame was past. At the next meeting, after Wells described her encounter with Forman, Ross told his own story to the group. Afterward, Macnamara asked Ross if he'd be willing to work more closely with the organizers. With that, Ross became something he'd never been before: an activist.[60]

One of the first things he did was recruit his brother-in-law, Charlie Baker. As a *Washington Post* reporter later described him, Baker was a lean man "with an open, wide face, a small mustache, sparkling eyes and an easy smile." A CBL worker put the matter more succinctly: "Charlie was a charmer."[61] Born in Banks, Mississippi, in 1926, the second of three sons, he had an eighth-grade education and worked as a sharecropper until the age of eighteen. Like Ross, Baker moved to Chicago after serving in the army during World War II and found a job at Campbell's Soup Company. In 1948, Baker married Ross's younger sister Charlene.[62]

Baker had been the first of the two men to buy in Lawndale. He knew that he had few options, since in 1960, he recalled, "a colored person" couldn't venture into most white Chicago neighborhoods "and live," much less "buy a home" there. The seller, a white man named John Karras, showed him a two-flat for $26,500. Baker thought the price was high, but Karras told him that the building held three apartments: a large floor-through on the first floor and two smaller ones on the second. Baker was dubious about the double apartment setup on the second floor. "Shouldn't these people have two ways out?" he asked. Karras reassured him. "Put a crash panel in here. They could come right out through your kitchen."[63]

Baker and his wife decided to go for the deal. When he called to arrange the closing, Karras said that "we didn't need no lawyer because he was going to be fair with me." He even threw in something extra: he'd had the crash panel door installed on the second floor at his own expense. Baker paid his first monthly installment of $197 on January 20, 1961. He was so excited that he encouraged Ross to purchase his two-flat a few blocks away.[64]

Baker soon found that his first payment was not the total charge. With insurance and interest, he owed not $197 but $247 a month. Baker and Charlene moved into the back apartment of the second floor and rented out the front and the ground floor. Three months later, the housing inspector showed up. That's when Baker learned that crash panels had been outlawed in 1956. He had to correct the violation or pay a fine of $200 a day. Baker moved out the second-floor renters, thus cutting his income by $80 a month. Around the same time, Baker was told that his back porch required immediate repair. He brought the violation notice to Karras. "It is your house; you do your own repairs," Karras snapped. He did help Baker get a loan to rebuild the porch, which added to his monthly payment. Baker came to the same conclusion as Ross: "I was stuck." He got a second job driving a cab, and Charlene took a job as well. The situation was hard on their children, but the alternative was to lose the building. Baker carried on, wrangling with Karras over various fees and desperately trying to keep up his payments. When his brother-in-law told him about the group forming in Lawndale that wanted to do something about the situation, Baker eagerly joined them.[65]

The third resident to emerge as a CBL leader was Henrietta Banks. A stylish thirty-eight-year-old mother of seven, Banks sported two-toned, black-and-bleached-blond hair and had a dazzling smile made all the brighter by one of her front teeth—gold with a heart-shaped cutout in the center. When she smiled at you, "you would need sunglasses," one of her coworkers recalled.[66] Banks and her husband, Saul, migrants from Alabama, both held full-time jobs, Saul as a welder and Henrietta at a printing firm. In 1961, they paid $25,000 for their building, which the previous owner had sold to a speculator shortly before for $14,000. Although they enjoyed their home and kept it in "spotless" condition, the couple lived "in constant fear of missing a monthly payment" and losing the building. The Bankses paid their monthly charges without complaint until May 1965, when the contract seller turned over their contract paper to a new investor. By then the Bankses had paid their balance down to $19,000. But the new owner insisted that the outstanding amount was $22,000. When Mrs. Banks asked why they suddenly owed an extra $3,000, he told her, "I am not responsible for what happened with the other guys. The sale price is now $22,065." At that, this normally cheerful woman could not contain her rage. "One day . . . I am going to shove these very papers down your throat," she threatened her new creditor. Three years later, Banks was among those accompanying Ruth Wells on her second visit to Forman.[67]

Banks proved to be a "born organizer." In February 1968, she, along with Wells, Ross, and about a dozen others began going door-to-door to talk about contract sales. Many residents denied that they had bought their homes on contract, even though the CBL had proof that they had. Banks intuitively understood that her neighbors' responses were rooted in shame and fear, feelings that would vanish once they understood that this was a group and not an individual problem. "So I took my contract along with me and showed them how bad we got stung. . . . I felt that if I showed that thing I would bring some people out." Her decision to tell her own story first was the right one, and her method was quickly adopted by all the other CBL organizers. Ross described a typical encounter. After telling his own story, Ross would say, "'By the way, he paid [X amount] for this place.' This started the ball rolling. They would say: 'That dirty son of a bitch.'" Then Ross would explain that the Contract Buyers of Lawndale were trying to "get all the people similarly situated to organize" to pressure their contract seller to renegotiate the contract price. "'Do you think he will?' 'Yes, I think he will.'" Such reassurance was usually enough to bring another person into the organization.[68]

Ruth Wells, of course, was the fourth Southern-born resident to take the lead in the CBL. Wells struck most people as quiet and levelheaded, "a tall, dignified, forthright lady," as one of the college boys described her.[69] But she had also waged a lifelong struggle against surges of anger that she could not always control. The twelfth and youngest child of farmer parents, she had moved from Mississippi to Gary, Indiana, at the age of fourteen. She found work in a factory and then in an office. When she was laid off from her job, she tried to sign up for unemployment benefits and discovered that in Indiana a black woman seeking state aid was automatically sent to work as a maid in a white person's home. If she refused, she was considered to have turned down a legitimate offer of work and was therefore not eligible for unemployment payments. Wells was outraged. When the woman behind the counter offered her maid's work starting "today," she retorted: "Why can't your mamma do it? Why can't she be the maid?" Wells felt some satisfaction when the woman turned bright red, but she also knew that she would not be getting benefits in Indiana anytime soon.[70]

In 1952, she moved to Chicago, where she married James Wells, a Mississippi-born foundry worker. Wells worked at the Department of the Navy in suburban River Forest, and she pursued a number of outside interests as well. She belonged to a women's social group, the Nonchalants, which raised money for needy families. She was active in the Missionary Baptist Church. But once she and James bought their two-flat in Lawndale on contract, the demands of the building took up most of her time. By the winter of 1968, though, Wells's time—and her temper—were redirected into challenging the contract sellers of Lawndale.[71]

The group had one additional, invaluable resource, Jack Macnamara, whose efforts on behalf of the CBL had taken on a missionary zeal. The decisive moment for him had come in December 1967, when he arranged a dinner for the families of the students who had worked with him that summer and fall. He invited Reverend Robert F. Harvanek, his Jesuit superior, to address the gathering. Harvanek praised the community organization project as a worthy endeavor but added that he was keeping a close watch on it. If at any point the project needed to be "put out of existence," he assured the parents in attendance, he would do so. Macnamara was profoundly upset by Harvanek's comments, by the thought that months of grueling labor could be snuffed out in an instant. That night he lay awake, torn between frustration at his powerlessness and devotion to the vow of obedience he had taken as a Jesuit, which might require that he abandon the cause. By dawn he had come to a resolution. "I decided that . . . what I was doing could maybe get me killed, drive me crazy, get me kicked out of the Jesuits, and I just, for some reason, was willing to accept all of those consequences. Once I got to that point, I was at peace." From that moment on, Macnamara plunged into work for the CBL with "cadre-like" intensity. Soon the stress was showing. One observer noted that he "regularly works 18-hour days and now carries only 150 pounds on his six-foot frame." Another commented, "He's going to kill himself the way he's working. He looks terrible."[72]

Throughout 1968, Ross, Baker, Banks, Wells, and Macnamara drew more and more Lawndale residents into the CBL. Determined to pressure the sellers into renegotiations, the organizers first grouped CBL members by contract seller. Members would then picket their contract seller, both at work and at home. Since many sellers hid their identity behind land trusts, the CBL also picketed the banks that held these trusts, demanding that the banks either force the trust owners to renegotiate their contracts at a fair, FHA-appraised value or turn over the owners' names.[73]

The organization also picketed the Chicago offices of the Federal Housing Administration, although by this point the FHA had changed its policies regarding areas like Lawndale. In July 1967, in part as a response to the urban riots that broke out between 1964 and 1967, the FHA directed its local offices to consider all buildings in "riot or riot-torn areas" as "acceptable risks."[74] But this turnaround hardly made up for past injuries. As Charlie Baker told the Chicago press, "Since the FHA would not insure mortgages for us when we bought our homes, the federal government must share the blame." John McKnight seconded Baker's view. "As far as I'm concerned, the white racist institutions—particularly the old FHA—are even guiltier than the speculators," he said. "They created the conditions."[75]

Twice a week, every week, through the spring, summer, and fall of 1968, the CBL pickets were out in force. They made little headway. Most of Chicago's savings and loan institutions refused to turn over their records. One official told CBL members, "You don't deserve anything from me! Get out of my office!" The FHA was just as intransigent: "I don't know how anyone can say FHA was responsible for any local situation in Illinois. We have no area of responsibility there. . . . We were merely following policy," an administrator insisted.[76]

The most virulent resistance came from the contract sellers themselves. It sometimes took the form of crude threats, such as the West Side realtor who told a CBL member, "If you set one foot in here I'll blow your . . . brains out!" The sellers were particularly enraged by CBL visits to their neighborhoods. As pickets approached the home of contract seller Al Weinberg, he shouted to police, "They're passing out scurrilous literature. Arrest them; it's all a pack of lies!" In response to a reporter who asked exactly what part of the CBL's "fact sheet" was untrue, Weinberg became practically apoplectic. "If you ever come here again you better come out here with weapons!" he raged.[77]

Some of the reasons for the contract sellers' fury were obvious. The sellers felt they were being defamed; many had wives and children who were nearly hysterical "under the pressure" of this sudden notoriety.[78] But the sellers' anger went deeper than that. By now, most contract sellers in

Lawndale had softened their original harsh terms. Many of the contracts they held were on overcrowded and decrepit buildings (conditions that the sellers insisted bore no connection to the inflated prices they had charged). They were hard-pressed to find buyers for these properties—much less the black home buyers with middle-class incomes that had earlier constituted a ready market for Lawndale buildings. The drop in demand created a risk, since they dared not leave their buildings vacant—empty properties were often severely vandalized. Given this situation, most contract sellers no longer evicted after a missed payment or two. Indeed, approximately 60 percent of Lawndale's contract buyers now retained possession of their buildings even if they were up to six months behind in their payments.[79]

Besides, what was wrong with the way the sellers did business? After all, their work was based on bedrock American values, such as "the integrity of a contract" and "the legitimacy of profits the market will bear." After years of telling their customers that they were doing them a favor by offering them homes on contract, some had come to believe their own sales pitch. "I liked the people on the West Side," one man said. "I was good to them." He seemed genuinely shocked when confronted by angry CBL members. "I couldn't believe it when they said I had cheated people. I came home to my wife and said, 'Isn't this the American system, where we make as much profit as we can?' She said, 'yes, you're right.' Two days later she said, 'No, *you're* wrong and *they're* right.'" Ultimately, this contract seller agreed to renegotiate.[80]

Many contract sellers were bothered as well by the CBL's visible backing from Catholic institutions. Black anti-Semitism was a fact of life in formerly Jewish, currently all-black areas like Lawndale where the remaining white businessmen, of whatever degree of moral probity, tended to be Jews. "The general discontent with Jewish businessmen is growing stronger in the Lawndale community all the time," reported one Jewish community activist in 1967.[81] Lawndale's Jewish contract sellers seemed to feel that this "general discontent" was manageable as long as outside agitators did not stir it into something uglier. Now they were being publicly denounced by sanctimonious men in collars. The Catholic Church had no great commitment to justice for blacks, the sellers believed, while its long tradition of disdain for Jews was beyond dispute. To some, the CBL seemed just the latest manifestation of that sorry Catholic tradition of scapegoating Jews, in this case Jewish small businessmen.[82]

In the spring of 1968, the contract sellers of Lawndale united into the Real Estate Investors Association. They contributed up to $5,000 each—the precise amount determined by the number of contracts held—to pay for a common legal defense.[83] Their decision to form an interest group was in part a response to the general social situation, which had become even more charged. On April 4, 1968, Martin Luther King Jr. was assassinated. On April 5, black enclaves in cities across the country exploded in days of rioting. In Chicago, the worst of the violence, arson, and looting occurred in Lawndale—the neighborhood's third riot in four years. Many in the CBL were shocked by the riot's intensity. "I thought they was going crazy," Ruth Wells recalled. "The man that they rioted about didn't go for violence at all. . . . It didn't make no sense." But the sorrow of the community's older members had little effect on the area's young men. They smashed virtually every shop window along Madison Avenue, a major commercial strip, and set at least five enormous fires that engulfed three solid blocks of that street.[84]

That same day, April 5, 1968, attorney Irving Block sent Monsignor Egan his first official correspondence as the legal counsel for the Real Estate Investors Association. His letter informed Egan and the CBL that most of his clients were willing to "work out deals on an individual basis." But "today a new facet has been added." His clients had been visited by CBL members who indicated that "unless we capitulate entirely to their demands, . . . physical violence would be attempted. I take this opportunity of placing myself on record that these threats have been made," he lectured Egan. "On a day when the Negro community has apparently run wild and is looting and pillaging, it ill behooves any group to permit threats of this kind," he continued, warning that, "if there is picketing tomorrow and evidence of violence, we shall seek those responsible and demand retribution." Egan had a choice: "helping these people or seeking headlines." The nastiest aspect of the letter was a small detail at the bottom that Egan surely noted as the personal threat it was: "cc: Cardinal Cody."[85]

Block's threats convinced CBL members that they needed attorneys of their own. Unexpected help came from one John O'Connor, a banker and the owner of a Chicago trucking firm. O'Connor had read a series of articles in the archdiocese newspaper the *New World* that portrayed CBL members as "good hardworking people" whose activities were a perfect example of "self-help" in the ghetto. The paper's depiction of Macnamara,

Egan, Sister Andrew, and other Catholic activists in Lawndale as emblematic of "the spirit of Vatican II" served to legitimize the CBL for Catholics throughout the city—O'Connor among them. Touched by the CBL's situation, he decided that this was a group he wanted to support. Years later, Peggy Roach recalled the shock and pleasure of opening unsolicited mail from O'Connor that contained checks for five, sometimes ten thousand dollars. He followed the checks with a call to Macnamara, asking what else the CBL needed. Macnamara answered without hesitation. "We need forty lawyers."[86]

Three weeks later, the CBL got its attorneys. O'Connor had called Judge Harold Sullivan, a progressive Chicagoan who happened to be his brother-in-law and who was also shocked by the obvious injustice Lawndalers had suffered. Sullivan in turn invited all the progressive attorneys he knew to join a legal support group for the CBL. "We promise each participating member of our group a rewarding experience and the chance [to work toward] the removal of a basic root evil," he wrote.[87] The attorneys met with the CBL in the summer of 1968. They heard an impassioned plea. "We need help in Lawndale and we need it now," Clyde Ross said. "We aren't asking for any handout. We are only asking for a chance to . . . keep our neighborhood clean. . . . How can we keep our property up when we have to pay twice as much as white people for our homes, and then all this money is taken out of Lawndale and goes to . . . white suburbs?" He concluded on a personal note: "I'm 45 years old. . . . What chance do I have? . . . If you white people, who took the time to come down here tonight, help us—then we have a chance."[88]

The attorneys agreed to help. That summer, while CBL members continued their picketing, legal negotiations began. As the *New World* reported, the first meeting of the legal volunteers with Irving Block resulted in a verbal battle "punctuated by sharp complaints and recriminations from both sides." Block let loose. He accused the Catholic Church of fomenting the CBL's activities. CBL members denied the charge, insisting that "the black people of Lawndale . . . were the main power behind CBL." The result of the three-hour session was the renegotiation of the contract of a single home. At least "a precedent for . . . direct negotiation between buyers and contract holders was established," the *New World* concluded optimistically.[89]

While negotiations limped forward, the CBL pushed for change on other fronts as well. Here Egan played a major role.[90] Throughout the spring and summer Egan and Macnamara attended meetings of the Metropolitan Housing and Planning Council, where Macnamara was appointed to a subcommittee to work on legislation "relating to the prevention of economic exploitation of racial prejudice in residential real estate." Macnamara drafted a multifaceted law that would leave legitimate contract sales untouched, while providing solid, enforceable remedies for people who had purchased on contract at obviously exploitative terms.[91]

Thomas Foran, the U.S Attorney for northern Illinois, wrote to John Horne, the chairman of the Federal Home Loan Bank Board, formally requesting that the FHA intervene on behalf of the contract buyers of Lawndale. While he might have taken this action in any case, it didn't hurt that Foran was a close friend of Egan's. Although the two men started out as adversaries over the Hyde Park conservation plan, Egan had gradually won Foran over. "He was a regular visitor to our house. Marvelous to our children," Foran recalled. And although passionately opposed to Egan's views on urban renewal, he was "all the way with Jack" on the CBL.[92]

In his letter, Foran pointed out that the FHA was already involved in the issue because its discriminatory practices left Lawndale residents no choice but to buy on contract. He also castigated the Federal Savings and Loan Insurance Corporation (FSLIC). When some of the savings and loans that had given mortgages to the contract sellers—thereby enabling them to buy the properties that they immediately resold on contract—became insolvent, their holdings had been taken over by the FSLIC. By 1969, the national press would note that the cost of their insolvency to the FSLIC in insurance payments alone was $100 million. The "FSLIC now holds more slum real estate mortgages than any Chicago institution," the *Washington Post* reported.[93]

Foran offered a way for the FSLIC to salvage something from this debacle. He argued that the FSLIC could divest itself of these properties and aid the exploited contract buyers at the same time. It need only lower the mortgage amounts owed by contract sellers, "*if* those sellers in turn agree to renegotiate their contracts and to pass on the discount to the contract purchasers." Foran gave the FSLIC one more reason it might want to get rid of these mortgages as soon as possible. Savings and loan institutions had often granted mortgages to speculators—including men who "had hoodlum connections"—that were considerably higher than the buildings' worth. In return the savings and loans got "kickbacks" from the speculators. In short, Foran was now investigating several Chicago-area savings and loans for the crime of "misapplication of federally insured funds." The FSLIC would do well to get out now.[94]

In July 1968, the first of two public hearings on the repercussions of exploitative contract sales were held by the Public Welfare Committee of the Illinois House of Representatives. Assistant U.S. Attorney Thomas Todd "created a furor" when he disclosed Foran's plan to prosecute the savings and loans. The real drama of the hearings, however, came from CBL members who "poured out their financial tales of woe." Clyde Ross told how he struggled at day and night-shift jobs to make principal and interest payments that would eventually total $46,872. "If something isn't done soon to get these leeches off our backs, there's really going to be trouble here," he told the committee, his voice trembling with emotion. Macnamara stressed his belief in free enterprise but insisted that what had happened in Lawndale was "actually an unconscionable, large-scale, price-gouging racket." Representative James W. Carter noted that although all of the real estate agents and bankers involved in contract sales had been invited to the hearing, "none of them showed up." In contrast, hundreds of black Lawndale residents packed the room; many of them had sacrificed a day's pay in order to attend. Representative Robert E. Mann added that if the real estate and loan officers involved wouldn't come voluntarily, they should be subpoenaed and forced to testify.[95]

The committee's follow-up hearing, held in mid-November, was even more emotionally charged. This time the testimony was dominated by the speculators, finally forced to tell their story. Irwin Spector of the Real Estate Investors Association admitted that he had paid $14,000 for a Lawndale building that he promptly resold to Howell Collins, a black buyer, for $25,500. He also admitted that he owned fifty similar contracts. When Representative Mann called both the price and the profit "unconscionable," Spector was unrepentant. "In a free economy a house is worth what anyone will pay for it," he insisted. Mann challenged Spector's contention that he operated in a free economy. On the contrary, Chicago contained a dual housing market rich with possibilities for exploitation. "You knew there was a white market anxious to sell and a black market anxious to buy," he chastised. Spector's attorney, Irving Block, denounced the hearings as a "kangaroo court." Mann shook his finger in Block's face, telling him, "We are not going to continue to listen to your running commentary!" When Block kept raising objections, Representative Carter told Block to "Shut up!" or leave the hearing. "Outbursts from witnesses and legislative members as well as spontaneous applause and catcalls from the audience marked the proceedings in which charges and countercharges flew," a witness summarized.[96]

The vehement debate that characterized these hearings was an indication that the climate had become more favorable for the CBL's challenge to the sellers. In the 1950s and early 1960s, when contract selling was at its peak, talk of the federal government's complicity and demands that slumlords renegotiate fully legal housing contracts generated passionate opposition from business leaders and attorneys, who almost unanimously cast such arguments as an attack on the American way of free enterprise. By 1968, however, there was a smoother fit between the CBL's demands and the mood of white Chicago.

In part, this shift was due to the riots following King's murder, which, though they confirmed the hostile impression of blacks held by many white Chicagoans, signaled to others that immediate action was needed to remedy ghetto conditions. The CBL's demand that black owners should pay a fair price for their housing now seemed a reasonable alternative to a potential uprising. Even President-elect Richard Nixon's response to the April riots seemed to lend support to the CBL. "People who own their own homes don't burn their neighborhoods," he commented.[97]

By the end of the year, Chicago newspapers had largely come out in support of the CBL. The FHA should work with the CBL to renegotiate the contracts, the *Sun-Times* editorialized, since that would "encourage black capitalism, home ownership and economic self-sufficiency in black communities." Federal policies concerning home ownership, many only a few years old, now seemed "crass, blatantly discriminatory and, well, un-American," the *Sun-Times* added. Even the *Wall Street Journal* supported the CBL's analysis. "There is no doubt the restricted housing market and the resultant contract buying contributed to the emergence of the slum," the paper reported.[98]

Sympathy for the CBL, however, was not just a reaction to the riots. It also reflected the group's moral, even spiritual appeal. Although the energetic engagement of Catholic activists had been a catalyst for the creation of the CBL, when Wells, Baker, Ross, and Banks took charge, they brought with them the black Southern church's culture of resistance. They opened CBL meetings with a long, spontaneous prayer. Members then "testified" about their experiences as contract buyers. As *Atlantic Monthly* reporter James Alan McPherson noted, CBL members identified contract buying with "sin, renegotiation with salvation, and the League itself as God's instrument of salvation." The transformation unleashed in Lawndale was a product of the group's ability to fuse anger, economic analysis, and a sense of communal mission. Ruth Wells said that, before the CBL was organized, "I didn't even know my next-door neighbor." Now, CBL members constituted a vibrant and close community, linked and strengthened by religious faith. Speaking of the group's solidarity, Macnamara recalled, "There were people who turned down fantastic settlements, $10,000 and $12,000 settlements, until the seller would agree to renegotiate everybody's contract on the same basis."[99]

The CBL's spirit had a profound effect on white observers. Many of Chicago's liberal Catholics—and even those who did not identify themselves as liberal—had been horrified by the white Catholic resistance that had met Martin Luther King's 1966 open occupancy marches. Michael Gecan, for example, started out "working class and conservative." His outlook shifted as he learned about the civil rights struggle from his Jesuit teachers. But the real change for him came with King's marches. "I saw people, whites who looked like me, stoning the marchers, and it was a tremendous eye opener," Gecan said. "We lived violence all the time but this was different. This wasn't just like guys on your turf or you're on their turf. This was murderous, completely uncontrollable." When he heard a call for volunteers to organize in Lawndale, he responded.[100]

While work with the CBL allowed many young Catholics to make up for "Cicero"—the shorthand term for the several neighborhoods where whites had attacked black marchers—it also gave them an outlet for their religious yearning. "I think we were stunned by how great the CBL members' liturgy was," Gecan recalled. Maureen McDonald, another volunteer, similarly told how impressed she was when she first heard contract buyer Howell Collins, "a little bit of a fella," deliver an opening prayer at CBL meetings. "He could quote his Scripture. You know, Catholics never read the Bible, so it was wonderful to listen to how he could take that Scripture and apply it to life in Lawndale." "They really took to the religious dimension," another white observer said of the "lapsed Catholics" working for the CBL. "I remember . . . some of them saying that CBL was church for them. It was the only real religion they had felt for a long time."[101]

Chicago's liberal Jews, too, flocked to support the CBL. Their spokesman, Rabbi Robert J. Marx, the founder of the Jewish Council on Urban Affairs (JCUA), believed that the struggles of black ghetto residents had an automatic resonance for Jews. "We need not remind our people of the constraints of ghetto living," he wrote. The white mob behavior he had witnessed during King's Chicago marches was particularly upsetting. "What I saw in Gage Park seared my soul," he wrote. The rage of the neighborhood's whites demonstrated "how the concentration camp could have occurred, and how men's hatred could lead them to kill."[102]

That the CBL was a black organization challenging mostly Jewish slum landlords undoubtedly complicated this direct Jewish identification with blacks as fellow victims of oppression, but it did not diminish liberal Jewish support. For Marx, a desire to confront Jewish slumlords had been a major spur to his creation of the JCUA.[103] By the mid-1960s, organized Jewish challenges to Jewish slum landlords had cropped up in cities around the country. Even though, as one prominent Jewish scholar explained, Jewish holdings in black ghettos represented "an infinitesimal fraction of the American Jewish economy" (in fact, "Negro banks may well be the major slumlords" in these areas, he noted), they loomed large symbolically. Not only were Jewish slumlords' activities immoral; they also threatened the urban-centered black-Jewish political alliance that was the basis of any political power Jews might hope to wield.[104] Marx was keenly aware of this national debate. When Macnamara contacted him early in 1968 with information about the CBL's campaign against Moe Forman, therefore, he was eager to help.[105]

Marx also viewed the CBL's battle as an opportunity to grapple with the larger issue of what he called the "interstitial role of the Jew—his being caught between larger social forces which all too often . . . press him into marginal endeavors." In April 1968, Marx wrote an essay, "The People in Between," that used the figure of the Jewish slum landlord to examine the workings of institutional anti-Semitism. How was it, Marx asked, that Jews so often functioned as the hated symbol of governing powers to which they were only marginally connected? The answer was that, since Jews were neither part of the masses nor part of their society's elites, they had historically been used by those elites to fulfill "certain vital yet dispensable functions." To illustrate his point, he referred to Poland, where Jews were barred from owning land but were granted the right to collect taxes and sell liquor. When tensions arose between the Polish state and the peasants, Poland's ruling class could distract the peasants by turning them on the Jews. Similarly, in the United States, Jews were excluded from the real sources of power—the senior management of banks, utilities, and insurance companies was overwhelmingly gentile—but were welcome to act as urban middlemen, that is, as ghetto merchants or contract sellers.[106]

Marx argued that this interstitial role turned Jews into the visible symbols of exploitation. But there was such a thing as "positive interstitiality," he pointed out. "The advantage of this role is that freedom to criticize is unhindered by . . . external institutional ties." The key was for Jews to become aware of their position. Then they would see how power really operates and thereby discover new ways to challenge oppressive institutional control. In short, American Jews must "deal with their slumlords and contract sellers, just as the archdiocese must deal with its Ciceros." If they did so, Marx believed, they could demonstrate "that freedom is Judaism, that Passover is not 3,000 years old—that it is today, and that we are part of it."[107]

Undoubtedly, some of Chicago's Jews supported the CBL because they were embarrassed by the contract sellers and eager to distance themselves from such socially marginal operators. "They were ashamed of them, wanted no part of them, even though some of them were big Israeli bond donors and all that kind of stuff," recalled Warren Lupel, then a young attorney working with Irving Block to defend the contract sellers.[108] But for many members of the Jewish community, their motives went beyond embarrassment. The Human Relations Commission of Skokie, Illinois, a heavily Jewish suburb of Chicago, passed a resolution "fully supporting and endorsing" the aims of the CBL. The Chicago Board of Rabbis stated its "vigorous moral opposition to the exploitation of blacks and specifically to any exploitative practices that may be involved in the contract sales in question." Several Jewish groups visited Jewish contract sellers to tell them that they had an ethical duty to do the right thing. Some of these sessions were "rather intense, with the rabbis and others refusing to leave, or to let the realtor leave for quite long periods," one observer reported. On rare occasions, these sessions produced results. "Rabbi, I have to talk with you. . . . I can't live with myself. My conscience can't take any more," one seller told Marx. He later renegotiated his contracts.[109]

The CBL's active discouragement of anti-Semitism further brought the two communities together. "Every once in a while someone would say something anti-Semitic, but it would just never go anywhere," Michael Gecan recalled. This was "partly because Rabbi Marx was around," but more centrally because "everyone knew that the issue was broader than that." Henrietta Banks confronted anti-Semitism head-on. As she wrote in a letter to the *West Side Torch*, a predominantly black newspaper, "several non-Jewish realtors" engaged in contract sales swindles, while the CBL received support "from several prominent members of the Jewish community. . . . I point this out to you for future reference so that it doesn't appear that the issue is a Jewish issue."[110]

While Chicago Jews could feel good about their willingness to confront their coreligionists, they might have felt a bit queasy about the coverage of the contract sales issue—especially in the Catholic press. The *New World* account of Al Weinberg's reaction to CBL leafleting, for example, included several photographs of the contract seller. One showed a pale, stoop-shouldered man in his fifties or sixties holding his dog, which the *New World* described as "a huge German Shepherd," on a short leash. Between the photos and Weinberg's verbal challenge to CBL members to bring their weapons next time they visited his street, the message was clear: Weinberg was a Northern version of Alabama's Bull Connor. Photos of the hunched, angry Weinberg contrasted with other, far more dignified images on the same page: the saintly, smiling Sister Andrew helping a black Lawndale couple apply for an FHA appraisal on their home and contract buyer Alan Frazier, whose portrait, apparently shot from a low angle, made him appear to loom tall, erect, and smiling.[111] For all that the CBL denied that a black-Catholic alliance was targeting depraved Jewish businessmen, this was precisely the message conveyed by the *New World* photographs.

The *New World* also hinted that the contract sellers were violent men. William Dendy, writing in the *New World,* described the steadfast courage of Macnamara and his college volunteers who supported the CBL "even when their lives were threatened" by "certain targets of their campaign."[112] In truth, physical attacks occurring in Lawndale were hardly the work of contract sellers, as the *New World* implied, but rather of some black residents who despised the white organizers as intruders into their community. As one black local recalled, Macnamara and his boys "were getting their asses kicked. There were more ass-whoopings that they took than people might want to talk about."[113]

On the whole, the young white volunteers had decent relationships with the community. Marc Young, a white Catholic who worked with Macnamara, described playing basketball with the local teenagers, eating meals together, and watching sitcoms in a "living room full of black folks from the neighborhood." Yet Lawndale was not transformed overnight from what it had been for years—a place where the "hate was so thick you could cut it with a knife."[114] Especially among the young, there was an undercurrent of violence that flared up periodically. "It was a very angry, violent time," Michael Gecan recalled. He recounted what happened to Bill Ford, one of the summer helpers, who had gone out to do some interviews. "Some guys caught him on a street. One said, 'Open your shirt.' Bill did and the guy cut his chest lightly. He said, 'What's my name?' Bill said 'I don't know.' So then the guy cut another mark into his chest, and said, 'Now what's my name?'" Bill got three or four letters sliced onto his chest before he was able to make it out. "Pablo was his name."[115]

Harassment of Macnamara's white helpers also took a more organized form. A group of black teenagers whom the college students nicknamed the "Mau-Maus" started showing up at Macnamara's apartment to threaten them. The challenge, the students understood, was based on "teenage testosterone turf grounds as well as on racial grounds." Nevertheless, "they scared us, those guys," recalled David Quammen, a Yale undergraduate who lived at Macnamara's that summer. "They were much more capable of violence than we were. . . . And we really didn't know how to deal with them. A Gandhiesque, white, well-meaning liberal shrug was not a particularly respected response."[116]

Macnamara refused to defend himself or to report any of the petty thefts to which he and the others were sometimes subjected. There was one member of Macnamara's household who was not intimidated by the

Mau-Maus, however. To Eddie Smith, a sixteen-year-old African American, the Lawndale toughs were not to be taken seriously. They were "just local gangbangers, just . . . nobodies," who saw the Presentation Church organizers as "vulnerable do-good honkies, and what's better than to take advantage of a bunch of do-good honkies?"

The fact that a black teenager had joined "Macnamara's band" went completely unmentioned in press accounts, which focused on the anomaly of young white men living in ostensible peace in the city's worst black ghetto. But Eddie Smith played a crucial role in the group's lives. Part of what won the white organizers' acceptance was the interracial mix of their household. "I was Jack's token black," Smith recalled. "That kind of made it seem OK to have white folks in the neighborhood, because they had a black kid that they were trying to send in the right direction."[117]

Smith had come to Macnamara in a circuitous way. Originally from Cleveland, Ohio, he had been a difficult child, causing endless trouble for his divorced mother, a nurse. "I was incorrigible. . . . Disrespectful to adults and very bullyish," Smith recalled ruefully. "I had a chip on my shoulder and I really didn't have a reason to have one." His behavior landed him in a youth detention center at the age of twelve. A year of incarceration did nothing to tame him. "I didn't need but two hours of sleep a day. The rest of the time I was into some crazy shit."

Smith converted to Catholicism as a teenager, mainly because he wanted access to the superior sports equipment at the Catholic schools. His new faith brought him into contact with Father Denano, who worked at Cleveland's Epiphany Church. Smith was fearless; by fifteen, he was already over six feet tall, a hulking, handsome young man full of uncontrollable rage. Nevertheless, he was awed by Father Denano, "a little Italian guy," as Smith called him, who was "just holy, holy, holy." Denano took it upon himself to watch over Smith. "He was always there for me," Smith said. "If I was in trouble at 3:30 in the morning, all of a sudden that fucking guy was standing there, looking me right in the face."

It was Denano who led Smith to Jack Macnamara. "He told me, 'You've got to get out of here. You're going to die or you're going to wind up in jail for a long time. Maybe a change of scene would do you some good. I got these friends in Chicago.' And that's how it all started," Smith recalled. Denano was convinced that a stay in Lawndale would encourage Smith's latent "do-gooder tendencies" and offer a worthy outlet for his considerable energy.

What he didn't realize was that Lawndale "was *way* worse" than Smith's former neighborhood in Cleveland. Smith attended Lawndale's Crane High School, which had a student body of over four thousand. "Our high school was jam-packed. . . . The teachers were trying, but there was so much going on in a classroom with forty-eight students that it was virtually impossible for them to do their job." The high school had great sports, though. Smith joined the football team, which won him respect on the streets: "I had a free pass, like everyone else on the team, to walk the neighborhood and do what we pleased."

On top of endless hours of research and organizing, Macnamara now had to serve as surrogate father to a troubled teenage boy. It was a challenge. Shortly before Smith was supposed to graduate, he attacked a teacher who commented that he was getting a diploma only because he was an athlete. Smith shoved the teacher off a second-floor balcony. "He was lucky he lived," says Smith. "I was lucky he lived too." The teacher didn't press charges, but Smith was forced to transfer to a new school just weeks before graduation.

Behavior of this sort was not easy for Macnamara to deal with, but in truth, some of Smith's rough ways benefited his group. Smith used his social and physical power to protect the nonviolent organizers he lived with. "Jack had been punched a couple of times, and it pissed me off," Smith said. When people hurt Jack, "I wanted to kill them!" When some local boys robbed the apartment, Smith made it his business to find out who was involved and then "deal with it." The local "nobodies" got "stomped in the face . . . eight or nine times by a guy, saying 'You remember them white boys upstairs? I like them white boys.'" This was enough to stop a repeat of the harassment, at least when Smith was around.[118]

Eddie Smith wasn't the only African American who looked after the white boys on Independence Avenue. Some older CBL members also saw to protecting Macnamara and his charges. One night a whole group went to the spot where the Mau-Maus hung out. As Macnamara recalled, "They warned them. They said, 'These people are very important to us. You guys stay away from that apartment.' And Mrs. Luceal Johnson said, 'If I see your black ass again over at that apartment I'm going to blow it off!'"[119]

The problem was that Smith didn't always act as a protector to his white housemates. Smith admitted that he "had so much rage" that he couldn't always direct it. After King's murder, he was one of the boys who ran amok in the streets. "I felt like somebody needed to pay," he recalled, like "somebody needed to be shot." Since there was nobody "to reach out to," he joined his friends in looting.[120] Occasionally Smith even turned his anger on Macnamara. His fury, he claimed, was triggered by Macnamara's "mild-mannered meekness. It bothered me that it was OK if we were disrespected." One day Smith hung Macnamara out their building's third-floor window. "I had him by one wrist, and I had him out the window. And I said something stupid about, your life is in my hands." To Smith's amazement, Macnamara "didn't even get scared." Smith pulled him back in. "I spent the rest of my time trying to make that up to him. He didn't even try to throw me out!"

Smith's violence was inexplicable, even to himself. "I don't come from privilege but I come from a good, solid family background. For some reason, I wanted to act like I was from the other side, which I wasn't." But Smith had been subjected to his share of violence. He spent much of his childhood with his mother's family in Talladega, Alabama, a "very racist environment." He remembered one incident in particular from the time he was five or six. As he and his friends were playing at a creek, a white man approached the boys and asked where they were from. When Smith "sassed" him in response, "he lifted me up by my neck and slammed my face down into the rocks. . . . He just kept slamming my face down, and then he tried to drown me."

Smith experienced violence in Cleveland, too. Once he found himself in a white area of the city pursued by some white boys, "and they got me. And there was a grown man. . . . This fucking guy picked me up by my balls." He told the ten-year-old, "You keep your fucking jig nigger ass out of here or I'll kill you, you black bastard. Nigger, I'm going to let you go this time, but just remember the time that a white man gave you something. I'm giving you your fucking life.'" Smith got the message: you don't "cross certain boundaries."

Despite his explosive character, Smith had a certain charm that won over teenagers and adults alike. Egan liked to call Smith "my bonnie little lad." Smith, like the rest of the Macnamara boys, got five to ten dollars a week to live on, but Egan would often slip him some extra money: "He'd come over and hug my neck. . . . And I'd go home and find three bucks in my pocket, which was great!" The older ladies of the CBL also doted on Smith. Henrietta Banks and Ruth Wells "loved me to death. They heard all the bullshit and they couldn't believe it. They thought I was just misunderstood." Smith felt particularly nurtured by Macnamara: "As much as I wanted to grow, he would allow it. I think he wanted me to keep my blackness as close to my heart as I could."

This is not to say that Smith didn't feel ambivalence about his life with Macnamara's group. He worried that if his friends found out where he lived, it would "totally disturb" his image. Sometimes Smith led Black Power rallies at Crane High School. "I'd stand in front of a podium with my fist up in the sky for revolution. *That* was the image I wanted. *Not* me living with some white boys." The Catholic experience, too, was confusing. "You spend a couple of years with Jack Macnamara, you get a little bit confused about religion, and about what God really means." Smith saw Macnamara as someone who tried to live like Jesus, that is, like a Jew—a positive association, given the boy's experiences in Alabama, where the Jewish shopkeeper, unlike the other white shopkeepers, gave equal credit to his black customers and treated them with warmth and respect. "So it really confused me. Knowing that Christ was a Jew, why were Catholic guys saying these bad, negative things about Jews, making jokes about them? I was like, 'Oh God, I think I'll be a Muslim.'"[121]

For all concerned, the experiment in interracial living and organizing was eye-opening. In the summer of 1968, Egan told a reporter that among the many benefits of the CBL was "the superb education" the college students had received, and he was right in more ways than he realized. For Michael Gecan, "as violent and tough as everything was, it was in that moment that people felt that racial and religious unity was a possibility."[122] For the white boys, life with Smith, a "rough-edged" teenager with a "gleaming smile," was both challenging and enlightening. Smith could have been speaking for all of them when he said, "Some of us were closer than others, but we were all friends. Even I wanted some change in this world, and this was as good a place as any to start."[123]

In spite of a year of activism, by the end of 1968 the CBL's campaign to pressure the sellers to renegotiate their contracts was stalling on all fronts. Only a single major contract seller had agreed to cooperate. U.S. Attorney Thomas Foran's plea to FHA and FSLIC officials had gone nowhere.[124] The lawyers Judge Sullivan had rallied to help the CBL were proving ineffectual since the law, they explained, was on the sellers' side. On the legislative front, Macnamara spent months working with the Metropolitan Housing and Planning Council to draft a law to aid the buyers, only to find that the other members of the committee opposed any provisions that would have retroactive power.[125]

The CBL's tactics also bore little fruit. For the most part, the pickets failed to shame the sellers into renegotiating. On the contrary, many felt that simply to clear their names, they had to stand firm against the CBL. "There were family issues, at least for Moe Forman," recalled attorney Warren Lupel. "Members of the family saying, 'Daddy, were you doing these horrible things?' or 'Is this true what they're saying about you?'" Any seller who considered renegotiating was rallied by Irving Block. He "never minded picketing in front of his office," Lupel said, but "Block was upset when there was picketing in front of his home . . . because that affected Ann, his wife."[126]

The sellers expressed their sense of persecution in an advertisement they took out on November 1, 1968, in enemy turf—the *New World.* "Will all Chicago-area small businessmen be subjected to this same shameful harassment?" the advertisement began. Contract buyers had been "perfectly satisfied with their properties" until outside "agitators" based in the Presentation Catholic Church "incited the contract purchasers by telling them they had been 'exploited.'" Since then, the contract sellers had faced relentless harassment. They suffered pickets around their homes, "outrageously insulting pamphlets" distributed to their neighbors, and even anonymous phone calls warning them to "get out of Lawndale if you want to live." The sellers had tried to be reasonable. "Because pressure of this type, no matter how unethical or illegal, has an effect on one's family," they had "offered to submit the whole situation to the American Arbitration Association," to no avail. "*The Contract Buyers Association rejected this offer, instead demanding the right to renegotiate contracts on their own terms!*" Although the *New World* published this advertisement, the editors were not impressed by its arguments. "The old bromide about outside agitation . . . sounds like it rolled up from the plantations 100 years ago. The members and officers of CBL live in Lawndale," the *New World* responded in an editorial.[127]

The CBL was under severe financial strain as well. With no tool at its disposal other than moral suasion, it sorely needed a reliable source of funding to continue its work. For a brief moment over the summer it seemed that its financial problems might be over. Gordon Sherman, the president of Midas Muffler, had announced that he wished to donate a quarter of a million dollars to an organization that would help the people of Chicago. He got in touch with John McKnight, a likely source of progressive contacts. McKnight decided that Sherman should meet Monsignor Egan and he set up a dinner to bring them together.

Egan came to the dinner exhausted after a long day of meetings, but when he realized the nature of Sherman's quest "the tiredness left me immediately and my mind cleared." The money would best be spent, he said, by funding "a tough, responsible people's community organization" in Lawndale. He suggested something "built in the manner of The Woodlawn Organization and directed by Mr. Saul Alinsky" that would reinvigorate the CBL and ensure its longevity and financial security. A week later, Egan and Sherman met with Alinsky, who said he would consider the proposition. To Egan's shock, Alinsky then held a second, private meeting with Sherman and convinced him that the money should go not toward Lawndale but to funding something Alinsky had long dreamed of: a permanent training institute for community organizers.

Egan was outraged by the betrayal. "When I learned about what happened I was furious and that nearly broke the fine relationship between Saul and me," he recalled. Egan eventually accepted Alinsky's action, on the grounds that the training institute was also a reasonable use of Sherman's charitable funds.[128] But the CBL, meanwhile, remained in financial straits. To address the problem, the CBL reconstituted itself into two entities: the Contract Buyers League, an all-black organization headed by Ruth Wells, Henrietta Banks, Clyde Ross, and Charlie Baker, and the Gamaliel Foundation, a mostly white nonprofit "advisory" organization devoted to raising money to support the CBL's activities.[129]

The creation of the Gamaliel Foundation in December 1968 as a separate fund-raising organization went some way toward answering the CBL's financial problems. The foundation was headed by Jack Macnamara, who once again petitioned his Jesuit superior, Father Harvanek, for permission to continue working in Lawndale. Macnamara's promise to obey whatever decision Harvanek made could not hide his less than complete confidence in his superiors' judgment: "Even if Christ's representatives in the institutional Church operate irrationally and close-mindedly, I will be happy to submit myself enthusiastically."[130] Harvanek granted the extension. For the time being the CBL would have a full-time, passionately committed organizer and fund-raiser in addition to its staff of four.

Yet this organizational realignment, and Macnamara's continued involvement, did not compensate for the meager results of the CBL's long year of effort. Members were growing dispirited over their inability to move the sellers. As Charlie Baker told a reporter: "We are . . . losing faith in the white man who says that the legal system can be changed. We are losing faith in those who say that justice can be achieved within the framework of the law."[131]

The CBL therefore decided to embark on a new tactic, what Baker called the "big holdout."[132] Members would withhold their monthly contract payments until the sellers agreed to renegotiate. The idea arose spontaneously from the group. After another long day on the picket line, members recalled, "one of the women" said "the only thing we should do is hold the money."[133] It was an extremely risky strategy, since contract sellers could easily evict the buyers and repossess their homes. But enacted en masse, it was also a brilliant strategy, since most of the contract sellers still held mortgages on the properties; without the monthly payments, the sellers risked defaulting on their own mortgages.

The organizers laid the groundwork for the payment strike through one-to-one discussions with members, who, once they understood the principle of a holdout, were all for taking action. Many had been "almost compulsive" about making their payments. To hold payments back was to profoundly alter their long-standing deference to the sellers. They geared themselves for a showdown that might well involve, in one Gamaliel worker's words, "the spectacle of thousands of black men, women, and children being evicted from their homes as winter approaches." The CBL organized its "anti-eviction" teams.[134] The stage was set for the thing Chicagoans feared most: a confrontation in the streets.

NINE

THE BIG HOLDOUT

The Contract Buyers League was born as a West Side organization, but by the end of 1968 the group had been flooded with new members from the South Side. One of the most significant byproducts of the "big holdout" was that it promised—or threatened, from some perspectives—to unite black Chicago.

Black South Siders, more established and upwardly mobile than the more recent, working-class West Siders, had initially kept aloof from the housing struggles in Lawndale. But Sidney Clark changed all that. Originally from Memphis, Clark had come to Chicago at the age of ten, moving with his family into the Altgeld Gardens housing project on the far South Side. In 1958, Clark joined the Chicago police force, making detective seven years later. When the department created a Gang Intelligence Unit in 1967, he volunteered to join. "I didn't have sense enough to be afraid," he said of that decision. "I wouldn't run from a fight. And if you thought you were tough, that's all right, so did I." Before long, he won two citations for bravery: the first for saving the life of a teenage gang member, the second for capturing an armed robber.

Clark married his childhood sweetheart, Julia, and they had two sons. He worked hard to create a stable domestic life for his family. When the boys started elementary school, Clark joined the Parent-Teacher Association, soon becoming its president. By the early 1960s, he recalled, he was "a young married man seeking to get further and do better as far as buying a home." It was with great anticipation that he and Julia purchased a new house in a South Side development created by Universal Builders. The main housing developer in the area, Universal had sold over a thousand newly constructed homes to African Americans. Its salesmen made the process simple. Customers went to see the models on Eighty-seventh Street and decided on the style they preferred; then a salesman took them around to various sites where the house could be constructed. The new house could then be purchased on contract.[1]

The Clarks soon noticed problems with their spanking new home. The basement was unfinished. The walls were thin and quickly developed cracks. The Clarks' dissatisfaction didn't crystallize, however, until early in 1968, when Sidney read about the CBL in the *Chicago Sun-Times*. As he followed the story—the inflated prices, the differences between contract sales and conventional mortgages, and the fact that West Siders had been forced to buy on contract because of racially biased mortgage policies— something clicked for him. He realized that for all of their Chicago sophistication, he and his South Side neighbors had fallen into the same trap. They, too, had been cut off from conventional mortgages and pressured into purchasing homes on contract at inflated prices. Clark began talking to his neighbors, who proved remarkably easy to organize. Universal Builders had built the community, and now that community came together. By the summer of 1968, South Siders were beginning to join the Contract Buyers of Lawndale. The organization accommodated them by changing its name to the Contract Buyers League.[2]

The sudden influx of newcomers produced some tensions. Veteran members resented the whiff of condescension they occasionally sensed from South Siders, who considered themselves superior to the "rural" people of the West Side ghetto. They doubted that the South Siders would have the courage to withhold their monthly payments and risk their new homes. Some, including Macnamara, were not even sure that it made strategic sense for Clark and his neighbors to participate in the payment strike. While the West Siders had run into a brick wall in their efforts to compel their sellers to renegotiate, as of November 1968, Universal Builders still seemed open to discussing the South Siders' grievances.[3]

Against all expectations, Clark and the other South Siders became among those most passionately committed to the payment strike. As Clark saw it, "the bottom line was that the money that we paid for our homes was inflated compared to Caucasians buying similar homes under similar circumstances."[4] As someone who had always followed the rules, Clark was infuriated by this injustice.

On December 1, in an impressive show of unity, over six hundred of the two thousand CBL families withheld their payments. The result was an almost giddy sense of emancipation. As one CBL member explained, the group "got a real kick out of not paying those crooks another cent till we get our renegotiations."[5] By January 1969, the payment boycott was making national news. Charlie Baker, who had emerged as the group's spokesman, told a reporter that CBL members were not worried about an immediate threat to their homes. Even if a seller filed an eviction order immediately, it would take another month at least for the courts to schedule the eviction. Besides, Baker pointed out, "With [the sellers'] records, I don't believe they want to go to court." If any seller dared to actually evict, the CBL would place a twenty-four-hour-a-day picket around the building. "That house will never be sold again," he assured another reporter.[6]

The CBL's anger and defiance were matched by the sellers' fury. The West Side contract sellers retained Irving Block as their counsel, took out full-page advertisements in which they presented themselves as the victims of Catholic Church "agitators," and hunkered down for a long legal battle. Universal Builders was even more enraged when its South Side customers joined the payment strike. The company was a family affair, run by the Samuelses and the Turoffs. Both families were Jewish and saw themselves as decent, liberal supporters of civil rights; they were shocked to find themselves placed in the same category as the low-class, panic-peddling slumlords of Lawndale. Publicly humiliated by accusations of racism, they lost any inclination to negotiate. Once the "big holdout" began, they immediately sought legal means to force the resumption of monthly payments. Intent on separating themselves from the West Siders, they turned for legal help not to Block but to a family friend, attorney Burt Weitzenfeld, and Michael Turoff, the son of Universal Builder co-owner Lee Turoff. Michael was uneasy about taking on the case; it was like a doctor operating on his own family. But he couldn't stay away either. Michael considered his father "the most moral, decent person" he knew. It hurt to see him "devastated by the charges that he was a cheat."[7] Turoff and

Weitzenfeld were determined to fight the CBL, as well as the thirty or so attorneys who had, in their view, been foolhardy enough to lend their services to the group.

As the CBL launched its payment strike, the group's attorneys were working to discover if there was any way the law could help their clients. Leading the effort was Thomas Boodell Jr., a recent Harvard Law School graduate who had been practicing "nuts and bolts" litigation at his father's prestigious Chicago law firm. Sharply aware that "the world was erupting" around him, that people were "marching in Alabama," he sought a way to participate. He consulted a colleague he knew from Catholic Social Action circles, who referred him to Monsignor Egan. Boodell was immediately impressed by the CBL and its goals. "I spent my days walking the streets talking to people and going through the records" to figure out "how this real estate market worked," he recalled. He cobbled together fellowships from the Adlai Stevenson Institute of International Affairs and the American Bar Foundation and used the funding to research the CBL's legal options.[8]

Boodell also helped the CBL to attract several new attorneys. The most important of these was Tom Sullivan, whose slight build and restrained demeanor belied his well-deserved reputation as a tough and brilliant litigator.[9] A star at Jenner and Block (no relation to Irving Block), one of the most prestigious and well-connected law firms in the city, Sullivan was convinced that the group had a case. While the other attorneys asserted that the law could do nothing to help CBL members because a valid contract is untouchable in law—"It is a shame that this is all legal. But there is no legal remedy," they told Macnamara—Sullivan insisted otherwise. "I would be extremely surprised if there was nothing that could be done," he said. "In fact I would be amazed if there's not."[10] Sullivan had something very specific in mind: just five months earlier, in June 1968, the U.S. Supreme Court had issued a major decision in the case of *Jones v. Mayer*. Although the ruling did not deal specifically with contract law, its focus on civil rights—and more profoundly, on the meaning of freedom in a land still dominated by racial segregation— convinced Sullivan that with some creative work it could apply to the situation faced by the CBL.

The case involved a complaint filed in September 1965 by Joseph Lee Jones, an African American, against the Alfred H. Mayer Company, a St. Louis–area construction firm that had refused to sell him one of its new homes. Jones's attorneys argued that the company's refusal to sell to him solely because Jones was African American subverted his basic rights. To support their claim, they cited the Civil Rights Act of 1866, which stated: "All citizens of the United States shall have the same right . . . as is enjoyed by white citizens . . . to inherit, purchase, lease, sell, hold, and convey real and personal property." For a century, that part of the act, known as Section 1982 of Title 42, had been interpreted as barring only *state*-sanctioned obstructions to blacks' equal access to property. In Jones's suit, the lower courts supported this long-standing interpretation: since Section 1982 applied only to governmental acts of housing discrimination, Jones could not use it to challenge the discriminatory actions of the privately owned Mayer Company.

Jones appealed, and the Supreme Court agreed to hear the case. In a startling victory for the plaintiff, the Court ruled that, although the Mayer Company was privately owned, its discriminatory actions did in fact fall under Section 1982. The ruling did more than challenge the accepted reading of that section; it also invested the Thirteenth Amendment, which had abolished slavery, with new force.

To resolve the question of the reach of Section 1982, the Supreme Court read the original congressional debates surrounding the Civil Rights Act of 1866. The act's authors, the Court found, had not drafted Section 1982 to bar only state-sanctioned racial discrimination in matters of property. Instead, they had crafted the act under the authority of the Thirteenth Amendment to ensure that those formerly held in bondage were granted "freedom"—which they defined as equality in society and before the law. The abolition of slavery did not mean that people of African descent could no longer be held as property yet could still be treated as a separate and inferior caste in all other respects. Instead, the act's authors argued that "all badges and incidents of slavery" would be abolished only when formerly enslaved individuals were guaranteed the same "fundamental rights" enjoyed by all U.S. citizens.

What precisely did these fundamental rights consist of? The Court quoted the unambiguous words of Senator Lyman Trumbull, the sponsor of the 1866 act. Free people were entitled to "acquire property, to go and come at pleasure, . . . to enforce rights in the courts, to make contracts, and to inherit and dispose of property." When the Thirteenth Amendment abolished slavery, Trumbull asserted, it also empowered Congress to "destroy all . . . discriminations in civil rights against the black man; and if we cannot, our constitutional amendment amounts to nothing."

The 1968 *Jones v. Mayer* decision reiterated Trumbull's original intent. The denial of any of the fundamental rights of free citizens, the Court wrote, whether by "state or local law" or private "custom, or prejudice," was unconstitutional, as it maintained the "badges and incidents of slavery." The Court also detailed the contemporary relevance of the Civil Rights Act of 1866: "Just as the Black Codes, enacted after the Civil War to restrict the free exercise of . . . rights, were substitutes for the slave system, so the exclusion of Negroes from white communities became a substitute for the Black Codes. And when racial discrimination herds men into ghettos and makes their ability to buy property turn on the color of their skin, then it too is a relic of slavery." The Thirteenth Amendment would be "'a mere paper guarantee' if Congress were powerless to assure that a dollar in the hands of a Negro will purchase the same thing as a dollar in the hands of a white man," the Court asserted. "At the very least, the freedom that Congress is empowered to secure under the Thirteenth Amendment includes the freedom to buy whatever a white man can buy, the right to live wherever a white man can live. If Congress cannot say that being a free man means at least this much, then the Thirteenth Amendment made a promise the Nation cannot keep."[11]

This dramatic ruling encouraged Tom Sullivan to pursue ways to use *Jones v. Mayer* to support the CBL. His boss, Albert (Bert) Jenner, a nationally known attorney and the head of Jenner and Block, approved the idea of Sullivan's working up a complaint. Jenner was a Republican, but he was also a committed civil libertarian who was fascinated by precedent-setting litigation. The CBL struggle piqued his interest. These are "hard-working people, trying to own a home," he said, and "they're getting screwed while they're trying to do it."[12]

Jenner did have some conditions. He insisted that Boodell and some other attorneys share the burden with Jenner and Block: "I can't spare all these lawyers from our office to work on it full time." There was also the matter of fees. The firm wanted to charge the CBL its standard fifteen dollars an hour. Jack Macnamara said that that was out of the question. The company then offered to represent the CBL for twenty-five dollars per family. Again, Macnamara said no. Finally, after Sullivan met personally with CBL members, an accommodation was reached. Jenner and Block would represent the CBL in a suit in federal court. The cost would be zero. Ultimately, "Sullivan said, 'Okay, we'll do it,'" Boodell recalled, "not knowing any better than I did that this would be a monster."[13]

Sullivan, Boodell, and a young Jenner and Block attorney named John Stifler completed a draft of their complaint in December. But Sullivan wasn't satisfied and brought in William Robert (Bob) Ming Jr., one of the nation's foremost civil rights attorneys, to review it.[14] A native black Chicagoan, Ming had served as special assistant corporate counsel and then assistant attorney general in Illinois, worked for the Office of Price Administration in Washington (where his colleagues included the young Richard M. Nixon), taught at the University of Chicago Law School, and started his own firm. Throughout, he devoted himself to the civil rights struggle. Ming was part of the NAACP's "brain trust," fought restrictive covenants and wrote about the biased loan policies of the FHA, and successfully defended Martin Luther King Jr. from income tax evasion charges in Alabama—as his assistant Ellis Reid recalled, Ming convinced Alabamans that "they hated taxes more than they hated Dr. King." He contributed to every major legal brief involving school desegregation, including *Brown v. Board of Education.*[15]

By the late 1960s, however, Ming's glory days were largely behind him. His daily working life was that of a Chicago insider. Back in 1955, he had helped to organize the black vote for Richard J. Daley's first mayoral run, a move that led to Ming's law firm becoming the city's counsel. In 1966, Ming participated in the "summit meeting" between Martin Luther King's Chicago Freedom Movement and the city's business, political, and labor leaders. There he had irritated King by claiming that "the Negro is protected" by Chicago's 1963 open housing ordinance. In short, as Ellis Reid recalled, Ming worked "both sides of the street."[16]

Playing both sides might have had its costs. Ming often ended his workdays at about 4:30 p.m., when he'd help himself to the contents of his heavily stocked office liquor cabinet. In the early evenings he could be heard recounting stories of his military service during World War II or of his encounters with famous civil rights leaders. "He was a bullshitter. He was a drunk," one of his former aides recalled, but "he could be very charming." And his formidable legal skills remained intact. As John McKnight noted, "He was probably, next to Thurgood Marshall, the most prominent black constitutional lawyer in the country."[17]

Ming agreed to revise the complaint. Sullivan was thrilled with the result. "Now it sings," he told Boodell and Macnamara. "You can't read it without wanting to do something for the plaintiffs." Ming also offered his services to the CBL. He and attorney Aldus Mitchell teamed up with Sullivan, Boodell, and John Stifler to do what everyone said could not be done: challenge legal contracts on the basis of civil rights.[18] On January 6, 1969, the attorneys filed a complaint in U.S. District Court against the West Side contract sellers, *Charles and Charlene Baker et al. v. F & F [Fushanis and Forman] Investment et al.* Two weeks later they filed a second complaint against the South Side builders that sold new homes on contract, *Sidney and Julia Clark et al. v. Universal Builders Inc., et al.*

Both suits charged that the contract sellers had violated the 1866 Civil Rights Act and the intent of the Thirteenth Amendment by exploiting residential segregation and the resulting artificially created black housing shortage for their own financial gain. The defendants also faced charges of conspiracy, unconscionability, usury, and fraud. The West Side sellers faced the additional charge of blockbusting.[19] The CBL's attorneys proposed a range of relief for the contract buyers, including having their installment contracts reformed to reflect fair market value; having them declared void, with the sellers compelled to return to the buyers all that they had paid, plus 6 percent interest and minus a fair market rental for the years that the buyers had lived in the property; a payment of $25,000 in punitive damages to each plaintiff; or a payment to each contract buyer of twice the amount that the buyer had paid on his or her installment contract. In all, the attorneys asked for approximately $40 million in damages.[20]

Many CBL members were elated. "I had read who Bert Jenner was. . . . Oh boy, he was a big man," Ruth Wells enthused. "A firm like that wouldn't come in unless we had a pretty good fight."[21] Others were uneasy about the sudden leadership role of prominent Chicago attorneys in what had been a grassroots struggle. Saul Alinsky had a saying: "If it's in the hands of the lawyers, it's out of the streets."[22] And the initial effect of the two federal lawsuits was exactly what Alinsky predicted: media attention immediately shifted from the CBL's payment strike to the lawsuits. The suits could "set a nationwide precedent by outlawing discriminatory practices by private businesses," the *Chicago Sun-Times* reported, adding that they had been prepared by "some of the most distinguished attorneys in Chicago." John McKnight told reporters that the suits could be the first real challenge to the "tangled web of urban racism" underlying the country's real estate system. Bert Jenner called the suits "pioneering litigation . . . that has never been tried before in the courts of this land." But privately, some attorneys had a different assessment, fearing that the suits, if lost, could undo the gains already made. As Boodell recalled, "People were calling me up and saying, 'boy, oh boy, . . . if you go too far, you're going to ruin the precedent of *Jones v. Mayer.*'"[23]

The CBL's attorneys had their work cut out for them. Although both suits were complex, the West Side suit (*Baker v. F & F Investment*) initially seemed the more demanding of the two. It named dozens of contract sellers as defendants, including several—Moe Forman, Lou Fushanis, Jay Goran, Gerald Crane, W. F. Smith, the Peters brothers, and Arthur Krooth— my father had battled.[24] The complaint accused them of exploiting Chicago's "custom" of segregation, using scare tactics to convince whites to flee changing neighborhoods, and taking advantage of the "artificial scarcity" of black housing that was created by segregation and by discriminatory FHA loan policies.[25]

The suit also named banks and savings and loan institutions as defendants, since they had provided money to the contract sellers while refusing loans to black prospective home purchasers. The defendant loan institutions knew that the mortgages they granted to the sellers would be used to buy property exclusively for the purpose of resale at "unconscionable" markups to blacks. They often made loans "in excess of value of mortgaged property" based on "false and excessive appraisals." They sometimes closed these loans "at the same time and place" as the execution of installment contracts. The fourteen financial institutions cited in the suit included General Federal Savings and Loan and the Chicago National Bank, both of which my father had fought a decade earlier.[26]

CBL attorneys cited *Jones v. Mayer*'s understanding of the Thirteenth Amendment—that "a dollar in the hands of a Negro" must "purchase the same thing as a dollar in the hands of a white man"—to make an obvious point. By selling homes to a captive market of black buyers "at prices far in excess of [the properties'] cost and value," the defendants "diminish[ed] the purchasing power of Negro citizens' money in comparison to the purchasing power of non-Negro citizens" and in effect collected "a race tax" from the plaintiffs. As a result of racial segregation abetted and exploited by the defendants, the plaintiffs were compelled to inhabit the city's worst housing and to pay exorbitant prices for that privilege. Their segregated neighborhoods contained inferior parks and schools. Though insurance rates were high, fire and police protection was inadequate. Garbage pickup, street maintenance, and public transportation were also worse than elsewhere in the city. The plaintiffs paid more for food, clothing, and building repair, and they suffered from the discriminatory application of city building codes.

Because the defendants overcharged the plaintiffs and then entrapped them in contracts that gave them no equity in the properties until most or all of the price had been paid, the plaintiffs could not sell their properties without suffering a grave financial loss. Therefore they were "required, in many cases against their wishes, . . . to remain, in involuntary financial servitude, as residents" of the West Side, even though the area had become "an undesirable place" in which to live and to raise children. "Plaintiffs have suffered discrimination solely on the basis of their Negro race and loss and impairment of their civil rights as guaranteed by the United States Constitution and the statutes of the United States," the complaint summed up. "They have been subject to the aforesaid indicia and badges of slavery as a direct . . . result of the wrongful conduct of defendants as alleged herein."[27]

The West Side sellers' attorney, Irving Block, expressed his initial reaction to *Baker v. F & F Investment* in a short note to Tom Sullivan. If not for "the tremendous respect that I have for members of your firm," he wrote, "I would think I was reading a fairy tale." But privately, Block wasn't laughing. This federal suit was based "not only on sound principles of law but also on logic," he wrote in a circular to the Real Estate Investors Association.[28] His anxiety probably increased when the case was randomly assigned to Judge Hubert L. Will, one of the most liberal judges in Chicago.

Also worrisome was the fact that the two sides were profoundly mismatched in terms of money and manpower. "We had a four-lawyer office, and half a dozen major law firms in Chicago were representing the CBL, for free," recalled Block's assistant, Warren Lupel.[29]

Block filed several motions to dismiss the suit. He argued that although *Baker* had been brought as a class action it did not fit that bill. The CBL complaint was "an artificial tying together of separate claims by separate plaintiffs against separate defendants and requiring separate proofs."[30] The suit should also be dismissed because the five-year statute of limitations had expired. The injuries allegedly suffered by most of the plaintiffs had occurred in the 1950s and early 1960s, when they signed their contracts—too long ago to be tried. Finally, Block challenged the plaintiffs' claim that *Jones v. Mayer*'s interpretation of Section 1982 was relevant to the actions of West Side contract sellers. *Jones v. Mayer* determined that Section 1982 barred all racial discrimination, whether private or public, in the sale or rental of property; that was well and good. But Section 1982 did not apply to Block's clients, who, after all, never refused to sell to the plaintiffs because of their race. The plaintiffs could only charge the contract sellers with "hypothetical" discrimination. They would have to make the unprovable claim that if the sellers had sold homes on contract to whites they would have charged them less. Such an argument, if given legal backing, would produce chaos. It would mean that "every non-white citizen has a cause of action in Federal Court to either reform or rescind each and every transaction" involving the purchase of real estate. He need only make the "simple allegation that he was charged more than a white person *would have been* charged" for the same parcel.[31]

Judge Hubert Will disagreed. He ruled that the case qualified as a class action.[32] He also dismissed Block's argument about the statute of limitations. He ordered that a notice be placed in Chicago newspapers "addressed to all members of the Negro race" who bought Chicago residential real estate on contract since January 1, 1952, from any of the suit's defendants. All such people were eligible to be part of a class action suit as long as they were still making payments on their contracts as of January 6, 1964 (exactly five years before the suit was filed).[33]

Most importantly, Judge Will rejected the defendants' claim that Section 1982 as interpreted in *Jones v. Mayer* did not apply to them because they never refused to sell to an individual because of his or her race. According to Will, the Civil Rights Act of 1866 was intended to ensure that "our economy be undifferentiated as to the race of a man." Therefore the very "existence of a black market distinct from a white market was the de facto vestige of what the Congress of 1866 intended to abolish." The law did not narrowly prohibit specific behaviors, such as the overt refusal to sell an item to an African American. It prohibited any actions that targeted blacks for unequal treatment and thereby placed them at a systematic economic disadvantage. Will saved his most scathing words for the sellers' argument that they couldn't be accused of discrimination against blacks, since it could not be proven that they would have sold property to whites at lower prices. Will dismissed this argument as "ridiculous." It would mean that the 1866 Civil Rights Act "allows an injustice so long as it is visited entirely on negroes."[34]

In March 1969, there was more good news for the CBL. The Justice Department filed a friend of the court brief supporting the West Side suit—or, more specifically, opposing the sellers' motion to dismiss it. Jerris Leonard, assistant attorney general in charge of the Civil Rights Division, told the press: "This is a very important case, and our interest is further sparked by the possibility of establishing a law that could be applied nationally." He praised the CBL's members for their "valiant effort to right a wrong." Their "lawful and orderly method," he commented, "has not gone unnoticed." As Leonard elaborated to a *New York Times* reporter, "Anybody who rakes a profit based on racial discrimination should have to pay it back with interest." He echoed the complaint's radical language, calling such gains a "race tax."[35]

The Justice Department memo was widely hailed. Attorney General John N. Mitchell called it the federal government's "first effort to break massive northern housing segregation." The *Wall Street Journal* believed it could establish the principle that "Negroes have a right to go into a Federal court and sue for damages when they've bought homes, appliances, groceries, clothing or other items on less favorable terms than whites get." Leonard's "determination to obtain this new self-help economic tool for Negroes apparently complements President Nixon's idea for helping blacks establish their own businesses," the *Journal* enthused.[36]

Irving Block saw the hypocrisy of the Justice Department's position. He was one of several attorneys to point out that, because the FHA had discriminated against blacks, the U.S. Justice Department had "unclean hands" and should not be allowed to enter the case on the side of the plaintiffs. Thumbing his nose at the Justice Department's grandstanding, Block filed a motion in April 1969 asking that federal loan and insurance agencies be added as *defendants* in the West Side (*Baker*) suit.[37]

Despite Block's efforts, Will's final ruling on the defendants' motions to dismiss, which was delivered in May 1969, gave the CBL's members a sweeping victory, upholding their claim that the sellers could be charged with violating their civil rights. One part of Will's decision may have given Block some satisfaction, however: his dismissal of the count titled "Unconscionability, Fraud, Usury, and Breach of Implied Warranties." Will ruled that the actions of the sellers alleged here—such as concealing accurate appraisals of the properties' value, the prices that they had recently paid for the properties, and the properties' building code violations— were not actionable offenses: "Statements as to value of property are ordinarily considered mere expressions of opinion, and for that reason, are not sufficient to warrant a rescission of the contract, even though they are false." The words were surely familiar to Block, since Will was quoting the Illinois appellate court decision in *Coleman v. Goran*—the case concerning Jay Goran's sale of a house worth $3,000 to William and Wilma Coleman for $12,000 that Irving Block had won on appeal back in 1960.[38]

More than anything, Will's decision revealed how times had changed. In 1960, when Block won the *Coleman v. Goran* appeal, he had represented normality and reason, while his opponent, Mark J. Satter, appeared to be the wild-eyed extremist. Now the situation was reversed. Jenner and Block's attorneys represented the mainstream, while Irving Block seemed to symbolize his clients' crude, obsolete racial brutishness. In the spring of 1969, a number of different attorneys still defended individual contract sellers— including several who, like Block, had done so for a long time.[39] Yet now, as one observer noted, these attorneys "did not want to be mentioned. . . . They were happy for the publicity to be directed against Block."[40] Block seemed to have a knack for drawing negative press. Late in 1968, for example, he stated that "some of these people can't get mortgages because they are no good!" In response, one black Chicago newspaper called Block a "racist."[41]

To Block's assistant, Warren Lupel, such charges were unfair, of a piece with the way the sellers were pilloried in the press. "None of the people we represented were angels," he said, but "that doesn't mean they're not entitled to be defended based upon the actual facts." Instead, in Lupel's view, Block and his clients were condemned well before the facts could be presented.[42] Still, the CBL case had its satisfactions. "When Block appeared in court with Albert Jenner on one side of him and Tom Sullivan on the other, he used to love it," Lupel recalled. "He would do things that these brilliant men could not deal with. For example, I can remember distinctly the courtroom being jammed with people before Judge Will. . . . And Block would put his arm around Jenner, and he'd say, 'My good friend Bert and I were just talking about this, Judge.' And Jenner would go, 'Oh God, how can this man call me a friend? How am I going to face these people?' He used to do things like that just to bug them."

For Block as well as Lupel, the West Side suit offered an opportunity to battle the attorneys of a prestigious firm and to challenge their self-righteousness. "The Jenner and Block attorneys never proffered to their clients that they represented the very lenders who refused these people loans for racist reasons," Lupel said. As with the Justice Department, "the hypocrisy was obvious." Jenner could squirm away from Irving Block in order to "get his arm off him," but he thought "it was perfectly acceptable that he represented [in unrelated suits] the First National Bank that wouldn't give these people two cents to buy real estate."[43]

All the same, Block seemed passionately committed to justifying the sellers' actions. When some considered negotiating with the CBL, Block "yelled and shouted at any suggestion that a compromise be reached."[44] No doubt he simply wanted to win his case. Yet Block also seemed to be carrying on a running argument with someone who was no longer there to answer back. When the *Wall Street Journal* asked for Block's views on contract selling, he responded, "I see nothing unholy in speculation." But no one had called speculation "unholy"—certainly not the *Wall Street Journal*. "Unholy alliance" had been a pet phrase of my father's; he used it routinely to describe the relationship between mortgage and insurance companies that shut off the flow of credit to changing neighborhoods.[45] For years after my father's death, Block no longer had him to debate, but he kept the argument going nevertheless.

Initially, Block remained engaged with his deceased friend and opponent by helping my mother settle my father's estate and by looking after my brother David. Then, in 1966, Block hired a new secretary. Her previous boss was Mark J. Satter. Working for Block represented quite a change for Sandy Gatto. "I don't think Block would have fought for the underdog the way your dad did. Not saying anything against him, it's just that he had a different type of practice," Gatto told me. But she liked Block personally: "Irving Block was a nice, nice man. He came across gruff but he was like a pussycat." Block even helped out her family. One of Gatto's aunts found herself in the same predicament as my mother, inheriting a building in a slum neighborhood that she couldn't afford to maintain. "It was a large apartment building," Gatto recalled, but Block took it off her hands. Her aunt received "practically nothing" for it, but she didn't complain. "She was just happy to be out of it." Gatto felt that when Block sold my mother's buildings to speculators, his actions were similarly well motivated. "I don't think Irving Block would ever do anything intentionally to hurt your family," she said.[46]

Block was undoubtedly confident that in turning my father's buildings over to the only people he believed capable of running them, he had done nothing wrong—no matter what Mark Satter argued.[47] But there was one person that he remained unable to convince. On July 12, 1968—coincidentally, the three-year anniversary of my father's death—my mother, Clarice, went to see Block about a legal matter, only to find him in the midst of a meeting with the Real Estate Investors Association. My mother now lived a quiet life. We had moved to the first floor of a two-flat in Skokie; my aunt, uncle, and cousin lived on the second. My mother had recently undergone additional cancer surgery. She worked part time at a Jewish community center and was grateful for the health insurance that the job provided. On her way out of Block's office that day, she passed picketers from the Contract Buyers League. In a small act of rebellion, Clarice took one of their leaflets and mailed it to my brother David, then at Oxford University. "If Dad were here he very well might have been the attorney for the Contract Buyers League," my mother wrote. "I'm certain that Irv Block is being paid handsomely for his efforts" on behalf of the Real Estate Investors Association. "I like him—but you know which side he has always been on. In our dealings he saw nothing wrong in handing our property over to one of his pet realtors or speculator friends who promptly resold it at a good profit."[48]

Block never got the chance he wanted to fully vindicate his clients—or himself. On June 9, 1969, he died of emphysema. "It was quite unexpected and sudden," Lupel recalled. "I had been to visit him the day before, and he was sitting up, his feet dangling, and he was fine."[49] For someone who got such joy from winning, it was particularly ironic that although Block had been in court almost daily for several months, he died while the biggest case of his life was still in the pretrial period.

The West Side sellers didn't have long to wait for a new champion. By July 1969, attorney George Feiwell had replaced Block as their main counsel. Like Block, Feiwell was an attorney who would fight, and fight hard, for his clients.[50] Structurally, Feiwell's position was similar to Block's. As CBL supporter Alan Boles noted, "Jenner and Block was very much of a silk stocking operation," while Feiwell was a "gritty, grubbing single practitioner."[51] Feiwell was young, healthy, extremely energetic, and committed to stay for the long haul. He knew the case was complicated. It was about to get more so, in part because of the community action that had precipitated the federal suits in the first place—the "big holdout."

Although the South Side *Clark v. Universal* case, which mainly targeted one company rather than scores of disparate individuals and institutions, appeared to be more straightforward, this assessment soon proved incorrect—in part because of Universal's legal strategy. Its attorneys immediately went on the offensive. First, Weitzenfeld and Turoff filed their own suit charging the South Side CBL with conspiring to interfere with a contractual obligation (that is, inducing its members to withhold payments on valid installment contracts). Bert Jenner got the suit dismissed.[52] The company then moved on to the next weapon in its legal arsenal: eviction filings. Because of the stipulations of Illinois's eviction statute, the Forcible Entry and Detainer Act, such proceedings were difficult to challenge in court. Those served with eviction notices were allowed only two defenses: (1) they did not receive the notice or (2) they had in fact made the payment. Arguments providing the context of a failure to make a payment were not allowed. By January 10, Universal had initiated thirty forcible entry and detainer suits. Ten days later, the number rose to sixty. [53]

There were several reasons for Universal's aggressive posture. As noted, the CBL's case against the South Side sellers—primarily Universal Builders—was less clear-cut than that against their West Side counterparts. West Side contract sellers routinely charged their buyers about double the worth of their buildings. In contrast, Universal's markups mostly ranged between 20 and 35 percent, and in some cases they were considerably less.[54] Universal also claimed to sell on contract only as a service to its customers. As executive Richard Samuels would tell reporters, "I'd prefer not to sell houses on contract. But if I didn't, I wouldn't be able to provide housing for hundreds of families that need it." He resented the blurring of West Side sellers' policies with those of his more reputable company. It was "a myth," he said, "that if you miss one payment you're out. You have to miss a lot more than one payment." In thirteen years of business, he claimed, Universal had never considered evicting a tenant until the CBL payment strike.[55]

While Universal's guilt seemed less obvious, the payment strike posed a greater financial threat to Universal Builders than to the West Side sellers. On the West Side, the holdout predominantly threatened the contract buyers, who had invested large amounts of money into homes that they now might lose, rather than the sellers, many of whom had already received from the buyers more money than the buildings were worth. On the South Side, the sellers were in greater jeopardy. Many contracts were for recent sales on which Universal still owed considerable amounts on its own mortgages. As Universal president Lee Turoff would explain to the press, he owed almost $2 million in construction mortgages. If the payment strike continued, he would face "financial ruin." He had no choice but to evict so that he could get paying tenants into the buildings.[56]

Universal's threats of eviction managed to accomplish what West Side sellers' legal arguments did not: they motivated the CBL's lawyers to pressure the group to call off its payment strike. The CBL attorneys claimed that they did so to avoid getting tied up in hundreds of eviction suits. In truth, most of the attorneys had been against the holdout from the start. There were early inklings of an attorney-community conflict when Tom Sullivan asked Macnamara if the CBL would end its strike if the attorneys advised them to. Macnamara replied that that was out of the question—the group made its own tactical decisions. To the CBL, the strike was a weapon to get their contracts renegotiated. It seemed to be effective: now that the sellers were facing their own mounting mortgage, insurance, and tax bills, more CBL members, at least on the West Side, received invitations from their sellers to "come down and talk."[57] As Charlie Baker exulted to a cheering crowd of CBL members, "We, not our enemies, are now in the driver's seat. Now we're going to let them do the sweating, while all that payment money piles up. We're going to win, and they better believe it."[58]

Their attorneys viewed the matter differently. "I can't advise you to have a payment strike because of the risks involved," Boodell told them. For those who missed the legalese, he put the matter plainly: "No, for God's sake, don't do that! They'll kick you out of your houses!"[59] Despite this danger, CBL members did not want to end the strike. They were ultimately convinced to do so only when their attorneys explained that the strike's continuation threatened the success of the two federal suits. In the spring of 1969, the lawyers were engaged in nearly daily court battles simply to prevent the suits from being dismissed. One of the arguments they used to justify their pro bono involvement was that the CBL, unlike "radical" groups, was willing to use the law rather than break it. The payment strike, which was undeniably extralegal, undercut this argument. The eviction issue, on top of this, tipped the balance. In a settlement negotiated by their attorneys and Judge Will, the strikers agreed to resume monthly contract payments. In return, the sellers would put a portion of these payments into an escrow fund to be repaid to the buyers if they won their cases. The South Siders accepted these terms on March 4, 1969, and the West Siders on April 3, 1969.[60]

Many CBL members were unhappy about ending the strike after only three months. As one woman told an interviewer, she had agreed to resume her payments only because "Jack and Baker and all them said this is what we had to do." Some of the attorneys began to sense that they had acted prematurely. As one acknowledged, "There was a general feeling among the people that 'we do not want to do this,' that 'we are being pushed by the lawyers.'"[61] Perhaps most upsetting was the sellers' seemingly vindictive reaction to the end of the strike. Several demanded that buyers pay not only the money withheld but also "permissive delinquencies" that the sellers had overlooked for years. When some buyers were unable to pay their debts on the spot, the sellers began eviction proceedings against them.[62]

Among the first to receive an eviction notice were Chester and Julia Fisher, a South Side couple. In May they appeared in court to contest their eviction. They admitted that they had received a notice and that they had not made the payments demanded; therefore the judge directed the jury to rule in favor of Rosewood Corporation, the Universal Builders subsidiary that had brought the charge. The Fishers were ordered to vacate their home. Their attorney, Marshall Patner, was not allowed to address the circumstances surrounding the couple's refusal to make their contract payment.[63]

Most of the CBL's attorneys felt that cases such as the Fishers' were a waste of time. Tom Sullivan, for example, did not want to become "entangled" in the issue. But Patner disagreed. A rolypoly, cheerfully disheveled man who was then in the midst of establishing a public interest law firm, Patner was a first-rate legal theorist who was familiar with the workings of contract sales. He also knew a lot about the state's eviction law, which he had long considered unjust and possibly unconstitutional.[64]

Working with a young volunteer attorney named Jeffrey Fitzgerald, Patner had come up with a plan to challenge the forcible entry and detainer statute: he would represent an evicted CBL family and raise in court the unconscionable terms of their installment contract. His defense would be ruled off limits, and the family would lose their case. Once they lost, however, Patner could appeal to the Illinois Supreme Court. There he would argue that the statute, by barring his clients from raising relevant defenses in court, denied them due process as well as equal protection under the law. In short, he would show that the law was unconstitutional and had to be modified or overturned. A successful challenge to the forcible entry statute would have huge repercussions. In addition to getting a one-sided law off the books, it might push the sellers to negotiate. As Fitzgerald explained, once the law was declared unconstitutional, evictions would stop, which "would put such pressure on the banks and sellers that they'd settle the main case."[65]

The eviction filed against Chester and Julia Fisher was Patner's test case. As expected, his arguments were ruled "not germane," and the Fishers lost. Patner then appealed, and by the late spring of 1969, the case was on its way to the Illinois Supreme Court. The Jenner and Block attorneys were not pleased. They felt that having the CBL represented by more than one group of attorneys would only sow confusion.[66] But the CBL's members felt differently. They welcomed Patner's determination to fight the forcible entry law, which, whatever its theoretical justification, handed the sellers the power to throw people out of their homes while denying them the dignity of their "day in court." The forcible entry or eviction statute had been the sellers' most powerful legal weapon. Now, the possibility that it could be overturned put the payment strike in a new light. In a matter of weeks, Patner's legal strategy became part of an "agonizing debate" among CBL members over whether they should resume the strike.[67]

They knew the risks involved. Carrying on with the payment strike would mean going against their attorneys' advice and facing the possibility of what one CBL member called "an ugly, harsh, sickening thing—to come home and see your things put out." On the other hand, if their organization was simply subsumed into a lawsuit it might well "die on the vine." Many also resented having been pushed to resume their payments while the sellers, for the most part, still refused to negotiate. Universal Builders claimed to be ready to talk, but as Sidney Clark said, from the company's point of view, "sitting down and talking meant simply 'you give the money to us that you already owe us and should have paid us and you get back on track and you start making your payments and keep your mouth shut.'" Clark felt that paying the sellers was not only personally humiliating but tactically unwise. "If you are giving them money," he told CBL members, "you are giving them the ammunition to fight us with."[68]

When the CBL finally voted on the issue, the results were overwhelming. As one member recalled, the desire to renew the strike "was just like a ball of fire. It was stronger than the first time." Starting July 1, 1969, members would again withhold their payments. The goal remained the same: to push the sellers to renegotiate. But this time around, the league would also publicize the gross disparity between the legal remedies available to the sellers through the forcible entry statute and those available to the buyers. This publicity, it hoped, would provide a more favorable political context within which Marshall Patner's legal challenge could proceed. CBL members also felt that "a delay in justice is a denial of justice." They pointed out that the law gave the sellers automatic relief, while they were forced to go through years of uncertain legal battles. In the meantime, every inflated monthly payment they made kept them mired in poverty.[69] The strike would give them the immediate redress—both symbolic and material—that the system denied them.

The renewed payment strike had one more goal: to give the contract buyers their day in court. They planned to use the opportunity to describe the realities of their lives. "Talking back" to judges was illegal, but to the CBL it was just. As Jack Macnamara noted, the judges were "intimately familiar with the style of life" of the sellers, but had no understanding of the pressures faced by the contract buyers. Such ignorance led to attitudes like those of one Chicago Circuit Court judge who repeated stories land-lords had told him about their no-good tenants: "There are people who are professional deadbeats, who constantly spend their money on booze and T.V. instead of on the good things of life like . . . rent [here the judge sat back and laughed at his own joke]. What are you to do about these professional deadbeats?"[70]

CBL members were determined to tell their side of the story. Once court eviction proceedings began, the strikers started to go in without lawyers and defend themselves. "Some of these ladies would make a lawyer look really bad anyhow," Ruth Wells recalled. "I've seen the court reporter crying after one of these ladies started talking." One CBL member explained to the judge that she would happily make her monthly pay-ments, but only if her contract was made more fair. The judge interrupted. "Young lady, I'm sorry to say this, but somebody has led you down the wrong path. . . . And I know who." Before he could berate her further, she cut him off. "You are right, Your Honor. They misled us in Mississippi. I came here to get a better place to raise my family. And when I came here . . . they misled me and cheated me again. All I wanted was to buy a . . . home, and I was cheated. I was misled worse here . . . 'cause there they don't hide their hand. I came to get justice. And you are sitting there agreeing with me, and at the end you are going to shake your head and say 'There is nothing I can do, my hands are tied.'" Wells, who accompanied this woman to court, recounted the story's conclusion. As predicted, the judge said: "I'm sorry, but my hands are tied." He gave the woman thirty days "to pay up or get out." The contract buyer remained unrepentant. "She said she wasn't going to put up or get out," Wells noted.[71]

Telling it to the judges sometimes won benefits, such as temporary stays of eviction orders. It gave CBL members a sense of power in a setting that had formerly intimidated them. They were proud to achieve better results when they argued their own cases than when they relied on attor-neys, and they were energized by encounters with judges who were shaken by their stories or who expressed regret about the role that the law forced them to play.[72]

Their rebellious stance also fostered a renewed sense of excitement and solidarity—feelings that had waned during the months of legal wrangling over the federal suits. Some of the excitement stemmed from members' concrete economic gains. "They loved it when [one of the leaders] would get up and announce the grand total [of money withheld] each month," Macnamara recalled. "I loved it, too." One CBL member said: "I felt that if we held out long enough, I'd have enough money to get another house."[73] More profoundly, the members' commitment to risking, for one another's sake, something as important as the homes they had struggled to hold on to created a sense of boundless possibility. As Charlie Baker said at one meeting: "If a thousand people get together and do one thing, who is going to stop them? It's like when Moses was leading the people away from Pharaoh. As they were going through the desert, the people were mumbling that it was a trick. . . . [But] they got to the other side and the sea fell back on Pharaoh. The same thing happens today. All you got to do is believe. If you all stick together, there's not a thing the real estate man can do."[74]

Once the strike resumed, CBL meetings again became packed, emotional celebrations of solidarity. At an August 1969 meeting, a Mr. Coleman, a member whose seller had agreed to lower his monthly payments from $200 a month to $127 a month, compared his victory to a religious awakening. "This is like telling that you've found the Lord," he told the group. "It's such a burden off of you that you can't keep it to yourself, you want to tell everyone about it." Attorney Bob Ming spoke about the federal lawsuits, explaining that they were "an effort to remove one of the vestiges of slavery. Not all of them, just one of them. If we remove one at a time, we'll ultimately get rid of all of them." The most emotional moment came during an impassioned speech by Clyde Ross. He described his discovery that, while other neighborhoods paid $31 a year for insurance, the common rate in Lawndale was $170. "That $170 that this man robs from you can be used to rehabilitate your house," he pointed out. But instead, "he takes it away from you, and spreads this poison image that you can't keep up your house! . . . They've cheated us about much more than money. . . . We've been cheated out of the right to be human beings in this society." He added, "In the final analysis, you are the ones going to pay for what you neglect. Your child is the one going to go in the alleys looking for leadership. Your child, not his!" But now, with the CBL, "we have a chance," he exhorted the crowd. "Stand on your own two feet! Be a human being! Fight for what you know is right! Fight!"[75]

By October 1969, 552 CBL families were again withholding monthly payments. Of these, 261 were threatened with eviction. Those who were brought to court under the forcible entry statute could buy time by appealing their judgments; they could not be evicted until their appeal was decided. There was a catch, however. They had to post a bond, which in most cases was set high enough to ensure that the landlord or seller would have his or her income covered for a year—the time estimated for the appeal process to go through the courts. For delinquencies on charges of $200 a month, for example, the bond was generally set at $2,400 to $3,000. In CBL eviction cases, however, judges set appeal bonds at $5,000 or even $7,500. To raise that sum, the evictee was given five days. In the first week of October alone, the CBL posted $71,000 in appeal bonds. For an organization that raised most of its money through solicitations of nonmembers, this was a staggering sum. It was clear that the CBL would be bankrupt well before all its members could appeal their evictions.[76]

It was against this backdrop that Macnamara once again invited Father Robert F. Harvanek, the provincial superior of the Chicago Province of the Society of Jesus, to dinner at his Lawndale apartment. Two years earlier, Harvanek had upset Macnamara by saying that he would not hesitate to end the Presentation Parish Community Organization Project if he felt it necessary. This time the mood was better. Several CBL members were present. They were magnetic, eloquent, and extremely knowledgeable, even quoting the Bible to place their struggle in what they saw as its proper religious context. When the evening ended, Macnamara recalled, "I just had a good feeling." But he could hardly have expected the phone call he received just one hour later. It was from one of Harvanek's assistants, "a really conservative, straightlaced Jesuit." Harvanek believed that the contract buyers had been unfairly treated and should have a chance to appeal their eviction rulings. Therefore the Society of Jesus would make $100,000 available for the posting of bonds. The Jesuits understood that if the appeals were lost the money would be lost as well, but they were willing to take the risk. Their grant was a concrete demonstration of their enthusiasm for the CBL's efforts to "achieve justice within the framework of this nation's legal system" and evidence of their faith in the ability of the U.S. judicial system to "rectify" its flaws.[77]

"I thought I'd died and gone to heaven," Macnamara recalled. Harvanek had made a bold and impressive move. After a yearlong study, the Jesuits had recently decided, in Harvanek's words, to "give our social apostolate the same priority as our education apostolate." Now Harvanek acted on that new priority. His superior, Pedro Arrupe, supported the appeal bond donation wholeheartedly. "No words of praise which I could pen can adequately express my admiration for the spirit of Christian charity which impels the Chicago Province to jeopardize its own possessions in order to win for others their human rights," Arrupe wrote.[78]

In December, Macnamara held another dinner for the Jesuit brass at his Lawndale apartment. In addition to CBL members, Macnamara invited some white supporters, including U.S. Attorney Thomas Foran and Midas Muffler chief executive Gordon Sherman. Once again, the evening was a success, this time filled with the spirit of ecumenism. "Gordon Sherman, who of course was Jewish, starts out his little spiel to these guys, you know, 'Jack and I are not of the same persuasion but we are of the same faith,'" Macnamara recalled. "I loved it, it really captured what we were all about." Within weeks, the Right Reverend John Edwards, chair of the Conference of Major Superiors of the Jesuit order, announced that the U.S. Jesuits would contribute an additional $150,000 toward the CBL's bond fund. As Edwards explained, "We believe in the soundness of the strategies of the exploited black home purchasers, and in the importance of our efforts as churchmen to do everything in our power to eradicate every form of racial injustice." The announcement made national news and further legitimized the CBL's struggle.[79]

Even the lawyers were won over. By the end of 1969, Tom Sullivan had agreed to work with Marshall Patner to fight the constitutionality of the forcible entry and detainer statute. Sullivan acknowledged that CBL members' grassroots pressure had "goaded" him to attempt legal innovations. "We'll go out and try to find the way," he told a CBL meeting. "But in a sense you are leading us." Tom Boodell Jr. encouraged the group to "keep prodding, and we'll keep on doing what we can." He had come to understand that to CBL members the harsh, one-sided provisions of the forcible entry statute were "an example of what white people would do to you."[80]

There was one person, though, who was not moved by the CBL's renewed payment strike. And unfortunately, Judge Hubert L. Will was of immense importance to its struggle.

• • •

Judge Will's background predisposed him to sympathize with the CBL. The Milwaukee-born son of a German Protestant pharmacist, he had chosen to study law because he believed that as an attorney he could help make society "efficient, useful and just." The brilliant professors and fellow students he encountered at the University of Chicago Law School, as well as the rise of Hitler in Germany, solidified his progressive convictions. After graduation Will went to Washington, D.C., where he helped draft a proposed national health bill in 1939. He served in the armed forces during World War II and then joined the American Veterans Committee, a group established as a progressive alternative to the American Legion. He was a donor to the Chicago Urban League, a member of the National Housing Conference, and a resident of Hyde Park, which both he and his wife were committed to maintaining as a stable interracial neighborhood. He was also an early supporter of Mayor Richard J. Daley, who rewarded Will's aid in the 1955 election by nominating him for the federal bench in 1961.[81]

Will's deep-seated racial liberalism was certainly a factor in his initially positive response to the CBL's actions. He later acknowledged that he might have been "overly tolerant, overly sympathetic" to the buyers at the start of the case because of his desire to "reconstruct the past hundred years." His empathy for the CBL also derived from his familiarity with Chicago's history of "panic peddling." In February 1969, Will had encouraged the West Side sellers to settle the federal civil rights suits rather than tie up the court's energies in a lengthy trial. "The spread [between what the sellers paid and what the buyers paid] is sufficient to make it clear that these were exorbitant prices," he noted, so why not settle? He surmised that the low price the sellers originally paid was a "scare price which they got from the white owner . . . by terrorizing him." Another time, Will commented that "nobody can dispute that in the availability of houses there has not been a free market." When the sellers' attorney angrily retorted that Will was prejudging the case, the judge stood by his words: "I am telling you what they will be able to prove. . . . I do not think it does any good for me to act as though I have been dead for the last 20 years."

Even deeper than Will's liberalism, however, was his commitment to the justice system itself, his belief that the law applied equally to all. The CBL's payment strike was, of course, based on precisely the opposite belief, that "the law operates differently for rich people than for poor people," as they wrote to Will. In November 1969, over one hundred CBL members showed up in Will's courtroom, and twenty came to the bar to speak directly to him. "Them books you got don't fit no black man's case," one man said. Another added that the law ignored poor black people, "unless we are out in the streets . . . breaking windows downtown." Only then, he continued, would the law "find some remedy for us."[82]

Will disagreed. He felt that the idea behind the resumed payment strike—that the legal system was inherently unjust but could be swayed by external pressure—was an insult. "You have not been denied things because of the color of your skin," he lectured one CBL member.[83] He was willing to accept the legal brief filed by Marshall Patner that put the constitutionality of the forcible entry and detainer law up for judicial review. But when CBL members and their attorneys asked Will to issue an injunction that would temporarily halt all evictions until Patner's appeal was decided, he refused. Indeed, he could not—to issue an injunction concerning a matter being heard in a different court lay entirely outside his judicial authority. If the CBL wished to change the law, they could lobby Congress to pass a new one. In the meantime, Will would enforce the law currently on the books. Instead of delaying, Will ruled that those who had been served with notices had five days to pay up—through either rent or appeal bonds—or face eviction.[84]

Will made his ruling on November 21, 1969. Three days later, thirty-five CBL families—all South Siders—who ignored the order to pay up were served with eviction notices.[85] Then on December 11, approximately one year after the first payment strike was announced, movers sent by Universal Builders removed furniture from the home of a CBL member, Elizabeth Nelson. The company could hardly have chosen a worse target. Nelson lived in her six-room house with nine children. One was her seventeen-year old son, Nathaniel. The other eight were the orphaned children of her late sister. Nelson, a forty-four-year-old widow, worked nights so that she could devote her days to caring for these children. She had offered to bring her payments up to date, but Universal would not accept them because she refused to cover the legal fees Universal had paid to start proceedings against her. Now she planned to resist their efforts to evict. "I've paid too much money just to walk off and leave here like this. I have too many children to be set out in the street with no place to go." It would be an uneasy Christmas for her family, she told reporters, but she was determined. "The only way we'll get anything for the colored people is to fight for it; we want fair prices like anyone else."[86]

Nelson need not have worried. Within hours, an angry crowd of CBL members and supporters moved her furniture back into her house. She and her children had a place to sleep, at least in the short term.[87] After a lull during the Christmas holiday, Universal made a second eviction attempt on January 5, 1970, this time against Mr. and Mrs. Joseph H. Gibson. A World War II combat veteran who worked at the Ford Motor Company, Gibson did not take kindly to the attempt. Responding to his wife's frantic call that their furniture was being hauled out by moving men, he "charged through the front door, shouting 'Get out of my damn house!'" Gibson struck one of the movers, who immediately fled. By now two hundred CBL supporters had arrived at the scene. They quickly moved the Gibsons' furniture back into their home.[88]

Newspaper reports of hundreds of black Chicagoans rushing to the defense of widowed foster mothers and World War II combat veterans were emotionally affecting. For white Chicagoans, however, they also raised fears of violence. Charlie Baker hinted as much. "So far, we've been non-violent," he commented. "We hope to remain so, but we don't know. Some people won't stand for being kicked out of their homes." The result was what the CBL hoped it would be—a groundswell of demands that the evictions be halted. Monsignor Egan asked the federal courts to stop the evictions, at least until the Illinois Supreme Court could rule on the forcible entry statute's constitutionality—a ruling that he hoped would be expedited. "When people who are being exploited have no financial resources, time is of the essence. . . . Justice has already been delayed too long."[89] The Reverend Thomas Diehl, acting provincial of the Jesuits' Chicago Province, sent telegrams to President Nixon, Illinois governor Richard Ogilvie, and Mayor Daley asking that all evictions be halted until the CBL's federal suits were decided. "The courts should protect the human rights of the contract buyers, not just the legal rights of the sellers, while the complaints are being adjudicated," he argued, adding that the federal suits might "become a landmark decision comparable to the school desegregation one."[90] The *Chicago Sun-Times,* the *Chicago Daily*

News, Chicago Today, and WLS-TV recommended that Universal voluntarily halt the evictions until either the state or the federal cases were heard. "Children in the street, furniture in the yard—it all smacks of the strife of the Depression Thirties," said the *Daily News.*[91]

Sheriff Joseph Woods, head of the countywide sheriff's office, which had jurisdiction over court-ordered evictions, was also eager to slow or halt the process. "I'm not in any great rush to stir up any trouble," he told reporters. But after a hiatus of several weeks he announced on January 28 that the evictions of 101 contract buyers would start the next day.[92] On January 29, Woods supervised the eviction of Mr. and Mrs. Johnnie Moss and their four children. Just three weeks earlier Woods's force of twenty-five sheriff's deputies had failed to dislodge the Gibsons. This time he was better prepared. Almost two hundred helmeted deputies, most carrying "truncheons and gas masks," massed in an early morning snowstorm to evict the Mosses.

It was a disaster. The deputies dragged furniture out of the Mosses' home. They dumped the family's plastic Nativity scene in the bushes and chased their dog into the yard, where it pranced around the deputy sent to control it. A crowd of over two hundred CBL members and supporters confronted the deputies. Among them were Father Egan and Rabbi Robert J. Marx. "This is ridiculous, that they're moving these people out," Marx told reporters. "Legally what the sheriff is doing is right. But the law protects a bad system."[93]

Chicago's progressive clergy were not the only ones making their presence felt that morning. CBL member Joe Gibson was barely able to contain a group of "angry young men" who taunted the sheriff's deputies with shouts of "We are going to have barbecued pig!" Some in the crowd admitted that they would not hesitate to use violence to defend their homes. As one South Sider told the *Chicago Defender,* "They ain't going to come in my door. I've got a couple of guns and I'll blast them. I've got four kids to protect. They ain't going to get me out of my home until they kill me."[94] Suddenly two shots were fired—both by security guards who were posted inside the Moss house to prevent the return of the family's furniture. The crowd responded by smashing the building's windows and loudly threatening to burn the place down. The guards abandoned the property, and the crowd moved the Mosses' furniture back inside. Newspaper photographers caught the slight, pale figure of Monsignor Egan among those lugging it through the snow.[95]

The result was that Johnnie Moss, a man whom reporters described as "so busy trying to pull himself up by his bootstraps" that he'd never had time for a civil rights march, now faced jail for living illegally in his own home. In 1960, Moss had paid $3,500 down for a building costing $31,950, which the CBL appraised as worth $25,000. When Moss tried to switch to a mortgage, Universal said it would cost him an additional $1,000. Moss had worked for seventeen years at Borden Ice Cream; his wife held two jobs to help with their contract payments. "I knew it was coming," Moss said of the eviction, "but I didn't fear it. When you work so long to get a little money you get tired" of injustice. He predicted more strife to come. "This is just the beginning," he told the *Chicago Defender.* "If the members of the CBL have to go further than this next time, they will."[96]

Sheriff Woods was stunned to see clergy lending support to what he considered a lawless mob. He was especially angry at Egan, whom he singled out as one of the radicals. He telephoned Cardinal Cody "to complain about Father Egan's activities," the *Daily News* reported. He also expressed his rage to the judge who had signed the eviction orders. After that day's fiasco, he would carry out no further evictions, he said, unless the courts were willing to back up those he'd already attempted. He also would no longer mobilize hundreds of deputies to ensure that angry crowds did not thwart the evictions. "I'll handle these evictions in the usual way by sending one deputy and movers," he said. "The court cannot order more." He added that the "futile" attempt to evict the Mosses had cost the county's taxpayers $25,000.[97]

Unfortunately, Woods was not at liberty to make such decisions, as he discovered two weeks later when he was sued for $7 million by Universal for refusing to carry out court orders. Since Illinois law held that a sheriff who flouted the court could be held in contempt and made liable for damages, Universal was on solid legal ground. Woods was left to sputter, "I never did say I would not evict. I said I would not evict with an army, and I said I would not evict until the court takes care of" the previous eviction attempts. Woods had no choice but to proceed to the next people in line—the South Side family of Robert and Alice Durham. But this time, as promised, he would send only a single deputy and a team of movers. The job of protecting the movers and maintaining order would be left to "the police in the city where the eviction is located."[98]

Woods's call to the police was a canny move in a struggle that, like most struggles in Chicago, was more political than ideological. Woods was a Republican. The sheriff's force was countywide and under the control of Republicans, while the Police Department, a Chicago institution, was part of the Democratic machine. This helps explain why Mayor Daley refused the pleadings of CBL supporters to stop the evictions: as long as they were carried out by the sheriff's force and not the city's, they would damage the image of a Republican whom Daley wanted out of office in any case. It also explains why Woods now insisted that the Chicago police play a role. It was the only way for him to put the political "tinderbox" of the evictions back into Daley's yard.[99]

As Woods and Daley tussled over questions of jurisdiction, Robert and Alice Durham appealed their eviction. They further argued that the forcible entry and detainer requirement that they post a $2,500 appeal bond discriminated against the poor.[100] Their case was added to the other appeals.

Meanwhile, on February 10, a three-judge panel—composed of Will, Luther W. Swygert, and Bernard M. Becker—once again denied the CBL attorneys' request for a temporary injunction to halt the evictions until the forcible entry appeal was decided. The CBL had agreed to end its strike almost a year earlier, Judge Will reminded them. It chose to break that agreement and renew the strike because it felt justice wasn't moving fast enough. On the contrary, Will wrote, "The case was being handled on an expedited emergency basis." The payment strike was nothing more than "a strong-arm, extra-court activity." Those facing eviction could always "alleviate their distress by making the payments as originally agreed in the District Court proceedings."[101]

Resuming payments as a means of avoiding eviction may have seemed logical to Judge Will. But not to CBL members, who saw the strike as the only way to pressure the sellers into renegotiating, and perhaps more importantly, to dramatize the broader legal discrimination against black homeowners. Even the threat of eviction no longer fazed the CBL. As Sidney Clark noted, "Many of us had reached the point" of telling Universal, "'you know what you can do with your house.'" As one of the group's attorneys put it, Judge Will "couldn't see past the fact that people were living in these houses without paying for them. . . . He didn't see that it was a big emotional deal if you had to pay money to this bastard," that is, to one's contract seller.[102]

The strike had become an equally emotional issue for the sellers, who felt increasingly aggrieved and isolated. Reporters now wrote glowingly about CBL solidarity. For example, a January 1970 article in *Business Week* praised Walter and Fay Clay—a couple who for a decade "never missed a payment" on their contract—for their courage in refusing an offer of a $10,000 discount. "The man was willing to renegotiate my contract, but he wouldn't do the same for other CBL members. . . . We fight together," Fay Clay explained. But the Clays' "man," seller Al Weinberg, read their steadfastness very differently. "It's not a question of negotiating with CBL. If you don't negotiate on their terms, you're out. It's unconditional surrender or nothing," he said.[103] To the West Side sellers, the payment strike— especially one supported by huge donations from the Jesuits—was another example of their victimization by the CBL, which adamantly refused every move they made toward one-on-one resolutions of the conflict. Universal shared the West Side sellers' view that the payment strike was merely the CBL's attempt to win by forcible tactics what they could not win in court. "Egan came to make demands. 'Either you renegotiate the contracts or we go on payment strike,'" Michael Turoff recalled. "We said, 'We'll discuss any individual contract, but we've done nothing wrong, so we won't change them all. . . . You go on strike, and we'll evict!'"[104] For Turoff and his father, the heart of the matter remained the issue of personal integrity. As Lee Turoff insisted, "I want to be vindicated in the courts. I've been accused of cheating and overcharging and I'm not guilty."[105]

Lee Turoff believed that the underlying issue was something even uglier: the stereotype, in his son Michael's words, that "Jews aren't fair and they cheat people." The tone of some of the media coverage contributed to the Turoffs' anger. Famed *Chicago Daily News* columnist Mike Royko described Universal Builders' executives as "people who have, as Algren put it, 'dollar signs for eyes.'" While the contract buyers "want only that which homeowners have always wanted—to own their own home," he wrote, "the dollar-eyes crowd wants nothing more than the preservation of their right to fleece somebody." Although Royko might not have known that Universal's owners were Jewish, the Turoffs and Samuelses could easily read anti-Semitism into such coverage. And sometimes there was more than just inference. When a white Catholic CBL aide called Michael Turoff a "kike," the Turoffs had their proof that anti-Semitism permeated the CBL. The aide's profuse apologies did little to assuage their anger.[106]

The charged politics surrounding the religion of the Samuelses and the Turoffs were further complicated by conflicts within Chicago's Jewish community. Many Jewish Chicagoans felt that it was important for them, as Jews, to back the CBL. Rabbi Robert Marx, Gordon Sherman, and Marshall Patner, as well as the Chicago Board of Rabbis and the eight Jewish organizations that had petitioned President Nixon on the CBL's behalf, all understood their support as part of a Jewish tradition of social justice. Jews supported the league on a grassroots level as well. Some worked in the CBL office; others joined the picket lines.[107] For many, the issues raised by the contract buyers' struggle seemed straightforward. As Gordon Sherman wrote to Rabbi Marx, "The irresistible power of the C.B.L. effort is that it is specific, noble, but safe for any timid liberal. The villains are clear; even the government is after them now."[108]

The South Side case seemed to muddy this clarity. When one liberal synagogue voted to contribute to the CBL's appeal bond fund, one of the synagogue's most prominent members insisted that the league's analysis of the South Side case was full of errors. He would henceforth withhold his contributions to the synagogue, and he suggested that others do the same. By the spring of 1970, the head of the Jewish Federation of Metropolitan Chicago was voicing fears that the involvement of Jewish organizations in the struggle would "create further confusion and division in our community."[109]

Debates about the proper Jewish response to the CBL led some Chicago Jews to think through the implications of their religious and ethical heritage as a "people in between." For the Samuelses and the Turoffs, the results of this debate were achingly personal. "People stopped talking to my father at the synagogue," Michael Turoff recalled. The humiliation left him breathless with anger thirty years after the fact.[110]

In late February 1970, Sullivan, Ming, and Boodell reported to CBL members that "after days of intense negotiations" they'd finally "hammered out a plan." Worried by the increasing pace of South Side evictions, the attorneys pointed out that Universal had a right to evict buyers who broke their contract by withholding payments—even if those buyers later resumed payments. Under the proposed plan, CBL members would resume meeting their contractual obligations. In return, the South Side sellers would "concede that [their] contract is in full force" and "no effort will be made to evict." Universal would also put a portion of the contract buyers' payments into an escrow account pending the Illinois Supreme Court's decision on the forcible entry and detainer appeal. But the South Side members rejected the proposal overwhelmingly, and so Sheriff Woods returned to his task. In six days he attempted to evict five South Side families. In each case, his deputies were thwarted by up to three hundred protesters. There was no violence, newspapers reported, only because the "sheriffs left peacefully when confronted."[111]

The CBL was able to block these evictions because it had advance notice of where they would occur. "We'd meet in the office by four o'clock in the morning," Wells recalled, and "get the strategy together" for the day. Staffers would wait for a phone call from "friends" inside the sheriff's office, who would tip them off about the location of the day's evictions. This would activate a highly effective phone tree, which alerted members early in the morning that an eviction was to happen—"Pharaoh is riding"—at a given address.[112] In this way hundreds of supporters were able to arrive at eviction sites at about the same time as the sheriff's deputies. Eventually Woods figured out the trick, and on March 23, after realizing that CBL members had "staked out" a South Side eviction site, he changed plans at the last moment. For the first time, Woods took his deputies to the West Side, where he planned to evict the family of Mr. and Mrs. Curtis Green.[113]

West Siders had been confident that evictions would not be tried in their neighborhood, in part because of white fears of gang violence. Sure enough, Woods's fourteen deputies immediately faced a volatile situation. The twenty-five protesters who arrived shortly after the deputies quickly swelled to a crowd of several hundred. Woods's badly outnumbered deputies called for police backup but were refused. Woods called the governor of Illinois, warning him that National Guard troops might be needed. After a mostly verbal confrontation that lasted several hours, Woods and his men had no choice but to retreat. "To put it mildly, I'm chagrined," he told reporters, complaining about the Chicago police. The evictions were not his idea, he reminded them; he had no choice but to enforce the orders.

Otherwise, he fumed, "I'll be sitting in my own pokey for contempt of court."[114]

That was the last time Woods would allow himself to be left "high and dry." He came up with a new strategy to compel Chicago police support for his men. Henceforth, he would have the sellers' attorneys request that all trespassers be removed from their property before his deputies arrived. The Chicago police were responsible for dealing with trespassing violations. Daley's police would now be forced to clear the crowds gathered at eviction sites. If they failed to do so, they would face their own citations for contempt of court.[115]

Woods's ploy had an immediate effect. On March 30, 1970, one hundred Chicago policemen, backed up by fifty additional reinforcement officers, sealed off the entire block of 9500 South Emerald. The police line kept approximately two hundred CBL supporters at bay. This enabled Woods's one hundred deputies and twenty-nine movers to evict four South Side families—their first successful evictions since the start of the strike.

Among the four was the family of Sidney Clark. Ironically, Clark was on active duty while his wife and two sons were moved out of their home. "I find this eviction very disgusting," he told reporters. "These families can't get two police officers to come and investigate a burglary. And then you have one company—Universal Builders—that can get 200 policemen to do this. I think this is very wrong." Michael Turoff, who was on the scene, disagreed. "We have people waiting to buy these homes. We are going to protect the property here." Charlie Baker was also present. He noted bitterly that Woods and the Chicago police "sent an army out here. . . . It's a damn shame. We can't raise a defense in court."[116]

Once Woods found a way to compel the Chicago police to aid in the evictions, the back of the strike was broken. On Tuesday, March 31, twelve more South Siders were evicted. A freak snowstorm halted evictions for a few days, but they started up again early the next week. "A common sight was dazed and lost-looking children and mothers with babies, standing in the 30-degree weather, around a hodge-podge of home furnishings in the mud, spewing from the doors of homes to the sidewalks . . . as far as the eye could see," one reporter noted on the day that twelve families were evicted. Clarence Darr, a fifty-five-year-old janitor who was left homeless with his wife and three children, stated simply, "We're being cheated and getting no consideration from the law." Steelworker Arthur Williams, also evicted, commented, "Where to now? Maybe back to the ghetto." He added, "We paid taxes . . . and now the tax money is spent to kick us out." Even the West Side sellers' attorney, George Feiwell, was disturbed by the sight of families and their belongings tossed into the streets. "It looked like the Warsaw Ghetto to me. I didn't like to see poor blacks treated that way," he commented years after the fact.[117]

There were sporadic acts of resistance. Twenty-seven people were arrested, mostly for disorderly conduct after a crowd pelted the police with rocks and snowballs and attempted to overturn a police car. Among those arrested was the Reverend George Clements, a prominent black Catholic who warned police that there would be "300,000 to 400,000 people demonstrating" the next time they attempted an eviction. But no mass protests materialized, and the sheriff pressed on. "I never thought I'd see this— wholesale evictions," a "dazed" CBL member commented. "Maybe now it will wake people up to the fact that nobody gives a damn."[118] Meanwhile, four South Side homes left vacant after their inhabitants were forced out went up in flames. Arson was suspected in all four cases and confirmed in one. Universal was upset but not surprised: their receptionist said that the company had "been plagued with telephone threats of arson" for months. Charlie Baker told reporters, "We don't know anything about it and we sure didn't have anything to do with it," but the implications were obvious. However disciplined its members, the CBL could not control the feelings aroused by the evictions, especially among younger and more volatile people, white as well as black.[119]

Worried by the escalating violence, the CBL again petitioned Mayor Daley to stop the evictions, restore families to their homes, and pressure the sellers to negotiate. Daley agreed to broker the matter, and, after two days of intensive talks between Universal and the CBL, announced a resolution. Apparently Daley had used his standard combination of flattery and perseverance until the two sides agreed. "I'd like to say something in favor of the mayor, this great mayor," one CBL leader said afterward. "He doesn't want anyone to leave these meetings, and he just keeps on hollerin' at you till you get an agreement."[120]

In this negotiation, as in the summit meeting four years earlier with Martin Luther King Jr., Daley's goal was not to remedy the problems facing black Chicagoans but to stop the social upheaval, which was making the city look bad. Daley admitted as much. The CBL-Universal agreement would "remove the unfortunate sight of people being evicted from their homes and will return the South Side to normalcy," he declared. Not surprisingly, the agreement was similar to the one proposed by the CBL attorneys a month earlier: if payments were resumed, the evictions would stop and families already evicted would be allowed to return to their homes as long as they, too, continued their monthly payments. Some of that money would go to an escrow account, where it would be held pending the outcome of the forcible entry appeal. Universal would not discuss renegotiating contracts, but it would work with CBL members who wished to switch from an installment contract to a bank mortgage.[121]

Just days later, on April 15, the Illinois Supreme Court ruled on the forcible entry and detainer case of *Rosewood v. Fisher.*[122] The original law had prohibited the mention of "matters not germane" to the eviction proceedings, preventing plaintiffs from raising issues about the "validity" of the contracts they had signed, including charges that the contracts were "unconscionable," "usurious," "extracted and induced by fraud," and "in violation of the civil and various constitutional rights of the defendants." Now the court, in what the Chicago press called a "landmark decision," ruled that the defenses concerning contracts raised by CBL members *were* relevant to the eviction proceedings. The case of Chester and Julia Fisher, as well as all other cases in which "defensive pleadings germane to the issue were stricken," was to be sent back to Cook County (Chicago) Circuit Court so that new hearings could be held.[123]

The press was eager to draw a positive moral from the Illinois Supreme Court decision. As a *Chicago Sun-Times* editorial enthused, the ruling "restores faith in the reliance on due process of law to promote social stability."[124] The rapturous media failed to grasp the narrow application of the judgment, which simply stated that, if one had bought a house on contract and if the validity of that particular contract was currently being questioned in a legal suit, then defenses relating to problems with that contract could be raised in forcible entry and detainer cases. Although such cases could be reheard, there was no guarantee that the judges would ultimately decide in the defendant's favor. Broader issues, such as whether the statute's requirement of a high bond as a precondition of appeal discriminated against the poor, were not addressed. Only one reporter seemed to get close to the mark, offering a relatively sober assessment of *Rosewood.*

The Illinois Supreme Court handed the Contract Buyers League "a major legal victory," he wrote. However, given that only a portion of those evicted had raised issues about their contracts' validity in court and that even those who had might not have their evictions stopped by the judges who reheard their cases, he predicted that the decision would not change the outcome of "most of the CBL cases in which evictions have been made or ordered." As Universal attorney Burt Weitzenfeld commented, "After all this turmoil, we are right back where we started."[125]

On the same day as the court ruling, South Side CBL members rejected the Daley-brokered settlement with Universal Builders. Some may have believed that the *Rosewood* decision would give them a better chance of fighting eviction notices in court. But the deeper issue was South Siders' fury that the agreement placed no pressure on Universal to renegotiate. "It's like a robber promising to stop beating me . . . if I turn over my wallet to him," one buyer complained. Another pointed out that Universal agreed to speak with them only because of the pressures of the strike. "If we drop our payment boycott, we will be back where we started 22 months ago—and all our struggle and suffering since then will go out the window."[126]

Sheriff Woods immediately grasped that for him the *Rosewood* decision changed nothing. "I have no choice but to proceed with the evictions unless [the families] pay or post an appeal bond," he told reporters. On April 21, Charlie Baker was evicted after 120 deputies sealed off his entire block. The next day eight more South Siders were evicted. During the "rock and bottle-throwing melee" that ensued, five sheriff's deputies were injured and twenty demonstrators were arrested.[127]

In the face of this chaos, increasing numbers of South Side CBL members quietly accepted Daley's proposed deal with Universal. Sidney Clark was appalled. "If you just wanted your little piece of meat and to hell with everybody else, then that's what you get," was his view of those who settled. He became the leader of a smaller group within the CBL that opposed negotiating with Universal. The press reported that the CBL was in the midst of a split. Baker denied it, admitting only that the CBL "has too many leaders." But the division was real.[128]

Left to right: Maroon editor David Satter, Irving Block, and former *Maroon* editor Robert F. Levey in front of Cicero Circuit Court, September 1966. Chicago Maroon *photograph. Reprinted with permission*

Rosa Downing contrasts the home of her landlord, L. J. Epstein, with the living room wall of her apartment in his building at 3901 W. Jackson. She, Ruby Kirk, and other tenants succeeded in getting Kirk named receiver of the building. Photo is from 1969. *As published in the* Chicago Sun-Times *LLC. Reprinted with permission*

Monsignor John J. Egan with neighborhood children in front of Presentation Church, 1968. *Tribune* file photo by Leonard Bartholomew. Chicago Tribune *file photo. All rights reserved. Used with permission*

Jack Macnamara with some of the Presentation Church Community Organization Project volunteers, summer 1967. *Left to right:* Macnamara, Tom Mackie, Ken Blessing, Bill Koffel, Bob Peck, Joe Speier, and Peter Welch. *Photo courtesy of Joe Speier*

Henrietta Banks and Jack Macnamara speak with passersby, 1968. *The* Jesuit Bulletin, *December 1968. Reprinted with permission*

Clyde Ross and Ruth Wells, 1972. Photos by Lee Balterman. *Copyright Lee Balterman. Used with permission*

Charlie Baker, 1970. Sun-Times *photo by Jim Klepitsch. As published in the* Chicago Sun-Times *LLC. Reprinted with permission*

Ruth Wells and Contract Buyers League member Charles Davis (*far right*) work with volunteers at a Wednesday night CBL meeting. *Photo by Lee Balterman. Copyright Lee Balterman. Used with permission*

Sidney Clark (now Sidney Sharif), 1970. Chicago Tribune *file photo. All*

Judge Hubert L. Will, 1976. *Photograph by Fredric Stein. Reprinted with permission*

Sheriff's deputies surround the front yard of evicted CBL member Johnnie Moss, January 29, 1970. *As published in the* Chicago Sun-Times *LLC. Reprinted with permission*

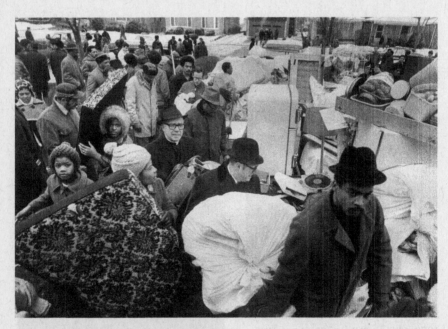

CBL members and neighbors return furniture to home of Johnnie Moss, January 29, 1970. Priest in center of photo, facing camera, is Monsignor Egan. Man in front of Egan, facing away from camera, is Rabbi Robert Marx. *Copyright* Chicago Tribune Company. *Reprinted with permission. All rights reserved*

CBL supporters cheer after thwarting an eviction attempt on Chicago's West Side, March 23, 1970. *As published in the* Chicago Sun-Times *LLC. Reprinted with permission*

South Emerald Street on March 30, 1970, when four CBL families were evicted from a single block. *As published in the* Chicago Sun-Times *LLC. Reprinted with permission*

Mayor Richard J. Daley and attorneys William R. Ming Jr. and Burton Y. Weitzenfeld announce an agreement between Universal Builders and the CBL, April 10, 1970. *As published in the* Chicago Sun-Times *LLC. Reprinted with permission*

South Side CBL members look on as Sol Diamond of Midstate Homes, s*eated at right,* signs agreement to reduce contract balances and switch them to regular mortgages, June 12, 1970. Seated next to Diamond, *right to left,* is CBL member Charles Davis and Dempsey J. Travis. *As published in the* Chicago Sun-Times *LLC. Reprinted with permission*

The battle between Mayor Daley and Sheriff Woods kept pace with the evictions. When Woods called for police backup during Charlie Baker's eviction, Mayor Daley attacked him publicly. "The sheriff has 1,400 deputies on his payroll and it's about time he lived up to his responsibilities," Daley said. "Evictions are the constitutional obligation of the sheriff. Let's quit kidding the public. Look at his budget, with his 1,400 deputies." Woods fired back, "I never pay much attention to him. Why should I defend myself against such an outburst?" He hinted that Daley and the entire Chicago judiciary were corrupt. He told a South Side CBL member that to end the evictions Daley need only make his preference known to the judge. "Then the order would go from the mayor to the judge, and from the judge to the sheriff."[129] Meanwhile the *Chicago Daily News* tallied the cost of the evictions thus far: $300,000 to the sheriff's office, $123,000 to the Chicago police. Total cost to the city and to the state of Illinois: over $500,000. Total number of successfully completed evictions: twelve.[130]

Emotions were running almost as high in Judge Will's courtroom, where Will was deliberating on the federal suits and several related eviction cases. The *Chicago Tribune* reported that Will had become "the target of vicious letters, telegrams, and telephone calls" as a result of public perception that he was responsible for the evictions.[131] In addition to fending off hate mail from CBL supporters, he engaged in shouting matches with attorneys representing the contract sellers. One day Will became so angry at George Feiwell that he stormed off the bench. "I thought Will would send me to prison" for contempt of court, Feiwell recalled.[132]

There was rage on both sides. In early May, Feiwell "went nuts" after Will reprimanded him in court, saying "I will not permit you to be a Shylock." Feiwell presented a petition filed by forty-eight of the seventy-five West Side sellers demanding that Will dismiss himself from that case because he was prejudiced against Jews. Will explained that he hadn't realized that the term "Shylock" had a Jewish reference until he reread Shakespeare's *Merchant of Venice*. "First I am accused of being unfair to the plaintiffs because they are Negroes . . . and now I am accused of being unfair to some of the defendants because they are Jewish," an exasperated Will told the *Chicago Defender*. He was even blunter about his feelings in court: "I feel I'm in *Alice in Wonderland*. Or I'm locked in an asylum with a bunch of insane people."[133]

This was the context for a ruling that Will handed down on May 14, 1970.[134] At issue was a motion by the sellers to exclude from the federal suit all plaintiffs still withholding their payments. As Will saw it, CBL members reserved the right to go on a payment strike yet were unwilling to face the consequences. The CBL had petitioned several courts requesting injunctions to stop the evictions until either the federal cases or the state eviction lawsuits were settled. Each court had denied the request. Each ruled that, "until it is determined through the submission of evidence and a trial . . . whether plaintiffs were in fact discriminated against in the purchase of their homes, plaintiffs cannot have the relief they seek." To grant them such relief, all agreed, would amount to punishing the sellers before they had been tried for a crime.

Furthermore, the court had arranged an agreement to end the holdout soon after it commenced in the spring of 1969. The CBL's renewed strike therefore constituted "a continuing violation and contempt of an order of this court." Will noted that "a court may refuse relief to a party who acts in open contempt of the court's orders," and that was exactly what he was going to do. Plaintiffs had twenty days to resume their payments along the lines stipulated in Will's original agreement. Those who did not would be barred from participating in the federal suits.[135]

It was left to Tom Boodell Jr. to spell out to CBL members the full implications of Will's order. You must make your payments, he told them. If you refuse, the consequences are serious. First, "you will be dismissed from the federal case"; if the CBL won agreement that its civil rights were violated and that payment of damages are called for, "you will not receive any benefit." Second, "you may be evicted from your house." Third, even after eviction, "you may be liable for rent" for all the months on payment strike. That is, strikers might end up having to pay back the sellers *and* losing their home. Fourth, the sellers might try to "collect their attorneys' fees under the contract provisions giving them the right to do so." Finally, some sellers had "other rights under their contracts which they could assert against you"—claims that "might involve you in additional legal problems."[136] In short, league members who continued to withhold payment would face eviction, bankruptcy as a result of potentially lengthy court actions taken against them by the sellers, and exclusion from the federal suit that many now saw as the best way to pressure recalcitrant sellers to renegotiate.

Judge Will gave the strikers until July 2 to pay up. The CBL debated the issue till the last possible moment. On July 1, its members voted to end the strike. They would place their hopes in the federal suits. If they had to resume payments to the sellers in order to be part of those suits, they were willing to do so.[137]

It would be easy to see the end of the payment strike as confirmation of Saul Alinsky's warning about the threat that legal battles pose to grass-roots movements. With the end of the payment strike and the shift in focus to winning the federal suits, the CBL's energy indeed waned.[138] But co-optation is too simple a framework to understand what happened to the CBL. Social movements thrive on a collective energy that is short-lived and unstable by definition. For two years, the collective momentum of the CBL enabled its members to take heroic stands and make extraordinary personal sacrifices. The pressure of attorneys notwithstanding, the league was unlikely to sustain the emotional power that characterized its early years.[139]

Then, too, the CBL simply did not have the resources to prevent hundreds of potential evictions enforced by armies of deputies and police officers in locations all over the city's South and West sides. Its members, moreover, were traumatized and exhausted by the two-year-long battle. One woman said she abandoned the strike after her husband threw a "tantrum" because he was so upset about the house: "He takes it out on all of us—me and the children." Another buyer described the physical and emotional strain of fighting the evictions: "I spent many a . . . day and night moving people back. I'd leave my job. I was feeling ashamed taking all that time off. I was a nervous wreck. And I had hurt my back moving people back in." Worst of all was the effect on his children, who were worried about being tossed out. "They'd say 'Where are we going to stay? Are we going out on the street?' This is why their grades went down."[140]

Although the CBL did not manage to force a renegotiation of all members' contracts, it achieved a number of victories. First, against the advice of one of the top legal firms in the city it challenged the legality of Illinois's eviction law—and won. Though *Rosewood v. Fisher* was narrow in its application to existing suits, it did create the right to raise defenses in court, thereby alleviating one of the core inequalities embedded in the Forcible Entry and Detainer Act. The state eviction law's imbalance in favor of land-lords was further altered in a second CBL eviction suit, *Hamilton Corporation v. Alexander*, which was decided two years after *Rosewood*. (Hamilton Corporation, like Rosewood, was a subdivision of Universal Builders.) The *Hamilton* case originated in the complaint of the Durhams, the couple who claimed that the eviction law was biased against the poor because it denied the right of appeal to people who were unable to post a sizable appeal bond. In 1972, the Illinois Supreme Court agreed, declar-ing the forcible entry and detainer law to be invalid to the extent that it required such a bond in order for an appeal to take place.[141]

Second, the payment strike did push a number of contract sellers, particularly on the West Side, to renegotiate. Before the big holdout, a whole year of activism—1968—resulted in fewer than a dozen renegoti-ated contracts. By June 1, 1970, the number of West Side contracts rene-gotiated had risen to seventy. By the end of 1970, 106 contracts had been renegotiated, at an average savings of $14,000 per family.[142] Some smaller contract sellers settled for something close to the CBL's original "fair price" formula—the price that the seller paid for the property, plus a fair profit markup of 15 percent. The experiences of the CBL's leaders show the range of results produced by the holdout. Henrietta Banks had her con-tract balance of $19,000 reduced to $7,000, an amount she then covered with a legitimate mortgage; her total savings, including interest payments, were close to $18,000. After Clyde Ross's seller, John Karras, defaulted on his mortgage, Ross reached a settlement with the bank that saved him over $20,000 in principal and interest. By the end of 1967, Ruth and James Wells had already paid their $23,000 contract balance down to $8,000; fol-lowing the strike the Wellses got a bank mortgage for the balance and owned the building in full by 1974. After being evicted from his building in 1970, Charlie Baker moved back in and lived there for two years with-out paying. Ultimately Baker abandoned the building and bought another in a different neighborhood, one of several CBL members who used the money saved during the holdout to start over somewhere else.[143]

Finally and perhaps most significantly, the strike led to the addition of the Federal Housing Administration (FHA) as a defendant in the West Side suit. When Irving Block, outraged by the federal government's friend of the court brief supporting the CBL, countered by attempting to have the

FHA and the Federal Savings and Loan Insurance Corporation (FSLIC) added to the list of defendants, his motion was denied. By the summer of 1970, however, CBL attorneys had spent a year negotiating with FHA authorities in the hope that they would help resolve the situation by making low-interest, discounted mortgage money available to league members. When the FHA refused to do so, the league's attorneys finally accepted that, on this issue at least, they agreed with the contract sellers. On August 14, they amended the West Side suit in order to add George Romney, secretary of the Department of Housing and Urban Development; the FHA and the FSLIC; the Veterans Administration, which, like the FHA, insured mortgage loans (for veterans only); and the Federal Home Loan Bank Board as defendants. Instead of focusing only on the middlemen, they would now target the federal programs that were largely responsible for the nationwide racially biased mortgage squeeze that the contract sellers exploited.[144] Some months earlier, Sidney Clark had told the *Chicago Defender* that the "FHA is responsible for all these black people being evicted from their homes" because "they set the pattern" by refusing to insure loans to blacks.[145] At last, that view was incorporated into the West Side suit.

The CBL's initiatives were not equally successful for everyone. On the South Side, the holdout led to some settlements, though not with Universal Builders. Twenty-five South Side CBL families had purchased new homes on contract from the one other South Side seller involved in the suit, a smaller operation called Midstate Homes. When discussions with Midstate faltered, Dempsey Travis, who had organized the nation's black banks and mortgage companies into the United Mortgage Bankers of America, got involved.

Travis had not been idle since the days he founded the Sivart Mortgage Company. His actions in support of black home buyers had recently culminated in his acceptance—after a three-year struggle—into the Mortgage Bankers Association, an action that finally integrated the white mortgage banking industry.[146] Throughout 1969, Travis closely followed press reports on the CBL and spoke out on its members' behalf. "Their situation is a byproduct of institutional racism," he told a *Chicago Tribune* reporter. When the South Side evictions began, Travis joined the crowds in the streets. He observed the spectacle of "families' belongings being carried out and set in the mud."[147] He decided that if there was any way he could help he would do so.

His chance came when Sol Diamond, the head of Midstate Homes, agreed to talk about a settlement with his South Side buyers. After nine days of negotiations, Diamond made his offer: if the strikers agreed to pay the money they had withheld, Midstate would reduce their remaining contract balances by 14 percent. It would also complete the paperwork required to shift the families from contracts to mortgages free of charge. Average savings for these families would range from $3,000 to $5,000.

There was one problem. Diamond would discount the contracts only if he could be sure that the remaining balance would be paid in full by a bank mortgage. But interest rates had risen since most CBL members had purchased their homes. Travis now had to "do the impossible"—conclude the deal with Diamond by finding mortgages for his contract buyers at interest rates at least a point below the going market rate. By the summer of 1970, Travis finally lined up the money. Most of it came from black insurance companies that agreed to discount their interest rates. "It was different with the white institutions," Travis commented. "They showed no sense of social obligation to the contract buyers."[148]

Travis believed that his deal with Midstate would serve as a model for resolving the conflict with Universal. It followed "a good principle in business that when a cash consideration is made available, the seller agrees to discount." Diamond was also happy with the agreement: "I don't have any more collection problems, the people will get a bargain, I get some of my money out—everybody gains." He added that he was through with the housing construction business: "With all my costs, I was lucky if I got 3 percent on my money. Now I'm going to take my money and loan it to Penn Central at ten and a quarter." Universal would do well to follow suit. "At this point," Travis said, "nobody is making any money and everybody is losing." According to Travis, Universal had "70 vacant homes and many of them have been vandalized. There is no reason for this going on, and I think Universal agrees."

Travis was wrong, however. He had overlooked the hurt, outrage, and wounded pride that lay behind some contract sellers' refusal to negotiate. Universal Builders, which held five times as many contracts as Midstate, rebuffed his efforts. They insisted that their prices were discounted to start with. They would not, under any circumstances, discount further.[149]

While many contract buyers benefited by joining the CBL, some did not. Approximately seventy CBL families—Sidney Clark's among them—

permanently lost their homes. After being evicted on March 30, Clark was served with a warrant for owning an unregistered gun and for possession of stolen property (a .38 caliber revolver) that sheriff's deputies had found while clearing out his house. He was also placed "on limited duty," that is, demoted to a desk job. Clark vowed to move back into his home, but that proved impossible. On July 13, his building went up in flames. By the time he and Dempsey Travis arrived at the scene all that remained was a "burned-out hulk." The building had seen three fires in the months since his eviction, and it was one of at least half a dozen Universal-owned homes of CBL evictees that were burned or bombed. The destruction was apparently an effort to ensure that Universal would be unable to resell the properties of those they evicted. But the arson and bombings, whoever was responsible for them, ensured a loss not only for Universal but for the families who harbored hopes of one day regaining their buildings.[150]

The stress of these losses may have exacerbated the growing rift within the CBL. Its most extreme manifestation was the alliance of Sidney Clark's small group with Sherman Skolnick, a white "self-trained legal expert." In June 1970, Skolnick created a "fact sheet" titled "Who Represents the Contract Buyers League?" It alleged that Jenner and Block had volunteered to represent the CBL precisely in order to ensure the group's failure, thereby protecting the firm's banking interests.[151] Then in August, Sidney Clark and eight other South Side residents filed a lawsuit alleging that a Catholic conspiracy underlay the CBL. The suit, which was drafted by Skolnick, claimed that the Chicago archdiocese, represented by Cardinal Cody, owned the land upon which Universal built its homes. To protect this investment, the archdiocese and various donors established the Gamaliel Foundation, which pretended to aid the league while secretly working to "cool off South Side C.B.L. members" and "force them to resume making payments to contract sellers." The plaintiffs asked for $10 million in damages for the "fraud" they claimed had been perpetrated.[152]

The factual basis for the suit was shaky, to say the least. Not surprisingly, the suit was quickly dismissed. Skolnick "did not know as much as we thought he did," one supporter noted ruefully.[153] The willingness of Clark and eight others to embrace Skolnick's conspiratorial worldview was a reflection of their bitterness and desperation. They had risked everything and won nothing, they felt, betrayed by a series of convoluted arguments presented by authorities in whom they had initially placed their trust.

Although Skolnick's assertions were nonsensical on their face, they were symbolically an accurate map of something that some in the CBL sensed but could not quite define: the dense web of connections between those in control that lies at the heart of institutional racism. After 1970, the battle against institutional racism, as embodied by the FHA, banks and savings and loan institutions, and the real estate agents, builders, and attorneys who exploited the racially biased credit shortage these larger entities created, shifted to the courts. Its outcome would rest with people who, it was true, had personal, social, political, and financial ties to many of those they were committed to defeating. For those with a conspiratorial mindset, there was much to fuel their suspicions.

By the end of 1970, many of the CBL's most powerful supporters had left the city. Some, like Jack Macnamara, had personal reasons for moving away. Macnamara's intense commitment to the league—as well as his struggles to raise Eddie Smith while living in an apartment packed with twenty-year-olds—had taken a toll both physically and emotionally. Briefly hospitalized for exhaustion in December 1969, Macnamara went back to work a few weeks later, but he continued to struggle with overwork and the complete lack of privacy in his life.[154]

Then in August 1970, Macnamara attended the wedding of one of the daughters of John O'Connor, the Catholic banker and trucking company owner who had been a steadfast financial supporter of the CBL. There he met the bride's twenty-three-year-old sister, Peggy, and his life was transformed. The two were "smitten with one another immediately," a friend of Macnamara's recalled. Macnamara was then in the midst of pushing for ordination, but their connection was too strong. Three months later, Macnamara left the Jesuits. "I have thought, I have prayed and, as you know, I have consulted," he wrote to his superior, Father Harvanek. Yet nothing changed his sense that his love for Peggy was so deep that it had to be part of God's plan. Macnamara, released from his vows, married Peggy and shortly thereafter moved with her to New York City.[155]

Jack Egan, too, was exhausted. Since his "exile" to Lawndale in 1966, Egan had used his unflagging energy and political savvy to transform Presentation parish into a vital center of spiritual life and political activity. Egan had provided the CBL with meeting space in his church, given speeches on its behalf, and sent a constant stream of personal notes to the mayor, the head of the city police department, the managers of the city's television stations, and anyone else he believed could aid the CBL. He had joined picket lines and barricaded himself in homes scheduled for eviction—sometimes bringing high-ranking and slightly anxious white officials with him. He had also struggled to win Cardinal Cody's support for the group. "I am happy to report to you that the Contract Buyers League is moving ahead responsibly and quite successfully," he wrote to Cody in a typical missive. Over two thousand families had affiliated with the league, and the "spiritual content of their approach is having a profound influence on the individual and family life of those involved."[156]

But as Ruth Wells recalled, Cody "wouldn't have nothing to do with us. We would write him and we would call him and you wouldn't get no response." Instead, he worked behind the scenes to stop Catholic funding of the CBL.[157] He also continued his crusade against Chicago's Catholic social action institutions. Back in 1967, Cody had delegitimized the eminent Catholic Interracial Council as an official Church agency. Shortly thereafter he had replaced Egan's activist-oriented Office of Urban Affairs with a new "Office of Inner City Apostolate," whose work consisted, one critic noted, exclusively of "scheduling some meetings, handling grants, and collecting some information on the inner city."[158] In 1969, Cody reined in the Interreligious Council on Urban Affairs (IRCUA), slashing its funding by three-quarters and cutting the number of Catholics on the board from twelve to three; Egan was among those dropped. Since the IRCUA had been funded largely by the Catholic Church, Cody's actions effectively destroyed the organization and weakened ecumenical activism in Chicago for years to come. In spring 1970, Rabbi Robert Marx, who had mobilized progressive Jews to support the CBL, was forced out of his position as director of the Chicago division of the Union of American Hebrew Congregations. His equivalent on the Protestant side, the Reverend Edgar Chandler, resigned as executive director of the Church Federation of Greater Chicago. Although the federation's president insisted that "there was absolutely no pressure on Chandler to resign," Rabbi Marx wasn't so sure. He believed that he, Chandler, and Egan—the core leadership of the IRCUA— were all forced out "directly as a result of the CBL battle."[159]

Throughout 1969, Egan had devoted himself to Presentation parish, the Contract Buyers League, and the Association of Chicago Priests, a group created as a counterweight to Cody's overwhelming ecclesiastic authority.[160] Then in April 1970, Egan was hospitalized because of a heart condition. When the Reverend Theodore Hesburgh, president of the University of Notre Dame, ran into Egan later that spring, he was shocked at his frail appearance. On the spot, he invited Egan to Notre Dame for a year: Egan could rest and also contribute to the university's new program on pastoral theology. It would be Egan's first break from pastoral and activist labor in twenty-eight years, and he could not deny that he needed it. With Hesburgh's agreement, he brought along his assistant Peggy Roach, who had over the years become indispensable. Their work together constituted a cominstry, in Egan's view.[161]

Appointed for one year, Egan remained with Roach at Notre Dame for thirteen years, returning to Chicago only after Cody's death in April 1982.[162] Egan's appointment as director of the Chicago Archdiocese's Office of Human Relations and Ecumenism in 1983 was one of the first acts of Cody's successor, Cardinal Joseph Bernardin. Egan told reporters that he was "ecstatic." "Chicago's Maverick Monsignor Returns to the Fold after Years in Exile," the *Chicago Tribune* exulted.[163]

The departure of Egan, who provided political and institutional shelter for the CBL, and of Macnamara, who devoted every ounce of his strength to organizing the movement, was disheartening for CBL members. Also unsettling was the fate of CBL attorney Bob Ming, whose passion and eloquence had figured so importantly in the CBL's legal struggles.[164] It came as a shock when the famed civil rights litigator was charged in April 1970 with a federal crime—failure to file income tax returns from 1963 through 1966. In November, after a trial in which Judge Julius J. Hoffman refused to allow Ming's attorney to present a single exhibit for the defense, Ming was sentenced to sixteen months in prison. Five months after he started serving his sentence, Ming suffered a stroke and a skull fracture. Shortly thereafter, on June 30, 1973, while on furlough from his prison term, Ming died at the Veterans Research Hospital in Chicago. He was sixty-two years old.[165]

Ming's attorney, Ellis Reid, "discounted that there was any connection" between his client's tax suit and his representation of the CBL. Instead, Reid was sure that Ming's jailing was a direct result of his challenges to President Nixon's authority. In 1968, Ming had aggressively lobbied against Clement Haynsworth, Nixon's pick for the Supreme Court. Ming also worked to defeat G. Harrold Carswell, Nixon's next nominee. Shortly after that, Reid recalled, an IRS agent he knew dropped him a bit of information. "Bob Ming is going to jail," the agent said. Perhaps there was a glimmer of justice in the end. "Ironically, [Ming] rallied enough to watch some of the Watergate hearings on television," an *Ebony* reporter noted.[166]

One last change of guard involved Judge Hubert Will. In June 1970, Will gave "enthusiastic approval" to a suggestion from CBL attorneys that was designed to streamline the unwieldy West Side case: rather than having to present evidence on all 3,000 West Side contracts, they could focus on a "random sample" of 470. This would be Will's last significant action in regard to the CBL. In September he resigned from the case. When Will met privately with Rabbi Marx to discuss the matter, Marx jotted down Will's explanation of his decision. Will left the contract buyers' suits because, "although he knew more about the case than any other judge would, he felt that the time had come for a new judge. At one time or another everyone involved in the case had been angry at Judge Will and he felt that new blood would help."[167]

Despite Will's opposition to the payment strike, his resignation was a blow. His May 1969 ruling supporting the CBL's right to try its federal suits had given Section 1982 of the 1866 Civil Rights Act the broadest possible interpretation.[168] There was no way to know if the two judges assigned to take up the federal suits would agree. The situation did not look promising. Judge Frank McGarr, assigned to the West Side case, was a "politically active Republican." As Tom Boodell Jr. recalled, "He told us right in the beginning that he would not have written the same opinion as Judge Will." Judge J. Samuel Perry, assigned to the South Side case, had grown up in Alabama but lived most of his adult life in a western Chicago suburb. He "had a reputation as something of a populist, with sympathy for the underdog," recalled Jenner and Block attorney John C. Tucker. The crucial question, Tucker knew, was whether or not "an Alabama populist" was "still from Alabama."[169]

THE FEDERAL TRIALS

In August 1971, Judge Samuel Perry announced that the *Clark v. Universal* trial would commence the following March. Black Chicagoans greeted the news with mixed emotions. Some, like Ruth Wells, remained optimistic, hopeful that the federal suits might return hundreds of thousands of dollars to Lawndale and South Side residents. Others were less sanguine. The massive preparation for these trials was a "joke," they said, because "there's no justice for the Negro."[1]

With Bob Ming in prison, Tom Sullivan and Tom Boodell assumed the lead in preparing the federal suits. They were joined by John C. Tucker, a white Chicagoan who had recently tried a case against the Federal Savings and Loan Insurance Corporation. Now that the FHA, the VA, and the FSLIC had been added as defendants in the West Side suit, his knowledge could prove useful. Tucker quickly became passionately committed to both cases. In part his enthusiasm grew out of his experiences with CBL members, the most "attractive, engaging, sympathetic people" he'd ever had as clients. Primarily, though, it was the moral force of the issues at stake that drove the Jenner and Block attorneys to give the suits their all. "You just felt as though there was a terrible injustice going on that needed to be addressed," Tucker recalled.[2]

The task was challenging, to say the least. The centerpiece of both suits, the violation of civil rights, required proof of racial discrimination, but adducing such proof was tricky. The case against Universal, for example, did not fit easily within the traditional model of racial discrimination, in which an African American is refused a service routinely available to a white person. In such an instance, discrimination is obvious. Because Universal built in an all-black area, however, there were no whites with whom one could compare the company's treatment of its black customers.

Sullivan's group chose another approach. They would argue that Chicago had two housing markets: one for whites and one for blacks. The end result of discriminatory practices by a wide range of actors from banks to white homeowners was that blacks were confined to a small section of the city. Racism thus artificially limited the supply of black housing, which in turn artificially raised its costs. Both the West Side and the South Side defendants took advantage of this situation by selling homes in the black housing market at prices higher than those for comparable buildings sold to whites, and on terms that were more onerous. The lawyers would charge Universal and the West Side sellers not with *creating* a discriminatory situation but with *exploiting* a preexisting condition of racial discrimination for financial gain.[3]

It was a risky argument. By the early 1970s, many attorneys accepted that "traditional" or overt racial discrimination in the sale of housing was barred by Section 1982 of the Civil Rights Act of 1866. They agreed as well that the 1968 *Jones v. Mayer* ruling had affirmed the section's applicability to the actions of private individuals as well as public authorities. But the CBL attorneys hoped to extend its reach even further, to argue that their "exploitation" theory of discrimination—wherein it was illegal to exploit a preexisting discriminatory situation for economic profit—was also barred by Section 1982.

To bolster their position, the attorneys looked to Judge Hubert Will's 1969 ruling, which affirmed that the purpose of Section 1982 was to ensure that the U.S. economy "be undifferentiated as to the race of a man." Will had implied that exploiting economic conditions created by racial discrimination was just as illegal as engaging in direct discrimination. "Defendants present the discredited claim that it is necessarily right for a businessman to secure profit wherever profit is available, arguing specifically that they did not create the system of *de facto* segregation which was the condition for the alleged discriminatory profit," he wrote. "But the law in the United States has grown to define certain . . . ethical limits of business enterprise. . . . For it is now understood that under s. 1982 as interpreted in Jones v. Alfred H. Mayer Co., there cannot in this country be markets or profits based on the color of a man's skin." Will concluded that "there is no reason to distinguish a refusal to sell on the ground of race and a sale on discriminatory prices and terms."[4]

Sullivan, Boodell, and Tucker would use Will's understanding of the "ethical limits of business enterprise" and his condemnation of sales made "on discriminatory prices and terms" as the basis of their arguments. If successful, their suits might do more than force the remaining contract sellers to renegotiate. They could also establish legal precedents for challenging other profits derived from racially divided markets. As Tucker explained, "There was a 'race tax' on many products besides real estate. Commodities like groceries, medicine, furniture, and gasoline cost substantially more in many black inner cities than in white areas of the same cities." Merchants in black neighborhoods insisted that they charged more in order to make up for higher risks of credit, vandalism, and theft. But there was little evidence to support their claims. What was indisputable, though, was that merchants diminished the purchasing power and economic well-being of African Americans by charging blacks higher prices.[5] If the contract buyers prevailed, they would bring the nation one major step closer to abolishing markets based on race, to enabling a black person's dollar to buy what a white person's could. The consequences could be immense.

To make claims this sweeping, the contract buyers' legal team needed concrete, legally compelling data to prove what had been common knowledge for at least a decade—the existence of a dual housing market.[6] Analysis of the financial transactions at issue in the two suits was a massive undertaking, however. Each of the 475 West Side CBL members who made up the "random sample" of that case's 2,600 plaintiffs had to describe their financial histories in exhaustive detail; the interview questionnaire alone was forty-four pages long. The property records of plaintiffs who were not in the random sample also had to be compiled as part of an effort to uncover the full histories of every parcel of property in their community. To contextualize all of this material, Jenner and Block staffers and CBL volunteers tracked down every property in the West Side's black sections that was held under a land trust. The complete histories of the 30,000 properties so identified then had to be laboriously extracted from the banks holding those trusts. The raw data on these land parcels were then transferred to computer cards so that they could be dissected by social scientists trained in sampling and data analysis. A worker had to make 199 entries on a computer card in order to record the history of a single property; the completion of one card took three hours of labor. Maps also had to be prepared so that financial patterns revealed by the data could be visually displayed. This was the preparatory work for the West Side case alone; the South Side case required similarly mountainous research.

Here the contract buyers' attorneys received help from an old friend. In 1969, John McKnight had taken a job as head of the Center for Urban Affairs at Northwestern University. There he assigned one of his students— a sociologist and former civil rights activist named Andrew Gordon—the task of analyzing the data on housing discrimination that CBL staffers collected from black contract buyers. Using Northwestern's massive mainframe computers to tabulate immense amounts of information, Gordon was able to demonstrate a "pretty set pattern" of discrimination. "The data spoke for itself," he said.[7]

The information gathering that CBL attorneys depended upon was largely carried out by a staff of approximately twenty college students who donated their time. Despite the often mechanical nature of suit preparations, these volunteers understood the importance of their task. Greg Colvin called the research "exciting"; Alan Boles said that his time with the CBL was "the most interesting year of my life." They valued the opportunity to work with committed activists like Ross and Wells and with prominent attorneys like Tom Sullivan. In the fall of 1970, several of them moved from Macnamara's apartment to a building owned by Ruby Kirk. "She was delighted to have us," Boles recalled. "She called us her 'college boys,' and we painted her apartment and fixed it up." Colvin remembers the heady feeling of going from dinner meetings with high-powered attorneys in downtown Chicago to nights in Lawndale, where the young men would fall asleep to the music of Aretha Franklin coming through the walls of the neighboring apartment. Kirk often invited the boys to dinner. "She would serve us soul food, which was way cool to eat back then," Boles said. The college students knew nothing of the tortured history of their home at 3901 West Jackson. To them, it was, in Colvin's words, "a fine, functional building" in which to live.[8]

On April 12, 1972, *Clark v. Universal* went to trial. Sullivan, Tucker, and Boodell brought in Karl E. Taeuber, the nation's top authority on residential segregation, who used census data to demonstrate what "most citizens of Chicago knew to be true"—that Chicago was among the most highly segregated cities in the nation. Blacks lacked freedom to live where they wished, Taeuber demonstrated; therefore, there was a dual housing market in Chicago. To prove that Universal took advantage of this dual market to overcharge blacks, the plaintiffs' attorneys brought in five experienced appraisers, who showed that Universal homes were priced at 16 to 35 percent higher than the prices whites paid for comparable buildings.[9]

In response to Universal's claim that it sold on contract as a service to customers who could not get mortgages, the plaintiffs countered that the company sold this way for one reason only—financial gain from a captive market. The practice of contract selling allowed it to charge higher interest and keep the equity until the entire price for the building had been paid. It also enabled Universal to obscure the fact that its prices were significantly above market value: if black clients had purchased their homes with a mortgage, a building appraisal would have been a precondition for obtaining the loan, and that appraisal would have revealed that Universal was overcharging.[10]

The lawyers' careful documentation indicated that Universal had exploited a discriminatory situation for financial gain. What would clinch their case, they believed, was evidence that Universal had engaged in "traditional" discrimination as well. And they found it. Before developing communities on the South Side, Universal had built near-identical settlements in the all-white Chicago suburb of Deerfield, Illinois. Although building costs in Deerfield were slightly higher, Universal sold those homes for considerably less than it charged on the South Side. They believed that even under a narrow reading of Section 1982—one requiring proof that

Universal sold the same product to whites at a different price from what it asked of blacks—Universal had engaged in racial discrimination.

To drive home the point the plaintiffs called on Richard Freeman, an economist at the University of Chicago who specialized in the statistical analysis of the economics of racial discrimination. Freeman agreed that the only way that Universal could get away with the high prices and harsh conditions it imposed on its South Side buyers was by exploiting a dual housing market based on race. He testified that Universal's Deerfield operations were "extremely important" because they showed "the exact same seller operating in two markets." The fact that Universal phased out the Deerfield operations in order to sell exclusively to African Americans in Chicago confirmed the greater profits to be made there. The "essential reason" for the greater profits was "not the differences in the way the houses were put together—the costs are about the same—but rather the race of the buyer," he concluded.[11]

The CBL attorneys suffered some setbacks. Judge Samuel Perry excluded Freeman's testimony from the jury because "discrimination is not a technical matter," a claim that presumably reflected his belief that Freeman's statistical supporting material was over the jury's head. Perry also barred evidence about Universal's Deerfield sales, ruling the price comparison not relevant because the suburban settlements were "miles away" from Universal's city properties. But on the whole, the CBL attorneys remained optimistic about the presentation of their case. About six weeks after the start of the trial, on Friday, May 19, they completed their arguments. Universal attorneys Burt Weitzenfeld and Michael Turoff then requested a directed verdict, that is, asked Judge Perry to dismiss the case. Their request implied that the plaintiffs' case was so weak that the defense need not even bother to refute it. Tucker, Sullivan, and Boodell never seriously considered the possibility that Perry would grant the defendants' request.[12]

The following Monday morning, Tucker noticed that "something was odd" in the courtroom. Usually there was one armed U.S. marshal stationed to keep order in the court, but today there were almost a dozen. After Judge Perry entered and the assembled court personnel, jury, and bystanders took their seats, the marshals remained standing, facing the audience. At this point Tucker was suddenly overcome by the realization of what was about to happen. Perry was going to dismiss the case. He had summoned extra armed marshals because he feared that when he did so Contract Buyers League members—many of whom were middle-aged, churchgoing women who had sat through weeks of tedious hearings dressed in their nicest clothes—would riot.

"They should have," Tucker thought. Perry, speaking rapidly, his eyes "glued to the paper as though he were afraid to look up," dismissed the case and exonerated Universal Builders. Although the "counsel for the plaintiffs have not painted a pretty picture of the defendants, . . . that picture is a picture of exploitation for profit, and not racial discrimination," he insisted. Where the plaintiffs saw a "conspiracy to discriminate against plaintiffs because of their race or color," Perry saw the operation of the same "law of supply and demand" that leads to "boom towns in time of war and dying ghost towns in time of peace." Seemingly misunderstanding the exploitation theory of discrimination, Perry declared that "nowhere in the six week trial is there one scintilla of evidence that the defendants . . . ever refused to sell to a white person or a black person . . . any house, or refused to sell one or the other at a higher or lower price, absolutely no positive evidence of discrimination in this record."[13]

In a particularly punitive touch, Perry imposed conditions that were intended to discourage the plaintiffs from appealing. If the plaintiffs appealed and then lost, he said, they would have to pay the costs of the trial. "With that the judge rose and fled," Tucker recalled, "just as Tom Sullivan began objecting to the shameless effort to coerce the plaintiffs into waiving their right of appeal." When Sullivan continued voicing his objections to the court reporter, Perry returned in a huff and "angrily ordered" the reporter to stop taking down Sullivan's arguments.

"It was over. Utterly dejected, we gathered up our papers," Tucker said. One of the Jenner and Block paralegals started to cry, and several contract buyers gathered around to comfort her. They "spoke of God's will" and affirmed their faith that "God would give them the strength to endure this" and to "keep on fighting." Tucker lacked this comforting sense of ultimate justice. "I felt more tired than I have ever felt in my life," he recollected.[14]

However shocking Perry's decision was to Tucker, some CBL supporters had expected a ruling of this sort. As soon as Judge Perry "started talking about 'the Negras,'" legal assistant Maureen McDonald said, she knew that the contract buyers "didn't stand a chance." Clyde Ross agreed. "I knew from the beginning . . . that we'd have trouble, because Judge Perry kept telling us how fair and unprejudiced he is," he told reporters. "You know what that usually means." As for whether or not to appeal, Perry had made it "a risky business," Ross noted. "All our members are poor people." But accepting defeat would only worsen the already bitter mood among the community's young people. "They called us fools when we decided to . . . go through the courts," he said. "What do we tell them now?"[15]

The question was settled when league members voted overwhelmingly to appeal the ruling. Their brief was largely composed by Richard T. Franch, a newcomer to the Jenner and Block team. Unlike Tucker, Boodell, and Sullivan, Franch had no personal relationships with CBL members. He was also a free-market conservative who opposed governmental interference in the economy. However, as Franch noted, "I represent clients and it doesn't matter what my personal views are." His meticulous appeal brief, prepared with Tucker's assistance, succinctly contested Perry's dismissal of evidence about Universal's Deerfield sales and his barring of the plaintiffs' expert witness. His most important argument addressed Perry's insistence that the plaintiffs had no "cause of action" under the Civil Rights Act of 1866 unless they could prove that Universal had engaged in traditional discrimination—that is, that Universal had sold homes to white buyers on the South Side for prices lower than blacks had paid for similar buildings. Franch responded that such a condition was nonsensical. "If plaintiffs were required to adduce such proof, their case would involve proving a contradiction: that there is a rigid segregation, resulting in a dual market, but that whites bought in the Negro market." This inherent contradiction was among the reasons that Judge Will had earlier rejected the same argument as "'obnoxious' in result and 'ridiculous' in logic." According to Will, the plaintiffs were not required to prove traditional discrimination at all. They were required only to prove that the defendants sold to blacks at prices higher than whites paid for comparable housing and that they could do so because racial discrimination limited the black housing supply.[16]

On October 24, 1973, Tucker argued the appeal before a panel headed by Judge Luther Swygert, "a big man with white hair and a white beard" who was, as Tucker knew, "an unapologetic liberal." His reassuring presence may have contributed to Tucker's fine verbal performance. He was "absolutely brilliant in the argument," Franch recalled. "I was sitting there, practically crying" by the time he concluded.

Tucker left the hearing feeling "dangerously confident." Nine long months later, on July 26, 1974, the ruling was handed down. "It was as complete a victory as we could have asked for," he exulted.[17] The court of appeals attacked Judge Perry's decision on numerous grounds, from his exclusion of evidence about Universal's pricing policies in suburban Deerfield, which it called "an abuse of discretion," to his imposition of conditions designed to discourage an appeal, which it condemned as an "unwarranted" action that "cannot be tolerated." The core issue, however, was "the conflict as to the scope of Section 1982." The judges did not agree with the narrow application of the traditional theory of discrimination. The language of Section 1982 was "broad yet clear": all citizens have the same right as whites to purchase property. Congress "plainly meant to secure that right against interference from any sources whatsoever, whether government or private." *Jones v. Mayer* similarly concluded that Section 1982 "must be accorded 'a sweep as broad as its language.'"

Thus the defendants could not "escape the reach of Section 1982 by proclaiming that they merely took advantage of a discriminatory situation created by others," the appeals court ruled. There was "no justification" for the defendants' argument that they would have sold their homes at the same prices and terms to white buyers. Such an argument, based on the theoretical existence of "whites who elected to enter the black market and purchase housing in the ghetto . . . at exorbitant prices," clearly "ignores current realities of racial psychology and economic practicalities." To accept the defendants' claim that they "would have exploited whites as well as blacks" would "be tantamount to perpetuating a subterfuge behind which every slumlord and exploiter of those banished to the ghetto could hide by a simple rubric: The same property would have been sold to whites on the same terms."

The appeals court concluded by eloquently restating the Supreme Court's interpretation of the Civil Rights Act of 1866 in *Jones v. Mayer*: "When a seller in the black market demands exorbitant prices and onerous sales terms relative to the terms and prices available to white citizens for comparable housing, it cannot be stated that a dollar in the hands of a black man will purchase the same thing as a dollar in the hands of a white man. Such practices render plaintiffs' dollars less valuable than those of white citizens—a situation that was spawned by a discarded system of slavery and is nurtured by vestiges of that system. Courts in applying Section 1982 must be vigilant in preventing toleration of this deplorable circumstance." Reversing Perry's judgment, the court ordered that a new trial be held, in which the defendants would be required "to articulate some legitimate, nondiscriminatory reason for the price and term differential" revealed in the first trial.[18]

The CBL's attorneys didn't have much time to celebrate the ruling. Judge Frank McGarr, assigned to the West Side case, had not been willing to set a trial date until the South Side appeal had been decided. Now he proposed spring 1975. The lawyers, whose attention had been focused exclusively on the South Side case, begged for an extension. It was granted. The West Side trial would begin on November 19, 1975. The contract sellers of Chicago's West Side would finally have their day in court.

By the time the West Side trial began, the corrupt practices of slum landlords and speculators in black urban areas had become so egregious—and widely reported—that the plaintiffs and their attorneys felt confident of receiving a sympathetic hearing. Indeed, since January 1969, when the CBL's suits were originally filed, exploitative practices in the urban housing market, both in Chicago and nationally, had grown ever more outrageous.

By the early 1970s, Chicago's Lawndale community was experiencing something that would make little sense in an ordinary market—a severe housing shortage coupled with a rush by many property owners to dump their deeds for almost any price. The housing shortage was a direct result of the exploitative practices of the city's contract sellers, whose repeated sale of already run-down properties had left buildings so decayed that the city was forced to demolish them. Of the several hundred West Side properties owned by Lou Fushanis at the time of his death in 1963, for example, almost 70 percent were torn down by the city as uninhabitable by 1970. In 1960, the city had condemned a total of 143 slum buildings. In 1968, it demolished ten times that number, 1,421, displacing 3,630 families. "I ordered four buildings torn down this morning," housing court judge Franklin I. Kral told reporters in March 1969. "They had 100 apartments. It makes you sick. But they were unlivable." The situation only deteriorated.

In 1972, the city pulled down 1,682 buildings, and it expected to break that record in 1973. As the *Chicago Tribune* reported, "Chicago's buildings are dying so quickly that the city's wrecking crews can't keep pace."[19]

The city's demolition backlog meant that abandoned buildings scarred poor neighborhoods. Lawndale was particularly hard-hit. By 1972, there were over 230 "decaying hulks" in Lawndale, while the next worst area—the black South Side neighborhood of Woodlawn—contained 130. These buildings were frequent settings for violence and crime. "There's been a death, two rapes, three fires, and still nothing has been done," a neighbor noted of an abandoned building at 734–6 South Independence Boulevard—just down the block from the apartment that had housed Jack Macnamara and his Presentation parish college organizers a few years before. While some Lawndale residents struggled to maintain their property, their efforts only resulted in what observers described as a "heartbreaking" sight: "a neat, newly sandblasted house whose owner tries to hold on with a white picket fence, striped awnings, flowers in the window. And next door and across the street are abandoned hulks, . . . boarded and burned, menacing the neighborhood."[20]

This terrible state of affairs inspired the *Chicago Tribune* to launch yet another investigation of the city's worst slumlords. Its 1973 top ten list included Gerald Crane, who was a defendant in the CBL's West Side suit. Six others on the list were financially interlinked and also named in the suit. They were Victor Spector, who had owned slum properties in the city since the 1940s; Gilbert Balin, who managed many of Spector's buildings; Al Berland, who owned many properties with Balin; Berland's childhood friend and frequent business partner Lou Wolf; Wolf's brother-in-law Joseph Berke; and the person who acted as all of these men's attorney, financier, and hidden partner, Moe Forman.[21] As assistant corporate counsel Timothy O'Hara noted, "They're all connected, and they pass the buildings around." Moe Forman "is a partner in almost everything. . . . He pays real estate taxes on hundreds of buildings in Lawndale. But he claims he does it only as a favor for friends." No one understood that the slums were owned by "just one group," O'Hara added. "It appeared to be diversified ownership. [But] they were organized." All together, the *Chicago Tribune* noted, their "massive slum operation" encompassed two thousand buildings.[22]

In the early 1970s, these men sometimes continued to make money the way they always had—by buying buildings cheap, mortgaging them with savings and loan companies for as much as or more than their worth, and then selling them on contract.[23] Profiteering around racial change followed a traditional pattern. As the number of black residents increased in Austin, a Chicago neighborhood west of Lawndale, savings and loan institutions redlined the area. For example, in 1974 a white married couple, both professors at the University of Illinois, sought a mortgage to purchase a house in Austin. Their mortgage application was turned down by seven banks, with no explanation. By refusing to grant mortgages to people seeking to buy in Austin, no matter what their credit history, banks and savings and loans were effectively turning Austin over to speculators who had ready access to credit. Fleeing whites took what they could get for their houses. Many sold for $10,000, only to see their former homes listed for sale on contract shortly thereafter for $25,000. The neighborhood became known as a "realtors' paradise." The number of real estate dealers working there skyrocketed, from forty in 1962 to three hundred a decade later.[24]

But big profits on contract sales were possible only if one could find buyers willing to pay grossly inflated prices, and that was no longer the case in Lawndale. While Austin witnessed the start of a familiar cycle of exploitation, Lawndale operators presided over that cycle's stark conclusion. Instead of making their money through evictions and resales, they now proposed to turn the titles over to their buyers—as long as these buyers were able to pay the remainder of the original, inflated price, or something close to it. The speculators' strategy was to help long-term contract buyers find mortgages that would enable the buyers to pay off their debt. That way, the sellers could "dump" a washed-out building and quickly get the maximum amount of cash. Of course, the strategy could succeed only if mortgage money was made available. And here circumstances worked in the sellers' favor. By 1968, in a historic reversal, the FHA had begun insuring mortgages in "older, declining areas" of the nation's cities—that is, in many black urban neighborhoods—making mortgages in such areas easier to acquire.[25]

There were a number of reasons for the FHA's turnaround. One was the need to defuse the tensions revealed by the urban riots of the mid-1960s. Others were linked to a change in the agency's structure. From its inception in the 1930s, the FHA had been an independent agency that insured mortgages based on principles that were both fiscally conservative and racially discriminatory.[26] But in 1965, the FHA's independent

status ended. That year President Lyndon Johnson created the Department of Housing and Urban Development (HUD) as a cabinet-level
agency, and the FHA was incorporated into the larger HUD bureaucracy.
HUD's explicit goal was to promote home ownership not just for whites
but also for blacks and other minorities long excluded from FHA support.
The FHA was brought closer into line with HUD goals in 1968, when Congress passed the Housing and Urban Development Act, which included a
number of initiatives designed to enable urban and low-income people
to purchase homes. The FHA was assigned to administer Section 223(e),
which dramatically increased the availability of mortgages for minority
and low-income buyers in urban areas. It did so not by lending such funds
directly but by fully insuring the mortgages made by banks, savings and
loans, or mortgage companies. FHA insurance now made the risk of lending in urban areas close to nonexistent, since the government would
cover the loss on any defaulted loan.[27]

With loans readily available, Lawndale contract sellers increasingly
helped their buyers convert the balance of their debt to FHA-insured
mortgages. Ironically, these contract negotiations effectively accomplished
what Charlie Baker had warned against at the start of the CBL's payment
strike: they allowed the contract seller to get out with all his cash and left
the buyer to pay off the full mortgage. There were occasional reductions
made to the original contract price, and these could be significant. For
example, Al Berland sold Oliver Bass the title to his two-flat for $10,000,
even though Bass had originally agreed to pay the inflated price of
$17,500. But such deals were generally given only on a building that was
so decayed that even the lower price was far more than it was worth.
When Bass got title to his home, the building was in violation of numerous city codes and under threat of demolition. It needed a new roof, a
new rear porch, new windows, and a new heating system. To pay for all
this, Bass, who earned $139 for a fifty-three-hour workweek at a candy
company, had to take out an additional loan of $29,000.[28]

Al Berland went to great lengths to ensure that his contract buyers got
FHA-insured loans. He even offered them help in filling out the loan
forms. More precisely, he worked with a pair of corrupt mortgage brokers
to falsify credit records for the applicants. By the time Berland was caught
in 1970, he had obtained $250,000 in federally insured loans. Under depo-
sition, he explained how they did it. If a contract buyer "had 10 children,"

they wrote down "two children. If he made $100 a week, they put $200, you know, to put it through." Judge Hubert L. Will, who presided over the case, fined Berland $10,000 and gave him four years' probation for filing false credit reports with the FHA. If the fraud had continued, Berland could easily have taken the FHA for $1 million.[29]

When the contract sellers were unable to unload their decrepit properties for a high price, they turned to another method to extract a profit. This scheme involved stripping the buildings of their mortgages. Its victims were not contract buyers but the savings and loan institutions that had financed the purchases in the first place.

At the time of their original buying spree, Lawndale contract sellers had acquired their buildings from whites on the cheap and then immediately mortgaged them—often for more than they were worth—to generate cash to buy more properties. They were able to do so because of the accommodating largesse of some of Chicago's savings and loan institutions. In the 1950s, for example, First Mutual Savings and Loan president Austin Waldron had a cozy relationship with Lou Fushanis, Joseph Berke, and other Lawndale speculators. Although he wouldn't lend to blacks moving to the area, he was happy to give unusually high mortgages to white contract sellers. Speculators paid high rates for these loans.[30] During the early years, when contract sellers routinely collected monthly payments that were up to three times higher than what they owed on their own mortgages, the arrangement worked smoothly. The speculators were easily able to pay their mortgages, purchase new buildings, and reap high profits.

But by the late 1960s, the system began to falter. Buildings were in such a sorry state that buyers were increasingly likely to put $100 down, make a few months of high payments, and then, overwhelmed by the avalanche of expenses necessary to make their new homes livable, abandon the properties. Without steady contract payments, Lawndale's contract sellers had no intention of continuing to pay their own mortgages. Instead, they defaulted on their loans, dumping hundreds of crumbling, overmortgaged buildings back onto the lending institutions. Since the near-ruined buildings were now worth only a fraction of the original loans, the institutions essentially lost their loan money, amounting to millions of dollars.

These losses pushed First Mutual to the point of collapse. Desperate to recoup something, the company offered the buildings for sale, at "rock bottom prices," to whoever would take them. The scavengers who gathered to buy were often the same men who had dumped them in the first place. In one day alone, Moe Forman turned six slums over to First Mutual; five of the six ended up back in his hands, with Gil Balin as copartner. Al Berland dumped approximately sixty buildings onto First Mutual and then repurchased them at a fraction of their former worth.[31]

By 1968, First Mutual was out of business, and 659 of its defaulted mortgages—worth $7.8 million—landed with the Federal Savings and Loan Insurance Corporation (FSLIC), the governmental agency that insured savings and loan deposits. Many of these debts had been owed by Lawndale's worst contract sellers. They included $756,920 in delinquent mortgages owed by Berke, $280,000 by Berland, $502,323 by Forman's F & F Investment company, $28,945 by Forman himself, and $241,658 by Fushanis's estate.

Stuck with the ownership of rotting slums on the city's West Side, the FSLIC, like First Mutual before it, offered the buildings for sale at whatever it could get. In a typical example, it sold one Lawndale building, on which it inherited a $36,000 defaulted mortgage, to Lou Wolf—for $3,500. Since Wolf was a client of Forman's and co-owned buildings with Forman, Joseph Berke, and Al Berland, turning a building over to Wolf essentially amounted to returning the property to the "massive slum operation" that had milked it in the first place. In this particular case, as in numerous others, the FSLIC—that is, American taxpayers—took the $32,500 loss.[32]

Some observers found it difficult to understand why Forman and his circle were so eager to reclaim the buildings they had so recently shed. "Slums don't pay. If there was a conspiracy, it was stupid," claimed Pierre DeVise, an urbanologist who taught at the University of Illinois in Chicago. In fact, the "stupid" one was probably DeVise. As the *Tribune* commented, "Such disbelief . . . has been the slumlords' greatest ally." For those ruthless enough to stomach the consequences, it was easy to make profits out of buildings for which one paid cash and on which one owed nothing. As Timothy O'Hara pointed out, "If you're not making repairs . . . you are making 100 percent profit."[33]

Of course, owners' refusal to maintain their buildings was nothing new. From the beginning, professional slumlords like Forman, Balin, Berland, Berke, and Wolf had been loath to make repairs. Forman was a regular in housing court when the *Chicago Daily News* investigated it in 1963; he remained so when the *Chicago Tribune* conducted its investigation in 1973. That year, in addition to contesting over forty code violation suits charged against him personally, Forman appeared in housing court about four times a day to get continuances on code violations filed against Berland, Wolf, or other clients.[34]

However, O'Hara noted a growing trend among slum landlords: to "avoid paying gas bills until your tenants freeze." Leaving one's building without heat during Chicago's winters was of a different order from refusing to fix faulty wiring or broken windows. It indicated a new phase in their operation, in which the goal was not to get money from tenants but to force them out altogether. For tenants, the results could be lethal. After her nineteen-month-old son, Scott, died of pneumonia, Mary Miller told reporters: "We had to huddle together around the stove and pile on coats and blankets. But it didn't do any good." Every time she complained, "the landlady would say 'If you don't like it get out.'" In the winter of 1969, three babies died over a three-week period because their West Side slum apartments had gone unheated. Their deaths confirmed the insight of the *Chicago Tribune*'s investigative reporters, who noted that, "when someone has to die in this shabby shell game played for money, it is usually a child."[35]

Slumlords' eagerness to rid their buildings of tenants was part of yet another profit-making scheme. It involved the manipulation of the Illinois Fair Plan, which was established in the aftermath of the 1968 riots to ensure that black neighborhoods were covered by fire insurance. As a result of the Fair Plan, buildings in Lawndale were now insurable for the same amount as those on the city's North Side Gold Coast. Slumlords realized that they could insure their rotting, neglected structures for twenty to thirty times what the buildings were worth. Of course, as one observer noted, they "aren't worth anything unless you burn them"—but if you didn't mind arson, then "even an abandoned building could be turned into a $60,000 windfall."[36]

Al Berland didn't mind. By August 1970, fires had broken out in forty-seven of his buildings and he had collected $350,000 in insurance. In one case, a tenant saved the lives of his four children by dropping them one at a time from a second-floor window. In another, Berland and Wolf were observed entering a property they owned at 715 South Lawndale "carefully" carrying some liquid in a bucket. The two men left "in a hurry" and shortly thereafter the building went up in flames. Later that day the police found Berland at his paint store, still wearing the clothing described by a witness. The witness later withdrew from the case "after his car caught fire mysteriously in front of his home." Chicago police sergeant John Moore, an arson expert, said that in his department Berland was known as "a torch."[37]

Gil Balin was also linked to an arson inquiry. According to newspaper accounts, he was charged in an indictment with conspiracy to commit arson. On January 12, 1972, a man reportedly posed as an exterminator so that he could carry large quantities of flammable liquids into a building that Balin managed on the city's South Side. A resident noticed an odd smell, and when he investigated he found gasoline poured about the top floor, along with an open-faced electric toaster that was stuffed with paper and attached to a timer. The tenant and the janitor pulled the timer's plug just minutes before it was set to go off, thus averting what fire investigators predicted would have been a "holocaust." Although the top floor was vacant, seven families lived in the building's first two floors. Investigators later determined that the third floor and its railings had been soaked with thirty gallons of gasoline. (It has proved impossible to determine whether Balin was acquitted or convicted, or if the charges were eventually dropped.) The owner, Victor Spector, had a $65,000 insurance policy on the structure. Police noted the striking similarity between this arson attempt and the events preceding a fire that had destroyed another building owned by Spector. In the latter case, witnesses saw men claiming to be painters carrying containers full of flammable liquids into the building just days before it went up in flames. The $25,000 insurance claim Spector filed was paid without question.[38]

Like Spector, Balin filed for $60,000 in insurance for fire losses on a Lawndale address that he bought in 1967 for $2,260. As Balin commented, "I have a lot of unprofitable ventures. They turn out good." Balin had told his tenants that he wanted them out. The building had suffered no fewer than five fires in the month before the final blaze. When Fair Plan officials hesitated to pay the claim, Balin sued for the money. Lou Wolf also had an unusually large number of fires in his properties. In one case he filed a $30,000 claim on a building he had purchased for $1,600. Wolf ultimately collected over $500,000 in fire insurance and used the money to purchase a cluster of bars and boutiques in the city's fashionable Lincoln Park neighborhood, a small empire that police investigators jokingly referred to as "Lou's Piece of the Rock."[39]

The fire that Berland and Wolf set at their 715 South Lawndale building received citywide news coverage in 1970. But in 1973, when *Chicago Tribune* reporters looked into the matter, they found that the case had "languished" under both state's attorney Edward V. Hanrahan and his successor, Bernard F. Carey. "Carey's staff said they were unaware of the existence of the case," the *Tribune* reported. By then, Berland and Wolf had collected over $800,000 in fire insurance. Only the renewed attention brought by the *Tribune*'s 1973 investigation prompted indictments. In January 1974, the two were finally found guilty of arson to defraud an insurer and conspiracy to commit arson. The prosecuting attorney called them "the personification of greed and avarice" and condemned their "unimaginable crime—pouring gallons and gallons of gasoline into a building where people live and setting fire to it for money." They were sentenced to 1½ to 4 years in prison.[40]

Perhaps one reason Berland and his cohorts went free for years despite crimes of this magnitude was the old problem of Chicago's understaffed and often incompetent city agencies. In 1973, as in 1963, Chicago's housing court judges heard forty cases a day, averaging about eight minutes per case; no records were kept that would enable a judge to single out chronic offenders.[41] The group also reaped the benefits of having friends in high places. In May 1973, Judge Franklin Kral resigned as the supervising judge of housing court after admitting that he'd received a $1,000 "discount" on a $3,000 purchase of paint and wallpaper from Al Berland's paint store. The Illinois Judicial Inquiry Board noted that the deal was made "in chambers, in cash, and with no record" and brokered by Moe Forman. Kral did not believe he was "guilty of any impropriety" and even moved to have the charges dismissed. As the board noted, Kral's motion was "disturbing because it seems to say that the conduct described is 'time honored and accepted' . . . and should be dismissed as 'business as usual.'"[42]

Kral was suspended without pay for two months. There was plentiful evidence, however, that his interaction with Forman and Berland was in fact "business as usual" for many housing court judges.[43] Indeed, profiting off slums sometimes occurred even among those whose job it was to prosecute people who did just that. In 1972, Arthur B. Mendelson, one of the city's assistant corporate counsels, owned at least four West Side slums. In one of his buildings, two tenants died in a fire. In another, three children were treated for lead poisoning. In yet another, residents went without gas for heat or cooking for almost two weeks. Mendelson owed $10,000 in unpaid property taxes, as well as $735 in unpaid water bills. He regularly showed up in his white Chevrolet to collect the rents.

Some city officials were embarrassed by the revelation. One pointed to Mendelson's conflict of interest: "He is working for the same office that is prosecuting slum landlords. . . . He also owes money on water bills, and [he] is collector for water bills." Mendelson's boss was distressed by the news. "It is clear that the entire buildings code enforcement efforts are rendered suspect when an assistant corporation counsel is involved in any conduct of slum properties," he said.[44]

What happened? Nothing. Citing "reorganization," the Housing Division of the State's Attorney's Office dropped the case against Arthur Mendelson, suggesting that it could be reinstated at some later date.[45]

Although justice was not served, these widely publicized scandals lent weight to the charges of corruption and conspiracy in the West Side suit. Then in 1972, a real estate scandal of national magnitude gave additional confirmation of the abuses pervading the housing market. Involving the newly merged FHA and HUD, it was so massive in scope that it made the doings of Chicago slum landlords look picayune. The scandal involved the abandonment and ruin of over 240,000 units of housing nationwide— enough to house over one million people. In Detroit alone, more than 25,000 houses had been abandoned—about 10 percent of the city's housing stock. The cost to the U.S. government was estimated at close to $4 billion, in preinflationary, early-1970s money. James M. Alter, chair of the Governor's Commission on Mortgage Practices, commented, "Outside of Watergate and Viet Nam, there is no greater scandal than in FHA and HUD housing. The cities are rotting and nobody seems to be responsible."[46]

This FHA-HUD scandal was actually a series of scandals involving the exploitation of several different programs that had been created as part of the Housing and Urban Development Act of 1968. U.S. cities were most affected, however, by the misuse of the FHA's 223(e) program, the one explicitly created to extend FHA mortgage insurance to low-income urban areas.[47]

The Section 223(e) program should have been a godsend to American cities. A buyer of limited income but sound credit history could now apply for a mortgage to buy a home with as little as $200 down. Mortgage bankers were willing to lend the remainder of the purchase price to the qualified buyer, since their mortgage loan was 100 percent guaranteed by the FHA. In theory, both the buyer and the lender knew that the home was sound and the price fair because the FHA guaranteed loans only after inspection of the premises. In thirty years the buyer would have paid off his or her mortgage, becoming the proud owner of an investment that could be passed on to the next generation. And if, for some reason, the buyer defaulted on the loan, the mortgage company was protected from loss. It would secure the defaulted building from vandalism and collect the remainder of the loan from the FHA insurance pool. The FHA would then sell the vacant but protected building to another buyer.[48]

But the program did not work out as planned. As noted, some contract sellers took advantage of newly available FHA-guaranteed mortgages to "settle" with contract buyers and get the full, grossly inflated price—or something close to it—for their properties. Section 223(e) also became the linchpin of an entirely new scheme of exploitation. Much like the contract-sale scenario, this new scheme enabled speculators to buy low from whites and sell, at a triple to quadruple markup, to blacks.

It worked like this. First, the "suede-shoe boys," as the real estate speculators were colloquially called, scoured urban neighborhoods looking for decayed buildings that they could buy for the lowest possible price— say, $5,000. Next, they bribed FHA appraisers to value the buildings at vastly inflated rates. A typical corrupt FHA appraisal might claim that the speculator's crumbling $5,000 house was actually worth, say, $20,000. With the corrupt appraisal in hand, the speculator could easily sell his slum building for quadruple its worth. Now, rather than selling the building on contract, he could recoup the full price immediately with an FHA-insured mortgage. So what if the price seemed high? The mortgage lender couldn't lose: after all, $20,000 was the property's appraised value, and more importantly, the loan was 100 percent guaranteed. As one broker explained, once the speculators "saw how they could get a mortgage commitment far in excess of [their purchase] price, zoom, it was wide open." The gold rush had begun.[49]

All that the speculator needed was someone to buy the building. He enticed buyers by emphasizing the low down payment—often no more than $200—rather than the high final cost. In Chicago and other cities, people eager to buy buildings on such terms were easy to find. They were usually black or Hispanic, and always low-income. Given the desperate housing shortage facing low-income families, an offer of a home of one's own for a $200 down payment was often irresistible. The speculators made the procedure seem quick and easy. They did all the paperwork, sometimes even lending the buyers the down payment. The speculators made sure that the purchasers—many of whom lacked the resources to carry their buildings' dramatically inflated prices—qualified for an FHA-insured mortgage by doubling or tripling their stated income, while hiding their debts. This fraudulent activity was shockingly blatant. Many speculators simply picked up blank tax forms and filled in whatever income they felt the mortgage companies might require. The mortgage companies didn't ask too many questions about these loan applications for the simple reason that the mortgages were fully insured. The creditworthiness of the borrower was of no relevance, since the company would never lose money on FHA-insured loans.[50]

Since mortgage companies made their profits through the exorbitant service fees they charged on FHA loans, they made money on every sale, with no risk whatsoever.[51] The mortgage companies got away with high service fees because banks and savings and loans continued to redline "changing" and all-black areas and refused to make conventional mortgage loans there. While FHA-insured loans had long been a supplement to normal mortgage activity, they now became the only mortgage activity in town. And the companies made even higher profits on FHA-insured mortgages when these actually defaulted. This was because, in addition to service fees, the lenders also charged interest rates of 7 to 9 percent; if the borrower defaulted within the first year of ownership, the FHA paid the mortgage company the entire value of the loan, plus 7 percent interest and all the service fees, within one year instead of over thirty years. If large numbers of homes were sold to buyers likely to default, the mortgage companies stood to make a lot of money.[52]

And large numbers of homes were sold. In the early 1970s, white working-class neighborhoods across the country were once again flooded with speculators who terrorized residents into selling low. Instead of using the traditional scare phrase "The blacks are coming," speculators adopted a subtler, more up-to-date slogan: "This is an FHA area." Everyone knew that it meant the same thing. Using racial anxieties to convince urban whites to sell their homes was profitable not only to the mortgage companies and the speculators but also to the banks and savings and loan companies that had originally made mortgage loans to local whites. Many older white residents had bought their homes in the 1940s and 1950s, when mortgage rates were extremely low. Now that inflation was pushing up interest rates, lenders had every reason to want to close those mortgages out. "In a community like this, older people had 3½ and 5½ percent mortgages," one West Side resident explained in 1972. "The banks were unhappy about that. It was bad money. It is worth it to clean out a whole area if you can get 8¾ percent," that is, the current conventional mortgage rate. She summed up the situation: speculative real estate brokers like to "keep people hating each other and fighting each other and moving" because when they are doing so, "everybody makes so damn much money."[53]

The person who did not profit was the low-income home buyer. The experience of Beulah Perkins, a young African American wife and mother, was fairly typical. In 1971, she got an FHA-insured mortgage that enabled her to purchase an $18,000 home in Austin for $200 down. The building had passed an FHA inspection, but once Perkins moved in, a number of problems became apparent. There were holes in the living room walls, and a section of the kitchen wall had been knocked out. The windows were installed improperly, making the house difficult to heat. The basement flooded every time it rained. There were numerous code violations. In addition to her high monthly mortgage payment, Perkins was responsible for thousands of dollars in repair bills. Yet either because of cosmetic coverups made by her seller or because of outright fraud, the FHA had failed to note these flaws. The newspaper headline about her story summed up the situation: "Her Dream Home a 'Nightmare.'"[54]

By 1972, similar abuses of FHA programs were reported in Boston; New York; Newark; Philadelphia; Wilmington, Delaware; Miami; Detroit; St. Louis; Seattle; Los Angeles; and Lubbock, Texas.[55] A *New York Times* reporter noted that FHA-guaranteed loans were being given on "substandard" buildings that lacked "such essentials as adequate heating and plumbing." The confluence of inflated mortgage payments and high repair costs meant that the low-income buyer never had a chance. As an investigator in Los Angeles explained, "Many of these families are so thrilled to have a house that they will take a second job, do without a new car, . . . anything to afford the house. After six months, however, after their child falls through the floor or the pipes burst and cause water to flow everywhere, they say to themselves, 'Why should I put up with this?' and abandon the house."[56]

This was precisely the situation facing Perkins. She became so financially stressed that abandoning her home increasingly seemed like the best option. Hers was one of fifty-six similar cases that the Organization for a Better Austin (OBA) documented in the area. "FHA is creating the slums of the future," organizers noted. Chicago-area FHA director John Waner concurred. "Even if a house is in good shape, you can't let people over-mortgage themselves," he explained, because to pay back their inflated loans they would cut corners by taking in additional tenants and deferring building maintenance. "That's the beginning of the ghetto, the slum. The very thing the woman ran away from, she has now created."[57]

Waner was one of many to note that mortgage companies, like the contract sellers in their heyday, were inordinately eager to foreclose on their buyers' overpriced homes. "If the buyer defaults on the first payment or the second payment, the mortgage company throws him into foreclosure immediately in order to pick up the windfall money," he explained. "The more FHA buyers who default, the higher the mortgage bankers' yield." Mortgage companies sometimes pushed buyers to default. "If the buyer missed last month and comes in with this month's payment, they'll tell him, 'I'm sorry, I won't take it,'" Waner said. The FHA's own records backed Waner's claim. These showed that the foreclosure rate on 223(e) FHA-insured mortgages was not double, or even quadruple, but an astonishing seven times that of conventional loans. The repossessed buildings sometimes ended up back in the hands of the speculators, who then started the cycle anew. In a clear replication of the contract sales scenario, there were cases of buildings resold as many as six times in an eighteen-month period. New York City's Assistant U.S. Attorney Anthony Accetta described the social and emotional costs that such statistics suggested. "I don't see how anyone who is black or Puerto Rican could have faith in the white system after being shaken down like this and then losing his house two months later," he said.[58]

The results of the scam could be seen in "the bombed-out appearance of many central cities, where block after block of structurally sound housing has been abandoned," New York Times reporter John Herbers noted in

1972. Of course, while the scandal meant ruin for some, it meant huge profits for others. In Chicago, the FHA paid out at least $42 million to real estate speculators and corrupt mortgage firms. In Brooklyn, such operators received $250 million from the FHA. In Detroit, which was hardest hit by the scandal, FHA insurance payments amounted to a shocking $375 to $500 million. As Brian Boyer observed, in return for this immense payout to Detroit's mortgage brokers and speculators, the U.S. government received "a deserted slum and the concomitant problems of rampant heroin addiction and the highest big city murder rate in the U.S.A."[59] Later generations had a simpler—and distorted—explanation for the desolation they saw in Detroit and other black urban areas. The devastation was caused, they insisted, by "the riots."[60]

By the spring of 1972, reports in Chicago, Detroit, and Philadelphia finally led to Justice Department investigations and U.S. Senate hearings on the FHA scandal. After initially denying reports of corruption, HUD secretary George Romney acknowledged that "the abuses are more prevalent than has previously been evident." He added that the FHA programs were "so poorly conceived and so incautiously developed that we estimate the federal government will [soon] have more than 240,000 units in default— and with little resale value except at catastrophic levels of loss." The companies exploiting FHA policies were not marginal. In New York, top officials of three of the largest mortgage lenders in the region were convicted of housing fraud. In Brooklyn alone, the U.S. Attorney's Office produced a five-hundred-count indictment asserting that "real estate speculators, brokers, lawyers, appraisers and bribed FHA employees conspired in the scheme" to get FHA insurance on slums sold at inflated prices. In Chicago, indictments were in the works for approximately thirty defendants, half of whom were FHA officials. In Detroit, there were forty-three indictments naming ninety-three defendants. Among them was one FHA appraiser accused of arson and another who claimed not to be aware that buildings had to be up to code to qualify for an FHA-insured loan. By 1975, Justice Department investigations into "allegations of collusion, kickbacks, bribery and falsification on Federal statements of a building's worth" had led to charges against 752 defendants and the conviction of almost 500 people. There were ongoing investigations in seventeen cities. Yet informed observers believed that the corruption uncovered thus far was only the beginning.[61]

Despite all of this, community groups did not want to end the FHA program. "We don't want to kill FHA, we want to clean it up because we had contract buying before which is pretty damn bad or worse," one Chicago activist explained. What the groups sought were basic safeguards, and the steps recommended by the House Committee on Government Operations in 1972 seemed a reasonable start. The committee had suggested that the FHA refuse insurance to mortgage companies with large numbers of defaulted homes. It urged the attorney general to create a housing fraud strike force modeled after organized crime strike forces. It asked that any mortgage banker currently under investigation for fraud be barred from doing business with HUD during the course of the inquiry.[62]

Yet shockingly, by 1975 HUD had instituted none of these suggestions. As a result, the exploitation of FHA programs became even more entrenched.[63] That year an exposé by the *Chicago Tribune* detailed another striking misuse of FHA funds. The scandal concerned the mortgage companies' failure to properly secure most of the approximately 3,600 vacant homes in the Chicago area now owned by the FHA. According to FHA rules, if a company wanted to collect FHA insurance on a defaulted loan, it had to first empty the property and then ensure that the vacant building was properly sealed. The guidelines were quite specific. They included: "Securing windows and doors to prevent unauthorized entry, boarding and screening them in areas where it is a common practice to do so; replacing broken glass to protect the interior against vandals and weather; protect the plumbing and other operating systems against damage by freezing . . . and care of lawns . . . to preserve neighborhood appeal."[64]

The FHA paid the mortgage companies anywhere from $400 to $2,000 per building to perform these tasks. For legitimate firms, this sum was entirely adequate to cover the cost of cleaning and securing the vacant properties. Many corrupt mortgage companies, however, turned these payments into yet another means of plunder. They pocketed the money and never put even a board in place to protect the property. Vandals quickly stripped the vacant buildings of plumbing, light fixtures, copper wire, and anything else of resale value. The neighborhoods were left with a haven for gangs and a potential site of arson. By the time government inspectors finally checked the properties they hoped to resell, they often found little more than "a pile of rubble." There were cases in which the

FHA continued to pay for services on buildings that were long since destroyed.[65]

Chicago-area FHA director John Waner collected cartons of proof that mortgage companies were charging for services they never performed. He sent the material to his superiors in Washington, D.C., along with a request for a more thorough investigation. He received no response. His was one of hundreds of attempts by local FHA directors to stop the unethical misuse of the program. All were stonewalled. *Chicago Tribune* reporters explained why: "Mortgage companies have so much influence in the HUD and FHA administration that it has become impossible to act against even the most unscrupulous."[66] A later report commissioned by HUD confirmed the *Tribune*'s findings.[67] In the fall of 1975, Chicago activists confronted HUD secretary Carla A. Hills about why nothing had been done to discipline corrupt companies. She responded that the HUD report offered merely "a recommendation"; she could not act, she claimed, until the case against the companies was more thoroughly documented.[68]

Stonewalling on racial issues was also commonplace in mid-decade Chicago. In 1975, Richard J. Daley, seventy-two years old and recovering from a recent stroke, won his sixth four-year term as mayor of Chicago. Daley built much of his support by placating the anxieties of the white working class. His continuing hold on power was one sign of the city's refusal to deal with issues of racial justice. (Many also attributed Daley's victory to the Democratic machine. It was "the ultimate in precinct power," commented the solitary Republican in Chicago's City Council. "They could have elected a gorilla.")[69]

Contributing to the quashing of racial issues were the actions of Daley's friend Cardinal Cody. By 1975, Cody had spent a decade undermining the city's many institutions of Catholic social activism. In July 1975, Reverend Andrew M. Greeley described the results. "Some of our best men have been driven from the priesthood. The laity have been ignored and in great part alienated. The poor have been dismissed in the name of a religion that must pay for itself," he mourned.[70]

The struggle for racial integration in Chicago had been all but abandoned. In November, just as jury selection for the West Side case was about to begin, a *New York Times* headline summed up the situation: "Chicago Is the North's Model of Segregation." The city's public schools were more segregated than they had been in 1965. Its black residents were so thoroughly confined to the city's West and South sides that they were invisible to the white population. When a report noted that the number of people perishing in fires was far higher in Chicago's black ghettos than elsewhere in the city, the fire commissioner reacted with disbelief. "What ghetto? What slums? I think our people live pretty nicely in Chicago. We don't have ghettos or slums." According to the *New York Times*, "A torpor hangs over race relations in Chicago."[71]

Yet to the attorneys trying the West Side case, the housing scandals and sorry racial statistics of recent years only increased the relevance of the upcoming trial. It would open just as FHA corruption, redlining, and racial segregation were once again in the news. It would present irrefutable proof about the sordid activities not merely of conspiring slum landlords but of the federal agencies whose practices provided the captive market that slumlords exploited. It would argue that such practices constituted an assault upon the plaintiffs' civil rights. If there was ever a time when such arguments were relevant, that time was now.

Jury selection began on November 19, 1975. Because this was a civil trial, only six jurors were required, along with six alternates. Since the trial took place in the Northern District of Illinois, which was about 70 percent white, there were few African Americans among the potential jurors, and the defendants' attorneys used peremptory challenges to eliminate every one of them. The best that the plaintiffs' attorneys could get was one African American man as a first alternate. There was a good chance that he might replace one of the six white jurors, an elderly man whose lungs had been damaged in World War I during a poison gas attack. "It seemed like he could hardly breathe and I thought, this guy's never going to last," Tucker recalled. Instead, the man made it to court every day for the entire four-and-a-half-month trial. Black contract buyers would have their day in court—before a four-man, two-woman, all-white jury.[72]

Other developments that threatened to undermine the suit were less apparent. In many ways, the trial that began on December 2, 1975, was a shadow of the original suit filed six years earlier. As a result of numerous out-of-court settlements, only 199 of the original 2,600 plaintiffs remained.[73] Of the far smaller group that would testify, most had not been active members of the Contract Buyers League. CBL leader Charlie Baker had withdrawn from the suit, having fallen out with the other members of the group. Ruth and James Wells replaced him as the lead plaintiffs in the case now known as *Wells v. F & F Investment*.[74] Many of the most notorious West Side contract sellers were also no longer in the case. In the year before the trial, Moe Forman settled with his buyers, as did Lou Wolf, Victor Spector, Al Weinberg, and many others. The details of the settlements are unknown, though evidence indicates that these men wrote off a portion of the balance they were owed and got the buyers FHA-backed mortgages to cover the rest; in return, the buyers agreed to drop their suit. The administrators of Lou Fushanis's estate filed for dismissal on the grounds that the estate was insolvent; their petition was granted.

Of the original 150 defendants—of whom 119 were contract sellers and the remainder various federal agencies and savings and loan institutions—only six remained, all contract sellers (ironically, only three of them concentrated on the West Side; the others sold mostly in South Side areas).[75] "They were probably the worst, but they also had the most properties to lose," Boodell said of the six who had chosen not to settle. Some among them also hoped to vindicate themselves in court. "Gerald Crane didn't think he had done anything wrong. John Karras didn't think he had done anything wrong," Feiwell's assistant attorney, Daniel Meenan, explained. "I don't think they felt they were doing any favors for anybody, but I don't think that they felt they violated anybody's civil rights."[76]

The jury was asked to judge these men—all middle-aged or elderly real estate sellers—on the puzzling charge of "conspiracy to violate the Civil Rights of the Plaintiffs in the sale of used residential property." Al Berland, then about fifty years old, had a goofy air; he appeared too dim to do anyone harm. Jay Goran was a short, excitable fellow. He testified in a voice crackling with barely controlled rage, and one day he broke down in tears on the witness stand as he described his efforts to care for his disabled son. His former partner, Gerald Crane, was a dignified and extremely well dressed gentleman of about sixty whose profound self-confidence was somehow contagious. In contrast, Joseph Berke was shockingly disheveled, his clothes so old and ill-fitting that it was difficult to believe that he had ever made significant amounts of money. John Karras's regal bearing hinted at the fact that he had been an all-star football athlete in college. The Reverend Wallace Reid, the white minister of a black Pentecostal church on the city's South Side, was a red-faced, 280-pound glad-hander who insisted that there was no conflict between his ministerial and his real estate practices. "He that provides not for his own hath denied the faith and is worse than an infidel," he recited on the stand. It was hard to imagine that these disparate individuals had acted in concert with one another.[77]

Of the most significance, however, was the disappearance of the federal housing agencies from the suit. Since August 1970, when the CBL attorneys had added the FHA, VA, FSLIC, and Federal Home Loan Bank Board (FHLBB) as defendants in the West Side suit, the Justice Department had fought back ceaselessly. The CBL complaint argued that as a result of the racially discriminatory policies of the FHA, VA, and FHLBB, "plaintiffs had to purchase homes in segregated areas from real estate speculators under installment contracts at exorbitant prices." The FSLIC was implicated in the contract sale scheme because it had taken over several savings and loan institutions that were initially among the defendants in the case and because it now held the installment contracts of some of the plaintiffs.

The Justice Department's defense of the FHA and VA hinged on the question of timing. While FHA or VA redlining may have pushed the plaintiffs to buy on contract, once they signed their contracts their interaction with the federal housing agencies was finished. Since the plaintiffs made their initial contract purchases before January 6, 1964, and the federal agencies were not added as defendants until 1970, the charges against them were filed too late to fall within the five-year statute of limitations. As for the FHLBB, Congress had explicitly granted that institution immunity from lawsuits. It should therefore be dismissed from the case.

Judge Frank McGarr accepted the Justice Department's argument about the FHLBB's immunity but dismissed its argument about the statute of limitations. The federal agencies could have avoided further injury to the plaintiffs if they had offered mortgage insurance in their area at *any time* during the life of the contracts, McGarr ruled. Had they done so, the plaintiffs could have refinanced their buildings, potentially reducing their monthly costs and freeing them from the installment contract relationship.[78]

The Justice Department appealed, but in December 1973 the U.S. Court of Appeals upheld McGarr.[79] At this point the FSLIC decided to settle. John Tucker negotiated the deal. "We actually made some very good settlements with the FSLIC," he recalled. "The amount we ultimately agreed on was not many dollars per home, but in total it was a significant sum, a portion of which provided a much-needed contribution to CBL's expenses."[80]

The FHA and VA did not follow suit. Instead, HUD secretary Carla Hills hired a new attorney, Chicagoan James C. Murray Jr., in early 1974.[81] Murray knew that the U.S. Civil Rights Commission was on record as stating that the FHA and VA discriminated in their loan and insurance policies. As he saw it, however, the evidence was anecdotal. His job was to unearth the data that would prove conclusively whether or not the FHA and VA were redlining Chicago in the period under question. With the case fast coming to trial, he had little time to lose.

First, Murray familiarized himself with the FHA and VA mortgage insurance programs. The VA, he learned, appraised individual properties and then granted mortgage insurance only if it determined that the property did not exceed "reasonable value"—that is, was not overpriced. It may have been this stipulation, rather than racial discrimination by the VA, that made the program of little use to black veterans. (For example, when a plaintiff in the CBL case applied for a VA-insured loan on a contract property selling for $24,000, he was told that, based on its own appraisal, the VA would guarantee a loan of only $12,000—far too little to allow him to purchase with a mortgage.) Next, Murray located the VA and FHA offices that held the appropriate records and then tracked their loans. He put colored pins in maps of the city in order to see whether VA- and FHA-insured loans were being made in white, mixed, and all-black Chicago census tracts.[82]

The results were unambiguous. "What came out of that effort was clearly that the Veterans Administration was not discriminating based on race," Murray recalled. "They were appraising property in mixed areas and in all-black areas of the city of Chicago." Murray called Richard Franch and presented his evidence about the VA. "I want you to dismiss them," he said. Faced with the evidence, Franch caved. In May 1975, just months before the case went to trial, the VA was dismissed.

The FHA was a different story. At the Chicago regional office Murray found "blue books" that contained the FHA's valuation of every neighborhood in Chicago. Inside there were actual red lines drawn around certain areas. Some were even annotated with notes such as "I don't know whether or not blacks live here." Murray had to admit that this did not look good.

The blue books strongly indicated that FHA officials were "marking out" certain neighborhoods, he recalled, and thereby "racially redlining portions of the city of Chicago." Moreover, once he charted the loan data for the FHA, just as he had for the VA, the evidence was indisputable: the FHA did not insure mortgages in Chicago's black or changing neighborhoods. Murray started to ponder "possible damages that the government might be subjected to" as a result of the forthcoming trial.

But then he made an important discovery. Starting in January 1965, he found, the FHA did insure *some* mortgages in Chicago's black and changing communities. Not many, to be sure, but Murray's proof of even a handful of FHA-insured loans in such areas was enough to invalidate the charge of a policy of wholesale racial discrimination.[83]

This discovery turned out to be decisive. Murray knew that the Contract Buyers League had added the FHA to the list of defendants on August 11, 1970. In order for the FHA's behavior to fall within the five-year statute of limitations, there had to be proof that the agency was still racially redlining portions of Chicago on or after August 11, 1965.[84] But according to Murray's data, the FHA had stopped across-the-board redlining in January 1965. The FHA's alleged behavior thereby fell outside the statute of limitations by seven months. Had the FHA been included in the original CBL complaint, filed on January 6, 1969, then the agency could have been brought to trial. But the one-and-a-half-year delay in adding the FHA to the suit changed everything. On August 5, 1975, Judge McGarr granted Murray's motion to dismiss the FHA. "And that's how the FHA got out" of the CBL case, Murray said. "It was not because they were totally innocent. It was the fact that it was too late to file against them."[85]

The dismissal of the federal housing agencies was a hard blow to the plaintiffs. Their attorneys nevertheless approached the trial in a spirit of optimism. John Tucker in the lead, assisted by Thomas Boodell and Richard Franch, felt that their case in this trial was if anything stronger than it had been for the South Side Universal suit. There, markups had been around 20 percent—high, but not outrageously so. The contract sellers on trial here sold their properties to black buyers at an average markup of 76.8 percent.[86]

They also had reason to be confident given the legal team on the other side. George Feiwell and his assistant, Daniel Meenan, who represented

Crane and Karras, were smart and aggressive, but Berke, Berland, and Reid each had their own attorneys. As Meenan noted, "Frankly, the lawyers other than Feiwell" were "not exactly eminent members of the trial bar." On the whole, they let Feiwell do the talking. The exception was Jay Goran, who represented himself as attorney pro se and who spoke frequently and emotionally. His opening statement was a typically baroque affair in which he managed to convey both condescension and hostility toward his black customers. Although it might look like he had taken advantage of "colored" people, he told the jury, "things are not always as they appear." He gave his black customers an opportunity to buy with low down payments, even though he was taking a "fearful chance." It was much like his experiences during World War II: "In Okinawa, I saw many dead Japanese. In death, they looked like children. But in life, with a gun in their hands, they were heinous."[87]

The fight would be tough, to be sure. The defendants would argue that their inflated prices were explained by one simple fact: the properties were sold to poor people on credit, not with cash (that is, not with a mortgage), and credit purchases cost more; that the plaintiffs were African Americans was mere coincidence. Tucker, Boodell, and Franch would present the jurors with a more complicated picture. The essential context for contract sales, they would argue, was Chicago's dual housing market. Knowing that black families had limited options, the defendants charged their black buyers outrageously high prices and created unusually harsh terms, in violation of Section 1982 of the Civil Rights Act of 1866, which stated that all citizens "have the same right as is enjoyed by white citizens" to purchase property. By conspiring to sell homes at prices far higher than market rate to blacks who had no other options, they denied the plaintiffs' civil rights and so deserved to be found guilty.

Tucker presented his case systematically. First, he called on Karl Taeuber to once again establish the existence of a dual housing market in Chicago.[88] To make his point, Taeuber used the "segregation index," which measures the degree to which a city's racial residency patterns conform to the actual racial proportion of its inhabitants. If a city is 10 percent black and its neighborhoods are also 10 percent black, then that city has a segregation index of zero: its black population is spread throughout the city in proportion to its numbers. If the city contains neighborhoods that are 20 percent black, then 10 percent of that city's black residents would have to move to an area where the black population is underrepresented in order for an "even" racial composition to be achieved. Such a city would have a segregation index of 10. In the United States, segregation indexes under 30 are considered quite low. Cities with such indexes are not viewed as segregated. Cities with segregation indexes of 30 to 60 are considered moderately segregated. Cities with indexes over 60—meaning that, in order for the city to have a racial residency pattern in proportion to its black population, 60 percent of the black residents would have to move to areas where blacks were underrepresented—are considered highly segregated. A segregation index of 100 would indicate complete racial ghettoization. It would mean that the entire black population of a city lives in entirely black neighborhoods.

In 1950, Taeuber reported, Chicago's segregation index was 92. In 1960, it was 93. In 1970, it remained at 93. Statistically, Chicago had achieved something shockingly close to absolute ghettoization of its black population. Chicago was not simply segregated—it was hypersegregated. This level of segregation was not explained by personal preference, Taeuber emphasized. Nor was it a function of economics. The ghettos were not poor neighborhoods that contained black people because blacks happened to be poor. In 1960, the majority of Chicago's blacks and whites had "middle-range" annual incomes. Specifically, 63 percent of nonwhites had annual incomes of $3,000 to $10,000, as compared with 66 percent of whites who fell within this range. "The economic level of blacks as compared to whites does not explain the high degree" of segregation, Taeuber concluded.[89] His testimony made two key points. First, the defendants were wrong to insinuate that the plaintiffs, because they were black, were therefore low income. Second, it was racism, and not the unfettered workings of a free market, that confined black Chicagoans of all economic classes to all-black ghettos.

The plaintiffs' second expert witness, John F. Kain, was a professor of economics, professor of regional planning, and chairman of the Department of City and Regional Planning at Harvard University. His research confirmed that racial segregation created "tremendous excess demand in the black market . . . and a particularly strong demand in . . . transitional neighborhoods" at the boundaries of existing black areas. This powerful demand "creates the opportunity for large monopoly profits to be made by those individuals who shift units from White to Black ownership," he explained. In short, speculators sold homes at "greatly inflated" prices because pent-up demand allowed them to get away with it.[90]

The plaintiffs had thus shown that theoretically a real estate seller could take advantage of the enormous demand in Chicago's black housing market to charge black customers grossly inflated prices. Their next step was to prove that the defendants did just that. They brought in Neil Renzi, an experienced real estate appraiser. Renzi had created "retrospective appraisals" of a dozen representative properties in the case. To do so, he inspected each property internally and externally. He compared each plaintiff's property with three others of similar age, size, and layout that were located in nearby white neighborhoods, had comparable amenities, and had been sold around the same time as were the plaintiffs' properties. He then used tax revenue stamps to determine the sale prices of all the properties. (When a property is sold, a tax stamp is affixed to the deed indicating the transfer taxes that have been paid. Since the transfer tax is based on the price of the property, tax revenue stamps can be used to determine a property's sale price.)[91] His conclusions were damning. In a typical example, he compared one of Jay Goran's properties to three "comparables," all located within a few blocks of Goran's building. The comparables sold for $7,500, $8,250, and $10,000. The fair market price for Goran's property, Renzi concluded, would have been $8,500. Goran had sold it to the Atkinsons, a black family, for $15,900.[92]

Feiwell attacked Renzi's credentials. He pointed out that Renzi's previous experience with retrospective appraisals had been confined to wealthy white suburbs where racial change was not an issue. He noted that "Renzi was 8 years old in 1955 and did not at that time know the market conditions" of Lawndale. He asked Renzi why he even took this assignment, given his limited knowledge of the area. Goran also interrogated Renzi. The down payment on the Atkinson property had been only $100. Didn't Renzi know that there were no mortgages available in this community in 1961? Was he suggesting that Goran should have sold this property for $8,500, with a down payment of only $100? Renzi admitted that he did not know of any other transactions in 1961 in which a three-bedroom, 2¼-bath house with garage sold for $100 down, even if the total asking price was $15,900.[93]

Goran's words only highlighted the fact that he was operating in a market in which he had a great deal of power over his black customers, since other forms of financing were not available to them. This context was further elaborated by Scott Tyler, a broker and appraiser who had extensive real estate experience on the city's West and South sides. He presented more "comparables," that is, retrospective appraisals that demonstrated that the defendants typically charged their black customers double the market rate. They could do so, Tyler explained, because the FHA was not insuring mortgages in these areas. Tyler knew this for a fact, since he had worked for the FHA in the 1950s. His job was to handle the assignments of appraisers at the local FHA office, and he observed that "there were no appraisal assignments in racially changing neighborhoods" such as Lawndale. Tyler allowed that there were black-owned savings and loan institutions in Chicago that loaned to creditworthy African Americans "to the extent that they could." Unfortunately, their resources were limited. "They probably controlled only fourteen to fifteen million dollars," which could not accommodate Chicago's million-plus black population. It was discrimination by the FHA and the savings and loan industry, and not black people's inherent lack of creditworthiness, that forced them to buy on contract.[94]

Goran fought back by presenting an appraiser of his own. Steven Horvath's training as an appraiser was not particularly strong; in college, he had taken a single course, Principles of Real Estate, that included a section on appraisals. But Horvath did have real-world experience. He had worked for Jay Goran for twenty-two years. As he described it, his job had been to "go out and look at these buildings and report back the condition and the area [in which they were] located and what I thought . . . the value of the property was." He estimated that during his years with Goran he had appraised some three thousand buildings. He spent several days on the stand describing properties that he claimed were comparable to those Goran sold. In a typical example, Horvath's "comparables" indicated that a building Goran sold on contract in 1957 for $17,900 had a market value of about $15,000 when Goran purchased it two years earlier. In short, Horvath's figures challenged the plaintiffs' claim that Goran's prices were outlandish.

In the course of cross-examination, though, Horvath's claim fell apart. When Boodell asked how he determined the prices of the Goran comparables, Horvath replied that he simply drew upon his experiences and recollections. He didn't compare the square footage of the comparable buildings. He didn't check their age. He didn't determine the precise year in which they had been sold. He didn't see what other homes in the neighborhood were selling for. Most crucially, he didn't look at the tax revenue stamps to determine the previous sale prices of the homes that Goran purchased, even though they were the necessary starting point of any comparable appraisal. Indeed, when tax revenue stamps were consulted a different picture emerged. The property Goran sold on contract in 1957 for $17,900 had been purchased by its white former owner in 1954, for $7,000. Goran bought the property from that white owner a year and a half later, in 1955, for $8,000. "This information does suggest that the value of the property in '55 when Goran purchased it would be $8,000 and not the $15,000" that Horvath claimed, Boodell observed.[95]

Despite Horvath's efforts, then, there was overwhelming evidence that Goran and the other defendants purchased properties from whites in "changing" neighborhoods for close to market value and then sold them at enormous markups to blacks. What remained to be proven was the meaning of those inflated prices. Were they the result of greedy operators brutally exploiting a captive market? Or were they the logical and prudent actions of businessmen acting in a risky environment?

Of course, the defendants could not exploit a captive black housing market if such a thing did not exist. Feiwell and Meenan therefore spent a great deal of time insisting that black Chicagoans faced no real restrictions in choosing housing. They brought in Sherman Shapiro, the senior vice president and staff economist for the Federal Home Loan Bank Board of Chicago, who insisted that there was not—and never had been—a dual housing market in the city. "There's no doubt in my mind [that Chicago] was a free, open, highly competitive market," he claimed. He acknowledged that a black person moving to a white neighborhood in Chicago might not have it easy. "His neighbors might not talk to him, kids may throw snowballs at him," he said, in a remarkable trivialization of white Chicagoans' history of threats, vandalism, arson, firebombings, and riots against the first blacks to move to their neighborhoods. He acknowledged that Chicago was not racially integrated and that blacks had far lower rates of home ownership than whites, but he traced this to blacks' personal preference. "Some like blonds, some like brunettes, some like to live in Skokie, some like to live someplace else," he said by way of explanation.[96]

The defendants also presented testimony by housing expert Pierre DeVise. He claimed that in Chicago there was no racial segregation, only racial "separation" that was best explained by individual "preference." "The fact that the City of Chicago is highly separated racially has practically no significance," DeVise declared. For proof that Chicago's African Americans had plentiful housing options, DeVise pointed to the numerous abandoned buildings in black neighborhoods. These abandoned properties demonstrated "the ravages of excess housing construction in Chicago," DeVise argued—an odd statement in a period when the severe housing shortage facing low-income Chicagoans was regularly in the news.[97]

Even if there was such a thing as a racially divided housing market, the defendants could not have exploited it because, the defendants testified, they were remarkably blind to race. Gerald Crane could not recall if he bought his properties from blacks or whites; nor was he aware of whether the neighborhoods in which he purchased buildings for resale were black or white; nor did he have any idea if the areas he operated in were undergoing racial change. Goran and Berland also testified that they had no recollection of whether the people they purchased from were white or black. Reid explained that he couldn't identify the race of his customers because he was the sort of person who "didn't pay attention to race." Berke was sure that his customers included whites as well as blacks. John Karras alone admitted that he bought "primarily" from whites and sold "primarily" to blacks.[98]

The only dual market that the defendants would acknowledge was that of cash versus credit. They took the risk of selling to people whose incomes were too low to allow them to get mortgages, and to cover their risk they charged higher prices.[99] Steven Horvath supported the sellers' insistence that all of their customers were bad credit risks. "Nothing except [bad] credit would prevent black people from going into institutions and obtaining a loan," he insisted, contradicting the statement of his employer, Jay Goran, that mortgages were simply not available in the areas where he sold properties.[100]

To counter such testimony, Tucker had to show that the plaintiffs' inability to get conventional mortgages was a result of systematic racial discrimination rather than their individual lack of creditworthiness. The most direct way to do so would have been to describe the racially discriminatory FHA policies that had made it nearly impossible for African

Americans to get mortgage loans. FHA discrimination was a verifiable fact. The agency itself admitted that it refused to offer mortgage insurance in most black neighborhoods and in all racially changing ones before 1965—that is, during the heyday of contract selling in Chicago. But the FHA had been dismissed from the case. Depending on how one interpreted the law, this could mean that no information about FHA redlining could be introduced at the trial.

The result was a running battle between John Tucker and George Feiwell—most of it outside of the jury's presence—over whether this crucial explanation for the plaintiffs' lack of access to conventional mortgages could be mentioned. The issue first blew up around the testimony of Scott Tyler. Feiwell argued that Tyler should not be allowed to testify about the ways that federal policies restricted blacks' access to mortgages, since the FHA was no longer in the case. "It's the not defendants' fault that the FHA would not finance in Lawndale," he added.

In this instance, McGarr ruled for the plaintiffs, permitting Tyler to discuss FHA redlining.[101] As the trial dragged on, however, McGarr increasingly sustained Feiwell's objections to testimony that mentioned the lack of FHA insurance in racially changing neighborhoods. In addition, McGarr made two midtrial rulings that worked against the plaintiffs. The first concerned the statistical information compiled by graduate students and faculty at Northwestern University's Center for Urban Affairs, who had used early-model computers to compare the housing prices and loan terms offered to black contract buyers with market rates, census statistics, and other public data. The results had powerfully supported the plaintiffs' claims of systematic discrimination. McGarr ruled the printouts inadmissible. "They are misleading," he insisted, and "they might be given unnecessary weight, since people feel computers are infallible." The second concerned the question of conspiracy. Although Berland, Berke, and Karras had worked closely together for years—as had Crane, Goran, and Reid—McGarr ruled that since he had "as yet seen no evidence" to support the charge of conspiracy, the issue was henceforth dropped. The defendants would be tried as separate individuals, and on one charge only—whether their business practices amounted to a violation of their customers' civil rights.[102]

But it was precisely this charge that was undermined by the limits McGarr placed on the plaintiffs' ability to contextualize their case. The problem flared up again during the testimony of Sherman Shapiro. When

Franch tried to get Shapiro to explain that FHA-insured loans required a down payment of only 5 percent of the property's appraised value, Feiwell objected and McGarr sent the jury out in order to allow the attorneys to debate the issue. Tucker pleaded with McGarr to permit Franch to continue. The defendants were presenting the plaintiffs' low down payments as proof of their poverty, Tucker argued, when in fact, if the FHA had insured loans in black or mixed areas, even plaintiffs who paid only a few hundred dollars down might have qualified for mortgages. Franch's right to elicit testimony about FHA policies was therefore crucial. "Your Honor knows . . . that in . . . [Chicago's suburbs] there were thousands of [white] people in this very period of time obtaining new housing, decent housing, with $400, $300, $500, $250 down, and FHA insurance," Tucker noted.

Feiwell argued that the point was moot since there was no way to know which particular plaintiffs would have qualified for FHA loans if they had applied for one. McGarr sided with Feiwell. "There is no evidence . . . that any plaintiffs weren't eligible for FHA or VA or applied for it . . . and therefore questions as to whether the institutions would or would not have made FHA or VA loans in those areas . . . is irrelevant," he ruled. Franch could question Shapiro, but not about FHA policies.[103]

Franch was allowed to elicit testimony about the discriminatory policies of Chicago's savings and loan institutions—but to no great effect. When Shapiro claimed that savings and loans lent to any creditworthy person, Franch got him to admit that his only evidence was the word of the lenders themselves. Franch then moved to strike Shapiro's testimony about the savings and loans' racial record: "It is clear that he is relying on hearsay and self-serving statements of the savings and loans, who obviously would not admit [racial redlining] even if they did. I think this is incompetent testimony." McGarr, however, let Shapiro's comments stand.

Franch tried again. He read a summary of testimony by mortgage broker Dempsey Travis that had appeared in a 1959 U.S. Civil Rights Commission report. "'Many mortgage institutions refuse to provide home financing for houses in mixed neighborhoods,'" Franch quoted Travis. "I don't agree with that," Shapiro responded. "'The 1959 Chicago survey showed that of the 243 associations in Cook County . . . only 21, including the two Negro associations in the city, had made loans [in black neighborhoods] during the preceding 12 months, and only one white association made an initial mortgage loan to a Negro family in a white area. Negro mobility was concluded to be limited to the resources of the Negro-owned institutions,'" Franch read. Well, clearly those savings and loans "found better loans to make," Shapiro responded. Finally Franch asked Shapiro directly: "Are you saying that the savings and loans actually made a significant amount of mortgage loans in racially changing neighborhoods during the period 1959 to 1969?" Shapiro was forced to grant that he was "not familiar with any of the data" on whom the institutions loaned to or which neighborhoods they loaned in. "I am not sure if they know either [since] those records are not kept," he said.[104]

Franch had essentially the same discussion with the over half a dozen savings and loans officials brought to the stand by Feiwell. Each testified under oath that his institution made mortgage loans to qualified individuals "irrespective of race, color, or creed" during the 1950s and 1960s. (The jurors were not told that most of these institutions had only recently been dismissed as defendants in the case.) Under questioning, each representative acknowledged that he couldn't say how many loans were made to African Americans because his institution kept no records of loans by race of borrower. "Verified no discrimination policy and, in fact, no records kept of whether mortgagee was Black or White," a juror summarized one official's testimony, apparently not realizing that the second part of the statement undermined the first—without records of where and to whom these institutions made their loans, they could not prove that they did not discriminate.[105]

Franch also got Shapiro to admit that if a property was significantly overpriced it would be next to impossible for a buyer to get a mortgage for it. According to Shapiro, savings and loans granted mortgages of 80 percent of a building's value. That would mean, Franch pursued, that if a property was put up for sale for $16,000 and the savings and loan association appraised its value as $10,000, the most that the association would lend on the property would be $8,000. "Correct," Shapiro responded. That would mean, Franch continued, that a buyer would be forced to make a down payment of the remaining $8,000 in order to purchase the property. "Correct," Shapiro said. Franch homed in for the logical conclusion. "So if a situation prevailed where the sale price [was] substantially in excess of the appraised value, people in that area would find it hard to get loans, wouldn't they?" "That is correct," Shapiro responded.[106]

Refusing to acknowledge the existence of dual markets or the policies of savings and loan institutions, the defendants repeatedly fell back on the same explanation for why the plaintiffs could not get mortgages: insufficient down payments. Overlooking the plaintiffs' long and extremely stable work histories, they claimed that their buyers had been unable to make adequate down payments because "they hadn't been on their jobs long enough."[107] The defendants also claimed that their customers were grateful for the chance to purchase property that their poor credit otherwise rendered out of reach. As Berke explained, his buyers were "glad for the opportunity" he gave them. In contrast, the plaintiffs emphasized their lack of choice in the matter. Laura Robinson told the jury that she purchased a property on contract from Jay Goran despite the high price because "everything that was put before her was too high, but she had to continue to live." Essie Green, who like her husband had a twenty-five-year work history, explained that she was twice turned down for mortgages before she purchased on contract from Berke with a $2,000 down payment. She bought in Lawndale because she "had no other choice"; "blacks couldn't live where they wanted to." Lester Barnes, who bought a run-down building from Rev. Reid on contract for $500 down, explained that he "had to be satisfied with the building as he had to have a place for his family" and also because "others were overcharging as well." Barnes's daughter also purchased a property on contract from Reid. This didn't mean that the family felt grateful. When Barnes saw the place that Reid sold to his daughter, he called it a "rat hole."[108]

Curiously, the most serious challenge to the defendants' claim that their African American buyers all happened to be bad credit risks came from the defendants themselves. Although they repeatedly stated that their price markups were justified because of the risks of selling on credit, they occasionally slipped and stated that their prices were firm, whether the property sold for cash or on credit. Under questioning by Tucker, Reid admitted that the peril of a credit sale was not the main reason for his high prices. "After all the other defendants have stressed 'credit' sale . . . the Reverend blows it," one of the jurors noted. Crane, too, acknowledged that, although "cash sales were relatively infrequent in the area" he worked, he did "sell for cash at the same price [as] credit." He also admitted that the people he sold to were good credit risks. Among the plaintiffs there was not one who he could positively say had defaulted on his or her contract.[109]

Underlying this debate over creditworthiness was a debate about virtue. Casting the contract buyers as shiftless spendthrifts whom no reputable savings and loan would trust, the defendants presented themselves as upstanding, creditworthy individuals who would never do anything like miss a mortgage payment. The claim was outrageous, especially given the fact that Berke's and Berland's refusal to pay their mortgages had led to the collapse of a savings and loan. The plaintiffs' attorneys therefore set out to contest it.[110]

Working in their favor were Al Berland's convictions for arson and for defrauding the FHA. This was why Berland's presence caused consternation among the other defendants and defense attorneys—an anxiety that sometimes bordered on the comic. Typical had been the argument over which defendants would sit near Berland and Lou Wolf when the case was still in pretrial hearings. First Goran protested being put in the same defendant group as Berland and Wolf. Then Feiwell piped in. "I don't want to be with those two guys. I want them at another table," he insisted. At this, James C. Murray Jr., then representing the FHA and VA, felt he had to intercede on the table location debate. "Well, Judge, if they're all asking for tables and everything else, the government would like its own table because we're not connected with either one of these people, and of course, I would like to have the American flag behind me," he deadpanned.[111]

As it turned out, Feiwell and Goran didn't have to worry. They asked Judge McGarr to bar any mention of Berland's criminal convictions, on the grounds that they would unfairly prejudice the jury against the other defendants. McGarr understood that Berland's conviction for FHA fraud was "intimately intertwined" with the issues in the case and that banning discussion of it would be "a windfall" for Berland. Nevertheless, he agreed that knowledge of the convictions would prejudice the jury, so he granted Feiwell and Goran's request.[112]

Tucker, Boodell, and Franch continued to hammer away at the defendants' morality. The defendants claimed that their access to mortgage money was a sign of their solid economic standing. The plaintiffs had a different explanation: the speculators' easy access to credit was the result of their collusion with savings and loan officials—a collusion that allowed both groups to exploit African American contract buyers. In contrast to the plaintiffs, who faced a brick wall when they sought mortgages, the defendants testified that they could get loans on buildings with remarkable ease. As Gerald Crane explained, he simply called the savings and loan institution, provided the address and a quick description of the property, and told the bankers how much he wanted to borrow on it. They always agreed, and they never asked him for the property's original price. They were generous because "they knew him at the savings and loan." Berland, Goran, Karras, Berke, and Reid all described similarly close relationships with specific institutions.[113]

A more troubling picture emerged in Tucker and Boodell's interrogation. All of the defendants routinely got loans on their recently purchased properties for well over 100 percent of their properties' value. The jury was presented with their application forms and saw that in case after case the amount listed under "price of purchase" was several thousand dollars higher than the actual sum paid for the property. After Berke testified that he had paid $11,000 for a building, for example, the plaintiffs' attorneys showed him a mortgage loan application in which the "price of purchase" was filled in as $16,000. The inflated price was not in Berke's handwriting; someone else had filled in the higher figure in an obvious attempt to justify the high mortgage loan.

Berke claimed to have no idea who that might have been. He did reveal that First Mutual Savings and Loan president Austin Waldron instructed him to complete only part of the forms. Waldron's lenient attitude really helped streamline Berke's paperwork; apparently Berke often signed blank loan applications, sometimes by the "handful." Reid said that there was nothing unusual about his practice of signing blank loan application forms on which "others" filled in a price. He claimed not to have noticed the words clearly printed at the top of the form, "Be Sure Application Is Completely Filled Out Before Signing." He testified that the savings and loans he worked with never asked him what he'd paid for his property or the purpose of the loan he was taking out on the property. In one case, Reid received a mortgage of $5,600 on a building he had purchased shortly before—for $500. Such testimony so disturbed Jay Goran that he told Judge McGarr that he had to speak to clarify the fact that he "took no bribes from savings and loans."[114]

The person who provided the most damning details about the relationship between the contract sellers and the savings and loans that funded them was John Karras. He got most of his mortgages from Service

Savings and Loan, whose president, William Szarabajka, he had known since he was fourteen years old, when Szarabajka had sponsored the young Karras's baseball team. But their intimacy was economic as well as personal. The two men created the Summit Investment Corporation, with Szarabajka as president and Karras as vice president. Karras admitted that the address of this "investment club" was the same as that of his real estate firm, Community Realty. He also admitted that some of the buildings he sold on contract were owned by the Summit Investment Corporation. This meant that the president of Service Savings and Loan was himself a contract seller who used the resources of his bank to loan his partner more money on his buildings than the buildings were worth. In short, Karras described a relationship of massive collusion. In 1969, a federally funded study had concluded that conflicts of interest were "more deeply embedded and institutionalized" in the nation's savings and loans than in any other sector of the economy. The "pervasive ancillary activities of management," who "may also be realtors, attorneys, . . . builders and developers doing business with the association" were particularly ripe for "excesses and abuses," federal authorities noted.[115] Summit Investment was a textbook example of such excesses.

The defendants offered a justification for why they were loaned thousands of dollars above what they had paid for their properties: rehabilitation. Crane explained that his business consisted of purchasing properties for cash, fixing them up, and selling them on contract. The repair work was the "key to the whole deal"; it justified his higher resale price and his acquisition of such substantial mortgage loans. Berland, Reid, and Goran also insisted that their dramatic markups and the high loans they received were attributable to the extensive repairs they made. Only Berke broke ranks when he admitted that he did not mention improvements to his buildings when he contacted his friends at the savings and loan.[116]

These claims too did not survive cross-examination. Many of the defendants provided no records of their repair costs.[117] Those who did produce building ledgers had to acknowledge that their repair costs were either nonexistent or negligible, or largely cosmetic.[118] For example, when Charles and Carrie Marie Simmons looked at a property for sale by Al Berland, they saw that the furnace was broken, the sewers were clogged, plaster on the first floor was crumbling, and the gutters needed to be replaced. The Simmonses' offer to purchase the place included a stipulation that Berland would be responsible for the necessary repairs. He made none of them. He did, however, repair a toilet on the first floor and the bathroom faucets on the second floor. He also presented the Simmonses with "five good gallons of Berland paint" so that they could fix up the first floor themselves.[119]

In the few cases where the defendants made significant repairs, they passed on the costs to their buyers. One day in 1957, for example, Vergia Handsbur came home to find that the front of the house had been sandblasted and tuck-pointed. She called Gerald Crane's office and was told that yes, Crane had indeed ordered the work to be done. Nonetheless, he sent Handsbur the bill. When he had the house painted shortly thereafter, he sent her the bill for that, too. "Man came out and said now that sandblasting and painting had been done, the building would pass inspection for the mortgage," Mrs. Handsbur explained. The mortgage was of no benefit to her: Crane was taking it out on the building in order to finance further property purchases. The Handsburs, meanwhile, were left to pay the $150 sandblasting charge and the $200 painting bill. Each added $10 a month to their already high monthly contract payments.[120]

At their most brazen, some of the defendants insisted that the high loans they received were a hedge against repairs they might have to make at some future date to help their contract buyers convert their outstanding balances to FHA-insured mortgages. Of course, by helping their buyers get FHA mortgages, they were ensuring that they would receive the full, inflated price for their properties. They nevertheless presented these final repair expenses as justification for the high prices they charged initially. For example, Berland described thousands of dollars in repair costs that he paid in order to get his properties to meet FHA requirements, as well as the $1,000 that his mortgage broker, Alexander Scott, charged him to process the FHA loans, as an explanation for his inflated prices. Berland had no documents to prove that he had made these FHA-related repairs. The jury also did not get to hear the full story behind his payments to Scott. Outside the jury's presence, Berland's lawyer asked that "any testimony on Alexander Scott's conviction for FHA fraud be excluded." McGarr agreed, ruling that the "indictment and conviction of Scott have nothing to do with the case."[121]

Apart from insisting on their moral probity and on the financial necessity of their actions, the defendants finally argued that they could not have violated the plaintiffs' civil rights, because they sold properties on contract, and at high prices, to white people as well. Of course, the 1974 Court of Appeals decision had explicitly rejected the argument that the sellers' exploitative behavior would be acceptable if it had been visited on whites and blacks alike. But when Tucker objected to the defendants' testimony about "white" sales on the grounds of the appeals court decision, McGarr overruled him.[122]

The color blindness of the defendants, who claimed to have no idea whether their customers were primarily black, vanished when they were asked about their white clients. Crane read the jury a list of twenty-two white couples to whom he had sold properties on contract. Under questioning, he acknowledged that many of the sales were actually to mixed-race couples. Goran's white sales were largely limited to families with Hispanic names such as "Ramos," "Colon," and "Villa." Reid admitted that out of 150 properties, some of which he sold numerous times, he could positively recall only one sale to whites; that was to Ronald and Alice Villa. When Tucker attempted to prove that the Villas and many other "whites" were actually Latinos, McGarr shot him down. "The court rules out allegations about other minorities. For purposes of this case the world is either black or white. The Villas are white," he determined.[123]

The plaintiffs' attorneys tracked down some of the defendants' white customers, who repeatedly turned out to be people of color. However, there were others whom they were unable to locate. Thus the jury never learned that the defendants created most if not all of their white sales out of thin air. For example, Crane's white list included Harry and Bernice Bernard, who were in fact black. In 1960 they had been so upset by Crane's treatment of them that they had hired an attorney, Mark J. Satter, to represent them in a suit they brought against him. (The first count of the complaint clearly stated, "The plaintiffs are members of the Negro race.") Crane's "white" buyers also featured Albert and Sallie Bolton, although Crane did say that he was "not certain" the Boltons were white.[124]

The plaintiffs' attorneys took two months to present their case. The defendants' response took another two months. Finally, on April 6, 1976, George Feiwell casually walked to the center of the courtroom and rested his hand on the rail. "Never thought we'd get there—we rest our case," he said. On

April 13, Judge McGarr presented his final instructions to the jury. Tucker had begged McGarr to include in his instructions the 1974 U.S. Court of Appeals ruling that there was "no justification" for the defendants' argument that they would have sold their homes at the same prices and terms to white buyers. McGarr refused to do so. He did, however, present a series of instructions that incorporated the basic structure of the plaintiffs' argument.[125]

The plaintiffs, McGarr told the jury, had to prove the following. (1) As a result of racial discrimination, a dual housing market existed in Chicago. (2) The existence of this dual market created an opportunity for the defendants to charge blacks more for housing. (3) The defendants took advantage of this opportunity and charged blacks prices for housing that were higher than what whites paid for similar properties. If the jury found that these three points were true, McGarr explained, the defendants had violated Section 1982, Title 42, which states that all citizens have the same rights as white citizens to purchase property. The burden of proof would then shift to the defendants. They would have to prove that "*no part* of this difference in price is due to the race of the buyer."[126]

With instructions this pointed, the plaintiffs had more than a fair chance of winning the case. Two and a half days later, on Friday, April 16—Good Friday—the jurors delivered their verdict. Although attendance had been sparse throughout the four-month trial, on that Friday the courtroom was packed with reporters and CBL members. John Tucker recalled the exact position of his body as he awaited the decision: "I was sitting with my elbows on the table in front of me, clasping my hands tightly together to try to keep them from shaking with tension." The jury foreman handed the verdicts to the clerk, who handed them to the judge, who read them to himself, and then returned them to the clerk.

"We, the jury, find for the defendant, Joseph Berke, and against the plaintiffs," the clerk read. Tucker thought fast. Berke was a sloppily dressed man who had acted as his own attorney. Perhaps the jurors felt sorry for him. Perhaps they were making an exception in his case because they didn't believe he had profited in the long run. Then the next verdicts were read. "We, the jury, find for the defendant, Al Berland, and against the plaintiffs. We, the jury, find for the defendant, Jay Goran, and against the plaintiffs. We, the jury, find for the defendants, John Karras and Sureway Investment Company, and against the plaintiffs." And so they continued.

Tucker rested his forehead in his hands. He struggled to follow the clerk's words despite the deafening noise inside his head, a "fizzing and popping like carbonated water." Through the static there was no mistaking the jury's decision. All six defendants were acquitted—"even the execrable Reverend Reid." The verdict was met by an eerie silence. "There was no outburst, not even a murmur," one of the jurors observed.[127]

George Feiwell was exultant. He told reporters that it was "poppycock" to blame the defendants for the fact that the contract buyers couldn't get mortgages. "Being poor is not a violation of anyone's civil rights," he insisted. The plaintiffs' attorneys were in shock. They went straight from the courtroom to Chicago's lakefront, where they sat together, struggling to regain their composure.[128]

Several factors probably went into the jury's decision. The exclusion of the federal agencies from the suit undermined, perhaps fatally, the case for a racially discriminatory dual housing market. Then, too, white attitudes toward racial justice had hardened by the 1970s, with many now believing that, far from suffering discrimination, blacks were getting too much "special treatment." Furthermore, the raging inflation of the decade made the prices that black contract buyers paid for their buildings in the late 1950s— an average of $25,000—seem reasonable. By the mid-1970s, comparable structures in white areas were worth double that amount. The length of the trial may also have hurt the plaintiffs. After weeks of tedious details about competing property appraisals, some jurors tuned out. While the attorneys droned on, jurors found themselves idly counting the squares of cross-hatching that decorated the courtroom ceiling.[129]

Yet the deciding factor might well have been the character of the jury's foreman. Francis McLennand was a white, middle-aged accountant from suburban Elmhurst. He kept a diary throughout the trial in which he recorded his perceptions. It reveals that McLennand had little sympathy for the plaintiffs, whom he ridiculed as simpletons, manipulated by CBL leaders. He also dismissed the plaintiffs' expert witnesses. They reminded him of the "Harvard intellectuals" who are "infiltrating the halls of Congress" and fomenting much "'do-gooding' nonsense."[130]

McLennand was far more comfortable with the defendants and their supporters. Berke was "a simple, straightforward type," he noted, while Karras positively exuded the "assurance & the confidence of maturity." The contrast between McLennand's assessments of various witnesses and those made by the plaintiffs' attorneys was striking. A Jenner and Block assistant, for example, described appraiser Steven Horvath's reaction to Tom Boodell's questioning as "the beginning of the Horvath collapse, unable to get the right answer with the right question." McLennand saw the same testimony differently. Horvath "has projected a high degree of integrity. Capacity for detail is outstanding."[131]

When the six jurors began their deliberations, half were sympathetic to the plaintiffs and at least one was so convinced of the defendants' guilt that he or she was angry about not being offered the chance to immediately assess financial damages. Yet McLennand steadfastly insisted that the overcharge suffered by contract buyers was "not a matter of civil rights, but supply and demand economics." The defendants' white sales were key to his argument. The jurors noted that there were over five thousand sales to blacks and at most only fifteen to twenty comparable sales to whites, but never mind. The existence of even a tiny number of such sales, McLennand argued, was proof that race had nothing to do with the defendants' practices. The defendants charged their customers the highest possible price, whoever those customers happened to be. Ultimately, the other jurors accepted this argument. These contract sellers "would have charged their own mother the going rate," they joked to one another.

In a posttrial interview, McLennand explained what he saw as the real issue in the case. His goal as a juror, he said, had been to ensure that the court's decision would help overturn "the mess Earl Warren made with *Brown v. Board of Education* and all that nonsense."[132]

That left the South Side case of *Clark v. Universal Builders,* which finally went to trial on November 5, 1979. After sixteen days, Judge Nicholas J. Bua delivered a ruling that exonerated Universal Builders. Bua claimed that the plaintiffs could not make a case under the traditional theory of discrimination because the homes that Universal sold to suburban whites were not comparable to those they sold to black Chicagoans. They could not prove that Universal overcharged their black clients because there was no proof that a standard percentage for profit in the building industry existed. Bua rejected the exploitation theory of discrimination as well. He conceded that the "plaintiffs have demonstrated . . . the existence of a dual housing market . . . in the City of Chicago," but they had not proved that this dual market necessarily presented the defendants with "the opportunity to extract unreasonable prices or terms which amounted to a tax on plaintiffs' race, or that the prices and terms charged were motivated by a discriminatory purpose or intent."[133] The plaintiffs' attorneys appealed, but their appeal was rejected, and the case finally put to rest, on April 19, 1983. One of the three judges rejecting the appeal was Luther Swygert, the same man who had written a ringing endorsement of the plaintiffs' exploitation theory back in 1974. He and the other judges found that an appeal was unwarranted since the U.S. District Court was not "clearly erroneous" in its judgments.[134]

Thus, the CBL lost both of its federal suits. But the hard labor that went into the cases was not in vain. It turned out that the key to challenging the nationwide denial of credit based on race lay not in the CBL attorneys' courtroom debates but in something far more prosaic—namely, the detailed financial information that had been provided by the "random sample" of 475 CBL members, who submitted to countless hours of interviews by the CBL's legal support staff; the land title investigations that were undertaken to contextualize it; and the transference of much of this information onto computer cards, thereby enabling it to be tabulated by researchers at Northwestern University's Center for Urban Affairs (CUA).[135]

Although the resulting data would be barred from the courtroom by Judge McGarr, it remained hugely important at the CUA, where the patterns of racial discrimination that it revealed became the "lens" through which other examples of housing discrimination were analyzed. In search of solutions, the CUA created a "housing group"—a high-powered assembly of community activists, researchers, progressive businesspersons, journalists, bankers, attorneys, seminarians, and graduate students—who soon produced a remarkable series of challenges to discriminatory federal housing policies.[136]

Among those receiving crucial support from the CUA housing group was activist Gale Cincotta. She had been living with her husband, an auto mechanic, and their six children in Austin, a neighborhood west of Lawndale, when "racial change" hit. Cincotta joined the Organization for a Better Austin, a community group dedicated to stopping "panic peddling." What really angered her, though, was the redlining of her neighborhood.

Convinced that this issue could not be addressed within the limits of a single community organization, Cincotta in 1972 helped to create National People's Action (NPA), the first national coalition of grassroots organizations devoted to housing issues, and the National Training and Information Center, which provides research support for community groups and training for community organizers.[137]

The NPA's first target was redlining, and the early documentation supporting their charges against redlining banks grew out of researcher Andrew Gordon's work for the CBL lawsuits at the Center for Urban Affairs.[138] Yet while Gordon's evidence strongly indicated that banks were engaging in racial redlining, the smoking gun was missing. At that point, John McKnight recalled, "Gale came up with an idea that was ingenious . . . *disclosure*."[139] Determined to harness federal regulatory power to stop redlining and promote community reinvestment, Cincotta proposed that banks be forced to disclose exactly where their mortgage loans were made. Once that information was public, she believed, legislation to end redlining would follow.

First there were numerous frustrating meetings between community activists and federal officials. As CUA researcher Darel Grothaus recalled, the banking industry "would always deny that they were doing anything. The industry would say, 'Well, show us that this is happening.' We'd say, 'We think it's happening, and we need to have disclosure. You need to show where you were getting your deposits and where you are making your loans.' 'Well, that's proprietary information.'" Finally, in 1974, after several years of meetings, picketing, and direct action protests by the NPA, the Federal Home Loan Bank Board of Chicago gave in. It agreed to provide the NPA with data on selected loans by zip code for the years 1971–1973.[140]

Armed with these data, the NPA turned again to the experienced researchers at the Center for Urban Affairs: Gordon and his students Darel Grothaus and Calvin Bradford. Once they correlated the banks' lending patterns with public records on racial residential distribution, Grothaus recalled, it was "clear as the nose on your face" that Chicago banks were practicing racially discriminatory mortgage lending. Grothaus then wrote the first local disclosure ordinance in the nation. Now all banks holding funds deposited by the city of Chicago were required to disclose where they made their loans.[141]

An article Grothaus wrote about disclosure came to the attention of Senator William Proxmire (D-Wisc.), who had just become chair of the

Senate Banking Committee. Proxmire met with Grothaus, Cincotta, and other NPA representatives, who were by now extremely knowledgeable about redlining and community reinvestment issues. Cincotta's group then worked with Proxmire to write, and secure the passage of, two landmark pieces of federal legislation: the Home Mortgage Disclosure Act (1975) and the Community Reinvestment Act (1977).[142]

The Home Mortgage Disclosure Act (HMDA) requires federally regulated banks to document the number and value of all mortgage loans granted by the institution. These reports must then be made available to the public. The Community Reinvestment Act (CRA) states that all federally regulated financial institutions "have a continuing . . . obligation to help meet the credit needs" of their local communities. They must prepare an annual report that describes how they are meeting those needs—including the credit needs of low- and moderate-income residents. By drawing on HMDA documentation, community groups can prove whether or not banks are fulfilling their CRA requirement.

The Home Mortgage Disclosure Act and the Community Reinvestment Act stand today as the crowning achievement of a long and painful battle that began back in the 1950s when African American contract buyers sought legal help for a trap they hadn't anticipated. By 1992, community groups had used the two acts to pressure financial institutions into $18 billion worth of reinvestments in over seventy U.S. cities. By 2004, the amount of money reinvested in local communities because of the laws came to approximately $1.5 trillion—almost half in affordable housing.[143]

John McKnight points out that the Contract Buyers League's determination to expose the machinations of the contract sellers and the loan institutions that funded them was the same idea that animated the HMDA and CRA: "If we could expose who was doing it and what they were doing, then we'd have the tools to get legislation to deal with it."[144] Change can occur in a circuitous fashion, and if there was ever an example of this, it is the contract sales struggle. In the end, the CBL story is one of triumph in the midst of loss. Even as their research was barred from the West Side trial, the information that CBL members and supporters gathered with such painstaking effort provided ammunition for underdogs engaged in an even more lopsided battle—one pitching Chicago community organizations against the nation's banking industry. And this time the underdogs won.

CONCLUSION

As I conclude this book in 2008, many of the injustices fought by mid-twentieth-century Chicago activists remain with us. Despite fair housing laws, prospective black home buyers are still "steered" away from white neighborhoods. Low-income African Americans in segregated neighborhoods remain subject to what CBL attorneys called a "race tax" and what my father referred to as the "million dollars a day cost of being black." As one recent study demonstrates, this "ghetto tax" means that the urban poor pay considerably more for goods and services ranging from food to auto insurance.[1]

The most striking evidence of the ongoing need to fight exploitative credit practices is the recent tidal wave of predatory lending known as the subprime mortgage crisis. Subprime loans were ostensibly made to people with less than stellar credit; to balance the risk of lending to such people, they carried harsher terms and higher servicing costs than prime loans. In fact, just as many contract buyers could have qualified for mortgages, so would an estimated 50 percent of those holding subprime mortgages have qualified for prime credit; "subprime" describes not a type of borrower but a type of loan, one that carries interest rates considerably higher than those of prime mortgages. The framework that enabled subprime loans to flourish was constructed by several obscure acts of

legislation passed in the 1980s, such as the Depository Institutions Dereg-
ulation and Monetary Control Act, which allowed subprime lenders to
exceed state caps on interest rates; the Alternative Mortgage Transaction
Parity Act, which legalized negative amortization, adjustable rate mortgages, and balloon payments—all methods that made high-priced subprime loans appear affordable; and the Tax Reform Act of 1986, which
created tax incentives for people who took second mortgages or "home
equity" loans, thereby helping mortgage companies convince Americans
that borrowing in this way was financially beneficial.[2]

Like contract sellers, subprime lenders pushed people to take on
more debt than they could handle. While contract sellers got away with
inflated prices because bank redlining left their customers with few alternatives, subprime lenders got borrowers to overmortgage themselves by
convincing them that prices would only continue to rise—and by working with handpicked property appraisers. Whether the borrower had the
economic wherewithal to carry the loan was of little concern to subprime
lenders, since the mortgage "paper" was quickly sold to Wall Street investment banks, who pooled large numbers of mortgages, categorized them
by levels of risk, and then used them as security for bonds sold to investors. Companies also garnered income from the "service fees" that they
charged on subprime mortgages, which could amount to as high as 15 percent of the loan's value. And those engaging in these practices were hardly
marginal. Countrywide Financial—which was by 2004 the largest origina-
tor of mortgages in the nation—became so enamored of the easy profits
to be made that it pushed customers into the subprime category, using
ruses such as automatically excluding cash reserves when tabulating borrowers' assets.[3]

Parallels with 1960s contract selling and the 1970s FHA scandals
abound. Subprime borrowers were persuaded to take on risky debts by
brokers who promised to "look out for their best interests." They were
often rushed through the loan closings, sometimes with no attorney present to explain the terms and represent their interests. Their mortgages
went into foreclosure at far higher rates than prime mortgages because
the interest rates were higher, but they also sometimes lost their property
after only one missed payment or as a result of accounting errors or arbitrary fees levied by the loan company. There was little incentive to help
borrowers avoid this fate because, as the Center for Responsible Lending

points out, foreclosure was "a profit opportunity for servicers and lenders," given the punishing late fees that they levied and given the fact that in almost all cases the lender was now merely servicing the loan, having long ago sold the mortgage itself off to a "faceless" Wall Street investor.[4]

"'Ghetto lending' practices of the 1960s have metastasized," is how one legal scholar sums up the early-twenty-first-century subprime mortgage meltdown: "We are all in the ghetto now."[5] While the crisis has damaged the entire U.S. economy, Home Mortgage Disclosure Act data suggest that, tragically enough, it was those who were just getting their foothold who were disproportionately hurt. Of all Americans, blacks and Hispanics were most likely to hold these dangerous overpriced loans. They were systematically targeted; inhabitants of moderate-income minority neighborhoods, where people were "house rich but cash poor," report being "bombarded" by mortgage brokers and home improvement contractors pressuring them to take out subprime home equity loans.[6] As one foreclosure prevention organization sums up, the subprime fiasco is having a "catastrophic effect on African American communities"; it could turn into "the largest drain of wealth" out of black America ever.[7] Yet now, as in the heyday of contract selling, peddlers of exploitative loans claim that they were merely trying to aid minorities in their quest for housing. Perhaps the saddest echo of all lies in the HMDA-based finding that between 2004 and 2006 the American city with the most residents holding subprime loans was—Chicago.[8]

One major cause of the subprime loan race gap is the fact that minority communities remain underserved by banks, and aggressive subprime marketers are only too eager to fill the vacuum. The Community Reinvestment Act was intended to address this very problem by compelling banks to provide loans in such neighborhoods. While the CRA has led to significant levels of investment in previously redlined communities, it is unfortunately also true that the banking industry has relentlessly fought to limit the reach of the CRA—aided by men such as former Republican senator Phil Gramm, who described the rules that the CRA imposes upon lenders as "an evil like slavery in the pre–Civil War era."[9] Since the CRA's provisions do not compel reinvestment in neighborhoods where the bank in question has no branches, it cannot by itself stop bankers' neglect of even solidly middle-class minority areas and has no effect at all on the predatory rates and practices of the storefront check-cash shops that stand in for banks in the nation's poorer communities.[10]

Yet there are reasons for optimism. The Community Reinvestment Act has impassioned defenders fighting to expand its reach—including former CUA analyst Calvin Bradford, who battles for community reinvestment to this day. The Home Mortgage Disclosure Act remains a critically important tool, enabling activists to determine which communities have been hardest hit.[11] Nationally, an array of consumer protection, community reinvestment, and municipal-community organization coalitions have arisen to help homeowners fight for their properties and to push Congress to take action. In July 2008, the Federal Reserve adopted new rules banning such practices as "coercing or encouraging an appraiser to misrepresent a home's value," "ignoring a borrower's ability to repay," and "penalizing homeowners for paying off their loans" early. As a Federal Reserve governor summarized in words that could easily have applied to the contract-selling scenario, "Abusive loans that strip borrowers' equity or cause them to lose their homes should not be tolerated."[12]

Finally, if Chicago remains a magnet for unscrupulous credit practices, it also remains at the forefront of challenges to them. The National Training and Information Center, the organization that Gale Cincotta helped to found in 1972, was among the first to document the emerging subprime crisis. In November 2007, the Illinois attorney general brought suit against One Source Mortgage, whose primary lender was Countrywide Financial, for using high-pressure sales tactics and for misleading its customers about the high interest rates it charged. In June 2008, the suit was expanded to include Countrywide Financial and its former CEO, Angelo Mozilo, who were charged with defrauding state borrowers through fake marketing pitches, hidden fees, and underhanded practices such as inflating borrowers' income to get them a higher loan—almost always without the borrowers' knowledge. As Illinois attorney general Lisa Madigan explained, "People were put into loans they did not understand, could not afford and could not get out of. This mounting disaster has had an impact on individual homeowners statewide and is having an impact on the global economy. It is all from the greed of people like Angelo Mozilo." In October 2008, after ten additional states joined in the suit against Countrywide, the company settled (without admitting wrongdoing). It agreed to provide $8.4 billion in loan relief, which will include reductions on principal balances and interest rates as well as the waiving of late fees and prepayment penalties. An estimated 400,000 borrowers will benefit. "We have created the first comprehensive, mandatory loan-modification program with the largest loan servicer in the country, and it is going to help homeowners stay in their homes," Madigan announced. The *New York Times* labeled the Countrywide deal "the largest predatory lending settlement in history."[13]

What of the Contract Buyers League? Judged in strictly monetary terms, it was a success. Participating families saw an average savings of $14,000— a hefty amount back in the early 1970s. As John McKnight observes, "The movement of contract buyers probably brought more economic benefit to more minority people than any single organizing effort of that time." Of course, success can't be measured simply by dollar signs; a movement's triumphs must also be measured by the fate of the community in which it originated and by its effects upon the lives of its participants. Here, the record is mixed. Although the contract sales battle brought significant savings to individual contract buyers who pressured their sellers to renegotiate, that money was too little and too late to save Lawndale. By 1986, Lawndale had a population of over 66,000 but only one supermarket and one bank. When sociologist William Julius Wilson described the hopelessness that results "when work disappears," he cited Lawndale as a community that "exemplifies" that process.[14] By then, the complex understanding of urban decline that the CBL fought to publicize had been thoroughly overshadowed by the more easy to assimilate drama of the Southern civil rights movement, on the one hand, and by the resurgence of "culture of poverty" analyses that blamed poverty on its victims, on the other.

In recent years, however, Lawndale and neighboring West Side communities have experienced something of a resurgence. In the 1990s, South Lawndale began to attract new immigrants; by 2000 the community was 83 percent Hispanic, almost half of whom were foreign born. While unemployment rates are high and schools remain seriously overcrowded, small businesses have returned and property values have appreciated. North Lawndale, which remains overwhelmingly African American, has also seen more businesses open and a rise in housing values. Supporting this resurgence have been networks of block clubs; indeed, North Lawndale residents are "far likelier" to participate in neighborhood groups than are residents of other Chicago or suburban areas. "Willingness to organize as a community distinguishes North Lawndale from many other inner cities," a recent study notes. This, too, is a legacy of the Contract Buyers League.[15]

The contested South Side neighborhood where Universal built its properties is now peaceful. It was a predominantly middle-class community dominated by single-family dwellings in 1960, when it had a black population of 12 percent; by 1980, when its population had become 98 percent African American, it remained overwhelmingly middle class. Today three-quarters of the area's residents own their own homes, and most have incomes comfortably above Chicago's median.[16]

While Chicago remains among the nation's ten most segregated cities, there has been progress on this score. The city experienced a 9.2 percent decline in residential segregation between 1980 and 2000—a rate that is below the national average decline of 12 percent, but significant nevertheless.[17]

What of the lives that were transformed by the twenty-year battle over contract sales? After their experience with Jay Goran in 1956, Albert and Sallie Bolton never purchased another home. They remained in Hyde Park as renters for another sixteen years, long enough for their four children to graduate from Hyde Park High School and from college as well—"every one of them," Mrs. Bolton says proudly. "I thank God for the storms he brought us through," she adds. "They just made us work harder and achieve what we wanted to achieve." After a decadelong struggle, Mary Lee Stevenson obtained ownership of the property she bought on contract at 3817 West Grenshaw. She lived there until she died in 1978. Her niece Bertha Richards also managed to hold on to her building. She and her family invested all they had in the handsome brick three-flat. But when Bertha's husband, Lawrence, died of a heart ailment at the age of 48, and her mother, Joeanna Williams, died shortly after that, following a long struggle with heart disease and diabetes, Bertha didn't want to live there anymore. She gave up the property in 1972. She eventually remarried and now lives in the single-family home that she and her new husband purchased with a mortgage. Richards still mourns the Lawndale building. "I loved it," she told me.[18]

In 1972, CBL activist Ruth Wells became the director of Citizens Alert, a community organization dedicated to monitoring complaints of police brutality. By 1974, her group had succeeded in persuading the Chicago Police Department to permit citizens to sit on its police brutality review board—an accomplishment that eluded Martin Luther King Jr.'s Chicago Freedom Movement. In 1976, the building she and her husband, James, had fought so hard to keep caught fire as a result of faulty wiring. "We had just put a new roof on, but the firemen had to cut a hole in it" to save the building, Wells recalled. She lived in a downtown hotel for a year while the building was repaired and then moved closer to her new job at the Office of the Village Clerk in Oak Park, a Chicago suburb. She also separated from her husband. In 1981, James Wells was diagnosed with lung cancer. Ruth took him back and cared for him for the final months of his life. She never remarried. Today she lives in an apartment complex in Oak Park.[19]

Clyde Ross became a lifelong activist. He succeeded in getting over-priced Lawndale-area insurance policies rewritten, and he worked hard on block club organizing. His devotion to the neighborhood was not enough to save his daughter from its dangers; she ended up battling drug addiction. Clyde and his wife, Lillie, eventually took legal guardianship of their grandchildren. Lillie died in the late 1990s. Today Ross still lives in the building he bought on contract from John Karras. He remains rightfully proud of the CBL's success in enabling him and many others to obtain full ownership of their properties.[20]

Sidney Clark, who lost his home during the "big holdout" and shortly thereafter suffered the death of one of his sons, experienced a spiritual awakening: "I really did begin to question my spirituality, what gave me motivation. That's when I began to transition from being I don't know what to being a Moslem." Today, he is Sidney Sharif. "If you think all this life is is a fistful of dollars, then you've lost already. Life has more to offer than things of monetary value. This is what you will learn when you decide to involve yourself in struggling with the real issues in life," he believes.[21]

The organizers who supported the CBL remain committed to social justice. Jack and Peggy Macnamara returned to Chicago in the early 1970s. Jack ran his own company, the Fred Busch Foods Corporation, until he retired in 2004. He and Peggy have seven children and eight grandchildren. Macnamara still serves on the board of the Gamaliel Foundation,

which has become the second-largest training center for community organizers in the nation. In 2006, he directed a feasibility study to investigate
the possibility of opening a Cristo Rey Jesuit high school on Chicago's West
Side; also serving on the planning committee were Clyde Ross and Ruth
Wells. Cristo Rey schools provide a curriculum of academic excellence
and leadership development for their students, 98 percent of whom go on
to college. Groundbreaking for the new school, Christ the King Jesuit College Preparatory School, was in June 2008.[22]

Most of the young people who worked with Macnamara in Lawndale
found the experience transformative. Two of them, Michael Gecan and
Mark Splain, became professional community organizers. Another, David
Quammen, became an award-winning author of mostly nonfiction works
about nature and science. His first novel, *To Walk the Line*, is a thinly
veiled account of his work with the CBL and of his friendship with Eddie
Smith. Several others became attorneys. One, Peter Welch, served in the
Vermont State Senate and in 2006 was elected the United States representative for Vermont. "Many of Peter's political ideals were shaped by his
work in Chicago, where he witnessed firsthand the effects of racial prejudice and learned that people working together can bring about needed
changes," his congressional biography reads.

Eddie Smith graduated from college and then ran a successful company called Bo's Trucking. But he engaged in illegal activities as well, and
ended up in prison for four years. When he got out, some of his gangster
friends told him, "Bo, you know what, you still ain't a bad looking guy.
Maybe you ought to be a movie star." Smith trained as an actor and a
stunt man and has been in numerous films, both mainstream and Christian. In several he has played a bodyguard—a role he can perform with
a certain authenticity given his experiences in Lawndale. He remains
grateful for the guidance he received from Jack Macnamara during his
troubled teenage years. He now worships as he did in his youth—as a
Baptist. "I believe in God and I believe that God is brilliant and that bless-
ings flow from above," he told me.[23]

Chicago's committed organizers created a lasting legacy. Saul Alinsky
died of a heart attack in 1972, at the age of sixty-three. Jack Egan heard the
news on his car radio on one of his many drives between Notre Dame and

Chicago. He pulled to the side of the road, called Nick von Hoffman, and wept. The Industrial Areas Foundation, which Alinsky began in the 1940s as a training institute for community organizers, continues to thrive. As of 2006, sixty community organizations counted themselves as IAF affiliates.[24]

Jack Egan never stopped fighting for justice, nor did his warmth and concern for the men and women he counseled and challenged ever flag. While most Chicagoans viewed his years at Notre Dame as an "exile," they were nothing of the sort to Egan and his indispensable partner, Peggy Roach. The two made Notre Dame the home base of the Catholic Committee on Urban Ministry (CCUM), which under their leadership became a "ministry to the ministers" who devoted themselves to empowering the poor. The group developed numerous diocesan urban programs, helped to make social action an acceptable part of seminary field training, and was a major force behind the creation of several national urban research and community funding institutions. As organizer Tom Gaudette recalled of one CCUM meeting, "This was where you met everybody: the unions, the gays, the women who wanted to be cardinals, . . . the poets, the workers, the prisoners. This was the real Church, the working Church. . . . It was a marriage between the Church and the real world." By 1975, the membership had grown from a few dozen people to over three thousand.[25]

On his return to Chicago in 1983, Egan continued to be an organizing dynamo. He created the Council of Religious Leaders of Metropolitan Chicago. He convinced the head of Alinsky's Industrial Areas Foundation to move the organization's headquarters from New York to Chicago. He helped to launch United Power for Action and Justice, an organization dedicated to unifying the resources and moral authority of Chicago's diverse religious communities. Egan also worked with Rabbi Robert Marx to create the Chicago Interfaith Committee for Worker Justice, aimed at renewing ties between religious groups and the labor movement. It quickly expanded into a national organization; by 2001, the National Interfaith Committee for Worker Justice had sixty chapters. Egan never stopped fighting exploitative credit practices that entrapped the poor. Starting in 1999, he battled the payday loan industry, which makes quick loans to low-income people at interest rates of up to 521 percent. In May 2001, Egan died of a heart ailment at the age of eighty-four. Shortly thereafter the coalition against exploitative payday loans that he helped to create was renamed the Monsignor John Egan Campaign for Payday Loan Reform. In 2005, the Egan Payday Loan Reform Act was passed by the Illinois General Assembly.[26]

Dempsey J. Travis recounted the story of his work with the Contract Buyers League in his autobiography. Since then he has written numerous books on black history, music, culture, and politics. He is the president of Travis Realty Company and a self-made multimillionaire. John L. McKnight continues to work with Northwestern University's Center for Urban Affairs, which is now called the Institute for Policy Research. He has helped spur research on health, law enforcement, urban disinvestment, child welfare services, and much more. Realtor John W. Baird, former president of the Metropolitan Housing and Planning Council, was among a group of Chicagoans who came up with the idea of providing rent vouchers for low-income people that would allow them to rent where they liked at subsidized prices. The idea was picked up by legislators and led to the Section 8 federal housing program. While the program is based on renting and therefore does not build equity for its participants, in 2004 alone Section 8 vouchers helped house approximately two million people. It has been called "the most successful public-and-private housing partnership in the history of the United States."[27]

The West Side contract sellers felt vindicated by the outcome of the CBL trial. Jay Goran died in the late 1990s, but his wife, Gertrude, remains proud of his triumph over "all the big shots" at Jenner and Block. Goran's former partner, Gerald Crane, was "unethical," Gertrude believes, but not her husband. Lou Wolf ended up in prison a second time for a scheme involving real estate taxes. Moe Forman and his wife, Mildred, both died in the late 1990s. The Reverend Wallace Reid was shot dead in his home by one of his contract buyers (not a plaintiff in the West Side suit) a few years after the trial's conclusion. As of 2001, Gilbert Balin was busy buying properties that were in foreclosure or available through "scavenger" tax sales, although he now interrupted his labors for intermittent monthlong trips to Europe. His son and daughter resided in the Gold Coast, Chicago's most exclusive neighborhood.[28]

The federal suits remained fresh in the memories of the attorneys who tried them. John Tucker admits that "twenty-six years later, I still haven't gotten over the verdict in the Contract Buyers League case." George Feiwell believes that corrupt savings and loan executives were "the real culprits" in the CBL's West Side suit. Warren Lupel, who worked with Irving Block to defend the contract sellers of Lawndale, named his son after Block. Michael Turoff, who represented Universal, still feels bitter about his years of struggle to clear his father's name. After discussing the matter with me, he said, "I hope to never discuss it again with anybody ever." But recently he ran into the son of Arthur Green, a man who had worked with Sidney Clark to organize the South Side members of the CBL. Green's son, Albert, told Turoff, "What happened happened a while ago—it was between our parents and not us." And he shook Turoff's hand.[29]

My mother, Clarice Satter, lived with her family in a two-flat in the Chicago suburb of Skokie until 1973. That year she remarried and moved to Evanston, Illinois, where, unbeknown to her, she lived across the street from one of the contract sellers her husband had taken to court in 1958.[30] She died of cancer in 1983. David Satter, my brother, became a well-known writer and journalist who specializes in Russian history and politics. His 1967 essay on welfare recipients has been incorporated into several books on Martin Luther King Jr.'s Chicago crusade.[31] Paul Satter never seemed to have fully recovered from our father's death. He has too many ideas about the workings of history to take on a full-time job, so he drives a cab to support himself while he reads and develops his theories. To cope with the loss of our father, Paul spent many years going through his papers, carefully arranging them in about a dozen large scrapbooks, which he kept on a shelf in his apartment. My sisters, Julietta and Susan, don't have many memories of their father. Nor do I, his youngest child. One summer I saw the dozen heavy scrapbooks that Paul had created out of my father's papers and asked what they were. Paul told me that he would have shown them to me anytime—I only needed to ask. I started to have nightmares about my father's papers, that they were destroyed in the rain or blown away by the wind while I cried uncontrollably. And then, to stop the nightmares and to uncover the mysteries of my family, I opened the scrapbooks and began to read.

NOTES

ABBREVIATIONS

ARCHIVES

CCCC Office of the Clerk of the Circuit Court of Cook County Archives, Chicago
CHS Chicago Historical Society
CPL Chicago Public Library
JBA Jenner and Block Archives, Jenner & Block, LLC, One IBM Plaza, Chicago
NARA National Archives and Records Administration—Great Lakes Region
UND University of Notre Dame Archives
UIC Manuscripts and Archives, Richard J. Daley Library, University of Illinois, Chicago
WLA, LUC Women and Leadership Archives, Mundelein College Archives, The Ann
    Ida Gannon, BVM, Center for Women and Leadership, Loyola University, Chicago

INDIVIDUALS

DS David Satter
JM Jack Macnamara
MJS Mark J. Satter

NEWSPAPERS

CA *Chicago American*   **GA** *Garfieldian*
CC *Chicago Courier*   **LAT** *Los Angeles Times*
CDD *Chicago Daily Defender*   **NW** *New World*
CDN *Chicago Daily News*   **NYT** *New York Times*
CST *Chicago Sun Times*   **WP** *Washington Post*
CT *Chicago Tribune*   **WSJ** *Wall Street Journal*

All of Mark J. Satter's columns, articles, manuscripts, radio and television transcripts, and speeches, and all correspondence to or by Mark J. Satter are in the Mark J.
Satter Papers (unless otherwise noted). These papers are being donated to the Newberry Library, Chicago, where they will be housed in its Midwest Manuscript Collection.

All interviews are by the author. In cases where the interviewees have given permission, these too will be donated to the Newberry Library. All newspaper articles
concerning Jack Macnamara or the Contract Buyers League are in Jack Macnamara
Papers (unless otherwise noted).

INTRODUCTION: THE STORY OF MY FATHER

1. "Mark Satter," *CDN*, July 14, 1965.

2. Lois Wille, "Credit Reform Fanfare and Flop," *CDN*, Jan. 23, 1965; L. F. Palmer Jr. and Paul Hunter, "Law Backs Housing 'Racket': Contract Buyers at Mercy of Sharpies," *CC*, Nov. 10, 1962; "Federal Curbs Urged on Wage Assignments: Attorney Fights Racket," *CDN*, Nov. 6, 1961.

3. Following Charles Abrams's *Forbidden Neighbors: A Study of Prejudice in Housing* (New York: Harper and Row, 1955) and Kenneth T. Jackson's *Crabgrass Frontier: The Suburbanization of the United States* (New York: Oxford University Press, 1985), numerous urban historians have shown that FHA redlining made it impossible for most African Americans to buy homes with a mortgage. Instead, they were forced to deal with speculators, who bought "low" from whites and sold "high" to blacks. But historians missed a critical point. Given that blacks could not get mortgages, how were they able to buy at high prices? One way was through contract selling, as will be detailed below.

4. Warren W. Lehman, "Speculation in Color: Racial Transition in Chicago" (unpublished ms.), 4–7, MJS Papers; see *Albert Bolton and Sallie Bolton v. Gerald H. Crane and Jay Goran*, Superior Court of Cook County, docket 57s6577, filed May 3, 1957, CCCC.

5. MJS, "Land Contract Sales in Chicago: Security Turned Exploitation," *Chicago Bar Review*, March 1958; see MJS Speech, "Mr. Chairman, Reverend Ministers, Dearborn Real Estate Panel, and Guests," March 26 and 27, 1958.

6. Norris Vitchek, as told to Alfred Balk, "Confessions of a Block-Buster," *Saturday Evening Post*, July 14–21, 1962, 18.

7. Letter, MJS to Jim [Hurlbut], July 18, 1962.

8. Ibid.

9. On the monetary loss to African Americans caused by unequal access to credit from Reconstruction-era sharecropping through the 1990s, see Dalton Conley, *Being Black, Living in the Red: Race, Wealth, and Social Policy in America* (Berkeley: University of California Press, 1999), 25–27. For early-twentieth-century Chicago, see Allan H. Spear, *Black Chicago: The Making of a Negro Ghetto, 1890–1920* (Chicago: University of Chicago Press, 1967), 118, 181, 227. On the disproportionate impact of the early-twenty-first-century subprime mortgage crisis on African Americans, see "Risk or Race? Racial Disparities and the Subprime Refinance Market" (Report of the Center for Community Change, prepared by Calvin Bradford, May 2002); "ACORN Study Shows Predatory Lending Is Leading to Foreclosures in Communities Nationwide," www.acorn.org/index.php?id=4174&tx_ttnews, accessed Sept. 12, 2007; "Racial Disparity Found among New Yorkers with High-Rate Mortgages," *NYT*, Oct. 15, 2007; "What's Behind the Race Gap?," *NYT*, Nov. 4, 2007; Kai Wright, "The Subprime Swindle: How Banks Stole Black America's Future," *Nation*, July 14, 2008. On federal credit discrimination against twentieth-century African American farmers, see "U.S. Will Pay Black Farmers for Loan Bias," *NYT*, Jan. 25, 2003; "Restitution for Black Farmers," *NYT*, July 27, 2004; "Black Farmers' Refrain: Where's All Our Money?," *NYT*, Aug. 1, 2004; "Bias Suits by Farmers Could Cost Billions," *NYT*, June 29, 2008.

10. Contract selling has been given only a page or two in the few published works that mention it at all. For example, see W. Edward Orser, *Blockbusting in Baltimore: The Edmondson Village Story* (Lexington: University of Kentucky Press, 1994), 91–92; Arnold R. Hirsch, *Making the Second Ghetto: Race and Housing in Chicago, 1940–1960* (Chicago: University of Chicago Press, 1998 [1983]), 32–33. To date, the most extended published discussion of contract selling is James Alan McPherson's "'In My

Father's House There Are Many Mansions—and I'm Going to Get Me Some of Them Too': The Story of the Contract Buyers League," *Atlantic Monthly,* April 1972, 52–82.

11. See Ann Stull, "Housing Speculators," *Community,* July 1958, for a clear explanation of speculators' profits; Lehman, "Speculation in Color," 5; and MJS, "Attorney Reveals Unethical Actions in Property Sales," *CDD,* all in MJS Papers. Also Vitchek, as told to Balk, "Confessions"; Favil Berns interview, June 10, 2001.

12. MJS to Jim [Hurlbut], July 18, 1962, 2, his italics.

13. His *Chicago Defender* column ran from Dec. 27, 1958, through March 26, 1960. His Greater Lawndale Conservation Commission column ran Oct. 1958 until Feb. 1961. Only scattered transcripts remain of the radio program *The Cost of Your Dollar.* In addition to transcripts for Jan. 14, Jan. 23, March 4, and Oct. 4, 1962, see letter, William G. Clark, Attorney General, State of Illinois, to MJS, Feb. 5, 1962, which refers to my father's recent comments on Wesley South's radio program, all in MJS Papers.

14. "Explains How Speculators Prey on Changing Areas: Lawyer Tells City Club Here of Fantastic Profit on Housing," *CDN,* May 2, 1960; "Warns of Speculators: Residents Told: 'Don't Push Panic Button,'" *Southeast Economist,* March 17, 1960; letter, MJS to Adlai Stevenson, n.d.; "Debate Contract Selling at GLCC Meeting," *GLCC News Notes,* July 23, 1958, all in MJS Papers.

15. For the "culturally deficient" school, see Nicholas Lemann, *The Promised Land: The Great Migration and How It Changed America* (New York: Vintage, 1992).

16. David A. Satter, "West Side Story: Home Is Where the Welfare Check Comes," *New Republic,* July 2, 1966, 16, 17.

17. Letter, MJS to Helen [Dorn], May 29 [1965].

18. *William H. Coleman and Wilma R. Coleman, His Wife, v. Jay Goran, and W. F. Smith,* Abstract of Record, Appellate Court of Illinois, First District, April term, A.D. 1960, 47992, MJS Papers; *William H. Coleman and Wilma R. Coleman, His Wife, v. Jay Goran, Gerald H. Crane, and W. F. Smith,* Superior Court of Cook County, docket 58s20591, motion to strike and motion to dismiss plaintiffs' suit, filed Dec. 29, 1958, 2–3.

19. Sanford D. Horwitt, *Let Them Call Me Rebel: Saul Alinsky, His Life and Legacy* (New York: Vintage Books, 1992 [1988]), 423 (italics in text).

20. See Spear, *Black Chicago;* Milton Rakove, *Don't Make No Waves, Don't Back No Losers: An Insider's Analysis of the Daley Machine* (Bloomington: Indiana University Press, 1975).

21. McPherson, "'In My Father's House,'" 78, 68; see Jeffrey Michael Fitzgerald, "The Contract Buyers League: A Case Study of Interaction between a Social Movement and the Legal System" (Ph.D. dissertation, Northwestern University, 1972).

CHAPTER ONE: JEWISH LAWNDALE

1. MJS, untitled autobiography, 11.

2. Louis Wirth, *The Ghetto* (Chicago: University of Chicago Press, 1928), 247; Erich Rosenthal, "This Was North Lawndale: The Transplantation of a Jewish Community," *Jewish Social Studies* 22 (1960): 68.

3. Charles Bowden and Lou Kreinberg, *Street Signs Chicago: Neighborhood and Other Illusions of Big-City Life* (Chicago: Chicago Review Press, 1981), 168; Rosenthal, "North Lawndale," 69, his italics; see Wirth, *Ghetto,* 247.

4. Rosenthal, "North Lawndale," 70–72; Irving Cutler, *The Jews of Chicago: From Shtetl to Suburb* (Urbana: University of Illinois Press, 1996), 213, 218–19.

5. Benjamin Ginsberg, *The Fatal Embrace: Jews and the State* (Chicago: University of Chicago Press, 1993), 78, 83–84; John Higham, *Send These to Me: Jews and Other Immigrants in Urban America* (New York: Atheneum, 1975), 190.

6. Cutler, *Jews of Chicago*, 63.

7. MJS autobiography, 9; Lakeside Directory of Chicago (Chicago City Directory), 1912, 1916, 1923, 1928, CHS.

8. MJS autobiography, 15.

9. Ibid., 16–17; Charlie Satter interview, Dec. 26, 1999, 2.

10. MJS autobiography, 17.

11. Joseph Satter interview, Aug. 18, 2001.

12. Cutler, *Jews of Chicago*, 129; see Lizabeth Cohen, *Making a New Deal: Industrial Workers in Chicago, 1919–1939* (Cambridge, U.K.: Cambridge University Press, 1990); Robert S. McElwaine, *The Great Depression: America, 1929–1941* (New York: Times Books, 1984).

13. Theresa Rubinson interview, July 22, 2001; David Satter interview, Feb. 2, 2001; Charlie Satter interview.

14. MJS autobiography, 18–23; Charlie Satter interview, 14.

15. MJS autobiography, 25.

16. People's Junior College clippings, MJS Papers.

17. MJS autobiography.

18. Rubinson interview.

19. Ellen Schrecker, *Many Are the Crimes: McCarthyism in America* (Princeton: Princeton University Press, 1998), 15; Mari Jo Buhle, Paul Buhle, and Dan Georgakas, eds., *Encyclopedia of the American Left* (Urbana: University of Illinois Press, 1992), 151.

20. MJS autobiography, 35; also see 31.

21. Michael Denning, *The Cultural Front: The Laboring of American Culture in the Twentieth Century* (London: Verso, 1997), 4–21, 64–77.

22. Clarice Komsky's high school yearbook, MJS Papers; Beverly Froikin interview, Feb. 11, 2001.

23. MJS autobiography, 29.

24. Deborah Horn interview, Feb. 11, 2001; David Satter interview, Feb. 1, 2001, 48.

25. MJS autobiography, concluding epigraph.

26. David Satter interview, Feb. 8, 2001; "Mark J. Satter," Freedom of Information and Privacy Acts file 100-397933, Federal Bureau of Investigation.

27. "Mark J. Satter," FBI file.

28. Wallace condemned Truman's Loyalty Board program. He called for an end to discrimination in the United States (the abolishment of school segregation and Jim Crow laws, the reform of immigration laws, and the promotion of equal rights for women); improvement of the quality of daily life for working people (a minimum wage for farmworkers, national health insurance, public day-care programs, a minimum national pension of $100 a month for people over sixty); and public control of large banks and essential industries such as railroads and gas and power utilities. John C. Culver and John Hyde, *American Dreamer: The Life and Times of Henry A. Wallace* (New York: Norton, 2000), 437, 433–34; also see 438, 481, 504.

29. Culver and Hyde, *American Dreamer*, 418, 435, 440–41, 501, 503; "Mark J. Satter," FBI file; telegram, Henry A. Wallace to MJS, Feb. 22, 1948, MJS Papers.

30. Thomas I. Emerson, "The National Lawyers Guild in 1950–51," *Guild Practitioner*, 60; "Mark J. Satter," FBI file.

31. Emerson, "National Lawyers Guild," 60. The proof of the NLG's disloyalty, HUAC claimed, was that the NLG opposed HUAC. The NLG responded by putting out its own pamphlet, titled *The National Lawyers Guild: Legal Bulwark of Democracy*, but it was too late. Schrecker, *Many Are the Crimes*, 224–26; Emerson, "National Lawyers

Guild," 63–65. "Half of us were spies" is from the Eugene Crane interview, June 26, 2001. Also see "Mark J. Satter," FBI files, 1953.

32. William Peters, "Race War in Chicago," *New Republic,* Jan. 9, 1950, 10–12; also see Report of the Chicago Commission on Human Relations (CHR) to Mayor Martin H. Kennelly, Dec. 10, 1949 (author's copy provided by Ed Holmgren; copy also in Chicago Municipal Reference Library); Arnold R. Hirsch, *Making the Second Ghetto: Race and Housing in Chicago, 1940–1960* (Chicago: University of Chicago Press, 1998 [1983]), 201.

33. "Mark J. Satter," FBI files, 1953, 10–23.

34. "Mark J. Satter," FBI files, 1955, 67–68, and 1961, 100.

35. Les Brownlee interview, Feb. 17, 2001. (Brownlee had originally published with his first name spelled as "Lestre" but later changed it to "Lester" and used the shortened form "Les.") Also see Sam Bassov interview, July 16, 2002; Warren Lehman, "Goodbye, Mark" (unpublished ms.), 2, MJS Papers.

36. Favil Berns interview, June 10, 2001, 4.

37. "Satter 'Worked with' Post Story Author," *GA,* July 25, 1962.

38. Ibid.

39. Paul Satter interview, Jan. 17, 2001.

40. "'I Wrote Post Article, but I'm No Blockbuster,' Declares Satter," *GA,* Aug. 1, 1962.

41. Lawndale Conservation Community Council, "A Comprehensive Plan for Urban Renewal in the North Lawndale Community," Aug. 11, 1966, 7, in CJEG-Egan I, box 54, UND; Hirsch, *Second Ghetto,* 193; see also Dempsey J. Travis, *An Autobiography of Black Chicago* (Chicago: Urban Research Institute, 1981), 128.

42. Alphine Wade Jefferson, "Housing Discrimination and Community Response in North Lawndale (Chicago), Illinois, 1948–1978" (Ph.D. dissertation, Duke University, 1979), 66, 69, 80; also see Chicago Urban League, "Housing in Chicago—A Preliminary Look," Feb. 21, 1958, and Chicago Urban League Community Services Department, "Urban Renewal and the Negro in Chicago," revised July 31, 1958, author's copies provided by Ed Holmgren.

43. Jefferson, "Housing Discrimination," 82; Amanda Irene Seligman, "Block by Block: Racing Decay on Chicago's West Side, 1949–1968" (Ph.D. dissertation, Northwestern University, 1999), 69–70.

44. Letter, MJS to Miss Jane Weston, March 8, 1962.

45. Paul Satter interview.

46. Bowden and Kreinberg, *Street Signs Chicago,* 173.

47. Rosenthal, "North Lawndale"; Jefferson, "Housing Discrimination," 62; Joseph Satter interview.

48. Steven M. Avella, *This Confident Church: Catholic Leadership and Life in Chicago, 1940–1965* (Notre Dame: University of Notre Dame Press, 1992), 215–17.

49. David Satter interview, June 1, 2002, 4–5.

50. See Cutler, *Jews of Chicago,* 242–44.

51. "Chicago Housing Called Midwest's Most Segregated," *CST,* Dec. 7, 1962, 38. This quote has been wrongly attributed to Saul Alinsky.

52. Jefferson, "Housing Discrimination," 72, 74.

53. "Phony Names, Land Trusts Used to Profit from Squalor," *CT,* May 6, 1973; "Lawndale Is Exploited," *CT,* May 7, 1973.

54. Berns interview, 33, 34.

55. Ibid., 35.

56. Ibid., 46, 34; also see 36, 48.

57. Wirth, *Ghetto,* 239–40.

58. "Phony Names."

59. Examination of Joseph Berke, Jan. 16, 1976, in "Abstract of Testimony in First Trial," *Ruth and James Wells v. F & F Investment,* 69c15, 3136, box 4, JBA. My thanks to Tom Sullivan for making this abstract available to me.

60. Ibid., 3112.

61. "Direct Examination of Al Berland," Jan. 12, 1976, in "Abstract of Testimony," *Wells v. F & F Investment,* 69c15, 2611, box 4, JBA.

62. "Fushanis Collapses and Dies," *CDN,* May 24, 1963.

63. "Lawndale Is Exploited"; "Direct Examination of Al Berland," Jan. 12, 1976, in "Abstract of Testimony," *Wells v. F & F Investment,* 69c15, 2614, 2646–51, 2660–67, box 4, JBA.

64. "Lawndale Is Exploited."

65. Ibid.; "Phony Names."

66. "Lawndale Is Exploited."

67. "'The Slums' Tightening Stranglehold on Chicago's Future," *CT,* May 20, 1973; "Lawndale Is Exploited."

68. "Staff Report," Aug. 3, 1959, Greater Lawndale Conservation Commission (GLCC) Papers, box 11, folder "August 1959," CHS, for early address of Fushanis's Friendly Loan. The company had moved by 1963; see "Here Are City Slumlords," *CDN,* May 21, 1963.

69. "Here Are City Slumlords."

70. Berns interview, 17, 24.

71. Ibid., 4.

72. Bassov interview; "Woman Names 10 in Bank Theft," *CA,* Aug. 25, 1956; "Hold Woman in Bank Loss," *Daily Tribune,* Aug. 25, 1956; "Woman's Story of $467,228 Bank Loss," *Chicago Sunday Tribune,* Aug. 26, 1956; "Why Did She Juggle $467,228?," n.p., n.d.; "Spinster Who Took $467,332 from Bank Gets Probation," *CA,* Feb. 2, 1958; "$467,332 Bank Theft Forgiven," *CDN,* Feb. 7, 1958, all in MJS Papers.

CHAPTER TWO: THE NOOSE AROUND BLACK CHICAGO

1. Arnold R. Hirsch, *Making the Second Ghetto: Race and Housing in Chicago, 1940–1960* (Chicago: University of Chicago Press, 1998 [1983]), 3–4, 17–23; St. Clair Drake and Horace R. Cayton, *Black Metropolis: A Study of Negro Life in a Northern City* (New York: Harcourt, Brace, 1945), 576–80; Amanda I. Seligman, *Block by Block: Neighborhoods and Public Policy on Chicago's West Side* (Chicago: University of Chicago Press, 2005), 30–31.

In 1939, before the World War II black migration, the Black Belt was already densely overcrowded, with 252,201 people living in a 4.2-square-mile area. See Robert C. Weaver, "Race Restrictive Housing Covenants," *Journal of Land and Public Utility Economics* 20, no. 3 (Aug. 1944): 187. Also see Steve Bogira, "Hate, Chicago Style," *Chicago Reader,* Dec. 5, 1986, 1; John T. McGreevey, *Parish Boundaries: The Catholic Encounter with Race in the Twentieth-Century Urban North* (Chicago: University of Chicago Press, 1996), 103.

2. Hirsch, *Second Ghetto,* 22–23.

3. Elaine Tyler May, *Homeward Bound: American Families in the Cold War Era* (New York: Basic Books, 1988), 13, 170; Drake and Cayton, *Black Metropolis,* 576–80.

4. Hirsch, *Second Ghetto,* 28–29.

5. Sallie Bolton interview, Oct. 11, 2001.

6. Ibid.; *Albert Bolton and Sallie Bolton v. Gerald H. Crane and Jay Goran,* Superior Court of Cook County, docket 57s6577, filed May 3, 1957, CCCC.

7. MJS, "Land Contract Sales in Chicago: Security Turned Exploitation," *Chicago Bar Record,* March 1958.

8. Bolton interview.

9. "Notes on the Deposition of J. Goran in the Case of Albert Bolton and Sallie Bolton," March 6, 1958, 11, in IAF (Alinsky) Papers, folder 163, UIC; Bolton interview.

10. Lestre Brownlee, "Chicago: America's Most Segregated City," 1958, 25, MJS Papers.

11. Allan H. Spear, *Black Chicago: The Making of a Ghetto, 1890–1920* (Chicago: University of Chicago Press, 1967), 14–15, 20.

12. Ibid., 21, 211–12; Alan B. Anderson and George W. Pickering, *Confronting the Color Line: The Broken Promise of the Civil Rights Movement in Chicago* (Athens: University of Georgia Press, 1986), 48.

13. Spear, *Black Chicago,* 12, 208–11.

14. Anderson and Pickering, *Color Line,* 46.

15. Ibid., 46–47, 464, n. 10. See also Robert C. Weaver, *The Negro Ghetto* (New York: Harcourt, Brace, 1948), 216–17. On dual housing market profits, see W. Edward Orser, *Blockbusting in Baltimore: The Edmondson Village Story* (Lexington: University of Kentucky Press, 1994), x–xi, 4–7; Robert O. Self, *American Babylon: Race and the Struggle for Postwar Oakland* (Princeton: Princeton University Press, 2003), 114–15, 264–65.

16. Wendy Plotkin, "Deeds of Mistrust: Race, Housing, and Restrictive Covenants in Chicago, 1900–1953" (Ph.D. dissertation, University of Illinois at Chicago, 1999), xii, 18.

17. Clement E. Vose, *Caucasians Only: The Supreme Court, the NAACP, and the Restrictive Covenant Cases* (Berkeley: University of California Press, 1967), vii.

18. Plotkin, "Deeds of Mistrust," 266–67. The barrier they posed to blacks was perhaps more psychological than actual, since enterprising whites in "restricted" areas were willing to break the deed restrictions when black demand—and consequently the prices that blacks were willing to pay for housing—got high enough. See Robert C. Weaver, "The Villain—Racial Covenants," in John H. Bracey Jr., August Meier, and Elliott Rudwick, eds., *The Rise of the Ghetto* (Belmont, Calif.: Wadsworth, 1971), 116–17.

19. Spear, *Black Chicago,* 26; see also 221–22.

20. Kenneth T. Jackson, *Crabgrass Frontier: The Suburbanization of the United States* (New York: Oxford University Press, 1985), 196, 204–6. In the late 1940s, when city rents averaged $93 a month, veterans could purchase a home in Levittown with no down payment and monthly mortgage payments of $56 a month (May, *Homeward Bound,* 69). For low down payments on new homes in the mid-1950s, see Self, *American Babylon,* 114.

21. Jackson, *Crabgrass Frontier,* 207, 217, 200, see also 197.

22. The maps were created by the Home Owners' Loan Corporation (HOLC), a New Deal agency that helped middle-class homeowners stave off foreclosure by refinancing their mortgages. The FHA adopted HOLC's appraisal methods and probably its actual maps as well. See Jackson, *Crabgrass Frontier,* 195–204, 215.

23. Charles Abrams, *Forbidden Neighbors* (New York: Harper, 1955), 231–32, 234.

24. Ibid., 232; Arnold R. Hirsch, "Choosing Segregation: Federal Housing Policy between Shelley and Brown," in John F. Bauman, Roger Biles, and Kristin M. Szylvia, eds., *From Tenements to the Taylor Homes: In Search of an Urban Housing Policy in Twentieth-Century America* (University Park: Pennsylvania State University Press, 2000), 209; Weaver, *Negro Ghetto,* 218–20.

Beginning in 1944 with the G.I. Bill of Rights, the Veterans Administration guaranteed mortgage loans for veterans, and in 1950 it established its own direct loan program. Between 1947 and 1960, the U.S. government insured over one million mortgage loans for veterans in the suburbs and over 800,000 in the cities. Of those insured in northern cities, the vast majority went to white veterans (Dempsey J. Travis, *An Autobiography of Black Chicago* [Chicago: Urban Research Institute, 1981], 157; Jackson, *Crabgrass Frontier,* 204).

25. Arnold R. Hirsch, "Containment on the Home Front: Race and Federal Housing Policy from the New Deal to the Cold War," *Journal of Urban History* 26, no. 2 (Jan. 2000): 162.

26. William R. Ming Jr., "Racial Restrictions and the Fourteenth Amendment: The Restrictive Covenant Cases," *University of Chicago Law Review* 16, no. 2 (Winter 1949): 226–27. Also see Ellis E. Reid, "Earl, Bob, and Me," *Law School Record of the University of Chicago Law School* 37 (Spring 1991): 6.

27. Hirsch, "Choosing Segregation," 211–12. On the origins of the idea that African Americans cause neighborhood decline, see Calvin Bradford, "Financing Home Ownership: The Federal Role in Neighborhood Decline," *Urban Affairs Quarterly* 14, no. 3 (March 1979): 321–25.

28. Raymond A. Mohl, "The Second Ghetto and the 'Infiltration Theory' in Urban Real Estate, 1940–1960," in June Manning Thomas and Marsha Ritzdorf, eds., *Urban Planning and the African American Community: In the Shadows* (Thousand Oaks, Calif.: Sage, 1997), 67, 69.

29. Travis, *Black Chicago,* 154, 157.

30. "Wants to Be No. 1 Banker, Period," *CST,* Sept. 24, 1970; Travis, *Black Chicago,* 128–29.

31. Travis, *Black Chicago,* 128–29, 157, 159.

32. Ibid., 139–40.

33. The statistics for commercial banks and life insurance companies were even more dismal. The Dearborn survey found that over the past year "not even a token number" of mortgages were lent to blacks by the 141 commercial banks and 229 life insurance companies in Cook County (*Hearings before the United States Commission on Civil Rights: Housing* [Washington: United States Printing Office, 1959], 738–39).

34. To address the mass write-off of black homeowners by insurance companies, Travis also called for federal prosecution of insurance companies that refused insurance to people "solely on account of race, creed, color, and national origin" (*Hearings before the United States Commission on Civil Rights,* 742).

35. Travis, *Black Chicago,* 148; also see 146.

36. Hirsch, *Second Ghetto,* 40, 58; also see 27.

37. Ibid., 56; Bogira, "Hate, Chicago Style."

38. Hirsch, *Second Ghetto,* 40.

39. Ibid., 54–55.

40. Ethel Johnson described their ordeal: "We barricaded the doors with furniture and put a mattress behind it. We crawled around on our hands and knees when the missiles started coming in through the windows. . . . Then they started to throw gasoline-soaked rags in pop bottles. They also threw flares and torches. As fast as they came in either the fireman or the policeman would step in to put them out. They were in and out of the house all the time. . . . The crowds didn't leave . . . until daybreak" (Hirsch, *Second Ghetto,* 59).

41. Whites gathered by the hundreds in front of these families' homes, where they engaged in hostile chants such as "Bring out Bushman," "Get the rope," and "String him up" (Hirsch, *Second Ghetto,* 75).

42. Ibid., 53–54; Homer Jack, "Cicero Nightmare," *Nation,* July 28, 1951, 64–65.

43. Arnold R. Hirsch, "Massive Resistance in the Urban North: Trumbull Park, Chicago, 1953–66," *Journal of American History* 82, no. 2 (September 1995): 534, 538. Also see D. Bradford Hunt, "Trumball Park Homes Race Riots, 1953–54," in James R. Grossman, Ann Durkin Keating, and Janice L. Reiff, eds., *The Encyclopedia of Chicago* (Chicago: University of Chicago Press, 2004), 206.

44. John W. Baird, "Statement to the Metropolitan Housing and Planning Council," Springfield, Ill., May 8, 1963, MHPC 74–20, box 2, folder 292, UIC.

Of course, many MHPC members were motivated by sincere outrage over decayed housing conditions. As one recalled, "You wouldn't believe how bad the slums were then. I saw families living in basements with wet dirt floors and six-foot ceilings. No heat, no electric lights, nothing. People were living in coal sheds and shacks and under stairways. There were rats everywhere" (Paul Gapp, "The 1st Lady of Slum Clearance Is Saying Goodby," *CT*, Dec. 2, 1973).

45. Hirsch, *Second Ghetto*, 104; also see 105–12.

46. Ibid., 125, 259.

47. As the preamble to the act stated, slums "cause an increase in the spread of disease, crime, infant mortality and juvenile delinquency, and constitute a menace to the health, safety, morals and welfare of the residents" (Hirsch, *Second Ghetto*, 113–14).

48. Ibid., 113–14.

49. John H. Sengstacke, "Are We Telling the Urban Renewal Story?," in *Renewing Chicago in the '60s* (lecture and discussion series sponsored by the University of Chicago and the Metropolitan Center for Neighborhood Renewal, 1961), 60, in author's possession. This pamphlet was loaned to me by Ed Holmgren.

50. Blacks were disproportionately displaced by urban renewal projects in part because they happened to inhabit deteriorating housing in central locations. Yet even controlling for all other factors, race remained a deciding factor in the choice of urban renewal sites in Chicago (Hirsch, *Second Ghetto*, 273–74).

51. Hirsch, *Second Ghetto*, 124, 223; Martin Meyerson and Edward C. Banfield, *Politics, Planning, and the Public Interest: The Case of Public Housing in Chicago* (New York: Free Press, 1955), 87. Also see Jewel Bellush and Murray Hausknecht, "Urban Renewal: An Historical Overview," in Bellush and Hausknecht, eds., *Urban Renewal: People, Politics, and Planning* (Garden City, N.Y.: Anchor, 1967), 13.

52. Hirsch, *Second Ghetto*, 223–24.

53. Between 1948 and 1963, slum clearance forced the relocation of 13,043 families, of whom approximately 80 percent were black. Similarly, the construction of public housing—ostensibly to house these displaced families—actually *displaced* another 12,035 families, of whom approximately 75 percent were black (Hirsch, *Second Ghetto*, 306, n. 76).

54. Bellush and Hausknecht, "Urban Renewal," 11–13.

55. Ibid. For a similar assessment made at the time, see Lestre Brownlee, "Decentralizing Negro Is a Thorny Problem," *CA*, April 26, 1958, MJS Papers. Also see Hirsch, *Second Ghetto*, 122–23.

56. Hirsch, "'Containment,'" 167–68.

57. Hirsch, "Choosing Segregation," 216.

58. Hirsch, *Second Ghetto*, 136; Peter H. Rossi and Robert A. Dentler, *The Politics of Urban Renewal: The Chicago Findings* (Glencoe, Ill.: Free Press, 1961), 48.

59. The construction of expensive new housing in place of existing structures would be "an effective screening tool" for "cutting down [the] number of Negroes," Kimpton wrote. As he jotted on a University of Chicago Board of Trustees meeting outline, "Tear it down and begin over again. Negroes" (Hirsch, *Second Ghetto*, 153; also see 149, 160).

60. MHPC plan quoted in Hirsch, *Second Ghetto*, 150, my italics.

61. Ibid.; John W. Baird, "The Role of Business in Urban Renewal," in *Renewing Chicago in the '60s*, 43.

62. To receive the funding, localities' programs had to include proof of the extent of area "blight," a detailed plan for the new land uses proposed, a plan for housing those dislocated, and a means of ensuring citizen participation in the renewal process. The act also established several programs that offered mortgage insurance to low- or middle-income families who were displaced by urban renewal developments (Roger W. Caves, "Housing Act of 1954," in Willem van Vliet, ed., *The Encyclopedia of Housing* [Thousand Oaks, Calif.: Sage, 1998], 252; Bellush and Hausknecht, "Urban Renewal," 15). It made an extremely stingy allocation for public housing—140,000 units nationally by 1958. This was shockingly inadequate, considering that in Chicago alone an estimated 43,418 families and 15,250 individuals were displaced between 1948 and 1961 by urban renewal and conservation programs. See Amanda Irene Seligman, "Block by Block: Racing Decay on Chicago's West Side, 1948–1968" (Ph.D. dissertation, Northwestern University, 1999), 50.

63. Hirsch, *Second Ghetto*, 272; also see 271. See Baird, "Role of Business," 43. Also see Rossi and Dentler, *Politics of Urban Renewal*, 58; letter, MHPC to Daley, Oct. 17, 1957, 2, in IAF (Alinsky) Papers, folder 188, UIC.

64. "City Forges Powerful Weapon in Its War against Blight," *CDN*, June 25, 1956, in IAF (Alinsky) Papers, folder 105, UIC; "How Anti-Slum Drive Has Brought Results Already," *CDN*, June 15, 1963, in MHPC 74–20, box 46, folder 1, UIC; Hirsch, *Second Ghetto*, 34.

65. "Cardinal O.K.'s Code on Housing," *CDN*, April 18, 1956, and "City Forges Powerful Weapon in Its War against Blight," both in IAF (Alinsky) Papers, folder 105, UIC; "How Anti-Slum Drive Has Brought Results Already."

66. Brownlee, "Decentralizing Negro Is a Thorny Problem."

67. Hirsch, *Second Ghetto*, 159, 150–51, 161; Thomas M. Landye and James J. Vanecko, "The Politics of Open Housing in Chicago and Illinois," in *The Politics of Fair-Housing Legislation*, ed. Lynn W. Eley and Thomas W. Casstevens (San Francisco: Chandler, 1968), 70.

68. Milton Rakove, *Don't Make No Waves, Don't Back No Losers: An Insider's Analysis of the Daley Machine* (Bloomington: Indiana University Press, 1975), 116. Chicagoans were free to elect a Republican committeeman as well, but since the city was overwhelmingly Democratic, Republican committeemen had little power. The situation was reversed in Chicago's suburban areas.

69. Ibid., 260; also see Drake and Cayton, *Black Metropolis*, 114–15; James Q. Wilson, *Negro Politics: The Search for Leadership* (New York: Octagon Books, 1960), 36; Adam Cohen and Elizabeth Taylor, *American Pharaoh: Mayor Richard J. Daley: His Battle for Chicago and the Nation* (Boston: Little, Brown, 2000), 94.

70. Cohen and Taylor, *American Pharaoh*, 96–97.

71. Dempsey J. Travis, *An Autobiography of Black Politics* (Chicago: Urban Research Press, 1987), 199, 207, 213; Arnold R. Hirsch, "The Cook County Democratic Organization and the Dilemma of Race, 1931–1987," in Richard M. Bernard, ed., *Snowbelt Cities: Metropolitan Politics in the Northeast and Midwest since World War II* (Bloomington: Indiana University Press, 1990), 75–77.

72. Hirsch, "Cook County," 75–77.

73. Ibid., 79.

74. Travis, *Black Politics*, 236; Hirsch, "Cook County," 80; Landye and Vanecko, "Politics of Open Housing," 75–78.

75. Fourth Ward alderman Timothy Evans recalled, "Holman's vicious attacks against Despres enabled Holman to get the largest slice of Daley's patronage pie within the black wards. . . . The next day after the speech [attacking Despres] had been delivered . . . Holman would . . . go to Daley and say, 'I stood up for you, Daley. Now I want the next series of judicial appointments for my people; I want specific jobs in city hall, etc.' . . . Holman was prepared to take the Uncle Tom lumps publicly as long as he could produce for his people privately" (Travis, *Black Politics*, 237).

76. Travis, *Black Politics*, 237; Hirsch, "Cook County," 80.

77. Arvarh E. Strickland, *History of the Chicago Urban League* (Urbana: University of Illinois Press, 1966), 163.

78. Travis, *Black Politics*, 268; Wilson, *Negro Politics*, 141–42; Hirsch, *Second Ghetto*, 246–48; Hirsch, "Cook County," 72.

79. Travis, *Black Politics*, 260–64.

80. Ibid., 268; also see 267.

81. Ibid., 303.

82. Warren W. Lehman, "Speculation in Color: Racial Transition in Chicago" (unpublished ms.), 4–7, MJS Papers.

83. Favil Berns interview, June 10, 2001, 7; MJS, speech, "Mr. Chairman, Reverend Ministers, Dearborn Real Estate Panel, and Guests," March 26 and 27, 1958, 4; MJS, speech, "Human Relations Committee of the City Club," March 11, 1958; also see "Excerpts from a Speech by Mark J. Satter to the Human Relations Committee of the City Club," IAF (Alinsky) Papers, folder 163, UIC.

84. Minutes of meeting of the Housing Advisory Committee of the Chicago Commission on Human Relations, Oct. 16, 1957, MJS Papers; Berns interview, 7.

85. Jeffrey Michael Fitzgerald, "The Contract Buyers League: A Case Study of Interaction between a Social Movement and the Legal System" (Ph.D. dissertation, Northwestern University, 1972), 277, 285; also see 271–78; William Dendy, "Judge Orders CBL Eviction Trial Tuesday," *NW*, Feb. 21, 1969.

86. Berns interview, 9.

87. Ann Stull, "Housing Speculators," *Community* 17, no. 11 (July 1958), MJS Papers. This article focused on my father's work on the Boltons' case and others like it.

88. Berns interview, 10.

89. *Albert Bolton and Sallie Bolton v. Gerald H. Crane and Jay Goran*, Amended Complaint in Chancery, 57s6577, filed July 28, 1958, 1–3, CCCC.

90. Ibid., 7–8.

91. Ibid., 3, 6, 2. The complaint admitted that the Boltons had fallen behind on a contract payment and had been served with a forcible entry and detainer, or eviction, notice. My father and Berns also admitted that the law offered little remedy to the Boltons, since Illinois's Forcible Entry and Detainer statute accepted only the "highly technical defense" that those served with an eviction notice did not receive the notification. Nevertheless, they requested that the eviction be stopped and that Goran be forced to account for the mysterious fees he had charged since the sale. They asked that the articles of agreement for warranty deed that the Boltons had signed be altered to reflect the true value of the property. They asked, in short, that the Boltons be given the opportunity to buy the property for the price that Goran and Crane had paid so recently—$4,300, plus interest. If that was outside the court's power, then it should render the contract sale void and return to the plaintiffs all the money they had paid thus far.

92. Lehman, "Speculation in Color," 7; MJS, "Land Contract Sales in Chicago."

93. Lehman, "Speculation in Color," 5; MJS, "Attorney Reveals Unethical Actions in Property Sales," *CDD*, April 26, 1958; Norris Vitchek as told to Alfred Balk, "Confessions of a Block-Buster," *Saturday Evening Post*, July 14–21, 1962, 19; Berns interview.

94. Lehman, "Speculation in Color," 5; also see MJS, speech, "Dearborn Real Estate Panel," March 26 and 27, 1958, 6–7.

95. "4 Die: Mother Grabs, Loses Baby in Fire," *CA,* Jan. 20, 1958, MHPC 76–102, box 5, folder 1, UIC.

96. "4 Die in Fire in Illegally Built Rooms," *CT,* Jan. 21, 1958; "4 Die: Mother Grabs"; "3 Adults, Infant Die in South Side Fire," *CDN,* Jan. 20, 1958, all in MHPC 76–102, box 5, folder 1; "Charge Two, Fire Jury Asks," *CT,* Jan. 31, 1958, in IAF (Alinsky) Papers, folder 49, UIC.

97. "Burning Sacrifices," *CST,* Jan. 27, 1958; "Slum Owners Surrender in Probe of Fire," *Chicago Sunday Tribune,* Feb. 2, 1958, IAF (Alinsky) Papers, folder 49, UIC.

98. W. N. Sutherland, "4 Points Offered to Halt Slum Fires," *CA,* Jan. 29, 1958; "Burning Sacrifices"; "They're All Guilty," *CDD,* Jan. 27, 1958, all in IAF (Alinsky) Papers, folder 49, UIC.

99. "Slum Fire Verdict: It's Manslaughter," *CDN,* Jan. 30, 1958; "Charge Two, Fire Jury Asks," *CT,* Jan. 31, 1958; "Lenders Map Plan to Aid Slum War," *CDN,* March 4, 1958.

100. "Sees Danger in Slum Proposal," *CDD,* Feb. 3, 1958, IAF (Alinsky) Papers, folder 49, UIC.

101. "They're All Guilty"; see "Burning Sacrifices"; "Charge Two, Fire Jury Asks."

102. "4 Die: Mother Grabs."

103. "Charge Two." This explains why Alice Butler had initially told authorities that she had obtained a permit for the conversion ("4 Die in Illegally Built Rooms").

104. "Slum Fire Verdict"; "Charge Two."

105. MJS, speech, "Talk Prepared by Mark J. Satter for Delivery before City Club of Chicago, Monday, May 2, 1960, Farwell Hall, Central YMCA"; letter, MJS to Paul Gapp, Oct. 31, 1960, 4; letter, MJS to Jim [Hurlbut], July 18, 1962, 5.

106. "Loan Bankers Make Slums, Says Lawyer," *CA,* March 12, 1958, MJS Papers; MJS, speech, "Human Relation Committee of the City Club," March 11, 1958. Also see "Excerpts from a Speech by Mark J. Satter to the Human Relations Committee of the City Club," IAF (Alinsky) Papers, folder 163, UIC; MJS, speech, "Dearborn Real Estate Panel," March 26 and 27, 1958.

107. MJS, speech, "A Talk Prepared by Mark J. Satter for Delivery at South Shore Temple, Friday, October 31, 1958," 8; also see "Talk Prepared by Mark J. Satter for Delivery before Decalogue Society of Lawyers, July 17, 1958."

108. MJS, speech, "Talk Prepared by Mark J. Satter for Delivery before Catholic Conference for Interracial Justice, Loyola University, August 29, 1958."

109. See MJS, speech, "Talk before Alpha Phi Alpha Fraternity at Good Shepherd Congregational Church," March 23, 1958.

110. "Hear Atty. Mark J. Satter Expose the Conspiracy between the Mortgage Bankers and Insurance Underwriters to Deliver the Property of Negroes into the Hands of the Exploiters," the meetings' handbills exhorted. MJS Papers.

111. MJS, speech, "Dearborn Real Estate Panel," March 26 and 27, 1958.

112. Ibid.

113. "Second Suit Charges Fraud in Sale of Flats to Negro," *CDN,* Feb. 4, 1958; "Hits Gouge of Negroes on Homes," *CST,* March 27, 1958; MJS, "Lawyer Reveals Unethical Actions in Property Sales," *CDD,* April 26, 1958; "Suit Charges Excessive Realty Sales Overpayment," *CDN,* June 2, 1958; Stull, "Housing Speculators"; "Pair Sue, Accuse Realtor in Housing Transaction," *CA,* Aug. 13, 1958; "Postpone Eviction of Negro Family," *CDN,* April 22, 1959; "Real Estate Speculation Foe Appeals," *CDN,* Aug. 5, 1959; "Lone Lawyer Pioneers a New Way to Fight Blockbusting Racket," *House and Home,* Oct. 1959, all in MJS Papers.

114. "Lone Lawyer Pioneers." Also see MJS, speech, "Talk by Mark J. Satter Prepared for Greater Lawndale Commission," June 17, 1958, 5; Stull, "Housing Speculators"; letter, Mrs. Clayton to Mark Satter, Oct. 20, 1958, in which she thanks him for saving the home of Clarence Glenn.

115. As my father stated in a typical speech, "I take the simple stand that . . . value for real estate should be the same to one man as another" (MJS, "Human Relations Committee of the City Club," March 11, 1958).

CHAPTER THREE: JUSTICE IN CHICAGO

1. He argued that "in usual circumstances" the real estate broker brings together the buyer and the seller of property, the mortgage banker provides the funds so that the buyer can pay the seller in full, and the attorney ensures that the client gets the title to the property. "Between each of these men and his client . . . there is a relationship of the most sacred trust. But the moment . . . a Negro man seeks to purchase . . . all these elements of honesty and trust break down." The mortgage banker "arbitrarily and capriciously refuses to make loans to Negro people." Instead of guarding their clients' interests, the real estate broker and the attorney conspire against them to grab "a commission for themselves of two and three times the very cost of the houses involved." See MJS, speech, "Talk Prepared by Mark J. Satter for Delivery before Catholic Conference for Interracial Justice, Loyola University, August 29, 1958."

2. "Postpone Eviction of Negro Family," *CDN*, April 22, 1959; *Sallie Bottom and Jessie Jackson v. Frank Bishofberger and Iloe Bishofberger*, Superior Court of Cook County, docket 59s6201, filed April 11, 1959, CCCC.

3. According to the complaint, Lewis bought the property with a $500 down payment and a $3,000 mortgage, on which he paid $50 a month. In turn, the Sheltons paid Lewis $1,000 down and $100 a month. They also paid all taxes, insurance, and maintenance costs of the property (*Henry Taylor Shelton, Elizabeth Shelton, Charles B. Wilburne, Mary E. Wilburne, and Willie L. Wilburne v. A. B. Lewis*, Circuit Court of Cook County, docket 58c11408, filed Aug. 13, 1958, CCCC; MJS, speech, "Catholic Conference for Interracial Justice," Aug. 29, 1958, 6).

4. *Johnnie James and Marylue James v. Charles M. Peters, Jr. and Arthur Krooth*, Superior Court of Cook County, docket 59s9666, filed Aug. 4, 1959, CCCC; *Johnnie James et al. v. Charles M. Peters et al.*, "Report of Proceedings," 59s9666, 9, CCCC.

5. The couple also did not realize that Charles Peters, the brother of Warren J. Peters, was part of a notorious family of real estate agents who had been speculating in "racially changing" Chicago neighborhoods since the early 1940s ("Real Estate Speculation Foe Appeals," *CDN*, Aug. 5, 1959; *James v. Peters and Krooth*, "Report of Proceedings," 9; also see "Here Are City Slumlords," *CDN*, May 21, 1963, and MHPC, "Housing Code Violations by Warren J. Peters and Associates," MHPC 74-20, box 14, folder 164, UIC).

6. The precise amount of the remaining balance was either incorrectly cited or in dispute, but sources state it as between $10,000 and $10,800. See "Real Estate Speculation Foe Appeals"; *James v. Peters and Krooth*, "Report of Proceedings," 9, 14, 34, 35, 37; "Answer of Krooth to Petition for Injunction," June 24, 1959.

7. "Charges Trickery in Sale of Home," *CDN*, April 12, 1958; "Charges $6000 Real Estate Gyp," *CDD*, April 12, 1958; "Real Estate Case Ruling Is Hailed," *CDN*, Nov. 25, 1960; *Mary Moore v. Harold A. Pinkert, Joseph M. Dvorak, Anthony Broccolo, and George Kotas*, Circuit Court of Cook County, docket 58c5038, filed April 9, 1958, CCCC.

8. This is why approximately 90 percent of slum property in Chicago was held in land trusts by the early 1960s. See Nicholas Shuman, "Land Trusts Worth While,"

CDN, April 28, 1960; Dean Schoelkopf, "Land Trust Law Shields Slumlords," *CDN,* May 28, 1963.

9. The real estate speculators' complicated systems of trusts and corporations also made it easier for them to evade housing court summonses. See Pamela Zekman and Jerry Thornton, "Winning Con Game in Slums," *CT,* May 11, 1973.

10. Quote is from *Shelton v. Lewis,* 58c11408, Second Amended Complaint in Chancery, but nearly identical phrasing is in all of my father's contract sale cases.

11. Rose Helper, *Racial Policies and Practices of Real Estate Brokers* (Minneapolis: University of Minnesota Press, 1969), 191–94, 196; also see 122, 200. The Chicago Real Estate Board represented only "realtors," who were the elite of Chicago brokers, but their guidelines set the moral and ideological tone for the profession as a whole. See Helper, *Racial Policies,* 88.

12. Ibid., 30–31. Although it was difficult to get the initial interviews, once the men agreed to speak to her "they spoke openly and emotionally, pounding on the desk at times and swearing."

13. Ibid., 166–67.

14. Ibid., 30, 45, 75, 89, 91, 111, 170, 174–75.

15. Ibid., 90, 174; also see 88–91.

16. Ibid., 119; also see 122, 138, 201.

17. Ibid., 118, 99, 69, 80. Many realtors did acknowledge class differences among blacks. They praised the "respectable and prosperous" class who cared for their property. See Helper, *Racial Policies,* 59.

18. Ibid., 78, 136, 78, 163; also see 137–38. See Amanda Irene Seligman, "'Apologies to Dracula, Werewolf, Frankenstein': White Homeowners and Blockbusters in Postwar Chicago," *Journal of the Illinois State Historical Society* 94, no. 1 (Spring 2001): 82.

19. Norris Vitchek as told to Alfred Balk, "Confessions of a Block-Buster," *Saturday Evening Post,* July 14–21, 1962, 18; Helper, *Racial Policies,* 156, 62; Gertrude Goran interview, April 17, 2001.

20. Helper, *Racial Policies,* 162, 173; Seligman, "Apologies," 70–72, 85–88. Also see anti-Semitic quotes in report, Chicago Commission on Human Relations (Augustine J. Bowe, Chairman) to Mayor Martin H. Kennelly, Dec. 10, 1949, on Peoria street riot, given to me by Ed Holmgren but also in Municipal Reference Library, Chicago, 21, 26, and especially 27; William Peters, "Race War in Chicago," *New Republic,* Jan. 9, 1950, 10–12.

21. Helper, *Racial Policies,* 174, 89.

22. As Helper explained, the speculator "does what other real estate men do not want to do, or do not think they should do, or will not admit they are doing—act as a go-between for the white seller and the Negro buyer in an area still white or nearly so" (*Racial Policies,* 172–73; also see 175–76).

23. Ibid., 183, 184; also see 190.

24. Ibid., 174.

25. Meyer Levin, *The Old Bunch* (Secaucus, N.J.: Citadel Press, 1985 [1937]), 304–5.

26. *Harry Bernard and Bernice Bernard, His Wife, v. Gerald H. Crane,* Superior Court of Cook County, 60s5047, filed March 18, 1960, Deposition of Bernice Bernard, 13, CCCC; "Phony Names, Land Trusts Used to Profit from Squalor," *CT,* May 6, 1973.

27. Goran interview.

28. Favil Berns interview, June 10, 2001, 25; see Helper, *Racial Policies,* 172, 176.

29. Michael Kalika, "Realtor Defends 'Buying on Contract' for the Public," *Lawndale Times,* June 19, 1958; see "Debate Contract Selling at GLCC Meeting," *GLCC News Notes,* July 23, 1958; "Urge Loan Groups Run by Negroes," *CDN,* June 18, 1958, all in MJS Papers.

30. Examination of Jay Goran, early Jan. 1976 (dates illegible on copy), in "Abstract of Testimony in First Trial," *Ruth and James Wells v. F & F Investment*, USDC docket 69c15, 1947, see 2085, in box 4, JBA. Crane made this pitch, as did speculator Lou Fushanis. See *Bernard v. Crane*, 60s5047, "Deposition of Bernice Bernard," 7; John Culhane, "His First Day 'Selling' Slums," *CDN*, May 25, 1963.

31. Culhane, "His First Day 'Selling' Slums."

32. Berns interview, 49, 54, 51.

33. Helper, *Racial Policies*, 64, 107; Lestre Brownlee, "Decentralizing Negroes Is a Thorny Problem," *CA*, April 26, 1958, in MJS Papers.

34. Arnold R. Hirsch, *Making the Second Ghetto: Race and Housing in Chicago, 1940–1960* (Chicago: University of Chicago Press, 1983), 182; Ellen Herman, *The Romance of American Psychology* (Berkeley: University of California Press, 1995), 174–237.

35. Frank T. Cherry, "Southern In-Migrant Negroes in North Lawndale, Chicago, 1949–59: A Study of Internal Migration and Adjustment" (Ph.D. dissertation, University of Chicago, 1965), 117; James N. Gregory, *The Southern Diaspora* (Chapel Hill: University of North Carolina Press, 2005), 108; also see 103–7.

36. See testimony of Chicago Urban League president Edwin C. Berry, *Hearings before the United States Commission on Civil Rights: Housing* (Washington: United States Printing Office, 1959), 843.

37. Berns interview, 48.

38. Vitchek as told to Balk, "Confessions," 19; also see Helper, *Racial Policies*, 78, and Hirsch, *Second Ghetto*, 61.

39. Ann Stull, "Housing Speculators," *Community* 17, no. 11 (July 1958), MJS Papers.

40. This attorney had purchased a property that his clients were interested in, inflated the price, resold the property to the clients on contract, and then convinced his clients to pay him an additional fee of $1,000 for saving them money. See *Boysie Coleman and Mearlee Coleman v. Samuel A. Aronfeld*, Circuit Court of Cook County, docket 58c7239, filed May 22, 1958, CCCC.

My father reported the threats to Bob Schultz, a *Chicago Daily News* reporter. "Satter said that the publicity he's had in the D[aily] N[ews]; his articles in the Bar Association Review; his appearance before a number of groups . . . (and the attendant publicity in local papers)—has got a lot of the real estate speculators sore. He thinks many of these people are out to get him—either his reputation or, perhaps, personal harm," Schultz told his editor. See "Memo City Desk," July 2, 1958, *Chicago Sun-Times* clipping morgue under subject "Mark J. Satter." My thanks to Amanda Beeler and Mike Sneed for making this memo available to me.

41. Berns interview, June 10, 2001, 16, 26, 7; Les Brownlee interview, Feb. 17, 2001.

42. MJS, speech, "Dearborn Real Estate Panel," March 26 and 27, 1958, 9.

43. "Notes on the Deposition of J. Goran in the Case of Albert Bolton and Sallie Bolton," 12, 8, 2, 7, 9, 11, 5, IAF (Alinsky) Papers, folder 163, UIC.

44. *Albert Bolton and Sallie Bolton v. Gerald H. Crane and Jay Goran*, Superior Court of Cook County, docket 57s6577, filed May 3, 1957, "Motion to Dismiss," CCCC.

45. MJS, speech, "Talk Prepared by Mark J. Satter for Delivery before City Club of Chicago," May 2, 1960.

46. *Shelton v. Lewis*, 58c11408, "Motion to Strike Third Amended Complaint."

47. *James et al. v. Peters et al.*, 59s9666, "Report of Proceedings," 27–28.

48. *Moore v. Pinkert et al.*, 58c5038.

49. "Home Payment Chain Drags Man to Grave," *CDN*, Aug. 13, 1960; "'Let Buyer Beware'—Home Sale Ruling," *CDN*, June 14, 1960.

50. *William H. Coleman and Wilma R. Coleman, His Wife, v. Jay Goran, Gerald Crane, and W. F. Smith,* Superior Court of Cook County, docket 58s20591, filed Dec. 16, 1958, "Complaint in Chancery," CCCC.

51. *Coleman v. Goran, Crane, and Smith,* 58s20591, "Motion to Strike and Motion to Dismiss Plaintiffs' Suit."

52. *Coleman v. Goran, Crane, and Smith,* 58s20591, "Amended Complaint in Chancery."

53. *Coleman v. Goran, Crane, and Smith,* 58s20591, "Motion to Strike Amended Complaint in Chancery."

54. *Coleman v. Goran, Crane, and Smith,* 58s20591, Order, Dec. 7, 1959.

55. MJS, "Brief and Argument for Appellants," *Coleman v. Goran and Smith,* Appellate Court of Illinois, First District, Jan. term, 1960, 47992, 8–9, 11, 18, 16, 17, MJS Papers.

56. *William H. Coleman and Wilma R. Coleman, His Wife, v. Jay Goran and W. F. Smith,* Gen. No. 47,992, Appellate Court of Illinois, First District, Second Division, June 14, 1960, 168, *North Eastern Reporter,* 2nd series, 168 N.E. 2d 56.

57. "'Let Buyer Beware'—Home Sale Ruling"; "House Deal 'Fraud' Rehearing Sought," *CDN,* June 15, 1960. My father petitioned for a rehearing, but the petition was denied. See 26 Ill. App. 2d 288, *William H. Coleman and Wilma R. Coleman, His Wife, v. Jay Goran and W. F. Smith,* Gen. No. 47,992; also see MJS to Professor Schaffer and Professor Howery, Nov. 22, 1960, MJS Papers.

58. *Mary Moore, Appellant, v. Harold A. Pinkert et al., Joseph M. Dvorak, and George Kotas,* Appellees, Gen. No. 48,015, Appellate Court of Illinois, First District, Third Division, 28 Ill. App. 2d 320; 171 N.E. 2d 73; 1960 Ill. App. LEXIS 532; "Real Estate Case Ruling Is Hailed," *CDN,* Nov. 25, 1960.

59. Bertha Richards interview, April 8, 2002, 13, 12; also see 19–20. See Dempsey J. Travis, *An Autobiography of Black Chicago* (Chicago: Urban Research Institute, 1981), 86, for detail about face masks. A third sister, Lillie Cruscoe, was also among the founders of King David M. B. Baptist Church.

60. Richards interview, 2–3.

61. Ibid., 3, 18; *Mary Lee Stevenson et al. v. Louis Lidsker, Nathan Elkin, Moe M. Forman, Morris Gans, and the Chicago National Bank, a National Banking Association,* Circuit Court of Cook County, docket 58c7254, filed May 24, 1958, CCCC. The other plaintiffs were listed as follows: "Jessie Jeter, Lillie M. Jeter, his wife, Tony Murry and Pinky Murry, his wife, Joeanna Williams and Bertha L. Richard and Lawrence P. Richard, her husband, and Reginald Kent, on behalf of themselves and on behalf of Davis, Wilson, Williams, Pleasant, Mattox, Wheeler, Causey, Godlen, Milan, Harris, Patterson, Griggs, Wragg, Roebuck, J. E. Davis, S. Williams Vega, Tolston, Copeland and Anderson."

62. Richards interview, 9; Warren Lehman, "Speculation in Color" (unpublished ms.), 11, MJS Papers; *Stevenson et al. v. Lidsker et al.,* 58c7254.

63. Lehman, "Speculation in Color," 12.

64. *Stevenson et al. v. Lidsker et al.,* 58c7254; "Notes on a Case to Be Filed in the Circuit Court of Cook County, Plaintiffs Mary Lee Stevenson, Jesse Jeter," IAF (Alinsky) Papers, folder 163, UIC.

65. Richards interview, 10, 9, 21.

66. *Stevenson et al. v. Lidsker et al.,* 58c7254, 5–6, 12; Lehman, "Speculation in Color," 12; "Suit Charges Excessive Realty Sales Overpayment," *CDN,* June 2, 1958. My father's arguments were highly contextual. He hoped that a full understanding of his clients' situation might enable the court to see them as people who were "particularly subject to exploitation" and who could thereby be offered legal protection without "bringing into question profits legitimately made in a really free market" (Lehman, "Speculation in Color," 13).

67. "Suit Charges Excessive Realty Sales Overpayment"; *Stevenson et al. v. Lidsker et al.*, 58c7254.

68. Nicholas Shuman, "Negroes File Suit Alleging Gouge," *CDN*, Feb. 2, 1961; also see "Suit Charges Plot in Negro Realty Deals," *CT*, Feb. 3, 1961.

69. NARA, Records of the District Courts of the United States, Record Group 21, Northern District of Illinois, Eastern Division (Chicago), 1819–1994, Civil Records, 1871–1972, Civil Action Case Files, 1938–1969, Case File 61c178, *Mary Lee Stevenson et al. v. General Federal Savings and Loan Association et al.*

70. *Stevenson and Kent v. General Federal Savings and Loan*, USDC 61c178. I have greatly condensed this case. See docket for full arguments on both sides.

71. Mike Royko, *Boss: Richard J. Daley of Chicago* (New York: Dutton, 1971), 64; also see Milton Rakove, *Don't Make No Waves, Don't Back No Losers: An Insider's Analysis of the Daley Machine* (Bloomington: Indiana University Press, 1975), 221–32.

72. Letter, MJS to Jim [Hurlbut], July 18, 1962. Other sources indicate that racism played a role in at least some parts of the Chicago judiciary during these years. "The white prosecutors and judges who occupied the vast majority of . . . positions in the criminal courts told each other racist jokes every day, using exaggerated imitations of the defendants who appeared before them," one attorney recalled of the "overtly racist world of the Chicago criminal courts in the early 1960s" (John C. Tucker, *Trial and Error: The Education of a Courtroom Lawyer* [New York: Carroll and Graf, 2003], 12, 13).

73. Sallie Bolton interview, Oct. 11, 2001, 6, 9, 14, 17, 5.

74. The judges wrote that "a party in possession of his mental faculties is not justified in relying upon representations" of a property's value (Appeal from Superior Court, *Coleman v. Goran and Smith*, docket 47992, 6).

75. "Home Payment Chain Drags Man to Grave."

76. Richards interview, 11, 23, 22.

77. Letter, Julio Vivas to *House and Home*, April 15, 1958, requesting copy of their journal containing article about MJS, in GLCC Papers, box 6, folder "April 1–17, 1958," CHS. The GLCC publicized the suit filed by Mary Lee Stevenson, Joeanna Williams, and five other families against Moe Forman and his associates. "Top news in the area is a suit brought against a group of real estate operators [charged] with buying and selling real estate to Negroes at highly inflated prices," a GLCC news column noted, in MJS Papers.

The GLCC was an offshoot of the North Lawndale Citizens Council, the organization founded by the Jewish People's Institute in 1950 in response to the JPI's realization that the area was going through a "radical racial transition." See Introduction to the GLCC Papers, CHS; also see Alphine Wade Jefferson, "Housing Discrimination and Community Response in North Lawndale (Chicago), Illinois, 1948–1978" (Ph.D. dissertation, Duke University, 1974), 80–84; Amanda Irene Seligman, "Block by Block: Racing Decay on Chicago's West Side, 1948–1968" (Ph.D. dissertation, Northwestern University, 1999), 69–81.

78. The GLCC staff reported one "tangible result" of the meeting: the real estate operators of Lawndale were now organizing a group called the "Investors' Association for the Education of the People" (Harry Gaynor interview, Aug. 15, 2001; Raymond J. Carlyle, "Weekly Report," April 16–21, 1958, GLCC, box 6, folder "April 1–17, 1958," CHS). On Weinberg's contract selling activity, see "Realtor Orders CBLers' Arrest: Police Refuse," *NW*, March 29, 1968, and Exhibits 1 through 6, appended to *Contract Buyers*

League v. F & F Investment, 69c15, in C-ROA (Peggy Roach) Papers, box 2, folder "Peg/Contract Buyers League," UND. (Roach's papers have now been moved to WLA, LUC.)

79. He pointed out that their excuses for refusing mortgages to black Chicagoans were shabby. "I have heard it said that Negro people will not make the regular payments. Do the mortgage bankers know that for every $100 a month that a speculator pays to them, a Negro man pays between $200 and $300 a month?" ("Talk by Mark J. Satter Prepared for the Greater Lawndale Commission, Tuesday, June 17, 1958, at Sears YMCA," 1–4; "Debate Contract Selling at GLCC Meeting," *GLCC News Notes,* July 23, 1958, both in MJS Papers).

80. *GLCC News Notes,* July 23, 1958, 2; Michael Kalika, "Realtor Defends 'Buying on Contract' for the Public: Realtors Call Satter's Attack of Exploitation of Local Negroes Unfair, Misleading," *Lawndale Times,* June 19, 1958, in MJS Papers.

81. "Urge Loan Groups Run by Negroes," *CDN,* June 18, 1968; also see *GLCC News Notes,* July 23, 1958, 2, MJS Papers.

82. Carlyle, "Weekly Report," April 16–21, 1958 (date on this folder is inaccurate since the report contains information about the GLCC panel meeting of June 17, 1958), GLCC Papers, box 6, folder "April 1–17, 1958," CHS.

83. See MJS, "So You're Buying a Home," *GLCC News Notes,* July 1958 through January 1961, MJS Papers.

84. Letter, MJS to Miss Jane Weston, AFSC, March 8, 1962; transcript of MJS on *South Side Lights,* Oct. 4, 1962. Also see letter, MJS to Mr. Albert Jedlicka, March 27, 1962.

85. Hirsch, *Second Ghetto,* 204, 159; see letter, Vivas to Mr. Claude J. Peck, n.d., in GLCC Papers, box 11, folder "August 1959," CHS.

The GLCC initially hired my father to represent the new corporation in its land purchasing efforts, but he quickly had a falling out with the corporation and was fired. For details, see Minutes, GLCC Board of Directors Meeting, Aug. 25, 1959, GLCC Papers, box 11, folder "August 1959," CHS; "Report, GLCC Fact-Finding Committee Re: Lawndale Redevelopment Corporation," Sept. 10, 1959, in GLCC Papers, box 11, folder "Sept. 1–22, 1959," CHS.

86. Transcript of MJS on *South Side Lights,* Oct. 4, 1962; letter, MJS to Albert Jedlicka, March 27, 1962.

87. GLCC Report of Executive Director, Oct. 9, 1962, 4, 9, in GLCC Papers, box 19, folder "October 1962," CHS; Julio Vivas, *Report of Executive Director,* 8th Annual Report, 1964, 1, in GLCC Papers, folder 121, UIC.

88. Julio Vivas, *Report of Executive Director,* 1964.

89. Mrs. M. Berman, "Staff Report," and Minutes, Staff Meeting, August 17, 1959, in GLCC Papers, box 11, folder "August 1959," CHS.

90. Seligman, "Block by Block," 245–46; Jefferson, "Housing Discrimination," 101, 123.

91. Seligman, "Block by Block," 246–49; also see accounts in GLCC Papers, box 6, folder "April 1–17, 1958," CHS; Jefferson, "Housing Discrimination," 124, n. 95.

92. Jefferson, "Housing Discrimination," 122–23.

93. Ibid., 127–28, 152–54, 159; Seligman, "Block by Block," 159.

94. Jefferson, "Housing Discrimination," 152, 155. When angry black parents complained that "this sardine-can, half-time education is putting our children farther and farther back in their schedule of learning," school administrators blandly responded that there was no problem: their children would be able to receive a whole day's education in half a day (Seligman, "Block by Block," 166, 174). This claim was particularly unlikely given that many African Americans in Lawndale came from Mississippi, where their children received grossly inferior educations, thereby entering the Chicago public school system at a serious educational disadvantage. See Les Brownlee, "Schools, Jobs Lure Migrants," reprint from *CA*, "Pilgrims with Shopping Bags," 1962, MJS Papers.

95. Jefferson, "Housing Discrimination," 116.

96. Ibid., 121.

97. Ibid., 124; also see 152; "Rabbi to Quit West Side Area, Calls It Too Perilous," *CDN*, July 2, 1958, GLCC Papers, box 7, folder "July 1–24, 1958," CHS; Erich Rosenthal, "This Was North Lawndale: The Transplantation of a Jewish Community," *Jewish Social Studies* 22 (1960): 67, 76.

98. The note continued, "For a few lousy dollars commission you devaluate every building in our block. . . . Four of us property owners have pledged to get even with you even if it costs our lives. . . . As for that nigger who bought this place we will see how much guts he has when we start working on him" (Adolph J. Slaughter, "Urge Mayor to Act in Racial Flare-Up," *CDD*, Aug. 15, 1959; "FBI Requests Letter Sent to Real Estate Man," *CT*, Aug. 15, 1959; GLCC Board of Directors Meeting, Aug. 25, 1959, 2; "Cops Guard Site of Racial Tension," *CDN*, Aug. 7, 1959, all in GLCC Papers, box 11, folder "August 1959," CHS).

99. Gaynor rented an apartment in his own building to a black physician and his wife in the spring of 1957. In response, hundreds of whites mobbed his building and smashed twenty-one of the building's windows. The Gaynors' insurance company immediately canceled their insurance, a group of men fired eleven shots through the Gaynors' windows, and the family received numerous bomb and kidnapping threats. Although the police eventually quieted the block, they didn't protect the Gaynors. On May 6, 1958, the back of their building was bombed. "My little daughter's room is in back, and she could have been killed," Gaynor told reporters (GLCC Board of Directors Meeting, Aug. 25, 1959, 2, and "Urge Mayor to Act in Racial Flare-Up," both in GLCC Papers, box 11, folder "August 1959," CHS; Harry Gaynor interview, August 15, 2001; Jack Mabley, "Landlords Defy Bigotry: Now They Need Police Guard," *CDN*, July 23, 1958, GLCC Papers, box 7, folder "July 1–24, 1958," CHS).

100. "Negroes and the Changing Neighborhoods," *CDN*, Aug. 17, 1959, and "The Negro in a Chicago of Transition," *CDN*, Aug. 24, 1959, both in GLCC Papers, box 11, folder "August 1959," CHS. For more white responses, see "Nasty Bag of Fear Tricks Used to 'Bust Up' Blocks," *CDN*, Oct. 16, 1959; "'We Can't Keep Running,' Chatham Residents Moan," *CDN*, Oct. 21, 1959.

101. The Lawndale state of crisis was shown by the 1960 census, which reported that 40 percent of its buildings were substandard. It estimated that 82.1 percent of its housing was owned by absentee landlords, supporting my father's claim that 85 percent of the homes in Lawndale were sold to African Americans on contract. Median family income was $4,981, compared with the city average of $6,738. Where the city's unemployment rate average was 3.1 percent, Lawndale's male unemployment rate was 10 percent and its youth unemployment rate was 25 to 50 percent. The schools were grossly overcrowded, and the numbers of families on public aid were growing (Jefferson, "Housing Discrimination," 85, 153).

102. Memo, John A. McDermott, Catholic Interracial Council, "Background Information on the Meeting of Lawndale's Religious Leaders," Aug. 16, 1961, 3, and "Lawndale Clergymen in Christian Action," Minutes of Meeting of January 25, 1962, 3, in C-ROA (Peggy Roach) Papers, folder "Lawndale," UND (now at WLA, LUC).

CHAPTER FOUR: REFORM–ILLINOIS-STYLE

1. MJS, "A Public Utility Concept of Housing Today: A Path towards Savings" (unpublished ms.), 1.

2. MJS, speech, "Talk Prepared by Mark J. Satter for Delivery before Catholic Conference for Interracial Justice, Loyola University, Friday, August 29, 1958." Since he made this point repeatedly, I've merged two examples to form this quote; see 2, 9.

By accepting laws that were fundamentally unfair, he argued, society encouraged dishonest behavior. Individuals "accommodated" to unjust laws by adapting their actions to fit "the jungle code imposed upon [them]." But "just as men will 'accommodate' themselves by wrongful acts to oppressive laws, so will men 'accommodate' themselves by compliance with standards of honesty once these oppressive laws are removed" (MJS, "Wage Attachment and 'Accommodation,'" *Summons* [DePaul University Law School], Jan. 1964, 2–3). Also see MJS, "An Argument for Abolition of Wage Attachment," *Illinois Bar Journal,* Aug. 1964, 1037; letter, MJS to Mayor Richard J. Daley, Dec. 5, 1960, 6, for his argument that laws should be based on the realities of daily life rather than on tradition.

3. See "Arrest Spurs Credit Racket Drive," *CDN,* April 14, 1961, and "Credit Racketeer Drive Beefed Up," *CDN,* April 17, 1961.

4. They were kindred examples of how "the Negro [is] robbed and cheated at every turn in his dealings with white operators of real estate and of goods," my father wrote to a *Daily News* reporter (MJS to Al Jedlicka, March 27, 1962, 1).

5. MJS, "Wage Assignments and Garnishments Cited as Major Cause of Bankruptcy in Illinois," *Personal Finances Quarterly Report,* Spring 1961, 50. Pennsylvania outlawed all wage garnishment. My father's first article on the topic was "The 'Worker' Petition in Bankruptcy and Illinois Law Regarding Wages," *Chicago Bar Journal,* April 1959.

6. Letter, MJS to Maurice Fischer, Dec. 14, 1960; letter, MJS to Harry [Schaudt], March 24, 1960, 2; Nicholas Shuman, "Death of a Nobody Spurs Move to Reform Time Payment Laws," *CDN,* July 9, 1960.

7. Letter, MJS to Maurice Fischer, Dec. 14, 1960.

8. The Fair Credit Practice Board confirmed her findings. While the items sold were often inconsequential, merchants could "make more money out of garnishments than out of selling goods by ballooning the original note with attorney's fees, court costs and other add-on fees." See "She Protects Your Paycheck," reprinted from *Inland News,* May 1960, in booklet, *Consumer Credit,* prepared by the Chicago Commission on Human Relations, at the Municipal Reference Library, CPL; Nicholas Shuman, "How Pitchmen Bilk New Bankrupts Here," *CDN,* Jan. 27, 1961. Also see MJS, "Illinois: Consumer Credit Jungle," *Loyola Law Times,* Jan. 1961; Nicholas Shuman, "Find Boss, Union Let Workers Down," *CDN,* Feb. 8, 1961; Shuman, "Death of a Nobody"; "More Buyer Protection Urged in Credit Abuses," *CST,* Jan. 26, 1965; "Defender of the Bankrupt Fights Garnishee!" *Muhammad Speaks,* March 12, 1965.

9. MJS, "'Worker' Petition in Bankruptcy"; letter, MJS to Irv Kupcinet, Jan. 30, 1962. Also see Lois Wille, "Credit Fanfare and Flop," *CDN,* Jan. 23, 1965; "Lawyer Fights to Salvage Victims of the Vultures," *Muhammad Speaks,* March 5, 1965; Nicholas Shuman, "How Pitchmen Bilk." Also see letter, MJS to Marty Faye, *ABC News,* Jan. 19, 1962.

Many noted that garnishments could lead to permanent unemployment. See "22 of 188 Men in Survey Blame Wage Assignment for Job Loss," *Human Relations News,* Feb. 1961, 3, GLCC Papers, box 15, folder "Feb. 6–28, 1961," CHS; Les Brownlee, "Dixie

Exodus May Bankrupt Illinois," *CA*, 1962 (reprint of Brownlee's series "Pilgrims with Shopping Bags"), author's possession. Also see Nicholas Shuman, "Greedy Vultures Find Easy Prey in Chicago's Installment Jungle," *CDN*, Jan. 21, 1961; letter, MJS to Daley, Jan. 5, 1960; "House OKs Credit Control Bill," *CDN*, April 11, 1961.

10. Most large companies had agreements with their unions that three garnishments justified firing the worker. Many small ones followed suit. Employers fired such workers in part because the wage assignment law gave the merchant the right to sue the employer if he or she did not divide the paycheck and pay what the merchant claimed was due. See "One Man Works—Another Man Collects His Pay," *Voice of 743*, Dec. 1960, MJS Papers. Also see letter, MJS to Bill [M. W. Newman], Feb. 25, 1963, and M. W. Newman, "Credit Law Reform Plans under Fire," *CDN*, March 23, 1963.

11. Nicholas Shuman, "Negroes File Suit Alleging Gouge," *CDN*, Feb. 2, 1961.

12. Wille, "Credit Reform Fanfare and Flop."

13. MJS, "The 'Worker' Petition in Bankruptcy"; MJS, "All That Money Can Buy," *CDD*, Jan. 20, 1959; also see columns of Jan. 29, 1958, Jan. 5, 1959, Feb. 23, 1959, Feb. 28, 1959, March 2, 1959, all in MJS Papers.

14. "Call Parley to War against Credit Gyps," *CDN*, Feb. 17, 1960; see Harry Schaudt, "The Tragedy of William Rodriguez," *CDN*, Feb. 8, 1960; Shuman, "Death of a Nobody"; "Urges State Repeal Creditors' Garnishee Law," *CDN*, Feb. 15, 1960.

15. Letter, MJS to Harry [Schaudt], March 24, 1960; also see letter, MJS to Ed Kandlik, Oct. 31, 1963; Sylvia Porter, "Too-Tough Laws on Garnishment Hike Bankruptcies," *CDN*, June 23, 1963.

16. "4 Curbs Proposed for Credit Abuses," *CST*, Nov. 30, 1960.

17. Ibid.; letter, MJS to Abner J. Mikva, Oct. 5, 1960, 4.

18. Letter, MJS to Ely M. Aaron, Nov. 23, 1960.

19. Alvin C. Adams, "Lawyer Blasts Firm's Proposal," *Chicago Defender*, Feb. 4–10, 1961. My father provides more detail on his charges in letter, MJS to Ely M. Aaron, Nov. 23, 1960, and letter, MJS to Daley, Dec. 5, 1960. Also see letter, MJS to Kupcinet, Jan. 30, 1962; Lewis Hunter, "Credit Can Bury You," *CC*, Nov. 6, 1962; Paul Gapp, "Credit Racketeers Target of Plan," *CDN*, n.d. (probably mid-April 1961).

20. "Calls Credit Law Proposals 'Fraud,'" *CDN*, Dec. 2, 1960; "Kup's Column," *CST*, Jan. 30, 1961, 26. The committee's chairman, Ely Aaron, tried to smooth things over. Mark Satter ought to be able to disagree with some of the committee's proposals "without making a lot of charges," he told the press (Alvin C. Adams, "Inland Denies Charge," *Chicago Defender*, Feb. 11–17, 1961). The Inland Steel representative on the mayor's committee, Dorothy Lascoe, also defended herself. "There's no solution but compromise," she said, adding that although the continuing garnishment provision saved bookkeeping costs for employers, "the debtor would save on attorney fees, too" (Paul Gapp, "Credit Reformers' Bickering Assailed," *CDN*, Jan. 14, 1961).

21. Transcript, MJS on *City Desk*, probably June 1961. Paul Satter made an audiotape of our father's appearance on this television show, which is its only surviving evidence. No date is given, but from the discussion I gather it ran in June 1961, just before the new laws were passed.

22. Nicholas Shuman, "New Credit Laws Put Heat on Gyp Retailers," *CDN*, July 1, 1961; Robert G. Schultz, "Senate Unit Delays Credit Control Bill," *CDN*, June 1, 1961; "Hails Credit Curb as Boon to Poor," *CDN*, July 5, 1961; also see Jack Lind, "Debtors Here Now Have a Chance to Be Heard; Go to Court under New Reform Law," *CDN*, n.d. (probably 1962).

23. Letter, MJS to *New City*, Dec. 4, 1962, 2; transcript of tape, MJS on *City Desk*, probably June 1961; "Attacks New Laws on Pay Seizure," *CDN*, June 29, 1961.

24. "Arrest Spurs Credit Racket Drive"; "Credit Raid Nets Suburb Salesman," *CDN,* May 24, 1961. I have been unable to determine the outcome of these cases.

25. "Senate Unit Delays Credit Control Bill," *CDN,* June 1, 1961; "Agree to Delay Garnishments: New Bureau Tackles Vending Fraud," *GA,* n.d., both in MJS Papers.

26. "17 File Suit against Vending Machine Firms," *Southwest News-Herald,* Aug. 10, 1961, MJS Papers.

27. "Agree to Delay Garnishments"; "Victim's Report on Vending Racket," *GA,* July 19, 1961; Sharon Bobbitt, "3 Agencies Out to Halt Vending Machine Racket," *GA,* July 6, 1961; "Residents Complain of Shady Vending Machine Proposition," *Southwest Side News,* July 13, 1961; "Check Vending Device Selling Abuses," *Saturday Times,* July 22, 1961; Sharon Bobbitt, "Slick Vending Racketeers Keep 'Just Inside' the Law," *GA,* July 19, 1961; Sharon Bobbitt, "Vending Machine Victims in Court," *GA,* Aug. 9, 1961; "Vending Machine Buyers Win Delay in Payments," n.p., Aug. 1961, all in MJS Papers.

28. "Vending Machine Buyers Consider Group Action," *GA,* possibly Aug. 2, 1961; also see "Agree to Delay Garnishments"; Harry W. Swegle, "Prospect Helps Spring Trap on Vending Firm Salesman," *CDN,* Aug. 9, 1961; Jack Mabley, "Psychology No Help to Sales Gyp," n.d. (probably Aug. 1961; gives humorous account of Detective Garcia's entrapment of a vending machine salesman); "Find Vending Devices Not Up to Code," *GA,* July 26, 1961, all in MJS Papers.

29. For individual cases, see V*ito Jonus v. Harmony Systems,* 61s13362, filed July 18, 1961; *Edmund Gable and Helen Gable v. Harmony Systems,* 61s14691, filed Aug. 7, 1961; *Edwin F. Holda v. Harmony Systems Inc., now known as Buffett, Inc., and Standard Finance Corporation,* 61s16100, filed Sept. 30, 1961, all in Superior Court of Cook County, CCCC; for joint action case, see *John D. Gibbs et al. v. Harmony Systems,* 44 Ill. App. 2d 37; 194 N.E. 2d 369; 1963 Ill. App. LEXIS 674; also see *John D. Gibbs et al. v. Harmony Systems, Inc., et al.,* Circuit Court of Cook County, 61c10866, filed Aug. 4, 1961, CCCC; also see Bobbitt, "Vending Machine Victims in Court."

30. "Vending Victims Lose Appeal," n.p., n.d.; "Court Weighs Vending Sale Scheme Feb. 5," *North West Suburban,* Jan. 17, 1962, both in MJS Papers.

31. "Court Weighs Vending Sale Scheme Feb. 5"; "Get Time to Reply in Court: 200 Buyers Claim Machines Sold Illegally," n.p., Nov. 16, 1961, MJS Papers.

32. As my father's appeal brief described it, the fraud they perpetrated was particularly ugly. By posing as potential employers, the defendants tried to "exploit the natural deference . . . of a 'job applicant' toward his 'employer.'" The vending machine sellers and finance companies were obviously conspiring. They worked closely together and appeared to be jointly owned. The defendant companies never denied the plaintiffs' charges of co-ownership (MJS, "Brief and Argument for Appellants," *John D. Gibbs et al. v. Harmony Systems, Inc., Overland Bond and Investment Corporation et al.,* 48863, Appellate Court of Illinois, Aug. term 1962, 9, 6, MJS Papers).

33. Ibid., 21.

34. Ibid., 23–24. He argued that the court had an opportunity to prevent such despoiling in the future. It should interpret the right to employment as a "property right" and, as such, "deserving the mantle of protection of a Court of Equity." He cited an 1890 statement by Brandeis and Warren: "The right to life has come to mean the right to enjoy life—the right to be let alone; the right to liberty secures the exercise of extensive civil privileges; and the term 'property' too has grown to comprise every form of possession—intangible as well as tangible." Now the Court should "extend that still growing concept of right of property." Courts already grant "protection to interference with the fruits of labor," he argued. "That right should be further defined by this Court, so that a . . . needed area of protection can be clearly set forth" (24–25).

35. *Gibbs v. Harmony,* 44 Ill. App. 2d 37; 194 N.E. 2d 369; 1963 Ill. App. LEXIS 674, Oct. 7, 1963; "Court Weighs Vending Sale Scheme Feb. 5."

36. *Gibbs v. Harmony,* 44 Ill. App. 2d 37, Oct. 7, 1963, 5–6.

37. "Vending Machine Victims Still Fight to Void Contracts," *GA,* Jan. 9, 1963.

38. "Hail Effect of Credit Reforms," *CDN,* Oct. 19, 1961; Hugh Hough, "Why Many Here File for Bankruptcy," *CST,* Jan. 27, 1963. Also see M. W. Newman, "Credit Law Reform Plans under Fire," *CDN,* March 23, 1963.

39. Lois Wille, "Success Takes a Licking," *CDN,* Jan. 23, 1965; also see "Tells How to Halt Credit Gouging," *CDN,* March 23, 1963, for King's account; "Credit Reform Law Called Failure," *CC,* Aug. 24, 1963.

40. Lois Wille, "Credit Reform Fanfare and Flop."

41. As Dorothy Lascoe explained: "The dealer says, 'In the month you had the car you got it in such bad shape that it's now worth only $200 instead of $1500.' . . . So he garnishes the man's pay for $1300, on a wreck of a car that was worth nothing in the first place. Then he finds another gullible buyer and sells it for $1500 again" (Wille, "Credit Reform Fanfare and Flop").

42. Wille, "Credit Reform"; Wille, "Success Takes a Licking." My father said that "Representative Little of Aurora" also owned a small-loan company; see letter, MJS to Bill (M. W. Newman), Feb. 25, 1963.

43. MJS to Bill [M. W. Newman], Feb. 25, 1963, 3; MJS, "Outlaw Garnishments," *Focus/Midwest,* July 1963.

44. His relationship with the *Daily News* began in 1958, when Paul Gapp covered his first contract sales lawsuits. Soon other *Daily News* reporters were interviewing him regularly. Reporters Paul Gapp, Bob Gruenberg, and Nick Shuman—who called my father "the best source I ever had"—became his friends. Others who worked with him included Georgie-Anne Geyer, Lois Wille, Harry Swegle, and M. W. Newman, who remembered my father as "a very intense, driven man" (Nicholas Shuman interview, Jan. 9, 2001; M. W. Newman interview, Jan. 10, 2001).

45. Fischer showed his respect by nominating Mark Satter for the Lane Bryant Award for Volunteer Service to the Community, a national honor, in 1960. See letter, Jerome E. Klein, Director, Lane Bryant Annual Awards, to "Candidate," June 1960, MJS Papers.

46. Favil Berns interview, June 10, 2001.

47. For example, see Robert Gruenberg, "A Plan to Ease Court Backlog," *CDN,* Aug. 6, 1960, and letter, MJS to Robert Gruenberg, Aug. 17, 1960; MJS to Maurice Fischer, Dec. 14, 1960, and "One Million Underdogs" series, *CDN,* Jan. 1961; MJS to Paul Gapp, Oct. 3, 1960, and Paul Gapp, "Renewal Officials Assail New Group," *CDN,* Oct. 7, 1960; MJS to Paul Gapp, July 16, 1964; letter, MJS to Bill [M. W. Newman], Feb. 25, 1963, and M. W. Newman, "Credit Law Reform Plans under Fire," *CDN,* March 23, 1963. Also see Warren Lehman, "Goodbye, Mark" (unpublished ms.), MJS Papers.

48. "Nasty Bag of Fear Tricks Used to 'Bust Up' Blocks," *CDN,* Oct. 16, 1959; Harry W. Swegle interview, Jan. 25, 2001.

49. "How to Erase Panic in Changing Areas," *CDN,* Oct. 24, 1959; Amanda Irene Seligman, "'Apologies to Dracula, Werewolf, Frankenstein': White Homeowners and Blockbusters in Postwar Chicago," *Journal of the Illinois State Historical Society* 94, no. 1 (Spring 2001): 76 and 91, n. 28.

50. Judon's employer told him to settle his debt or lose his job. He sent Judon on to his own attorney, Leonard Harris. By now Judon had additional debts for a gold watch and for children's clothing. Harris arranged a loan for Judon from Commonwealth Loan Company, which charged him high interest. The money was sent directly

to Harris, who then made weekly payments to Judon's creditors and of course to him-self as well (letter, MJS to Maurice Fischer, Dec. 14, 1960).

51. Letter, MJS to Maurice Fischer, Dec. 14, 1960.

52. Nicholas Shuman, "'Speculators' Get Quick Profits—Here's the Record," *CDN*, Jan. 24, 1961; also see Shuman, "How Sharpies Bilk Unfortunates Here," *CDN*, Jan. 23, 1961.

53. "Mortgage Credit Refusals Squeeze Minorities Here," *CDN*, Jan. 25, 1961. Shu-man noted that Chicago's new migrants were particularly vulnerable. In Puerto Rico, peddlers were trusted members of the community. Among Native Americans, the cul-tural value placed on harmony made it difficult to turn down persistent salesmen. "Often they will buy things they don't need and can't afford just to be pleasant," explained the director of Chicago's American Indian Center. In the rural South, a late payment meant the denial of credit by that merchant in the future—not the garnishment of one's wages. Shuman also described the costs of the racket. In 1960, gar-nishments took $14.5 million of workers' earnings in Illinois, while processing costs alone cost businesses $9 million a year (Shuman, "Greedy Vultures Find Easy Prey").

54. Shuman, "How Pitchmen Bilk New Bankrupts Here," *CDN*, Jan. 27, 1961. This article drew heavily upon Shuman's earlier article about Mark Satter's ideas, "Bank-ruptcy No Cure-All," *CDN*, Oct. 8, 1960. Shuman's "Bankruptcy" article in turn restated information my father had first presented in MJS, "'Worker' Petition in Bankruptcy."

55. "Daily News Honored for Local Coverage," *CDN*, Oct. 16, 1961, 3.

56. Alfred Balk interview, Feb. 18, 2001.

57. My father said these exact words to another reporter, but Balk recalls that he gave him a similar lead. Quote is in "'I Wrote Post Article, but I'm No Blockbuster,' Declares Satter," *GA*, Aug. 1, 1962; also see Balk interview; letter, Alfred Balk to David A. Satter, Dec. 27, 1967, DS Papers.

58. Balk interview.

59. Norris Vitchek as told to Alfred Balk, "Confessions of a Block-Buster," *Satur-day Evening Post*, July 14–21, 1962, 15–19.

60. Chicago Commission on Human Relations, "Selling and Buying Real Estate in a Racially Changing Neighborhood," June 14, 1962, GLCC Papers, box 19, folder "June 1–15, 1962," CHS; "Block Busting Tale Told by Human Relations Report," *Hyde Park Herald*, July 25, 1962, IAF (Alinsky) Papers, folder 88, UIC; letter, MJS to Jim [Hurlbut], July 18, 1962; MJS to Mayor Richard J. Daley, Feb. 19, 1964.

This was the second time my father worked with the commission, a city agency ded-icated to combating racial tension. The first time, in October 1957, he had described the dangers of contract selling, stressing the racial dynamics at play. Contract sellers' "conspiracy to defraud" was "usually perpetrated against Negroes who are particularly susceptible because of the tight housing market in the Negro community," he empha-sized. Unfortunately, while the CHR included antiracist activists, it was dominated by mortgage bankers and urban renewal proponents—among them Julian Levi. This may be why the CHR downplayed my father's warnings about the harm contract sales did to African Americans, stressing instead that such sales "compound[ed] problems of land clearance by inflating prices out of relation to values." The consumer education booklet that the CHR later released on the topic failed to acknowledge that contract selling had anything to do with race, concluding simply that "*the person entering into a contract to buy should do so with great caution.*" Like the city's courts, the CHR said "buyer beware," ignoring the fact that some buyers in Chicago—African Americans—had no other option if they were to buy at all. See Chicago Commission on Human Relations Housing Advisory Committee Minutes, Oct. 16, 1957, MJS Papers; Chicago Commission on Human Relations, "Questions and Answers on Housing," preliminary draft, Jan. 1958, MHPC 74–20, box 23, folder 728, UIC. For a history of the decline of the CHR as a force fighting racism, see Alan B. Anderson and George W. Pickering, *Confronting the Color Line: The Broken Promises of the Civil Rights Movement in Chicago* (Athens: University of Georgia Press, 1986), 55, 64; Arnold R. Hirsch, *Making the Second Ghetto: Race and Housing in Chicago, 1940–1960* (Chicago: University of Chicago Press, 1998 [1983]), 246.

61. CHR, "Selling and Buying," 9; Ben Holman, "Ask Training for Negro Home Buyers," *CDN,* July 20, 1962; "Installment Home Buying," *CDD,* July 26, 1962. The *Defender* also called for the exposure of "Negro real estate sharpies . . . who are taking advantage of their own people."

62. "Seek Racial Policy for Real Estate," *CT,* Aug. 10, 1962.

63. The show featured my father's words of advice to his fellow attorneys. "When our people come to us already enmeshed in problems of obligation far beyond their apparent ability to carry . . . the obligation of the lawyer remains strong nevertheless to . . . help these people, even though it may appear that by the letter of the law there is no help there," he said. "Our responsibility to the community does not end when people have made mistakes. If anything, our responsibility only then has its real beginning" (tape, *The House on Congress Parkway,* part 2, *Dateline Chicago,* Sept. 29, 1963). A member of my family made an audiotape of the second installment of the program, but not the first. Part 2 makes references to the first installment, however. Also see references to the show in L. F. Palmer and Paul Hunter, "Million Dollars a Day Cost of Being Black," *CC,* Nov. 3, 1962. Also see condolence note, John Gibbs, NBC News Chicago, to Mrs. Satter ("He provided the spirit and drive for our two documentaries about the slum house on Congress Parkway"), in MJS Papers.

64. "There is a total absence of protection given by the courts to folks who buy property on contract," the *CC* quoted my father. "Many mortgage and banking interests have entered into a conspiracy to see to it that Negroes pay from $2 to $3 for every $1 worth of shelter" (L. F. Palmer and Paul Hunter, "Law Backs Housing 'Racket,'" *CC,* Nov. 10, 1962). Also see Palmer and Hunter, "Million Dollars a Day Cost of Being Black," MJS Papers.

65. Lehman, "Goodbye, Mark," 7 ("Probably almost everything that's been written about Chicago speculators can be traced back to Mark Satter—the *Chicago Daily News* series on Panic Peddling, the T.V. documentary *House on Congress Parkway,* the public hearings of the Chicago Commission on Human Relations, and the *Saturday Evening Post* article on speculators, and the less known work of many others").

66. Letter, MJS to Jim [Hurlbut], July 18, 1962; MJS, "Will Probe Bring an End to 'Block-Busting' Racket?" *Chicago Defender,* Aug. 4–10, 1962; also see letter, MJS to Mr. Lloyd General, Aug. 1, 1962.

67. Len O'Connor comments, July 20, 1962, in Len O'Connor Papers, box 31, folder "Scripts, July 1962," 1–2, CHS; CHR press release, July 20, 1962, 2, GLCC Papers, box 19, folder "July 1962," CHS.

68. Gershon Braun, interview, July 28, 2002. Braun, my cousin, recalls watching the program.

69. The plumbing fixture fine had been publicized in the *Chicago Tribune,* which was never friendly to my father's work, under the headline "Mark Satter Fined $25 in Housing Court." To add further insult, the *Tribune* said, "Also given a suspended fine of $25 . . . was the Friendly Loan Corp.," run by contract seller Lou Fushanis, one of my father's long-standing targets. See "Mark Satter Fined," *CT,* Feb. 16, 1961, in GLCC Papers, box 15, folder "Feb. 16–28, 1961," CHS; letter, Ritz (Maurice) Fischer to MJS, July 23, 1962. On my father's feelings about the show, see Les Brownlee interview, Feb. 17, 2001, and Braun interview. Also see Seligman, "Apologies to Dracula," 71.

70. Letter, Clarice Satter to "Whom It May Concern at NBC"; also see letter, Jim Hurlbut to Clarice Satter, Aug. 2, 1962, MJS Papers.

71. "'I Wrote Post Article, but I'm No Blockbuster,'" *GA,* Aug. 1, 1962; also see Seligman, "Apologies to Dracula."

72. Letter, MJS to Nicholas Shuman, May 8, 1961; also see letter, MJS to Irv Kupcinet, Jan. 30, 1962, 2; letter, MJS to *New City,* Dec. 4, 1962; MJS to Bill [M. W. Newman], Feb. 25, 1963; MJS, "Outlaw Garnishments."

73. Letter, MJS to Shuman, May 8, 1961; also see Alvin C. Adams, "Inland Denies Charge," *Chicago Defender,* Feb. 11–17, 1961; letter, MJS to Richard J. Nelson, Feb. 13, 1961. My father also accused "several disconnected groups of Negro men" of soliciting funds from men who exploit blacks. These groups knew "full well that the great bulk of men who traffic in the Negro community are vulnerable to such money solicitation and of course that these men are also possessed of the funds which they have taken from the Negro people. The matter of the solicitation is cloaked in all form of virtuous endeavor" (letter, MJS to Jim Hurlbut, March 8, 1962). Also see letter, MJS to Al Jedlicka, March 27, 1962.

74. Dempsey J. Travis, *An Autobiography of Black Politics* (Chicago: Urban Research Press, 1987), 268.

75. Arvarh E. Strickland, *History of the Chicago Urban League* (Urbana: University of Illinois Press, 1966), 201, also see 200; Adam Cohen and Elizabeth Taylor, *American Pharaoh: Mayor Richard J. Daley: His Battle for Chicago and the Nation* (Boston: Little, Brown, 2000), 435. Korshak's cousin Ted owned a slum property. He claimed to be not particularly close to Marshall but admitted that "there is only one Korshak family in Chicago, and we're all part of it" (Mike Royko, "A Landlady vs. City Hall," *CDN,* Nov. 17, 1971). Also see Mike Royko, "Mr. Korshak's Memory Is Bad," *CDN,* Nov. 23, 1971.

76. Strickland, *Chicago Urban League,* 209.
One of the Chicago Urban League's stranger bedfellows was Charles Swibel, or "Flophouse Charlie." Swibel began his career working for Isaac Marks, one of Chicago's biggest slumlords. After making his fortune running skid-row flophouses—where Swibel refused to rent rooms to blacks, in violation of Illinois law—Swibel was appointed by Mayor Daley to the board of the Chicago Housing Authority. Yet CUL president Edwin Berry considered Swibel to be a close personal friend. Chicago progressives were often shocked to find Swibel at the parties Berry hosted in his home. While Swibel might not have influenced Berry, it was also true that Berry's friendship had no apparent effect on Swibel's understanding of race and housing. After years of maneuvering behind the scenes, Swibel became head of the Chicago Housing Authority in 1967. The result was what one would expect out of a public housing authority run by a slumlord. A 1982 federal study reported that, under his leadership, the CHA became one of the "worst" managed public housing authorities in the nation. Swibel ran the CHA for the sole purpose of the "acquisition of as many Federal . . . dollars as possible for the creation of patronage jobs and financial opportunities." Retaining him as CHA head, the report concluded, was "unconscionable." See James R. Ralph Jr., *Northern Protest: Martin Luther King, Jr., and the Civil Rights Movement* (Cambridge: Harvard University Press, 1993), 292, n. 72; John McKnight interview, July 6, 2001; Cohen and Taylor, *American Pharaoh,* 199; Arnold R. Hirsch, "The Cook County Democratic Organization and the Dilemma of Race, 1931–1987," in Richard M. Bernard, ed., *Snowbelt Cities: Metropolitan Politics in the Northeast and Midwest since World War II* (Bloomington: Indiana University Press, 1990), 78.

77. Transcript of MJS on *South Side Lights,* Oct. 4, 1962.

78. Sanford D. Horwitt, *Let Them Call Me Rebel: Saul Alinsky, His Life and Legacy* (New York: Vintage Books, 1992), 6; also see 14, 28, 194–95.

79. Ibid., 8–9. Saul had a younger brother who died very young; the death made his mother even more protective of him.

80. Ibid., 6–15, 23–33, 46–55, 79, 105.

81. Bernard O. Brown, *Ideology and Community Action: The West Side Organization of Chicago, 1964–67* (Chicago: Center for the Scientific Study of Religion, 1978), 19, 85.

82. Horwitt, *Call Me Rebel*, 383; Kris Ronnow interview, Sept. 26, 2003; also see Peter H. Rossi and Robert A. Dentler, *The Politics of Urban Renewal: The Chicago Findings* (Glencoe, Ill.: Free Press, 1961), 226, n. 1, and 233. See Horwitt, *Call Me Rebel*, 80–81, for an example of Alinsky and his organizers practically shaking down local businesses for financial support; also see 183.

83. See Horwitt, *Call Me Rebel*, 277–78, for example.

84. Ibid., 166; also see 175–76.

85. Marjorie Frisbie, *An Alley in Chicago: The Life and Legacy of Monsignor John Egan*, commemorative ed. (Franklin, Wisc.: Sheed & Ward, 2002), 22–26; John T. McGreevy, *Parish Boundaries: The Catholic Encounter with Race in the Twentieth-Century Urban North* (Chicago: University of Chicago Press, 1996), 42–44; Steven M. Avella, "Reynold Hillenbrand and Chicago Catholicism," *U.S. Catholic Historian* 9, no. 4 (Fall 1990): 353–70.

86. Frisbie, *Alley in Chicago*, 22–26; McGreevy, *Parish Boundaries*, 42–44; Avella, "Reynold Hillenbrand," 353–70.

87. Frisbie, *Alley in Chicago*, 22, 9, 34.

88. Ibid., 34, 29; also see 36–37. "Wary appraisal" is a quote from Frisbie, not Egan.

89. Carl R. Rogers, "The Necessary and Sufficient Condition of Therapeutic Personality Change," *Journal of Consulting Psychology* 21, no. 2 (1957): 96.

90. Frisbie, *Alley in Chicago*, 68; also see 47–70; Peggy Roach interview, Oct. 13, 2001, 4; Thomas O'Gorman, "An Interview with Patty Crowly, Co-Founder of the CFM," *U.S. Catholic Historian* 9, no. 4 (Fall 1990): 457–67.

91. "Samuel Cardinal Stritch," www.stritch.edu/content.aspx?id=1992 accessed May 7, 2008; also see Frisbie, *Alley in Chicago*, 2, 47, 69, 75.

92. McGreevy, *Parish Boundaries*, 85–86; also see 92.

93. Nicholas R. Shuman, "600 Students Get Facts to Wage Race Bias War," *CDN*, Dec. 9, 1958; 1958 Bishops' Statement on Race, author's copy provided by Peggy Roach (copy in Peggy Roach Papers, WLA, LUC).

94. Hirsch, *Second Ghetto*, 96, also see 59, 84–86; McGreevy, *Parish Boundaries*, 93.

95. McGreevy, *Parish Boundaries*.

96. Homer Jack, "Cicero Nightmare," *Nation*, July 28, 1951, 65. See Hirsch, *Second Ghetto*, 194, for more on white Catholic commitment to home ownership.

97. McGreevy, *Parish Boundaries*, 93; also see 17–19; Hirsch, *Second Ghetto*, 187–99.

98. McGreevy, *Parish Boundaries*, 128, 98.

99. Horwitt, *Call Me Rebel*, 270; also see 270–74; Frisbie, *Alley in Chicago*, 71–82.

100. Horwitt, *Call Me Rebel*, 305–8.

101. Frisbie, *Alley in Chicago*, 78–79.

102. Rossi and Dentler, *Politics of Urban Renewal*, 225–26; Horwitt, *Call Me Rebel*, 308.

103. Frisbie, *Alley in Chicago*, 95; also see "Hyde Park Is on the Move," *CDN*, April 23, 1959.

104. John Egan, "More Housing . . . Less Segregation," *NW*, May 16, 1958. The article was ghostwritten by Nicholas von Hoffman, but Egan served as the public face of the opposition. See Horwitt, *Call Me Rebel*, 372; Rossi and Dentler, *Politics of Urban Renewal*, 225–35; Hirsch, *Second Ghetto*, 165.

105. Press release, "Cardinal's Conservation Committee Replies to Remarks of Mr. Fred Kramer," July 11, 1958, 1, IAF (Alinsky) Papers, folder 188, UIC; William J. Gleeson, "Interracial Commission Examines Housing," *NW*, Sept. 5, 1958, 10; see Rossi and Dentler, *Politics of Urban Renewal*, 228.

106. Frisbie, *Alley in Chicago*, 100–101.

107. Many agreed with social conservatives like Foran that Egan had overstepped the boundaries of priestly duty. See letter, Daniel Cantwell to Jack [Egan], May 26, 1958, Cantwell Papers, box 20, folder 3, CHS.

108. Frisbie, *Alley in Chicago*, 98, 104–5.

109. Horwitt, *Call Me Rebel*, 373.

110. Ibid., 374; Frisbie, *Alley in Chicago*, 99.

111. Horwitt, *Call Me Rebel*, 323–24, 374–75; "Hyde Park Is on the Move." Also see Rossi and Dentler, *Politics of Urban Renewal*, 233.

112. M. W. Newman, "S.W. Side Gets Tough in War on Panic Peddlers," *CDN*, Sept. 2, 1960; Newman, "What Happens When White Neighbors Refuse to Panic," *CDN*, Sept. 3, 1960.

113. Frisbie, *Alley in Chicago*, 152; also see Horwitt, *Call Me Rebel*, 435.

114. For example, von Hoffman's response to an article in the *Christian Century*, May 10, 1960, claimed that the OSC was "an interracial organization" (22).

115. M. W. Newman, "How a S.W. Side Community Works for Racial Peace," *CDN*, Sept. 1, 1960; Horwitt, *Call Me Rebel*, 356, 430.

116. Horwitt, *Call Me Rebel*, 359; also see 357.

117. Harry W. Swegle, "Citizen's [*sic*] Aim Jab at Blockbusters," *CDN*, n.d.; Newman, "S.W. Side Gets Tough." Press reports said that the loans were made to "young couples," but Horwitt, *Call Me Rebel*, explains that, at least initially, these loans were "available only to whites" (426–27).

118. The square block detailed in "Selling and Buying Real Estate," on which twenty-nine out of thirty-three parcels were sold to black buyers on contract by 1961—including at least six sold by Gerald Crane and Jay Goran at huge markups—was barely a mile from the center of the OSC's territory. See Newman, "How a S.W. Side Community Works for Racial Peace"; CHR, "Selling and Buying," 2.

119. Horwitt, *Call Me Rebel*, 358, 430–31. Ironically, one of the actions that convinced the area's remaining whites to leave was a demonstration by black mothers organized by another Alinsky organization, TWO.

120. Ibid., 376, 385, 393–99; P. David Finks, *The Radical Vision of Saul Alinsky* (New York: Paulist Press, 1984), 144–46.

121. Arthur M. Brazier, *Black Self-Determination: The Story of The Woodlawn Organization* (Grand Rapids, Mich.: William B. Eerdmans, 1969), 38.

122. Nicholas Shuman, "Woodlawn to Parade for Credit Reform," *CDN*, March 3, 1961.

123. Ibid; Brazier, *Black Self-Determination*, 40.

124. Horwitt, *Call Me Rebel*, 407.

125. Transcript of MJS on *South Side Lights*, Oct. 1962; also see Brazier, *Black Self-Determination*, 45.

126. Brazier, *Black Self-Determination*, 39; Fink, *Radical Vision*, 149, 147.

127. Horwitt, *Call Me Rebel*, 423. When Alinsky learned that the University of Chicago wanted to demolish a mile-long, one-block-wide swath of housing in Woodlawn, he and von Hoffman felt that the "strip of land" coveted by the university was "of limited importance compared with the larger issues facing blacks in Woodlawn." In 1960, they even offered Julian Levi a deal: if he withdrew his opposition to Alinsky's funding application for a community organization in Woodlawn, Alinsky would withdraw his opposition to the university's plan. On the other hand, Alinsky warned, if Levi continued to oppose his fund-raising efforts, he would turn the "university's land grab in Woodlawn" into a public issue. It was only after Levi rejected the cease-fire offer that Alinsky decided to use the "land grab" to mobilize Woodlawn's residents. TWO protests ultimately resulted in a delay in Levi's urban renewal plans (Horwitt, *Call Me Rebel*, 376–78, 391–92; Fink, *Radical Vision*, 157).

128. Alinsky had been aware of the contract sales problem at least since 1958. Throughout that year his organizers closely followed my father's contract sale crusade, poring over his legal suits and taking detailed notes on his speeches. See typed reports in IAF (Alinsky) Papers, folder 163, UIC.

129. Brazier, *Black Self-Determination*, 43, 45.

130. Horwitt, *Call Me Rebel*, 423.

131. Fink, *Radical Vision*, 148.

132. See Charles M. Payne, *I've Got the Light of Freedom: The Organizing Tradition and the Mississippi Freedom Struggle* (Berkeley: University of California Press, 1995).

133. MJS, "A Public Utility Concept"; letter, MJS to Chicago City Missionary Society, Nov. 22, 1964. Also see Paul Gapp, "Study Proposes Handling Rental Housing as Public Utility," *CDN*, July 5, 1964, and letter, MJS to Paul Gapp, July 16, 1964.

134. Letter, MJS to Martin Farrell, Nov. 5, 1962. On Farrell and Alinsky, see memo, von Hoffman to Saul Alinsky, "Visit from Father Farrell," Sept. 17, 1958, IAF (Alinsky) Papers, 85–3, folder 1–9, UIC.

135. Letter, MJS to Paul Gapp, July 16, 1964; also see Gapp, "Study Proposes Handling Rental Housing as Public Utility."

136. Letter, MJS to Al Jedlicka, March 27, 1962.

CHAPTER FIVE: THE LIBERAL MOMENT AND THE DEATH OF A RADICAL

1. Favil Berns interview, June 10, 2001, 15, 31, 55, 32, 21, 18.

2. "Summary of the Report on Major Violators of the Building and Housing Code" and "Minutes of Meeting of the Code Enforcement Committee," MHPC, Oct. 17, 1962, both in MHPC 75-104, box 3, folder 7, UIC; Betty Flynn, "Slumlords Neglect Paintwork, Plaster and Children Suffer Lead Poisoning," *CDN*, May 31, 1963; Flynn, "Lead Poisoning Cases Spur New Appeal to Health Board," *CDN*, June 5, 1963.

3. Statement, John W. Baird, President, MHPC, Oct. 23, 1959, "File—Statements—MHPC," MHPC 74-20, box 24, folder 291, UIC.

4. "Recommendations for Making Code Enforcement Part of Total Plan to Maintain the City," draft 5, Jan. 15, 1963, 1–2, in MHPC 75-104, box 3, folder 7, UIC. See "Special Study of Housing Cases," June 30, 1946, MHPC 75-104, box 3, folder 5, for more background.

5. Lestre Brownlee, "Decentralizing Negro Is a Thorny Problem," *CA*, April 26, 1958, MJS Papers; Arnold R. Hirsch, "'Containment' on the Home Front: Race and Federal Housing Policy from the New Deal to the Cold War," *Journal of Urban History* 26, no. 2 (Jan. 2000): 158–89.

6. "Fair housing" and "open occupancy" were generally used interchangeably, though the former sometimes referred to legislation that prohibited realtors, but not private owners, from racial discrimination in the sale or rental of property. See Thomas M. Landye and James J. Vanecko, "The Politics of Open Housing in Chicago and Illinois," in *The Politics of Fair-Housing Legislation: State and Local Case Studies*, ed. Lynn W. Eley and Thomas W. Casstevens (San Francisco: Chandler, 1968), 87.

7. "Recommendations for Making Code Enforcement," Jan. 15, 1963; "Resolution," June 12, 1963, MHPC 75-104, box 3, folder 7; John Baird, "Statement of the Metropolitan Housing and Planning Council," May 23, 1963, MHPC 74-20, box 24, folder 295, UIC.

8. Prospectus, Fair Housing Service for Greater Chicago, April 1959, and Prospectus, Fair Housing Service of Greater Chicago, second draft, May 12, 1959, in Daniel Cantwell Papers, box 20, folder 5, CHS; HOME, *For All the People: The Right to Choose a Home* (pamphlet), Cantwell Papers, box 20, folder 4, CHS. Also see memo, John A. McDermott to Members of the Steering Committee, NCRR, Jan. 30, 1963, Cantwell Papers, box 14, folder "CCRR," CHS. For a list of those sponsoring open-occupancy legislation in 1965, see "Rally at State Capital Urges Open-Occupancy Measure," *CST,* May 19, 1965.

9. John W. Baird interview, Feb. 13, 2004; *Baird and Warner, Inc., 1855–1980: Celebrating 125 Years in Real Estate* (pamphlet, Baird and Warner, 1980).

10. Baird interview.

11. Statement made by John W. Baird, Aug. 9, 1962, GLCC Papers, box 19, folder "August 1962," CHS.

12. MJS, speech, City Club, Farwell Hall, Central YMCA, May 2, 1960.

13. MJS, speech, Vernon Missionary Baptist Church, Nov. 5, 1961, 5; also see MJS, "All That Money Can Buy," *CDD,* Feb. 6, 1960.

My father argued that in the absence of fair mortgage loans, open-occupancy legislation would benefit only "already economically secure families." He was correct. The pro-open-occupancy organization Freedom of Residence, for example, sent its members a report titled "100 Serious Cases of Housing Injustices," which listed high-income African Americans (earning over $10,000 a year). The injustice was that white bigotry prevented these well-to-do families from renting or purchasing property in various Chicago neighborhoods. The housing needs of moderate-income black families were entirely ignored. See Donald Frey, "100 Serious Cases of Housing Injustices," in Cantwell Papers, folder 6, Housing 1962–June 1963, CHS.

14. He offered his alternative solutions: "First, . . . savings and loan associations whose funds are insured by the Federal Government must, as a condition for continued insurance, show that their mortgage funds are invested in Negro areas in the same proportion as . . . [in] white [communities]. Existing law is sufficient to base a finding of discrimination should it be shown . . . that existing Negro communities are regularly blacklisted." Second, the courts must take action when "the value of a home triples as the Negro husband and father approaches." He concluded, "Add to available mortgaging, and honest pricing, a job security and freedom from garnishment of his wages," and black Chicagoans "will need no condescending 'open occupancy' laws." He added that while white-led open-occupancy groups "strut across the stage of self-proclaimed virtue," black Chicagoans show not the "slightest interest" in their proposals. "The burden of survival in the jungle society around them simply leaves no time for vicarious pleasures" (MJS, "Open Occupancy Legislation—Who Are the Hypocrites?" [unpublished manuscript]).

15. Ibid. See letter, MJS to *Community Magazine,* Sept. 26, 1962, for an early effort to get the essay published; letter, Richard Christiansen to MJS, July 6, 1965, for its final rejection.

16. "Debate Contract Selling at GLCC Meeting," *GLCC News Notes,* July 23, 1958, 2, MJS Papers. The details of how Moe Forman bought the Richards-Williams property with a loan from People's Federal are in a draft letter, MJS to [John] Ducey, April 28, 1961, in Bertha Richards file, MJS Papers. Also see *Mary Lee Stevenson et al. v. Louis*

Lidsker, Nathan Elkin, Moe M. Forman, Morris Gans, and Chicago National Bank, Circuit Court of Cook County, 58c7254, filed May 24, 1958, CCCC.

17. Letter, MJS to Walter Rojek, Dec. 15, 1960; letter, Rojek to MJS, Dec. 16, 1960; letter, Rojek to MJS, Feb. 13, 1961. My thanks to Bertha Richards for providing me with copies of this correspondence.

18. As president of the Dearborn Real Estate Board, Travis attempted to present an alternative perspective to the white media. He responded to the *Chicago Daily News* 1959 "Panic Peddlers" series, for example, with some historical perspective. "We advocate open occupancy, the only way to relieve our city of its title, 'most segregated large city,'" he said. "In contrast, you will find documented in the minutes of the Chicago Real Estate Board for April 4, 1917, a plan setting forth the policy of filling up one block with Negroes before permitting them to move into adjoining blocks. The realtors laid the ground rules for blockbusting 43 years ago." He added, "the term 'realtor' means for white only in Chicago. No Negro ever has been accepted. Color and not competence is the basis for membership in the Chicago Real Estate Board." See "How to Erase Panic in Changing Areas," *CDN,* Oct. 24, 1959, in CJEG-Egan II, box 29, UND.

19. At the 1958 GLCC panel, Al Ropa had encouraged African Americans to set up their own savings and loan associations. "Many of you people save your money outside your own community," he lectured the almost entirely black audience. "Bring that money in to Lawndale and set up your own association. If you don't have confidence in your own community, nobody else will" ("Urge Loan Groups Run by Negroes," *CDN,* June 18, 1958).

20. Dempsey J. Travis, *An Autobiography of Black Chicago* (Chicago: Urban Research Institute, 1981), 157–59.

21. Travis, *Black Chicago,* 160.

22. "The Battle Mounts," *CDN,* March 28, 1968. The other two banks were Lawndale National and Cosmopolitan National. Moe Forman eventually put the title to Joeanna Williams's property in a trust with Exchange National Bank; see letter, Moe Forman to MJS, Feb. 20, 1962, in Richards's file. Exchange National also held the property in question in *Henry Taylor Shelton et al. v. A. B. Lewis,* Circuit Court of Cook County, 58c11408, filed Aug. 13, 1958, CCCC.

23. Travis, *Black Chicago,* 160.

24. "Discuss Mortgages," *Bulletin,* in IAF (Alinsky) Papers, folder 85, UIC. The quote refers to the Travis Investment and Securities Company, which I assume is a subsidiary of the Sivart Corporation.

25. Travis, *Black Chicago,* 159. Specifically, African Americans controlled thirteen banks, twenty-seven savings and loan associations, four mortgage banks, and fifty life insurance companies ("Segregated Money: Negroes Seek to End Alleged Discrimination in Home Mortgage Field," *WSJ,* Oct. 25, 1962, in IAF [Alinsky] Papers, folder 85, UIC). In 1962, black-owned banks collectively held $71.3 million in assets, which constituted .0260 percent of total assets held by U.S. banks. See Armand J. Thieblot Jr., *The Negro in the Banking Industry* (Philadelphia: University of Pennsylvania Press, 1970), 195–96.

26. While these institutions could offer blacks "a new, if limited, source of mortgage money themselves," they would also compete with white institutions for black dollars. "This competition, it is reasoned, will prompt the white institutions to give more consideration to Negro mortgage applications" ("Segregated Money").

27. Ibid.; Travis, *Black Chicago,* 158.

28. Travis, *Black Chicago,* 159.

29. "Lack of available mortgage money for Negroes is forcing us into the hands

of unscrupulous speculators in Negro housing who are just out to make a fast buck," one UMBA member explained in 1962, shortly after the MHPC's John W. Baird's public insistence that the "extension of additional mortgage funds to Negroes" would not solve the contract sales problem ("Segregated Money"; Statement by John W. Baird, Aug. 9, 1962, GLCC Papers, box 19, folder "August 1962," CHS).

30. Quoted in Karen Orren, *Corporate Power and Social Change: The Politics of the Life Insurance Industry* (Baltimore: Johns Hopkins University Press, 1974), 127. Orren doesn't name the person she is quoting, but based on the description it is obviously Travis ("Chicago's leading black mortgage banker" and "in 1966 the first black man to be admitted to the Mortgage Bankers Association" [126]).

31. Landye and Vanecko, "Politics of Open Housing," 75–79; Dempsey J. Travis, *An Autobiography of Black Politics* (Chicago: Urban Research Press, 1987), 234–35.

32. Landye and Vanecko, "Politics of Open Housing," 80–83; John W. Baird, "Statement of the Metropolitan Housing and Planning Council Presented to the Executive Committee of the House of Representatives," May 8, 1963, MHPC 74-20, box 24, folder 292, UIC.

33. Travis, *Black Politics,* 242; Landye and Vanecko, "Politics of Open Housing," 84; Adam Cohen and Elizabeth Taylor, *American Pharaoh: Mayor Richard J. Daley: His Battle for Chicago and the Nation* (Boston: Little, Brown, 2000), 305–6, 431.

34. Landye and Vanecko, "Politics of Open Housing," 84; Georgie Anne Geyer and Harry Waldo Swegle, "More and Better Black Faces, Daddy: Good-by Mister Charlie," *Chicago Scene,* Sept. 1963, 10–16.

35. Daley also drew on another recent CHR study to justify his new support for the municipal ordinance—"Selling and Buying Real Estate in Racially Changing Neighborhoods." In Daley's view, which was perhaps colored by the analysis of his friend Len O'Connor, the report proved that whites also suffer in areas of racial change. If the City Council added an anti-panic-peddling provision to the ordinance, then white aldermen could tell their constituency that it would be for their own good because it would end the blockbusting tactics that whites despised (Landye and Vanecko, "Politics of Open Housing," 84–87).

36. Ibid., 89–99.

37. James C. Murray Jr. interview, April 4, 2006; Cohen and Taylor, *American Pharaoh,* 306, 430–31; James R. Ralph Jr., *Northern Crusade: Martin Luther King, Jr., Chicago, and the Civil Rights Movement* (Cambridge: Harvard University Press, 1993), 115 and 279, n. 68.

38. "Terms of Agreement with CBS" (italics in original), MHPC 75-104, box 3, folder 7, UIC.

39. John Culhane, "Life in the Chicago Slums," *CDN,* May 20 and 21, 1963; "Exclusive: The Story of Chicago's Slums," *CDN,* May 20, 1963. The entire series can be found in MHPC 80-49, box 14, folder 6, UIC.

40. "Here's What Slumlords Have to Say," *CDN,* May 22, 1963. "Do you think I go over there and throw garbage out the window?" slum owner Charles Bernstene asked. "I would be glad to have you spend a week in my office and if you don't go to the nuthouse after that you are a better man than I am." John Culhane, "Tenants, Too, Help Make Slums," *CDN,* May 27, 1963; "Slum Rent Gouge Study Continues," *CDN,* June 1, 1963.

41. Ron Chizever, "A Contract Buyer Left Out in Cold," *CDN,* June 3, 1963.

42. Dean Schoelkopf, "The Slum Operators: A Day in Court," *CDN,* May 22, 1963; Richard T. Stout, "'To the Fullest Extent'—Slumlords Get Off Easy in Court," *CDN,* May 23, 1963.

43. Dean Schoelkopf, "Housing Court Opens 1st Time with 2 Judges," *CDN,*

June 6, 1963; Dean Schoelkopf, "Levy $7500 Fines Against Slumlords," *CDN,* June 7, 1963; "Urge Stiffer Fines to Combat Slums," *CDN,* June 5, 1963.

44. The MHPC's legislative proposals had mixed results at best. The bill that would have required those selling property to file an affidavit declaring that the buildings were free of code violations passed the Illinois House. It was defeated in the Senate, however, "after a drastic amendment was mysteriously tacked onto the bill" by its sponsor, State Senator Arthur Swanson (R-Chicago). "I'm going to let the whole bill die," Swanson told another state senator. A bill requiring banks to name owners of land trusts within ten days of receiving a notice about code violations and one requiring that code violations be posted on building entrances passed. The Illinois legislature also passed a law stating that landlords could not evict tenants simply because the tenants complained about possible code violations. Unfortunately, "no penalties were written into the bill," reporters noted ("Anti-Slum Bill Killed by Senate," *CDN,* June 27, 1963; Ron Chizever, "Slum Tenants Get Some New Protection," *CDN,* July 13, 1963; see "City to Issue 'Open Ownership' Warnings," *CDN,* Sept. 17, 1963). Swanson later opposed a 1965 open-occupancy measure, proposing instead a bill supporting "property owners rights" (to discriminate in the sale of their property). See "Rally at State Capital Urges Open-Occupancy Measure."

45. "Realtor, Civil Crusader Differ on Slum Cause," *GA,* June 26, 1963.

46. Memorandum to Saul D. Alinsky from Nicholas von Hoffman, "What the City of Chicago Does in Housing," April 8, 1958, 22–29, in IAF (Alinsky) Papers, folder 82, UIC; Maurice Fischer, "Schools, Taxes, Slums in the News," *CDN,* May 25, 1963.

47. "Libonati: Slumlord Behind in His Taxes," *CDN,* June 10, 1963. For another example, linking a deputy bailiff (process server) and the cousin of Chicago's assistant corporate counsel to a building judged "unfit for human habitation," see "Deputy Bailiff Moonlights as Slum Building Boss: Process Server Gets Served," *CDN,* June 8, 1963. Also see Maurice Fischer, "Slum Investments Tarnish Sheen of Ballplayers," *CDN,* April 28, 1962.

48. Memorandum to Alinsky from von Hoffman, "What the City of Chicago Does in Housing."

49. Paul Gapp, "Renewal Officials Assail New Group," *CDN,* Oct. 7, 1960. On Bass and Bernstene, see "Convict Slumlord of Code Violations," *CDN,* June 5, 1963; on Bass and Winkler, see "Slumlord Winkler Facing Eviction," *CDN,* June 28, 1963.

50. Letter, MJS to Paul Gapp, Oct. 3, 1960; letter, MJS to Len O'Connor, April 19, 1961. On loans to minority home owners, see MJS's notes, "From the Chicago Daily News, Saturday, October 29, 1960," and "Proposal to Harry N. Osgood," MJS Papers.

51. When reporter Paul Gapp published a *Daily News* article on the topic a few days after receiving my father's letter, he presented urban renewal proponents' criticism of the Income Property Owners Association—but not my father's critique of urban renewal proponents. See Gapp, "Renewal Officials Assail New Group," *CDN,* Oct. 7, 1960. Undeterred, my father wrote a letter on crash panels to Len O'Connor. "I am ready to supply you with detailed figures involving property sold . . . in this manner in every part of our city now occupied by minority peoples. . . . The need for help by the minority people is desperate beyond description," he wrote (MJS to Len O'Connor, April 19, 1961). O'Connor then invited my father onto his show and smeared him as a slumlord.

52. Berns interview, 22, 58–62.

53. Robert Lerner, "Fight 'Crash Door' Law," *Sunday Star,* March 5, 1961, see *Adolph Kaukus and Vera Kaukus and Income Property Owners Association v. City of Chicago,* 61s4145, both in MHPC 80-49, box 4, folder 1, "Crash Panel Court Case," UIC. Berns's coattorneys were Samuel Bass and Harry G. Fins.

54. "Judge Knocks Out Glass Panel Code," *CDN*, Dec. 14, 1961; "Glass Panel Exits Upheld by Judge," *CST*, Dec. 15, 1961, in MHPC 80-49, box 4, folder 2, UIC.

55. The court also pointed out that the facts of this particular case did not support the legal challenge. For details, see docket 37293, agenda 46, Nov. 1962, *Adolph Kaukus et al., Appellees, v. The City of Chicago, Appellant*, and *Adolph Kaukus and Vera Kaukus v. City of Chicago, Defendant Appellant*, 37923, Supreme Court of Illinois, Appeal from Superior Court, "Brief and Argument of Amici Curiae," both in MHPC 80-49, box 4, folder 2, UIC.

56. Chicago Property Owners Association, "Questions and Answers," MHPC 75–104, box 2, folder 7, UIC. The MHPC knew that small landlords would have difficulty deconverting their apartments. As head of the Cardinal's Conservation Committee, Monsignor John J. Egan had warned them about the problem in 1956. While he supported the new codes, he also insisted that they be justly implemented. "The small landlord may not find it easy to secure the money necessary to make his property conform to the law. It is to be hoped that every form of assistance will be extended to people who find themselves in those positions." No such assistance was offered ("30 Groups O.K. Proposed City Housing Code," *CT*, April 18, 1956, and "Opposes Weakening of Housing Code," *NW*, June 25, 1956, in IAF (Alinsky) Papers, folder 105, UIC; MHPC Code Enforcement Committee, "Code Enforcement Statement," July 28, 1964, MHPC 76-36, box 1, folder 1, UIC).

Favil Berns summed up the IPOA view of the situation: "The funds from urban renewal helped the Democratic Party here get control of everything. They controlled every single office. They controlled the judiciary, they controlled the U.S. District Attorney's office, they controlled every facet of state government even. That was the benefit of urban renewal" (Berns interview, 22).

On slumlords and the IPOA, see Ron Chizever, "End of the Road for a Slumlord," *CDN*, May 20, 1963; "Slumlord Winkler Facing Eviction"; "Here Are City Slumlords, *CDN*, May 21, 1963; "Convict Slumlord of Code Violations."

57. John Culhane, "Fiery Death Trap Had a Slum Record," *CDN*, June 5, 1963, in MHPC 74-20, box 46, folder 1, UIC.

58. Fischer, "Schools, Taxes, Slums in the News."

59. John Culhane, "I Was Hired to Sell Slums to Negroes," *CDN*, May 24, 1963; Culhane, "His First Day 'Selling' Slums," *CDN*, May 25, 1963.

60. Culhane, "His First Day 'Selling' Slums."

61. Fushanis's will was rejected by the probate court in 1963. This made it difficult for Fushanis's partner, Moe Forman, to get the $300,000 that he claimed Fushanis owed him ("Fushanis Collapses and Dies," *CDN*, May 24, 1963; Ron Chizever, "Will of Fushanis Is Thrown Out," *CDN*, July 1, 1963; "Lawndale Is Exploited," *CT*, May 7, 1973).

62. As he pointed out, the "giant resources of our government" did nothing to stem community decay until there was "nothing left but to buy giant tracts and invite in the bulldozers, with resultant displacement [and] destruction of community fabric." Why couldn't these resources be drawn upon earlier, "at a point at which the community fabric can yet be saved, and a community of small household owners, which are the genuine backbone of any stable city, be backed in its own efforts to rebuild the city"? (MJS, speech, Vernon Missionary Baptist Church, Nov. 5, 1961, 13–14). He was still making these arguments in 1963. The "same city government which took no responsibility in preventing the purchasers from being exploited in their original purchase" and which "had withdrawn help in the form of repair loans" then "condemned [the black purchaser's] property . . . and . . . pushed him off the land empty-handed" ("City Takes Best Land from Negroes, Says Satter," *CDD*, Dec. 4, 1963).

63. Transcript of MJS on *South Side Lights*, Oct. 4, 1962.

64. Sandy Gatto interview, July 13, 2002, 4.

65. David Satter interview, June 1, 2002, 1. The gossip column "Chicago Informer" by J. G. Velna was published in the *National Informer*. My copy is barely legible and does not have the date. For a similar entry about my father by Velna, see his column of July 14, 1963.

66. Gatto interview, 4.

67. David Satter interview, 19–20; Berns interview, 8.

68. David Satter interview, 20.

69. Letter, MJS to Helen [Dorn], Jan. 11, 1965; Paul Satter interview, Jan. 17, 2001, 15; Berns interview, 12; also see David Satter interview, June 1, 2002, 7.

70. Letter, MJS to Helen [Dorn], May 29, 1965; David Satter interview, Feb. 1, 2001, 60–61; David Satter interview, June 19, 2001; Harry Gaynor interview, Aug. 15, 2001. My father described his problems with corrupt building managers in "'I Wrote Post Article, but I'm No Blockbuster,' Declares Satter," *GA*, Aug. 1, 1962.

71. On Gilbert Balin and Forman, see "Lawndale Is Exploited."

72. David Satter interview, Feb. 1, 2001, 7, 48.

73. David Satter interview, Feb. 2, 2001, 60; Berns interview, 6; "Mark Satter, Beaten Up, Robbed," *GA*, April 3, 1963. My thanks to Amanda Seligman for locating the *Garfieldian* article about my father's robbery, which occurred on March 23, 1963, at 3901 W. Jackson.

74. See letters, MJS to Maurice Fischer, Dec. 14, 1960, and Aug. 2, 1962.

75. My father was also drawn to the welfare issue because of personal experience. Lawndale contained an unusually large number of people on public aid. My father probably had many welfare recipients among his tenants because he kept his rents at what he considered a fair price, which was $90 a month for four rooms, in contrast to the $90 for one room that was more typical of the area. Since public aid recipients were forbidden to spend more than $90 a month on housing, they were directed to rentals in that price range—including my father's buildings. See "'I Wrote Post Article.'" On welfare rates in Lawndale, see Alphine Wade Jefferson, "Housing Discrimination and Community Response in North Lawndale (Chicago), Illinois, 1948–1978" (Ph.D. dissertation, Duke University, 1979), 115; Lawndale Conservation Community Council, "A Comprehensive Proposal for Urban Renewal in the North Lawndale Community," 8–9, in CJEG-Egan I, box 54, folder "Program of Community Action," Aug. 11, 1966, UND.

76. M. W. Newman and Nicholas Shuman, "ADC Keeps Children, Women Alive, Barely," *CDN*, Aug. 29, 1961; Newman and Shuman, "Illegitimacy—How Our Costs Rise," *CDN*, Aug. 30, 1961; Les Brownlee, "Pilgrims with Shopping Bags: Chicago Picks Up the Check," 1962 reprint, *CA*, MJS Papers.

77. Many also noted the economic pressures caused by unscrupulous credit practices. "Wage assignments and garnishments by credit sharpies have caused many people—especially Negroes—to go on relief," said one social worker. "The cards are stacked." Brownlee, "Pilgrims with Shopping Bags" and "Dixie Exodus May Bankrupt Illinois," 1962 reprint, *CA*, MJS Papers.

78. Les Brownlee, "Schools, Jobs Lure Migrants," 1962 reprint, *CA*, MJS Papers.

79. MJS, "A New WPA—Alternative to Chaos," *Labor Today*, Aug.–Sept. 1964, 17–18; also see letter, MJS to Fischer, Aug. 2, 1962, and letter, MJS to Irv Kupcinet, Jan. 30, 1962.

My father's perspective was common in the 1930s, when New Deal agencies first extended relief to black Americans. "Employment itself is a human need," claimed a 1935 article in *Opportunity*, the magazine of the National Urban League. "Relief alone is pauperizing Negro families and is therefore doing more harm than good." Article cited in Mary Poole, *The Segregated Origins of Social Security* (Chapel Hill: University of North Carolina Press, 2006), 182.

80. MJS, "A Plea for a Reborn WPA," *Panorama Magazine* (*CDN*, magazine supplement), Aug. 1, 1964. Also see MJS, "A New WPA—Alternative to Chaos," *Labor Today,* Aug.–Sept. 1964, 18; MJS, "Jobs vs. Dole—A Suggested Approach" (unpublished manuscript); "Talk Prepared by Mark J. Satter for Delivery before Lawn Manor Hebrew Congregation," Dec. 20, 1963.

81. St. Clair Drake and Horace R. Cayton, *Black Metropolis,* vol. I, rev. and enl. ed. (New York: Harper and Row, 1962), xli–xlii, xlix; Arnold R. Hirsch, *Making the Second Ghetto: Race and Housing in Chicago, 1940–1960* (Chicago: University of Chicago Press, 1998 [1983]), 29. Also see Daniel Seligman, "The Battle for Chicago," *Fortune,* June 1955, 123, 208; Adam Green, *Selling the Race: Culture, Community, and Black Chicago, 1940–1955* (Chicago: University of Chicago Press, 2007), 10–11.

82. A study by the Bureau of Jewish Employment stated that "98 percent of the white collar job orders received from over 5,000 companies were not available to qualified Negroes." Virtually all of the fastest-growing industries in Chicago excluded blacks, while the industries that accepted them—the metal and food production industries— were declining rapidly (Drake and Cayton, *Black Metropolis,* xxxvi, xlvii).

83. A new WPA program would benefit the general population as well. "Giant public projects" could create a "permanent shortage in the labor pool. Direct competition for labor between government and industry will be a strong incentive to an economically healthy America" (MJS, "A Plea for a Reborn WPA"). Also see MJS's review of Searle F. Charles, *Minister of Relief: Harry Hopkins and the Depression* (ms.).

84. Letter, MJS to Ritz [Fischer], Feb. 6, 1964; letter, MJS to *New Republic,* Feb. 7, 1964; letter, MJS to *Harper's* magazine, Feb. 21, 1964; letter, MJS to George, Feb. 24, 1964.

My father emphasized welfare's effect on men. He never considered whether joblessness would have the same deleterious influence on mothers with young children. He did not see that mothers who were responsible for young children were not "idle." He never acknowledged that among most Americans, wage earning was not a valued cultural norm for women, nor did he specifically call for employment opportunities for the women who made up the bulk of welfare recipients. He did not note that black women who worked for wages were often so underpaid that waged work did not bring them independence.

85. The pressing need was for a "radical reassessment of our practices . . . with regard to . . . home ownership, financial practices, welfare programs, job opportunities, [and] wage collection laws," he concluded. Specifically, he called for a new WPA to create jobs, the passage of federal laws outlawing wage garnishment to protect wages, and federal policing of all financial institutions to stop the denial of mortgage and improvement loans to black neighborhoods, thereby making home ownership and home improvement possible (MJS, "Jobs vs. Dole—A Suggested Approach").

86. Letter, MJS to Helen [Dorn], Jan. 27, 1965; letter, MJS to Helen [Dorn], Jan. 11, 1965.

87. David Satter interview, June 1, 2002, 18.

88. Letter, MJS to Helen [Dorn], Jan. 11, 1965; Gatto interview, 6.

89. MJS, "Home Finance and the Foreclosure Racket," *Labor Today,* April–May 1963, 20–21; also see MJS, "Outlaw Garnishments," *Focus/Midwest,* Jan. 1963; MJS, "Wage Attachment and 'Accommodation,'" *Summons,* January 1964; Gatto interview.

90. He broke down the then-common distinction between the "rabid" and the "respectable" right, pointing out that "respectable" corporations such as Boeing

Aircraft funded rabidly right-wing films such as *Communism on the Map*, which depicted Communism as successful in every nation except the United States, West Germany, Formosa, and Switzerland (and which was seen by ten million Americans). The nation was in a downward spiral, he argued. The "timid and the fearful [are] laying the groundwork for the respectables [on the right]. The respectables [are] financing the rabid and the rabid in turn [are] further muzzling the timid and the fearful" (MJS, speech, "America's Vicious Right Wing," delivered at Sachar Lodge, B'nai B'rith, Dec. 18, 1963).

91. MJS, "An Argument for Abolition of Wage Attachment," *Illinois Bar Journal* 52, no. 12 (Aug. 1964): 1037; letter, MJS to Ed Kandlik, Oct. 1, 1963; letter, MJS to Maurice Fischer, Aug. 2, 1962. He also addressed the fact that "poor people can't afford lawyers" (letter, MJS to Kandlik, Oct. 1, 1963). He suggested the creation of a "form of 'workingmen's compensation' . . . where on a mass basis, the profession can provide services of a higher caliber than any one individual can afford, but at a price within the ability of even the poorest workingman" (letter, MJS to WTTW-TV, Feb. 9, 1962).

92. MJS, speech, to Nu Beta Epsilon Fraternity, n.d.; see transcript, *The House on Congress Parkway*, part 2, MJS Papers; also see MJS, "Expanding the Scope of the Lawyer's Responsibility in Changing Communities," *Illinois Continuing Legal Education* 1, no. 3 (July 1963): 87–96.

93. In addition to cases described in chapter 3, see *Boysie Coleman and Mearlee Coleman v. Samuel A. Aronfeld*, Circuit Court of Cook County, docket 58c7239, filed May 22, 1958, CCCC; *Louis Chapman and Catherine Chapman v. Gerald H. Crane, as Trustee under Trust No. 7441*, Superior Court of Cook County, docket 62s20927, filed Sept. 26, 1962, CCCC; "Ask Judge to Halt Family's Eviction," *CDN*, Sept. 27, 1962. See also "Law Can't Help, but Judge Does," *CDN*, Sept. 28, 1962.

94. Gatto interview, 27, 28; David Satter interview, June 1, 2002, 11–12.

95. Letter, MJS to Helen [Dorn], Jan. 11, 1965; also see letter, MJS to Helen [Dorn], Jan. 27, 1965.

96. Letter, MJS to Helen [Dorn], Jan. 27, 1965.

97. David Satter interview, Feb. 1, 2001, 26; Paul Satter interview, 28–29.

98. David Satter interview, Feb. 1, 2001, 23; Gatto interview; Paul Satter interview, 31, 34.

99. Letter, Clarice Satter to MJS, June 1, 1965.

100. David Satter interview, Feb. 1, 2001, 27–28.

101. Letter, John J. King to MJS, June 1, 1965; letter, John Egan to MJS, Feb. 12, 1965; letter, Ritz Fischer to MJS, June 3, 1965; letter, John J. King to MJS, June 9, 1965; letter, Egan to MJS, June 4, 1965.

102. "Lawyer Fights to Salvage Victims of the Vultures," *Muhammad Speaks*, March 5, 1965; also see "Defender of the Bankrupt Fights Garnishee!" *Muhammad Speaks*, March 12, 1965, MJS Papers.

103. Letter, Clarice to MJS, May 24, 1965; letter, MJS to Clarice, May 26, 1965; letter, MJS to Clarice, May 27, 1965.

104. Letter, MJS to Clarice, May 22, 1965.

105. "It has for twenty-five years been my belief that in a money society such as ours, virtually no man will break out of the binds of financial inadequacy unless money (investment) works for him. Even now, I believe our investments will improve, and within a few years the buildings will start to bring to the family a regular monthly return. Not only you and Paul, but Julie, Susan and Beryl must look to an education, and this can be [a] great help there, and after," my father wrote (letter, MJS to David, June 6, 1965).

106. Letter, MJS to Helen [Dorn], May 29, 1965; Gatto interview, 21.

107. Paul Satter interview, 29.

108. This account is based on David Satter's recollections about our father's death, which he wrote in 1967, DS Papers.

109. Letter, Mrs. Mark Satter to Mayo Clinic, Aug. 4, 1965; Paul Satter interview, 31.

110. Letters, Paul to MJS, May 25, 1965; June 1, 1965; and n.d. (after June 1, 1965).

111. David Satter interview, Feb. 1, 2001, 29; Paul Satter interview, 43.

112. Letter, Leon Despres to Mrs. Mark J. Satter, July 13, 1965; see telegram, Richard J. Daley to Mrs. Mark J. Satter, July 13, 1965. Other letters expressing shock at my father's death include Elmer Gertz to Mrs. Mark Satter, July 23, 1965; Erik Ekdahl to Mrs. Mark J. Satter, July 13, 1965; Seymour Simon to Mrs. Mark J. Satter, July 15, 1965; Norman N. Eiger to Mrs. Satter, July 16, 1965. Many described his death as a loss to the entire city; see Abner J. Mikva to Mrs. Satter and Children, July 16, 1965; Irving S. Steinberg to Clarice, n.d.; Arthur K. Young to Mrs. Mark J. Satter, July 13, 1965; John Gibbs to Mrs. Satter, n.d.; Thomas J. Boodell to Mrs. Satter, July 28, 1965.

113. "Mark Satter," *CDN*, July 14, 1965.

114. Warren Lehman, "Goodbye, Mark" (unpublished ms.), 3, MJS Papers.

115. "Here Are City Slumlords," *CDN*, May 21, 1965; MJS condolence book.

116. See "Linked to Chicago's Slums," and "Phony Names, Land Trusts Used to Profit from Squalor," *CT*, May 6, 1973.

117. Wesley South interview, April 13, 2001, 8.

CHAPTER SIX: KING IN CHICAGO

1. Edmund J. Rooney, "A Night of Shame on Pulaski Road," *CDN*, Aug. 14, 1965, and Michael McGovern, "Our Reporter Tells of Own Beating," *CDN*, Aug. 14, 1965, in CUL Papers, 76–116, box 165, folder 7, UIC; Alan B. Anderson and George W. Pickering, *Confronting the Color Line: The Broken Promises of the Civil Rights Movement in Chicago* (Athens: University of Georgia Press, 1986), 163; M. W. Newman, "West Side Story: A Look at Chicago's Newest Ghetto," *CDN*, June 6, 1966.

2. Lawndale Conservation Community Council, "A Comprehensive Plan for Urban Renewal in the North Lawndale Community," Aug. 11, 1966, 8–10, 12–13, CJEG-Egan I, box 54, folder "Program of Community Action," UND; M. W. Newman, "West Side Story: A Look at Chicago's Newest Ghetto," *CDN*, June 6, 1966.

3. Lawndale Conservation Community Council, "A Comprehensive Plan," 8–9; Alphine Wade Jefferson, "Housing Discrimination and Community Response in North Lawndale (Chicago), Illinois, 1948–1978" (Ph.D. dissertation, Duke University, 1979), 115.

4. M. W. Newman, "West Side Story: Viet War Brings Jobs to Ghetto's Unskilled," *CDN*, June 7, 1966; Lois Wille, "The West Side: Poverty Fighters List Their City Hall Gripes," *CDN*, June 10, 1966.

5. M. W. Newman, "West Side Story: A Look at Chicago's Newest Ghetto," *CDN*, June 6, 1966; Lawndale Conservation Community Council, "A Comprehensive Plan," 9–10, 12, 13.

6. This problem had been obvious at least since 1963. According to Wesley South, that year my father had worked with him to expose the addresses of white, often Jewish precinct captains whose Lawndale addresses turned out to be a local hotel. See Wesley South interview, April 13, 2001.

7. Lois Wille, "Poverty Fighters List Their City Hall Gripes." After the 1968 riots, columnist Mike Royko quipped that the West Side state senators were "Bernie Neistein,

Sam Romano, Tom McGloon and Zygmunt Sokolnicki . . . an inspiring foursome had they gone on TV Friday night and pleaded with their black constituents to cool it, baby" ("City in a Bind," *Look*, Aug. 6, 1968).

8. IRCUA, "Criteria to Guide Funding of a Community Organization Enterprise," Feb. 1967, in Red Squad Files, box 189, folder 1042, CHS; also see Margery Frisbie, *An Alley in Chicago: The Life and Legacy of Monsignor John Egan*, commemorative ed. (Franklin, Wisc.: Sheed & Ward, 2002), 195, 111–12.

9. John J. Egan, "Housing and Community Action," address to the National Catholic Conference on Interracial Justice, Omaha, Neb., Aug. 28, 1965, in CJEG-Egan I, box 50, folder "Father Egan's Talks," UND; also see Kris Ronnow interview, Sept. 26, 2003; John J. Egan, "Archdiocese Responds," *Church in Metropolis*, Summer 1965.

The IRCUA attempted to raise $450,000 to fund community organizing in Lawndale, but in June 1965 its application for federal antipoverty funds was turned down. It had been opposed by Sears and by Inland Steel, which feared that the money might be used to bring in Alinsky. The result, Rabbi Robert J. Marx said, was that when riots broke out in Lawndale shortly thereafter, "there was no real indigenous leadership ready to act effectively in the time of crisis" ("Chicago Clergy Gives $20,000 to Riot-Torn Slum," *NYT*, Aug. 20, 1965). Also see "Religion-Race Group Submits 5-Point Program," *CST*, Sept. 11, 1965, Daniel Cantwell Papers, box 14, folder "Chicago Conference on Religion and Race," CHS.

10. "A Report from the JCUA," Rabbi Robert J. Marx Papers, box 11, folder 1, CHS.

11. "Jews Are Warned on Tension in Negro Ghettos," *NYT*, Nov. 4, 1964; Robert J. Marx, "Judaism and Open Housing," Marx Papers, box 11, folder 1, CHS; Lou Kreinberg interview, June 15, 2001. Also see James Alan McPherson, "'In My Father's House There Are Many Mansions—And I'm Going to Get Me Some of Them Too': The Story of the Contract Buyers League," *Atlantic Monthly*, April 1972, 60.

Fushanis may have intentionally misled people about his ethnicity. One of his buyers described him as "a tall Irishman"; historian Alphine Wade Jefferson asserted that "Lou Fushanis was Jewish." I gather that Fushanis was Greek both because this is what he told *Daily News* reporter John Culhane and because his body was taken to the Adinamis Funeral Home, which served the Greek American community. See "Fushanis Collapses and Dies," *CDN*, May 24, 1963; John Culhane, "I Was Hired to Sell Slums to Negroes," *CDN*, May 24, 1963; Jefferson, "Housing Discrimination," 74.

12. Sanford D. Horwitt, *Let Them Call Me Rebel: Saul Alinsky—His Life and Legacy* (New York: Vintage Books, 1992), 380–81, 383. There were always some Protestant leaders who supported Alinsky, however. See P. David Finks, *The Radical Vision of Saul Alinsky* (New York: Paulist Press, 1984), 167.

13. Bernard O. Brown, *Ideology and Community Action: The West Side Organization of Chicago, 1964–67* (Chicago: Center for the Scientific Study of Religion, 1978), 18–19, 35–47, 85.

14. Franklin I. Gamwell, "The West Side Christian Parish: A History of Its Decline" (unpublished ms., 1969, in author's possession), 18–19, 21.

15. James R. Ralph Jr., *Northern Protest: Martin Luther King Jr., Chicago, and the Civil Rights Movement* (Cambridge: Harvard University Press, 1993), 59.

16. Ibid., 42; Horwitt, *Call Me Rebel*, 469.

17. King quoted in Harvard Sitkoff, *The Struggle for Black Equality, 1954–1980* (New York: Hill and Wang, 1981), 187–88.

18. Frisbie, *Alley in Chicago*, 174–76; also see Gamwell, "West Side Christian Parish," 19; Brown, *Ideology and Community Action*, 61; Kreinberg, "A Report from the JCUA," 3.

19. Sitkoff, *Struggle for Black Equality*, 192–97.

20. Ibid., 142–43.

21. In 1961, a white mob in Montgomery, Alabama, lobbed Molotov cocktails—homemade bombs made by pouring gasoline into bottles—into a black church packed with people of all ages who had gathered to support the Freedom Riders. In fall 1962, a deadly riot broke out at the University of Mississippi, where at least 2,000 white students, augmented by unknown numbers of older whites, tried to stop a black man, James Meredith, from registering for classes at the all-white school. Here, too, rampaging whites lobbed Molotov cocktails, as well as rocks and bricks, and fired rifles, not only at buildings that they believed might be harboring Meredith but also at law enforcement troops. The white mob wounded 160 marshals, including 28 by gunfire. They also murdered two men: a reporter, who was shot in the back, and a local jukebox repairman, who was shot in the head by a stray bullet (Taylor Branch, *Parting the Waters: America in the King Years, 1954–63* [New York: Touchstone Books, 1988], 458–59, 664–69).

22. Sitkoff, *Struggle for Black Equality,* 154; also see *Report of the National Advisory Commission on Civil Disorders* (New York: Bantam, 1968), 35–37.

23. Dempsey J. Travis, *An Autobiography of Black Politics* (Chicago: Urban Research Press, 1987), 344; also see David J. Garrow, *Bearing the Cross: Martin Luther King, Jr., and the Southern Christian Leadership Conference* (New York: Vintage, 1986), 439.

24. Ralph, *Northern Protest,* 35, 38–39.

25. Ralph David Abernathy, *And the Walls Came Tumbling Down* (New York: Harper and Row, 1989), 362–63.

26. Evans learned the price of supporting King when he tried to get a loan to repair his church. His application was turned down for seven years in a row. "I know you must be well aware that Mayor Daley can stop any structure in Chicago that he wants to," Evans was told by one of the brokers who rejected him (Travis, *Black Politics,* 346, 354–55). Also see Ralph, *Northern Protest,* 79–80.

27. Abernathy, *Walls Came Tumbling,* 378, 372–73; Henry Hampton and Steve Fayer, *Voices of Freedom: An Oral History of the Civil Rights Movement from the 1950s through the 1980s* (New York: Bantam, 1990), 300–302; Ralph, *Northern Protest,* 76.

28. Garrow, *Bearing the Cross,* 455.

29. Ibid., 444; also see Abernathy, *Walls Came Tumbling,* 367; Ralph, *Northern Protest,* 38–39.

30. Branch, *Parting the Waters.*

31. Anderson and Pickering, *Color Line,* 183, 176; also see Ralph, *Northern Protest,* 38–39, 48; Abernathy, *Walls Came Tumbling,* 366–67; Hampton and Fayer, *Voices of Freedom,* 298.

32. The NAACP report found 87 percent of Chicago's black children went to predominantly black schools, 12 percent attended mixed schools, and only 1 percent attended predominantly white schools. White elementary schools averaged 669 students; black elementary schools averaged 1,275 students. See Anderson and Pickering, *Color Line,* 76–77, 84–86.

33. Ibid., 106, 88–89, 113–20, 123, 130–34, 141–43.

34. Ibid., 156–60. On Raby, see Taylor Branch, *At Canaan's Edge: America in the King Years, 1965–68* (New York: Simon and Schuster, 2006), 241.

35. Anderson and Pickering, *Color Line,* 174, 164.

36. Ibid., 177–80.

37. Al Raby summed up the dismay of CCCO and SCLC supporters. "We are shocked at this shameless display of naked political power exhibited by Mayor Daley in intervening at the highest level—not to bring Chicago into compliance with the Civil Rights Act, but to demand federal funds regardless of how they are used," he told reporters. "Mayor Daley ostensibly supported the Civil Rights Act and all the Democratic congressmen from Illinois . . . voted for it. Yet they are the first to squeal like stuck pigs when the bill is enforced in the North" (Ibid., 179–81).

38. Ibid., 182–83, 187.

39. John McKnight interview, July 6, 2001, 31, 11, 9, 6, 8, 12–13.

40. Ibid., 21, 13; also see "John McKnight," *Chicago* magazine, Nov. 1985, 205; Chicago Commission on Human Relations Housing Advisory Committee Minutes, Oct. 16, 1957, MJS Papers.

41. McKnight interview, 24, 22; "John McKnight," *Chicago* magazine.

42. McKnight interview, 26; Wille, "Poverty Fighters List Their City Hall Gripes."

43. "I had a way of explaining it," McKnight said. "I would sit down with people and I would put these numbers down. Okay we start with $10,000. . . . I even had some play money that I used in the office to show how the profits were made." He added, "Mark was the tribune, . . . the Joshua, trying to blow down the walls with his horn." Mark's analysis was "correct," but "he needed to find somebody who'd pick up the ball, which is what I did, that's my little contribution" (McKnight interview, 25, 21).

44. Ibid., 32, 34. On the "lunatic streak" in Bevel, see Branch, *At Canaan's Edge*, 12.

45. Abernathy, *Walls Came Tumbling*, 370–71; also see Travis, *Black Politics*, 352; Adam Cohen and Elizabeth Taylor, *American Pharaoh: Mayor Richard J. Daley: His Battle for Chicago and the Nation* (Boston: Little, Brown, 2000), 361.

SCLC organizers did not realize that King and Abernathy's apartment buildings were not typical of the area. While large rental units were common in New York City, most Chicago housing was on a smaller scale—generally two-flat apartments. As reporters noted, despite Lawndale's roughness, "90 per cent of the apartment buildings on the side streets are clean, comfortable two-flats." McKnight seconded this view. King and Abernathy "just happened to be on the main strip where the apartment buildings are," he recalled. But other than that street, "most of those blocks only have apartment buildings on the corners. They anchor the corner and everything else is two- or three-flats" (Newman, "A Look at Chicago's Newest Ghetto"; McKnight interview).

46. Anderson and Pickering, *Color Line*, 189.

47. Ibid., 188–90; Garrow, *Bearing the Cross*, 456–57.

48. Anderson and Pickering, *Color Line*, 191; Robert J. Marx, "Religious Communities and Urban Power Structures," speech delivered Oct. 11, 1966, at the University of Michigan, 5, in Marx Papers, box 8, folder 6, CHS; Ralph, *Northern Protest*, 63–64; M. W. Newman, "Dr. King's Slum Formula," *CDN*, June 9, 1966.

49. Anderson and Pickering, *Color Line*, 193; Ralph, *Northern Protest*, 72, 63–64; Newman, "Dr. King's Slum Formula"; Jerry Lipson, "What Slum Volunteers Are Told about Roots of Negro Ghettos," *CDN*, July 9, 1966, CUL Papers, 76-116, box 129, folder 58, UIC.

50. Abernathy, *Walls Came Tumbling*, 376, also see 370; Anderson and Pickering, *Color Line*, 190.

51. Ralph, *Northern Protest*, 62; Anderson and Pickering, *Color Line*, 185; Garrow, *Bearing the Cross*, 448.

52. "Dr. King Wins Housing Victory," *CST*, Jan. 26, 1966, in MHPC 76-102, box 6, folder 5, UIC; Abernathy, *Walls Came Tumbling*, 371; Garrow, *Bearing the Cross*, 459; "Dr. King's Landlord Faces Probe," *CST*, Jan. 27, 1966.

53. Anderson and Pickering, *Color Line*, 191; also see Ralph, *Northern Protest*, 78.

54. Branch, *At Canaan's Edge*, 442.

55. Ralph, *Northern Protest*, 86; Travis, *Black Politics*, 353; Raymond R. Coffey, "King Late for Slum Battle," *CDN*, Jan. 28, 1966; Frank Sullivan, "Two-Front Attack Slated in Chicago's War on Blight," *CST*, Feb. 11, 1966. The threat to withhold welfare payments from slum landlords was timeworn. The tactic was first announced in 1961 and was revived in 1963. See "County Spurs Drive to Withhold Slum Rents," *CDN*, May 24, 1963.

56. Ruth Moore, "The 'Chicago Plan' for Fighting Slums Is Told by Weaver," *CST*, May 27, 1966.

57. Travis, *Black Politics*, 354. As if to prove this point, one of King's closest associates in Chicago, attorney Chauncey Eskridge, had his building written up for code violations. See Ralph, *Northern Protest*, 267, n. 100.

58. Under a new program, some contract buyers could apply to the Department of Housing and Urban Development for repair loans; those earning under $3,000 a year might also be eligible for repair grants of up to $1,500. These loans, however, required "months of negotiation" ("Countering Blight: Help for Homewners' Repairs," *CST*, Aug. 7, 1967).

59. The CDA's units would be rented to families with incomes of $5,400 to $11,000, well above Lawndale's median income of $4,981 (Moore, "The 'Chicago Plan' for Fighting Slums").

60. Lois Wille, "West Side Story: 2 Forces Fight Slum Misery," *CDN*, June 8, 1966.

61. Ralph, *Northern Protest*, 86, 270, n. 123; Wille, "2 Forces Fight Slum Misery."

62. Garrow, *Bearing the Cross*, 491; Ralph, *Northern Protest*, 45; Travis, *Black Politics*, 346–47.

63. Charles M. Payne, *I've Got the Light of Freedom: The Organizing Tradition and the Mississippi Freedom Struggle* (Berkeley: University of California Press, 1995), 365; Newman, "Dr. King's Slum Formula."

64. Ralph, *Northern Protest*, 54, 62–63; also see 89–90.

65. Anderson and Pickering, *Color Line*, 177–78; Ralph, *Northern Protest*, 52, 91, 98.

66. Anderson and Pickering, *Color Line*, 195, 199–201; Garrow, *Bearing the Cross*, 479.

67. Garrow, *Bearing the Cross*, 473–74, 479.

68. Sitkoff, *Struggle for Black Equality*, 214.

69. Garrow, *Bearing the Cross*, 488.

70. Abernathy, *Walls Came Tumbling*, 373; Ralph, *Northern Protest*, 106–7; also see Garrow, *Bearing the Cross*, 489–90; Travis, *Black Politics*, 362.

71. Hampton and Fayer, *Voices of Freedom*, 306; Travis, *Black Politics*, 362–66. Cody's statement had been written by Monsignor John J. Egan, who also "harried" Cody into taking part in the rally (Frisbie, *Alley in Chicago*, 187).

72. "Program of the Chicago Freedom Movement, July 1966," in David J. Garrow, ed., *Chicago 1966* (New York: Carlson, 1989), 104–9.

73. The AFSC supported open occupancy legislation. Since Chicago already had a fair housing ordinance, Moyer had used direct action to spur the passage of an open occupancy law in suburban Oak Park. Ironically, the Oak Park office that Moyer picketed was a branch of Baird and Warner, whose head, John W. Baird, vigorously championed open occupancy. "They always liked to catch us because then they could say we were hypocrites," Baird recalled. His firm had instituted training programs for its salesmen forbidding them to practice racial discrimination. However, there were always some salesmen that "we couldn't get . . . to go along" because they had been "inculcated by the philosophy of the old real estate industry," he said. "We still do this [training] with . . . salesmen . . . right now," Baird told me in 2004. John W. Baird interview, Feb. 13, 2004.

On Moyer's crusade, see Anderson and Pickering, *Color Line*, 197–98; Ralph, *Northern Protest*, 99–101; Mary Lou Finley, "The Open Housing Marches, Chicago

Summer '66," in Garrow, *Chicago 1966*, 47, n. 1; Arnold Rosenzweig, "Negroes Denied Homes," *Chicago Defender*, May 29–June 3, 1966.

74. Ralph, *Northern Protest*, 100–101.

75. Bevel cast West Siders' disinterest as a product of their ignorance (Finley, "Open Housing Marches," 9).

76. Lipson, "What Slum Volunteers Are Told," *CDN*, July 9, 1966; Finley, "Open Housing Marches," 3–4; also see Ralph, *Northern Protest*, 102.

77. Finley, "Open Housing Marches," 7–8; see 10–11 for similar quotations.

78. Ibid., 8, 12.

79. Robert E. Cook, executive vice president of the IAREB, quoted in Anderson and Pickering, *Color Line*, 217; also see Rose Helper, *Racial Policies and Practices of Real Estate Brokers* (Minneapolis: University of Minnesota Press, 1969), 179–80; Amanda Irene Seligman, "Block by Block: Racing Decay on Chicago's West Side, 1948–1968" (Ph.D. dissertation, Northwestern University, 1999), 198–99; "Human Factors Cause Slums, Realtors Say," *CDN*, July 9, 1966; "Rally at State Capital Urges Open-Occupancy Measure," *CST*, May 19, 1965, in Ely Aaron Papers, folder 25, UIC.

80. Edward Rutledge, "Threat to the Great Society: Anti-Fair Housing Referenda," *Journal of Intergroup Relations* 4, no. 4 (Autumn 1965): 3, 7, 8, 10.

81. Ibid., 3–19.

82. Beth J. Lief and Susan Goering, "The Implementation of the Federal Mandate for Fair Housing," in *Divided Neighborhoods: Changing Patterns of Racial Segregation*, ed. Gary A. Tobin (Newbury Park, Calif.: Sage, 1987), 233; Douglas S. Massey and Nancy A. Denton, *American Apartheid: Segregation and the Making of the Underclass* (Cambridge: Harvard University Press, 1993), 191–92.

83. Allen J. Matusow, *The Unraveling of America* (New York: Harper and Row, 1984), 206; Ralph, *Northern Protest*, 174; also see Branch, *Parting the Waters*, 679; Lief and Goering, "Federal Mandate," 231–32.

84. Matusow, *Unraveling of America*, 206–7; Ralph, *Northern Protest*, 174–76; "Human Factors Cause Slums, Realtors Say."

85. Ralph, *Northern Protest*, 107–9; Anderson and Pickering, *Color Line*, 208–9.

86. Finley, "Open Housing Marches," 14, 20, 15; Anderson and Pickering, *Color Line*, 220.

87. Ralph, *Northern Protest*, 176.

88. Travis, *Black Politics*, 374; also see Brown, *Ideology and Community Action*, 49–50.

89. Brown, *Ideology and Community Action*, 56–57; Anderson and Pickering, *Color Line*, 213.

90. Ralph, *Northern Protest*, 112; also see Travis, *Black Politics*, 376–77; Anderson and Pickering, *Color Line*, 214; Finley, "Open Housing Marches," 17.

91. Garrow, *Bearing the Cross*, 493–94; Anderson and Pickering, *Color Line*, 211–12; Brown, *Ideology and Community Action*, 54.

92. Brown, *Ideology and Community Action*, 57–58.

93. Anderson and Pickering, *Color Line*, 213–14; Travis, *Black Politics*, 378.

94. Hampton and Fayer, *Voices of Freedom*, 310; Travis, *Black Politics*, 379; Anderson and Pickering, *Color Line*, 214. On the roots of black mobilization against Northern police brutality, see Martha Biondi's wonderful study *To Stand and Fight: The Struggle for Civil Rights in Postwar New York City* (Cambridge: Harvard University Press, 2003), 60–78.

95. Robert Marx, "Chicago Summer: Another Analysis," *New City*, Sept. 1966, 9; Mike Royko, *Boss: Richard J. Daley of Chicago* (New York: Dutton, 1971), 151.

96. Ralph, *Northern Protest,* 92, 78; also see Garrow, *Bearing the Cross,* 497.

97. Garrow, *Bearing the Cross,* 498.

98. Anderson and Pickering, *Color Line,* 223; Hampton and Fayer, *Voices of Freedom,* 311.

99. Ralph, *Northern Protest,* 120–21, 128; John T. McGreevy, *Parish Boundaries: The Catholic Encounter with Race in the Twentieth-Century Urban North* (Chicago: University of Chicago Press, 1996), 188; Anderson and Pickering, *Color Line,* 224; also see Travis, *Black Politics,* 381–82.

100. Ralph, *Northern Protest,* 120; Anderson and Pickering, *Color Line,* 224.

101. Anderson and Pickering, *Color Line,* 224; Ralph, *Northern Protest,* 121; Travis, *Black Politics,* 381–83, 362; Finley, "Open Housing Marches," 22; Hampton and Fayer, *Voices of Freedom,* 311–12; Brown, *Ideology and Community Action,* 59.

102. Anderson and Pickering, *Color Line,* 225.

103. Ibid., 227.

104. Ralph, *Northern Protest,* 124; Anderson and Pickering, *Color Line,* 228; Travis, *Black Politics,* 386–87.

105. Anderson and Pickering, *Color Line,* 228; Hampton and Fayer, *Voices of Freedom,* 313–14.

106. Finley, "Open Housing Marches," 9.

107. Anderson and Pickering, *Color Line,* 228–30, 232; Finley, "Open Housing Marches," 22–23.

108. Ralph, *Northern Protest,* 148–49; Anderson and Pickering, *Color Line,* 232.

109. Anderson and Pickering, *Color Line,* 225–26; Ralph, *Northern Protest,* 126–27.

110. Ralph, *Northern Protest,* 142.

111. There had been discussion of a possible Cicero march for months, but no decision had been made when Jackson made his announcement (Finley, "Open Housing Marches," 23; Anderson and Pickering, *Color Line,* 229, 201).

112. Hampton and Fayer, *Voices of Freedom,* 318; "Cicero Teens Bludgeon Youth with Baseball Bat," *Chicago Defender,* May 28–June 3, 1966; Brown, *Ideology and Community Action,* 63.

113. Anderson and Pickering, *Color Line,* 229–30.

114. McKnight was among the few commentators to voice skepticism about the gathered dignitaries. "It is of perhaps some significance to note who was not in attendance," McKnight scribbled in his notes for the day. "Particularly notable as nonattendants were the Chicago Negro aldermen and Congressman William Dawson. Here, at a moment of great meaning for the Negro community, their elected political representatives were not even present, and they were not present because they were irrelevant: the Mayor could make any decisions that were necessary without them" (McKnight, "The Summit Negotiations," in Garrow, *Chicago 1966,* 112; see "Participants in the Conference on Open Housing," in Garrow, *Chicago 1966,* 93–94; Cohen and Taylor, *American Pharaoh,* 402).

The account that follows draws upon John McKnight's report on the summit negotiations. McKnight did not tape-record the proceedings, but he took detailed notes during the sessions that he then dictated into a tape recorder as soon as the sessions finished for the day. David Garrow warns that "while quotation marks have been used to indicate that a particular person is speaking, the words within the marks are the essence of their point rather than the precise spoken words" (Garrow, *Chicago 1966,* 111).

115. Anderson and Pickering, *Color Line,* 239–40; McKnight, "Summit Negotiations," 115.

116. McKnight, "Summit Negotiations," 116. McKnight had been working with

Stayman since 1965 on the problem of mortgage redlining; see McKnight interview, 26; Wille, "Poverty Fighters List Their City Hall Gripes."

117. Abernathy, *Walls Came Tumbling*, 386–87; McKnight, "Summit Negotiations," 116.

118. Anderson and Pickering, *Color Line*, 244–45; also see McKnight, "Summit Negotiations," 123–24.

119. McKnight, "Summit Negotiations," 132–33.

120. Ibid., 133–34.

121. Anderson and Pickering, *Color Line*, 255–57. It is the "Chicago real estate dealers who should be enjoined, and not the demonstrators," King noted. Daley called upon the Chicago City Council to pass a resolution praising his injunction. Alderman Leon Despres denounced the resolution, but it was passed by the City Council, 45 to 1 (Travis, *Black Politics*, 392–94).

122. Anderson and Pickering, *Color Line*, 258–59; Ralph, *Northern Protest*, 166.

123. McKnight, "Summit Negotiations," 147–54.

124. Ibid., 141, 138.

125. Ibid., 139–40, 142–43, 145.

126. Anderson and Pickering, *Color Line*, 272–73, 276; Brown, *Ideology and Community Action*, 69–70.

127. Ralph, *Northern Protest*, 203; Abernathy, *Walls Came Tumbling*, 399; Anderson and Pickering, *Color Line*, 269.

128. Hampton and Fayer, *Voices of Freedom*, 317; Anderson and Pickering, *Color Line*, 274.

129. Brown, *Ideology and Community Action*, 65, 70.

130. Travis, *Black Politics*, 401–2; Anderson and Pickering, *Color Line*, 277.

131. Anderson and Pickering, *Color Line*, 277, says forty-two whites were arrested; I am going with the figure of thirty-two, which was cited in "Guards Bayonet Hecklers in Cicero's Rights March," *NYT,* Sept. 5, 1966. Other details are taken from Travis, *Black Politics*, 401–2.

132. Hampton and Fayer, *Voices of Freedom*, 318; Travis, *Black Politics*, 403.

133. Travis, *Black Politics*, 403; "Guards Bayonet Hecklers"; Ralph, *Northern Protest*, 199.

134. Ralph, *Northern Protest*, 191–92; also see Matusow, *Unraveling of America*, 206–7.

135. Ralph, *Northern Protest*, 192–94; also see Anderson and Pickering, *Color Line*, 140, 277–78.

136. Garrow, *Bearing the Cross*, 533, 535; Anderson and Pickering, *Color Line*, 281–82, 295, 300.

137. Anderson and Pickering, *Color Line*, 306, 299–301.

138. "Survey Bares Ghetto Tragedies," *CDD*, Sept. 6, 1966, CUL 76-116, box 129, folder 58, UIC.

139. Ralph, *Northern Protest*, 90.

140. Payne, *I've Got the Light*, 3–4.

141. By 1966, SCLC and SNCC members had worked jointly on civil rights projects for years. The membership of the two groups often overlapped. James Bevel exemplified those links. He was one of the founding members of SNCC. In 1961, he joined the SCLC as its youth training specialist, and thereafter he remained involved with both organizations. Bevel's leadership would seem to guarantee that SNCC organizing principles would be followed in Chicago as they had been in Mississippi. Unfortunately, by 1966, Bevel seems to have lost the wisdom of SNCC in favor of empowering

select leaders and encouraging "manliness" and individual responsibility—perhaps a reflection of his personal trajectory toward psychological solutions that would culminate in the 1990s with his embrace of the far-right conspiracy theorist Lyndon LaRouche. Timothy Noah, "Bevel's Second Children's Crusade," *Slate*, posted April 10, 2008, www.slate.com/id/2188857, accessed Sept. 8, 2008.

142. Although this choice was emblematic of their own naiveté about how power really operated in Chicago, leaders instead castigated black West Siders for being "far from understanding the closed housing market as one of their key problems"—a deficiency the organizers hoped to remedy as the "educational processes of the Movement progressed." Finley, "Open Housing Marches," 9.

143. "Notes on Resident Participation in Chicago," 1966, in CJEG-Egan I, box 54, 24, UND.

CHAPTER SEVEN: THE STORY OF A BUILDING

1. David A. Satter, "The West Side, and the Plight of the Urban Poor," *Chicago Maroon Magazine*, March 4, 1966.

2. Letter, George W. Beadle to Mr. Satter, March 21, 1966, DS Papers.

3. *Housing Affairs Letter*, April 8, 1966, 3; letter, Peter G. Burns, Director of Community Renewal, Ottawa, Canada, to The Editor, *Chicago Maroon*, March 1, 1967. Also see letter, Richard J. Watson, North City Corporation, Philadelphia, to David Satter, April 21, 1966; letter, Bruce Tunell to David A. Satter, July 11, 1966, all in DS Papers.

David's article was brought to their attention after excerpts were published in the prestigious *Journal of Housing*. See letter, Fred Vogelsand, Assistant Editor, *Journal of Housing*, to David A. Satter, May 13, 1966, DS Papers. The Cincinnati Real Estate Board publication the *Realtor* also published an excerpt, under the flattering headline "Housing Expert Comments on Housing the Poor." See *Realtor*, June 1966.

4. David A. Satter, "West Side Story: Home Is Where the Welfare Check Comes," *New Republic*, July 2, 1966.

5. Letter, Anne N. Barrett, Houghton Mifflin Co., to David A. Satter, June 28, 1966; letter, David A. Satter to Anne N. Barrett, July 1, 1966; letter, Joseph Alsop to Mr. Satter, June 29, 1966. Also see letter, Esther S. Yntema, Senior Editor, Atlantic Monthly Press, to David A. Satter, June 9, 1966, all in DS Papers.

6. Joseph Alsop, "Removing a Poverty Carcinogen," in his column "Matter of Fact," *Washington Post*, March 1, 1967. Alsop concluded with an attack on the provisions that he felt made welfare damaging to its recipients. These were suggestions that many welfare recipients agreed with, such as ending the "lunatic provision" that made families ineligible if the husband was present, provisions that punished people who earned extra money by throwing them off welfare, thus practically outlawing "self-improvement, job-seeking, [and] learning good work habits," and finally, welfare clients' treatment not as "free citizens" but as "'cases,' to be handled by caseworkers."

7. In a recent example, at a 1966 legislative hearing landlord Jacob Feldman admitted that, in one of his buildings, he recovered his entire investment plus 100 percent profit in three years; in another, he collected $42,500 in rents but paid out only $2,400 in maintenance. When accused of making "excessive" profits, Feldman had a succinct answer: "That's why I bought the building." He added that he felt a 50 percent profit on his investment was justified "given the headaches involved" in running a slum building (Ed Kandlik, "City Slum Owners Tell 'Woes,'" *CDN*, June 2, 1966).

8. Charles Abrams's *Forbidden Neighbors* (New York: Harper, 1955) explained the FHA's racially biased insurance policies. Nicholas Shuman's "One Million Underdogs" series, which ran in the *Chicago Daily News* from Jan. 23, 1961, through Jan. 27, 1961, clearly explained both bank redlining and the ways that speculators exploited the credit squeeze to make immense profits.

9. For example, see "Exclusive: The Story of Chicago's Slums," *CDN*, May 20, 1963.

10. He hinted that the "dirty" apartment was rented by a welfare recipient, but his description of her behavior—her storing of crumpled paper in a cloth bag but her practice of shoving of actual garbage onto the floor—indicates that her problem was mental illness, not welfare.

11. Betty Flynn, "A Slum Home CAN Be Clean," *CDN*, May 23, 1963; for a similar story, see Dean Schoelkopf, "10 Realty Men Face Quiz in Slum Probe," *CDN*, May 31, 1963, both in MHPC 80-49, box 14, folder 6, UIC. Note that here, too, the clean slum apartment was inhabited by an ADC recipient and her five children. In Representative Robert Mann's opinion, this woman's housekeeping did not invalidate the larger question of how the building in which she lived was maintained. "Some of the places we visited were not fit for human habitation," Mann commented, adding "I was impressed by the conscientious effort some tenants were making to maintain clean apartments." Also see John Justin Smith, "Random Garbage and the Chicago Slums," *CDN*, May 23, 1963, in which Smith describes being "startled" to discover a clean apartment on the second floor of a slum building.

12. Lois Wille, "West Side Story: 2 Forces Fight Slum Misery," *CDN,* June 8, 1966.

13. David Satter interview, Feb. 1, 2001, 58–59. Rumors that Mark Satter was a slumlord are mentioned in Warren Lehman, "Goodbye, Mark" (unpublished ms.), MJS Papers.

14. David Satter interview, June 1, 2002, 6; Satter interview, Feb. 1, 2001, 58.

15. Perhaps he should have described a real slum landlord instead of a composite, but at eighteen, David admitted, he "was not too well versed in some of the canons of the journalistic profession" (interview, June 1, 2002, 6). David never hid his essay's origins from those close to him. As columnist Joseph Alsop went from being a letter-writing fan to a friend and mentor, David told him that his reportage was based on his father's buildings. Alsop wasn't bothered by this detail, or perhaps, as David recalled, Alsop "didn't really hear what I was saying," since "he then wrote a column in which he said that I had set out to expose slum landlords, but in fact had changed my mind, which made it more of a story of course, but it was not true" (Satter interview, June 1, 2002, 20).

16. Satter interview, June 1, 2002, 5–6, 22.

17. Ibid., 2, 6. "The key there was that [Mark Satter's] buildings included apartments of different sizes. With different sizes there were different rents. And some of the . . . apartments . . . were accessible to low-income tenants or people on welfare," who caused problems. "The welfare recipients were leaving all the time, often without paying," David recalled (5).

18. David Satter interview, June 19, 2001. David had one other reason to view his piece as a vindication of our father's views. The last essay our father wrote on the topic of welfare, "Jobs versus Dole," was rejected by numerous journals, including the *New Republic.* See letter, MJS to Ritz [Fischer], Feb. 6, 1964; letter, MJS to *New Republic,* Feb. 7, 1964; letter, MJS to George, Feb. 24, 1964.

19. MJS, "A Plea for a Reborn WPA," *CDN*'s *Panorama,* Aug. 1, 1964; MJS, "A New WPA—Alternative to Chaos," *Labor Today,* Aug.–Sept. 1964, 17–19.

20. MJS, "Jobs versus Dole—A Suggested Approach," unpublished ms, my italics.

21. Satter, "West Side Story."

22. David Satter, 'The Institution of Relief as an Alienating Factor among Nonwhites on the Near West Side of Chicago" (unpublished undergraduate paper, Nov. 30, 1965), 16, 19, and teacher comments on the paper, 19, 20, DS Papers.

23. Satter interview, June 19, 2001; Satter interview, June 1, 2002, 11; see also Warren Lupel interview, June 25, 2001, 4.

24. David E. Gumpert, "Editors Have Day in Court," *Chicago Maroon*, Sept. 30, 1966, 3.

25. The bills are included in my father's probate file, no. 65 P 7747, CCCC.

26. Satter interview, June 1, 2002, 5.

27. My mother told me about the fire and her struggles with the building manager on March 30, 1972, when I was thirteen years old. I wrote the story down in my journal and then forgot about it. One day in 2006, when I was finishing this manuscript, I decided to take a look at my old journals. I randomly opened one of them to the page on which my mother told me this story. My 1972 account included details of how much my mother was paid for her buildings. It is on pages 52–53 of my diary for the period Feb. 6, 1972–July 4, 1972.

28. Letter, MJS to Helen [Dorn], Jan. 11, 1965. On efforts to sell the Kilbourn apartment, see letter, Clarice to MJS, May 22, 1965; letter, MJS to Clarice, May 25, 1965; letter, Clarice to MJS, May 28, 1965.

29. I am assuming a price of $50,000 for the building at 3846–48 West Congress Street because another six-flat about four blocks away (at 3626–28 West Lexington) was valued at that amount in the 1950s. See "Razing of Hovel Stymied for 5 Years," *CT*, May 7, 1973. My parents might have paid less since they purchased the building in the 1940s. However, my father remortgaged the building several times to finance his other purchases, so the debt probably went up over the years.

30. This entire story is recorded in my journal, March 30, 1972 (see n. 27, above).

31. Satter interview, June 1, 2002, 8–9.

32. I pieced these transactions together from the property records for 348 South Kilbourn, which show Margaret Balin's ownership as of November 5, 1965, the placing of the property in trust with Exchange National Bank that same day, and a contract sale of the building on February 21, 1966, for $13,000, notarized by Moe M. Forman. There is some confusion about this property, however. On March 10, 1969, my mother wrote to Irving Block to tell him that someone had contacted her about the Kilbourn Avenue building. She was taken aback because, as she wrote Block, "the Kilbourne Ave. bldg. was sold in 1966, I believe. Needless to say, it was a giveaway." This could mean that the building was sold in a transaction that was separate from the $2,000 package sale that Irving Block negotiated for her other buildings. When my mother told me about the buildings in 1972, I wrote that she had sold three buildings, not four. But that could have been confusion on my part. In any case, the building ended up in Balin's hands, and the eventual contract sale of the building was negotiated by Moe Forman. On Balin's business relationship with Forman, see "Slumlords Hide Empire in Legal Maze of Names, Sales," *CT*, May 6, 1973.

Gil Balin, of course, knew Mark Satter. He had been the manager of Mark's buildings and he had attended his funeral. During the fall of 1966, Balin became one of the last targets of the Chicago Freedom Movement when some of his tenants organized against him. For details, see *Urban Affairs Weekly Reports*, AFSC Chicago Regional Office, Oct. 30, 1966, and Nov. 20, 1966, in AFSC Papers, Philadelphia.

33. Satter, "The West Side"; Satter, "West Side Story."

34. David Satter, "West Side Story."

35. David never wrote again on the topic. His "West Side Story" essay is cited in the major historical work on Martin Luther King Jr.'s Chicago crusade as evidence that it was "virtually impossible . . . for landlords to make a profit from their slum holdings." See James R. Ralph Jr., *Northern Protest* (Cambridge: Harvard University Press, 1993), 271–72, n. 129.

36. When the GLCC tried to step up code enforcement against neighborhood slum landlords in 1958, L. J. Epstein was a frequent target. The GLCC housing enforcement officer noted of an Epstein building: "Entire building shows absolute lack of maintenance or care of any kind." See "Violation Summary against L. J. Epstein and Company," in GLCC Papers, box 6, folder "June 1–16, 1958," CHS. The complaints against Epstein were ongoing. See, for example, letter, William E. Bonner to Epstein Realty, Oct. 27, 1959. A partial list of the violations Bonner found in two Epstein buildings included no heat, no hot water, cockroach infestations, and broken windows (GLCC Papers, box 11, folder "Oct. 23–31, 1959," CHS). Also see "Two-Front Attack Slated in Chicago's War on Blight," *CST,* Feb. 11, 1966.

37. Ruby Kirk interview, Aug. 21, 2001.

38. Ibid.

39. Ibid.; Lois Wille, "Ruby Kirk the Slum-Fixer," *CDN,* May 3, 1969.

40. Kirk interview; Wille, "Ruby Kirk the Slum-Fixer"; "Slum Tenants Buy Building," *CDD,* July 29, 1970, MHPC 76-102, box 5, folder 1, UIC.

41. That same year the Kate Maremont Foundation, a private group, also got federal financing to purchase and renovate a single four-story, fifty-eight-apartment complex (Wille, "2 Forces Fight Slum Misery").

42. Alan B. Anderson and George W. Pickering, *Confronting the Color Line: The Broken Promise of the Civil Rights Movement in Chicago* (Athens: University of Georgia Press, 1986), 305; Wille, "2 Forces Fight Slum Misery."

43. During these years my father repeatedly begged judges to appoint receivers for the properties of Chicago's worst contract sellers. He was ignored. See any of his cases cited in this book.

44. Lois Wille, "Slumlords Flee," *CDN,* March 25, 1969.

45. Wille, "Ruby Kirk the Slum-Fixer"; "Slum Tenants Buy Building."

46. Kirk interview; Wille, "Ruby Kirk the Slum-Fixer."

47. "Slum Tenants Buy Building"; Kirk interview; Alan Boles interview, Jan. 20, 2005, 19.

48. Wille, "Ruby Kirk the Slum-Fixer"; Boles interview.

49. Wille, "Ruby Kirk the Slum-Fixer."

50. Boles interview.

51. Letter, Irving Block to David Satter, March 8, 1966, DS Papers.

CHAPTER EIGHT: ORGANIZING LAWNDALE

1. Margery Frisbie, *An Alley in Chicago: The Life and Legacy of Monsignor John Egan,* commemorative ed. (Franklin, Wisc.: Sheed & Ward, 2002), 171; also see Charles Dahm, *Power and Authority in the Catholic Church: Cardinal Cody in Chicago* (Notre Dame, Ind.: University of Notre Dame Press, 1981), 3–4, 17.

2. Joseph H. Fichter, "Chicago's Archdiocesan Office of Urban Affairs," *America,* Oct. 23, 1965, Margaret (Peggy) Roach Papers, WLA, LUC. Egan was on the Executive Committee of the Chicago Conference on Religion and Race, on the Board of Directors of the Community Renewal Foundation, and on the Board of Governors of the MHPC; he was also a leader of the Interreligious Council on Urban Affairs and a member of the Mayor's Advisory Committee of the Community Renewal Program, among other responsibilities.

3. "Put to Pasture? Controversial Priest Here Gets a Parish," *CDN,* Jan. 14, 1966, Roach Papers, WLA, LUC; also see Frisbie, *Alley in Chicago,* 172–73.

4. Frisbie, *Alley in Chicago,* 177–78.

5. Egan, "Housing and Community Action," talk given to the National Catholic Social Action Conference and the NCCIJ, Omaha, Aug. 28, 1965, 4, 10, 5, his italics, in CJEG-Egan I, box 50, "Father Egan's Talks," UND.

As Egan summarized elsewhere, if people's living conditions "prevent them from living a total human life, we have to exert everything we can to remove these obstacles." Poor education, lead paint on the walls, or overpriced housing that drained a family's resources were all properly religious concerns, therefore ("The City, the Church," *Chicago Tribune* magazine, Nov. 17, 1968, Margery Frisbie Papers, WLA, LUC).

6. Egan warned that religious activists would pay a price for challenging the powerful: "The prestige of the priest, minister, or rabbi . . . can be put to use in the cause of right, or at least in the cause of right as it is dimly seen by weak and sometimes myopic human beings." But once the clergy uses this prestige "contrary to people's cherished way of doing things," that respect will evaporate. "The policeman will doff his cap to you as you walk by him on a corner near your church. . . . But as you walk by him in a downtown civil rights parade, don't count on the hat-doffing" (Egan, "Problems of the Urban Church in the Twentieth Century," address to the National Presbyterian Center, Washington, D.C., February 7, 1966, in Roach Papers, WLA, LUC).

7. Frisbie, *Alley in Chicago,* 191; also see 177–78.

8. Ibid., 178–79; also see Jack Macnamara interview, July 30, 2001, 14.

9. "Deposition of Monseigneur [*sic*] John Egan," Sept. 23, 1969, *Contract Buyers League v. F & F Investment,* USDC 69c15, 10, in CJEG-Egan II, box 112, folder "CBL Complaint and Counterclaim: J. Egan Deposition," UND.

10. Frisbie, *Alley in Chicago,* 180.

11. Ibid., 180–81; Mark Splain interview, March 26, 2004, 8–11; also see Sister Mary Sharon Rose, "Operation Powder Keg," *BVM Vista,* Sept. 1967, 30, in Roach Papers, WLA, LUC.

12. Jeffrey Michael Fitzgerald, "The Contract Buyers League: A Case Study of the Interaction between a Social Movement and the Legal System" (Ph.D. dissertation, Northwestern University, 1972), 81–82; Frisbie, *Alley in Chicago,* 181–82.

Fitzgerald wrote his dissertation when the CBL was in the midst of a legal battle; for that reason he used pseudonyms for everyone he wrote about. Their true identities, however, are easily discernable; I also double-checked with Fitzgerald that my assumptions about who was who were correct. See Jeffrey Fitzgerald interview, March 29, 2002. In this chapter and the following two, therefore, I have taken the liberty of using the real names of those whom Fitzgerald describes with pseudonyms.

13. Macnamara interview, Feb. 22, 2001, 7, and Macnamara interview, July 30, 2001, 1–13.

14. Macnamara interview, July 30, 2001, 14–15; "Macnamara's Band Scores a Hit," *Jesuit Bulletin,* Chicago Province, Dec. 1968, 4–6, JM Papers.

15. David Quammen interview, March 9, 2004, 6; Macnamara interview, April 12, 2001, 5–6.

16. Maureen McDonald interview, Aug. 10, 2001, 6.

17. Splain interview, 14–15, 1; Macnamara interview, April 12, 2001, 27. By the summer of 1968, organizers' pay had risen to ten dollars a week. See "Seminarian Fights Lawndale Gyps," *CA,* July 19, 1968, JM Papers; also see "Presentation Community Organization Project Financial Report, June 1–Dec. 31, 1967," CJEG-Egan II, box 112, folder "CBL Correspondence," UND.

18. Sidney Lens, "Jim Crow–Northern Style," *Liberation,* Dec. 1956, 14, describes "worn-out Jewish areas." Ernest Scribner, "Shadow of a Gunman Over the 24th Ward," *Chicago Scene,* April 1963, describes Lawndale's former Jewish population as "very poor." In 1964, Lois Wille wrote that North Lawndale collapsed once its population shifted from "middle-income Jews to low-income Negroes" (Wille, "The Gap in City Planning," *CDN,* Jan. 14, 1964). She also describes Jewish Lawndale as "white and prosperous" in Wille, "Political Feelers Start to Go Out for Plums in Poverty War Pie," *CDN,* April 8, 1965. The "finest in the nation" quote comes from "CBL—What It's Done," *NW,* May 31, 1968. Two white CBL organizers also described white Lawndale as prosperous; see Alan Boles, "Black Homeowning," *New Republic,* Dec. 13, 1969, and Rolland Smith, "Jesuits and the CBL," *Christian Century,* Feb. 25, 1970. The only counter to this rosy picture came from a black writer who actually grew up in Lawndale. He noted accurately that Lawndale was "already in an advanced state of decay when whites abandoned it" (W. Joseph Black, "The Renewed Negro and Urban Renewal," *Architectural Forum,* June 1968, 61).

19. Rose, "Operation Powder Keg," 32.

20. Macnamara interview, April 12, 2001, 4–5; William Dendy, "Self-Help Program Works in Lawndale," *NW,* Feb. 9, 1968.

21. Fitzgerald, "Contract Buyers League," 81–82.

22. Macnamara interview, April 12, 2001, 7; Lois Wille, "Battle Mounts against 'Race Tax,'" *CDN,* March 23, 1968; "Seminarian Fights Lawndale Gyps."

23. If their building had been purchased with a mortgage, Arbertha could have sold it after her husband's death and used the proceeds to purchase something cheaper. But in 1959, the FHA refusal to insure loans to most black home purchasers meant that the Arberthas had no choice but to buy on contract—which meant that Arbertha did not own the building. Now she had to keep up the monthly payments or lose everything she and her husband had invested into the property (Wille, "Battle Mounts").

24. Discovery Deposition of John R. Macnamara, *Baker et al. v. F & F Investment,* USDC 69c15, 25, JM Papers. Occasionally Presentation organizers heard Lawndale residents complain that "they were on the contract," as they complained that they were "on ADC," but Macnamara hadn't grasped the implications of their words. In fact, Macnamara and his organizers assumed that Lawndale's most pressing issue was urban renewal. Rumor had it that there was a plan to let Lawndale decay so that the city could get "Model Cities" money to tear it down, displace local blacks, and start over (Fitzgerald, "Contract Buyers League," 83–84).

25. Deposition of John R. Macnamara, 26; John McKnight interview, July 6, 2001; Macnamara interview, July 30, 2001, 22.

26. Macnamara interview, July 30, 2001, 22; Deposition of John R. Macnamara, 42; "Seminarian Fights Lawndale Gyps." Also see Wille, "Battle Mounts."

27. Splain interview, 15; Macnamara interview, April 12, 2001, 7; Macnamara interview, July 30, 2001, 24. Also see CBL flyer, "Evils of Contract Buying," 1968, which contains the real estate history of twenty Lawndale buildings, in C-ROA (Peggy Roach) Papers, box 2, "Peg/Contract Buyers League, Chicago," UND (Roach's papers have since been moved to WLA, LUC). The eight-block area was bounded by Independence on the east, Pulaski on the west, Flournoy on the north, and Arthington on the south.

28. Frisbie, *Alley in Chicago,* 192. Frisbie doesn't cite a source for these statements, but Egan said something similar to a reporter around this time. "From the very beginning . . . we were warned by almost everybody that this extremely difficult and complicated endeavor could not succeed. We were told that the power against us was too great; however, we knew it was the power of greed and selfishness and exploitation by men without scruples who lived luxuriously on the misery of the poor" and who must be challenged, Egan said (William Dendy, "CBL Tells It Like It Is to State Committee," *NW,* July 12, 1968).

29. Egan deposition, 73, also see 13. See material on Mark J. Satter's campaign in IAF (Alinsky) Papers, folder 163, "Land Contract Sales—Case Notes and Speech Excerpts," UIC. Despite Egan's initial hesitancy, he had clearly hoped to revive my father's crusade against exploitative contract selling. In the late 1960s, he sent a copy of "Suit Charges Excessive Realty Overpayment," *CDN,* June 2, 1958—the first article to appear about my father's suit on behalf of Mary Lee Stevenson, Joeanna Williams, and their neighbors against Moe M. Forman—to U.S. attorney Thomas Foran along with a note, "Tom—is not this a legitimate area of interest in your new task. JE" (CJEG-Egan II, box 112, folder "CBL Correspondence," UND).

30. Michael Gecan interview, July 19, 2002, 17; also see 16; Fitzgerald, "Contract Buyers League," 275. Macnamara agreed: "Yes, rumor is that holders of the secret land trusts were members of the Democratic machine" (Macnamara interview, July 30, 2001, 25, 26).

31. Macnamara interview, July 30, 2001, 22–23; also see Splain interview, 13.

32. Macnamara interview, April 12, 2001, 5; also see Memo, Dr. Ross P. Sherer, Loyola University, to Egan, Sept. 25, 1967, in CJEG-Egan II, box 112, folder "CBL Correspondence," UND; Splain interview, 12–13; Memo, John R. Macnamara, S.J., to Rev. Thomas Diehl, S.J., Re: Report on Visit to Eastern Colleges, Dec. 8, 1967, in CJEG-Egan II, box 112, folder "CBL Correspondence," UND; Gamaliel Foundation, "Progress and Prospects" (unpublished report), Sept. 1970, 4, JM Papers. Among the students who received college credit for organizing in Lawndale (via Chicago's Loyola University) were James Devanney, Thomas Mackey, Mark Splain, William Ryan, Peter Welch, and Marc Young. See "Economic Miracle Delights Lawndale," *CST,* March 7, 1968.

33. Gamaliel Foundation, "Progress and Prospects," 50.

34. "Remarks by Mike Gecan," Contract Buyers League Reunion, June 21, 1997, 2, 4, JM Papers; Gecan interview, 3–5. As Gecan explained, success depended "not just on the merits of the case" but on whether "you know everything there is to know" about your topic. Also see William Dendy, "Self-Help Program Works in Lawndale," *NW,* Feb. 9, 1968.

35. Splain interview, 15.

36. Macnamara interview, April 12, 2001, 9; Ruth Wells interview, June 14, 2001, 4; also see James Alan McPherson, "'In My Father's House There Are Many Mansions—and I'm Going to Get Me Some of Them Too': The Story of the Contract Buyers League," *Atlantic Monthly,* April 1972, 56.

37. Wells interview, 3; McPherson, "'In My Father's House,'" 55; Fitzgerald, "Contract Buyers League," 94–95.

38. Fitzgerald, "Contract Buyers League," 94–95; Wells interview, 25–26, 66–67; Alphine Wade Jefferson, "Housing Discrimination and Community Response in North Lawndale (Chicago), Illinois, 1948–1978" (Ph.D. dissertation, Duke University, 1978), 183–84; *Contract Buyers League v. F & F Investment,* Exhibit 1, in C-ROA (Peggy Roach) Papers, box 2, folder "Peg/Contract Buyers League Chicago," UND (now in WLA, LUC); Ruth Wells, "Housing Workshop Task Force: Will the Church Do What Needs to Be Done?" Aug. 1971, CJEG-Egan II, box 111, folder "Peg-CBL," UND.

39. Wells interview, 9–10; McPherson, "'In My Father's House,'" 54–56.

40. Wells, "Housing Workshop Task Force," 2–3; Fitzgerald, "Contract Buyers League," 95; McPherson, "'In My Father's House,'" 55.

41. Fitzgerald, "Contract Buyers League," 36, 38, 95; Macnamara interview, April 12, 2001, 11.

42. Wells interview, 4–5; McPherson, "'In My Father's House,'" 58; Fitzgerald, "Contract Buyers League," 97.

43. McPherson, "'In My Father's House,'" 58.

44. CBL "Progress Report" (unpublished report), Nov. 20, 1968, JM Papers.

45. Fitzgerald, "Contract Buyers League," 98–99.

46. See McPherson, "'In My Father's House,'" 59. The case of Mr. and Mrs. Howell Collins was typical. They paid the inflated price of $25,500, plus the highest rate of interest allowed at that time by Illinois law. If the Collinses had been charged a fair price of $15,000 for the building (the contract seller had purchased it a few months earlier for $14,000), they would now owe $570. Instead, after nine years of payments the Collinses still owed over $17,000 on the building. See "Contract Buyers Plan Big Holdout," *West Side Torch*, Nov. 30–Dec. 13, 1968, JM Papers.

47. Memo, Contract Buyers of Lawndale to Moe Forman, Feb. 21, 1968, in news release, Feb. 20–21, 1968, CJEG-Egan II, box 111, "CBL Materials," UND. I am quoting a memo to Forman from Feb. 21, but I am assuming that the same words or words very similar to them were said during the February 3 meeting. For a more detailed chronology of early attempts to reach Forman, see Feb. 21, 1968, news release, 2.

48. Wells interview, 9.

49. Fitzgerald, "Contract Buyers League," 98–99; also see Memo, Contract Buyers of Lawndale to Moe Forman, Feb. 21, 1968, in news release, Feb. 20–21, 1968.

50. Fitzgerald, "Contract Buyers League," 105; CBL news release, Feb. 21, 1968, 2.

51. CBL news release, Feb. 21, 1968, 2; "Jesuit Launches Campaign against Home Contract Gyps," *NW*, Feb. 16, 1968.

52. Although Forman didn't address the group, Egan did. "The people of our community have too long suffered the inequities of the 'contract sales system,'" he told them. It is a "vile system . . . born of the desires of evil men to make money feeding on the fear of white people and the need [of] Negro people to buy homes in a closed housing market."

Forman agreed to renegotiate contingent on FHA refinancing. The story of the CBL's first confrontation with Forman is documented in CBL news release, Feb. 20–21, 1968; "Economic Miracle"; J. M. Kelly, "Fair Minded Should Support Fight against Contract Sales," *NW*, March 1, 1968; "Students Help Negroes Cut Home Costs," *CST* (Chicago Sun-Times Service—might have been published in *Woman's World*), March 10, 1968, JM Papers; Fitzgerald, "Contract Buyers League," 146.

53. "Nun Helps Lawndale Home-Buying Program," *CDN*, April 2, 1968; CBL "Progress Report," Nov. 20, 1968.

54. The CBL's rapid growth was not attributable to the magnitude of the exploitation its members endured. After all, exploitative contract sales had been well documented for a decade. If the exploitation was extreme, so was its complexity and the consequent difficulty of formulating a response to it.

55. Clyde Ross interview, Aug. 3, 2001, 10, 19, 5; also see Clyde Ross, "Grass Roots," Working Paper 5, Adlai Stevenson Institute, in CJEG-Egan II, box 111, folder "CBL News Clips," UND.

56. Ross interview, 20, 24–25. On Campbell Soup factory conditions, see Carmen Teresa Whalen, *From Puerto Rico to Philadelphia: Puerto Rican Workers and Postwar Economies* (Philadelphia: Temple University Press, 2001), 53, 158.

57. Fitzgerald, "Contract Buyers League," 22–23.

58. Ibid., 22; "CBL Tells It," *NW*, July 12, 1968; Exhibit 1 of *Contract Buyers League v. F & F Investment*.

59. Fitzgerald, "Contract Buyers League," 36.

60. Ross interview, 1.

61. "Home Buyers Fight Contract Racket," *WP,* Aug. 4, 1969; McDonald interview, 12.

62. Discovery Deposition of Charles Baker, Sept. 30, 1969, for *Baker v. F & F Investment,* 69c15, 3–15, JM Papers.

63. Ibid., 152–53, 16–19.

64. Ibid., 31–32, 49.

65. Ibid., 53–55, 58–61, 86, 181, 95.

66. Alan Boles interview, Jan. 20, 2005, 8.

67. "Economic Miracle"; Fitzgerald, "Contract Buyers League," 20, 30, 100–102.

68. "Home Buyers Fight Contract Racket"; Fitzgerald, "Contract Buyers League," 100–102.

69. Marc Young interview, July 2, 2005, 7; see Jefferson, "Housing Discrimination," 182, for more descriptions of Wells.

70. Wells interview, 6, 50, 56–57, 60, 66.

71. Ibid., 1, 27, 8, 57–58, 46, 41.

72. Macnamara interview, July 30, 2001, 17; letter, Macnamara to Very Rev. Robert F. Harvanek, S.J., Nov. 18, 1970, 2, CJEG-Egan II, box 112, "CBL Correspondence," UND; Greg Colvin interview, Feb. 3, 2005, 10; "Economic Miracle"; "Seminarian Fights."

73. Wille, "Battle Mounts"; "Nun Helps"; William Dendy, "CBLers Renew Fight against Slumlords," *NW,* May 3, 1968; Dendy, "CBL Steps Up Campaign, Bids for Bank Support," *NW,* May 17, 1968.

74. Gamaliel Foundation, "Progress and Prospects," 9–10.

75. "Home Buyers Set Strike," *CDD,* Nov. 21, 1968; Wille, "Battle Mounts." Also see "Negroes Plan to Withhold Home Money," *CT,* Nov. 21, 1968.

76. "CBL Pickets Large Savings and Loan Firm," *NW,* May 24, 1968; "Eviction Orders Served in Home Contract Fight," *NW,* Dec. 6, 1968. Also see Fitzgerald, "Contract Buyers League," 104; "CBL Steps Up"; Gecan interview, 6.

77. "Death Threat Made on Life of CBL Student," *NW,* March 22, 1968; "Realtor Orders CBLers' Arrest: Police Refuse," *NW,* March 29, 1968; also see "CBLers Renew Fight."

78. Fitzgerald, "Contract Buyers League," 149.

79. Joseph A. Nowicki, "Appraising in the Ghetto," *Real Estate Appraiser,* Sept.–Oct. 1969, 5–9.

80. Fitzgerald, "Contract Buyers League," 234: McPherson, "'In My Father's House,'" 59, JM Papers.

81. *JCUA Newsletter,* Jan. 1967, 4, in Robert J. Marx Papers, box II, folder 5, CHS; also see Jefferson, "Housing Discrimination," 134, 136.

82. See Michael Turoff interview, Oct. 15, 2001, and Warren Lupel interview, June 25, 2001; William Dendy, "CBL, Slumlords Meeting Sets Precedent Here," *NW,* June 14, 1968; also see the Real Estate Investors Association advertisement, "Will All Chicago-Area Small Businessmen Be Subjected to This Same Shameful Harassment?" *NW,* Nov. 1, 1968.

83. Fitzgerald, "Contract Buyers League," 489, n. 24.

84. Wells interview, 47; also see Ross interview, 8; "1500 New Troops Here," *CDN,* April 6, 1968 (see map showing areas of greatest violence).

85. Letter, Irving Block to John Egan, April 5, 1968, in CJEG-Egan II, box 112, "CBL Complaints and Counterclaim," UND.

86. Macnamara interview, July 30, 2001, 27–29; McDonald interview, 17; Frisbie, *Alley in Chicago,* 199; also see "Lawndale Drive Now Paying Off," *NW,* June 12, 1968; Dendy, "Self-Help Program Works" and "Here's How Nun-Realtor Helps Poor Caught in Contract-Buying Trap," *NW,* March 29, 1968.

87. Fitzgerald, "Contract Buyers League,"160; also see Macnamara interview, July 30, 2001.

88. William Dendy, "Legal Committees Form to Support CBL Workers," *NW,* Aug. 16, 1968. Dendy's article says that they met for the first time on Aug. 9, 1968. However, a group of attorneys working for the CBL also met on June 8, 1968, at Loyola University (Dendy, "CBL, Slumlords Meeting," *NW,* June 14, 1968).

89. Dendy, "CBL, Slumlords Meeting." Dendy doesn't identify the attorney who attacked the Catholic Church, but I am assuming it was Irving Block based on Fitzgerald's description of him as the person who made the most outrageous and public comments about the CBL. See Fitzgerald, "Contract Buyers League," 161.

90. As Macnamara recalled, Egan's approach to social change was always divided between his understanding that people must fight their own battles and his instincts as a "political animal" that insider connections were the way to make things happen in Chicago (Macnamara interview, July 30, 2001, 28).

91. See "An Act Relating to the Prevention of Economic Exploitation of Racial Prejudice in Residential Real Estate," attached to Minutes of the Code Modernization Committee, April 24, 1968, MHPC 76–102, box 2, folder 1, UIC; also see Minutes, MHPC Code Modernization Committee, March 6, 1968, same folder.

92. Frisbie, *Alley in Chicago,* 101, 197.

93. "Home Buyers Fight Contract Racket"; also see Nowicki, "Appraising in the Ghetto," 9, and Boles, "Black Homeowning."

94. Letter, Thomas A. Foran to John E. Horne, May 31, 1968, CJEG-Egan II, box 112, "CBL Correspondence," UND, my italics; also see Fitzgerald, "Contract Buyers League," 157. Foran pointed out that while the FHA had stopped redlining areas like Lawndale, action on behalf of the CBL would help make that change in policy "retroactive," thereby enabling "those people who were the first ghetto residents to seek the advantages and responsibilities" of home ownership to pay a fair price for their homes. "It is the ultimate premise of the American economic system that the market permits the purchase of a commodity at a fair price," he wrote.

95. Dendy, "CBL Tells It Like It Is"; "Probe Sought on Lawndale Sales," *CDN,* July 9, 1968; "Tell Contract Buying Scheme," *CDD,* July 9, 1968; "Ten S & L Firms Are Probed in Housing Fraud," *CT,* July 9, 1968.

96. William Dendy, "State Committee Queries Home-Contract Realtors," *NW,* Nov. 22, 1968; "How to Buy a $15,000 House for $44,820," *CST,* Nov. 16, 1968.

97. "Slum Clearance," *WSJ,* Jan. 2, 1969; also see Leon M. Despres, "The Chicago the Delegates Won't See," *Progressive,* Aug. 1968, 27; Monsignor John J. Egan, untitled talk (beginning "Since the group has been over the basic territory . . ."), CJEG-Egan I, box 50, "Father Egan's Talks," 3, UND.

98. "End Home-Contract Gouge," *CST,* Nov. 23, 1968; "Slum Clearance." Also see McPherson, "'In My Father's House,'" 59.

99. McPherson, "'In My Father's House,'" 64, 56, 66. See "Chicago Blacks Fight a Race Tax," *Business Week,* Jan. 24, 1970, for story of Mr. and Mrs. Clay, black Lawndale residents who refused a $10,000 settlement offer from Al Weinberg because Weinberg would not make similar offers to his other contract buyers.

100. Gecan interview, 2–3. It helped that Macnamara was closely associated with Egan. Gecan's family had been part of Our Lady of the Angels parish. He had grown up hearing his mother praise the "wonderful sermons" Egan had delivered there. See Gecan's CBL reunion speech, 1.

101. Gecan interview, 20; McDonald interview, 14; Fitzgerald, "Contract Buyers League," 129; also see Jefferson, "Housing Discrimination," 200–201.

102. Robert J. Marx, "Judaism and Open Housing," n.d., Marx Papers, box 11, folder 3, CHS; letter, Robert J. Marx to "My dear friend," Aug. 5, 1966, Marx Papers, box 11, folder 1, CHS.

103. Dawn Turner Trice, "Activist Retiring after Fighting for So Many Causes," *CT,* Aug. 20, 2001; Robert J. Marx and Louis Kreinberg, "The Jewish Council on Urban Affairs: A Progress Report," 2–3, Marx Papers, box 11, folder 1, CHS.

104. "Jews Are Warned on Tensions in Negro Ghettos," *NYT,* Dec. 4, 1966, CUL 76-116, box 129, folder 58, UIC. Also see Hillel Levine and Lawrence Harmon, *The Death of an American Jewish Community: A Tragedy of Good Intentions* (New York: Free Press, 1992), 184–93, for an account of confrontations between rabbis and Jewish slumlords (with a decided bias toward the Jewish slumlords).

105. Letter, Marx to Macnamara, March 1, 1968, in CJEG-Egan II, box 112, "CBL Correspondence," UND; Fitzgerald, "Contract Buyers League," 151.

106. Robert J. Marx, "Chicago Summer: Another Analysis," *New City,* Sept. 1966, 10; Marx, "The People in Between," April 13, 1968, 1, in Marx Papers, box 8, folder 7, CHS. The latter article was later published in *Dimensions,* Spring 1969. Also see Beryl Satter, "'Our Greatest Moments of Glory Have Been Fighting the Institutions We Love the Most': The Rise and Fall of Chicago's Interreligious Council on Urban Affairs, 1958–1969," *U.S. Catholic Historian* 22, no. 2 (Spring 2004): 33–44.

107. Marx, "People in Between," 12, 1; Marx, "In Accordance with Maimonides' Principle That the Highest Form of Charity . . . In Response to Our Fears about Black Power," 2, in Marx Papers, box 11, folder 5, CHS; also see Marx, "Religious Communities and Urban Power Structures," 4, delivered Oct. 11, 1966, in Marx Papers, box 8, folder 6, CHS; letter, Marx to "My dear friend," Aug. 5, 1966.

108. Lupel interview, 6.

109. Fitzgerald, "Contract Buyers League," 150–51; McPherson, "'In My Father's House,'" 61.

110. Gecan interview, 20; "Contract Buyers Cite Support from Jewish Realtors," *West Side Torch,* shortly after its Aug. 22–Sept. 5 issue, 1968 or 1969 (the clipping is undated, but Banks' letter refers to the Aug.–Sept. issue), JM Papers.

111. Photos accompany articles "Realtor Orders CBLers' Arrest" and "Here's How Nun-Realtor Helps," *NW,* March 29, 1968, CJEG-Egan II, box 111, folder "CBL News Clips," UND.

112. Dendy, "CBL—What It's Done . . . Where It's Going," *NW,* May 31, 1968.

113. Eddie Smith interview, Nov. 16, 2003, 27.

114. Young interview; Fitzgerald, "Contract Buyers League," 127.

115. Gecan interview, 11. This incident is also described in David Quammen, *To Walk the Line* (New York: Knopf, 1970), a lightly fictionalized account of Quammen's experiences working with Macnamara in Lawndale.

116. Quammen interview, 3; see also 14.

117. Smith interview, 26. There was another black youth whom Macnamara looked after for a time, but Smith recalled little about the other teenager. See Macnamara interview, July 30, 2001.

118. Smith interview, 1–3, 5–9, 15, 23, 27, 34.

119. Macnamara interview, April 12, 2001. See Gecan interview, 11, for a similar story.

120. Smith interview, 10. Smith added that the riot "was the most amazing thing

I've ever seen in my life. The whole street—from Madison Avenue to Ashland Avenue—was in flames. We didn't dare go past Ashland, because that became very white. . . . I was running right next to a guy who got his brains blown out by the cops. And when he got hit in the head by the slug, he picked up more speed . . . and then he tilted over and died. . . . I think he was dead on his feet. He just spurted out past all the rest of us that had jewelry and furs and all the other stuff that we stole from the stores."

121. Ibid., 1–2, 5, 7, 11–13, 20, 22–23, 25, 31–33.

122. "Msgr Egan Outlines Major CBL Objectives," *NW,* May 31, 1968; Gecan interview, 20.

123. Young interview, 3; Smith interview, 25. David Quammen was so moved by his experiences living with Eddie Smith that he wrote a novel, *To Walk the Line,* largely about their relationship.

124. They refused to offer across-the-board discounts to contract buyers, instead insisting upon deciding which buyers were "deserving" of discounts on an individual basis. The resulting bottleneck meant that very few contracts were renegotiated through the FHA and FSLIC (Fitzgerald, "Contract Buyers League," 12, 57; McPherson, "'In My Father's House,'" 59, 67; "Economic Miracle."

125. William Dendy, "Land Trust Bill Dies in Senate Committee," *NW,* July 26, 1968.

126. Lupel interview, 9, 6; also see Fitzgerald, "Contract Buyers League," 62.

127. "Will All Chicago-Area Small Businessmen" (paid advertisement), emphasis in original; "Facts Contradict Charges in Real Estate Investors' Ad," *NW,* Nov. 1, 1968. The sellers' accounts of harassment were not fanciful. Some of the CBL's young organizers were not above making harassing telephone calls to the sellers. See Quammen, *To Walk the Line,* 35–36; Smith interview, 17–18.

128. "Egan reminiscence on Alinsky and Sherman," Frisbie Papers, box 1, folder 4, WLA, LUC; also see McKnight interview, July 6, 2001; Sanford D. Horwitt, *Let Them Call Me Rebel: Saul Alinsky, His Life and Legacy* (New York: Vintage, 1992), 517–18.

129. McPherson, "'In My Father's House,'" 67; Deposition of John Macnamara, 102; Gamaliel Foundation, "Progress and Prospects," 13, 16.

130. Letter, John R. Macnamara to the Very Rev. Robert F. Harvanek, Oct. 7, 1968, CJEG-Egan II, box 112, "CBL Correspondence," UND.

131. "Home Buyers Set Strike," *CDD,* Nov. 21, 1968.

132. "Contract Buyers Plan Big Holdout," *West Side Torch,* Nov. 30–Dec. 13, 1968, JM Papers.

133. Fitzgerald, "Contract Buyers League," 206–7.

134. Ibid., 229; "15 Home-Payment Boycotters Receive Eviction Notices," *National Catholic Reporter,* Jan. 1, 1969; "Eviction Orders," *NW,* Dec. 6, 1968.

CHAPTER NINE: THE BIG HOLDOUT

1. Sidney Sharif interview, June 16, 2001, 12–13, 5–6 (Clark later changed his name to Sharif); "Evicted Contract Buyers Aren't Giving Up Hope," *CT,* April 4, 1970; James Alan McPherson, "'In My Father's House There Are Many Mansions—and I'm Going to Get Me Some of Them Too': The Story of the Contract Buyers League," *Atlantic Monthly,* April 1972, 67.

2. Jeffrey Michael Fitzgerald, "The Contract Buyers League: A Case Study of Interaction between a Social Movement and the Legal System" (Ph.D. dissertation, Northwestern University, 1972), 184–86; Sharif interview, 1. Although Fitzgerald reports that a "significant number" of South Siders did not join the CBL until September, the CBL had changed its name to accommodate South Siders by July 1968; see Contract Buyers League flyer in letter, Clarice Satter to David Satter, July 13, 1968, DS Papers.

There is evidence that Universal homes were sold at about 35 percent (or $6,500) above the price of comparable units in white neighborhoods; see *Sidney Clark and Julia Clark et al. v. Universal Builders Inc. et al.*, U.S. Court of Appeals for the Seventh Circuit, 72-1655, Plaintiffs-Appellants' Brief, 25, JBA. However, Fitzgerald notes that charges of price inflation against Universal were nowhere near as clear-cut as those against the West Side sellers, in part because the homes Universal sold were newly constructed and therefore did not have a prior price to which their current price could be compared. See Fitzgerald, "Contract Buyers League," 185.

3. Fitzgerald, "Contract Buyers League," 182, 187, 207–8. On tensions between South Siders and West Siders, see interviews with Ruth Wells (June 14, 2001), Sidney Sharif, and Maureen McDonald (Aug. 10, 2001). These tensions dated back at least to the Depression years; see St. Clair Drake and Horace Cayton, *Black Metropolis: A Study of Negro Life in a Northern City* (New York: Harcourt, Brace, 1945), 577–79.

4. Sharif interview, 6.

5. Fitzgerald, "Contract Buyers League," 238; also see 207, 213.

6. "15 Home-Payment Boycotters Receive Eviction Notices," *National Catholic Reporter*, Jan. 1, 1969; D. J. R. Bruckner, "Ghetto Escalates War on Housing Specula-tors," *LAT*, Jan. 20, 1969.

7. Michael Turoff interview, Oct. 15, 2001, 5–7.

8. Thomas Boodell Jr. interview, Aug. 20, 2001, 3.

9. Once the CBL announced its payment strike, Judge Harold Sullivan decided that only the very best legal talent could defuse this potentially explosive situation. He contacted Tom Sullivan, explaining that the CBL's payment strike constituted a "big emergency with possible evictions." He asked if he could send Macnamara and Boodell to speak with him about whether a legal case could be made on the CBL's behalf. See McPherson, "'In My Father's House,'" 68; "Hope Marks CBL's Third Birth-day," *CST*, Jan. 22, 1971; Alan Boles interview, Jan. 20, 2005, 1–2, 7; Jack Macnamara interview, July 30, 2001, 30; Fitzgerald, "Contract Buyers League," 172.

10. Fitzgerald, "Contract Buyers League," 165; also see 172; McPherson, "'In My Father's House,'" 68.

11. *Joseph Lee Jones v. Alfred H. Mayer Co.*, 88 S. Ct. 2186 (1968), in 88 *Supreme Court Reporter*, 2199, 2203, 2194, 2205. A reading of the act as barring only state-sanctioned racial discrimination in matters of property would have been more conso-nant with the Fourteenth Amendment's provision of "equal protection of the laws" to "all persons." But the legislation was written in 1866, two years before the passage of the Fourteenth Amendment; it was created under the authority of the Thirteenth Amendment, which potentially granted it a broader purview. As the *Supreme Court Reporter* summarized, "Neither adoption of the Fourteenth Amendment nor subse-quent readoption of Civil Rights Act of 1866 were meant to limit application of Act to state action." It also noted that the Civil Rights Act of 1968 "had no effect" upon Sec-tion 1982. See 2188.

12. Macnamara interview, 30. Jenner served as senior counsel to the Warren Commission investigating the assassination of John F. Kennedy and was a member of the Presidential National Commission on the Causes and Prevention of Violence ("Jen-ner and Block Tries a Little Management," *American Lawyer*, May 1989; also see "Albert E. Jenner," *LAT*, Sept. 19, 1988).

13. Boodell interview, 10, 8; Macnamara interview, 30, 32.

14. John C. Tucker, *Trial and Error: The Education of a Courtroom Lawyer* (New York: Carroll and Graf, 2003), 264; McPherson, "'In My Father's House,'" 69, 68.

15. Ellis E. Reid, "Earl, Bob, and Me," *Law School Record of the University of Chi-cago Law School* 37 (Spring 1991): 6; Ellis Reid interview, Aug. 17, 2001, 6; also see

William R. Ming Jr., "Racial Restrictions and the Fourteenth Amendment: The Restrictive Covenant Cases," *University of Chicago Law Review* 16, no. 2 (Winter 1949): 203–38.

16. Reid interview; Reid, "Earl, Bob, and Me"; also see John McKnight, "The Summit Negotiations," in *Chicago 1966,* ed. David J. Garrow (New York: Carlson, 1989), 124, 127; also see John C. Tucker interview, July 17, 2001, 5.

17. Boles interview, 5; John McKnight interview, July 6, 2001. Also see George Feiwell interview, June 18, 2001.

18. Tucker, *Trial and Error,* 264. Boodell officially became "additional Counsel" to the CBL suit in April 1969, but he was involved in the suit from the start. See docket sheets, 69c15, *Baker et al. v. F & F Investment et al.,* USDC, Eastern District of Illinois, Eastern Division, ascension number 021-74-A242, location number 369814, box 2, also see ascension number 021-01-0005, location number NARA, box 1, and ascension number 021-82-0225, location number V4837, box 1, 9, NARA.

19. They were also charged with violating federal and Illinois state antitrust laws (because they conspired to keep housing prices artificially high) and with violating federal securities law (because they solicited their customers through false and misleading advertising).

20. *Contract Buyers League et al. v. Universal Builders et al.,* USDC for Northeastern District of Illinois, Eastern Division, 69c115, in CJEG-Egan II, box 111, folder "CBL Materials," UND; *Contract Buyers League et al. v. F & F Investment et al.,* USDC for the Northern Division of Illinois, Eastern Division, 69c15, in C-ROA (Peggy Roach Papers), box 2, folder "Peg/Contract Buyers League," UND (Roach's papers have now been moved to WLA, LUC), and in JM Papers; McPherson, "'In My Father's House,'" 68; "Contract Buyers Lose Suit," *CT,* April 17, 1976.

In May 1969 the defendants' motion to dismiss the Contract Buyers League as a plaintiff was granted. Thereafter the two cases were known as *Baker v. F & F Investment* and *Clark v. Universal Builders.* To simplify matters I refer to the cases as *Baker* and *Clark* from the start. See *Contract Buyers League et al. v. F & F Investment et al.,* 69c15, May 21, 1968, 300 F. Supp. 210 (1969), 230.

21. Fitzgerald, "Contract Buyers League," 262; also see 173. I have replaced Fitzgerald's pseudonym with the attorney's real name in this quote.

22. Quoted in McKnight interview.

23. "Contract Home Buyers File a Civil Rights Suit," *CST,* Jan. 7, 1969; William Dendy, "Lt. Gov. Simon Gives Support to Contract Buyers League," *NW,* Feb. 7, 1969; Boodell interview, 11. See "CBL Wins Legal Skirmish," *CDD,* Oct. 13, 1970, for more on Jenner's strong support for the CBL's suit; also see Bruckner, "Ghetto Escalates War on Housing Speculators."

24. The defendants also included L. J. Epstein, who had gotten possession of my father's building at 3901 West Jackson, and Alvin Shavin, the Lawndale landlord who had welcomed Martin Luther King Jr. as a tenant in 1966. See docket sheets for 69c15. In an irony that few could appreciate, the CBL's attorneys also subpoenaed journalist Alfred Balk, the author of the 1962 *Saturday Evening Post* exposé "Confessions of a Block-Buster," in order to pressure him to reveal the identity of "Norris Vitchek." Although sympathetic to the CBL, Balk refused to name the speculator, insisting that he was entitled to shield his source under the free speech provisions of the First Amendment. The U.S. Circuit Court ruled in Balk's favor, and the CBL's attorneys appealed the decision. In 1973, the Supreme Court let the circuit court's ruling stand, an action widely heralded as a victory for freedom of the press ("Editor Is Backed on Secret Source," *NYT,* Feb. 20, 1972; "Court OKs Protection of Source," *Miami Herald,* Dec. 9, 1972; "Shielding News Source in Civil Trial Permitted," *LAT,* May 8, 1973; Alfred Balk interview, Feb. 18, 2001).

25. Like many of my father's suits, *Baker* also stressed the "gross inequality of bargaining position and power" between the "unsophisticated and uneducated" buyers and the "sophisticated" sellers (Complaint, *Contract Buyers League v. F & F Investment*, 69c15, 7, 9, 10, 11, 12, JM Papers).

26. Ibid., 13. The defendants also included "assignees," that is, people who purchased contract papers at "substantial discounts" from the sellers. Several individuals, including Moe Forman, Al Berland, and John Karras, were charged as both "defendant-seller" and "defendant-assignee" since they both sold buildings on contract and bought discounted contracts from one another.

The details were laid out in a lengthy "Exhibit 1," a copy of which is in C-ROA (Peggy Roach) Papers, box 2, folder "Peg/Contract Buyers League," UND (now at WLA, LUC). It listed all the contract sellers, who loaned them the money for their initial purchases, the dates they bought the buildings, what they bought them for, the dates they sold the buildings on contract to black plaintiffs, and the price they charged. The data were consistent and damning. Lou Fushanis, Moe Forman, and John Karras were among the owners of an installment contract signed by Ozirea Arbertha and her mother, Blanche Peeler. The original building had been purchased by one of the three men in May 1959 with a loan from First Mutual, for $15,000; it was sold to Arbertha and Peeler three months later for $28,000. Jay Goran used a loan from Supreme Life Insurance to purchase a building for $14,820 in May 1959; less than three weeks later he sold it on contract to Emmanuel and Elizabeth Ross, a black couple, for $21,000. Goran's old partner W. F. Smith bought a building for $9,000 on March 5, 1960, and sold it on contract to Willie Nelson, a black man, one week later, for $18,500. The list went on until the property transactions of sixty-five plaintiffs in the suit were similarly described.

27. Complaint, *Baker v. F & F Investment*, 69c15, 4, 17, 9–10, 19–20.

28. Letter, Irving L. Block to Thomas P. Sullivan, Jan. 8, 1969, in JM Papers; Fitzgerald, "Contract Buyers League," 509, n. 15. Fitzgerald says that the circular was written by the Real Estate Investors Association, which Block represented. I think it is fair to assume that Block either wrote it or supported its assertions.

29. According to Lupel, the CBL's attorneys immediately demanded that Block produce, among other documents, the original appraisals made when his clients first applied for mortgages to purchase Lawndale properties. Feeling "besieged with discovery," Block asked several partners in large firms to co-counsel with him. The first five firms he approached wouldn't touch the case. The sixth agreed to lend Block one attorney (William Dendy, "Federal Judge Begins Hearing on CBL Suit," *NW,* Jan. 17, 1969; Warren Lupel interview, June 18, 2001, 1–2). On Judge Will, see Tucker, *Trial and Error,* 113.

30. Opinion by Judge Will, *Contract Buyers League v. F & F Investment,* 69c15, USDC for Northern District of Illinois, Eastern Division, March 28, 1969, in *1969 Trade Cases,* 86,699.

31. Opinion by Judge Will, *Contract Buyers League v. F & F Investment,* 69c15, USDC, N.D. Illinois, E.D., May 21,1969, 300 *Federal Supplement* 210 (1969), 218–20, 215–16 (his italics). I have combined Will's response to the statute of limitations argument with his earlier response about the class action argument in order to streamline the narrative. No meaning is lost.

32. While the individual installment contracts contained somewhat variable terms, "the logic of the complaint is that the . . . inequity of any particular contract is the result of a greater scheme of exploitation involving . . . the contracts executed by the other plaintiffs." Will added that since the plaintiffs allegedly suffered fraud and discrimination because of their lack of financial resources, it followed that they could "protect their civil rights in the courts" only through "combining their financial resources." (Opinion by Judge Will, *Contract Buyers League v. F. & F Investment*, March 28, 1969, 86,698.)

33. Block claimed that the alleged injury to the plaintiffs occurred at the moment they signed their contracts. Will instead supported the plaintiffs' argument that the injury continued as long as the plaintiffs continued to pay on their contracts. See "Notice to Negroes Who Bought Residential Homes," in C-ROA (Peggy Roach Papers), box 2, folder "Peg/Contract Buyers League, Chicago," UND (now at WLA, LUC); Opinion by Judge Will, *Contract Buyers League v. F & F Investment*, March 28, 1969, 86,700.

The CBL was thrilled with this victory. As Charlie Baker explained, the rulings "open the door for potential savings of at least $60 million for an estimated 7,000 black home buyers in Chicago" ("Justice Dept. Joins Suit with Contract Buyers," *National Catholic Reporter*, April 9, 1969).

34. Opinion by Judge Will, *Contract Buyers League v. F & F Investment*, May 21, 1969, 215–16.

35. "U.S. Rights Expert Watches Case Here," *CA*, Feb. 13, 1969; William Dendy, "Washington Official Here to Look at CBL," *NW*, Feb. 14, 1969; "U.S. Backs Negroes' Suit to Recoup 'Blockbusting' Profits in Chicago," *NYT*, March 29, 1969. Also see "U.S. Joins Negro Suit over Homes," *CT*, March 29, 1969.

36. McPherson, "'In My Father's House,'" 70; "Negroes Could Sue Home Dealers, Stores for Bias under Plan," *WSJ*, March 31, 1969; also see "U.S. in Suit to Aid Cheated Negroes," *Cincinnati Post and Times Star*, March 28, 1969, and "U.S. Joins Negro Suit over Homes," JM Papers.

It took months of effort by U.S. Attorney Thomas Foran and Assistant U. S. Attorney Thomas Todd to convince Leonard to consider the CBL's situation. The Justice Department knew that the CBL lawsuit could target federal agencies, since the Federal Housing Administration and the Federal Savings and Loan Insurance Corporation were guiltier than any of the defendants of creating the scaffolding of residential segregation that ensured black economic inequality. This knowledge prompted Leonard to finally file the amicus curiae. The deal was the following: if the CBL's attorneys held back in the short run from adding federal agencies to the lawsuit, then the Justice Department would support the CBL. Thomas Todd offered to draft the Justice Department brief. He wrote a forty-three-page document, including ten pages that were "really scathing about the FHA." But Leonard's assistant slashed Todd's draft. "The ten pages I had on the FHA had been dismissed in a sentence," Todd recalled, adding that "this was Leonard's doing." Yet the Justice Department was ready with its press release touting its accomplishment almost before the brief was completed. "They said this was an indication of what the Administration was going to do to help black people," Todd noted. "But the brief said absolutely nothing. It got them a million dollars' worth of publicity" (McPherson, "'In My Father's House,'" 68–70).

37. "U.S. Throws Its Power behind Blockbusting Suit," *CST*, March 29, 1969; also see "U.S. Joins Negro Suit over Homes"; Fitzgerald, "Contract Buyers League," 507, n. 6; docket sheets, 69c15, 8, 11, 21.

38. Opinion by Judge Will, *Contract Buyers League v. F & F Investment*, May 21, 1969, 225.

39. Michael Kalika, David L. Jorgenson, and Jay Goran were among the attorneys for the defendants listed in Opinion by Judge Will, *Contract Buyers League v. F & F Investment*, March 28, 1969, 86, 697–98.

40. Fitzgerald, "Contract Buyers League," 161. I've replaced Fitzgerald's pseudonym, "Hook," with the real name "Block."

41. "Contract Buyers Plan Big Holdout," *West Side Torch,* Nov. 30–Dec. 13, 1968, JM Papers; also see Fitzgerald, "Contract Buyers League," 108, for CBL member confronting Block on television about this comment.

42. "Some of the most outrageous things would be said in court" about their clients, Lupel recalled. "And Block was an advocate, and a damn good one, and would not allow . . . these things to be said about the men that he knew for most of his professional life. And they would try to shut him up and he wouldn't accept it" (Lupel interview, 4, 3, 8).

43. Ibid., 5–7.

44. Fitzgerald, "Contract Buyers League," 480, n. 24.

45. David Garing, "Slum Clearance," *WSJ,* Jan. 2, 1969. For examples of my father's use of the term, see Paul Gapp, "South Siders Left Groaning as Insurance Rates Zoom," *CDN,* Nov. 12, 1958, and "Talk Prepared by Mark J. Satter for Delivery before Catholic Conference for Interracial Justice," August 29, 1958. According to Lupel, Block often thought about my father. "I met your father when I first started [at Block's office]," Lupel told me, "and Block talked about him often after his death" (Lupel interview, 4).

46. Sandy Gatto interview, July 13, 2002, 14; Gatto interview, April 25, 2002, 4.

47. Block may have felt that, if logic alone wasn't enough to support his position, there was my father's fate to consider. Block was intimately aware of the price my father paid for his politics. It was Block who, as my mother's attorney, wrote to the University of Chicago to beg for financial aid for my two brothers: "Mr. Satter was a practicing attorney without any partnership affiliation. At the time of his death . . . his financial affairs were in an extremely precarious condition. . . . There are, as you know, a total of five children, and . . . there are considerable doubts in my mind as to whether the two Satter boys will be able to continue with their education, even with the assistance of the University. There is no source of income other than Social Security." (Moved, perhaps, by Block's description of my family's plight, the University of Chicago gave my brothers scholarships shortly thereafter.) Letter, Clarice Satter to Robert J. Charles, Director of College Aid, University of Chicago, Sept. 1, 1965; letter, Irving L. Block to the University of Chicago Office of Admissions and Aid, Aug. 9, 1965, MJS Papers.

48. Letter, Clarice Satter to David Satter, July 13, 1968, DS Papers.

49. Lupel interview, 11.

50. Boodell interview, 19.

51. Boles interview, 2; also see Boodell interview, 19.

52. The suit is *Hamilton Corp. v. Clark,* 69c210. See Fitzgerald, "Contract Buyers League," 269, 195; Gamaliel Newsletter, Feb. 5, 1969, JM Papers.

53. Fitzgerald, "Contract Buyers League," 271–74, 277, 286; William Dendy, "Judge Orders CBL Eviction Trial Tuesday," *NW,* Feb. 21, 1969; Dendy, "CBL Files Court Suit on Realtors," *NW,* Jan. 10, 1969; Bruckner, "Ghetto Escalates War on Housing Speculators."

54. While Mrs. Nelson, the first person whom Universal tried to evict, paid $19,450 for her home, the CBL estimated the building's true value at $19,000 ("Contract Buyers Dig In for Fight," *CDN,* Feb. 4, 1970). Some markups were more substantial. Isaac Thompson paid $23,200 for his home, but it was appraised at only $18,250. Isaac and Jessie Preston's home cost $30,695 on contract but was appraised at $24,575. See "2 More Evictions Blocked by Contract Buyers Group," *CST,* March 21, 1970. For price markup range of 20–35 percent, see Jeffrey Michael Fitzgerald, "The Contract Buyers League and the Courts: A Case Study of Poverty Litigation," *Law and Society Review* 34, no. ¾ (Winter 1975): 68.

55. Universal insisted that its profits averaged less than 10 percent. The CBL

made them appear greater, Universal argued, because it confused the issue by adding in tax fees ("Home Sale on Contract Defended," *CDN,* April 4–5, 1970; "High Profit Charge Denied by Builder," *CT,* April 4, 1970).

56. "Home Sale on Contract Defended"; also see "Revised Meeting between Rabbi Marx and Judge Will," Nov. 10, 1970, Robert Marx Papers, folder 11–12, CHS.

57. Fitzgerald, "Contract Buyers League," 245, 230. They were not alone in viewing the tactic as effective. By January 1969, housing activists from Detroit, Cleveland, and Indianapolis were in Chicago to study the payment strike (Garing, "Slum Clearance").

58. Dendy, "Lt. Gov. Simon Gives Support to Contract Buyers League"; also see "Contract Buyers Rebel—and Hold Out $136,000," *CDN,* Jan. 30, 1969; Bruckner, "Ghetto Escalates War on Housing Speculators."

59. Boodell interview, 5.

60. Fitzgerald, "Contract Buyers League," 195–96.

61. Ibid., 209. I have replaced Fitzgerald's pseudonyms with the real names and inserted internal quotes in the second quote.

62. Ibid., 196.

63. William Dendy, "CBL Legal Battle with Realty Firm Goes On and On," *NW,* May 23, 1969.

64. Fitzgerald, "Contract Buyers League," 322. That Patner was Jewish and aware that some of the sellers were also Jewish might have contributed to his interest in the case. Patner also already had a professional acquaintance with one CBL member, Sidney Clark. After Clark and his colleagues in the Chicago Police Department's Gang Intelligence Unit compiled evidence to put gang members in prison, it was often Patner who showed up to represent them. Sharif interview, 11; Boles interview, 13; Jeffrey Fitzgerald interview, March 29, 2002, 2; McPherson, "'In My Father's House,'" 73–74.

65. Fitzgerald interview, 8; Fitzgerald, "Contract Buyers League," 317–18; "Suit Here Could Halt All Illinois Evictions," *CDN,* Jan. 3–4, 1970.

66. McPherson, "'In My Father's House,'" 73; Fitzgerald interview, 8.

67. Fitzgerald, "Contract Buyers League," 190; Macnamara interview, April 12, 2001, 17–18; Fitzgerald, "Contract Buyers League," 318.

68. Fitzgerald, "Contract Buyers League," 389, 220; Boles interview, 3; Sharif interview, 9.

69. Fitzgerald, "Contract Buyers League," 210, 217; "The Contract Buyers League Story," Nov. 21, 1969, JM Papers.

70. Fitzgerald, "Contract Buyers League," 276, 218.

71. Ibid., 306–8; also see "9 Contract Buyers Ordered Evicted," *CST,* Dec. 19, 1969.

72. Fitzgerald, "Contract Buyers League," 308–9.

73. Ibid., 222, 213.

74. Ibid., 222–23. This speech was made during the first payment strike, but Fitzgerald reports that it was typical of the sorts of speeches made during the second as well.

75. Transcription of taped CBL meeting, August 1969, author's possession and in JM Papers.

76. "Homebuying Unit in Money Bind, Vows Sit-In," *CST,* Oct. 3, 1969; "Jesuits Aid Contract Buyers," *CDN,* Oct. 8, 1969.

77. Macnamara interview, July 30, 2001, 17; news release, "Statement of the Very Rev. Robert F. Harvanek," Oct. 8, 1969, JM Papers.

78. Macnamara interview, July 30, 2001, 17; "Jesuits Aid Contract Buyers"; letter, Pedro Arrupe, S.J., to Very Reverend Robert F. Harvanek, Sept. 24, 1969, CJEG-Egan II, box 112, "CBL Correspondence," UND.

79. Macnamara interview, July 30, 2001, 18; "Blacks Get $250,000 to Battle

Evictions," *Chicago Today*, Dec. 31, 1969, JM Papers. See also "Jesuits Give $150,000 to Chicago Black Group," *LAT*, Dec. 31, 1969; "Jesuits Aid Contract Buyers"; "Jesuits Aid CBL Appeal Bond Fund," *NW*, Oct. 10, 1969; "In the Jesuit Tradition," *CDN*, Oct. 27, 1969. Ultimately, the courts did not permit the CBL to use the "lump-sum appeal bond" offered by the Jesuits, and the money was returned (McPherson, "'In My Father's House,'" 74). The boost that the Jesuits' actions gave to the CBL's legitimacy was nevertheless extremely valuable. See "What's Happenin' at CBL," July 1, 1970, JM Papers.

80. Fitzgerald, "Contract Buyers League," 322–24, 336; also see 261.

81. "The Unfinished Oral History of Judge Hubert L. Will," http://www.fjc.gov/servlet/tGetInfo?jid=2588, 19–20, accessed Dec. 29, 2003; Jon Will interview, Jan. 27, 2004. When the American Legion gave an award to Governor Orval Faubus, who sent the National Guard to Little Rock Central High School in order to prevent nine black students from attending, the American Veterans Committee instead presented an award to the nine students for their bravery. Will was among the founders of the AVC's umbrella organization, the World Veterans Federation (Jon Will interview).

82. Fitzgerald, "Contract Buyers League," 442, 445, 431, 341–42.

83. Ibid., 443, 342; also see "CBL Evictee Return Near?" *CDN*, April 9, 1970. Will tried to be scrupulously fair to all sides. When the realtors asked that any person withholding monthly payments be dismissed from the federal suit, Will said no. He would not rule that "you cannot have the question of the deprivation of your civil rights considered because you engaged in a tactic with which this court happens to disagree" (Fitzgerald, "Contract Buyers League," 439).

84. "Judge Denies Writ Barring Home Evictions," *CST*, Nov. 13, 1969; "Meeting Buoys Contract Home Buyers," *Chicago Today*, Nov. 26, 1969; "Evictions Are Ordered for 32 in the Contract Buyers League," *CST*, Nov. 25, 1969; Will interview. Also see docket sheets, 69c15, 41, 46.

85. "Evictions Are Ordered for 32 in the Contract Buyers League"; "Meeting Buoys Contact Home Buyers"; docket sheets, 69c15, 41.

86. "She's Evicted—but Returns," *CDN*, Dec. 12, 1969; "Evicted Mother Back in House," *NW*, Dec. 19, 1969; "Contract Buyers Dig In for Fight," *CDN*, Feb. 4, 1970; "'Weathers' Eviction," *Chicago Defender*, May 2–8, 1970. Early press reports described Mrs. Nelson as a divorcee. Later ones described her as a widow. See "Arrest 7 in CBL Evictions," *CDD*, March 31, 1970.

87. "Contract Buyer's Friends 'Undo' Eviction," *CST*, Dec. 12, 1969.

88. Bob Cromie, "Contract Buyers Are Angry," *CT*, Jan. 7, 1970; "Contract Buyers Bar Sheriff's Evictions," *CST*, Jan. 6, 1970; "Cold Foils Evictions in Buyer Fight," *CDN*, Jan. 6, 1970. Gibson's fury was in part a result of years of unfair treatment. In the early 1950s, he'd paid $5,000 down to a South Side real estate agent who was then convicted of selling property he didn't own. Gibson lost the $5,000. In 1959, he paid $3,000 down to Universal Builders for a home priced at $24,000, only to learn that at the time of purchase the building had been appraised at $15,000.

89. "Priest Asks U.S. to Halt Evictions," *CDN*, Dec. 31, 1969.

90. Bob Cromie, "Jesuits Back Contract Buyers," *CT*, n.d. (probably around Jan. 7, 1970); Rev. Thomas Diehl, Letter to the Editor, *CDN*, Feb. 5, 1970, JM Papers.

91. "Postpone the Evictions," *CDN*, Feb. 2, 1970; see "Justice for Black Home-Buyers," *CST*, Jan. 8, 1970; "Eviction Appeal Needs Settling," *Chicago Today*, Jan. 9, 1970; Joel Daly commentary, WLS-TV, Jan. 29, 1970. That spring there were more such pro-CBL editorials. See "Stop Evictions!" *CDD*, April 1, 1970; "Kup's Column," *CST*, April 1, 1970, all in JM Papers.

92. "Woods in No Hurry to Resume Evictions," *CST*, Jan. 23, 1970; "Evictions Set in Buyer Dispute," *CT*, Jan. 28, 1970.

93. "How It Looked to the Family Inside," *CST,* Jan. 30, 1970; "Angry Crowd Foils Eviction," *CDN,* Jan. 29, 1970; "Rout Guard, Foil Eviction," *CDD,* Jan. 29, 1970.

94. "Eviction 'War' Feared: Raiders Provoke Violence," *Chicago Defender,* Jan. 31–Feb. 6, 1970; "Crowd Foils South Side Eviction," *CST,* Jan. 30, 1970.

95. "Rout Guard, Foil Eviction"; Arthur Siddon and Stanley Ziemba, "Sheriff Calls Off Eviction," *CT,* Jan. 30, 1970.

96. "Contract Buyers Dig In for Fight," *CDN,* Feb. 4, 1970; "Eviction 'War' Feared."

97. "Next Move in Evictions Up to Judges," *CDN,* Jan. 30, 1970; "Sheriff Bars 'Army' Evictions," n.d., CJEG-Egan II, box 111, folder "CBL News Clips," UND; "No Forceful Evictions: Woods," *CST,* Jan. 31, 1970; "CBL Eviction Try Postponed," *NW,* Feb. 6, 1970.

98. "Sheriff Is Sued by 7 Realty Firms," *CST,* Feb. 18, 1970; Fitzgerald, "Contract Buyers League," 502, n. 13; "Contract Buyers' Eviction Moratorium Over: Woods," *CST,* March 17, 1970; also see "Woods Will Evict Family to Avoid Rap," *CDN,* Feb. 20, 1970.

99. Fitzgerald, "Contract Buyers League," 502, n. 13; "CBL Chief Evicted—for 5 Minutes," *CDN,* April 21, 1970; "Evictions and Prudence," *CST,* March 19, 1970.

100. "Top Court Rejects Contract Buyer Suit," *CST,* Feb. 28, 1970.

101. The decision is quoted in an advertisement, "Payment or Eviction? The Truth about the Contract Buyers League Strike," n.d. (approximately Feb. 19, 1970), JM Papers. The three judges decided not to take a position on the constitutionality of the Forcible Entry and Detainer Act; they would await the decision of the Illinois Supreme Court. See docket sheets, 69c15, 49; "Contract Buyer Eviction Ban Refused by Panel of 3 Judges," *CDN,* Feb. 11, 1969; "Contract Home Buyers Lose Plea for Writ," *CST,* Feb. 12, 1970.

102. Sharif interview, 9; Fitzgerald, "Contract Buyers League," 326, 189.

103. "Chicago Blacks Fight a 'Race Tax,'" *Business Week,* Jan. 24, 1970.

104. Turoff interview, 2. The Turoffs and Samuels insisted in an advertisement that ran in the *Chicago Sun-Times* that the CBL hopes "to coerce us economically and thus force us to knuckle under to their demands. This we will not do." "Payment or eviction? The truth about the Contract Buyers League Strike." Universal said that CBL members "have developed into a mob" that has "attacked and abused the judicial process" ("Contract Buyer Eviction Ban Refused by Panel of 3 Judges").

105. "Home Sale on Contract Defended."

106. Turoff interview, 9; Mike Royko, "Dollar-Eyes Have It Again," *CDN,* n.d., in CJEG-Egan II, box 112, folder "CBL Correspondence," UND; McDonald interview, 8–9.

107. Robert J. Marx, "The People in Between," Marx Papers, box 8, folder 7, CHS; Boles interview. Marx's JCUA contributed $5,025 to the CBL. See letter, Charlie Baker to Robert J. Marx, July 7, 1970, Marx Papers, folder 11-2, "Contract Buyers League," CHS.

108. Letter, Gordon B. Sherman to Robert Marx, April 17, 1969, CJEG-Egan II, box 112, folder "CBL Correspondence," UND.

109. Letter, James P. Rice to Bob (Robert S. Engelman), May 28, 1970, Marx Papers, folder 11–2, CHS; also see letter, Arthur W. Brown Jr., published in *Pathfinder,* n.d., Marx Papers, box 11, folder 2, and letter, Marx to Maurice N. Eisendrath, March 23, 1970, Marx Papers, box 11, folder 3, CHS.

110. Turoff interview, 10.

111. Letter, Thomas P. Sullivan, William R. Ming Jr., and Thomas J. Boodell Jr. to "Dear Client," Feb. 26, 1970, CJEG-Egan II, box 112, "CBL Correspondence," UND; "2 Eviction Attempts by Sheriffs Blocked," *CT,* March 20, 1970. Also see "Early Solution Seen in Home Evictions," *CST,* Feb. 27, 1970; "Contract Buyers' Eviction Moratorium Over: Woods."

112. Wells interview, 15; McPherson, "'In My Father's House,'" 75. Also see Fitzgerald, "Contract Buyers League," 349; Larry Green, "Evictions 'Tipoff' Bugging Sheriff," *CDN* (?), n.d. (before April 15, 1970), JM Papers.

113. "Buyers Co-Operation in Evictions Sought," *CDN,* March 24, 1970.

114. "100 Police Join Eviction Attempt," *CDN,* March 23, 1970; also see McPherson, "'In My Father's House,'" 74–75. See Surveillance Report, Chicago Police Department "Red Squad," March 26, 1970, for a description of how the CBL tried to keep eviction information out of the hands of local gang members, who they feared would "incite violence" (Red Squad Files, box 230, folder 1134–1, CHS).

115. "Sheriff Refuses to Delay CBL Evictions," *CST,* March 25, 1970.

116. "Police Seal Block, Evict 4 Families," *CDN,* March 30, 1970; "Arrest 7 in CBL Evictions," *CDD,* March 31, 1970.

117. "Woods Raiders Evict 12," *CDD,* April 1, 1970; "12 More Evictions on the S. Side," and "Police Evict 12 More," *CDN,* March 31, 1970; "Deputies Evict 12 More Contract Buyers," *CT,* April 1, 1970; Feiwell interview.

118. "12 More Evictions on the S. Side"; "200 Police Evict 4 CBL Families," *CST,* March 31, 1970; "Woods Raiders Evict 12"; "Deputies Evict 12 More Contract Buyers."

119. "Report Arson in Contract Buyer House," *CT,* March 26, 1970; "Fires Hit 4 Eviction Area Houses," *CST,* March 26, 1970. On white radicals fighting police, see "6 More CBL Families Evicted," *CDN,* April 22, 1970; Fitzgerald, "Contract Buyers League," 351.

120. Fitzgerald, "Contract Buyers League," 380; see "CBL to Protest at City Hall," *CST,* April 5, 1970; "Daley to Mediate CBL Clash Today," *CDN,* April 10, 1970.

121. "CBL Eviction Pact Detailed," *CDN,* April 10, 1970; also see "Attorneys Draft Terms of Pact Ending CBL Evictions," *CST,* April 10, 1970; "Pact to End Evictions Signed," *CT,* April 11, 1970.

122. *Rosewood Corp. et al. v. Chester J. Fisher et al.* consolidated 156 appeals of early forcible entry and detainer actions against CBL members as well as the appeal of a previous, similar case (*Alexander et al. v. Hamilton Corporation*). See *Rosewood v. Fisher,* 46 Ill. 2d 249, Supreme Court of Illinois, April 15, 1970, *Federal Reporter* 263, *North Eastern Reporter,* 2nd series, 836–37; Fitzgerald, "Contract Buyers League and the Courts."

123. See *Rosewood v. Fisher,* 837, 838, 840. The court added, "It does not escape us that the construction we have placed upon the act may interfere with the summary aspects" of it. "But the right of such [contract] purchasers to be heard on relevant matters, . . . as well as the desirable purpose of preventing a multiplicity of suits, is . . . superior to the desire to provide a speedy remedy for possession" (839).

124. "Protecting the Home-Buyers," *CST,* April 17, 1970.

125. David Reed, "Victory for CBL in Supreme Court," *CST,* April 16, 1970; "Remands 2 Evictions to Lower Court Here," *CT,* April 16, 1970; also see *Rosewood v. Fisher,* 838.

126. Gus Savage, "New Plan May Save CBL from Questionable Pact," *Southwest Citizen,* April 16, 1970, JM Papers; also see Contract Buyers League press release, April 13, 1970, in Chicago Urban League Papers, 77-54, box 3, folder 3, UIC. The notice was released two days before the CBL officially rejected the pact, but it commented on the aspects of it that it found problematic: "The original intent of the withholding of monies . . . was to effect renegotiation of the contracts. . . . The sellers state flatly that they will not discuss reducing contract prices. [But] this is actually what we have been suffering for—not refinancing."

127. "Home Buyers Reject Pact with Seller," n.d., Red Squad Files, box 230, folder 1134–2, CHS; "CBL Chief Evicted—for 5 Minutes"; "150 Deputies Evict President of Contract Buyers League," *CT,* April 22, 1970; "20 Arrested as Crowd Hurls Rocks, Bottles during Evictions," *CT,* April 23, 1970. A crowd of over a hundred people came to Baker's defense. Baker finally vacated his apartment by moving to the second-floor unit in his building, where his daughter and son-in-law were tenants and thus not part of the eviction battle.

128. Sharif interview; "CBL Split: Report Collapse of Pact Ending Evictions," *CST,* April 17, 1970; also see "5 More CBL Evictions on South Side," *CDN,* April 24, 1970; "CBL Chiefs Split," *CST,* April 24, 1970.

129. "CBL Chief Evicted—for 5 Minutes"; "Sheriff Criticizes Chicago Police," *CT,* April 23, 1970; "6 More CBL Families Evicted," *CDN,* April 22, 1970; also see "20 Arrested as Crowd Hurls Rocks"; "Woods Evicts CBL Head: Daley Raps Joe Wood," *CDD,* April 22, 1970.

130. "Evict! How High the Cost?" *CDN* photo essay with text, April 23, 1970.

131. Fitzgerald, "Contract Buyers League," 441. "I get telephone calls from United States Senators, from the Mayor, . . . from rabbis, etc. etc.," all blaming him for delaying the resolution of the CBL issue, Will said.

132. Feiwell interview, 4; also see "Court Threatens to Enjoin CBL Evictions," *CST,* April 29, 1970; Boodell interview.

133. Daniel Meenan interview, July 23, 2001, 12; "Ask Judge Will Quit CBL Case," *CDD,* May 7, 1970; "Sellers Ask Judge to Quit CBL Case," *CST,* May 29, 1970; Fitzgerald, "Contract Buyers League," 447–48.

134. The evictions continued in early May. See "Priests Help CBL Widow Move Back In," *CST,* May 7, 1970; "Tenants Included in CBL Evictions," *CST,* May 9, 1970; "New Evictions on South Side," *CDN,* May 4, 1970; "Crippled Man Evicted on South Side," *CDN,* May 4, 1970; "The Curse of Contract Buying," *Ebony,* June 1970; "Evict 14 S. Side CBL Families," *CST,* May 5, 1970. Also see "Evictions Mount in CBL Struggle," *CDD,* May 5, 1970; "26 Evictees Who Went Back Named in Trespass Warrants," *CST,* May 20, 1970. Several CBL members filed reports of police brutality. See "U.S. Begins Rights Probe in CBL Member Evictions," *CT,* May 3, 1970.

135. Will added that the CBL's contempt of court was worsened by the organization's claims that the court moved "more slowly for black citizens than . . . for whites." In fact, he wrote, the courts dealt with the CBL's complaints "with exceptional speed and expedition." Indeed, "the only substantial delay . . . has resulted from the payment strike which strike plaintiffs seek to justify on the ground that the courts are delaying justice to them" (*Charles and Charlene Baker v. F & F Investment,* 69c15, USDC, Memorandum Opinion, May 14, 1970, 7–9, in CJEG-Egan II, box 111, folder "Peg-CBL," UND).

136. Letter, Thomas J. Boodell Jr. to clients, June 23, 1970, CJEG-Egan II, box 112, "CBL Correspondence," UND.

137. Ibid.; also see "What's Happenin' at CBL," July 1, 1970, and "What's Happenin' at CBL," June 1, 1970, JM Papers.

138. McPherson, "'In My Father's House,'" 81. In early 1970, when the payment strike was at its height, up to six hundred people attended weekly meetings. A year later, organizers were lucky to get one hundred people to attend.

139. Fitzgerald, "Contract Buyers League," 458–59; Fitzgerald, "Contract Buyers League and the Courts," 185.

140. Fitzgerald, "Contract Buyers League," 389–90.

141. *Hamilton Corporation et al. v. James B. Alexander et al.,* 53 Ill. 2d 290 N.E. 2d 589: 1972 Ill. LEXIS 281, Nov. 30, 1972; also see Fitzgerald, "Contract Buyers League and the Courts," 191.

142. "What's Happenin' at CBL," June 1, 1970; "What's Happenin' at CBL," Jan. 1, 1971; see "What's Happenin' at CBL," July 1, 1971 (by then, 155 contracts had been

renegotiated), all in JM Papers. For a detailed breakdown of the savings of several families, see "CBL Merry Christmas and New Year," Dec. 1, 1972, in CJEG-Egan II, box 112,
folder "CBL Correspondence," UND.

143. Fitzgerald, "Contract Buyers League," 398–99, 507–8, n. 17, 402–3, 387; Ruth
Wells, "Housing Workshop," Aug. 1971, 2, CJEG-Egan II, box 111, "Peg-CBL," UND;
Wells interview, 36. On settlements by contract sellers Weinberg, Smith, Stein, and
Karras, see docket sheets, 69c15, 84, 88, 94, 113.

144. "U.S. 'on 2 Sides' of CBL Dispute," *CDN*, Sept. 9, 1970; Fitzgerald, "Contract
Buyers League," 507–8, n. 6; also see docket sheets, 69c15, 65, 84.

145. "CBL Fears 'Cop Collusion,'" *CDD*, May 20, 1970.

146. For details on the difficult process he went through to gain acceptance, see
Dempsey J. Travis, *An Autobiography of Black Chicago* (Chicago: Urban Research Institute, 1981), 159–61.

147. "How One Man Fought to Aid Contract Buyers," *CT*, Aug. 16, 1970; Travis,
Black Chicago, 170.

148. Travis, *Black Chicago*, 170–71; also see "Pact to End Evictions Signed," *CT*,
April 11, 1970; "Daley Tells Terms of Pact to End CBL Evictions," *CST*, April 11, 1970; "CBL
Okays Mortgage Plan," *CDD*, April 14, 1970; "South Siders Fail to OK Eviction Pact,"
CDN, April 15, 1970; "$100,000 Mortgage Fund Available to Contract Buyers," *CST*,
June 19, 1970. Travis referred to the head of Midstate Homes as Louis Diamond, but
the press reported his name as Sol Diamond (see Travis, *Black Chicago*, 170, and "Con-
tract Buyers and Home Sellers Sign an Accord," *CST*, June 13, 1970).

149. "Contract Buyers and Home Seller Sign an Accord"; "CBL Getting Second
Break in Two Weeks," *CDN*, June 19, 1970; "How One Man Fought to Aid Contract Buyers." Also see "CBL under Negotiation," *Directions* (Sivart Publication), Summer 1970,
CUL 76–116 (Chicago Urban League Papers), box 59, folder 28, UIC; letter, Julian H.
Levi to Sydney Clarke (*sic*), May 6, 1970, CUL 77-54, box 3, folder 3, UIC, where Levi
notes the economic benefits to all sides of refinancing CBL homes with low-interest
mortgages. "The reasoning here . . . is based on hard economics," he writes, adding that
he understands that "stubbornness on either side can make the effort meaningless."

150. "Contract Buyers Seek Agreement to Regain Houses, Avoid Arson," *CST*,
July 14, 1970; also see McPherson, "'In My Father's House,'" 72, 73, 76; "Eviction
Halt Is Agreed On in CBL Pact," *CST*, April 9, 1970; "CBL Evictee Return Near?" *CDN*,
April 9, 1970; "Evicted Cop, CBL Leader, Moves Back In, Vows to Stay," *CDN*, May 25,
1970; "9 South Side Homes Ripped by Dynamite," *CST*, Feb. 1, 1971; "Fires Hit 4 Evic-
tion Area Houses," *CST*, March 26, 1970; "Evictions, Arson in Struggle," *Chicago
Defender*, May 2–8, 1970.

151. As proof, Skolnick pointed out that Albert Jenner was a director of the United
Bank of America in Chicago, and shockingly, at one time Illinois Supreme Court justice
Thomas E. Kluczynski, who ruled on the Rosewood Corporation eviction case, was a
stockholder in the bank. Jenner and Block had to crush the CBL, because if the group
won, "the resulting effects would or could cause numerous Chicago-area banks to
close their doors," Skolnick argued (Sherman H. Skolnick, "Who Represents Who in the
Contract Buyers League?" June 6, 1970, JM Papers).

152. Terry Shaffer, "Cody Named in CBL Suit for $10 Million," *CDN*, n.d.; "Cody
Charged in Suit by Contract Buyers," *CT*, Aug. 26, 1970; "Contract Buyers Name Cody in
$10 Million Fraud Suit," *Chicago Today*, Aug. 25, 1970, all in JM Papers. The suit named as
defendants Archbishop John Cardinal Cody as well as Charlie Baker, Jack Macnamara,
Tom Sullivan, Albert E. Jenner, William R. Ming Jr., Gamaliel donor Gordon Sherman, the
Gamaliel Foundation, and several other prominent CBL members or supporters. Most
CBL members "expressed the opinion that it is most unfortunate that the splinter group

[of nine former CBL members] has separated themselves from the Contract Buyers League and allowed their dissensions to reach the proportions that it has" ("A Bit of Confusion and Frustration," "What's Happenin' at CBL," Sept. 1, 1970, JM Papers).

153. "Cody Dismissed in CBL Suit," *CST,* Oct. 22, 1970; Fitzgerald, "Contract Buyers League," 505, n. 8. The Catholic Archdiocese did not own any of the homes sold by Universal Builders. It did have a tenuous historical connection to land upon which some Universal homes had been built. The connection was the following. In 1930, Martin Dawson died. His will donated twenty-four lots of vacant land to the Catholic Bishop of Chicago. In February 1959, the Catholic Bishop of Chicago sold the lots to Chatham Town Homes, Inc., a subsidiary of Universal Builders. The land formerly owned by Martin Dawson thus became a small part of Universal's land holdings. The Catholic Bishop of Chicago thereafter had no financial involvement with Chatham or with Universal Builders. The claim that the Gamaliel Foundation was funded and controlled by Cardinal Cody and the Chicago archdiocese was pure fantasy. Macnamara had incorporated the Gamaliel Foundation in December 1968, and the organization had no financial connection whatsoever with the Chicago archdiocese ("Chicago Archdiocese Denies Any Involvement in Chatham Homes," *NW,* Aug. 28, 1970).

154. Letter, Egan to Dr. Hanni, Dec. 15, 1969, CJEG-Egan II, box 112, UND; Boles interview.

155. Letter, Macnamara to Theology Council, Bellarmine, Aug. 26, 1970, CJEG-Egan II, box 111, "Peg-CBL," UND; letter, Macnamara to Father Harvanek, Nov. 18, 1970, CJEG-EGAN II, box 112, "CBL Correspondence," UND; McDonald interview, 29; "CBL Organizer Quits Jesuits," in "City Beat" column, *CST,* Dec. 3, 1970, CJEG-EGAN II, box 112, "Contract Buyers League, 1967–1976"; Macnamara interview, July 30, 2001, 36; letter, Macnamara to Edmond S. Sager, April 27, 1971, in CJEG-Egan II, box 111, "Peg-CBL," UND.

156. Letter, Monsignor John J. Egan to John Cardinal Cody, July 2, 1969, CJEG-Egan II, box 112, UND. Egan's notes to a wide range of Chicagoans about the CBL can be found in box 112, folder "CBL Correspondence." John McKnight describes how he and a Jesuit provincial were among those whom "Jack suckered into coming" to an eviction protest; see McKnight interview.

157. Wells interview, 17; also see letter, Charlie (of the Campaign for Human Development) to Jack Egan, July 26, 1971, and memo, William J. Kenealy to the Subcommittee on Legal Rights, Campaign for Human Development, May 21, 1971, in CJEG-Egan II, box 112, folder "CBL Correspondence," UND.

158. Charles Dahm, *Power and Authority in the Catholic Church: Cardinal Cody in Chicago* (Notre Dame: University of Notre Dame Press, 1981), 297, n. 19. Also see Alan B. Anderson and George W. Pickering, *Confronting the Color Line: The Broken Promise of the Civil Rights Movement in Chicago* (Athens: University of Georgia Press, 1986), 488–89.

159. "Church Federation Director Chandler Resigns His Post," *CST,* Sept. 22, 1968 (?), Red Squad Files, box 189, folder 1042, CHS; Margery Frisbie, *An Alley in Chicago: The Life and Legacy of Monsignor John Egan,* commemorative ed. (Franklin, Wisc.: Sheed & Ward, 2002), 199, 219. Marx's analysis was proven correct—in his own case at least—in 1985, when an official of the UAHC told Marx that the UAHC leadership had reacted "poorly" to Marx's program because they didn't control it. "Then, when your lay leaders spoke to [the UAHC] in wrath, because you had embarrassed contract holders, it was NECESSARY (!) to get you out of Chicago . . . not to punish you, but to protect us! . . . We who professed prophetic Judaism capitulated to [those] who objected to your practice of prophetic Judaism. . . . They were committed to a different set of 'profits'" (letter, Rabbi Erwin L. Herman to Bob Marx, Feb. 26, 1985, Marx Papers, box 11, folder 3, CHS).

160. The association originated in 1966, when shocked Chicago clergymen gathered to discuss Cody's summary demotion of Egan from head of the Office of Urban Affairs to a decrepit parish in Lawndale. "If he can get Egan, he can get any of us," one said. The association addressed issues ranging from retirement packages to celibacy. "They were interested in things affecting their lives as priests," Egan recalled. "It was the first time they . . . had the inspiration and courage to look into their own lives and to feel they might have something to say about it." Egan was elected to head the group, which met in Presentation Church, in 1969. It was soon besieged with requests from priests all over the nation who wished to start similar organizations (Dahm, *Power and Authority,* 28, 10; Frisbie, *Alley in Chicago,* 204–12). See "Priests, Blacks Join to Stem CBL Evictions," *NW,* Jan. 9, 1970, CJEG-Egan II, box 11, folder "CBL News Clips," UND, for account of the Association of Chicago Priests' support for the CBL.

161. Letter, Sister Ann Michele for Msgr. Egan to Arthur Green Sr., April 1, 1970, CJEG-Egan II, box 112, folder "CBL Correspondence," UND. Egan's friends knew that Peggy was "indispensable." They credited her with "writing Jack's stuff, keeping him straight, and putting him on the right planes" (Frisbie, *Alley in Chicago,* 226–27, 214).

162. Exactly why Egan, the consummate Chicago insider, stayed away for so long is not clear. Egan admitted that "Cardinal Cody felt I was the one who engineered the Association of Chicago Priests." Others speculated that Egan's support of the CBL had been "ruining Cody's relationship with the Mayor." See Macnamara interview, July 30, 2001, 25–26; Michael Gecan interview, July 19, 2002, 18; Fitzgerald, "Contract Buyers League," 466, n. 3; "Parish Battles Blockbusters," *CA,* July 14, 1969.

163. "Chicago's Maverick Monsignor Returns to the Fold after Years in Exile," *CT,* March 30, 1983. Also see Frisbie, *Alley in Chicago,* 205, 225, 259–60; Edward R. Kantowicz, "The Beginning and End of an Era: George William Mundelein and John Patrick Cody in Chicago," *Patterns of Episcopal Leadership,* ed. Gerald P. Fogarty (New York: Macmillan, 1989), 203.

164. Boles interview, 5.

165. "Ming Is Sentenced to 16 Months," *CST,* Nov. 20, 1970; "Ming Gets 16 Months in Tax Case," *CDN,* Nov. 19, 1970; "Ming Battles Tax Suit," *CDD,* April 15, 1970; Reid, "Earl, Bob, and Me," 7–8; "Ming, Crusading Lawyer, Buried in Chicago after Battle for His Dignity," *Jet,* July 19, 1973; "A Case of Black and White," *Ebony,* Dec. 1973 (the two accounts of Ming's death differ slightly). Ming had been sent to Sandstone Federal Penitentiary, a minimum-security prison in Minnesota. "It's where all the Chicago politicians are sent," John McKnight noted (McKnight interview, 9). Ming's wife, Irvina, was sure that their friend Hubert Will could use his pull to reduce the prison sentence, but to her eternal bafflement and anger, Will was helpless in the matter (Jon Will interview, 2).

166. Reid, "Earl, Bob, and Me," 7–8; "A Case of Black and White"; Reid interview. Also see Boodell interview, 22.

167. "What's Happenin' at CBL," July 1, 1970, and "What's Happenin' at CBL," Aug. 1, 1970, JM Papers; "Revised Meeting between Rabbi Marx and Judge Will, Nov. 10, 1970," Marx Papers, folder 11–2, CHS.

168. *Contract Buyers League v. F & F Investment,* 69c15, May 21, 1969, in 300 F. Supp. 210 (1969), 215.

169. Boodell interview, 24; Tucker, *Trial and Error,* 272; also see Fitzgerald interview, 10.

CHAPTER 10: THE FEDERAL TRIALS

1. See "Application for Funding," Contract Buyers League to Campaign for Human Development, 1971, 1, in CJEG-Egan II, box 112, folder "Contract Buyers

League," UND; Jeffrey Michael Fitzgerald, "The Contract Buyers League: A Case Study of Interaction between a Social Movement and the Legal System" (Ph.D. dissertation, Northwestern University, 1972), 411; James Alan McPherson, "'In My Father's House There Are Many Mansions—and I'm Going to Get Me Some of Them Too': The Story of the Contract Buyers League," *Atlantic Monthly*, April 1972, 82.

The CBL was now mostly an administrative organization dedicated to helping Jenner and Block attorneys gather information for the upcoming trials. Ruth Wells and Charlie Baker continued to work with the CBL, as did Clyde Ross, who simultaneously organized block and neighborhood organizations in Lawndale. Ross's activism garnered him a fellowship at Chicago's Adlai Stevenson Institute in 1971. He convinced large insurance companies to insure well-maintained Lawndale homes at the same rate as elsewhere, resulting in substantial savings for residents. Fitzgerald, "Contract Buyers League," 409; Clyde Ross, "Grass Roots," Adlai Stevenson Institute Working Paper no. 5 (1972), CJEG-Egan II, box 111, "CBL News Clips," and "What's New at CBL," Feb. 15, 1972, CJEG-Egan II, box 112, folder "CBL Correspondence," UND.

2. John C. Tucker interview, July 17, 2001, 6. In addition to the loss of Ming, another key attorney, John Stifler, was struck down with cancer; at the time of his death he was in his midthirties.

3. *Sidney Clark and Julia Clark et al. v. Universal Builders Inc. et al.*, U.S. Court of Appeals for the Seventh Circuit, 72–1655, Plaintiffs-Appellants' Brief, 7, JBA.

4. *Contract Buyers League v. F & F Investment*, 69c15, May 21, 1969, 300 F. Supp. 210 (1969), 216.

5. John C. Tucker, *Trial and Error: The Education of a Courtroom Lawyer* (New York: Carroll and Graf, 2003), 266.

6. For public acknowledgments of the city's dual housing market, see, for example, Monsignor John J. Egan, "More Housing—Less Segregation," *NW*, May 16, 1958; Chicago Commission on Human Relations, "Summary of a Public Hearing on Real Estate Practices in Racially Changing Neighborhoods," Aug. 9, 1962, GLCC Papers, box 19, folder "August 1962," CHS; John Baird, "Statement of the Metropolitan Housing and Planning Council, May 8, 1963," MHPC 74-20, box 24, folder 292, UIC.

7. Andrew Gordon interview, Aug. 13, 2001, 3; also see "What's Happening in Our Downtown Office," Sept. 30, 1970, CJEG-Egan II, box 11, "CBL News Clips," UND; *Clark v. Universal Builders*, Plaintiffs-Appellants' Brief, 12–13, JBA; Fitzgerald, "Contract Buyers League," 422–23.

8. Greg Colvin interview, Feb. 3, 2005, 5; Alan Boles interview, Jan. 20, 2005, 19, 30.

9. Tucker, *Trial and Error*, 275; *Clark v. Universal Builders*, Plaintiffs-Appellants' Brief, 14–15, 34, JBA.

10. See "Home Builders Accused of Gouging S. Side Buyers," *CST*, April 12, 1972. The plaintiffs pointed out that the South Side neighborhood where Universal operated was one of the few black areas in the city where it was possible to obtain mortgage loans. Builder Herbert Rosenfeld, who operated in the same part of the city and sold to the same basic clientele as Universal, sold 85 percent of his homes with regular mortgages and at prices that were comparable to those that whites paid in adjoining areas (*Clark v. Universal Builders*, Plaintiffs-Appellants' Brief, 35, JBA).

11. Freeman explained that, "normally, one does not think of a market divided into two parts within the same city. Normally, you think of two markets to be Japan, the United States—two separate markets where there might be two separate prices for the same . . . commodity. . . . But, in this case, *because of the race of the people*, the market is, in fact, divided into two parts. . . . If the black man could have gone into the white market ten blocks away and have bought a house at fair market value, . . . there would

not have been two prices existing in this market" (*Clark v. Universal Builders,* Plaintiffs-Appellants' Brief, 67–69, my italics, JBA; also see Tucker, *Trial and Error,* 274).

12. *Clark v. Universal Builders,* Plaintiffs-Appellants' Brief, 66, JBA; *Sidney Clark and Julia Clark et al., Plaintiffs-Appellants, v. Universal Builders Inc. et al., Defendants-Appellees,* 72–1655, U.S. Court of Appeals for the Seventh Circuit, 501F.2d 324; 1974 U.S. App. LEXIS 7462; 19 Fed. R. Serv. 2d (Callaghan) 521, 14, n. 21; Tucker, *Trial and Error,* 274.

13. Perry noted that, while Universal sold "almost exclusively on a contract basis, . . . this was perfectly legal, and is a customary way of selling homes. They had a right to do that." In contrast, he associated the contract buyers with criminal behavior. "From the evidence of violence that occurred, it is reasonable to assume that at least some of the plaintiffs participated in fire-bombing the houses belonging to the defendants," he asserted, citing no documentation whatsoever to support this claim (trial transcript, *Sidney Clark and Julia Clark et al., Plaintiffs, v. Universal Builders Inc. et al., Defendants,* 69c115, USDC Northern District of Illinois, Eastern Division, May 22, 1972, 5433–44, 5438, 5434, JBA; Tucker, *Trial and Error,* 276).

14. Tucker, *Trial and Error,* 276–77.

15. Maureen McDonald interview, Aug. 10, 2001, 20; "Judge Nixes CBL Homes Suit," *CDD,* May 23, 1972.

16. Tucker, *Trial and Error,* 277; Tucker interview; Richard Franch interview, March 20, 2006; *Clark v. Universal Builders,* Plaintiffs-Appellants' Brief, 74, 76, JBA.

17. Franch interview, 3; Tucker, *Trial and Error,* 279; also see Tucker interview, 20.

18. *Clark et al., Plaintiffs-Appellants, v. Universal Builders Inc. et al., Defendants-Appellees,* 72–1655, Oct. 24, 1973, argued, July 26, 1974, decided.

19. Lois Wille, "Top Threat to Housing," *CDN,* April 23, 1970; Wille, "Worst Housing Shortage!" *CDN,* March 22, 1969; "The Slums Tightening Stranglehold on Chicago's Future," *CT,* May 20, 1973; also see "City, Carey Purge Slumlords," *Chicago Today,* May 31, 1973, Harold Washington Library Center, CPL.

20. "The Slums Tightening Stranglehold"; "Very Young, Very Old Tragic Losers in Battle of the Slums," *CT,* May 6, 1973; Wille, "Top Threat to Housing"; also see Wille, "Worst Housing Shortage!"

21. "Phony Names, Land Trusts Used to Profit from Squalor," *CT,* May 6, 1973; also see "Nab Slumlord Enforcing Rent," *Chicago Today,* Jan. 10, 1974. On Spector's role in the West Side suit, see "Slumlord Guide—8 Steps to Profit," *CT,* May 8, 1973. As of March 20, 1975, Wolf, Forman, Berke, and Berland were still defendants in the CBL case. See *James and Ruth Wells et al. v. F & F Investment et al.,* 69c15, "Plaintiffs' Amended Pre-Trial Memorandum," 7. My thanks to Tony Lisanti, who provided me with a copy of this document.

22. Lois Wille, "How Slumlords Dodge the Law," *CDN,* April 21, 1970; "Lawndale Is Exploited," *CT,* May 7, 1973.

23. Wille, "How Slumlords Dodge the Law"; "Very Young, Very Old Tragic Losers"; "Winning Con Game in Slums," *CT,* May 11, 1973.

24. William E. Farrell, "Redlining, Whether Cause or Effect, Is No Help," *NYT,* Sept. 14, 1975 (I assume the couple was white because the article does not specify their race); "Parish Battles Blockbusters," *CA,* July 14, 1969, on microfilm at Harold Washington Library Center, CPL; "Panic Peddling Curb Is Voted by Illinois House Committee," *CST,* May 12, 1971; "Panic Peddlers Are Still Evading Human Relations Commission," *CT,* Jan. 21, 1971; "Her Dream Home a 'Nightmare,'" *Chicago Today,* Jan. 26, 1972, in MHPC 89-49, box 65, folder 10, UIC.

Austin is directly west of West Garfield Park, not Lawndale, but I describe the area as west of Lawndale because Chicagoans spoke of East and West Garfield Park as part of "greater Lawndale" since at least the late 1960s.

25. George R. Metcalf, *Fair Housing Comes of Age* (New York: Greenwood, 1988), 87.

26. Home buyers paid for FHA insurance—½ of 1 percent of the monthly interest on their mortgages went to the insurance pool, to "protect the money guy," or the mortgage lender. In return, the FHA insurance program enabled down payments for homes to decline dramatically. Until its incorporation into HUD, the FHA both supported itself on the ½ of 1 percent insurance fee paid by homeowners and created a large financial reserve (Brian D. Boyer, *Cities Destroyed for Cash: The FHA Scandal at HUD* [Chicago: Follett, 1973], 95–96).

27. Metcalf, *Fair Housing*, 87; George Bliss and Chuck Neubauer, "Thousands Abandon, Lose Homes," *CT*, June 22, 1975; Chris Bonastia, "Hedging His Bets: Why Nixon Killed HUD's Desegregation Efforts," *Social Science History* 28 (Spring 2004): 19–52.

28. William Clements, "Slum Loan: A Dream Shattered," *CDN*, June 2, 1970. For similar deals made by Moe Forman, see Lois Wille, "U.S. Housing for Poor Lags," *CDN*, April 25–26, 1970, and Wille, "How Slumlords Dodge the Law." For Baker's warning, see D. J. R. Bruckner, "Ghetto Escalates War on Housing Speculators," *LAT*, Jan. 20, 1969.

29. "Reveals Scheme to Swindle FHA," *CST*, Sept. 13, 1970; also see Mike Royko, "How to Get Badge, Gun," *CDN*, March 27, 1970; "Realty Broker Fined $10,000," *CDN*, June 17, 1970.

30. See testimony of Joseph Berke, Jan. 16–19, 1976, in "Abstract of Testimony in First Trial," *Ruth and James Wells v. F & F Investment*, 69c15, 3136–87, box 4, JBA; George Feiwell interview, June 18, 2001.

31. "Slumlord Guide"; "Lawndale Is Exploited."

32. "Slumlord Guide." That Berland, Balin, Forman, Berke, and Wolf were using the FSLIC as a conduit to strip buildings of mortgages was not immediately obvious, since they hid their ownership of the buildings, often putting them in land trusts. As Balin explained, "I don't want any buildings in my name, because when I go to court I don't like them to know that I own them." They also swapped buildings among themselves. Their complex webs of hidden co-ownership, designed to avoid code violation or other legal charges, came in handy when the group repurchased buildings from the FSLIC. "If we had known these people were working together, we would never have sold to them," moaned Thomas P. Sughrua, head of the FSLIC in Chicago. "But how in hell can you tell one guy's nominee from another?" See "Razing of Hovel Stymied for 5 Years," *CT*, May 7, 1973; "Lawndale Is Exploited"; "Slumlord Guide."

33. "Phony Names, Land Trusts Used"; "Slumlord Guide."

34. "Lawyer Quits Slum Cases," *CT*, May 22, 1973.

35. "Third Baby Dies in Cold W. Side Slum," *CDN*, Feb. 12, 1969; Wille, "How Slumlords Dodge the Law"; "Phony Names, Land Trusts Used."

36. "Big Profit in Insurance Claims Possible from Burned Out Hulks," *CT*, May 10, 1973; "Slumlord Guide."

37. "Reaps Insurance in 47 Slum Fires," *CST*, Aug. 2, 1970.

38. "Big Profit in Insurance Claims Possible"; "3 Indicted in Slum Arson," *CT*, May 5, 1973; "Very Young, Very Old Losers in Battle of the Slums."

39. "Big Profit in Insurance Claims Possible"; "How Slumlord Milked Building Nobody Wanted," *CT*, May 10, 1973. Insurance claims on properties owned by Berland and Wolf were made in the name of a man who had died years before. They didn't even bother to spell his name right. They also lied about their buildings' fire histories. But "incredibly," when Fair Plan insurance officials complained, Chicago police and firemen insisted that there was no evidence of a "burn-for-profit scheme." As a Chicago Fire Department Bureau of Investigation chief commented, "All the people in the neighborhood say everything is arson. It is the vandals and the kids, and the winos. I doubt very much that there is a conspiracy to burn buildings down" ("Big Profit in Insurance Claims Possible"). Also see "Long Fight to Bleed Slum Related," *CT,* May 9, 1973.

40. "Slumlord in Arson Case Gives Self Up," *CT,* May 15, 1973; "2 Guilty of Arson Charges in Torching of W. Side Building," *CST,* Jan. 30, 1974; "2 Slumlords Get Prison for Arson," *CDN,* April 19, 1974.

41. As Lois Wille noted, the result was that "bigtime slumowners . . . [were] often treated as lightly . . . as if they were little old ladies struggling to make a living from a two-flat." For every $100 in fines that could be charged, judges asked for $3.72—and 20 percent of even these were suspended (Wille, "Why Slumlords Go Free," *CDN,* April 22, 1970). Also see Wille, "How a Slum Landlord Beats City Housing Codes," *CDN,* March 24, 1970.

42. "No Favors Granted, Kral Tells Hearing," *CDN,* Dec. 18, 1973; "Judge Given a Discount Quits as Court Chief," *CDN,* May 24, 1973; "Judge Kral Action under Ethics Fire," *CST,* July 21, 1973; "Judicial Board Raps Kral on Gift from Slumlord," *CT,* Sept. 26, 1973.

43. "Judge Kral Begins 2 Mo. Suspension," *CDN,* Dec. 19, 1973. Kral became chief judge in housing court only after his predecessor, Robert A. Napolitano, was removed by the Courts Commission for "irregularities involving concessions at the Illinois State Fair" ("Slumlord Wins, Sells 2 Buildings to City," *CT,* Jan. 19, 1974).

44. His boss could be forgiven for not knowing that Mendelson owned slum properties, since he put the buildings' titles under phony names ("Alan Miller" or "Arnold Miller") or transferred ownership to his aunt or mother-in-law. Mendelson resigned from his position shortly after the revelations were made public ("Slumlord in the City Hall," *CST,* April 11, 1972; "Tell All, City Aide Accused of Slum Holdings Ordered," *CST,* April 11, 1972; "City Hall Aide Quits in Slum Exposé," *CST,* April 12, 1972).

45. "From Slum Lawyer to Official," *Chicago Today,* June 5, 1973. For more on city officials as slum landlords, see "Council Candidate a Slumlord," *Chicago Today,* May 30, 1973; "Duped by Slumlord, S & L Officials Say," *Chicago Today,* June 1, 1973. For a slumlord who ran as the West Side's candidate for Illinois state legislature despite having refused to respond to over twelve court summonses relating to code violations on his properties—and who was consequently ordered to be arrested on sight—see "Candidate Answers 2d Arrest Order," *CST,* March 2, 1974. Also see "Slumlord Wins, Sells 2 Buildings to City," all at the Harold Washington Library Center, CPL.

46. Bliss and Neubauer, "Thousands Abandon, Lose Homes"; also see Boyer, *Cities Destroyed,* 6–7, 142; "FHA Scandal Enmeshed in Red Tape," *CT,* June 23, 1975.

47. Also abused was Section 235, which tried to make housing affordable for low-income people by subsidizing interest payments on mortgages above the first 1 percent, and Section 236, which offered tax breaks for developers of multiunit rental apartments that included some low-income tenants. See Bonastia, "Hedging His Bets," 26; Walter Thabit, *How East New York Became a Ghetto* (New York: New York University Press, 2003), 179; Boyer, *Cities Destroyed,* 20–23.

48. "The Way It Ought to Be and the Way It Really Is," *CT,* June 22, 1975.

49. Boyer, *Cities Destroyed,* 107. Also see Thabit, *East New York,* 179; John Herbers, "Federal Agencies Press Inquiry on Housing Frauds in Big Cities," *NYT,* May 8, 1972.

50. "The mortgage companies have not been checking out credit information for low-income buyers," fumed John Waner, then head of the FHA Chicago-area office, in 1972. "They could care less" (Boyer, *Cities Destroyed,* 192; also see 98, 106).

51. Mortgage companies sometimes charged fees of up to 16 points—that is, 16 percent of the value of the loan (Boyer, *Cities Destroyed*, 96–97, 181; Calvin Bradford and Anne B. Shlay, "Assuming a Can Opener: Economic Theory's Failure to Explain Discrimination in FHA Lending Markets," *Cityscape: A Journal of Policy Development and Research* 2, no. 1 [Feb. 1996]: 80).

52. Boyer, *Cities Destroyed*, 96–97, 181–82; Bradford and Shlay, "Assuming a Can Opener," 80. The longer a loan takes to be paid off, the lower the percentage profit on the interest; conversely, the faster a loan is paid back, the higher the percentage of profit. Since the FHA had insured the loan in full, it was obliged to pay back the full amount in case of default, no matter how quickly that default occurred (Bliss and Neubauer, "Thousands Abandon, Lose Homes"). For statistics on the FHA's share of the housing market in the 1960s and 1970s, see John C. Weicher, *Housing: Federal Policies and Programs* (Washington: American Enterprise Institute for Public Policy Research, 1980), 112–13.

53. Boyer, *Cities Destroyed*, 181, 184, 186. The Austin resident quoted was Gale Cincotta, who became a leader in the anti-redlining movement. Also see Ron Dorfman, "Greenlining Chicago: The Citizens Action Program," *Working Papers for a New Society* 3, no. 2 (1975): 32.

54. "Her Dream Home a 'Nightmare.'"

55. Herbers, "Federal Agencies Press Inquiry"; "Dun & Bradstreet among 50 Named in Housing Fraud," *NYT,* March 30, 1972; Boyer, *Cities Destroyed*, 4.

56. William E. Farrell, "Housing Scandals Slowing Programs," *NYT,* Dec. 12, 1975.

57. "Her Dream Home a 'Nightmare'"; Boyer, *Cities Destroyed*, 194.

58. Boyer, *Cities Destroyed*, 192; "Dun & Bradstreet among 50 Named." See Bliss and Neubauer, "Thousands Abandon, Lose Homes" and "Burocrats [*sic*] 'Lose' Critical Study," *CT,* June 23, 1975, for more on mortgage companies' efforts to foreclose prematurely. These June 1975 *CT* articles were part of a weeklong series on the FHA scandals; the entire series can be found in MHPC 80-49, box 64, folder 3, UIC. Also see Herbers, "Federal Agencies Press Inquiry"; Thabit, *East New York,* 180.

59. Herbers, "Federal Agencies Press Inquiry"; Boyer, *Cities Destroyed*, 8, 142. Also see Bliss and Neubauer, "Thousands Abandon, Lose Homes"; Thabit, *East New York,* 180.

60. For typical Chicago examples, see Christopher Chandler, "'Shoot to Kill . . . Shoot to Maim,'" *Chicago Reader,* April 5, 2002; "In Chicago, Killing Keeps Up a Rapid Pace," *NYT,* Oct. 24, 2002; "From Projects to Progress in Chicago," *Business Week,* Oct. 27, 2003. Thomas J. Sugrue's excellent study *The Origins of the Urban Crisis: Race and Inequality in Postwar Detroit* (Princeton: Princeton University Press, 1996) tries to challenge conventional wisdom about "the riots" as the cause of Detroit's problems by detailing the twenty years of job flight and housing and employment discrimination preceding them. Yet his book, like many of the best postwar urban histories, concludes with a black urban riot, thus implying that the riot was the end point of Detroit's destruction. In fact, while the 1967 Detroit riot left 2,509 buildings looted and burned, the 1970s FHA scandal led to the abandonment of ten times that number of buildings. See Sugrue, *Origins of the Urban Crisis,* 259–71. Also see Amanda I. Seligman, *Block by Block: Neighborhoods and Public Policy on Chicago's West Side* (Chicago: University of Chicago Press, 2005), a meticulously researched study that nevertheless implies that riots alone are responsible for the numerous vacant lots on Chicago's West Side.

61. Boyer, *Cities Destroyed*, 6; also see 143, 177; "Dun & Bradstreet among 50 Named"; Farrell, "Housing Scandals Slowing Programs"; Jerry M. Flint, "Romney Says His Agency Can't Solve Housing Problem," *NYT,* March 28, 1972.

62. Gale Cincotta quoted in Boyer, *Cities Destroyed,* 187. Also see Cincotta quoted in Farrell, "Housing Scandals Slow Programs"; "FHA Homes Rot," *CT,* June 27, 1975.

63. The programs failed for a number of reasons. The original federal legislation (created by Democrats) grossly catered to private interests. The Republicans then turned the FHA into a patronage machine, stocking key positions with incompetent political cronies and firing experienced workers because of "cost-cutting" demands. The Nixon administration also subverted HUD-FHA programs because of fears that they would lead to residential integration, thereby angering Nixon's segregationist white supporters. For competing explanations of why these programs failed, see Flint, "Romney Says His Agency Can't Solve Housing Problem"; "FHA Scandal Could Be Nipped," *CT,* June 26, 1975; "FHA Homes Rot." For a more detailed analysis, see Bonastia, "Hedging His Bets." Also see the entire *Chicago Tribune* exposé, June 22–29, 1975, in MHPC 80-49, box 64, folder 3, UIC.

64. "Inspectors Lose Cool in Describing Wrecked Homes," *CT,* June 26, 1975.

65. Bliss and Neubauer, "Thousands Abandon, Lose Homes"; "Inspectors Lose Cool"; "The Way It Ought to Be."

The fate of one Chicago home gives a sense of the losses caused by mortgage companies' negligence. The building, at 5738 South Sangamon Street, had been sold with an FHA-insured mortgage for $20,000. The buyers defaulted and the FHA paid close to $20,000 to the mortgage company, plus an extra several hundred dollars for securing the building—a service the company never provided. By the time the FHA put the building up for resale, its sinks, bathtubs, toilets, and boiler had been stolen; all of its windows were smashed; and it was covered in stinking trash both inside and out. It was sold for $501, the cost of the lot on which the building stood. The federal government's loss on this single building was approximately $19,000. According to HUD's own records, it owned over 65,000 such abandoned single-family homes, as well as an additional 35,000 multifamily buildings. Its financial loss on these structures was stunning. The destruction of decent housing at a time of a housing shortage was heartbreaking ("FHA Scandal Enmeshed in Red Tape," *CT,* June 23, 1975; William E. Farrell, "Housing Agency Assailed as Chief Slumlord of U.S.," *NYT,* Dec. 11, 1975).

66. The most recent FHA commissioner and undersecretary of HUD in Washington, D.C., Sheldon Lubar, had headed Mortgage Associates, which, reporters noted, "turned over to the government more damaged and destroyed housing—after collecting FHA insurance on it—than any other mortgage company in the Chicago area." Lubar refused to act against companies that made fraudulent charges to the FHA. Consequently, the *Tribune* noted, the "drain of public money into the coffers of unscrupulous businessmen is a continuing process" in Chicago and nationally ("FHA Scandal Enmeshed in Red Tape"; also see Bliss and Neubauer, "Thousands Abandon, Lose Homes").

67. "Historically, H.U.D. has placed great reliance upon the principle that mortgagees function with great integrity," the report noted. HUD feels no need to act against corruption, the report continued, as long as "the mortgagee indicates a willingness to do better in the future." Of course, such willingness is "invariably" promised (Farrell, "Housing Agency Assailed").

68. Farrell, "Housing Scandals Slowing Programs." Also see Farrell, "H.U.D. Secretary Jeered by Chicago Homeowners," *NYT,* Oct. 21, 1975.

69. William E. Farrell, "Daley's Victory in the Primary More Than a Personal Triumph," *NYT,* Feb. 27, 1975; Farrell, "Chicago Is the North's Model of Segregation," *NYT,* Nov. 9, 1975.

70. William E. Farrell, "Cardinal Cody Is Assailed for Closing 4 Schools in Chicago Ghetto," *NYT,* July 27, 1975.

71. Farrell, "Chicago Is the North's Model of Segregation"; William E. Farrell, "Chicago, 'a City That Works,' Faces Some Hard Realities," *NYT,* April 1, 1975.

72. Tucker interview, 8; Tucker, *Trial and Error,* 281.

73. "What's Happening in Our Downtown Office," Sept. 30, 1970, states that there were 2,600 plaintiffs in the West Side case, out of which the property transactions of a random sample of 475 were analyzed. This document is attached to "What's Happenin' at CBL," Oct. 1, 1970, in CJEG-Egan II, box 111, folder "CBL News Clips," UND. Francis E. McLennand, "A Juror's Notes and Comments" (unpublished ms., in author's possession), 6, says that there were originally approximately 500 plaintiffs, but he might have been referring to the random sample of 475 people.

74. Docket sheets 69c15, *Baker et al. v. F & F Investment et al.,* USDC, Eastern District of Illinois, Eastern Division, ascension number 021-74-A242, location number 369814, box 2, also see ascension number 021-01-0005, location number NARA, box 1, and ascension number 021-82-0225, location number V4837, box 1, NARA. See McDonald interview, 28; Jeffrey Fitzgerald interview, March 29, 2002, 11; Boles interview.

75. McLennand, "A Juror's Notes," 5. Techically there were seven; M. E. Stein was listed as a defendant. However, he did not attend the trial, no evidence was presented for or against him, and he was dismissed by the jurors at the end.

76. Thomas Boodell Jr. interview, Aug. 20, 2001, 8; Daniel Meenan interview, July 23, 2001, 15–16; also see McLennand, "A Juror's Notes," 3–6.

77. McLennand, "A Juror's Notes," 6, 19; Warren Lupel interview, June 25, 2001, 10; Sandy Gatto interview, July 13, 2002; Meenan interview, 16; Franch interview, 6; Boodell interview, 4; Feiwell interview; testimony of Jay Goran, Jan. 5, 1976, 2288–89, in "Abstract of Testimony," *Wells v. F & F Investment,* 69c15, box 4, JBA; testimony of Wallace Reid, Feb. 5, 1976, 4601–2, in "Abstract of Testimony, Vol. 2," *Wells v. F & F Investment,* 69c15, box 4, JBA.

Much of what follows draws upon the "Abstract of Testimony" referenced above. The abstract cites page numbers that I assume refer to the full trial transcript and that I therefore cite as well. It is not always clear whether the abstract is quoting trial testimony directly or paraphrasing it. I am treating the material as a direct quotation unless I am certain that it is not.

78. The Justice Department also argued that the federal agencies—the FHA, the VA, and the FSLIC—had immunity from suits for damages under Section 1981 and 1982. McGarr dismissed this argument, ruling that 42 USCS 1982 is "an absolute bar to all racial discrimination in the sale or renting of property, private as well as public, federal as well as state," and that "damages were expressly recoverable under Section 1982" (*Charles and Charlene Baker et al., Plaintiffs-Appellees, v. F & F Investment Company et al., Defendants, Federal Housing Administration et al., Defendants-Appellants,* 72-2036, September term, 1973, U.S. Court of Appeals for the Seventh Circuit, 489F. 2d 829; 1973 U.S. App. LEXIS 6644, Oct. 25, 1973, argued, Dec. 6, 1973, decided, 1–4).

79. Ibid., 10–11. Since FHA redlining prevented the plaintiffs from refinancing—that is, from getting out of their installment contracts—"it would follow that a new injury was inflicted on the plaintiffs each day until the federal defendants abandoned their discriminatory policies. . . . Plaintiffs allege that the discriminatory policies continued at least through 1967, and the federal defendants seem to admit that they were in effect until 1969." The complaint against the FHA and the VA, filed on August 11, 1970, was thus "well within the limitations period." The Court of Appeals also denied the FSLIC's request to be dismissed. If the defendant savings and loan institutions had discriminated, then the FSLIC was also potentially liable since it was the legal successor to the failed defendant savings and loans.

80. Tucker interview, 7; Tucker, *Trial and Error,* 271. Of course, the FSLIC, which insured savings and loans and not mortgages, was more distant from the issues of the case than the FHA and the VA. Unlike these two agencies, the FSLIC did not itself practice racial discrimination and thus create the conditions for exploitative contract buying.

81. Murray's father was the alderman who had sponsored Chicago's 1963 open housing ordinance. Murray vividly recalled the ugly threats that neighbors made against his family as a result (James C. Murray Jr. interview, April 14, 2006).

82. Ibid. Also see testimony of Emma Halbert, Feb. 27–28, 1976, "Abstract of Testimony," 6122–54, and testimony of Vergia Handsbur, one of Gerald Crane's plaintiffs, who testified between Dec. 22, 1975, and Jan. 12, 1976, "Abstract of Testimony," 1406–7, JBA. The VA program was also much smaller than the FHA program. By 1960, when contract selling in Lawndale was at its height, the VA home loan program was making fewer loans nationally than at any time since its inception fifteen years earlier. See www.va-home-loans.com/history_VA_loan.htm, accessed April 26, 2006.

83. Murray interview. Most people say that the FHA began insuring mortgages in urban black neighborhoods in 1966; see Kenneth T. Jackson, *Crabgrass Frontier: The Suburbanization of the United States* (New York: Oxford University Press, 1985), 214–15. The early opening of loan insurance in Chicago could have been the result of the efforts of John McKnight, who had elicited promises from lenders at that time (see ch. 6).

84. The Court of Appeals decision was explicit on this point. "Of course, plaintiffs cannot recover any items of damage that accrued before August 11, 1965," the Court wrote (*Baker et al., Plaintiffs-Appellees, v. F & F Investment Company et al., Defendants, Federal Housing Administration et al., Defendants-Appellants,* No. 72-2036, September term, 1973, 9).

85. Murray interview; docket sheets, 69c15, 226; also see trial transcript, exchange between John Tucker and Judge McGarr, March 22, 1976, *Wells v. F & F Investment,* 69c15, 8040, JBA.

86. Tucker, *Trial and Error,* 282; "Contract Buyers Lose Suit," *CST,* April 17, 1976.

87. Meenan interview, 8; my transcription of Goran's statement, delivered on Dec. 4, 1975, from tape 325 of the West Side trial (69c15). My thanks to Tony Lisanti for making these tapes available to me.

88. Taeuber had a Ph.D. from Harvard and was a sociology professor at the University of Wisconsin. He and his wife, Alma F. Taeuber, were the authors of *Negroes in Cities: Residential Segregation and Neighborhood Change* (1965), a magisterial study that used the "segregation index"—a measure routinely used by economists, sociologists, and demographic experts—to analyze the process of racial neighborhood transition nationally.

89. Examination of Karl Taeuber, Dec. 2, 1975, and Dec. 4, 1975, 99, in "Abstract of Testimony," JBA; also see Douglas S. Massey and Nancy A. Denton, *American Apartheid: Segregation and the Making of the Underclass* (Cambridge: Harvard University Press, 1993), 19–23, 74–76. All the information that follows comes from the "Abstract of Testimony in First Trial," *Wells v. F & F Investment,* 69c15, box 4, JBA, unless otherwise noted.

90. Testimony of John F. Kain, Feb. 19, 1976, 5408–12, trial transcript (not abstract), box 3, JBA. To streamline the arguments in this lengthy trial, I have changed the order of some of the witnesses.

91. For a detailed explanation, see Robert Gilroth, Judy Meima, and Patricia A. Wright, *Tax, Title, and Housing Court Search* (Chicago: Center for Urban Economic Development, University of Illinois at Chicago, 1984), 37, JM Papers.

92. Testimony of Neil Renzi, Jan. 20, 1976, 3397–410, 3501–35.

93. Feiwell and Goran examination of Renzi, Jan. 20 and 23, 1976, 3604–11, 3688–90, 3761, 3839–40.

94. Scott Tyler testimony, Feb. 9–12, 1976, 4962–5240. Feiwell didn't challenge Tyler's claims about the FHA. Instead, he did something more damaging. "I nailed the guy with a contract sale. I thought they'd fold when I pulled the numbers out!" he recalled. Tyler admitted that he had bought a property at a tax sale for $12,000 and then sold it on contract to a black buyer who was "not particularly creditworthy" for $18,000. Although Tucker pointed out that "Tyler's one building was purchased as an isolated incident," his contract sale undoubtedly hurt his credibility. Despite Feiwell's humiliating surprise attack, Tyler presented two key building blocks of the plaintiffs' case. He described the FHA and savings-and-loan redlining that backed black buyers into a corner. He also presented half a dozen highly detailed, retrospective appraisals on properties that the defendants had sold at an average markup of 100 percent. Feiwell interview; also see Tyler testimony, 5075.

95. Testimony of Steve Horvath, March 11, 1976, 7161–76, 7519–20, and Boodell examination of Horvath, March 15, 1976, 7481, 7433, 7478–509, 7519–20. See Chicago Commission on Human Relations, "Selling and Buying Real Estate in a Racially Changing Neighborhood," 28, in GLCC Papers, box 19, folder "June 1–15, 1962," CHS, for details on Goran's purchase of properties on this block.

96. Testimony of Sherman Shapiro, March 22, 1976, trial transcript, 8012, 7959, in box 3, JBA.

97. Testimony of Pierre DeVise, April 2, 1976, trial transcript, 8138, 8144, 8254, in box 3, JBA; also see McLennand, "A Juror's Notes," 41–42.

98. Testimony of Gerald Crane, Dec. 11, 1975, 618, 656; testimony of Jay Goran, Jan. 5–12, 1976, 1988–91; testimony of Al Berland, Jan. 12, 1976, 2628; testimony of Wallace Reid, Feb. 2, 1976, 4226–33; testimony of Joseph Berke, Feb. 27–March 1, 1976, 6216–24; testimony of John Karras, Jan. 23, 1976, 3857.

99. For example, see Goran testimony, Dec. 31, 1975, 2073, 2105; Goran testimony, Jan. 5, 1976, 2310.

100. Horvath testimony, March 11, 1976, 7187. Horvath stated repeatedly that Chicago savings and loan institutions did not discriminate against blacks in any way. He knew this because he would telephone savings and loan institutions and ask if they loaned to blacks, and they always stated that they did. See Horvath testimony, 7608–10. Also see Shapiro testimony, trial transcript, 8011–13, 7958–59.

101. Feiwell and Tucker, Feb. 9, 1976, 4892–911; also see 4870–76.

102. McGarr ruling, Feb. 3, 1976, 4417 and 4438; also see McLennand, "A Juror's Notes," 23; McGarr order, Feb. 24, 1976, 5805; Gordon interview, 3.

103. Tucker, Feiwell, and McGarr, March 22, 1976, trial transcript, 8042, 8122. In their pretrial memorandum, Tucker reminded McGarr, the plaintiffs argued that "the FHA contributed to the acts of the defendant sellers . . . by cutting off access of mortgage funds to plaintiffs which forced them to buy on contract at unreasonable prices." McGarr replied that he was aware of "the original theory of your case. [But] when the case went to trial, the FHA was no longer in it" (trial transcript, 8045).

104. Franch and Shapiro, March 22, 1976, trial transcript, 7964, 8006–9; also see *Hearings before the U.S. Civil Rights Commission: Housing* (Washington: U.S. Government Printing Office, 1959), 740.

105. My transcription of tape 350 of trial testimony of April 2, 1976; McLennand, "A Juror's Notes," 35.

106. Shapiro testimony, March 22, 1976, trial transcript, 8027–29. Plaintiffs Golden and Vergia Handsbur described being caught in exactly this situation. They testified that they purchased a building from Gerald Crane in 1956 for $17,900, unaware that Crane had bought it only a month earlier for $8,500. Vergia Handsbur was uneasy about the terms of the contract sale, and so in June 1957 she went to First Federal, one of the city's black-owned savings and loans, to see if it would give her a mortgage that would enable her to buy the property outright. The bank refused. If she had paid $10,000 for the property, which was its approximate market value, it might have considered giving her a mortgage. But since she owed not $10,000 but $17,900, the bank could not make the loan. Vergia Handsbur went to the Veterans Administration and was refused there as well, for the same reason (testimony of Vergia Handsbur, Dec. 22, 1975–Jan. 12, 1976, 1395–411).

107. Goran testimony, Dec. 31, 1975, 2073, 2105. For examples of the plaintiffs' long work histories, see Handsbur testimony, Dec. 22, 1975, 1394, 1367–78; Frank Carpenter testimony, Feb. 3, 1976, 3914–15, 4342–54. The Handsburs and Carpenters also made extremely high down payments. The Handsburs put $2,500 down for a property that Crane purchased for $8,500. The Carpenters put $1,250 down for the property they purchased from Karras—whose out-of-pocket expenses for the building had totaled $226.84.

108. Berke testimony, Jan. 16–19, 1976, 3179; also see Reid testimony, Feb. 2, 1976, 4303–7; Laura Robinson testimony, Jan. 9, 1976, 2451; Essie Green testimony, Jan. 19, 1976, 3345, 3359; Lester Barnes testimony, March 5, 1976, 6707–28.

109. McLennand, "A Juror's Notes," 4, 20; Crane testimony, Dec. 19, 1975, 1149, and Dec. 15, 1976, 1013, 1056–57. Horvath, too, undercut the defendants' main argument. In the space of a few minutes, Horvath said that white people paid prices that were the same as or higher than what blacks paid; that "we priced our Negro price considering the credit sale," that is, they charged their black customers more because they sold to them on credit; and that the price they charged "was for cash or credit; it didn't make any difference" (Horvath testimony, March 16, 1976, 7616).

110. See Crane testimony, Dec. 19, 1975, 1179, for typical claim of creditworthiness. When Berke claimed to have never defaulted on a mortgage, Tucker showed the jury several documents proving that he had—even while his contract buyer continued to make regular payments (Berke testimony, Jan. 19, 1976, 3250–57).

111. Murray interview, 9. As Meenan recalled, although none of the defendants were "exactly likable, warm-and-fuzzy-type people," the person he was most uncomfortable around was Berland. "I knew enough about him and his background and I just had no use for him" (Meenan interview, 18).

112. McGarr ruling, Feb. 24 and Feb. 26, 1976, 5822, 5941, 5948.

113. Crane testimony, Dec. 12, 1976, 1060–64; also see Crane testimony, Dec. 19, 1976, 1176; Berland testimony, Jan. 12, 1976, 2692, 2817; Goran testimony, Jan. 5, 1976, 2293; Berke testimony, Jan. 16–19, 1976, 3136–39; Reid testimony, Feb. 5, 1976, 4617–20.

114. Berke testimony, Jan. 16–19, 1976, 3186–87; also see 3136–59, 3180–86; Reid testimony, Feb. 3, 1976, 4487, 4473–76, 4492; Goran request, Feb. 12, 1976, 5204–18.

115. Karras testimony, Jan. 26–27, 1976, 3856–62, 3904, 4047; "Abuses Battled in Savings Field," *NYT,* Nov. 22, 1971.

116. Crane testimony, Dec. 11, 12, and 15, 1975, 711, 1004, 1060; Berland testimony, Jan. 12, 1976, 2668–74, 2692–99; Berke testimony, Jan. 19, 1976, 3210–11.

117. For example, see Berke testimony, Jan. 16–19, 1976, 3129; Berland testimony, Feb. 26, 1976, 6007–20; Karras testimony, Jan. 26–27, 1976, 3918; Reid testimony, Feb. 3, 1976, 4417–37.

118. In contrast, the buyers' repair expenses were high, often starting with the cost of installing a furnace. Since the buyers' contracts specified that repairs were their responsibility, they bit the bullet and paid for them. See Crane testimony, Dec. 15, 1975,

900–910, 917–37, and Vergia Handsbur testimony, Dec. 22–23, 1976, 1374–4110, 1470, 1619, 1676; Maggie Davis testimony, Dec. 29, 1975, 1740; Mrs. Arydell Spinks testimony, Dec. 29, 1975, 1824.

119. Berland testimony, Jan. 12, 1976, 2669–71; Charles Simmons testimony, Jan. 12, 1976, 2831–61.

120. Vergia Handsbur testimony, Dec. 22, 1975, 1395–411.

121. Berland testimony, Feb. 26, 1976, 6001–21.

122. Tucker, *Trial and Error*, 283; also see Tucker objection during Reid testimony, March 4, 1976, 6572–84.

123. McGarr ruling, Feb. 6, 1976, 4682; also see McGarr comment, March 18, 1976, 7712; Crane testimony, Dec. 11, 1975, 668–82; McLennand, "A Juror's Notes," 43; Horvath testimony, March 18, 1976, 7313–14, 7694–711; Goran testimony, March 12, 1976, 7393–94; Reid testimony, March 4, 1976, 5291.

124. *Harry Bernard and Bernice Bernard v. Gerald H. Crane,* Complaint in Chancery, Superior Court of Cook County, 60s5047, filed March 18, 1960, CCCC; Crane testimony, Dec. 11, 1976, 668–82, and Dec. 12, 1976, 750.

125. McLennand, "A Juror's Notes," 43; Tucker, *Trial and Error*, 282–84.

126. McLennand, "A Juror's Notes," 48–49, my italics.

127. Tucker, *Trial and Error*, 283–86; McLennand, "A Juror's Notes," 59; also see docket sheets, 69c15, 261.

128. Richard Phillips, "Contract Buyers Lose," n.p., but probably *CT,* April 17, 1976, JM Papers; Boodell interview.

129. Tucker, *Trial and Error*, 287; McLennand, "A Juror's Notes," 3.

130. McLennand, "A Juror's Notes," 54.

131. Ibid., 24, 9, 30; Jenner and Block assistant comment on Horvath testimony, March 18, 1976, 7744.

132. Tucker, *Trial and Error*, 288; McLennand, "A Juror's Notes," 52–54; also see Fitzgerald interview. On June 22, 1976, the plaintiffs appealed, but the appeal was rejected in January 1977. See docket sheets, 69c15.

133. *Sidney and Julia Clark et al. v. Universal Builders Inc. et al.,* 69c115, USDC for Northern District of Illinois, Eastern Division, 1982 U.S. Dist. LEXIS 12678, May 3, 1982.

134. *Sidney and Julia Clark et al., Plaintiffs-Appellants and Cross-Appellees, v. Universal Builders Inc. et al., Defendants-Appellees and Cross-Appellants,* 82-1770, 82–1859, U.S. Court of Appeals for the Seventh Circuit, 706 F. 2d 204; 1983 U.S. App. LEXIS 28725, Nov. 10, 1982, argued, April 19, 1983, decided. The Court of Appeals did agree with Judge Bua that the case was "close" and therefore upheld his rejection of Universal's request that the plaintiffs pay the defendants' attorneys' fees. See letter, Carol R. Thigpen, Jeffrey D. Colman, and Charles L. Barker, Jenner and Block, to "Dear Contract Buyer," April 29, 1983, box 5, JBA.

135. See "What's Happening in Our Downtown Office," Sept. 30 1970, appended to "What's Happenin' at CBL," Oct. 1, 1970, CJEG-Egan II, box 111, folder "CBL News Clips," UND.

136. Gordon interview, 5–6. Some of its members wrote the lion's share of the legal brief in the 1976 Supreme Court ruling *Gatreaux v. Chicago Housing Authority,* which outlawed racial segregation in public housing, forced the Chicago Housing Authority to balance its previous policy of concentrating public housing units in all-black neighborhoods by putting future units in white areas, and opened white suburbs to public housing. When four hundred CHA tenants were subsequently moved to private, integrated apartments in Chicago and its suburbs, follow-up studies demonstrated their high rates of educational and occupational achievement relative to that of those left behind in the ghetto: "It has provided policymakers with strong empirical evidence that racial and economic integration can make a difference in the lives of inner-city blacks" (Adam Cohen and Elizabeth Taylor, *American Pharaoh* [Boston: Little, Brown, 2000], 549). See Leonard S. Rubinowitz and James E. Rosenbaum, *Crossing the Class and Color Lines: From Public Housing to White Suburbia* (Chicago: University of Chicago Press, 2000).

The CUA housing group also provided crucial support for whiz kid Ron Grzywinski, a progressive banker who was troubled by the fact that banks fled neighborhoods as soon as blacks moved in. In the early 1970s, the South Shore Bank had petitioned the controller of currency for permission to move out of Chicago's South Shore neighborhood because, it claimed, there was no deposit base left in the increasingly African American area. With help from the "numbers crunchers" at the CUA, South Shore Bank's petition to leave the neighborhood was denied. This was "the first successful challenge in the country to disallow movement out of a racially changing neighborhood," a CUA member recalled. Grzywinski went on to purchase South Shore Bank and run it as a new kind of bank—one devoted to community reinvestment as well as profit. By 1986, the bank's assets had more than doubled and its deposits had more than tripled. Today the institution, now called ShoreBank, is internationally famous as a paradigm of community development financing (Darel Grothaus interview, Dec. 6, 2001, 2–3; Judith Barnard, "Money Matters," *Chicago* magazine, Feb. 1977, 97–104; "Small Bank Revives Urban Area," *NYT,* Jan. 30, 1986).

137. Anne Witte Garland, "'We've Found the Enemy': Gale Cincotta," in *Women Activists: Challenging the Abuse of Power* (New York: Feminist Press, 1988), 38–39, 48; also see Grothaus interview, 5. The OBA was established in 1967 by Alinsky-trained organizer Tom Gaudette, who had taken time out that same year to advise young seminarians in Lawndale—including Jack Macnamara—on the basics of community organizing. See Lynne Navin, "Organization for a Better Austin," in Patricia Mooney Melvin, ed., *American Community Organizations: A Historical Dictionary* (New York: Greenwood, 1986), 140–41.

138. "I got the university to get my researchers interested in the [contract sales] issue and do the kind of documentation that was used by the Contract Buyers League suit. It was also used by Gale Cincotta and her movement to get that legislation through" (John McKnight interview, March 4, 2001, 8). CUA researcher Darel Grothaus adds, "The politics of the situation were completely run by Gale and the community organizers. But she recognized that we had something to contribute, that we could give a certain credibility because (a) we had documentation that we were developing and (b) the credibility of the university, of social science researchers. . . . While I'm proud of the work that we did, without that political carrier, it wouldn't have gone anywhere. It would have been a dusty report" (Grothaus interview, 8).

139. McKnight interview, 37, my italics.

140. Grothaus interview, 8; Gregory D. Squires, "Community Reinvestment: An Emerging Social Movement," in Squires, ed., *From Redlining to Reinvestment: Community Responses to Urban Disinvestment* (Philadelphia: Temple University Press, 1992), 10.

141. Grothaus interview, 8–9; Squires, "Community Reinvestment," 10. Just as my father had done in his 1960 lawsuit against General Federal Savings and Loan, Grothaus justified the ordinance by citing the original banking charters. These stated that federally chartered banks must serve community needs, not just depository needs but lending or credit needs as well. One couldn't determine if banks were living up to their charters, Grothaus argued, if there was no public disclosure of where loans were made.

142. As Cincotta's colleague Calvin Bradford recalled, Washington-area econo-mists would at first disdain Cincotta's testimony and then "surreptitiously open their pads and [begin] taking notes on how neighborhood economics really worked" (NTIC, "Gale Cincotta, 'Mother of Community Reinvestment Act' Dies,"www.ntic-us.org/currentevents/press/curr-obit-8-15-01.htm, accessed Jan. 7, 2002. Grothaus inter-view, 9; Kris Ronnow interview, Sept. 26, 2003, 15; Squires, '"Community Reinvest-ment," 10).

143. Squires, "Community Reinvestment," 10–12; editorial, "Banking on Local Communities," *NYT,* April 15, 2004; "U.S. Set to Alter Rules for Banks Lending to Poor," *NYT,* Oct. 20, 2004.

144. McKnight interview, 37. Peggy Roach also pointed out that "local efforts like the CBL . . . undergirded efforts to achieve the Community Reinvestment Act" (Margery Frisbie, *An Alley in Chicago: The Life and Legacy of Monsignor John Egan,* commemo-rative ed. [Franklin, Wisc.: Sheed & Ward, 2002], 197).

CONCLUSION

1. See "Firm Steered Home Buyers, Group Says," *NYT,* March 24, 2006; "Study Documents 'Ghetto Tax' Being Paid by the Urban Poor," *NYT,* July 19, 2006.

2. Kathe Newman, "Post-Industrial Widgets: Capital Flows and the Production of the Urban" (unpublished ms. in author's possession, currently under submission to the *International Journal of Urban and Regional Research*), 4, 11–14; "With Ads, Banks Ushered in Frenzy for Home Equity Loans," *NYT,* Aug. 15, 2008.

3. Bill Marsh, "Housing Busts and Hedge Fund Meltdowns: A Spectator's Guide," *NYT,* Aug. 5, 2007; Gretchen Morgenson, "Inside the Countrywide Lending Spree," *NYT,* Aug. 26, 2007. Subprime lenders had an incentive to peddle loans with adjustable interest rates and harsh prepayment penalties, since investment banks paid significantly more than face value for such loans. See Gretchen Morgenson and Geraldine Fabrikant, "Countrywide's Chief Salesman and Defender," *NYT,* Nov. 11, 2007.

4. Gretchen Morgenson, "Countrywide Subpoenaed by Illinois," *NYT,* Dec. 13, 2007; Newman, "Post-Industrial Widgets," 14, 29 (see 19–20 for statistics on subprime foreclosure rates); Morgenson, "Work Out Problems with Lenders? Try to Find Them," *NYT,* July 20, 2008; Morgenson, "Can These Mortgages Be Saved?" *NYT,* Sept. 30, 2007; Morgenson, "Dubious Fees Hit Borrowers in Foreclosures," *NYT,* Nov. 6, 2007. Also see Morgenson, "Blame the Borrowers? Not So Fast," *NYT,* Nov. 5, 2007.

5. Patricia J. Williams, "Movin' On Down," *Nation,* July 14, 2008, 9.

6. African Americans were 2.3 times as likely as whites, and Hispanics twice as likely as whites, to acquire subprime loans (adjusting for loan size and borrower income). See Vikas Bajaj and Ford Fessenden, "What's behind the Race Gap?" *NYT,* Nov. 4, 2007; Kai Wright, "The Subprime Swindle: How the Mortgage Industry Stole Black America's Hard-Won Wealth," *Nation,* July 14, 2008, 12; Newman, "Post-Industrial Widgets," 27, 23; "Acorn Study Shows Predatory Lending Is Leading to Fore-closures in Communities Nationwide," www.acorn.org/index.php?id+4174&tx_ttnews, accessed Sept. 12, 2007; "Risk or Race? Racial Disparities and the Subprime Refinance Market," a report of the Center for Community Change prepared by Calvin Bradford, May 2002, http://www.butera-andrews.com/legislative-updates/directory/Background-Reports/Center%20for%20Community%20Change%20Report.pdf, accessed Sept. 14, 2007.

7. Jessica Attie of the Foreclosure Prevention Project at South Brooklyn Legal Services, quoted on British Broadcasting Company (BBC) *NewsPod,* broadcast Sept. 19, 2007.

8. Erik Eckholm, "Black and Hispanic Home Buyers Pay Higher Interest on Mortgages, Study Finds," *NYT,* June 1, 2006; also see Morgenson, "Inside the Countrywide Lending Spree," and Morgenson and Fabrikant, "Countrywide's Chief Salesman and Defender"; Joe Nocera's scathing article "A Mission Goes Off Course," *NYT,* Aug. 23, 2008, which dissects Fannie Mae and Freddie Mac heads' bogus claim that their extensive subprime mortgage investments, which were made against the advice of their risk officers and which earned the two men approximately $30 million in 2007, were undertaken in order to open housing to low-income families; Morgenson, "Countrywide Subpoenaed by Illinois."

9. "Panel Clears Overhaul Bill on Banking," *NYT,* Sept. 12, 1998. In 2004, the Bush administration attempted to weaken CRA requirements for banks with assets between $250 million and $500 million—an exemption that would cover over 1,100 of the nation's banks (David W. Chen, "U.S. Set to Alter Rules for Banks Lending to Poor," *NYT,* Oct. 20, 2004). On recent efforts to undercut the CRA, see "Violating Your Way to an Outstanding Rating" (testimony of Calvin Bradford for the National Training and Information Center before the Subcommittee on Domestic Policy of the House Committee on Oversight and Government Reform, March 21, 2007, http://domestic policy.oversight.house.gov/documents/20070322180758-29796.pdf, accessed Nov. 16, 2007).

10. Bajaj and Fessenden, "What's behind the Race Gap?"; Mark Winston Griffith, "Banking at the Bottom," *NYT,* Oct. 9, 2005. During his 2008 presidential campaign, Senator John McCain blamed the Community Reinvestment Act for the subprime mortgage meltdown. For a succinct refutation, see Michael S. Barr and Gene Sperling, "Poor Homeowners, Good Loans," *NYT,* Oct. 17, 2008.

11. See Calvin Bradford, "Home Mortgage Disclosure Act: Newly Collected Data and What It Means," written testimony before the House Financial Services Committee, June 13, 2006, http://financialservices.house.gov/media/pdf/061306cb.pdf, accessed Aug. 23, 2008; Bradford, "Violating Your Way to an Outstanding Rating."

12. Steven R. Weisman, "Feds Set Rules Meant to Stop Deceptive Lending Practices," *NYT,* July 15, 2008. In 2007, a federal judge in Ohio dismissed fourteen foreclosure cases brought by Deutsche Bank when the bank was unable to provide the most basic documents proving ownership; since then, scores of additional foreclosure cases have been dismissed by federal judges for the same reason (Gretchen Morgenson, "Foreclosures Hit a Snag for Lenders," *NYT,* Nov. 15, 2007; Morgenson, "Foreclosures by Lender Investigated," *NYT,* Nov. 28, 2007).

13. Morgenson, "Countrywide Subpoenaed by Illinois"; Morgenson, "Illinois Suit Set against Countrywide," *NYT,* June 25, 2008; Morgenson, "Countrywide to Set Aside $8.4 Billion in Loan Aid," *NYT,* Oct. 6, 2008; also see Newman, "Post-Industrial Widgets," 19.

14. "John McKnight," *Chicago* magazine, Nov. 1985, 205; William Julius Wilson, *When Work Disappears: The World of the New Urban Poor* (New York: Knopf, 1996), 34–35.

15. Parisa Arash, Office of the Governor, State of Illinois, "North Lawndale: Profile of an Illinois Workforce Advantage Target Area" (Aug. 2002, available at http://www.illinois.gov/iwa/documents.cfm, accessed Aug. 18, 2008), 12, 20; "From Projects to Progress in Chicago," *Business Week,* Oct. 27, 2003. The adjoining communities of East Garfield Park and West Garfield Park, which have often been included as part of "greater Lawndale," continue to struggle from lack of investment and population decline, though there, too, housing rehabilitation and church-based community endeavors are ongoing. See Amanda Seligman, "North Lawndale," "East Garfield Park," and "West Garfield Park," and Christopher R. Reed, "South Lawndale," in James R. Grossman, Ann Durkin Keating, and Janice L. Reiff, eds., *The Encyclopedia of Chicago* (Chicago: University of Chicago Press, 2004), 252–53, 575–76, 769–70, 870–71.

16. Clinton E. Stockwell, "Washington Heights," *Encyclopedia of Chicago*, 858–59. Universal also built properties in sections of Auburn Gresham and Chatham, although most of the plaintiffs' properties were located in the eastern section of Washington Heights. The area's middle-class character may be at least partially attributable to the fact that mortgages were made to black buyers there. See Plaintiffs-Appellants' Brief, U.S. Court of Appeals for the Seventh Circuit, 72-1655, *Sidney Clark and Julia Clark et al., Plaintiffs-Appellants, v. Universal Builders Inc. et al., Defendants-Appellees*, 35–37, JBA.

17. "Midwest Areas Are Most Segregated in U.S., Study Reveals," *Jet*, July 9, 2001; "Milwaukee Is Most Segregated City: U.S. Census Analysis," *Jet*, Dec. 16, 2002; also see "Suit Says Chicago Housing Renewal Plan Perpetuates Segregation," *NYT*, Jan. 24, 2003.

18. Sallie Bolton interview, Oct. 1, 2001; Bertha Richards interview, April 8, 2002. Church obituaries for Richards, Williams, and Stevenson provided by Bertha Richards. Richards has little to say about Moe Forman, other than her guess that "he probably died cheating." But she refuses to cast the issue as racial. "The Bible says, 'Love you one another as I have loved you.' God made black ones, he made red ones, he made white ones, he made whatever he wanted to make, the Lord did that, we had no part in how he made us," she believes.

19. Ruth Wells interview, June 14, 2001; see "Ruth Wells," in www .thehistorymakers.com/biography.

20. Clyde Ross interview, Aug. 13, 2001; Maureen McDonald interview, Aug. 10, 2001.

21. Sidney Sharif interview, June 16, 2001, 23.

22. Jack Macnamara interview, Jan. 29, 2007; "Report on the Feasibility of a Cristo Rey Model High School in the Austin Neighborhood," January 2007, author's copy (courtesy of Jack Macnamara); "Chicago's Second Cristo Rey Model School Opens," June 27, 2008, http://www.jesuit.org/newsannouncements/news/716.aspx, accessed Aug. 24, 2008.

23. Eddie Smith interview, March 26, 2004. Smith played Peter Copeland in the Warner Brothers film *The Fugitive* and was Malcolm's bodyguard in the Paramount Pictures film *Ali*.

24. Sanford D. Horwitt, *Let Them Call Me Rebel: Saul Alinsky, His Life and Legacy* (New York: Vintage, 1992), 540; www.industrialareasfoundation.org, accessed Feb. 3, 2007; Margery Frisbie, *An Alley in Chicago: The Life and Legacy of Monsignor John Egan*, commemorative ed. (Franklin, Wisc.: Sheed & Ward, 2002), 287.

25. Frisbie, *Alley in Chicago*, 237–44; also see 226, 259.

26. Robert A. Ludwig, "The Final Chapter," in Frisbie, *Alley in Chicago*, 291, 295–96, 308–9; also see Samuel G. Freedman, "An Advocate Lends a Hand as Social Justice Goals Unify Faiths," *NYT*, June 16, 2007; "Msgr. J. Egan Payday Loan Reform Bill Will Protect Consumers from Predatory Pricing and the Cycle of Debt," press release, Feb. 4, 2005, Monsignor John Egan Campaign for Payday Loan Reform, http://www .citizen action-il.org/issues/payday/payday.html, accessed Jan. 26, 2007.

The last cause Egan took up before his death was a pressing question of "internal justice": women's ordination. "I look at my church and I am troubled," Egan wrote in May 2001. "Why are we not using to the fullest the gifts and talents of women who constitute the majority of our membership throughout the world? . . . It's not just a question of using women to fill in during an emergency. It is a matter, I believe, of social justice." His article on this topic was published in the *National Catholic Reporter,* June 1, 2001, and is reprinted in full in Frisbie, *Alley in Chicago,* 320–24.

27. See http://www.dempseytravis.com/, accessed Jan. 27, 2007; http://www.northwestern.edu/ipr/people/mcknight.html, accessed Jan. 27, 2007; John W. Baird interview, Feb. 13, 2004; "The War on Affordable Housing," *NYT,* Oct. 16, 2004.

28. Gertrude Goran interview, April 17, 2001; Warren Lupel interview, June 25, 2001, 10; John C. Tucker, *Trial and Error: The Education of a Courtroom Lawyer* (New York: Carroll and Graf, 2003), 290; USDC for N. D., Illinois, Eastern Division, *United States of America v. Capital Tax Corporation,* 04c4138, Jan. 4, 2007; phone conversation with Richard H. Balin, Sept. 21, 2001; phone conversation with Tamra Balin; Chicago telephone directory. On Balin's activities since the 1970s, see David Ibata, "Association Wins $363,826 in Fee Dispute," *CT,* Dec. 17, 1984; Tom Brune, "The Slum Brokers: Tougher Laws Would Save Real Estate," *CST,* May 23, 1990; "Investor Sentenced for Bilking HUD," *CST,* Aug. 13, 1991.

29. Tucker, *Trial and Error,* 286; George Feiwell interview, June 18, 2001; Lupel interview; Michael Turoff interview, Oct. 15, 2001, 13–14.

30. "Pair Sue, Accuse Realtor," *CA,* Aug. 13, 1958.

31. See James R. Ralph Jr., *Northern Crusade: Martin Luther King, Jr., Chicago, and the Civil Rights Movement* (Cambridge: Harvard University Press, 1993), 271–72, n. 129; Kathleen Connolly, "The Chicago Open-Housing Conference," in David J. Garrow, ed., *Chicago 1966: Open Housing Marches, Summit Negotiations, and Operation Breadbasket* (New York: Carlson, 1989), 91.

ACKNOWLEDGMENTS

My first thanks go to the approximately ninety people who sat for interviews, some of them multiple times. I hope that they are satisfied with my telling of their stories. My brother David Satter was particularly gracious and helpful. I could not have written this book without the guidance that David's detailed, always candid, and uncannily accurate memories provided. Several interviewees allowed me to pester them repeatedly for information, including John L. McKnight, Richard Franch, Jack Macnamara, and John C. Tucker. Jack Macnamara, Tom Sullivan, Bertha Richards, Ed Holmgren, Marilyn Shuman, and David Satter also provided me with invaluable documents. I am grateful to them all.

I have been fortunate to have a supportive work environment at Rutgers University–Newark. In 2001 I received a Metropolitan Research Award from the Joseph C. Cornwall Center for Metropolitan Research, then headed by Dennis Gale, which jump-started this book. I am grateful to my Cornell Center–funded research assistants, Yanique Taylor, Jerome Greg Taylor, and Andrea White. Thanks also to the Institute on Ethnicity, Culture, and the Modern Experience, run by Clement Price and Charles Russell at Rutgers–Newark, which provided me with a research assistant in the fall of 2002 and a desperately needed course release in the fall of 2004, and to my research assistants who were funded by the Rutgers–Newark Department of History: Charles Foy, Jennifer Mandel, Brennan Heffernan, Stephanie Jones-Rogers, Laura Troiano, Sebastian Mercier, and Tony Aschettino. Edward J. Kirby allowed me to take a sabbatical a year ahead of schedule so that I could complete my interviews. My colleagues in the Department of History have made work a pleasure. I've received invaluable support and guidance from Jan Lewis, Sallie Kasper, and especially from Christina Strasburger, who has been spectacular in every way.

My thanks to the Gay and Lesbian (LGBT) Faculty and Staff Organization at Rutgers–Newark, who provided community.

I am forever grateful to my brilliant friends Mia Bay and Kirsten Swinth, the two people who read my original, 600-plus manuscript and made sage suggestions for editing; to James Goodman, James T. Fisher, Alison Isenberg, Linda E. Fisher, and Kathryn Tanner, who also read early versions of the manuscript; and to Maggie Shiffrar, Donna I. Dennis, Martha Jones, Annette Gordon-Reed, D. Bradford Hunt, Len Rubinowitz, Rachel Hadas, and Jacqueline Goldsby, who read shorter portions. Thanks also to Jonathan Hyman and to Jacqueline Goldsby for their research tips.

I am greatly indebted to scholars of Chicago history, particularly Arnold R. Hirsch, Alan B. Anderson, George W. Pickering, and James R. Ralph Jr. Thanks to Amanda I. Seligman for her meticulous research and for her generosity in sending me a copy of her dissertation. I have relied heavily on Jeffrey Fitzgerald's wise, in-depth dissertation on the Contract Buyers League, and I am grateful as well for the insights he shared in his interview, including his suggestion that if I wanted to understand Chicago I needed to read Milton Rakove. I am indebted to James Alan McPherson's 1972 article on the Contract Buyers League, and last but not least, to the brilliant and engrossing writing of reporters at the old *Chicago Daily News,* particularly Nicholas Shuman, Lois Wille, M. W. Newman, and Paul Gapp.

My deepest thanks to Geri Thoma, who read several versions of the manuscript and always advised me wisely, and to my editor at Metropolitan Books, Sara Bershtel, who reorganized and cut and polished the manuscript until it shined. Also at Metropolitan Books I thank Riva Hocherman, for her numerous invaluable suggestions, and Megan Quirk, for her responsiveness, rock-solid dependability, and overall professionalism in seeing this project through to completion. I am grateful to the J. Anthony Lukas Prize Project of the Columbia Graduate School of Journalism and Harvard University Neiman Foundation, who granted this project an Honorary Mention for their 2004 Work-in-Progress Award for Exceptional Works of Nonfiction. The psychological lift of that honor helped me to persevere through the long and intense process of writing this book.

Thanks to the archivists who directed me through massive amounts of information on mid-twentieth-century Chicago, including Jeanie Childs at the Circuit Court of Cook County Archives and Sharon Sumpter at the University of Notre Dame archives, and to the librarians of Dana Library at Rutgers–Newark upon whose helpfulness and professionalism I have become utterly dependent. Thanks to Antony W. Lisanti for enabling me to listen to tapes of the "West Side" CBL trial.

I also wish to acknowledge old friends who have become like family: Ira Sheffey, Edith Lee, Kayla Lee Sheffey and Emma Lee Sheffey, Donna Bryan, Judith Berns, Beth Brewer, Alfred Thomas, Maggie Shiffrar, Mia Bay, and Kirsten Swinth.

In the summer of 2001 I interviewed Maureen McDonald, who worked with the CBL and on the group's legal suits on and off from 1968 until 1978. Maureen then turned and interviewed me. When I told her about my father's work and admitted that I wasn't sure how to retrieve his legal files, Maureen immediately offered to help, even walking me over to the archives at the Daley Center and helping me fill out the forms. When I had to return to New York City, Maureen kept track of the outstanding requests and retrieved the records. Thanks to her I was able to retrieve hundreds of pages of documentation that form the heart of this book. In short, I became one of the countless people who were the recipients of Maureen's warmth and generosity.

Maureen brought that same generosity of spirit to her job at the Cook County Public Guardian's Office. She was working late one evening in October of 2003 when a fire broke out at the Cook County Administrative Building. Maureen was one of six people to die in that fire. At her funeral, Cook County Public Guardian Patrick Murphy said that "the week of her death Maureen came into my office, planted her elbows on my desk, and demanded that I do something to stop the vultures who were taking homes from elderly residents who fell behind in their taxes. I told her that the state legislators were controlled by the business interests," he continued, "and that the chances of reform were therefore slim. But she said, 'Do it!' And now, Maureen, I will." May her memory continue to inspire action.

The person that truly made this book possible, of course, is my brother Paul Satter. As a teenager Paul took it upon himself to preserve our father's legacy. I hope that Paul is pleased with the book that has resulted.

INDEX

ABOUT THE AUTHOR

BERYL SATTER was raised in Chicago, Skokie, and Evanston, Illinois. A graduate of the Harvard Divinity School and Yale American Studies program, she is the author of *Each Mind a Kingdom,* and is a professor of history at Rutgers University in Newark. For her work in progress on *Family Properties,* Satter received a J. Anthony Lukas citation. She lives in New York City.